10,000 *GARDEN QUESTIONS*

Answered by 20 Experts

10,000 GARDEN QUESTIONS

Answered by 20 Experts

Fourth Edition

Marjorie J. Dietz, *Editor*

Originally edited by F.F. Rockwell

*New drawings for the fourth edition
by Ray Skibinski*

VOLUME II

DOUBLEDAY & COMPANY, INC.   GARDEN CITY, NEW YORK

Printed in the United States of America
Design by Jeanette Portelli

Contents

Section

10. The Home Vegetable Garden   749

Planning the Garden • Soil Preparation • Seed Sowing •
Maintenance • Exhibiting • Equipment • Miscellaneous •
Pests and Diseases • Specific Vegetables

11. Home-grown Fruits   894

The Orchard • Specific Tree Fruits • Dwarf and Espalier
Fruit Trees • Small Fruits • Cane Fruits • Nut Trees

12. House Plants   1000

General Culture • Decorating with House Plants • Miniature
Gardens • Specific Flowering House Plants • Annuals and
Biennials as House Plants • Foliage Plants • Gift Plants •
Shrubs • Ferns • Vines for Indoors • Cacti • Succulents •
Hardy Bulbs for Forcing • Hardy Spring Bulbs for Indoors •
Tender Bulbs for Indoors

13. Plant Troubles and Their Control   1137

Insects, Diseases, and Their Controls • Ornamentals and
Their Pests • Vegetables • Fruits—General • Specific
Fruits and Their Pests

14. Weeds 1330

General • Specific Weeds

15. Regional Garden Problems 1342

From Alabama to Wyoming

16. Sources for Further Information 1433

Books • State Agricultural Experiment Stations • Horticultural and Special Plant Societies • Botanical Gardens, Arboreta, and Public Gardens • Some Sources for Plants and Seeds

Index 1457

10,000 GARDEN QUESTIONS

QUESTIONS

Answered by 20 Experts

10. The Home Vegetable Garden

BY FAR THE most important reason for "growing your own vegetables" is that only by so doing can one be certain of getting vegetables of the finest quality. The local market gardener, who used to provide really fresh vegetables to neighborhood stores, is all but extinct. Vegetables that have to be shipped hundreds or thousands of miles before being graded and repacked for chain-store distribution lose much in quality and flavor. Many of the best quality varieties are never grown for market because they lack eye appeal, or do not mature uniformly so a crop can all be harvested at one time; or because they do not keep well when shipped. Lettuce is an example. The real quality varieties, such as 'Buttercrunch' and 'Oakleaf', are seldom if ever to be found in a market; the shopper must go without lettuce or be satisfied with the coarse and tasteless sorts which possess about as much flavor as a piece of aluminum foil. Such things as cantaloupes and tomatoes must be picked "firm" (a euphemism for "half-green") in order to be safely shipped to the wholesaler, and by him distributed to the retailer. They may "color up" by the time the consumer gets them, but they never gain their full flavor, or their full value as food. Sweet corn that is picked not more than an hour or two before it reaches the table is very different from the semiwithered article in the supermarket bins.

Even if one does not have space for a full-scale vegetable garden (say 50 × 30 feet), a supply from some of the most productive crops—such as tomatoes, pole beans, broccoli, bush squash, and lettuce—can be grown on a very small plot; or even in combination with garden flowers. In addition to getting better quality, the home gardener is likely to find —after deducting the cost of seed, fertilizer, spray materials—that he has made a dent in his food budget. Of course greater savings result from large gardens offering a surplus for freezing and canning.

Location

The location of the vegetable garden is important, but in the home garden plot there is not likely to be much choice as to where it can be placed or as to the type of soil to be selected. One thing, however, is absolutely essential—an abundance of sunshine.

The shade of a tall tree that casts a constantly shifting shadow upon the vegetable rows will not be too serious, but every square foot of the garden should get daily at least 5 or 6 hours of full sunshine, and preferably more. Asparagus and rhubarb, which make their most rapid growth in early spring, will stand considerable shade later in the season; lettuce in hot weather is rather benefited by slight midday shade, but as a general rule—the more sun the better.

Size of Plot

"How large a plot should I have to make it worthwhile to grow vegetables?"

That is a question often asked by the beginner, and it is a very sensible one. The answer, however, cannot be too definite. A well-worthwhile supply of quick-growing, closely planted crops—such as lettuce, onion sets for green onions, bush squash, carrots, radishes, mustard, cress, New Zealand spinach for a summer-long supply of "greens," and some tomatoes and beans (both bush and pole)—can be grown on an area as small as 10 × 10 feet or in a long border 5 × 20 feet.

A larger plot, however, is advisable, if it is at all possible to secure one. On many a small place a plot at least 10 × 25 feet can be provided for vegetables by the simple expedient of transplanting some of the existing shrubbery and possibly doing away with a shade-casting and root-hungry tree or two not really needed to maintain an attractive landscape planting around the house.

A plot 30 × 50 feet (or its equivalent) is recommended by government experts as desirable where the object of the gardener is to grow an important part of the family's food supply. Unfortunately the prevailing "lot" system used in subdividing suburban real estate makes it impossible, in many cases, to allocate even this moderate amount of space to home food production. But very often it is possible for the homeowner to obtain the use of additional land at a not-too-inconvenient distance.

Drainage

"Can vegetables be grown on wet ground?"

Drainage is another important factor in the growing of vegetables. Soil in which the average run of flowers and shrubs grow will prove suitable for the vegetable garden; but a boggy or a swampy location, in which the water has a tendency to remain after heavy rains, at less than 12 inches below the surface, should be drained before any attempt is made to employ it for vegetable gardening.

Low-lying ground that has a tendency to collect and hold surface water, but is not actually swampy, can often be made suitable for vegetable growing by the simple process of using raised beds in which to plant. Such beds—made up into shape and size convenient for planting—are formed by merely digging out paths 4 to 6 inches deep and distributing the removed soil over the surface of the beds. It is desirable, but not essential, to have the paths slope slightly to a low spot, so that surplus moisture draining from the beds into the paths will in turn be drained out of the paths.

Protection

Many a first-year gardener has seen much of his efforts go for naught because his plot was not adequately protected from mechanical injury—damage by dogs, rabbits, woodchucks, gophers, or children not trained to have a proper respect for plants. Without such protection the experienced gardener would not think of attempting to plant a garden where injuries from such sources are possible; but the average beginner will go gaily ahead and "take a chance"—only to regret it later.

Chicken wire with a 2-inch mesh, and at least 2 feet (and better 3 or 4) in height, supported by posts firmly set in the ground at intervals of 8 or 10 feet, will supply adequate protection. The lower edge of the wire should be buried 2 or 3 inches deep and firmly pegged down to prevent small animals from burrowing under it.

Such protection will of course make an additional item of expense the first year, but it is a worthwhile investment, and if kept in repair will last for many seasons. A 4-foot fence will also serve as a permanent and space-saving support for tomatoes, peas, cucumbers, or (with some additional support) for pole beans. It is quite worth its cost for this purpose alone. Only a 4-foot fence will offer much protection against pheasants, and a much higher one is necessary to discourage deer.

Equipment

The equipment required in caring for a moderate-sized vegetable garden need not be extensive or expensive, but it pays to have tools of the best quality.

For a small plot a spading fork, an iron bow rake, a hoe, a trowel, and a watering can are the essential implements. A hand duster or a small sprayer (preferably both) will be needed in the control of insects and diseases.

In addition to these tools for working the soil, an adequate supply of water, used intelligently, will increase the yields of many crops 50 to 100 per cent. Nobody wants to waste water, and methods for conserving it are emphasized in this section and in other sections as well.

What Vegetables to Grow

"What vegetables shall I grow in a small garden?"

In arriving at the answer to this question, several things must be considered.

How small is the garden?

What vegetables does the family like?

What crops will do well in your locality?

Is it planned to grow some crops for freezing and storing or only summer supplies?

Without knowing the answers to these questions, it is not possible to suggest a definite list of what vegetables to grow. It is possible, however, to give the beginner some guidance. Here are five lists that will help him.

I. Vegetables That Yield Most

(In proportion to space they occupy and the time required to grow them)

1. Tomatoes
2. Pole beans
3. Broccoli
4. Onions (from sets)
5. Beans, bush
6. Beets
7. Carrots
8. Chard
9. Chinese cabbage
10. Spinach, New Zealand
11. Mustard
12. Lettuce
13. Turnips
14. Cress
15. Cabbage
16. Radishes
17. Spinach
18. Bush (summer) squash

II. Requiring Least Space

1. Tomatoes
2. Pole beans
3. Beets
4. Carrots
5. Leeks
6. Turnips
7. Bush squash
8. Onions
9. Lettuce, leaf
10. Chard
11. Chinese cabbage
12. Beans, bush
13. Mustard
14. Radishes
15. Cress
16. Tampala

III. Requiring Considerable Space

(Look for varieties of some of these vegetables that have been bred for small-space gardens)

1. Broccoli
2. Cabbage
3. Cauliflower
4. Spinach, New Zealand
5. Corn
6. Eggplants
7. Peppers
8. Parsnips
9. Potatoes
10. Sweet potatoes
11. Peas
12. Cucumbers
13. Melons
14. Winter squash

IV. Short Season

(Can be followed by other crops)

1. Beans, bush
2. Beets
3. Early cabbage
4. Carrots
5. Cress
6. Lettuce

7. Mustard
8. Onions (from sets)
9. Peas
10. Radishes
11. Spinach
12. Turnips

V. Difficult to Grow in Many Regions

1. Cauliflower
2. Celery
3. Chinese cabbage
4. Cucumber
5. Muskmelons
6. Onions

7. Peas
8. Potatoes
9. Pumpkins
10. Spinach
11. Squash (winter varieties)
12. Watermelons

Plan Ahead

It will be seen from all this that the planting of a vegetable plot, if it is to yield maximum returns, is not merely a matter of walking into a garden center, picking out, more or less at random, a dozen or two packets of vegetable seeds, and then starting in at one end of the vegetable plot and sowing each as far as it will go.

A carefully thought-out plan for the vegetable garden should be made before any seed is bought—and this is even more important for a small plot than for a large one.

Making such a plan is not difficult, and it is a lot of fun—quite as interesting as solving a crossword puzzle. The first step is to make an outline plan, showing the shape and dimensions of the plot. It will help greatly if this is drawn to scale—say ½ inch equaling a foot for a small plot or ¼ inch or less a foot for a larger one. On the former basis, a garden plot 20 × 30 feet would be represented by a rectangle 10 × 15 inches. Each row of vegetables to be planted is then indicated. "Planting Tables" showing the proper distances between rows of the various

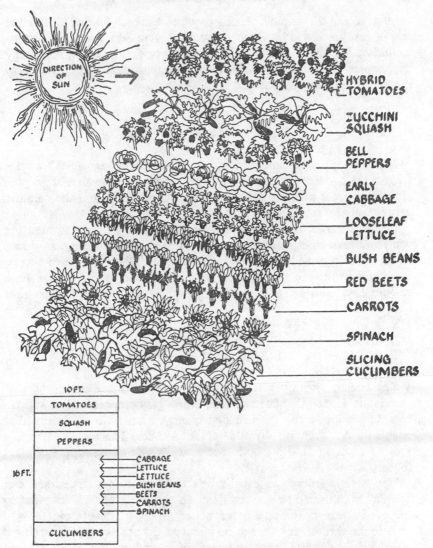

DIRECTION OF SUN

HYBRID TOMATOES

ZUCCHINI SQUASH

BELL PEPPERS

EARLY CABBAGE

LOOSELEAF LETTUCE

BUSH BEANS

RED BEETS

CARROTS

SPINACH

SLICING CUCUMBERS

10 FT.

16 FT.

| TOMATOES |
| SQUASH |
| PEPPERS |
| CABBAGE |
| LETTUCE |
| LETTUCE |
| BUSH BEANS |
| BEETS |
| CARROTS |
| SPINACH |
| CUCUMBERS |

Here is a vegetable garden that is ideal for a space-restricted lot and a small family. Ten feet wide by 16 feet long, it features easy-to-grow vegetables that will yield worthwhile produce. The early cabbage, lettuce, and spinach will not last all season, so their space can be filled by more bush beans, eggplant, or broccoli and lettuce (planted in early summer) for fall harvesting.

vegetables and the amount of seed required for each 50 or 100 running feet of row are issued by Cooperative Extension Services, State Experiment Stations, the United States Department of Agriculture, and many newspapers and magazines. The two plans reproduced here show how the finished planting plan should look.

Planning for Winter Supplies

In making up the planting plan, remember that if vegetables for winter use are wanted—for canning and for freezing—these should be provided for in the planting plan, although "surpluses" from the summer garden will give satisfactory results for small families.

If, for instance, canned tomatoes and tomato juice are wanted for winter, at least twice as many tomato plants should be set out as would be required to provide a summer supply alone. Beets and carrots to be stored for winter are not sown in early spring but planted in late June or July, thus utilizing space from which quick-growing early crops have been removed.

Preparing the Ground

The beginner with vegetables is very likely to make the mistake of planting in ground that has not been thoroughly prepared. Most vegetables, to produce a full crop of first quality, must have conditions that enable them to grow rapidly and without a check. This means extremely thorough soil preparation, both mechanically and in the supply of plant foods.

Very small gardens can usually be dug by hand, but larger ones can be quickly cultivated by power tillers. The longer in advance of planting the ground can be prepared, the better. Many gardeners dig the soil (where the earliest crops are to be planted) the preceding fall, turning it up roughly and thus getting the benefit of the pulverizing action of alternate freezing and thawing during the winter. A further advantage of digging in advance of planting is that many weed seeds have a chance to germinate. The tiny weed seedlings are destroyed when the soil is worked over before sowing or planting.

(Details of soil preparation and fertilizers will be found in Section 1.)

5/15 BUSH SQUASH (4 Hills acorn, 1 row zucchini)	24"
LEAF LETTUCE 4/10 LETTUCE 5/15	18"
TOMATOES (8 staked plants) 5/15	18"
KOHLRABI 4/10	18"
TOMATOES	18"
EARLY CABBAGE PLANTS 4/10	18"
PEPPERS (10 plants) 5/15 EGG PLANTS 5/15	18"
SPINACH 4/10	15"
LIMA BEANS 5/20	15"
SPINACH 4/10	15"
LIMA BEANS 5/20	15"
SNAP BEANS 5/15 LETTUCE 8/15	21"
SNAP BEANS 5/10 BEETS 7/20	12"
BEETS	6"
	6"
BROCCOLI 7/15 BEANS 7/10	12"
BROCCOLI 7/15	9"
SWISS CHARD 4/25	PARSNIPS 4/25	PARSLEY 4/25	18"
BEETS 4/25 ENDIVE 7/15	15"
BEETS 5/15	12"
CARROTS 4/25 CHINESE CABBAGE 8/1	12"
CARROTS 5/15	12"
RADISHES 4/10 CARROTS 7/1	12"
ONION SETS 4/10 CARROTS 7/1	12"

30 Feet

20 Feet

PLAN FOR A 20 × 30-FOOT GARDEN

A typical northern garden with suggested planting dates for regions where the average date of the last freeze is May 10 or thereabouts. Both seeds and transplants (tomatoes, eggplants, peppers, broccoli, and cabbage) have been used. Full advantage has been taken of all space by interplanting (lettuce sown April 10 and May 15 between rows where bush squash and tomatoes are to be planted about May 15, for instance). Space is also conserved by succession crops—snap beans after broccoli, lima beans after spinach, etc.

Sowing and Planting

"When should the vegetable garden be planted?"
In the well-arranged vegetable garden, planting is a more or less continuous operation from the time the frost is out of the ground until 6 to 8 weeks before hard frost is to be expected. The 3 most active planting periods, however, are very early spring, when the hardy, frost-resistant vegetables are put in; 4 to 6 weeks later, when the tender ones are planted; and 4 to 8 weeks later than this, when many crops for late fall and winter use are sown. North of the Mason and Dixon line these dates are normally:

Mid-March to mid-April for early, hardy crops.

May 1 to June 1 for tender crops.

Mid-June to late July for "succession" crops for fall and winter use.

The *hardy* vegetables include beets, broad or fava beans, carrots, turnips, lettuce, onions (sets, plants, or seed), leeks, radishes, parsnips, salsify, witloof chicory; the cabbage group (cabbage, broccoli, cauliflower); mustard, spinach, and chard; parsley; early celery; peas; potatoes.

The *tender* sorts include most beans; corn, tomatoes, eggplants, and peppers; the vine crops (squash, cucumbers, melons, and pumpkins); okra; sweet potatoes.

The *late* sorts (some of which are hardy and some tender) for fall and winter use include bush beans; beets, carrots, turnips, rutabagas; lettuce, Chinese cabbage; cabbage, broccoli, Brussels sprouts, kale.

Information covering the details of seed sowing, transplanting, and cultivating is given in Section 3.

Planning the Garden

Is it necessary to make a ground plan of the vegetable garden before planting? It will save time, seed, and mistakes later on. However, seasonal developments may make minor changes necessary.

Should plant rows run east and west? The direction of the rows is of minor importance. Other factors being equal, there is a slight advantage if the rows run from north to south.

When the land slopes from north to south, should the rows be made across the slope or down it? When the land slopes perceptibly so that there is a tendency for heavy rain to run down the slope instead of soaking in, rows should always be run across the slope. If this makes the rows too long, a path can be run down the center of the plot, cutting the rows in half. On steep slopes it is desirable to make a series of terraces, held in place by stone or permanent sod, so that the ground under cultivation will be fairly level.

In what direction is it best to plant a vegetable garden—north and south or east and west? It makes very little difference. What is more important is the location of the tall-growing vegetables with reference to the low-growing kinds. Plant the low plants on the east or south sides. Keep tall ones in the back where they will not shade the others.

Should root vegetables and leafy sorts be planted in alternate rows? Since the fertilizer requirements differ—the leafy vegetables need considerable nitrogen and the root vegetables require a higher percentage of phosphorus and potash—it is usually more convenient to group the two types rather than to plant them in alternate rows.

Shall I plant rows of tall vegetables between those which are low-growing? As far as is practicable, tall growers should be together at the north end of the garden and low growers at the south or east. Often, however, rows of lettuce, radishes, or other low growers can be grown between tomatoes or other tall growers and can be harvested before the latter attain much height.

My garden is 22 × 30 feet. Should the tall vegetables, like corn and climbing beans, be on the south side of the garden in order to prevent shading smaller plants? Always plant tall-growing vegetables on the north or west side of the garden, if possible.

On what sides of the garden should trees or shrubs be planted as a protection against winds? Ordinarily, on the north and west sides, unless prevailing spring winds are from some other direction.

Which vegetables are easiest to grow in a beginner's garden? Explain how to arrange beds. For vegetables that are easiest to grow, see the introduction to this section. It is not necessary to make beds in a vegetable garden. Practically all types of vegetables do best planted on the level surface. Merely mark off rows for sowing the seed after the ground is well worked and prepared. A narrow path can be left through the center or along the sides of the garden.

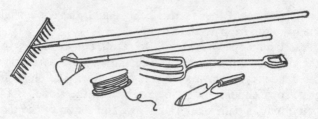

These tools—a rake, hoe, spading fork, trowel, and line for marking rows—are sufficient for most small vegetable gardens.

I have an area 50 × 15 feet. What is the best way to plant it? How can I obtain extra crops, earlier and later?   Plant the rows crosswise; 14 feet of carrots, beets, leaf lettuce, or other greens are enough for one planting. For beans and other vegetables of which larger amounts are wanted, plant two or three 14-foot rows. Keep tall-growing sorts, like tomatoes, corn, or pole beans, at one end, preferably north or west. Set out plants of as many vegetables as possible (such as cabbage, broccoli, lettuce, tomatoes, eggplant, beets) to get extra-early crops. Be ready to plant succession crops at once, when early crops are finished.

What are the so-called warm-weather plants?   Warm-weather plants will be killed by light frosts and cannot be placed in the garden until all danger of frost is past. The following may be grouped under this heading: beans (all types except broad beans), cucumbers, eggplant, muskmelon and cantaloupe, okra, peppers, pumpkins, squash, sweet corn, sweet potatoes, tomatoes, and New Zealand spinach. Seeds of tomatoes, however, can be sown as early as the soil is workable. They will germinate as soon as conditions are favorable. Transplants of tomatoes are tender. New Zealand spinach must be sown early, but it is often slow to germinate.

Where can I get a chart on how long it takes to grow various vegetables?   In pamphlets on vegetable growing issued by most State Experiment Stations or in vegetable gardening books. Most of this information is given in seed catalogs. The information is given with the description of each vegetable. (See individual vegetables, this section.)

What should I plant in a garden 90 × 90 feet?   For a garden of this size consult your State Agricultural Experiment Station or county agent of the Cooperative Extension Service. This size garden will permit growing unusual crops which would not be economical in smaller gardens.

What are the frost-hardy vegetables? The following vegetables survive light frosts: beets, broccoli, Brussels sprouts, cabbage, carrots, cauliflower, celery, chard, collards, dandelion, endive or escarole, kale, kohlrabi, leeks, lettuce, mustard greens, onions, parsley, peas, potatoes, radishes, roquette, spinach, and turnips; also broad or Windsor beans.

What crops can be grown on the edge of a city plot that gets hard in the hot summer and isn't very fertile? Can more than one crop be harvested during a year's time? Sweet potatoes, peanuts, bush beans for use dry, and soybeans. You would get only one crop of these. Any crop will take moisture. These will take the minimum amount of care.

What types of vegetables grow best in a sandy soil? While sandy soils are not recommended for commercial growing of some vegetables, satisfactory crops of most of them for home use can be obtained. The soil, however, must be kept well supplied with humus, and fertilizer in small amounts should be applied frequently. Water is usually the limiting factor on sandy soil.

What vegetables would grow best in ground that has never been cultivated before? This ground contains a lot of quackgrass. This would depend largely upon the character of the soil. Root crops—beets, carrots, parsnips—do not do as well on new ground as on land that has been worked for a few seasons. This is especially true of onions. Turnips, however, often do excellently on new soil. Corn and the various vine vegetables, if generously fertilized, should do well. Also, potatoes should do well if the ground is suitable for them. However, the quackgrass is likely to prove troublesome unless killed with dalapon two months before planting.

What is best to plant on newly cleared land? The soil is a little sandy. Would potatoes do well? (Rhode Island.) Potatoes need good soil. This is especially true of the 'Chippewa' variety. Snap beans, sweet corn, and sweet potatoes would probably be all right. Other vegetable crops are heavy feeders and would require very thorough soil preparation.

Which of the common vegetables can satisfactorily be grown in clay soil? Practically all of the usual home garden vegetables can be grown in a clay soil if it is properly handled. Root crops (carrots, parsnips) may be poor if grown in stiff clay loam.

What small vegetables can be successfully raised to mature before September 15 on the north shore of Cape Cod? (Northeast storms are

frequent and devastating.) Most of the frost-hardy plants, including cauliflower, broccoli, and turnips.

What could you recommend for a vegetable garden 50 × 100 feet in northern New England? This will make a very big garden which should produce a surplus for sale unless you decide to grow a large area —say one half—in potatoes. That leaves a lot of space for cabbage, broccoli, cauliflower, carrots, turnips, rutabagas, lettuce, Swiss chard, and sweet corn. If you grow tomatoes, you probably should have at least two dozen plants.

We own a vacant lot on a hillside—the soil is heavy yellow clay (brick clay). What sort of garden should we contemplate? Tomatoes do well enough. Since tomatoes do well on this soil, most other crops, except asparagus and melons, will do better. You will have to grow a short, stubby variety of carrot. You probably cannot grow parsnips. This soil needs considerable limestone, and the addition of plant refuse and coal cinders would tend to loosen it. Use limestone freely. Start out with a 25 × 25-foot garden and grow tomatoes, cabbage, broccoli, and Brussels sprouts as well as lettuce, carrots, and beets. Then add to it each year.

What vegetables would you recommend for the garden of a person who works all day and has a minimum of time to work in the garden? It isn't a question of which vegetable takes the least effort, but how big a garden you have. Radishes and turnips can be grown by sowing seed and forgetting them until it is time to pull them out of the weeds. Timely control of weeds when they are small will save much labor, regardless of the crop.

What kind of vegetables can be grown over a wire fence? Tomatoes, cucumbers, melons, squash, pole beans.

How can we garden at our summer home? We spend long weekends there in early spring, sometimes a week or more at Easter, and are "in residence" from mid-June, when school lets out, until Labor Day. Two or three weekends in the fall wind up the year. Your best solution is fall digging or tilling, after a light frost or two. Collect all the organic matter you can find—leaves, garbage, sawdust, etc., plus any plants left in the garden. If local farmers can spare manure, you are in luck. In the soil, work under all the organic matter you can. In the future, compost all table scraps and other available organic matter for use the following fall. Don't overlook the scraps from cleaning fish, hunting, etc., which add to the richness of a compost pile.

Let the tilled soil settle. Arrange to be there just before a hard freeze is expected. Rake the soil level and plant the seeds of any of the following crops your family will eat: beets, broccoli, Brussels sprouts, cabbage, carrot, Chinese cabbage, cress, endive, escarole, kale, kohlrabi, lettuce, New Zealand spinach, onion sets or top onions, parsley, parsnips, peas, radish, rutabaga, spinach, Swiss chard, and turnip. Seeds of tomato and 'Butternut' squash can be treated with captan or thiram to protect them from soil fungi and sown at the same time.

There is better than a 50 per cent chance that these seeds will survive the winter and begin growth before you can work the soil in the spring. If they fail, there is still time to seed all these crops before hot weather.

When the soil warms up and the danger of frost is past, plant seeds of warm-season crops such as snap beans, pole beans, sweet corn, cucumber, eggplant, okra, peppers, and melons.

Weeds will be a problem; ask at garden centers for information on the annual weed-control chemicals that can be used to spray the soil (after the first crop of seedlings in spring has been killed) and will keep the surface weed-free for up to two months.

Growing seedlings at home and carrying them to the garden on a spring visit (early for hardy vegetables; after the danger of frost for tender crops) is another way the problem of planting can be handled. They will transplant easily in peat-fiber pots (for most kinds) and in berry boxes filled with compost (for melons, squash, and cucumbers).

Rely heavily on mulches to conserve moisture and reduce weeds. Increase the organic content of sandy soils all you can. Save wood ashes from the fireplace as a soil amendment and fertilizer.

In the North, how late can vegetables be planted? Except in cold spots such as near the Canadian border, the following dates will give edible produce in 9 years out of 10:

June 15: Brussels sprouts, cabbage, carrots, and beets for fall use. *July 1:* Chinese cabbage, broccoli, carrots and beets for storage, sweet corn, cucumber, zucchini, and snap beans. *July 15:* rutabaga. *August 1:* turnips, endive, escarole, garden cress, kohlrabi, lettuce, radish, peas (use 'Sugar Snap' for highest productivity and 'Wando' for heat resistance), spinach. Even if immature when frost comes, many vegetables then are gourmet treats, i.e., baby carrots, finger-length zucchini, tiny snap beans.

ROTATION

Is rotation of garden vegetables important? If space permits, it is a good idea occasionally to give the whole garden a rest for a year or two, but space in a garden is too limited for any real benefit from moving crops just a few feet.

What is the difference between planting crops in "rotation" and in "succession"? Rotation cropping is the practice of planting, in a given area, different crops each year. Succession planting means following one crop with another in the same season—for instance, the planting of snap beans in the row from which early carrots have been harvested.

How do I rotate plantings of vegetables to get the most out of them? Simply change the location of the different vegetables from year to year. However, in a small garden most vegetables can be grown in the same spot for several years in succession, if the ground is kept fertile. Rotation in the home garden is of little or no advantage.

Can you suggest a rotation of crops for the small garden? If you can use a big enough area, a garden planted every other year or every third year makes a good rotation. During the vacant years the garden may be seeded to green-manure crops, which are plowed under or put into a permanent sod. If weeds are permitted to grow and are mowed down when they begin to blossom, they will make a good green-manure crop. Rotating the vegetable crops in a small garden, except in a limited way, is not practical.

SUCCESSION PLANTING

What vegetables can be planted in the same area in a current season, one following the other? (New York.) In general, any vegetable that is removed from the ground sufficiently early in the season can be followed by any other which will have time to mature. Crops which are out of the way in time to be followed by others are early cabbage and cauliflower, lettuce, peas, beets, radishes, carrots, kohlrabi, turnips, and spinach; also, onions from sets that are used green. These can be followed by peas (in cool regions only), late celery, and late plantings of lettuce, beets, carrots, and turnips; cabbage and cauliflower, and early varieties of sweet corn. Chinese cabbage, mustard, kale, and collards for late autumn and winter use can also be grown after early crops.

Define "intercropping." Is it desirable? It may be defined as the planting of rows of quick-growing crops, such as lettuce, radishes, or spinach, between widely spaced, slower-growing items, such as celery, peas, and tomatoes. Intercropping is desirable because, if carefully planned, it results in producing more food from small gardens.

What are the combinations for intercropping vegetables? In general, intercropping vegetables in the small garden gives less yield per square foot of space than extra-close planting without intercropping. There are some exceptions. Early cabbage and lettuce transplants, for instance, can be set between the rows where tomatoes are to be set out later. Bush beans can be planted between the rows where peppers and eggplant are to be set later. With close planting (12 inches between rows for many crops), the ground will be so completely covered that there is not room for another crop in between. In general, two crops can be grown on the same ground only when one of them will be removed *before the other needs the entire space;* or when long-season crops are widely spaced to permit intercropping.

How can I get the largest number of vegetables from a small plot of ground? By intensive culture. This implies careful planning, thorough soil preparation, adequate fertilization and irrigation, succession and companion cropping, proper selection of varieties, constant control of pests and diseases, and keen attention to details at all times.

Two gourmet lettuce varieties: the heat-resistant 'Oakleaf' (left) and 'Butter-crunch', a 'Bibb'-type lettuce that is heat-resistant. 'Royal Oakleaf' is an improved version of 'Oakleaf'.

What is the trick to intensive gardening? I have about 4 × 15 feet to devote to vegetables. There is no trick or magic involved. Lay out 3 rows, 13 feet long. Plant 1 row of beets, 1 row of carrots, to be followed by 2 rows of snap beans planted after their roots are out. Plant ½ row of radishes or onion sets to be followed by Swiss chard, and ½ row leaf lettuce to be followed by late turnips or other root vegetables. Plant a staked tomato at each end of each row, allowing 1 foot from the stake to the planting of other vegetables. A fence on the north edge can be used to grow pole beans or cucumbers.

Is the custom of planting beans, corn, and pumpkins in the same space a good procedure? While this practice is often followed on farms, in the home garden it is better to keep them separate. In the small garden pumpkins have no place unless they can be planted near the edge of the plot and allowed to run out over the grass or climb along a fence.

USE OF SPACE

How many square feet will I need to supply each member of my family with vegetables for one year? Much depends upon soil fertility, crops grown, methods of cultivation, as well as varying needs of different families. From 300 to 500 square feet per person would perhaps be a fair answer. This would include crops for storing and canning for winter.

What is the size of the smallest plot one can use for a vegetable garden? You can use a patio planter to grow radishes and lettuce; you can grow tomatoes and peppers in pots or tubs. An area 4 × 20 feet is practical.

Would it be worthwhile for us to have a garden in a space 10 × 17 feet? There are just two of us. Yes. Highly perishable crops like lettuce and greens are always worth growing. You can grow a large part of your green vegetables as well as a few tomato plants in this area if you plan carefully.

Which are the five or six most practicable vegetables for an inexperienced person to try to raise in a home garden (20 × 25 feet) in New England? Tomatoes, snap beans, onion sets, radishes, Swiss chard, carrots, beets, and head or leaf lettuce. Follow one crop with another. Snap beans could follow radishes and lettuce.

What vegetables shall I plan to grow in a medium-sized garden? Anything you like with the exception of kinds which are known to be uncertain in your locality (consult local growers or your State Experiment Station) and such space consumers as corn, potatoes, squash, and pumpkins. (See the Introduction.)

How would you plan a vegetable plot 60 × 90 feet using principally the ordinary, easily grown items: corn, beans, peas, potatoes, tomatoes, radishes, etc.? Use 30 feet of the 90 for potatoes and divide the remainder among other crops, giving most space to those the family likes best.

What is the best way a plot 50 × 200 feet can be utilized so that it will include a home 20 × 32 feet, a little orchard of about 18 trees, a vegetable garden, and space for housing chickens? The chickens and the orchard can occupy the back 50 × 100 feet, with the poultry house in the center. The area between the house and the orchard could be the vegetable garden. If the house used up 75 feet, it would still give you a 25 × 50-foot vegetable garden.

How can I plan my garden, which is 90 × 100 feet? My husband died and I want to make a garden for myself and two children. This is almost a quarter of an acre, which would require a tremendous amount of work unless you possess a small power cultivator or rotary tiller. An area 25 × 50 or 75 feet will give you all the vegetables you need for your family. You might use that much for the garden and use the other land for some crop like tomatoes, potatoes, or sweet corn which you could sell to the neighbors.

What is the most profitable crop on an acre lot (part sandy and part loam and clay)? I have raspberries and strawberries, corn, and most garden vegetables. (Ohio.) Any crop is profitable if it will grow in your locality and you have a market for your produce. Strawberries, with irrigation and mulching, are usually profitable. If your vegetables are good and you live in an area where you can sell good produce, a general assortment can be profitable. First, you must learn to grow the crop well, and then sell it to good advantage.

Which vegetables would you recommend for planting in a small area (10 × 12 feet) that would produce the best yield? Onion sets, leaf lettuce, carrots, beets, 6 staked tomato plants, and 2 rows of snap beans. Make more plantings after the first crops are finished.

What vegetables could I plant in a sunny place where I have dug an extra foot of border on my flower bed; also, in an old rose garden about 9 feet square? Radishes, leaf lettuce, carrots, and beets in the narrow border; staked tomatoes and snap beans in the rose garden. Plant the beans between the tomato plants.

What is the usual size of a backyard garden? What vegetables could best be grown in that size? What could be used for second-crop or succession planting? An average-size backyard garden would be 20 × 25 feet. This will grow most vegetables for a family of four and you will still have some left over that you can freeze. Lettuce, beans, beets, carrots, cabbage, tomatoes, and onions (from sets) are good to start with.

You can make several plantings of all these vegetables, except tomatoes. Rutabagas, turnips, spinach, and lettuce are good for the fall.

Would you advise planting a few vegetables in border flower beds? We have very little rainfall and must irrigate most of the year.   This is easily done. Plant tall vegetables north and west so they won't shade the low-growing plants. Keep the low-growing plants near the edges on the east or south side. Tomatoes can be set 2 feet apart and trained to stakes set alongside the plants. Low-growing plants can be set or planted in rows in the borders. Avoid crowding for vegetables which set pods or fruits. Parsley and chives make handsome edgings.

We are planning to convert some of our flower garden into a vegetable garden. Will you suggest suitable vegetables to plant against a brick wall 4 feet wide, facing south?   Tomatoes, pole beans (especially limas), and cucumbers trained on a trellis would do well in such a situation.

What vegetables can be grown in flower beds in limited space?   Half a dozen tomato plants scattered along the back of the flower beds, tied to stakes or grown in wire cages of wide mesh so they won't sprawl. Radishes and lettuce can be planted in the border toward the front. Asparagus can be planted so that the summer growth will serve as a background. Snap or pole beans can be planted between later-flowering plants. Rows of carrots and beets can be grown between rows of flowering plants, as they do not take much space. Onions can be grown from sets. There is always the possibility of growing a few cucumber vines in a tub or barrel in a vacant corner. Various herbs can be used as low edgings.

What steps must one take to start a home garden?   (1) Decide on your crops and how much you want of each. (2) Select the ground and make your plan. (3) Sow seed for the plants 5 to 7 weeks before you plan to set them outside. (4) Get your ground ready with lime and fertilizer. (5) Plant frost-resistant crops about 3 weeks before the last spring frost (usually about mid-May). (6) Get warm-weather plants started, to have them ready by the middle of May.

LOCATION

What exposure should I choose for my vegetable garden?   Providing the site is sunny, the precise exposure is less important than soil and other details. A southern or southeastern exposure will produce earlier crops. Even a northern exposure has advantages for cool-weather crops, such as late peas and summer lettuce.

What is the ideal location for a vegetable garden? A well-drained, gentle slope facing the east or southeast, in full sunshine throughout the day and protected by shrubbery or a fence on the north and northwest.

Can I have a successful vegetable garden in a low, wet spot on my grounds? The soil is rich. Vegetables must have good drainage. The only way you can successfully grow them in the location mentioned is to drain the area thoroughly by ditching or tilling, if necessary. (See Section 1 and the introduction to this section.)

What food plants can be planted in wet places such as undrained muck ponds, bayheads, etc.? Except for watercress, which prefers running water, there are no vegetables which will grow in undrained soil. Stay away from salt water. Make beds 4 to 6 feet wide and at least a foot higher than the paths to get rid of the free water. Then you can grow lettuce, carrots, beets, collards, and similar types of vegetables. If the soil stays fairly dry, celery, tomatoes, and beans will grow well.

Can my vegetable garden be made on the west side of my house? This is not a good spot for vegetables. Try to find a place that has full morning sunshine and as much sun in the afternoon as possible. The west side would do, however, if the garden is not too close to the house.

How much sunshine is necessary for vegetables? Vegetables need all the sunshine they can get. A minimum of 5 to 6 hours of direct sunshine per day.

What is the best vegetable to plant in the shade? There are none that will grow well without some sunshine. With partial shade, but sunshine in the morning, some of the leafy vegetables grow fairly well.

What vegetables are most suited to a shady garden? Will any of them yield successive crops, or is each good for only one crop? Vegetables, to amount to anything, must have sunshine during the morning. The leafy vegetables are the only ones that will stand any shade. If they will grow, they may be planted in succession.

What vegetables will grow close (5 feet) to the north side of a house? None.

I have a plot of 36 × 50 feet, one side of which lies in the shadow of my house. What vegetables (if any) can I plant in the shade? If the garden is to the south of the house, you will have little difficulty. If it's on the west side, your only chance is some greens that may grow in the shade. On the north side, forget vegetables.

We have a large space of fertile ground underneath our fruit trees which gets sunshine only part of the day. I have not planted anything that has grown satisfactorily. Will you please inform me as to which vegetables will grow well in partial shade? Leafy vegetables are the only ones that will do well. Your difficulty may be that the tree roots rob the vegetables of water and fertilizer.

Would it be worthwhile to dig up a partially shaded area to plant vegetables such as beans and tomatoes? No, absolutely not. Some of the leafy vegetables might make a fair growth but not tomatoes and beans.

How can I raise a vegetable garden surrounded by oak trees that are at least 25 feet in height? It is hardly worth trying unless the trees are 20 feet or more from the vegetable plot. Plants must get morning sun, at least, and the roots of the trees would rob the vegetables of water and nutrients.

What vegetables will grow near maple trees in dry earth? None. Maple roots are too competitive.

Our new home was built on land that formerly was occupied by many tall trees, mostly oaks. We have some trees left which shade all parts of our grounds at some part of the day. The soil is acid and heavy. We have turned over half of the backyard and removed stones, roots, etc. Some land was left rough; another section was planted with rye and vetch, and we intended to turn it under in the spring. Can you suggest vegetables which we might grow under these conditions? To grow good vegetables, stay at least 10 feet from the outer edge of the branches, where the vegetables will receive at least the morning sun. The biggest problem is to keep the roots of the growing trees from robbing the water and fertility from the vegetable plants. Put on sufficient pulverized limestone to sweeten the soil. If this soil is very heavy, it should have considerable leafmold or manure, or even coal cinders, mixed with it.

What flowers and vegetables will grow close to the shady side of a privet hedge? Most vegetables, if the privet does not rob the vegetables of water and fertilizer. The shading effect is not serious unless it is on the south side of the vegetable plants, where it may produce too much shade. Five to six hours of direct sunshine are essential.

Are there any vegetables that will grow and produce in a plot 4 × 20 feet, which gets only morning sun and is within a few feet of pine and birch woods? The main problem here would be water and nutrients for the vegetables. The shading is not so serious unless the spot receives less than five hours of direct sunshine. Probably frequent watering would be required.

How do you develop a hillside garden? This requires the building of terraces, the width of which will be determined by the steepness of the slope. The rows must run crosswise of the slope.

What vegetables can be grown in sandy soil where wind and salt spray attack them? We have grown kale, broccoli, and lettuce fairly well. What others would you suggest? This can be answered only by your experience. Any smooth-leafed vegetable, including asparagus, should grow well. Plants with hairy or rough leaves probably would be injured by any appreciable amount of spray.

What vegetables grow and produce best in sandy and decomposed granite soil? This depends on how well the soil has been fertilized previously. If the soil has some lime in it, most vegetables can be grown provided that sufficient water and plant nutrients are added. Dissolving a cup of a mixed fertilizer in 3 gallons of water and watering the plants with this every 2 weeks will help. These usually are good soils.

COMMUNITY GARDENS

I would like to plant a vegetable garden, but don't have the land. How can I start a community garden? The most important requirement for a community garden is land. In city areas, tour your neighborhood and check out vacant lots, particularly city-owned vacant sites and park areas. In the country, talk with farmers, private landowners, and church groups—also corporations and local planning authorities. The next most important need is a "leader"—someone with enthusiasm, plus a gift for planning and organizing.

The best location is one with easy access to a water supply. Secure a location that is not temporary. There's nothing more discouraging than cultivating a plot of land only to realize that it won't be available the following year.

Divide the land into equal-size plots, and allocate one plot to each gardener or family group. Don't expect to garden the entire area like one big happy family. Each person with his or her own plot to look after is a better system. Don't make the plots too large if you are beginning gardeners. A well-cared-for small plot will yield far more than a large area that is neglected.

Try to have everyone start on the same day, having paid a farmer to plow the ground. This gets everyone off to an enthusiastic start, and the experience of planting the seeds becomes pure pleasure. Leave room for pathways between plots. Toilet facilities and a handy shed to lock up equipment should also be considered. In areas with potential vandalism, it may be necessary to erect a fence.

Soil Preparation

DIGGING OR TILLING

What's the case for fall digging versus spring digging? Dig in the fall, leaving the ground rough. Winter weather breaks up clods and aerates the soil through freezing and thawing. Many overwintering insect enemies are turned up, and there is less liability of leaving air pockets in the turned soil. Light, sandy soils, however, can suffer from washing by winter rains and usually are best left until spring for tilling or digging.

When digging a sodded plot of ground for the first time, to be used for a vegetable garden (in the spring), how should the ground be treated? Plow or till in the fall, leaving the clods on an angle instead of turning them over flat. This is done to avoid leaving a layer of sod between the subsoil and the surface soil. If lime is needed, also apply that in the fall, raking it in lightly so that rains will not wash it into hollows and low spots. If the sod is heavy, the plot should be tilled or dug in the spring at right angles (if reworking is necessary) to the direction in which it was first dug, so that the decomposing sod may be more thoroughly broken up and mixed through the soil.

When should spring digging or tilling be done? Digging should not be undertaken in the spring until the ground has begun to dry up after spring frosts are out. A simple test is to squeeze a handful of soil into a firm ball. If this ball under pressure from the fingers crumbles apart readily, the soil is ready to work. If it tends to remain in a sticky mess, digging should not be attempted until it has dried out further.

Should the vegetable garden be spaded up after the harvest in the fall and then again in the spring before the new planting? Or is spading in the spring sufficient? Spading or tilling in the fall is advantageous on most soils, except very light, sandy ones. Ground prepared in this way in the fall will need much less work done on it in the spring to get it ready for seed sowing and planting.

*A power-driven rotary tiller can be a work-saver.
Use it to prepare the soil in the vegetable garden
and for mixing in fertilizers and organic matter.*

When should a new vegetable garden be tilled or dug? Any time before seed-sowing time. Heavy or medium soils are better tilled or dug in the fall; very sandy soils, in the spring. However, if you have missed out on fall preparation, don't hesitate to begin a new garden in the spring.

When should the established vegetable garden be tilled or dug? If the soil is at all clayey, it should be turned over in the fall and left in a rough condition all winter. Very light, sandy soils should be tilled or dug in early spring.

How deeply do you think the ground should be dug for a vegetable garden? As deeply as possible providing that (1) not more than an inch or so of infertile subsoil is turned up; (2) labor is available. From 8 to 12 inches is a fair depth, but a somewhat greater depth is by no means excessive as the ultimate goal.

Does deep preparation of the soil help to make long, sturdy roots? Yes indeed. All crops benefit from deep soil preparations. Onion roots have been traced to a depth of 5 feet. Parsnips may be grown that are 3 feet long, with roots extending deeper.

Should ground be more deeply worked in dry areas? In general, yes. Some sandy soils are exceptions. Especially in dry locations it is necessary to encourage roots to strike deeply in search of moisture.

Do you advise turning over old sod ground, not used for 15 years, in late fall? By all means. Leave the ground in ridges rather than turning it over flat; this will permit alternate freezing and thawing during the winter to pulverize it more thoroughly. If the ground slopes, dig it

In digging soil with a shovel or spading fork, thrust the blade or tines straight down instead of at an oblique angle. Cultivating while weeds are very small saves backbreaking "chopping" later when weeds reach full size. But easier than cultivating weeds is the application of mulches or, in very small gardens, planting vegetables close together so most weeds are crowded out. Those that do manage to appear can be pulled out by hand.

across the slope of the land to check any tendency to erosion. A rototiller may usually be rented to turn over small pieces of ground. These small machines do an excellent job. If your grounds extend to even as much as an acre or two and the actual creation of your garden is still ahead of you, the purchase of a rototiller is often a wise move.

LIME

What is the best ground conditioner? For most soils, raw ground limestone is the best conditioner, as it both improves the mechanical condition of the soil and corrects acidity. For most vegetables, however, lime should not be applied to alkaline soil. Under such conditions, gypsum or land plaster is better, as it will not make the soil more alkaline—as will lime. Ashes and sifted cinders improve the physical condition of any heavy soil.

Should lime be spread over a vegetable garden early in the spring or in the fall? It is much better, if possible, to apply lime in the fall after the ground is dug. Then cultivate it in so that heavy rains will not wash it away.

What are the relative lime requirements of the common vegetables? With few exceptions, most vegetables do best in a soil which is slightly acid—that is, a soil showing a pH reaction of 6 or 6.5 to 7. (See

Acidity, this section.) The vegetables most tolerant of a somewhat acid soil are potatoes, sweet potatoes, watermelon (to a somewhat lesser degree), eggplants, peppers, and tomatoes. Those least tolerant of acidity (and therefore most in need of lime) are asparagus, cauliflower, celery, leeks, lettuce, onions, and spinach.

PROBLEMS WITH SOIL

What soil treatment do you recommend for a lawn dug up for a vegetable garden? If the sod is very heavy, it may be desirable to remove the turf, cutting it as shallowly as possible and making a compost heap of the sod thus obtained. However, if the sod can be dug under (mixing it thoroughly with the soil so that it does not remain in unbroken lumps), that is preferable. On soil prepared this way, an application of 5 to 10 pounds per 100 square feet of a complete fertilizer should give good results the first year.

Do you think removing all the stones from a vegetable garden is a good idea? Our garden was cleared of every stone for about 10 inches down; lots of manure was spread over the ground in the winter. My theory is that the fertilizer sank too far into the ground, as there was no foundation, and was lost to the crop. The year before we had a fine crop —it was only the second time for using this garden. Removing stones is not at all essential, except that their absence makes it easier to work the soil. However, taking them out would not injure the soil or make fertilizers leach away more quickly. Roots of most vegetables go down 2 feet or more.

How can I prepare a 10-acre plot to good advantage? First, supply sufficient liming material to bring the pH up near the neutral point, and plant some cover crop to plow under. Then fertilize for the vegetable crops. Consult your county agent.

What types of vegetables can be grown in clay-loam soil? How can that kind of soil be made to grow any kind of garden? This is a cold, late soil, best suited to frost-hardy plants like members of the cabbage family. Such soil should be well limed and have organic material mixed with it. After a year or two of use it should be suitable for most vegetables.

Our vegetable garden has a rather heavy clay soil. What treatment would you advise? Manure, compost, and humus supplied by growing green-manure crops will all help to lighten a clay soil. Applications of lime or of land plaster (gypsum) will also help greatly in improving the mechanical condition and make it less likely to form hard lumps. Clay soil should never be dug or cultivated while wet.

I have never done any vegetable gardening; I want to dig up part of my lawn to plant a vegetable garden. There is only about 2 inches of topsoil; the rest is sand. How should I go about it?   Your problem is a difficult one, as very shallow soils are not the best for vegetable growing. Dig about 4 inches deep, breaking the sod up as thoroughly as possible and mixing it through the soil. If well-rotted manure can be obtained in the spring, apply a heavy coating—2 to 4 inches deep—and dig this under just sufficiently to cover it up so that the surface will be clear for planting. Lacking manure, apply a 2-inch layer of peat moss (available in 6-cubic-foot bales from garden centers). Your problem will be to keep the soil well supplied with humus to absorb and hold moisture; sandy soils dry out too rapidly. In using fertilizer, make frequent small applications while the plants are growing instead of putting it on in advance of planting, as is often done on heavier soils. Sandy soils require frequent watering.

How is newly spaded soil prepared for a vegetable garden?   If the soil is acid, lime should be added and cultivated in. Unless the soil is already in very good condition from previous applications of fertilizer, 4 to 5 pounds of complete fertilizer per 100 square feet is broadcast and raked in before planting. Before seed sowing, the surface of the soil should be gone over with an iron-toothed rake, removing all small stones and trash and leaving it as smooth and level as possible.

What is the best time to prepare the ground for early planting of potatoes, corn, and various vegetables?   As a general rule, it is best to prepare the ground for planting a month or more in advance. This is particularly true if sod or a green-manure crop is to be turned under. Advance preparation makes possible partial decay of the green vegetable matter before the vegetable crop is planted; otherwise, the decaying plant material will temporarily draw upon the nitrogen in the soil, thus robbing the planted crop, unless additional nitrogen is added when the crop is planted. Wherever very early planting is to be done, it is advantageous to till the ground the previous autumn if it is possible.

How do I prepare a former flower garden for a vegetable garden and what are the best vegetables for a beginner to grow?   A flower garden that has been well fertilized should be in excellent shape to grow vegetables. Thorough and deep digging and the application of a complete fertilizer will put it into condition. The vegetables that it would be advisable to grow will depend on the size of the plot and the gardener's experience (see lists in the introduction to this section).

If clay soil is turned over in the fall, how early can the first vegetables be planted in the spring? (Ohio.) Clay soils dug in the fall can usually be planted much earlier than if the preparation of the ground is left until spring. The hardy crops (see Introduction) can be put in just as soon as the soil is sufficiently dry to be cultivated and raked without sticking to the tools and forming hard lumps. Ordinarily this would be in early April, but will vary with the season.

Is it necessary to have different types of soil for the common vegetables, such as carrots, lettuce, cabbage, etc.? No. In a well-prepared garden plot practically the complete list of vegetables can be grown satisfactorily. It is important, however, that the soil be slightly acid. If it is too acid or too alkaline, many vegetables will not do well. (See Acidity, this section.)

We live near salt water; our soil is not very good. The only flowers that we seem to grow successfully are marigolds and zinnias. If this soil agrees with them, what vegetables could we grow? If protected from high winds and salt spray, most vegetables can be grown. Add as much organic material to the soil as possible—peat moss and seaweed, for example.

In our vegetable garden we always have excellent results with green beans, tomatoes, butter beans, cucumbers, but poor results with peas, carrots, spinach, beets, and turnips. The soil is sandy, with pine trees in an adjoining pasture. Does this experience suggest that something is lacking? (Texas.) This indicates that the soil may be low in lime, boron, and potash. A complete soil test should be made, and if calcium is low, some pulverized limestone (preferably dolomitic) should be spread on the surface when the soil is prepared.

Why did my carrots, beets, and turnips grow only to about one fourth their normal size? My flowers mostly stayed very short with small blooms. The ground hadn't been turned over in 75 years. Does it require some special care? Few vegetables (particularly the root crops) do well on soil not previously cultivated. With good culture you will undoubtedly see an improvement each year for two or three seasons. Other than the usual cultivation, the incorporation of humus, and fertilizing, the soil probably does not require any special treatment. For root crops, use fertilizers that are high in potash and phosphorus, and irrigate during dry spells.

FERTILIZERS

What is the difference between "fertilizer," "manure," and "plant food"? In a general sense, any material added to the soil which will aid plant growth is a fertilizer. As more commonly used, the term "fertilizer" refers to manufactured products in dry form sold in bags; "manure" refers to such animal products as cow, horse, or sheep manure. "Plant food," as usually employed, is an incorrect term; the only true plant foods are manufactured or developed *within the plant*. However, the term "plant food" is frequently employed as a polite word for fertilizer or manure.

What is the difference between organic and inorganic fertilizer? The former is made from animal or vegetable sources, such as bone or blood or cottonseed meal; the latter is made from mineral or synthetic substances, such as phosphate rock, nitrate salts, or potash salts.

What is meant by the term "complete plant food"? As used by manufacturers, a commercial fertilizer containing all three of the main elements which are required for plant growth, i.e., nitrogen, phosphorus, and potassium. "Complete fertilizer" is the correct term, rather than complete plant food.

What is the meaning of the three numbers which appear on every package of complete fertilizer, such as "5–10–5"? The first number always stands for the percentage of nitrogen, the second for the percentage of phosphorus, and the third for the percentage of potassium.

What is meant by "trace elements"? Do any complete fertilizers contain these? Trace elements are substances such as manganese, boron, sulfur, and iron, required for plant growth but in smaller quantities than the three main elements (nitrogen, phosphorus, and potassium) and usually present in most soils. Yes, most complete fertilizers do contain some of the trace elements, either in the raw materials from which the fertilizer mixture is made or they are added purposely to supply them. Since the law does not require manufacturers to declare the presence of trace elements on the bag, you must take this on faith.

What is the best all-round garden fertilizer—one which is of high, medium, or low percentage in plant nutrients? A medium-percentage fertilizer such as 5–10–5 or 4–12–4 is usually recommended for general garden use.

What is a "starter" or "transplanting" solution? This consists of a small amount of high-analysis chemical fertilizer dissolved in water. A cup is poured directly on the roots of plants when they are transplanted or a cup is poured directly on the seed for every 3 feet of row. An ounce of 13–26–13 fertilizer, or 3 ounces of a 5–10–5 fertilizer, in a gallon of water, makes a starter solution.

What is a "sidedressing" solution? This is the same as a starter solution, but sometimes made stronger, used to pour around the plants after they are well established and growing. Two to three times as much fertilizer is dissolved in the water. It gives a quick response and there is somewhat less danger of burning the plants than when a dry fertilizer is used.

How should nitrogen be applied to the soil? In a complete fertilizer, or in the form of ammonium sulfate, nitrate of soda, dried blood, or tankage, usually at the time of transplanting or in the early stages of plant growth, at the rate of 2 or 3 pounds per 100 square feet of row. Nitrogen helps in the development of leafy vegetables.

Sidedressings of fertilizer during growth are helpful to most vegetables. Fertilizer with high nitrogen is desirable for leaf crops, such as lettuce and Swiss chard. Seed- or fruit-producing crops, such as beans or tomatoes, require abundant potash.

When and how should phosphorus be applied to a vegetable garden? Apply phosphorus in a complete fertilizer, or in superphosphate, at the time of soil preparation, at the rate of 3 to 5 pounds per 100 square feet. Phosphorus *must* be worked into the soil as it does not move down from the surface.

When should I apply potash and in what form? In a complete fertilizer, 3 to 5 pounds, or in the form of muriate of potash 2 to 3 pounds, per 100 square feet. Or add this material to the manure or compost used in the garden. Potash is especially helpful in building up soils which do not grow good root crops or produce satisfactory stem plants, such as celery.

When should dried blood be used as a fertilizer?   Dried blood is used when an organic source of nitrogen is wanted. It is usually applied at the rate of 4 pounds per 100 square feet.

A sidedressing of fertilizer applied in a ring around the stem of young eggplant and cabbage.

What is "superphosphate," and what is its chief use in a vegetable garden?   Superphosphate is ground and treated phosphate rock that carries (usually) about 20 per cent phosphorus. ("Treble" phosphate carries about 45 per cent.) It is used in almost all complete fertilizers. On most new soils it can be applied separately in addition to other fertilizers, being thoroughly mixed with the soil in advance of planting, 4 to 6 pounds per 100 square feet.

Can a successful garden be made using only complete fertilizers and peat moss or humus without manure?   If manure is not obtainable, you can still have a successful garden by planting and turning under cover crops yearly, maintaining compost heaps to be used in the garden when rotted, and adding complete fertilizer when preparing the ground at planting time and as sidedressings during plant growth.

If manure and fertilizer are available, which do you recommend?   Use both: manure, when preparing the ground and when planting many crops; complete fertilizers, just before planting and as a sidedressing during the growth of the plants.

Is there a good general fertilizer for the vegetable garden?   Most fertilizer companies put out a "vegetable formula" fertilizer designed for use with most vegetable crops. This varies somewhat in different regions of the country. In general, a 5–10–5 mixture is a good all-purpose fertilizer for vegetables. For root crops, a 2–10–10 fertilizer, if available, is better; or supplement the 5–10–5 fertilizer with extra potash.

What are the food needs of different vegetables? While there are many special formulas made up for different vegetables that are grown on a commercial scale, in the home garden it is not practical to attempt to work out these differences. Homemade compost, plus a generous application of a high-quality complete fertilizer, will produce good crops. Where some special need exists, this can be provided for by an additional application of one of the several materials that carry nitrogen, phosphoric acid, or potash.

What is a good general fertilizer that can be used on potatoes, celery, tomatoes, and cabbage? A 5–10–5 or 5–10–10 fertilizer if your soil needs the extra potash. The first is better for cabbage and celery; the second is good for tomatoes and potatoes.

What fertilizer (grade of mixture) should be used on plants such as potatoes, tomatoes, corn (sweet), cabbage, and cauliflower? See the answer above. A general-purpose fertilizer can be supplemented by other materials for particular crops. For instance, lettuce, cabbage, and cauliflower during their early stages of growth are benefited by an abundance of nitrogen, and this can be supplied in the form of nitrate of soda or ammonium sulfate applied around the growing plants in addition to the general-purpose fertilizer which has been used.

What is the best way to fertilize new ground for vegetables? If the soil is acid, spread lime over the surface and apply at least 25 pounds of a 5–10–5 fertilizer on a 1,000-square-foot area before the ground is

There are different ways to apply fertilizer. The fertilizer can be broadcast over the ground and raked in (far left); dry fertilizer can be spread, about 4 inches from the root and stem area of plants, along rows; and liquid fertilizer, mixed according to directions on the container, can be applied to individual plants or groups of plants.

plowed or spaded. Then set all the plants and plant all the seed with starter solution.

How shall I fertilize a small space to produce the largest possible crops of different vegetables? (North Dakota.)   In areas where water is at a premium, it is difficult to use chemical fertilizer in the dry form. Keep the soil limed only if needed, and use animal manure if available. Then use a starter solution for setting the plants and when sowing. If more fertilizer is needed, use a sidedressing solution.

What can I do to enrich a vegetable garden plot 20 × 20 feet which has been planted regularly for 15 years and does not produce very good crops?   Very likely the soil is deficient in humus. If this is the case, commercial fertilizer alone will not produce good crops. Dig in a generous coating of compost or, if available, manure, applied 2 to 4 inches deep over the surface, or half that amount of compost.

Can you tell me the fertilizer necessary to make an active, producing vegetable garden soil out of former woodland?   This would depend upon the type of soil. It is best to make a test for acidity (see Section 1), then apply sufficient lime to bring the soil to a "slightly acid" condition—the best for most vegetables. Phosphoric acid is almost sure to be needed. Consult your local county Cooperative Extension agent or State Experiment Station for the general requirements of soil in your vicinity.

What should I use on a leaf soil in the woods to be able to grow a vegetable garden? I tried squash; the plants flowered but never produced any squashes; the blossoms all fell off. The same happened with cucumbers. Please tell me what kind of fertilizer to use.   The falling off of flowers without setting fruit usually indicates a deficiency in phosphoric acid and potash. Probably these should be used, in addition to a complete fertilizer, for two or three seasons, until the plant nutrients in your soil are more evenly balanced. Full sun is needed for all vegetables.

Does rotten manure have any effect on root crops, like scabbing or stunting?   Manure that is not thoroughly decomposed does sometimes make rough or scabby root crops. Other conditions, however, may be the cause. Potatoes grown in soil that is too heavily limed are almost certain to be scabby although no manure has been used on the ground for years.

Is there a connection between the type of fertilizer and the taste of vegetables or fruits?   Supposedly, no, but poor soil fertility will affect the flavor of fruiting vegetables such as melons.

I have room to place tomato plants between my rows of daffodils during the month of May. What would be the best fertilizer to use? Would

manure dug in be injurious to the bulbs? Manure can cause bulb diseases; use a complete fertilizer for the tomatoes. Superphosphate may be added, as this would not only help the tomato crop but would also be of decided benefit to the daffodils.

What causes tough-skinned and very small carrots and beets grown in the same ground that grows excellent tomatoes? Some deficiency in the soil, such as a lack of phosphorus, which builds strong roots. Apply superphosphate, 4 to 5 pounds per 100 square feet. If possible, have the soil tested by your county agent, who will give you advice on its improvement.

Our soil is sandy. What amount of fertilizer should we use? We have heard so much about the damage caused by too much fertilizer that we're confused. Sandy soil usually requires larger additions of humus and nutrients (in the form of compost—manure, if available—or fertilizer) than heavy soils. The method of application, moreover, is different. Sandy soils are likely to leach badly. Several light applications during the season give better results than one heavy application. Everything possible should be done to increase the humus content of sandy soil by using manure, humus in the form of compost, peat moss, or green crops for turning under.

What is the best time to fertilize a vegetable garden—fall or spring? Slow-acting materials such as lime and superphosphate may best be applied in the fall; or, if in the spring, as early and as far in advance of planting as possible. The more quick-acting materials (such as the ordinary "complete" fertilizer) and well-decomposed compost should be applied in the spring. The very quick-acting fertilizers, like nitrate of soda or sulfate of ammonia, and the somewhat slower dried blood or tankage is best used at the time of planting or applied around plants after some growth has been made.

Is it best to put stable manure on a vegetable garden in the fall or spring? This depends largely upon the condition of the manure. If thoroughly decayed, it is usually best to apply it in the spring. If in a fresh state, apply it in the fall or winter. If manure is applied long in advance of planting, there is a considerable loss of nitrogen, especially in light soils.

If a vegetable garden is covered with manure in the fall, is fall cultivation really necessary? Fall tilling is highly desirable unless there is danger of erosion. The manure will decay more thoroughly and evenly instead of merely drying out and it will also increase the bacterial action in the soil. Mixing the manure with the soil will also help retain nutrients. Earlier planting is made possible.

Is there anything I can do in the fall to improve a plot to be used for vegetables in the spring?   A heavy application of compost or manure dug into the ground in the fall will put it into good condition for spring planting. Even if manure or compost is not available for tilling or digging, leaving the ground in ridges and furrows will help put it into better mechanical condition. If lime is needed, fall is the best time to apply it.

Is it a good idea to use wood ashes on a vegetable garden plot? When is the best time to apply them?   Wood ashes contain potash and are also an excellent soil conditioner. Usually it is preferable to apply them in the fall, as they are not as quick-acting as most commercial fertilizers. However, if this cannot be done, they can safely be applied in the spring.

Do wood ashes on the ground make parsnips woody, and if not, what is the cause?   Wood ashes, which add both lime and potash to the soil, are excellent for almost all vegetables. It is much more likely that woody or fibrous parsnips are the result of conditions causing slow growth. All root crops, to be brittle and tender, must develop quite rapidly and without a check. Lack of sufficient nitrogen, or a prolonged period of dry weather, would cause a woody condition.

Is soot from a furnace motor stoker beneficial for a vegetable garden?   No.

Should coal ashes be used on a vegetable garden? If so, when?   Sifted coal ashes are beneficial to the physical condition of most soils, especially to heavy ones. The winter's supply of ashes, screened and spread over the surface as they are produced in the winter, can be dug or tilled under in the spring.

In growing vegetables, is there much difference in the results of broadcasting commercial fertilizer before planting or spreading it in the rows when planting?   Formerly, most fertilizers were applied by broadcasting before planting or in the row at the time of planting. The modern practice is to use ½ or ⅔ of the fertilizer in 1, 2, or 3 side-dressings along the sides of the rows during growth. This has been found to produce a bigger yield and to maintain growth at a more even rate of development—highly desirable for most crops.

How should fertilizing be done when transplanting vegetable plants from a cold frame to an open garden?   Fertilizer is applied about a week in advance and thoroughly mixed in with the top 3 or 4 inches of soil. Or compost or a complete fertilizer is thoroughly mixed with the soil in the bottoms of holes in which plants are to be set.

Should vegetables be fertilized after being sown or transplanted into an open garden? If so, when and how? If the soil is rich and fertile, this may not be necessary. Otherwise many vegetables, when about half grown, benefit from the application of a sidedressing. Use 3 to 5 pounds of fertilizer to each 100 feet of row. Spread it thinly down each side of the row, 3 or 4 inches from the plants, and cultivate in.

ACIDITY

What is meant by an "acid" soil? One in which the chemical reaction is acid instead of alkaline, as measured by the pH scale. This scale corresponds, in a way, to the thermometer scale for measuring temperature.

What is the meaning of pH? See the introduction to Section 1. A pH reading of 7 indicates the neutral point. Figures below pH 7 (pH 5.5, for instance) indicate the degree of acidity; figures above pH 7, the degree of alkalinity.

Is it worthwhile to have my soil tested before I plant vegetables? It is well to have the soil of an untried piece of ground tested before starting to improve its condition, especially if you have reason to think it is worn out or unfertile. Consult your county Cooperative Extension agent or State Agricultural Experiment Station about testing your soil and how to improve it.

How can I tell if my soil is acid? There are available inexpensive testing kits which anyone can use.

Do vegetables prefer acid or alkaline soil? Most vegetables are grown most successfully in slightly acid soil, i.e., soil with a pH of 6 to 7. Soil with a pH 5 to 5.6 will grow potatoes, sweet potatoes, watermelons; pH 5.2 to 6—eggplants, peppers, tomatoes; pH 5.6 to 6.8—beans, carrots, corn, parsley, parsnips, pumpkins, salsify, Swiss chard, turnips; pH 6 to 7.2—beets, broccoli, cabbage, cucumbers, endive, leaf lettuce, muskmelons, peas, radishes, rhubarb; pH 6.4 to 7.6—asparagus, cauliflower, celery, leeks, head lettuce, onions, spinach.

What vegetables are good for a very acid soil? We cannot raise peas. Potatoes, sweet potatoes, and watermelons. Liming the soil (see Soil Preparation) would make it suitable for peas.

What treatment is necessary when beans, carrots, and beets are stunted, but 10 feet away they grow fine and strong? If poor drainage is not the cause, there may be an extremely acid spot in the soil. A soil test would prove this. If not, an additional application of a complete fertilizer should correct the trouble.

What steps can I take to correct the condition of my vegetable plot, which is very acid? See the introduction to Section 1, and Soil Preparation, this section.

GREEN MANURES (COVER CROPS)

When a garden writer advises the use of "green manure," what is meant? Any crop grown for the purpose of digging or tilling it under to decay in the soil—and thus add humus—is called a green manure. Long used in farm practice, green manuring in the home vegetable garden is rapidly gaining favor.

Is the practice of green manuring worthwhile for the home garden? Most decidedly, especially in sections where it is difficult to procure animal manures. This is a good inexpensive way to build up the humus content of the soil.

Do you advise the use of green manures for conditioning a vegetable plot? Yes, by all means. By putting in a cover crop in late summer or autumn as soon as vegetable crops are harvested, and digging it under in the spring when 6 to 10 inches high, the humus content in the soil will be maintained. (See Section 1.)

What is the best way to handle a green-manure crop (rye) that has grown too tall to be dug under conveniently? Mow the tops and add them to a compost heap, or use for mulching; dig under stubble and roots, which will add considerable humus.

What is the best way to maintain garden fertility? One of the most important factors in maintaining fertility is to keep up the humus content of the soil. This can be done by using manure or compost, and by growing green crops whenever possible to be turned under to decay. (See Section 1.) After the soil is producing well, the practice outlined above, plus moderate yearly applications of a complete fertilizer, should maintain the fertility indefinitely.

What should I sow after plowing my garden plot in the fall? Unless the ground is tilled or spaded by the first of September (in the latitude of New York) there is little use in sowing a green-manure or cover crop where early planting is to be done. Rye and rye grass are the two most satisfactory crops for fall and winter growth to turn under for green manure. In the latitude of Washington, D.C., and farther south, these crops will make considerable growth during the winter months and can be sown in late September or early October.

Which makes a better green-manure crop for a vegetable garden—rye or rye grass? Both winter rye and perennial rye grass make excellent green-manure crops. Both can be sown any time from midsummer until frost, and are perfectly hardy through the winter. Rye germinates somewhat faster and makes a more rapid early growth. It is coarser and more difficult to dig under in the spring if the job is not done early. Rye produces more bulk in a shorter time than rye grass, but both are satisfactory. Rye continues to grow whenever air temperatures are over 40° F. during the winter.

Sowing a cover crop in the fall and turning it under in the spring is one way to increase the humus content in the soil, as this forkful of winter rye shows.

What is the best time to plant sweet clover and soybeans, and when should these two cover crops be turned under? Sweet clover, a biennial, may be sown early in the spring but will make a suitable growth for green manuring even if sown as late as mid-June. Turn under when it is 8 to 12 inches high, or any time before its stalks become hard; sow in midsummer to turn under the following spring. Sow soybeans after the danger of frost has passed and turn under any time after sufficient growth has been made and before their main stems begin to get hard.

What are several good summer and winter cover crops? Summer: cowpeas, soybeans, oats, buckwheat, and Hubam or annual sweet clover. Winter: rye, perennial rye grass, or (if sown not later than mid-August) crimson clover or vetch.

Is there any evidence that growing vetch on land will inoculate peas? Yes. The bacteria left in the soil from the vetch roots will help the growth of peas.

My vegetable garden is covered with leaves; because of furrows, it is difficult to rake them off. Shall I burn them or turn them under in the spring? By all means, plow or dig under the leaves instead of burning them. Anything which will decay that can be turned into the soil will help add humus.

What vegetables or flowers will grow in 100 per cent humus? A shallow pond drained many years ago is dry black humus that I am told should be mixed with topsoil, now hard to get. Undoubtedly topsoil mixed with the humus would improve it. Many humus-rich soils, however, will grow good crops of most vegetables, provided a complete fertilizer is applied. Such soils are used by many truck gardeners. Celery is the most productive crop on high organic soils. Try it for one season before adding topsoil and then use it only for such vegetables that may not do well in the humus.

Seed Sowing

SEEDS

How can I be sure that I am buying good vegetable seed? By making your purchases only from reliable firms that specialize in seeds. The great skill and effort that go into producing high-quality seeds are not apparent in the seed packet—only in the crop that results.

For how many seasons are vegetable seeds good? There is considerable variation in the length of time that different vegetable seeds maintain their vitality. Onions, okra, and parsnips, for instance, can be counted on for only one year. Beans, beets, members of the cabbage family, and most vine crops are good for three or four years.

Will seeds that are purchased for one season, and not used, germinate the following spring? If they have been stored in a dry place, they probably will germinate well except for those mentioned above. There is no treatment that will improve their germination but the germination can be tested before planting. (See below for method.)

I have considerable green bean seed left. Can it be used for the next planting season? The seeds usually germinate well for several years. However, to make sure that germination will be satisfactory, sprout a few of them on moist blotting paper (in a saucer) before planting them. The percentage of germination can then be accurately determined.

What vegetable seeds can the home gardener harvest without risking deterioration or cross-pollination? What steps can a gardener take with the more difficult varieties? This is a big question to answer here. In a dry season, with good, clear weather, many kinds can be grown. Tomatoes, beans, peppers, eggplants, lettuce, endive, and onions are self-pollinated. Most of the others are cross-pollinated, and for good seed would have to be hand-pollinated under bags.

What is the proper method of saving and treating seeds from a vegetable garden so they will grow the following year? In general, vegetable seeds are gathered as they begin to reach maturity, indicated by the seed pods turning brown and hard. They can then be spread out on trays or in flats until they ripen further. During this period they must be protected from moisture. When completely ripened, they are stored in tight containers. Short-lived seeds can be stored at below freezing temperatures. In regular storage, temperature and humidity combined must not exceed 100° F., i.e., at 60° F., humidity should not exceed 40 per cent; at 50°, not above 50 per cent.

INDOOR SOWING

What vegetable seeds can be started in a house, greenhouse, hotbed, or cold frame in the spring? Tomatoes, peppers, eggplants, early lettuce, celery, celeriac, early cabbage, early cauliflower, and early broccoli; beets also transplant readily, if a few extra-early ones are wanted; also, sweet potato vines.

What is needed in the soil to start vegetable seedlings indoors? The soil for starting seedlings need not be rich. The mechanical condition is more important. A mixture of ⅓ garden soil, ⅓ sand, and ⅓ peat moss or compost, thoroughly mixed and passed through a sieve, gives good results, but may carry damping-off disease. Therefore, the sterile soilless mixes, such as Jiffy Mix, Readi-Earth, etc., are more convenient. They can be bought at garden centers.

Is it possible to have any amount of success in starting vegetable seeds indoors if there is no direct sunlight? Seeds will start but will not progress satisfactorily unless they have long hours of direct sunshine. Fluorescent tubes can be used successfully to supplement daylight by turning them on at 4 P.M., off at 9 P.M. Without daylight, keep the tubes on 14 hours.

When is the best time to seed vegetables in a flat before transplanting them in the spring? This depends on what vegetables you are growing, whether they are hardy or tender, and the length of time these take from seed to food crop. In general, seeds are planted in flats in late February and early March to be set out in April and May. Cabbage and broccoli started in February can be set out in early April. Tomatoes started at the same time are transplanted first into 2- and then into 3- or 4-inch pots before they can be set out in May. Peppers and eggplant seeds, which are very tender, can be sown in March as the plants cannot go into the open garden until all danger of frost is past and the ground has warmed up.

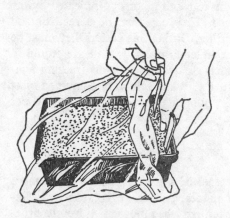

After sowing seeds, slip the flat into a plastic kitchen bag to retain moisture. Place the flat in a warm place out of direct sun. As soon as seedlings appear, remove the flat from its bag and place in sunshine or under fluorescent lights.

Should vegetable seedlings in flats, pans, or a seed bed be thinned before they are transplanted? If seeds are sown far enough apart, thinning will probably not be necessary. If the little plants are crowded, however, thinning is advisable, just as soon as they are well up.

What temperature should one have to start plants from seed indoors or in a greenhouse? Night temperature for hardy plants, 40° to 50° F.; for tender plants (tomatoes, peppers, eggplants), 50° to 60°. These are minimums; 5° to 10° F. higher will do no harm. To germinate the seeds, 60° for hardy plants (cabbage, etc.) and 70° for tender ones.

How can lettuce, tomatoes, peppers, cabbages, and other plants from seed be grown indoors? (New York.) To grow vegetable plants successfully indoors from seed you must have a very sunny window or a sun porch with a southern or southeastern exposure. Use fluorescent tubes to supplement sunshine during short days in late winter. Start hardy vegetable seeds (cabbage family, lettuce, etc.) February 15 to March 1 in flats of prepared soil. Start tender vegetables (peppers, eggplants, and tomatoes) about March 15, also in flats. Transplant to other flats when true leaves are formed and (for extra good plants) finally to small pots. Harden off the hardy vegetables outdoors in a cold frame from about April 1 to April 15 before setting in an open garden. Tender vegetables are hardened in a frame beginning about May 1. For other localities, seeds are started about 2 months before they can go out into a cold frame for hardening off.

Can vegetable seedlings be grown under artificial light? Fluorescent tubes can be used with the tubes about 4 inches above the upper leaves. If the seedlings are growing in a very cool basement, daylight white or warm white tubes can be used in combination with 4 20-watt incandescent bulbs spaced between the tubes. If the incandescent sockets are wired in series, instead of parallel, they will emit more red light (the color lacking in the fluorescent tubes).

Use an artificial soil medium such as vermiculite, calcined clay, perlite mixed with peat moss, or one of the packaged soilless mixes available from garden centers. Water whenever needed, but add a house-plant fertilizer (at about $\frac{1}{10}$ the strength recommended on the package) every time you water.

Before transplanting out-of-doors, harden the plants in a sunny window or cold frame for two or three days.

The seedlings growing in my south window grow spindly. What is wrong? Probably cloudy weather in March and April. Elevate the seed planter with a book. Or supplement daylight with a 60-watt incandescent light turned on all day during dark days and at 4 P.M. on clear days, off at 9 P.M. One bulb suspended 3 feet above flats will stimulate an area a yard square.

How should I label newly planted seeds? Each group of seeds planted should be labeled. Place a small wooden label with the name of

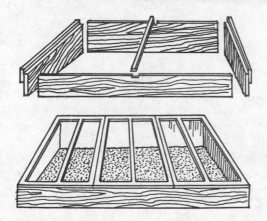

The use of a cold frame or a hotbed helps to get the vegetable garden off to an early start in the spring. (Above) Wooden sections for the frame before being assembled in the garden. (Bottom) Typical frame with a lightweight sash (cover), each 2 × 4 feet.

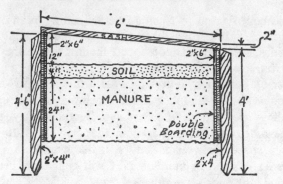

Cross section of a manure-heated hot-bed. Or use electric cables for the heat source.

the plant, variety, source, and planting date in a pan or at the end of a row in a flat or bed.

What is "bottom" heat? When is it used in growing vegetable seedlings? Warmth applied beneath the soil in which the seeds are grown, as by placing a flat of seeds on a heater or radiator. It is used to hasten the germination of tender or difficult seeds. *It should not be continued after seedlings are well up.* Soil readings above 90° are harmful. Insulate the top of a radiator if used: Direct heat could injure the seeds. A cardboard carton flattened out will do. Electric heating cables can be purchased at garden centers or from mail-order seed houses and can be regulated to exact temperatures.

End of cold frame marked with rows for seed sowing.

How long can newly sown seeds in pans, flats, or seed beds be kept covered from the light?   Until germination takes place. They must then be uncovered *immediately.*

How can I water young seedlings to keep them from being beaten down by the spray of water?   If grown in flats, pans, or pots, they should be watered *from the bottom,* by placing the container in a tray or pan partly filled with water. If grown in a seed bed or in an open garden, they should be watered with a very fine spray, but long enough to thoroughly soak the soil; water early in the morning, so they can dry off before night.

How can I heat a cold frame for early seed sowing?   You can grow your own plants (to be set out in a garden) in a one-sash hotbed built against a cellar window, if you have some heat there. Otherwise, 4 100-watt light bulbs placed in the sash along the sides and lighted on cold nights would give sufficient heat to keep the plants growing. Or buy electric heating cables from a garden supply center. You can cover the sash in late afternoon to hold in as much heat as possible from the sun. Grow the frost-tolerant plants first and the warm-weather plants later.

A temporary cold frame can be made in a jiffy with scrap lumber. The sash or covering can be plastic sheeting stapled to a wood frame.

How can I prevent seedlings in flats from turning to the light so that their stems are crooked?   Give them all the sunshine possible. If they still "draw" to the light, turn the flat or pan daily. (See the previous questions on supplementing daylight with artificial light.)

OUTDOOR SOWING

How should the ground be prepared for seed sowing of vegetables?   Spade or till. Lime, if necessary. Fertilize. Rake or harrow to a fine, crumbly surface immediately before the seeds are sown. The surface should be even. If in doubt, consult local gardeners or your county

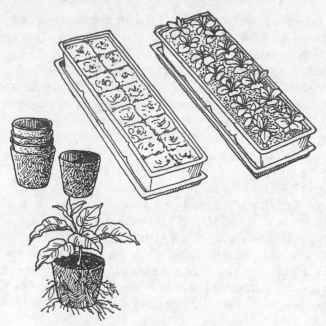

*For the lazy gardener: Preplanted
seed flats can be purchased that
require only water to initiate seed
germination. Other aids include
various kinds and sizes of peat
pots. The roots grow into and
through the peat so that the pot
and the plant are set out together
in open ground.*

agent through the Cooperative Extension Service in regard to your lime
and fertilizer needs.

**In planting seeds (in the open) for later transplanting to permanent
positions, shall I broadcast or plant in rows?**   Plant in rows so that you
will know where to look for seedlings and to facilitate weeding and
transplanting.

**Should vegetable seeds be treated with anything prior to being
planted?**   The only seed treatment home gardeners should be concerned with is a fungicide treatment. Peas, beans, corn, and similar
large seeds that are highly susceptible to rot diseases are best treated

with captan, a mild, protective, nonpoisonous fungicide. Some seed companies provide this service automatically for the seeds that need it; others will do it on request. Another harmful fungus disease is called "damping off," which attacks seedlings at the soil line, causing them to keel over and die. The disease is most troublesome indoors and is best prevented by using only clean, new containers and sterile soil mixes, or sterile planter pots such as Jiffy-7 peat pellets.

How can I hasten the germination of hard-shelled seeds like peas, New Zealand spinach, celery, and parsley? By soaking them in tepid water for 24 to 48 hours before they are sown. Then dry them off and sow at once. New Zealand spinach seed will not sprout in warm soil. Sow as early as the soil is workable.

What vegetable seeds are planted in the open garden in early spring? Peas, radishes, lettuce, cress, roquette, spinach, onions and leeks, parsnips, salsify, dandelions, early beets and carrots, kohlrabi, turnips, Swiss chard, fava or broad beans, and New Zealand spinach.

This well-developed eggplant seedling, with its roots growing through the peat pot, is ready to be planted—pot and all—in the open ground, if frost danger is past. Such tender vegetables as eggplant, pepper, and tomato are excellent subjects for peat pots.

Which tender vegetable seeds cannot be safely planted until the soil is thoroughly warm? Snap beans, lima beans, corn, cucumbers, squash, pumpkins, melons, and okra.

What is a trench, a furrow, a drill, and a hill? *Trench*—A ditchlike excavation 6 inches or more wide and a foot or more deep, made when spading soil. Or the term is also applied to deep drills in which celery or peas are planted. *Furrow*—The hollow between the ridges of soil thrown up in the process of tilling or of digging. Also, a very deep drill (such as a "furrow" for planting potatoes). *Drill*—A shallow mark in the soil in which seed is sown; usually less than an inch deep. *Hill*—A low, broad, flat mound in which seed is sown. Also, the spot where a few seeds are sown when the rows are not continuous but have spaces between a group of plants—as a "hill" of corn or of beans—even though the ground is perfectly level.

How can I get my seed rows straight? By stretching a stout cord taut between two stakes so that the cord lies along the ground where the row is to be made. In using the hoe to form the seed row, keep one side of the blade against the cord, which acts as a guide to the hoe. Or use a pointed stick, run along the cord for very shallow drills.

How should rows be fertilized before seeds are sown? In the intensively cultivated garden, it is better to broadcast the fertilizer over the surface and rake it thoroughly into the top 2 or 3 inches of soil a few days before seed is sown. Where rows are 2 feet or more apart, the fertilizer may be worked in only along the rows.

How deep should seeds be covered with soil? Not more than 2 to 4 times their own smallest diameter. For early sowings, and in clay soils, cover somewhat less than normal depth.

I planted lettuce and dandelion seed last spring and they did not grow. Why? Mustard seed did grow. The trouble may have been too deep planting. Lettuce seeds should be scarcely covered and sown in very well-prepared light soil. Lettuce seedlings cannot push up through a hard surface. Dandelion seeds also should be planted very shallowly. Often the germination is low. Mustard, which is an unusually strong grower, will generally sprout even under unfavorable conditions. Some lettuce seed, particularly 'Grand Rapids', will not sprout if covered. The seed must have light to germinate.

How thickly should vegetable seeds be sown? Small seeds, 4 or 5 times as thickly as the plants will finally stand. Thus, if turnips need 3 inches of space between the plants to develop, sow from 12 to 20 seeds per foot. This permits proper spacing after thinning out. Large seeds (such as pole beans or squash) may be sown 1½ to 2 times as thickly as plants are to stand after thinning.

Is it advisable to water vegetable seed rows after sowing? If the ground is at all dry, it is very much better to water the seed rows *before* sowing. After the drill is made, run a slow stream of water from a hose or watering can along the bottom. Let the water soak in, then sow the seed.

How early and how deep should vegetable seeds be planted? (Maryland.) In most parts of Maryland the planting of hardy vegetables (see the Introduction) can begin about the middle of March. This, however, will vary with the season. Practically all seed packets contain directions for when to sow and the depth of planting for the varieties enclosed. For more complete instructions, get the bulletin on this subject published by the State Agricultural Experiment Station at College Park.

What time should a garden be started in western Suffolk County on Long Island? For hardy seeds such as lettuce, between April 1 to the middle of the month, but peas and broad beans can be planted in mid-March.

Is there anything gained by planting by signs—such as the phases of the moon? Many gardeners believe so, but there is no scientific evidence to this effect. Planting by such a sign as "when white oak leaves are the size of squirrels' ears" (for corn) is quite different, as the size of leaves is determined by seasonal weather conditions.

Maintenance

THINNING

What is meant by "thinning" vegetables? This is the term applied to the practice of pulling out surplus seedling plants so that those left can have room to develop properly. In order to be sure of having rows without skips, gardeners sow extra seeds in the row. If germination is good, a surplus of plants is the result.

How can one tell how many plants to remove when "thinning out"? In directions for growing vegetables, the distance apart at which they should stand is given. Carrots, for instance, are usually thinned to about 2 inches apart; onions, 2 to 3 inches; beets, 3 inches; beans, 4 to 5 inches, etc.

Can any use be made of thinnings? Thinnings of many vegetables can be used. Young beets, for instance, make excellent boiled greens; small onions may be used as "scallions," for eating green. Baby carrots may be canned. Or the thinnings of many kinds may be used for transplanting, if additional plants are wanted.

After being thinned, my plants wilted badly; can anything be done to prevent this? Yes. First of all, begin thinning just as soon as seedlings are well up—the bigger they get, the more those left will be disturbed. Thin when the soil is moist, after a rain or a good watering. Cutting off surplus seedlings with a pair of sharp-pointed scissors avoids disturbing those left to grow and prevents wilting.

How soon should rows of small vegetable plants be thinned? Just as soon as the individual plants begin to crowd each other and before there is the slightest chance of their becoming "leggy" for lack of light and air.

Is more than one thinning advisable? With plants that grow closely in the row—such as onions from seed, carrots, and beets—two or three thinnings are often made as the plants grow; this leaves a margin of safety in case of injury or loss among the plants that are left.

TRANSPLANTING

How large should seedlings be before being transplanted? Seedlings should be transplanted as soon as they form their first true leaves (these are the third and fourth leaves to form) and before they become crowded in the flat, pan, or seed bed.

How often should vegetable seedlings grown indoors be transplanted before being set in the garden? Usually once—from the seed flat to a peat pot and then outdoors. However, there are seed-starting systems that avoid any indoor transplanting, such as Jiffy-7 peat pellets. These are pellets of compressed peat that expand to seven times their height when water is added to them. The peat is held in place by a netting. Two or three seeds are sown in a depression at the top, and on sprouting the weakest seedlings can be thinned out, leaving one strong seedling to grow into a healthy transplant. When transplanting time comes, you can plant pot and all into the garden, although gently removing the netting will ensure stronger root development.

What are the advantages of pot-grown plants over young plants cut out of the flat and planted in the garden? Pot-grown plants suffer little or no shock when they are set in the open garden, while plants removed from flats or seed beds have to recover from the disturbance to their root systems.

When are tender plants set out in the vegetable garden? When the ground warms up and the weather is settled. Tomatoes can be set out about May 15 to June 1 in the vicinity of New York; peppers and eggplants, a little later.

When can hardy vegetable plants be set in the open garden? Just about the time the last expected hard frost is past. Many beginners delay planting much longer than necessary.

How can I prevent newly set vegetable plants from wilting? Set after sunset or on a cloudy or rainy day. Water well after setting. If necessary, cover during the hours of high sun for a day or two, using newspapers or baskets. Uncover as soon as the sun is low.

Should newly transplanted vegetables be watered after the plants are set? Yes, they should be thoroughly watered. Leave a slight depression around the stem when planting and fill this with water.

When transplanting, does it help to trim back vegetable plants? Such plants as lettuce, cabbage and other members of the cabbage family, and beets may have their outside leaves trimmed back before setting. This practice is particularly helpful in setting plants which are apt to wilt.

What are Hotkaps? Are they useful in transplanting? Hotkaps are miniature paper tents to be set over seeds or young plants in the open garden to protect them from frost, wind, and insects during the early part of the season. They are of use in transplanting. They must be removed, however, before the plants are crowded; preferably, as soon as they are established and begin to grow after setting. Discarded plastic milk and other beverage containers can also be used (cut off the bottom of the container first; leave the top open for ventilation).

Hotkaps, available from garden centers, are miniature greenhouses for individual plants. With Hotkaps, tender seedlings grown indoors can be planted outdoors nearly 3 weeks earlier than normal. After a few weeks, tear a hole in the top of the tent to allow room for the growing plant.

If a late frost is forecast after setting young plants in the open garden, can anything be done to save the plants? Yes, they may be covered with Hotkaps, newspaper tents, or gallon-size plastic beverage containers (with their bottoms cut off) until the weather warms up.

CULTIVATION

Just what is meant by the term "cultivation" as used in garden articles and bulletins? Cultivation is the breaking up and stirring about of the soil around and between growing plants.

How do "deep" and "shallow" cultivation differ? Shallow cultivation means stirring the soil to a depth of 1 or 2 inches. Deep cultivation may penetrate the soil as much as 5 or 6 inches, but usually less.

Should plants be cultivated to the same depth throughout the season? No. Usually deep cultivation is given just after transplanting or when plants from seed are still small. As they grow, and the roots spread out into the space between rows, the depth of cultivation is reduced.

What tool do you recommend for hand cultivation? The scuffle hoe is the most useful tool for hand cultivation. Sometimes known as the Dutch hoe or the English scuffle hoe, this tool, with various minor modifications, is now manufactured in the United States.

How long should cultivating be kept up? The longer, the better; and at least until crops have neared maturity and pretty well cover the ground. If a mulch is used, stop cultivating as soon as it is in place.

How can I prevent heavy crops of weeds from developing among my vegetables? By using a mulch. The only other way is by clean cultivation, which takes far more time.

What is meant by "hilling"? Drawing the soil up around growing plants with the hoe for the purpose of (a) covering small weeds; (b) supporting the plants; or (c) blanching the stems to make them more tender.

What vegetables require hilling? In the home garden, very few (in farming, the practice is more general). Potatoes, corn, broccoli, and bush beans are often hilled for support; celery, leeks, and sometimes asparagus are hilled for blanching. As a rule—except in heavy soils—the less hilling, the better.

WEED CONTROL

Are weed killers available for vegetables? Yes, but since they can be used only on certain crops, read the directions on those sold in your local garden center for specific information.

What general procedure would you suggest for keeping down weeds in a vegetable garden?   Cultivate between the rows with a hoe or roto-tiller (the latter is practical only in a large garden) and remove weeds *by the roots* from the rows of seedling vegetables. Water thoroughly and then mulch with grass cuttings, hay, marsh hay, straw, or other available light material such as shredded sugarcane or ground corn cobs. Black plastic mulch is also highly effective and saves work. The prevention of weeds is much more practical than their removal after they are well established. Check your local garden center for chemical controls for annual weeds.

WATERING

Which vegetables need water in dry weather?   In prolonged droughts, all vegetables benefit from irrigation. Those most susceptible to drought injury are peas, celery, spinach, and lettuce.

Does it harm plants to water in the heat of the day?   Not if water is fed slowly and deeply into the soil from the end of a hose from which the nozzle has been removed. Lightly sprinkling the surface of the soil and the leaves in high sunlight in addition to deep watering reduces leaf

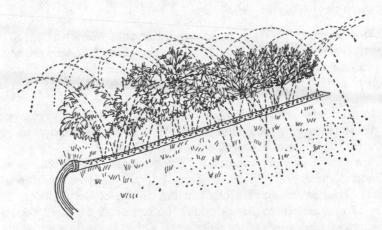

A sprinkler type of hose applies water through minute holes in a gentle spray that soaks the soil without packing its surface or spattering mud. Another type of perforated hose applies a trickle of water, without a spray, directly to the soil.

and soil temperature and may prevent the loss of seedlings. Growing crops are often watered with overhead irrigation in full sunshine, but early morning or evening is better, as less water is lost by evaporation.

Does irrigation tend to bring plant roots to the surface and thus weaken plants? Only if the watering is insufficient. If a "rain machine" or rotary sprinkler is used, it should be left on long enough in each area to really moisten the soil several inches deep, just as when watering slowly with a hose.

How often should an area be watered in dry weather? Often enough to keep the soil uniformly moist at all times to a depth of several inches. Fluctuating moisture is bad for tomatoes. It causes blossom-end rot.

How deep should the soil be moistened by watering? Water long enough to moisten the soil to a depth of at least 4 inches. One watering will then last a week to 10 days.

Some authorities contend that watering vegetable plants weakens their root systems and makes them "soft." Is this true? No. Lack of moisture is one of the biggest causes of poor results in a vegetable garden. If it is possible to get water to the vegetable garden, the crops harvested on watered areas will well repay the gardener for his effort and expense.

SUPPORTS

What supports do you recommend for pole beans? Use 8- to 10-foot poles driven 1 to 1½ feet into the ground and made into a "tepee," using 3 poles for each support. Plant the beans at the foot of each pole. If single poles are used, drive them at least 2 feet into the ground.

On what support shall I grow my lima beans? These will grow readily on a fence with additional wires or cords added above to give sufficient height. Poles can also be used. (See above.)

How shall I support tomatoes? Use tomato towers or cages—wire cylinders 5 to 6 feet high made from heavy mesh wire (6 × 6-inch mesh). Position the tomato plant in the middle of the cylinder. Side shoots from the tomato grow through the mesh and the plant becomes self-supporting, saving the gardener work. Other methods, such as staking (tying plants to 7-foot-long stakes) and using tripods, where tomato plants are tied to form a "tepee," are satisfactory, but more time-consuming. Staking tomatoes is not necessary, but it produces cleaner fruit, makes harvesting easier, and uses less space.

Do side shoots need to be pruned from staked tomatoes? When growing tomatoes up a single stake, pruning of suckers and side shoots is advisable, but the modern method is to use tomato towers (see previous answer), where all side shoots are allowed to grow. Providing that the soil is fertile and adequate irrigation maintains proper moisture in the soil, the growth of side shoots and suckers will not reduce crop yields.

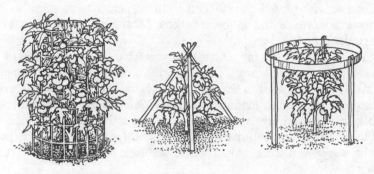

Three methods of supporting tomato plants. (Left) Within cylinders of heavy-mesh (about 6 × 6 inches) wire. The cylinders should be held upright by heavy stakes. (Center) "Tepee" and (right) hoop methods.

How shall I grow my tall peas to support them adequately? Peas can be planted along a 4- or 5-foot fence. Encourage vines to climb by setting cut brush as soon as vines begin to form. Set the brush *outside* the row of peas, on an angle to the fence. Netting for supporting peas is sold in garden centers for those who don't have access to a wood lot.

Should dwarf peas be supported? If dwarf peas are held up with a section of chicken wire or pea brush (cut about 3 feet long and driven firmly into the ground), they will bear more heavily and be easier to pick.

When brush is not available to support peas, what is the best substitute? A special coarse netting of cord, made for the purpose, is available. Sections of chicken wire will do, or buy special netting at garden centers.

Can vine crops be grown on supports and thus save ground space? Yes, cucumbers, melons, and even squash do well on trellises or fences.

MULCHING

What are the advantages of using black plastic as a mulch?   Black plastic is highly desirable with warm-weather crops such as tomatoes, melons, cucumbers, and peppers. Black absorbs heat, so black plastic warms up the soil early and helps to maintain that warmth even during periods of temperature fluctuation (such as cool nights), allowing plants to make rapid growth and yield earlier. The plastic also helps conserve moisture and suffocate weeds. Most garden centers offer biodegradable plastic.

What can be used for mulch in a vegetable garden in place of peat moss?   Peat moss is not a good mulch unless mixed with other materials. It is better used in the soil to supply humus. Moreover, there are many other materials that are less costly. Select a material locally available in your vicinity such as sawdust, ground corn cobs, buckwheat hulls, pine needles, salt marsh hay, bagasse (sugarcane waste), peanut hulls, seaweed, leaves, ground bark, or black plastic (see previous answer).

When should mulching be applied in the vegetable garden?   As soon as the plants are well started, the ground can be cultivated, weeds removed, area thoroughly watered, and mulch applied.

Is a summer mulch advisable in the vegetable garden?   It can be used successfully to keep weeds under control with crops that do not need frequent cultivation. It also serves to conserve soil moisture, to absorb rain where it falls, and to keep the soil beneath it loose and friable.

Can old newspapers be used as a mulch?   Yes, especially to form walkways between rows of vegetables to create a clean, weed-free walk area. Consider using strips of black plastic for your rows of plants and layers of newspapers between the plastic strips. The heavy newspapers will also effectively anchor the plastic to prevent damage by wind.

HARVESTING

How can I tell when vegetables such as onions, potatoes, beans, and squash are ready to pick?   This depends upon the purpose for which they are wanted—whether for immediate use, for storage, or for freezing. Onions can be pulled when small for green onions. For storage, they should be picked when the tops have fallen over. For pickling, you want them when they are an inch in diameter. For immediate use, potatoes can be used as soon as they are big enough to make it worthwhile to dig them. For storage, they should be dug when the vines are practically dead. For freezing, canning, or immediate use, snap beans should be picked before the pods show the location of the seeds. Cabbage and head lettuce should be picked when the heads are solid. Fruits should be picked green or ripe, depending on the use you wish to make of them. Green fruits, such as tomatoes, are best when they are full grown, just before they begin to turn color.

What vegetables can be gathered after frost?   There are two types: those that will withstand a light frost without being injured and those that will survive after fairly hard freezing. Among the former are cauliflower, lettuce, chard, celery, and such root crops as beets and carrots. Celery well banked up will stand fairly hard frost. The real tough ones, which resist quite heavy freezing, are Brussels sprouts, cabbage, kale, broccoli, parsnips, salsify, rutabagas, turnips, leeks, spinach, Chinese cabbage, and escarole.

How can one tell when melons are ripe?   As soon as they can be lifted easily from the stem.

When New Zealand spinach grows too fast and gets ahead of us, what can be done with it?   Use the tips for pot greens. Cut back the old stems to within a few inches of the crown to stimulate bushy new growth. It can also be frozen for winter use.

Our okra grew well, but was woody and tough. What was wrong?   You did not harvest it soon enough. Pods should be barely finger length.

When are edible soybeans ready to cook green? When are they harvested to be used dry?   As soon as the pods have filled out. They remain edible as green shell beans for about 2 weeks. After the pods turn brown, they must be dried for use as dried beans. Harvest these before the pods burst open, as this will result in the beans shelling out on the ground. Pull up the plants and strip off the pods into a basket. Keep in a dry, warm place until they shell out.

When should summer squash be picked?   When very young (about 5 to 6 inches long), less than half grown, and while the skin is very tender. Though edible when better developed, the flavor and texture are inferior.

When should sweet corn be picked?   When in the full milk stage, i.e., while its kernels can still be readily punctured with a thumbnail, releasing the juice, or "milk"—and as short a time as possible before it is to be cooked.

When should sweet potatoes be harvested?   After the first killing frost blackens the vines.

When are winter squash and pumpkins harvested?   Before frost.

WINTER STORAGE

Is there any simple and inexpensive method for the small gardener to use in storing vegetables for winter?   The simplest method for storing vegetables is in a bushel basket filled with dried leaves in a garage. Another method is pit storage. Dig a pit in a well-drained location. Place a layer of gravel or sand in the bottom. Line the pit with straw. Store your vegetables in the pit. Cover with straw and then at least 6 inches of soil, or deep enough to ensure safety from freezing in your climate. A 3- or 4-inch pipe sunk into the storage space and extending well above the ground gives ventilation.

How are root crops and cabbages stored outdoors in a barrel?   An excavation is made in a well-drained spot and a tight barrel is buried in an upright or tilted position with its top 6 to 10 inches below the ground level. Vegetables are packed in the barrel. The opening is covered with a bag thickly packed with dry leaves, peat moss, or sand. The soil is then filled in to a depth to make the contents of the barrel frostproof. (See illustration.)

How should vegetables be stored for winter use in a root cellar? How should a root cellar be properly constructed?   An ideal root cellar can be constructed by making a double wall, with an air space between, and an insulated roof. An 8-inch terra-cotta flue is placed in the bottom and run through a trench to a point well outside the root cellar, where it is brought up to the surface and hooded with a wind-operated ventilator several feet above the soil level. The roof also has a ventilator with a damper. The action of the wind forces air (which takes on the temperature of the soil) down through the terra-cotta duct to the storage. This maintains a constant temperature in the storage house and at the same time maintains good aeration. The root cellar must be well drained to prevent water from standing on the floor or from gathering in low spots.

What are the proper temperature and moisture conditions for fruit and vegetable storage?   The best temperature for winter storage of root crops, cabbage, and most fruits is 35° to 40° F. The cellar, pit, or other storage space should be dark, with a dirt floor, but well drained. Though humidity is needed, no water should collect and stand on the floor or in the bottom of the pit or barrel.

How do you store carrots, beets, and turnips to keep them from shriveling?   Store in a cool, dark place, 35° to 40° F., packed in sand or slightly moist peat moss, or in boxes covered with bags containing sand, leaves, or peat moss.

Can Chinese cabbage, leeks, kale, and celery be stored indoors?   Yes, in a basement room or root cellar at a temperature of 35° to 40° F. They will need moderate air circulation and plenty of moisture. Leave some dirt about the roots and pack closely in boxes placed on the floor. Kale can be kept growing in a covered cold frame in the garden through most of the winter.

How can squashes, pumpkins, and onions be stored?   These vegetables require dry storage. The vine crops should be "cured" for a week or two in a temperature of 80° to 85° F., then stored on a shelf in a dry cellar at 45° to 60° F. Onions should be kept in the dark, in a dry place, at 35° to 40° F. But cure them in trays or boxes, under cover, but with free circulation of air, for several weeks after harvesting.

How do I store sweet potatoes in order to keep them through the winter?   Sweet potatoes are dug when their vines are killed by frost and are handled with care to avoid bruising. Perfect tubers are cured at a high temperature (80° to 85° F.) for 2 weeks. They are then stored in a dry place at 45° to 50° F.

We have strong, healthy roots of French endive. We do not wish to force them until spring. How shall we winter the roots?   Leave them in the ground in the open garden. Dig when ready to force. Hard freezing does not injure French endive.

Where one does not have a place cold enough to keep potatoes from sprouting, is there any other method one can use to prevent them from sprouting while in storage during winter months?   A frostproof pit is

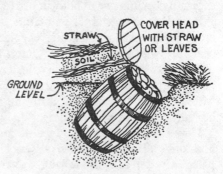

Traditional barrel type of outdoor storage pit. The cover must be tight to keep out moisture. Another method that works quite well is packing root crops (beets, etc.) among dry leaves in a bushel basket in the garage.

most satisfactory for storing potatoes. They need to be kept in the dark, just safely above freezing, in a humid but not too moist atmosphere. Otherwise, they will sprout; rubbing the sprouts off is of some benefit. Or they may be treated with a chemical "sprout inhibitor." Potatoes stored at temperatures *below* 42° F. will taste sweet. Bring out of storage into a warm room for a week before cooking.

What is the best way for a city gardener to store vegetables? Lacking better storage (see above questions), canning or freezing is the best answer, although drying has also become popular, and a number of food dryers are now commercially available.

My family dries beans for winter use. These dry beans are infested by worms which render them unfit for consumption. What can be done to remedy this condition? After drying the beans, place them on screened trays in a cold oven. Heat very gradually to 180° F. After 10 minutes at 180°, cool and store.

How are dried peas and beans stored for the winter? If possible, in airtight containers of tin or glass in a dry, cool room at a temperature from 45° to 60° F. Treat with heat before storing. (See above.)

Is sand the only suitable material in which to store cabbages and other crops in an outdoor pit? Vermiculite, peat moss, or buckwheat hulls can be used instead. These materials should be very slightly dampened.

Exhibiting

In what condition should vegetables be picked for exhibition purposes? In prime eating condition. The overgrown specimens often shown by beginners will not win prizes on size alone.

How should vegetables and fruits be prepared for exhibition? Root crops are washed. Tomatoes, eggplants, peppers, squash, apples, and pears are wiped and polished. Onion tops are cut off and outer, discolored skins are removed. Celery, leeks, and Chinese cabbage are washed and the roots are cut off neatly. Cabbage stems are removed, together with outer imperfect leaves. Strip the husk from a section of each ear of corn and cut it off near the base.

How can greens and the tops of root vegetables be kept fresh for exhibitions? Harvest well in advance and harden overnight in a cool place in water or sprinkle with water. If they are unwilted and of good color at the end of the hardening period, they will probably stand up through the show.

How are vegetables displayed in harvest shows? Try to have each exhibit made up of items of uniform size. The schedule usually calls for a specific number of potatoes, tomatoes, beans, etc. Select perfect specimens of uniform size and place each group neatly on a paper plate. Lay out pea or bean pods side by side where they can be counted and seen easily by the judges. Turn tomatoes stem end down; fruits, stem end up. Carrots, beets, and other roots may be displayed with their tops if they can be kept fresh, but they are usually shown with their tops removed.

Is it important to show only perfect vegetables in an exhibit? Yes, in order to win a prize each item shown must be of high quality, well grown, and well displayed. Uniformity of size is also important.

How shall I display a vegetable collection in a show? Make an arrangement of the vegetables, placing squash, melons, and other large items at the back center with corn, root vegetables, etc., radiating from the center. Smaller vegetables are placed in the foreground.

Equipment

What tools are needed for a vegetable garden? Only a few tools are needed for a small garden. The most important are a spade or a flat-tined spading fork, an iron rake, a hoe, and a hand weeder. It is highly desirable to have two hoes—one with a fairly large blade for "hilling" and heavy hoeing and one with a small, narrow blade for cutting out small weeds. In a vegetable garden of considerable size a rototiller is a great time-saver.

Is a spading fork essential equipment for a vegetable garden? Many people consider a spading fork indispensable. It is useful in breaking up the soil when digging and in lifting roots or other crops. If only a small number of tools are to be purchased, however, get a spade first and a spading fork later.

What sort of spade do you recommend for a vegetable garden? Most gardeners prefer a long-handled pointed spade with a diamond-pointed blade. The handle should reach to the top of your ear when held upright.

What sort of knife shall I use to cut asparagus? An asparagus knife with a fishtail blade is best for the purpose; it cuts stalks below the ground without injuring new stalks that are developing. However, it is not necessary to cut asparagus stalks. You can snap them off instead.

What type and make of power machinery do you suggest for tilling, cultivating, etc., to lighten hand labor and that is suitable to use in a garden 50 × 100 feet?   You might consider an electric-powered unit called a Soil Blender, which will churn up bare soil, but isn't effective on sod. Otherwise, there is no power machine particularly suitable for use in a plot as small as 50 × 100 feet, especially if the area is fenced in. Probably the nearest thing to it is a small-sized rototiller. It isn't worth owning for so small a garden. Rent it instead. This is for preparing the land, not for cultivating. It would be much more satisfactory to have the garden tilled or dug by hired labor and depend upon mulching to lessen the work of cultivating. However, the old-fashioned wheel hoe is still available from dealers in garden supplies.

What is a scuffle hoe?   A scuffle hoe is a tool used for cultivating the ground by using a backward and forward motion to destroy weeds and break up the surface soil. In purchasing a scuffle hoe, it is essential to select one with a sharp cutting blade.

Which is more useful in the vegetable garden—a wheelbarrow or a garden cart?   A garden cart with big wheels will carry many times the weight of a wheelbarrow but most carts are too large for average lots. If your space is limited, a small wheelbarrow will be more useful.

Are seed sowers worth buying?   Yes, they are very helpful to the vegetable gardener. There are a number of different sorts. A small hand sower helps to drop seeds evenly in flats, seed beds, and even in the garden.

What is the best piece of equipment for measuring the space between vegetable rows?   Secure a long, narrow strip of wood about 1 × 2 inches and 8 or 10 feet long. Mark it off at 3-, 6-, and 12-inch intervals with a heavy carpenter's pencil.

Are rotary sprinklers helpful in a vegetable garden?   As a rule, it is better to water slowly around plant roots with a hose, without a nozzle.

What is a "porous" hose, and how is it used?   This is a canvas hose to be attached to the end of the rubber hose. It can be obtained in 25- or 50-foot lengths. Water seeps through the canvas very slowly and is at once absorbed by the soil. It is especially good for watering vegetables in rows and in soaking the bottoms of drills before sowing seeds in very dry weather. A three-ply or two-ply plastic, perforated hose throws many fine jets of water along its length, watering a 25-foot or 50-foot row or length of border at one time.

Would creosote-treated fence posts affect vegetable plants very near them? No. The creosote will not spread through the soil.

Are Hotkaps worth using? Hotkaps, properly used, are of great assistance in getting an early start in the garden. Not only do they make possible earlier planting, they also furnish protection from insects and from wind and heavy rains while the plants are small and struggling to get a start. They are particularly useful in starting vine crops such as cucumbers and melons, and protecting tender plants such as tomatoes, eggplants, and peppers when they are first set out. Discarded gallon-size plastic jugs are especially useful for protecting tomato seedlings. For smaller seedlings, clear plastic jars used for food packing are convenient.

Miscellaneous

What edible foods can be raised in a basement or cellar and sold at a profit? As practically all vegetables require full sunshine for several hours a day, they cannot be successfully grown in a basement. Witloof chicory, a salad plant, can be grown in the dark from roots which have been produced by sowing the seed in early spring and gathering the roots in the autumn. A local market for this crop might be developed. Another possibility might be mushrooms, but this crop requires quantities of horse manure or a special mushroom compost handled in just the right way and would not prove feasible unless the manure were readily available.

How does one build and manage a cold frame? What vegetables can be kept in it for winter use? (Ohio.) See Cold Frames, Section 3. In a tight frame in a well-protected spot, lettuce can be grown until late December or January if the plants are started in August or September. Root crops, such as beets, carrots, and turnips, can be stored for the winter, but they should be covered with several inches of soil, leaves, or other mulching when the ground begins to freeze. Boards instead of glass are used to cover the frame when used for storing purposes. Celery taken from the garden on the approach of freezing weather, with the roots on and replanted in the frame close together, will blanch nicely and remain crisp for several weeks. Cabbage, Chinese cabbage, and cauliflower replanted in the frame may be held for several weeks longer than out-of-doors.

What vegetables would you suggest for raising in boxes, pots, and tubs on a city roof that is very high and exposed to the wind and sun?   Many roofs are too weak to support the load of enough soil for good growth, so use one of the soilless mixes that contains vermiculite, or use peat moss as a substitute. Parsley, onion sets, lettuce, herbs, peppers, eggplant, New Zealand spinach, cucumbers and bush squash, melons, and tomatoes would be some of the best vegetables to try.

What vegetables can be eaten from the garden in the winter? My basement is too warm for storage. (Michigan.)   About the only vegetables that can be used direct from the garden in cold weather in the North are parsley, Swiss chard, broccoli, kale, collards, and Brussels sprouts; these will stand quite hard freezing and can be picked through December and often into January. Also, parsnips, salsify, and leeks are hardy enough so that they are not injured by severe freezing. To use the latter during the winter, they should be heavily mulched to prevent the ground from becoming too hard to dig. The Jerusalem-artichoke is also perfectly hardy and the tubers can be dug and used any time they can be gotten out of the ground.

I have learned by experience that there are two kinds of fruits and vegetables. (1) Those that can stand shipping. (2) More delicious and delicate ones for home gardens. How can I select the latter?   A recent increase in the interest in home vegetable growing has focused attention on this point. Many of the leading catalogs now take these differences into account in their descriptions. Such phrases as long bearing season, for local market, high quality, etc., mean noncommercial varieties.

Is there any danger of germ contamination in having a vegetable garden over a septic-tank drainage system?   There is some question as to whether contamination may occur in soil over a septic-tank overflow field. In theory, it cannot. The natural drainage of the soil is, however, an important factor. If another location for the vegetable plot could be found, it would be better.

What is organic gardening?   Organic gardening or farming is the growing of vegetables without the use of chemical fertilizers or sprays. It is accomplished by keeping the soil limed to a near neutral pH and following a rotation of crops where a good leguminous crop like clover or a sod crop occupies the land 2 out of 3 or 4 years. Animal manures are used to maintain the fertility of the ground. Also, plant refuse is composted and applied to the soil. Organic fertilizers are also used. Although perfectly feasible in home gardens, the big question is whether organic gardening on a commercial scale could feed America's large population.

What kind of soil will produce the best vegetables containing the most vitamins and minerals; is commercial fertilizer necessary to obtain such vegetables? Any garden soil in good tilth. While commercial fertilizer is usually used, it is not essential; minerals exist in the soil.

Can we have a garden on a sandy soil that is full of ants? Most sandy soils, if improved with humus and fertilizer, will grow excellent vegetables. If ants have made nests or hills, they can readily be eliminated by treating the soil with diazinon according to directions.

Pests and Diseases

(See individual plants, and also Section 13.)

Specific Vegetables

ARTICHOKE, GLOBE (CYNARA SCOLYMUS)

In what section of the country can globe artichoke be grown successfully? As a winter crop, in California, between San Francisco and Los Angeles; on the Gulf Coast, and in the South Atlantic states. In the eastern states (as far north as Massachusetts) as a summer crop, the roots being mulched during the winter. Globe artichoke is a difficult crop for the home gardener, usually requiring two seasons to grow if started from seed.

How does one grow large globe artichokes? (Pennsylvania.) They cannot be grown satisfactorily in Pennsylvania, unless you can protect them against winter freezing or buy started plants in the spring. They require a fertile, well-limed soil; the plants are grown from offshoots from old plants. They are vigorous growers. The part used is the bud of the flower, which should be picked before it is open.

ARTICHOKE, JERUSALEM- (HELIANTHUS TUBEROSUS)

Can you tell me something about Jerusalem-artichokes grown as a garden root vegetable? The tubers are started like potatoes, from cut tubers set 18 inches apart. It is really an American sunflower and ought to be known by its Indian name of sun-root; it grows 5 to 6 feet tall. No attention is required until the roots are dug in late fall or early spring, when they must be thoroughly removed from the soil or the plants will spread and are likely to become a pest. Jerusalem-artichokes are best planted by themselves, outside the garden.

Are Jerusalem-artichokes desirable as a garden vegetable? They are easy to grow and produce a heavy crop of nonstarchy tubers. However, they spread rapidly and can become a weed. The plants are subject to black aphids and mildew, and so should be kept at a distance from choice flowering or vegetable plants.

What time of the year should Jerusalem-artichokes be dug? Does freezing improve them? Freezing does improve their flavor and therefore they should be dug as late as possible in the fall, during a winter thaw, or early the following spring before they have a chance to sprout.

How are Jerusalem-artichokes prepared for the table? They are boiled and served with cream or Hollandaise sauce or diced raw, chilled, and added to mixed salads. And in numerous other ways such as glazed, au gratin, etc.

ASPARAGUS

Where can I purchase roots or plants of asparagus? Most seed suppliers and garden centers offer asparagus roots in the spring. In many cases they are rather small. It is advisable to order about twice as many as needed and plant only the best.

How should a new asparagus bed be fertilized? See that there is plenty of humus in the soil, preferably by turning under a cover crop, compost, or manure during the fall before planting. When preparing trenches for planting, enrich thoroughly with compost or manure and superphosphate. Be sure that the pH is not below 6.5. If it is, add lime.

What is the proper procedure for starting an asparagus bed from plants? Since asparagus is to occupy the ground for a long time, it is well to have the land in good fertility and tilth and free of weeds. Asparagus does well in a fairly wide variety of soils, from sandy to moderately heavy; good drainage is important. In early spring, make trenches 4 or 5 feet apart and about 8 inches deep in well-prepared soil. The very deep planting that was formerly recommended is not now considered necessary; if the soil is heavy, planting shallower than 8 inches may be better.

Is it advisable to attempt to plant a bed of asparagus roots in the fall of the year? Early spring is better.

How many asparagus roots should be planted per person? Under favorable conditions, 10 plants or 15 feet of row may be expected to furnish asparagus for one person through the season. One-year-old plants are best to purchase.

If young asparagus is covered too much, would that stop its growing? Yes, especially if the soil is heavy and planting is deep. Eight inches is deep enough for asparagus roots, and the first covering should be only 2 inches, gradually working soil in as the plants grow.

If I transplant asparagus that has been cut before, can it be cut the first year after it is transplanted? It is not ordinarily best to move old asparagus roots, but if this is done, it would probably be best not to cut the first year. Good top growth is necessary to reestablish the crowns. After that, judgment can be based on the vigor of shoots as they come up.

Is it possible to purchase asparagus roots to plant in the spring and have the shoots to eat the following spring? If asparagus plants are set out in the spring, the shoots should not be harvested until the second spring following. Then they may be cut for a period of about 4 weeks and for a full crop the next year.

How late in the season can asparagus be cut? For an established bed, 8 weeks is about the usual cutting period. If the shoots become spindly, quit cutting so that good growth can be made for the following year. The tops have the job of storing food for next year's crop in the enormous root system underground.

I started an asparagus bed this year. Next year, when it's time to use the spears, how are they cut? Asparagus is best cut with a special asparagus knife just below the surface of the soil. Care must be exercised not to jam the knife into the crown or to injure the buds of shoots that may be coming up. The knife should be slipped down fairly close to the shoot that is being cut, and then tilted to avoid injury to other shoots. Some prefer simply to snap off the spears at ground level.

Is it necessary to bank or ridge asparagus each year? Most people prefer green asparagus to white or blanched; hence, banking is not necessary. Slight ridging may be effective in smothering young weeds just when they appear in the row.

Should asparagus be deeply cultivated? Asparagus should not be deeply cultivated as this practice damages the roots and crowns and so hinders growth.

How do I care for and harvest asparagus plants (roots) set out last spring? During the summer, pull the weeds and give shallow cultivation; mulch with manure or rich compost in autumn and work it lightly into the surface soil in early spring, keeping a little away from plants and remembering that their roots are shallow and spread horizontally. In the fall, when the old plants have lost their green color, cut the tops a few inches above the ground and destroy them.

Why do some authorities advise cutting asparagus stalks in the fall, while others prefer leaving them until spring to help hold the snow and form a winter mulch? Cutting the stalks in the fall before the seeds mature and sow themselves prevents an infestation of seedling plants in the bed. These may become troublesome weeds. If cut 6 or 8 inches high, the stems will help hold mulch or snow.

When should asparagus be fertilized and what fertilizer should be used? Once a year is often enough to fertilize the asparagus bed. It doesn't make a great deal of difference whether it is done in early spring or at the end of the cutting season, when plants are allowed to grow up. Fertilizing before cutting is generally preferred. In sandy soils, use a 5–10–10 fertilizer at the rate of 35 pounds per 1,000 square feet. In heavier soils, a 5–10–5 would probably do as well. Compost and manure are also first-rate for asparagus.

How does one apply salt to asparagus? Don't. In the old days farmers found that while asparagus could tolerate salt, weeds could not, and so it became known as an effective form of weed control. However, excessive salt buildup in your vegetable garden soil can be harmful. Instead, use a weed-smothering mulch to achieve weed control, such as layers of shredded leaves or other organic material.

How do you protect asparagus during the winter? It is root-hardy and needs no extra protection.

How often should asparagus beds be reset?   Never. If an old bed runs out, start a new one, using young plants.

Do asparagus crowns gradually come to the surface of the soil?   This is true, not because the crowns actually move, but because the new growth of the root stocks which make up the crowns is nearer to the soil surface than the old growth. This, however, is of little harm since most people prefer green asparagus. When they come within 2 or 3 inches of the surface, cultivation over the row before and after cutting is likely to injure the buds.

What is the best method to revive an old asparagus bed? The yield is light now and stalks are small.   If an asparagus bed is in good shape except for lack of fertilization, it can be revived by starting a good program of fertility maintenance. If the crowns have become spent or the stand is poor, it is better to start a new bed.

Is it practical to interplant between asparagus rows?   No. Roots of asparagus are not deep and spread horizontally. Interplanting would injure these spreading rootlets.

How are asparagus plants grown from seed?   For growing asparagus roots, select a fertile soil in good tilth. Mark out rows 18 inches apart. Sow seeds 2 inches apart in the row and cover ½ to 1 inch deep. Soaking the seed in water at room temperature for 3 to 5 days will hasten germination. Then plant at once, in late April or early May.

Does asparagus do well in the Deep South?   Asparagus is successfully grown commercially in South Carolina, but in such states as Florida and Louisiana it does not do well.

What causes asparagus to be tough and pithy?   Insufficient fertilizer; poor soil preparation; a pH below 6.5; allowing it to get too old before being cut.

How can I avoid asparagus rust?   Purchase seeds or roots of a rust-resistant variety such as 'Mary Washington'.

What is the control for asparagus beetle?   Dust with rotenone or methoxychlor.

What asparagus varieties are suitable for the Washington, D.C., metropolitan area?   'Mary Washington', which is partially resistant to asparagus rust, is the leading variety everywhere.

What is your opinion of 'Paradise' asparagus compared with 'Mary Washington'?   Indications are that 'Paradise' is very similar to a good strain of 'Mary Washington'. It cannot be expected to give a full crop a year ahead of other varieties, as is sometimes claimed.

BEAN, BUSH AND POLE (PHASEOLUS VULGARIS)

What is the difference between string beans, stringless beans, and snap beans? All older varieties of beans had strong, fibrous, stringy growths running the length of the pods. The removal of these strings was a tedious job. Many years ago, plant breeders began producing varieties in which these "strings" were eliminated. These were called stringless beans. Stringless beans are easy to break or "snap" into pieces; hence they are now called snap beans.

How should the ground be prepared and fertilized for planting snap beans and shell beans? Beans need a well-prepared, thoroughly drained soil. Use a 5–10–10 complete fertilizer, 2½ pounds per 100 square feet of row. Apply as a sidedressing, 3 inches from the row or hill. Beans do well on soil too poor for most other vegetables. Fertilizers high in nitrogen are to be avoided.

How are snap beans best grown in the home garden? Bush snap beans are planted after the danger of frost is fairly well past, 2 or 3 weeks after the last killing frost, or a week before tomatoes are set out. They will not withstand frost after they are above ground. They thrive in a wide variety of soil types. Leaf diseases are controlled by getting seed that is disease-free. Dusting is necessary in areas where Mexican bean beetles prevail.

How many plantings of snap beans shall I make each year? That depends on the length of your growing season. Beans require about 60 days to mature. The last planting should not be made later than 70 days before the first killing frost. Therefore, you can plant every 2 weeks until that date. If you make a planting May 1, you can plant 5 or 6 times.

Is there really a bean, either snap or lima, that can be planted early and will stand cool weather? Broad or Windsor (*Vicia faba*) beans resist frosts and are usually planted about the same time as peas. (See below.)

What varieties of yellow wax beans will ripen in rotation? All the bush beans ripen about the same time. They can be planted, however, for succession crops, at intervals of 2 to 4 weeks. You can grow the pole varieties and have beans over a longer period.

Do varieties of beans mix when planted in a garden near each other? Some degree of crossing in the field occurs among beans, differing with varieties and conditions. However, this would not affect the immediate crop. It might result in hybridization if seed were to be saved for the next year.

Can beans be grown in the same place two successive years?   Yes.

How and when should I plant 'Kentucky Wonder' or other pole beans?   Plant when the danger of frost is past. Where seasons are very long, a late planting can be made for fall. Sow seed along a fence or trellis, 3 or 4 seeds per foot and an inch or two deep. If a hill system is preferred, plant 6 to 8 seeds per hill; set poles at least 3 feet apart.

Can pole beans be grown successfully along a fence about 4 feet high?   Yes, on a wire fence. A higher fence is better. A little trellis can be set above the fence to allow for greater height of the plants. If the fence is of stone or boards, it will be desirable to use strings or chicken wire from the ground to the top of the fence.

When do you harvest kidney and other shell beans for use in the dry state? Should they be shelled right away?   Dry beans are harvested when the pods have matured and begun to dry up, but before they open and begin to drop the beans. One has to strike a happy medium for minimum loss from immaturity on the one hand and shattering on the other. Leaves ordinarily turn brown to a considerable degree. Vines can be harvested entirely and allowed to dry on a shed or garage floor, and then the beans can be flailed out. Of course, in small quantities they can be picked by hand. They will shell out easier after the pods have become dry.

How should I care for snap, lima, and soybeans in the fall so as to get seed for planting or winter eating?   Conditions in the Northeast are not very favorable for saving the seed of beans. Commercial production has moved to the West to irrigated areas where there is bright, dry weather at curing time. On a small scale, one can pick the pods, dry them, shell them, and put the seeds away. On a larger scale, the whole plant can be pulled when leaves begin to drop and taken in to a barn floor, garage, or other suitable place. Then they can be flailed out, cleaned, and put away. Plants from which seed is saved should be free of anthracnose and bacterial blight. Storing seed in a refrigerator will stop bean weevil and protect germination.

When bean vines turn yellow, is it an indication of too much water, cold weather, or lack of fertilizer?   This could be an indication of either lack of fertilizer or cold weather.

What beans for use green or dry are not bothered by the bean beetle?   There seems to be little difference in susceptibility of bean varieties to Mexican bean beetle. People are sometimes confused because there are early and late broods of the beetle with a period of relative immunity between. The beetle is not particularly difficult to control with methoxychlor or Sevin.

What is the best control for Mexican bean beetle?   Methoxychlor or Sevin dusted on the underside of the leaves when the grubs hatch from the orange-colored eggs. Don't dust until you see the grubs or beetles, as the dust does not last long. (See Section 13.)

What are the names of stringless bush beans, both green and wax?   'Green Pod', 'Tendergreen', 'Tenderpod', and 'Wade' for green; 'Pencilpod', 'Brittlewax', and 'Goldcrop' for the yellow.

What is the best green bean to plant for canning?   'Bountiful' is a heavy bearer. 'Tendergreen' is of better flavor and retains its tenderness even when quite fully grown.

What variety of green stringless beans would you recommend for freezing?   'Tendergreen', 'Topcrop', or 'Tenderpod'.

What beans are resistant to the blight?   Most modern varieties are bred for disease resistance.

In a small vegetable garden, would you recommend pole beans instead of bush beans?   The question of bush versus pole beans is largely one of choice. Bush beans are less trouble to take care of, bear considerably earlier, and succession plantings can be made to give a supply throughout the season. On the other hand, pole beans bear over a longer period of time, and a good many like the pole varieties such as 'Blue Lake', 'Romano', and the old 'Kentucky Wonder'. 'Burpee's Golden' is a distinct type, with yellow pods of fine flavor.

BEAN, LIMA (PHASEOLUS LIMENSIS)

Do large lima beans need to be planted right side up to grow?   Lima beans do not need to be planted right side up (or, more correctly, with the eye down). Experiment has shown small difference in results when planting in this way. But in heavy soil in the home garden, it is probably worth the extra trouble.

How can I grow lima beans successfully?   Lima beans (bush type) can be grown on well-maintained garden soil, being planted after the danger of frost is past. Seed at the rate of 3 or 4 per foot, 1 to 2 inches deep, with rows 2 to 3 feet apart. Dusting for Mexican bean beetle may be necessary.

How long will pole lima beans grow and produce?   Pole limas will yield edible beans over a longer period of time than bush beans—4 to 5 weeks, or even more, depending on climatic conditions.

When are lima beans ready to eat? When they are about full grown but still green. If they stay on the vines long enough to begin to turn white, they are usually too hard.

Do large limas require acclimating? No. Acclimating a stock of seed generally means breeding for adaptation to a specific soil and climate. Lima beans seem to be about as widely adapted as most of our vegetables.

How and when do you harvest lima beans? If left till dry, they mold; if green, they shrink. I have too many to go over them every day or so. Most gardeners prefer to harvest lima beans when tender—and then freeze or can them at this stage. Most of the dry lima beans are grown in western areas where conditions are particularly favorable for their production and curing. If left to mature in the garden, they can be harvested when the pods have dried, but if the climate or weather at this time is humid, there is likely to be trouble in drying and curing.

What can I do to pole limas to make them mature? Lima beans, especially the pole varieties, require a fairly long season for maturity of the crop—90 to 120 days. Thus, in northern climates it is important that they be planted as soon as possible after the danger of frost is past. They can be started earlier if Hotkaps are used. Or for bush limas, erect a plastic tunnel over the row.

Will pole lima beans mature in Massachusetts? The growing season in Massachusetts varies from 150 to 200 days. Pole limas require 90 to 120 days for maturing, so it is possible to grow them. The length of the season is measured between the average date of the last killing frost in the spring and the average date of the first killing frost in the fall.

I have been trying to raise pole lima beans for 3 years and have had no success. The vines grow 10 to 12 feet long with lots of bloom, but the beans fall off when they are about a half inch long. A few will get full-size pods but no beans. My garden is sandy loam and I use the best seed I can obtain; I also use a 5–10–10 fertilizer at the rate of about 1,000 pounds per acre, applied in the hill. What is wrong? Lima beans do not set well when there is a period of hot, dry, sunshiny weather with low humidity during the blossom period. Night temperatures below 50° F. cause blossoms to drop. One study showed that under certain conditions, where there is boron deficiency in the soil, applications of 15 pounds per acre of borax made increases up to 40 per cent in yield of limas. Whether this is directly associated with the set of the pods or with other factors is not clear. Use of a hormone spray, such as Blossom Set, is recommended. Factors such as insect injury and unbalanced nutrition are probably involved. Inoculating the seed with Legume-Aid before sowing is recommended.

How can I raise lima beans without blight? The best insurance against blight (including both anthracnose and bacterial) is the use of clean seed that has been grown in territory free from the disease. Some progress has been made in developing resistant strains. Cultivating beans when wet will spread anthracnose if it is present. Bean refuse in the garden is likely to harbor and carry over the disease.

Do Mexican bean beetles attack lima beans? Yes, very much so. Control by dusting with rotenone dust or methoxychlor.

BEAN, SOY- (GLYCINE MAX)

What type of soil is needed to grow soybeans? Soybeans are among the thriftiest of plants and will make the most of any soil in which they find themselves. But better soil means more and better beans.

Where can I obtain United States bulletins on the culture of soybeans? Publications of the United States Department of Agriculture can be obtained from the Superintendent of Documents, U. S. Government Printing Office, Washington, D.C. 20402.

Do soybeans require any special care? Soybeans should not be planted too deeply, about 1 inch. Rows should be 2 to 3 feet apart, 5 to 8 seeds per foot. Protect soybeans from rabbits and Japanese beetles.

Should soybeans be inoculated? When growing soybeans for the first time, it is wise to get inoculating material with the seed or from a seed store. They can be grown on the same soil for a year or so, and from that point on inoculation should not be necessary. Even though not inoculated, they will usually make a fair crop.

Are edible soybeans satisfactory in the home garden? Yes, if you have use for them and you like them. They are used as green shell beans or dry, but require 3 to 4 months to mature and more space than snap beans.

Is it feasible to grow edible soybeans as a green-manure or cover crop, to be plowed under after harvesting the beans? They will do, but snap beans grow faster as a cover crop for plowing under.

We had a lot of soybeans. It was a big job to pick them but far worse to shell them. Is there an easier way? Soybeans should be blanched in boiling water, 3 to 5 minutes, before shelling them out. This makes the process much less difficult. Or try the Japanese method: Drop the green pods into boiling water and boil them for about 15 to 20 minutes. Drain the water and sprinkle the pods with salt. Then take each pod separately and squeeze the beans into your mouth. (See also next question.)

How do you cook soybeans? Green soybeans may be scalded in the pods to make shelling easier. Shell, boil until tender (like limas), and serve buttered. *Baked:* Soak dried soybeans overnight; bring to a boil in fresh water and boil ½ hour; then use them as pea beans for baked beans. *Soy Loaf:* To one pint of cold, boiled (dried) soybeans, add a beaten egg, a cup of bread crumbs, 1 tablespoon chopped onion, 2 tablespoons tomato catsup, and salt and pepper to taste. Form into a loaf and bake for 1 hour. Serve with tomato sauce. *Salted:* Soak dried beans overnight; boil for 1 hour in fresh, salted water; spread in a shallow pan (after removing excess moisture) and roast in an oven at 350° F. until light brown; butter and sprinkle with salt. Or French fry dried, boiled beans in deep fat and sprinkle with salt.

BEAN, BROAD (VICIA FABA)

What soil is preferred by broad or Windsor beans? A heavy, well-drained soil, limed and manured or enriched with compost.

When should Windsor (or broad) beans be planted to bear before hot weather? Broad, Windsor, or fava beans thrive under cool conditions. They can be planted as soon as soil is dry enough to work, usually about the time that peas are planted. They mature in early summer, or in about 80 to 90 days.

How can black aphids be avoided on broad beans? Plant early, as soon as the danger of hard frost is past. Spray with malathion according to the directions on the package when first aphids appear; repeat as frequently as needed. Pinching off the growing tips of the plants where the aphids cluster is a control method that should appeal to organic gardeners.

BEAN, MUNG (PHASEOLUS AUREUS)

What is the botanical family and species of the small mung beans used by the Chinese for sprouts, and how do they compare with soybeans in protein and vitamin value? (California.) The small-seeded or green mung bean used for bean sprouts by the Chinese is *Phaseolus aureus*. Like other beans, the family name is *Leguminoseae*. The mung bean, although belonging to the same genus as our common field beans, is of a different species. The protein content of the mung bean is about the same, or slightly higher, than that of our common beans. The comparative figures on percentage composition are 23.3 and 22.7 per cent respectively. For soybeans, the protein value is about 50 per cent higher.

How do you grow bean sprouts used to make chop suey? Bean sprouts are usually produced by placing a layer of the dry seed on a rack in the bottom of a moist chamber, preferably in a large earthen jar. (The beans should not lie directly in water, hence the advice to place them on a screen or rack above the water.) The vessel should be covered to exclude light and maintain a moist atmosphere. A minimum of 5 to 7 days is the period usually required to produce sprouts 2 to 4 inches long. The room temperature will promote rapid sprouting. In the winter, water should be added twice daily; in the summer, preferably three times a day. Before placing the beans in the jar for sprouting, the seed should be thoroughly washed and the jar made sterile to prevent molding.

BEET (BETA VULGARIS)

How shall I sow beets and when? Sow as soon as the ground can be worked, in rows 12 to 15 inches apart, a dozen seeds to the foot, ½ inch deep. For late beets, sow deeper, up to 1 inch. If the soil is dry, water well before sowing.

What fertilizer should be used for beets? Beets require very fertile, well-limed soil, not deficient in potash and in good tilth. Apply compost or a complete fertilizer (preferably 5–10–10) at the rate of 3 pounds per 100 square feet of row.

Why are there spaces in the beet row where seed did not come up? Possibly the seed did not germinate because it was too old. Or damping-off organisms may have been at work. Use a seed disinfectant (captan or thiram) before planting to prevent damping off.

Is it profitable to transplant beets? I have never had them grow as well as the ones left in the row. However, I don't seem to be able to prevent the seed from coming up too thickly. Each beet seed (so-called) contains several true seeds, hence the thick growth of seedlings. Those thinned out may have been damaged at the roots, or when transplanted the taproot may not have been set vertically. When carefully transplanted, plants grow well.

Why do beets that are apparently healthy fail to produce large

roots?   Possibly because the plants are getting too much nitrogen and too little potash. Have your soil tested.

I have heard that beets need boron. Could I put some borax in a watering pot and add it to the soil that way? My beets were a failure. The carrots growing beside them were fine.   This may have been because of a lack of boron. One ounce of borax in 16 quarts of water will prevent it. The trouble may have been due to a lack of potash. Use wood ashes where you grow beets.

What variety of beets do you recommend for winter storage?   'Detroit Dark Red' is a standard variety for late keeping. 'Winter Keeper' or 'Lutz Green Leaf' are others. 'Winter Keeper' has the best flavor after long storage.

BROCCOLI (BRASSICA OLERACEA)

How is broccoli grown?   In exactly the same manner as cabbage. The spring crop is started in the house under fluorescent lights, or in a greenhouse or hotbed in early March, taken to the garden in mid-April, and harvested in June. The fall crop may be directly seeded in the garden about July 1 to 10, thinned out about August 1, and harvested in September or October.

How do you fertilize broccoli?   Broccoli requires a lot of nitrogen. If it is kept fertilized well, it will grow until freezing weather. Sidedress the plants every month or so.

Cabbage and broccoli, two important vegetables for the home garden, can be set out in seedling form as soon as frost is out of the ground. Sow seeds in early summer for a fall harvest or in mild climates in the fall for winter and early spring harvests.

What is the secret of obtaining early broccoli in the North? Grow your plants from seed sown indoors about March 1. Or buy young plants from a local grower and set them out as soon as the ground can be worked and danger of hard frost is over.

When should broccoli be planted? It can be started with plants set in the garden as early as the ground can be prepared. These plants will produce good broccoli all season in most regions. If a second crop for fall is wanted, sow seeds outside in May–June.

Is there any way to hurry along broccoli? I planted some late in April. September arrived and there still were no blooms. Up until severe freezing it was still growing, but there were no heads. Sow seed May 15 to June 1 and set out plants in July; or sow indoors in February or March for an early crop. Early strains are now available. 'Green Goliath' and 'Green Comet' are 15 to 20 days earlier than older varieties.

What treatment of broccoli plants will cause them to produce thick clusters of buds rather than sparse clusters? Plant in rich, deep, friable soil. Cultivate constantly. Water during dry periods and sidedress with nitrogen or liquid manure when plants are established. The side sprouts never produce heads as large as those that first form at the top of the main stalk, but they still taste good.

When and how should broccoli be cut? When flower heads have formed, but while florets are in tight bud. Cut with a sharp knife a few inches below the head. New heads will form from side shoots, and cutting can continue as heads form. Keep heads cut regularly.

How can I keep broccoli producing all summer? Keep the heads cut off as soon as they are ready to use. When cutting broccoli, cut 2 to 4 inches of stem. If cut too close to the heads, the plant will send out too many small side shoots rather than fairly large ones.

What is the cause of apparently healthy broccoli suddenly turning yellow and wilting? It could be caused by any one of a number of things: lack of water or food, cabbage yellows (a disease), or root maggots. (See Section 13.)

BROCCOLI RAAB (BRASSICA OLERACEA RUVO)

The fresh-produce department of our supermarket has recently been selling a vegetable called "broccoli raab" in the winter and spring. Can I grow this in my summer vegetable garden? Yes. Broccoli raab (also known as "sparachetti," "broccoli-headed turnip," or "Italian turnip") is an annual, a member of the cabbage family, and tastes more like mustard or turnip than broccoli. It is a cool-season crop as are most in the family. For late spring or early summer harvest, seeds must be planted in early spring, just as soon as the ground is workable. The plants grow about 18 inches high and must be harvested just as soon as the flower buds form, otherwise they quickly become tough and go to seed. Flower buds, foliage, and upper stems are all eaten after being boiled for a short time. Don't overcook. Serve with butter or oil and garlic.

BRUSSELS SPROUTS (BRASSICA OLERACEA GEMMIFERA)

When should you plant Brussels sprouts seed? Sow seeds May 15 to June 15. Set plants out about August 1.

What cultivation and type of soil are needed for Brussels sprouts? Set plants out in rich, friable soil; cultivate constantly; water in dry weather and sidedress with nitrogen or liquid manure during its early stages of growth.

How can I raise Brussels sprouts? They grow up, and I break off outer leaves, except a few on top. The little balls start, and there they sit! Try an application of liquid manure or water-soluble fertilizer when sprouts begin forming (see preceding answer). Pinching out the growing tip will often force heads to form.

Can Brussels sprouts be grown in the climate we have in St. Louis? Not too well. Seed should be sown in your area June 1, plants should be set out July 20 in cool soil, and watering should be frequent.

Should we cut the leaves off Brussels sprouts when heads start to form? Remove lower leaves only, to facilitate cutting of the sprouts.

My Brussels sprouts are beautiful plants, but the sprouts are loose and leafy. How can I get firm sprouts? (South Carolina.) Heat may be the cause of this trouble. Try an application of water-soluble fertilizer when sprouts begin forming.

When and how are Brussels sprouts harvested? Brussels sprouts are harvested by cutting the "sprouts" (like tiny heads of cabbage) off the stems with a sharp knife after the leaves have been broken off. The leaves will usually snap off easily as far up the stem as the "sprouts" are ready to cut.

CABBAGE (BRASSICA OLERACEA CAPITATA)

What kind of soil is suitable for cabbage?   In the home garden, cabbage can be grown successfully in a wide variety of soils. For commercial culture, a rather heavy loam is usually preferred, although early varieties are frequently grown on fairly light soil. All of the cabbage group are heavy feeders and do best when two or three applications of fertilizer are given during the growing season.

What kind of soil and fertilizer are required for growing cabbage successfully? (California.)   Any soil that will not bake too hard is suitable for cabbage. Frequent cultivation is essential. Fertilizers high in nitrogen are preferable when setting plants out, plus a sidedressing of nitrogen or liquid manure when they are half grown.

How can I make cabbage head early? (New Jersey.)   Set out in early April, choosing early varieties, as soon as the ground can be worked. Apply good fertilizer immediately. Sidedress with fertilizer high in nitrogen or liquid manure one month later. Water frequently in dry weather.

I cannot raise cabbage or cauliflower in my garden. Why?   If the soil is not poor, it may be infested with club root, which attacks cabbage and cauliflower. Try new soil in a different part of the vegetable garden. Dig to a depth of 12 inches; use plenty of compost or rotted manure. Cultivate frequently; water during dry spells; sidedress with nitrate of soda or liquid manure when the plants are established. Cabbage yellows, a disease, is another problem. Plant only yellows-resistant varieties.

Why do our cabbage and broccoli plants, carefully tended in newly turned soil that is rich and black, form foliage instead of heads? (Illinois.)   Probably a lack of lime, phosphorus, or potash. Boron deficiency can cause the heart to die out. You can see this by examining the leaves in the center of the plant.

I have been planting cabbages for four years, but they do not do well; they make long stems but few heads. What is the trouble?   The seed purchased may be of doubtful quality. The plants may be held out of the ground too long before being planted. The soil may be deficient in phosphorus and potash or may not be sufficiently cultivated. The weather may be too warm.

We have a small plot of Savoy cabbages. Some of them are large and some are very small. Why?   Evidently your seed was of uneven quality;

soil fertility may be spotty. Buy the best seed and distribute your fertilizer evenly.

Why do cabbage heads crack? How can I prevent this?   This is usually due to rapid growth during warm weather on early cabbage, causing premature formation of a seed stalk when the head is maturing. Heads should be cut as soon as they are full grown. With the fall crop, there is less difficulty. Loosening the roots by pulling or bending over the head to break the fibers on one side of the stem delays cracking.

When should cabbage seed be started? (Missouri.)   For a spring crop, 60 to 90 days before the danger of the last hard frost. For a fall crop, May 15 to June 20.

When is the best time to plant cabbage for early setting? (New Jersey.)   Sown indoors, 60 to 90 days before the danger of the last hard frost, usually late March to mid-April.

How is fall cabbage grown? When is it planted? (Missouri.)   Sow seed May 15 to June 20. Set out your plants August 1. Harvest before hard freezing.

How do you control worms on cabbage and other crucifers? Dust the foliage with rotenone dust, methoxychlor, or Sevin when the worms make their appearance. In the home garden, catching the yellow or white butterflies (which lay the cabbage worm eggs) with a net is helpful—and good exercise!

Cardboard or foil discs placed around the stems of cabbage plants prevent injury from root maggots.

What insects and diseases attack crucifers?   Root rots are the most serious diseases. Cabbage yellows is serious in some parts of the country but there are resistant varieties to overcome this disease. The main insect trouble is the cabbage worm, which eats the leaves, the harlequin plant bug, and aphids (plant lice), which suck the juices. On early cabbage the root maggot does much damage unless controlled by using cardboard discs around the stems when setting out your plants.

How can cabbage be stored for winter?   A few heads of cabbage can be stored by pulling the plants out by the roots and covering the head with a paper sack, tying the sack shut around the stem, and then hanging the head up by the roots. A cool cellar is best. For large quantities, cabbage should be stored in pits out-of-doors and covered with layers of straw and soil so it won't freeze.

What are good early and late varieties of cabbage?   *Early:* 'Jersey Wakefield', 'Golden Acre', 'Stonehead' hybrid. *Late:* 'Danish Ballhead'. *Red:* 'Red Danish'.

CARROT (DAUCUS CAROTA SATIVUS)

What soil is best for carrots?   Well-limed and aerated sandy loam soil. Incorporate plenty of humus. Unless loose and friable, roots will be tough and crooked.

Do carrots need plenty of water to grow large, or is fertilizer more important?   Carrots need a well-limed soil and average moisture conditions. Use a 5–10–10 fertilizer if the soil is poor.

Does the flavor of carrots vary with the condition of the soil? The carrots that I raised last year had a flat, unsavory flavor. They were grown in ground uncultivated for 10 years.   A well-grown carrot is sweeter than a stunted carrot. You may need more lime, humus, and potash in the soil. Too much nitrogen as well as continued hot weather will cause poor flavor.

How does the market gardener plant carrot seed and cultivate to keep down the weeds? What are the newest methods of carrot growing?   The market gardener's soil is freer of weeds because the ground is cultivated so much. The rows are thinned while the plants are still very small, and chemicals are used to control annual weeds, not later than 50 days before the carrots are harvested.

I can never get a good stand of carrots. Why?   Probably the ground bakes too hard. Try sprinkling some pulverized magnesium limestone over the seed before you cover them. Don't plant the seed too deep; barely covering from sight is sufficient.

How should carrots be planted for succession crops?   Make 3 plantings: early spring, early summer, and midsummer—mid-July to August.

Why doesn't carrot seed germinate?   It may be too old. Or it may be due to a lack of lime in the soil. Use pulverized magnesium limestone and sprinkle it over the seed in the row before covering with soil.

When is it best to thin out carrots? When the seedlings are about 2 inches tall. Thin them when the soil is moist—soon after a rain or a good watering.

How are carrots transplanted? This cannot be done satisfactorily. Anything that breaks off the main taproot causes them to produce branched or forked carrots.

Why do my carrots so often lack color? The soil may be too dense, contain too much nitrogen, or lack lime. On black soil, 20 to 50 pounds per acre (1 to 2 ounces per 100 feet of row) of copper dust will improve their color. Plant newer coreless varieties, which are solid orange in color.

What would make carrots (good seed) which grew rapidly very tough, even the baby ones? Probably a deficiency of potassium, or insufficient lime in the soil. Hard clay soil forces the roots to twist or "corkscrew." Fiber forms with each twist.

What makes forked carrots? Failure to pulverize thoroughly the soil in which they are to grow; the use of manure which is not well rotted; or perhaps allowing seedlings to grow too big before thinning, which is apt to make their roots twist around one another.

I have read about treating soil with borax for carrots. When advisable, how is it done? Is regular kitchen borax used? One ounce of ordinary borax to 16 quarts of water, poured along the row, is enough for 50 to 75 feet.

My carrots sometimes have many roots instead of one straight one; or sometimes they are full of little nodules like root bumps. How can this be prevented? This sounds like nematode injury. Try to grow them where carrots have not been grown before. Fall tilling will tend to minimize the trouble. A lack of lime sometimes causes forked carrots.

Carrots grown during the past season have sprouted many smaller roots from around the main root. The main roots are healthy, about 7 or 8 inches long, with as many as 6 or 8 smaller carrots all around the main stem. Only some of these in the same row showed this peculiarity, while others were normal. Soil tests were: slightly alkaline, good nitrogen content, deficiency in potash. A good dose of 20 per cent superphosphate was given the soil three weeks before planting in a sandy loam soil in southern Connecticut. What is the matter? Try some magnesium limestone as well as more potash. It is doubtful whether the high pH is due to lime in the soil.

Do carrots poison the ground? No, but they do use up nutrients which cause deficiencies for other crops. This is not poisoning, but it does affect later crops.

My carrots come up and grow very well until the first week in July, then their tops die down rather suddenly. About the middle or last of August, new shoots appear. The carrots get no bigger than my middle finger, although the tops look healthy. This has occurred every year for five years. Other things grow on. What is it? This sounds like leaf blight. Many commercial growers spray with Bordeaux mixture to control this disease.

What is the proper time to plant carrots for winter storage? (Iowa.) Plant seed June 1 to 20, for usual table size. If deluxe "baby" carrots (about half grown) are wanted, two or three weeks later.

We replanted the carrots in a box of soil in the cellar this fall. Now they are developing new tops and rootlets. Will the rootlets spoil the carrots for use as a raw vegetable? Not unless they make considerable growth, in which case they will be bitter. The soil should be air dried when used for storing roots. Very slightly dampened peat moss, sand, or vermiculite is better than soil for packing around roots in winter. Root crops will not start to grow if the temperature is kept below 40° F.

When shall I dig carrots for winter storage? Just before a hard freeze; early frosts do not injure them. Storing them too early can cause them to sprout.

At what stage of development should carrots be pulled for canning? In the "baby" stage—finger size—for best table quality.

What is the best carrot to plant on a rather heavy soil? 'Oxheart', 'Chantenay', 'Danvers', or 'Nantes Half Long'. Use plenty of magnesium limestone.

Can you name a good sweet variety of carrot for the home garden? There are many, such as 'Coreless Nantes', 'Sweetheart', and 'Short 'n Sweet'.

CAULIFLOWER (BRASSICA OLERACEA BOTRYTIS)

What is the best method for growing cauliflower? Get high-quality seed. For a spring crop in northern areas with cool, moist weather, sow indoors in February or early March. Set out your plants as soon as the danger of frost is over. The soil must be deep and very rich. Cultivate constantly and sidedress with a high nitrogen fertilizer. Fall crop: Sow seed June 1 to 15; set out plants in August.

Why didn't some of my cauliflower form heads, while Brussels sprouts and other cauliflower did? Both crops dislike high summer temperatures, which cause irregular growth.

What causes cauliflower heads to turn yellow or purple? The heads turn yellow or purplish if not protected from the sun. Pull leaves together over the top of the head as soon as it begins to form and tie them together at the tips to hold them in place. This will keep the heads perfectly white. 'Early Purple Head' and 'Royal Purple' do not require tying.

How do you bleach cauliflower? When I tie the heads together, they turn black and rot. I have been told to use lime, but I hesitated to do so. Do not tie the heads until they are about 2½ inches in diameter. Never tie too tightly or too closely over the head. Be sure the "curd" is dry when tied.

I planted cauliflower and grew nice, snowy-white heads, the first one in 62 days. When they were cooked, they turned a light brown color. What was wrong? Evidently your water contains a considerable amount of iron. Cauliflower should be steamed rather than boiled.

CELERIAC (APIUM GRAVEOLENS RAPACEUM)

How do I grow celeriac; what are its soil and light needs? Does it have to be blanched? How long can it be left in the ground? Is it subject to celery blight? Celeriac (also known as root celery or knob celery) is grown by the same methods as other celery, with about the same type of soil and light requirements. It doesn't need to be blanched and seems to be more resistant to disease than ordinary celeries, but it may require Bordeaux dusting. It can be left in the soil until the danger of freezing weather has passed. The roots will not freeze quite as quickly as the leaf stalks of ordinary celery. It does require good soil and ample irrigation to develop large, smooth roots of fine quality. These, with their tops removed, can be stored in sand or soil for the winter.

CELERY (APIUM GRAVEOLENS DULCE)

Can celery be grown in the home garden? If so, what variety is recommended? It *can* be grown, but requires so much care, patience, and space that most home gardeners prefer to buy it. 'Golden Self-

Blanching' is one of the best for the home garden, though—despite its name—it requires blanching. 'Fordhook' is another.

How should early celery plants be started?   Sow seed in flats of a soilless mix. Mark out rows ¼ inch deep and 2 inches apart or scatter the seeds over the surface. Sow seed 10 to 15 per inch; cover very lightly by sifting on not more than ⅛ inch of soil. Cover the flats with newspaper or plastic and water moderately. As soon as seedlings break ground, remove their covering. When seedlings are 1½ or 2 inches high, transplant them to other flats, spacing them about 2 inches apart. Firm well, with the crowns just about even with the soil but not above. Watering should be managed to give steady but not too rapid growth; temperature between 55° to 65° F. is about right. Plants should be hardened by watering sparingly.

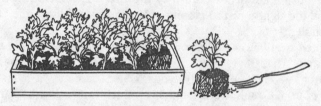

A flat of celery plants ready for transplanting into a garden.

What is the best time to start celery seed for early planting?   Celery seedlings start slowly and seed should be sown indoors 8 to 10 or even 12 weeks before setting outdoors. Celery will withstand moderate frost, and it may be put out about the average date of the last hard, killing frost, or 2 to 3 weeks before tomato-setting time. Celery plants for a fall crop may be started in a well-prepared outdoor seed bed about 8 weeks before field setting. Celery will withstand light frost but not hard freezing in the fall, and 100 to 125 days should be allowed from the time of setting out plants until harvest or storage.

How should celery be spaced and transplanted in the garden?   Celery plants should be dug with minimum breaking of the fine root system. In transplanting, avoid doubling up or bunching of roots; pack the soil firmly and set the plants at about the depth they were growing in the plant box or seed bed. If set too shallowly, roots are exposed; if too deeply, soil is likely to get into the crowns. Rows may be 2 to 3 feet apart and plants spaced 6 inches apart in the rows. For partial blanching, celery may be planted in rows 18 inches or 2 feet apart. For blanching with earth, 3 to 4 feet between rows should be provided.

What is the best kind of soil for celery? Should celery be planted in sun or shade? The soil best for celery should be fertile and well filled with organic matter. The soil range is from moderately sandy to sandy loam to moderately heavy soil, provided the other requirements are met. Muck or peat soils are especially suitable. Rich, well-maintained garden soil containing compost and/or rotted manure will give good results. It responds well to liberal applications of commercial fertilizer—up to 1 pound per 20 square feet. A 5–10–5 fertilizer will not be far wrong on most soils. On peat soils, a high potash fertilizer may be desirable. Celery does not do well under shady conditions.

How much water does celery require? A great deal. The root system of the celery plant is not spread far or deep and a liberal water supply is needed, more so than for most vegetables. The soil should be kept moist throughout the growing season.

Can an outdoor seed bed be used for late celery plants? Yes, but it should be well-prepared, rich, friable soil. If seed is sown thinly, transplanting may be omitted, but this uses up garden space. Watering is likely to be necessary, but it should not be overdone, so that the plants will not be soft and spindly. Good plants for setting out are about 6 inches high and should be managed so that leaf pruning will not be necessary. It takes about 8 weeks to grow the plants.

How do I grow and care for celery in Southern California? Celery is not likely to do well in the hotter, dryer parts of California, but a good deal is grown near the coast. Cultural methods are not greatly different from other places. Ample irrigation is likely to be necessary.

We grew our first celery this year. It seemed to thrive, became a good size, blanched well, but is hollow and tough. What does it need to grow large and tender? In the fall, the stalks were soft and stringy. The quality of celery is very much dependent upon favorable growing conditions, especially fertility and moisture. It is not likely to be good if the weather is hot and dry. Pithiness or hollow stalk is generally traceable to poorly bred seed. Stringiness varies widely with varieties, being more prominent in the 'Golden Self-Blanching' group than in the late green celeries. It is much more prominent where celery has been grown under unfavorable conditions of fertility, moisture, or heat.

How does one grow the celery that develops large hearts that will be used for braising or eating raw? The proportion of "heart" in celery depends a good deal upon variety. The 'Golden Self-Blanching' strains are good in this respect, the old 'Giant Pascal' are not as good, but a number of green celeries of high quality (such as 'Fordhook' and

'Utah') have been developed. The heart comes up and becomes more prominent late in the growth of the plant or even in the storage space (see below).

How should celery be blanched?   Commercial growers use boards or stout paper along the rows; home gardeners may slip a tube over each plant or tie paper around it. The old method of pulling up earth around the plants involves much washing in the kitchen. Only the stalks, not the foliage, are to be blanched.

I would like to know what causes celery blight. What can I do to check it?   Celery "blight" (there are three different leaf diseases) is controlled by faithful dusting or spraying with Bordeaux, taking special pains to cover the lower leaves, especially the undersides. The soil should be free from celery refuse, and it is best if the soil has not grown celery for a period of three years. Spraying or dusting may well begin in the plant bed, especially if disease has been troublesome in the past. Treatment every week or ten days is necessary, unless the season is very dry and disease is not developing.

What will prevent celery from rotting in the ground after it has been hilled up?   Celery for storing and hilling ought to be practically free from disease. Hilling should not be done until really cool weather, and the plants should be dry.

Cross section of celery stored in a trench for fall use, or later in mild climates.

How can celery be stored, and for how long?   The plants are lifted complete with roots (which are light and should be disturbed as little as possible) and replanted in a shallow trench, in boxes in a storage house or cool cellar, or in a cold frame. The roots should be kept moist but the stalks should be dry. The plants can be kept for many weeks. The temperature should be just above freezing.

CHAYOTE (SECHIUM EDULE)

What is chayote?   A perennial tropical vine native to America. It is grown as an annual in cooler climates, where 220 days may be counted on between killing frosts. Fruits, which are melonlike, are edible baked or steamed. The tuberous roots are also edible in climates where the vine is perennial and able to produce small tubers. Young shoots are also edible.

What is the culture for chayote? Plant the entire fruit on its side with the point slightly exposed where the vine is to grow; or plant shoots from the base of an established plant. A rich, well-fertilized soil is needed and a support on which the vine can climb. Fruit may be expected in late fall from spring planting in climates with at least a 220-day growing season.

Can chayote be grown in Maine? Not very well. Chayote is a tropical perennial vine. It may be grown in greenhouses, or as an annual for its fruit, in sheltered places where the growing season is at least 220 days between killing frosts.

CHICORY, WITLOOF, FRENCH ENDIVE (CICHORIUM INTYBUS)

Why does my chicory seed, planted in the spring, fail to come up? Much of the seed used in this country is often several years old. French seed should come up readily no matter how early it is planted. Buy seed from a reliable source.

How is chicory grown in the garden for winter forcing? Plant out-

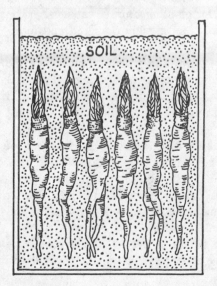

Cross section showing roots of Witloof chicory packed in a deep box of moist soil or peat moss and sand for forcing for winter salads.

of-doors in early spring in rows 18 inches apart; thin out to 4 inches apart; grow on through the entire summer. Summer foliage is not used but permitted to grow and feed roots. Dig the roots just before a hard freeze for forcing indoors.

How do I force chicory? What should be done with the roots saved for successive forcing? Dig the roots just before a hard frost and trim to a uniform length of 6 to 8 inches; cut the tops off just above the roots. Pack in a box, 12 to 16 inches deep, in peat moss and sand (or peat moss and loam), close together, and cover with 6 inches or more of soil. Place in a cool, dark cellar, water well, and cover with a board. When shoots appear at the surface, reach down through the soil and cut just above the roots with a sharp knife. Save the roots wanted for a second crop by planting—as above—in dry soil; do not water until ready to force the crop.

Growing chicory in the cellar, how do we take off the leaves—cut or tear them off? The chicory seems to be having good growth and the leaves are very good to eat. If the chicory is forced properly, you shouldn't have to remove any leaves. The "heads" are cut. If the outer leaves are loose, it is an indication that the soil above the crowns is too loose. This should be compact and firm. (See the previous question.)

CHINESE CABBAGE (BRASSICA OLERACEA PEKINENSIS)

How should the soil be prepared for planting Chinese cabbage? The soil should be well drained but moist, thoroughly prepared and fertilized, especially with nitrogen.

How is Chinese cabbage seed planted, and when? Sow where the plants are to grow, very thinly, in rows 18 to 24 inches apart. Thin to 3 inches apart, then to 6 or 8 inches. The fall crop is planted 2½ to 3 months before frost. Chinese cabbage is a cool-weather plant and must be grown quickly.

How can one keep Chinese cabbage from going to seed instead of heading? Plant in late midsummer for a fall crop; it doesn't like heat. Plant as late as possible to mature. Keep the soil moist, the plants growing without check—80 to 90 days from seeding to maturity. Newer varieties from Japan, i.e., 'Springtime', can be sown as early as the soil can be worked and will not go to seed.

Why does my Chinese cabbage not form heads? Please give some pointers on its cultivation. Chinese cabbage requires cool weather and short fall days to make heads. It should be grown on very fertile soil with lime and plenty of moisture. Thin to 8 inches.

What is the trouble with our Chinese cabbage? It grows well until ready to head, then begins to wilt; then the leaves begin to rot. This is probably due to a crown or heart rot. A specimen should be sent for diagnosis to your county agent at the Cooperative Extension Service, usually listed in phone books under the county government.

Why is our Chinese cabbage so buggy? Plant lice or aphids can be a nuisance on Chinese cabbage. Spray or dust the plants with methoxychlor or rotenone just as soon as lice appear. Repeat as frequently as needed.

CHIVES (ALLIUM SCHOENOPRASUM)

What are the soil and light needs of chives? They are easy to grow, but in view of the fact that the seed may not be too good, it is best to start with plants, dividing them into sections. They need a well-limed, loamy soil and full sunlight or light shade. Divide and replant old clumps every two or three years to prevent overcrowding.

Is it necessary to cut blossoms from chives in order to keep the tops (foliage) good for use? Removal of the flowers makes new growth easier to cut because old flower stems are tough. This also encourages the growth of new foliage instead of letting its strength go into seeds.

How are chives used in cookery? Young foliage and bulbs are used for flavoring in soups, salads, in cream cheese, in sour cream, on vegetables—wherever a very delicate onion flavor is desired.

CORN, SWEET (ZEA MAYS)

How is the ground prepared for corn planting? It should be thoroughly dug or tilled. Soil along the rows or in hills should be well pulverized when fertilizer is being added prior to planting.

How should corn be fertilized? Corn needs a 5–10–5 complete fertilizer and/or compost to make the soil fertile. Rotted manure is also good. Fertilize when preparing the ground a week or more before planting. In garden soil in good tilth, pour a cupful of starter solution over the seeds in a hill before covering with earth and omit other fertilizer.

Does sweet corn need lime? Corn likes a pH of 6.0 to 6.8; that is, slightly acid.

How should corn be planted? Either in rows 30 inches apart, 3 or 4 kernels to the foot, 1 to 2 inches deep, 3 or 4 rows being planted at once to ensure cross-pollination; or in hills or groups 3 feet apart each way, 5 or 6 seeds to the hill, planting always 2 or more rows of hills for cross-pollination.

When should sweet corn be planted? Plant sweet corn a week before the probable date of the last killing frost in the spring, if for an early crop; 10 days or so later for a main crop. A late planting (of early varieties) can be made 80 to 90 days before the probable date of the first fall frost.

Can corn be successfully started in pots indoors for transplanting? Yes, providing they are not kept too warm and set in the ground too early. This method has limitations but will give you earlier corn. Peat-and-fiber pots, 3 or 4 inches square, are better for this purpose than clay pots.

In order to have a supply of young corn fairly late into the fall, what is the latest date it should be planted? (New York.) July 4 to 15, depending on the length of the growing season (between last spring and first fall frosts) in the locality. This calls for using seed of an early variety.

Is there any advantage in planting sweet corn in blocks instead of single rows? When planting three varieties of sweet corn at one time for succession, it is better to plant a third of each of three rows in a little block than to have single rows of each variety. This makes for better pollination, since each row helps pollinate the others and so ears are better filled.

How should corn be cultivated? Cultivation should be frequent to control weeds, but should be shallow. Hill up as plants grow.

How many stalks of sweet corn are left to a hill? Usually only 3.

My sweet corn was a complete failure this season. It grew heavy, tall stalks but no ears. I planted 6 rows at a time, about 6 inches apart in a row. Rainfall was exceptionally heavy, which was the only unusual thing. What was wrong? (Soil analysis shows a deficiency of potash.) I used commercial fertilizer with a heavy percentage of potash and a small amount of nitrogen. The stalks were too close together. They should be a foot apart.

I have never succeeded in growing good corn. The stalks grow well but the ears are few and small. I buy seed from a good house and plant in accordance with instructions. I have planted the seeds in three widely separate locations; in fact, one garden is 7 miles away from the others. This sounds like too close planting or too much nitrogen and too little lime, phosphorus, or potash. The soil may be too dense below the tilled layer.

Last spring I planted corn (two kinds) and it tasseled when it was about 2 or 3 feet high. That was all we saw of the corn. Why? This sounds like an acid soil, dry weather, dark days, or a lack of fertilizer was the cause—possibly all four.

What is the cause of incomplete development of kernels on an ear of corn? All around the ear the kernels may be plump, sweet, and full of juice, but 2 rows or more may be dry and flat. Plant in blocks rather than single rows, in order to assure cross-pollination and development of every kernel. It may also be the result of the corn borer working in the stalk just below the ear.

Can the fact that my corn failed to produce one single ear, when planted in two 250-foot rows, as per directions, be due to the fact that the 3–8–7 fertilizer used was too poor in phosphate? The fertilizer should be O.K. Perhaps the stalks were too close together. Ten 50-foot rows would ensure better pollination than two 250-foot rows. Sometimes hybrid varieties set their pollen in one short period. If this period coincides with windless days, no pollen will fly.

Should suckers be removed from corn? If so, when? Nobody has been able to prove that there is any advantage in removing the suckers from sweet corn. From a physiological point of view, to do any good the suckers should be removed when they are not over 3 inches tall. Most people sucker corn when it is a foot high. This is too late and injures the parent plant when the suckers are removed.

How can I keep crows from stripping sweet corn after it is in ear? Hang up tin cans or other noisemakers. Scarecrows may help.

What can I do to control the corn borer? Dust the plants every 5 days with Sevin. They should be dusted from the top so that the dust gets into the axils of the leaves. Rotenone dust once a week is another control. All infested stalks should be burned in the fall as the pest winters over in the plant refuse.

How can I prevent the corn-ear worm from ruining the ears? You can put 10 to 20 drops of mineral oil containing rotenone on the silk about 3 days after the silk comes out of the ear. Or you can cut off the silk close to the ear every 5 days. Or grow varieties developed with close-tipped husks to prevent entry of the worm.

Is there any method of controlling corn smut during the growing period? There is no complete control except to remove and burn as soon as discovered and before powdery spores are released into the air to spread disease. Smut is a fungus growth that comes through the stem into the ear or tassel.

Are any varieties of sweet corn absolutely smut proof?   No. You might try spraying the plants with Bordeaux mixture when the ears are beginning to form. Be sure to destroy smutty ears before the powdery spores are released into the air.

What is hybrid sweet corn?   A hybrid is the first-generation progeny resulting from the crossing of two inbred lines. The breeder first works several years purifying and fixing the character of his inbred lines. He then crosses two of these, hoping to secure a combination of several desired characters and more vigorous growth.

What kind of sweet corn is the sweetest?   The sweetest sweet corn varieties are hybrids, known as "supersweets," but there are two types of "supersweets"—those that need isolating in order to retain their supersweet qualities, such as 'Early Xtra Sweet', and those that don't, called 'EV' (short for a gene known as Everlasting Heritage). The isolated sweet corns came first, and the 'EV' sweet corns are an improvement. 'EV' sweet corns, such as 'Kandy Korn EV' and 'Earliglo EV', not only require no isolation to retain their supersweetness, but they also stay sweet for up to 10 days after picking. Among white sweet corn, a variety called 'Silver Queen' has developed a reputation for being the sweetest, milkiest, tenderest sweet corn, and it requires no isolation. Even though it is not a "supersweet," it matches supersweets for flavor.

How can I get succession crops of sweet corn?   Take any one variety and make plantings every 2 weeks. If you make only small plantings (a dozen hills or so), make plantings every week. Or you can pick a group of varieties that will mature at different dates.

Where can I get seed for varicolored corn? (Michigan.)   Most seed houses carry various kinds, such as 'Rainbow'.

CRESS (CURLY CRESS, UPLAND CRESS)

I have tried in vain to establish watercress in our wet meadow, which often becomes dry in the summer. Are there substitute greens we can grow?   Watercress needs constant running water to grow properly, although it can be grown in rich, damp soil. As an acceptable substitute, obtain seed of curly cress, which has a peppery tang, or upland cress, which is more similar in flavor to watercress. The plants do best in the cool weather of spring and fall and mature fast, so seeds should be sown every few weeks to maintain a supply. In hot-summer regions, postpone sowings until late summer for fall use. Curly cress grows well indoors in a cool sunny window or under fluorescent tubes.

CUCUMBER (CUCUMIS SATIVUS)

How is cucumber seed planted? In the open ground after the danger of frost is past. Rows can be 4 to 5 feet apart, with a plant every 2 to 4 feet in the row. Many gardeners plant seeds too thick and fail to thin out. For an earlier harvest, sow seeds indoors in peat pots or outdoors under Hotkaps.

How are cucumbers fertilized? With plenty of well-rotted manure or compost placed under the soil in which the seed are planted, either in hills or rows.

How are cucumbers cultivated? Cultivate carefully for weeds until the vines spread, when hand weeding is necessary. Mulching between rows or hills can be used to keep weeds down.

How often should cucumbers be picked? To ensure production through their full bearing period, pick regularly (which may be daily, certainly every few days); the younger the better. If fruits are allowed to mature, the vines soon stop bearing.

Can cucumber plants be transplanted? Cucumbers can be started inside, 3 weeks ahead of garden setting, using any good greenhouse or plant-growing soil in peat pots. Sow 3 to 4 seeds per pot and thin out to 1 or 2; keep at a temperatue of about 65° F.; water moderately so plants grow vigorously but will not have started to vine before field setting. Care must be taken in setting them out not to disturb the root system, as they do not stand transplanting as well as cabbage or tomatoes.

Should cucumbers be trained upwards? If so, how? They can be trained on a fence or over a wall to save space, but are usually allowed to run over the ground. In small gardens, plant bush varieties.

Can cucumbers be planted near melons? Cucumbers can be planted close to melons without fear of "crossing." What causes melons to "taste like cucumbers" is exposure to cool or cold weather sometime during growth rather than cross-pollination.

Do cucumbers and muskmelons cross? No. However, the belief that they cross is widespread, and many experiences are related that seem to confirm it. The most carefully conducted and scientifically correct experiments have been made in vain attempts to cross them.

Should cucumbers be picked when their foliage is wet? What makes

cucumber vines turn yellow before all fruit is mature? Cucumbers are subject to several leaf and vine diseases which would probably be spread somewhat more freely when the plants are wet. These diseases are best controlled by rotation of land and by seed treatment as mentioned in the following question.

Why do cucumber vines die so soon? Because the fruits are not picked or because of diseases, such as bacterial wilt, scab, anthracnose, and angular leaf spot. Most reputable seed catalogs list the tolerance of varieties to these diseases. As cucumbers come up, they should be dusted with rotenone, pyrethrum, Sevin, or methoxychlor for striped beetles, which are carriers of bacterial wilt. Use of Hotkaps will protect small plants from the cucumber beetle, which spreads the wilt.

Where do cucumber beetles come from? Cucumber beetles pass the winter as adults. Some are in the garden under old cucumber or melon vines and unharvested fruits and some are in fence rows, ditch banks, wood lots, and rubbish piles near the garden. They come out of hibernation about May 1 and feed on weeds for a few days while waiting for the cucumbers and melons to come up.

My problem is growing cucumbers and squash. I can grow the plants but they get many empty blossoms; when the fruit comes on the plants and I get a few small ones, the plants start to die. I use plenty of well-rotted manure and give them lots of water when needed. What is the trouble? Probably wilt spread by striped cucumber beetles. (See the previous questions.) "Empty" blossoms may be male.

Are there wilt-resistant cucumbers? Some results have been achieved in breeding mosaic- and mildew-resistant strains, but so far none have been developed that are resistant to bacterial wilt. 'Burpee Hybrid' is resistant to both mosaic and downy mildew; 'Marketmore 70', to scab and mosaic. 'Gemini', an all-female variety, is resistant to five or more diseases. Of the pickling sorts, 'Pioneer', 'Mariner', and 'Wisconsin SMR18' carry multiple resistance.

Are there any advantages to growing all-female cucumbers? If so, how do the female flowers get pollinated? The advantage of an all-female cucumber is that most of the flowers are capable of producing fruit. Older varieties of cucumbers are generally "male dominant," meaning that they produce more males than females, and the males have a tendency to appear first. However, there are three kinds of so-called all-female cucumbers: The first kind is truly all-female and a normal cucumber vine with male blossoms must be planted nearby to ensure pollination. When seed suppliers sell this kind, they include seeds of a pollinator, stained a distinct color so you can recognize them. Another kind of all-female produces a small percentage of male flowers—sufficient to ensure pollination—and a third kind (which must be isolated) produces all-female flowers requiring no pollination whatsoever from a male flower, since it is self-fruitful. This third kind is mostly for greenhouse growing. In order to determine which is which when buying seed, check the catalog description or packet instructions carefully.

DANDELION (TARAXACUM OFFICINALE)

How do I grow dandelions? You can buy dandelion seed and sow it in rows in late summer and harvest them the following spring. They require a fertile soil that is well limed.

Would dried dandelion leaves make good winter eating? What about other edible weeds? Most of the common nonpoisonous weeds, if harvested when young, are quite nutritious from the standpoint of vitamins. They can be dried and used later. The main question is their palatability. Lawn grass and young alfalfa are very nutritious if you like them.

DASHEEN (COLOCASIA ESCULENTA)

I have heard about the "dasheen," the rival of the potato, and I wish to try it. Can you tell me of its cultural necessities and if it is possible to grow it at an altitude of nearly 5,000 feet with a relatively short season? No, it is a tropical plant.

EGGPLANT (SOLANUM MELONGENA ESCULENTUM)

How is the soil prepared for eggplant? The soil should be well drained and rather sandy, well worked with compost or rotted manure.

What is the secret of growing eggplants successfully? Don't grow the young plants too fast until the fruit is set. The use of Blossom Set will help. Grow them on well-aerated soil that is amply supplied with lime. Use plenty of compost in holes when setting out and keep well watered. If subjected to temperatures below 50° F., flowers will drop off and no fruit will set; the same result will occur at temperatures above 90° F.

What is the best way to grow eggplants? Buy young, healthy plants or raise from seed indoors in peat pots in a warm place under fluorescent lights. (See Seed Sowing.) Set out when the ground is thoroughly warmed up or earlier under the protection of Hotkaps. Set 2 feet apart in rows 2½ to 3 feet apart. Work in 5–10–10 complete fertilizer around each plant as it begins to grow. Cultivate often or mulch.

Why do the blossoms of eggplants continue to drop off? Care is taken that they do not get frostbitten; manure has been applied and the ground is kept cultivated, but the blossoms still will not hang on. You probably grow the plants too soft with fertilizer, or at too high or too low a temperature. Grow them slower, with less nitrogen.

What makes eggplants develop a rot all over them in spots while only half grown, resulting in practically no crop? This is a bacterial or fungus spot and is caused under conditions where the fruit tends to stay moist on the surface. This often happens on poorly prepared soil. Check soil acidity. It may need more lime.

Eggplant in this area was destroyed by a "wilt." Dust and sprays failed completely. Can any helpful information be given? (Kansas.) There is no control for eggplant wilt after it has once gotten into the plants. The prevention is to grow seedlings in soil which has not grown them before and set the plants in fields which have not grown eggplants for at least 10 years. Some varieties, such as 'Black Beauty', are more resistant than others.

How do you keep bugs off eggplants? Dust the plants with Sevin or methoxychlor if the bugs eat the foliage; or spray with malathion if plant lice are present.

Which are the best varieties of eggplant? 'Black Beauty' is the old standby but there are several hybrids with smaller fruits, such as 'Dusky', that bear earlier and more bountifully. 'Florida High Bush' is especially suited to the South.

ENDIVE AND ESCAROLE (CICHORIUM ENDIVIA)

How is endive grown? In the North, sow seeds about July 15 for fall use. When endive reaches maturity, it is usually blanched by tying the outside leaves around the heart, as with cauliflower. After being tied, the head can be covered with waterproof paper to prevent rotting. Endive is frost-resistant and provides salad greens late in the fall. It can be stored in a cool cellar like celery, where it blanches in the dark. Endive that is tied up will rot in wet weather, particularly if the soil is not well limed.

FENNEL (FOENICULUM VULGARE DULCE)

What is Florence fennel, and how is it grown? Florence fennel (or finocchio) is a celery-like vegetable with an anise flavor. It matures quickly (in 90 days) and is sown in garden rows, thinned to 6 inches, and grown without special attention until approaching maturity. Then it is hilled up by having the soil drawn high on either side of the row to blanch the stalks. The blanching process takes about 3 weeks.

GARLIC (ALLIUM SATIVUM)

How does one grow garlic? Garlic can be grown just like onions, either from the "cloves" (divisions of the bulb) or from seed.

How do you divide garlic to plant? I want to grow large bulbs. You divide the garlic bulb into cloves and plant the individual sections. The size of the bulb is determined by soil and weather conditions. A fertile soil in good physical condition with ample rainfall will produce large bulbs.

When is it best to plant garlic—spring or fall? It can be planted either time. Spring planting is best where the soil freezes.

How deep should one plant garlic? Cloves are planted with their tops ½ inch below the surface. Seed should be planted not over ¼ inch deep. Plant in moist but not wet soil so the ground over the seed does not bake.

Can I grow the garlic chives used in oriental cuisine? Yes. Garlic chives (*Allium tuberosum*) are very hardy and bear attractive fragrant white flowers in late summer so they can be grown in herb or flower gardens. Their bright green leaves are used to flavor many Chinese dishes. The plants do self-sow and may become weedy.

GOURD

Is there an edible gourd? A variety called "vegetable gourd" is described as ornamental (it is creamy white, mottled, striped with dark green) and of good eating quality.

Which kinds of gourds are suitable for bird houses? The ordinary dipper gourds as well as others of the *Lagenaria* genus.

How can I produce dipper-type gourds? I have heard that it is necessary to tape the neck of the gourd. Dipper-gourds culture is the same as for other gourds. The shaping of necks is not ordinarily necessary for dipper gourds, but if you want to modify their shape this could be done with string or wire.

Is there any fertilizer that will cause gourd plants to grow more rapidly?   The same provisions that are made for cucumbers and melons will work well with gourds. Use a 5–10–5 fertilizer or a combination of dried manure and a smaller amount of fertilizer, or compost and superphosphate.

How do you raise gourds?   Gourds are not particularly difficult to grow. They can be allowed to run on the ground but are better planted along a wire fence or provided with a trellis. Their general requirements are about the same as for cucumbers and melons—a moderately rich, well-fertilized soil with reasonable moisture supply. They thrive under a wide range of conditions, and most varieties of small gourds will mature in the northern part of the country. Seed is sown about 1 inch deep and plants are thinned to 2 or 3 feet apart, according to varieties. Dusting may be necessary to control the striped cucumber beetle. In northern climates, plants can be started indoors in peat-fiber pots under fluorescent lights. Shallow cultivation should be practiced to control weeds.

What is the earliest date gourds can be planted?   Gourds are planted at about the same time as cucumbers, 2 or 3 weeks after the average date of the last killing frost in the spring, or at about the time tomatoes are set out. Gourds will not stand frost.

How do you start gourds from seed?   Ornamental gourds are usually raised in peat-fiber pots from seed sown in April or May and transplanted in June. When the peat pots are set out in the ground, they quickly disintegrate but save the roots from being disturbed in the transplanting operation. Seed can also be sown outdoors when the danger of frost is past.

How can one take care of gourds after they are picked so that they will not decay?   Gourds should be thoroughly matured on the vines before they are picked. They will not stand freezing if they are still succulent. If by necessity they are taken at the immature state, they should be handled with the utmost care and allowed to dry and cure indoors, but mold is likely to attack them. Some recommend washing gourds, but wiping with a soft cloth is probably better. Disinfectant solutions may be of some service, but not too much. To keep gourds in their natural state, waxing is one of the best methods, using ordinary floor wax and polishing lightly. Some use shellac, but this changes the color and appearance. Some also like to decorate and paint them in simple or fanciful fashion. Stems should be left on the gourds, removing them from vines by cutting. Maturity may be judged by feeling them, but it is not wise to test with the fingernail. They should be dry and the stem should be withered.

What is a good spray to combat the stem borer of gourds? It is best to grow the gourds on ground where cucurbits (members of the squash family) have not been grown the previous year or where their refuse remains. Early summer squash may be used as a trap crop. When the borer is already at work in the vines, surgery is resorted to, cutting lengthwise of the vine with a thin knife to destroy the larvae. Then the cut portion is covered with earth and little harm is done to the plant. Methoxychlor spray or dust applied 3 or 4 times beginning in early summer may be effective in destroying the borers just after they are hatched.

HORSE-RADISH (ARMORACIA RUSTICANA)

How do you raise horse-radish? What kind of soil do you use? Horse-radish must be grown on a well-limed, sandy loam soil that has a subsoil which is well aerated to permit deep penetration of the taproot. The crop is grown from root cuttings which are set (large end up) 10 to 12 inches apart in rows 2 to 3 feet apart. The roots can be set in deep trenches and covered 2 inches over their tops. Set horse-radish roots in the spring for that season's crop.

I am interested in growing horse-radish. My plants that are 1 year old show no signs of root deterioration. However, plants that are 2 to 3 years and older show excessive dry rotting of the roots. To your knowledge, can this be remedied? This is a natural sloughing off of tissue which cannot be prevented. The best horse-radish comes from 1-year roots from small root cuttings that are planted every year.

When do you harvest horse-radish? Should it be dried before being grated? Horse-radish is harvested in the fall and the grating is done while the roots are in their natural fresh state.

KALE (BRASSICA OLERACEA ACEPHALA)

When and how is kale planted?   Kale is improved by cold weather and should therefore be sown in the open, about 2 months before freezing is expected. Seed should be thinly sown, as the plants will eventually stand 18 to 24 inches apart. While kale will grow almost anywhere, it will be of better quality on good soil.

How late in the season can kale be cut for table use?   Until heavy frost kills it, although in much of the North it survives the winter. Cut the bottom leaves first, before they get tough. Neglect of this point has given kale a worse name than this vitamin-richest of the potherbs deserves.

I have planted kale two different years. In all, about 3 plants have appeared. How do you make it come up?   Buy high-grade seed. Seed should be covered ⅜ to ½ inch, and the seed bed should never be allowed to dry out.

How can I keep kale in the garden from freezing? (Ohio.)   Kale is considered hardy in your area of the country and nothing but extremely low temperatures should cause damage. The leaves are improved by hard frost.

Can kale be kept green for table use during cold weather?   By taking up plants and growing them in a covered cold frame it is possible to have kale through most of the winter.

How should kale be cooked?   Kale can be chopped, boiled as a green, and served buttered. It can be cooked with ham hocks or ham, which flavors the kale. *Scalloped kale:* Boil chopped kale until tender. Drain. Mix with chopped hard-boiled egg. Place in a baking dish. Moisten with soup stock or bouillon. Cover the surface with slices of cheese and sprinkle with seasoned bread crumbs. Bake in an oven about 15 minutes, until heated through and the crumbs and cheese are browned.

KOHLRABI (BRASSICA CAULORAPA)

How should one plant and care for kohlrabi to get best results?   Plant early on a well-limed, fertile soil. Kohlrabi is easy to grow and should give no trouble on a good soil. On poor soil, some fertilizer and a complete fertilizer applied as a sidedressing should be used. Thin out to about 3 inches. Harvest when not over 2 inches in diameter.

How should kohlrabi be harvested?   Many gardeners plant kohlrabi but few eat it. Kohlrabi should be harvested while the bulb is still growing and tender. When growth stops, the bulb quickly becomes hard and woody in texture, bitter in flavor, and entirely inedible.

LEEK (ALLIUM AMPELOPRASUM PORRUM)

What is the culture of leeks? Leeks are grown from seed in well-limed, very fertile soil with ample water. They must be grown in full sunlight. Shade will not produce good growth.

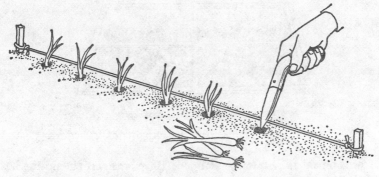

A dibble (planting gadget you can buy or make) is handy for setting out many seedlings, such as those of leeks and onions.

What is the proper way to transplant leeks? Make a trench 5 to 6 inches deep; enrich the bottom with old manure or compost and fertilizer. Set young plants (trimmed back, both tops and roots) in the bottom, 5 to 6 inches apart. As they grow, fill the trench and draw earth up to blanch them.

Part of my crop of leeks is still in the ground. I have been told they could be left there and used next spring. Is this information correct? (West Virginia.) Yes, this is true for the home garden where the appearance of the leaves is not so important. For market, the leaves will be ragged, which will hurt their sale.

LETTUCE (LACTUCA SATIVA)

How should the soil be fertilized for head lettuce? Lettuce has a scanty root system; therefore, it must have good soil with enough humus to hold the moisture so necessary for such a crop and to provide equally necessary nitrogen. Compost or rotted manure is needed and as much lime as is needed to counteract any acidity.

When can lettuce seed be planted outdoors? Loose-leaf lettuce should be one of the earliest crops sown and is preferred, for several reasons, by the average home gardener. Head lettuce should be started indoors and transplanted (after hardening off), so that the heads may be well grown before hot weather comes. The variety 'Buttercrunch' can be sown out-of-doors both early and late and will form loose heads.

Use a cold frame for early harvests of lettuce.

How soon should lettuce be thinned? How far apart should the heads be? Leaf lettuce, sown in the open, can be thinned a couple of times while still very small, until the final plants stand 8 to 10 inches apart. The larger head-lettuce varieties should stand 10 to 12 inches. Small varieties, such as 'Bibb' and 'Tom Thumb', which are among the best, need only about 6 inches.

How can I be sure to get good head lettuce? By growing it in ideal conditions; namely, a fertile soil, well drained but not dry, in a climate where the nights are cool and the days warm. Raise seedlings indoors or in a cold frame; harden off by gradual exposure to the outdoors; transplant them on a cloudy day and protect them from strong sunlight until well established in the garden.

How can I raise large heads of delicious, crisp, tender, loose-leaf lettuce? (Vermont.) You should have no trouble in your climate. Prepare soil with plenty of lime and well-rotted manure if available, and sow the seed as soon as the ground can be prepared in the spring; thin so that the plants stand 8 inches apart; or start seed indoors, sidedress with liquid fertilizer if needed. 'Salad Bowl', 'Green Ice', and 'Oakleaf' are good varieties of the type you describe.

How can I, with Missouri soil conditions and without replanting, raise

head lettuce rather than leaf lettuce?   Head lettuce requires a good, well-limed soil with ample moisture and cool nights. You can't grow head lettuce if the weather gets hot. Sow the seed as early as possible and thin the seedlings to stand 8 to 12 inches apart. See that the ground has plenty of humus—in the form of well-rotted manure, if available, and compost.

How can I get lettuce to grow faster?   Lettuce requires a limed soil with a good balance of nutrients, especially nitrogen in early spring. The soil must have a clean odor and drain easily. You probably need lime and humus.

How can head lettuce be grown for a small family to have plenty all summer?   You may not be able to grow head lettuce during the summer months because of hot days and nights. During the season of cool nights, you should have good heads by making plantings at 2-week intervals. 'Matchless' is a heat-resistant variety of head lettuce. Leaf lettuce is more nutritious and is usually grown during the summer months. 'Buttercrunch', a loose-head variety, does well in heat, as does 'Ruby'.

Why doesn't lettuce grow in our soil? (Pennsylvania.)   Perhaps you have insufficient lime in the soil or too little phosphorus. Have your soil tested and if necessary add lime to bring it up to pH 6 or 7. Use well-rotted manure or compost.

What makes lettuce heads rot in the center, and why does the first early crop seed before heading?   This may be due to a lack of available calcium or to one of the lettuce diseases that cause the heart to decay. Head lettuce goes to seed because of hot weather or other conditions that check normal growth. It needs cool nights to head well.

What causes "tip burn" in head lettuce?   Tip burn is usually caused by uneven growth where the leaves get too soft. It may be due to too little calcium in the soil or too free use of a fast-acting fertilizer such as nitrate of soda as a sidedressing, especially if hot sunshine follows a cloudy, moist spell.

Can lettuce seed be planted in the house?   Not unless you have good light and cool temperatures. The temperature should not be above 55° F. It can be grown in a cold room in a south window or under fluorescent lights.

I would appreciate suggestions for vegetable window boxes. Can lettuce be grown in pots or boxes?   Yes, if you have sunshine and the night temperature is not too high. Head lettuce requires cool nights to make it head. Leaf lettuce will grow in any window box. Keep the plants 6 to 8 inches apart. Use a soil with plenty of lime and humus in it. Fluorescent lights will help in the winter.

Where can I obtain lettuce seed which produces a plant for all winter? (Pennsylvania.) No varieties are hardy in the northern states unless grown in a greenhouse. 'Salad Bowl', 'Boston', 'Buttercrunch', and 'Oakleaf' are good varieties for a late fall crop. Endive, similar to lettuce and used for salads, is considerably hardier and should survive through fall and early winter in a cold frame.

Please recommend some lettuce varieties for the home garden, including some that are heat-resistant. 'Salad Bowl' and 'Green Ice' are the best of the loose-leaf type, which is easier to grow and gives a plentiful yield of leaves that are higher in vitamin content. 'Buttercrunch' has high quality, heads well, and resists heat. 'Royal Oakleaf' and 'Ruby' are especially heat-resistant.

What members of the lettuce family (or other salad greens) can be planted throughout the summer months? Use head lettuce in the early spring and late fall. 'Bibb' is a good very early variety. 'Oakleaf' is another. In summer, grow mustard greens and such heat-resistant lettuces as 'Ruby' and 'Salad Bowl'; in autumn, 'Salad Bowl', 'Oakleaf', and 'Buttercrunch' head lettuce and endive, which is frost-resistant. Witloof chicory can be forced indoors for winter salad. Other greens to add to the salad bowl in spring and summer along with lettuce are curly cress, roquette, and spinach.

What is 'Bibb' lettuce? 'Bibb' lettuce is a loose-heading or bunch-heading variety having very thick, smooth, dark green leaves quite different from any other type. It is especially adapted to growing in cold frames in the southern states during the winter months and makes a good spring lettuce in the open garden in the North. 'Burpee Bibb', 'Buttercrunch', and 'Tom Thumb' are very similar.

MUSHROOM

I would like to know about growing mushrooms in the cellar. How do you start a bed? Is there a special temperature you have to keep? Can you be sure of having nonpoisonous kinds? Use composted manure; pack in beds 6 inches deep; inoculate with pure-culture spawn; cover with an inch of soil; grow at 55° to 60° F. It sounds simple but is really very difficult. Write to your Agricultural Experiment Station for detailed information or purchase prepared flats or pots with the spawn already planted. Water and care for according to directions. Purchased spawn will not contain poisonous mushrooms.

How can a home mushroom bed be made under a front porch? You would have to close the area so that you could maintain conditions described in the answer to the previous question.

How can mushrooms be grown outside? You will have difficulty in doing this. Wild mushrooms grow only when weather conditions are favorable. You would have to provide those favorable conditions; therefore, mushroom growing in the open is not practicable.

How can I safely tell edible wild mushrooms? There are several regional as well as general books on the subject. One of the best is *The Mushroom Hunter's Field Guide,* by Alexander H. Smith, published by the University of Michigan Press, Ann Arbor.

MUSKMELON AND CANTALOUPE (CUCUMIS MELO)

Please give information on raising muskmelons. Muskmelons do well in lighter soils and need a warm, sunshiny season for maturing quality fruits. Seed can be sown out-of-doors, but in northern sections it is better to start seed indoors, using Jiffy-7 peat pellets to grow healthy transplants for setting outside after all danger of frost has passed. Start seeds 4 to 5 weeks before outdoor planting time. Set 3 to 4 feet apart, in rows 4 to 5 feet apart. Cultivate frequently; some pulling of weeds will be necessary after the vines spread. Black plastic mulch works well with muskmelons. Where the season is short, early varieties such as 'Harper Hybrid', 'Champlain', and 'Delicious 51' may be grown. Temperatures below 50° F. during growth reduce the sugar content of melons and decrease flavor.

How are muskmelons fertilized? They need a well-manured soil, light and thoroughly prepared, and a complete fertilizer. Two to 4 shovelfuls of well-rotted manure or rich compost are usually worked into the soil under each "hill" when planting.

When can I plant muskmelons? After the danger of frost has passed, about tomato-setting time. About the middle to the last of May in most of the northern states, or a few weeks earlier under Hotkaps or similar protection.

How can an early crop of muskmelons be achieved without starting it indoors? Use plant protectors such as Hotkaps. In this way, seed or plants can be put out 2 or 3 weeks earlier than would otherwise be ad-

visable. As plants begin to make growth, the protector should be torn
open at the top to provide ventilation.

*Cucumber, melon, and squash
seeds can be sown while frosts
are still possible if the seeds
are sown under Hotkaps or
similar protection. The Hotkaps will warm the soil, which
is necessary for germination.*

Can muskmelons be started indoors?   Yes, clay pots, paper pots,
peat-fiber or Jiffy-7 pots, or the like can be used with a good plant-
growing soil. Sow seed 3 to 4 weeks before setting out-of-doors. Grow
at a temperature of 65° to 70° F., watering to provide vigorous growth;
but plants should not start to run before they go to the garden. When
setting in the garden, do not disturb the roots.

How can I tell when muskmelons are ready to pick?   Most varieties
of muskmelon develop a yellowish color as they mature. Watch the
place where the stem joins the fruit. When this begins to crack and the
stem comes off cleanly and freely, the melons are ready to harvest.
Some varieties are not quite ready for the table at this stage but should
be kept a few days in a sunny windowsill until they become a little soft
at the blossom end. Varieties differ considerably in the application of
these tests. When ripe, the fruits must be refrigerated, as they can spoil
very fast.

**Can you please tell me how to grow good quality muskmelons? I
planted some last summer on a pile of old sod. I had melons, but they
were quite tasteless and flat.**   Lack of sweetness and flavor in muskmelons may be due to cool, moist weather during the maturing period
and to loss of leaves by disease. Active foliage is required to make sugar.
Varieties also differ in quality.

Our muskmelons grow only as large as an egg. Why?   There are
many possible reasons for this. This may be due to a lack of phosphorus
and lime in the soil. It may be due to a lack of water or the presence of
insects. On sandy soils, it may be a lack of fertility. If the vines are vigorous, it may be due to a lack of potash.

Can I raise muskmelons in the clayey but well-drained soil of this region? (New Jersey.) Yes. Add humus; do not plant until the soil is warm. Try the variety 'Hearts of Gold'.

How can I fight muskmelon diseases? Plant disease-resistant varieties. Treat seed with captan or thiram. When plants come up, they should be faithfully dusted for striped cucumber beetle. Keep free from weeds; some of them carry mosaic, which injures the crop.

How can I keep cantaloupe vines from wilting about the time the fruit starts to grow? This is due to the work of the cucumber beetle when the plants are young. As they feed on the foliage, they inoculate the plants with the wilt organism. A cold frame with mosquito netting over it placed over the plants until they are well started will keep the beetles off and thus prevent the wilt. Methoxychlor will control beetles.

I live on the north shore of Long Island; I should like to grow some melons. What kind is best? Growers on Long Island and in Connecticut have had good success with 'Delicious 51'. Other good varieties are 'Burpee Hybrid', 'Saticoy', 'Iroquois', 'Harper Hybrid', and 'Supermarket'.

What are the best varieties of muskmelons? Muskmelon varieties vary widely in their adaptation to regions. In the southern half of the country the 'Hale Best' group does very well, but it does not thrive under the cooler, more humid, conditions of the North. 'Mainerock' is both early and adapted to cool weather. 'Delicious 51' is a good early. 'Harper Hybrid', 'Burpee Hybrid', 'Iroquois', and 'Gold Star' all do well in various sections of the North.

OKRA (ABELMOSCHUS ESCULENTUS)

How much seed is necessary to plant 30 feet of okra? One half ounce of okra seed will plant 100 feet of row, usually enough seed in a packet for 25 or 30 feet. The plants should stand at least 12 or 15 inches apart.

How and when should okra be planted? I have been unsuccessful in trying to raise them. When the soil is well warmed—that is, about the same time as beans. The soil should not be acid, and better plants and pods will result if it is fertile. Okra needs, in addition, lots of sun and a location where there is little risk of cold winds.

What caused most of my okra to grow to immense size but to set only a few pods? In all probability, some fertilizer too rich in nitrogen has been used. Unfavorable weather conditions, however, may have been the cause. Long periods of rain often result in poor pollination.

In a fairly good soil where other vegetables grow well, for 4 years in succession, okra has done poorly. The leaves turn yellow, wither, and die. This sounds like either a disease working in the stems or root lice or other insects working on the fine roots. The soil should be well limed. Dig up a plant next time and see whether root lice are causing the trouble. They infest okra at times. Aphids are carried by ants. Treat the soil with diazinon before planting to get rid of ants.

At what size should okra pods be picked? When they are young and tender—finger length, and not too thick through. Large pods are too pithy and tough to be palatable.

ONION (ALLIUM CEPA)

What is the correct way to raise onions? Grow onions from sets for summer, or from seed or plants for winter storage. The soil should be well limed, fertile, and abundantly supplied with nitrogen; work in 5 pounds of a complete fertilizer to 100 square feet. Harvest when the tops begin to break over and die. Use small sets to prevent large neck and seed stalks.

What is the best way to grow onions in the small garden? From onion sets—very small onions which made their limited growth the previous season. These will furnish the early onions. They are available in early spring from garden centers and mail-order houses. Those for later use and winter storage can be grown from seed. The soil must not be acid and should be extra-well-fertilized.

For fall and winter use, is it best to plant seed, plants, or sets of onions? Sets for early onions, and plants for late onions for storage. Growing from seed is more difficult and uncertain.

When should onion sets be planted? How deep? As soon as the soil can be made ready in the spring. Push into prepared soil, leaving ½ inch above the top of the sets. If large onions are wanted, the sets should be 3 to 4 inches apart; for scallions or bunch onions, about 1 inch apart. Do not plan to thin out and use alternate onions for scallions, as this disturbs the roots of those left to form large bulbs.

What are onion sets? Onion sets are grown by sowing seed thickly, 50 to 60 pounds per acre, in drills or rows 2 or 3 inches wide. The seedlings should be grown on fairly clean soil. The tops will begin to turn yellow in July. When mature, they are pulled and the tops cut off.

They are piled in the field in shallow piles for a week if the weather is dry. Then they are stored under cover in shallow trays with good ventilation. Only varieties that store well as mature bulbs will keep as sets. Spanish types are worthless.

Please give the easiest way for the home gardener to raise onion sets for the following year. Or is it better to raise onions from seed in one season? For home use it is better to buy sets or plants in the spring and raise a crop of bulbs from these.

What is the proper way to grow onions from seed? Plant the seed in rows early in the spring as soon as the ground can be worked. Make rows 12 to 15 inches apart; sow 8 to 10 seeds per inch; cover ¼ inch deep; thin to stand 2 to 3 inches apart in the row. Use fertile, well-drained soil, liberally limed, then cultivate to keep out weeds. Watch for thrips on the young seedlings. Harvest when the tops begin to die after they break over. Cure thoroughly, under cover, before storing for winter.

What kinds of onion seed do I need for my market garden to supply good green onions all summer? What kind of fertilizer do they require? (Michigan.) 'White Portugal' and 'Evergreen Long White Bunching' are grown for this purpose, but any variety recommended for the northern states is good for growing green onions. In order to have them all summer it is necessary to make successive plantings of seed at 2- to 3-week intervals. An 8–6–6 fertilizer at the rate of 400 pounds to the acre, broadcast over the surface when the ground is prepared, should be ample for green onions.

Can I raise 'Bermuda' onions from seed? (Ohio.) Yes, but unless the seed is sown early (in a greenhouse) and transplanted, the onions will be much smaller than those sold in stores. The 'Sweet Spanish' types have all but replaced 'Bermuda'.

How and when should 'Bermuda' onions be planted to grow large? Get plants from a southern plant grower or from a seed supply firm. Set the plants, as soon as the ground can be prepared, in rich soil, and make provision for watering during dry weather.

How should 'Bermuda' onions be stored for best results? They store poorly. Use storage types instead.

What fertilizer is best to use in a sandy soil to grow big onions from sets? A 7–7–7 or an 8–6–6. Compost or well-rotted manure, plus a complete fertilizer (such as 5–10–5), usually give a satisfactory crop. Wood ashes are excellent for onions.

Do onions need lime? Onions should be grown on soil with a good lime content—not because the onion actually needs so much calcium but because the presence of lime helps to aerate the soil, enabling the plants to grow better.

What is the botanical name of the onion that bears little bulblets at the top?   This is the perennial tree (or Egyptian tree) onion, *Allium cepa proliferum*. It is winter-hardy.

What are "multiplier" onions good for?   The multiplier onion is probably a sport of the regular onion and is used for flavoring, just as regular onions are used. It is often confused with the species mentioned above.

What is the botanical name for shallots and how are they grown?   The shallot is *Allium cepa aggregatum*. It is propagated by planting the sections or cloves of which the large bulb consists.

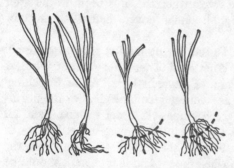

Onion seedlings ready for transplanting. Tops and roots (right) are trimmed back as indicated.

I had very bad luck with onions. They were no bigger than seed onions at the end of the season and the green onions were very thin. What was wrong?   If they did not stay green, it may have been due to thrips on the leaves, lice or maggots on the roots, poor soil, a lack of lime in the soil, or too much nitrogen.

Could onion seeds be sown in the fall, or in February? I'm especially interested in 'Sweet Spanish' types. (Missouri.)   Both seed and sets can be planted in the fall and winter months if the soil can be prepared properly. The large Spanish onions are usually sown in seed beds and then transplanted in the spring only.

Should blossoms of onions be cut?   If the flower stalk is cut, water might rot the bulb. If the flower stalks are forming, they can be recognized when the neck of the onion is small. They should be broken over (not cut) to prevent the neck of the onion from getting too large. A big-necked onion does not keep well in storage.

How do I grow large onions? When should they be taken up?   Their size depends on the weather, how well the soil has been prepared, adequate thinning (2 to 3 inches apart while plants are small), and keeping the crop absolutely free from weeds. Only large-type onions, such as the 'Sweet Spanish' varieties, produce big bulbs. Dig bulbs when they are large or when tops fall over.

What causes onion tops to fall over and turn brown?   This is normally the sign that the bulbs have attained maturity. The tops, then of no further service to the plant in manufacturing its food, naturally shrivel and collapse. If the onions are not matured, drought may be the cause, or thrips.

Does planting onions near gladioli increase the possibility of the latter being attacked by thrips?   It would not make much difference; if thrips are bad, it is because of weather conditions being favorable for their multiplication. Any crop that harbors thrips will increase their population for crops that follow. Control thrips with Sevin or diazinon according to the directions on the container.

How can I prevent onions from becoming sunburned?   White varieties sometimes sunscald or turn green. Gather as soon as their tops begin to die; spread out thinly, under cover, but with good ventilation until their tops dry up, then remove the tops.

How do I keep dry onions from sprouting in the winter months?   If onions are kept too warm in a room where the air is moist or where light enters, they will sprout. Some onions will sprout more than others because the bulbs have not been properly cured. Some varieties keep better than others. The best winter keeper of all is 'Spartan Sleeper', which can be stored at room temperature for 6 months or more before spoiling.

Please name some good varieties of onions for the home garden. *Early:* 'Crystal White Wax', 'Silver Skin' ('White Portugal'). *Midseason:* 'Yellow Globe', mild. *Late:* 'Southport White Globe', 'Sweet Spanish' types, 'Gigantic Gibraltar', all mild; 'Ebenezer', 'Yellow Globe', medium mild. Best storage onion is 'Spartan Sleeper'.

PARSLEY (PETROSELINUM CRISPUM)

How should parsley be grown? Does it tolerate shade?   Parsley does not do well in a shady place. As a matter of fact, there are very few vegetables that do, not even the ones that do not tolerate too much heat and drought. Parsley can be sown in good, friable, well-enriched garden soil as soon in the spring as the ground can be prepared. Make rows shallow and cover lightly with fine soil. Sow seed about 10 or 20 to the foot, or thicker if you want to use the thinnings. If sizable plants are wanted, they should be thinned to from 5 to 8 inches apart. Adequate water supply is important.

Should the parsley bed be covered during the winter? If so, what material should be used?   Excelsior or dry leaves or some other material that will not become wet and form a mat will keep the plants green well into the winter. Still better, transfer some of the plants to a tight frame; if the latter is reasonably frostproof, they should last through the winter.

My parsley plant stops growing when taken indoors, ball, root, and all, even though it stands with other plants that thrive. Why does it do this?   This sounds like the turnip-rooted parsley, which will become dormant. It is better to use the regular parsley, which is fibrous-rooted.

How can I successfully transplant parsley from outside beds for winter window gardening?   Soak the ground around the plants the day before you wish to move them. Dig the plants by leaving a small ball of soil around the roots and set in a window box in soil that has not been treated with chemical fertilizer. Trim off at least half of the outside leaves.

Why does my parsley, brought in from out-of-doors and potted, turn dark at the edge of its leaves and look as if it was dying?   Parsley brought in from out-of-doors should be cut back to the crown so it can make new growth. Old leaves will wither. Water sparingly at first, increasing as growth starts. Parsley requires several hours of sunshine a day to do well indoors. Young plants started in August are much better for winter use than old roots. All herbs grown indoors do better if fluorescent tubes supplement daylight.

Are the bottoms of parsley plants good to eat? If so, how would you use them?   The roots of turnip-rooted (or parsnip-rooted) parsley are edible. Use in soups.

How can I make my parsley seed germinate more quickly?   The natural germination period is long. Soak the seeds for 24 hours in tepid water before planting to soften the hard shells. After soaking, run tepid water through the seed to remove a natural chemical that slows germination.

PARSNIP (PASTINACA SATIVA)

How can I have long, fleshy, well-developed parsnips?   Soil for parsnips should be very well and deeply worked to a depth of 12 to 18 inches. If perfect roots are desired, all stone and hard clods must be removed from the soil, which should be enriched with compost. Plant seeds early in the spring in rows 18 to 20 inches apart, covering ¼ to ½ inch deep. Thin to 4 inches apart. Grow on through the entire season, cultivating the ground as needed. The crop will be ready in autumn and can be stored, or some can be left in the ground (as they are perfectly hardy) for digging in winter and spring.

How are exhibition parsnips grown? Deep holes, 4, 5, or 6 inches apart, are made with a crowbar, in well-prepared, pulverized soil. These are filled with sifted soil and compost and 3 or 4 seeds are planted on top of this. When seedlings develop, all but one are removed. Such roots are often 3 to 4 feet long when dug at the end of the season.

What variety of parsnip is best to grow? Though 'Hollow Crown' is the standard, 'All-American' is newer and preferable because the roots are thick but chunky, and so can be well grown without such deep preparation.

PEANUT (ARACHIS HYPOGAEA)

What is the proper time for planting and care, cultivation, and harvesting of peanuts? The nuts (removed from the shells) are planted an inch deep and about a foot apart in well-prepared, light soil. Manure and nitrogenous fertilizers are avoided. Rows should be 3 feet apart. Give clean cultivation until after the blossoms at the base of the plant (which are not readily found) are produced. Mulching around the base of the plant at this time is beneficial and helps keep down weeds for the balance of the season. Plant about the same time as the first sowing of sweet corn. At least 4 months are required to produce the crop.

What should one do to make peanuts give a better yield in sandy Michigan ground? This may be a water and a fertility problem. Perhaps the season is too cool for peanuts to grow satisfactorily. They require warm nights for a considerable period.

Do you think it is possible to grow peanuts successfully as far north as I live, in Spokane, Washington? The season in your part of the country should be amply long even if the seed is sown outdoors in the usual way, but night temperatures are unfavorable. While peanuts do not transplant readily, they can be started in small peat or Jiffy-7 pots and the young plants set out after the danger of frost has passed. The time gained results in a larger crop and is best in a region like yours with cool nights.

PEA (PISUM SATIVUM)

Are green peas very hard to raise?   In areas where hot weather, and especially hot nights, is likely to come suddenly, they are difficult. Peas are easy to grow if the soil is in good condition and the seed is planted very early in the season. Only one variety, 'Wando', will set pods in hot weather.

What sort of weather and climate do peas prefer?   Cool nights with bright, cool days.

What kind of soil, weather conditions, etc., are necessary for growing green peas in a home garden? What variety is best?   A good soil that is well limed and does not contain an excess of nitrogen. The subsoil should be open so the roots can penetrate it. Peas should be planted as early as possible to get them to set pods before hot weather. 'Little Marvel', 'Novella', and 'Green Arrow' are good dwarf varieties. 'Freezonian', 'Midfreezer', 'Mammoth Podded Extra Early', and 'Lincoln' are good 2½ footers. 'Alderman' and 'Sugar Snap' (edible-podded) are excellent tall ones. Only the variety 'Wando' will set pods in hot weather.

Do garden peas require a new soil to do their best?   Not unless the soil is infected with root diseases. Lime will work wonders for peas. Don't overfertilize them. Use a starter solution. Water in dry weather.

What fertilizer is necessary to produce a good growth of peas?   If the soil is properly limed and generally fertile, you do not need any fertilizer. In a garden, a starter solution poured on the seed when it is planted should be enough.

What particular soil feeding do peas need? I have good loam soil that produces excellent beans, tomatoes, etc., but peas do not do well. The plot is well manured each year although I haven't used any commercial fertilizer.   You may need some lime. Also the soil may have too much nitrogen. Peas must be planted as early as the ground can be prepared.

Is hen manure good fertilizer for growing peas? What causes pods to dry up instead of maturing properly?   No. Peas do not need the nitrogen that is present in the chicken manure. If peas grow too rapidly because of too much nitrogen and water, the pods may start to grow without being fertilized and will dry up, as there is no seed in them. Hot weather also causes them to shrivel.

When should peas be planted, both smooth and wrinkled sorts?   Either type may be sown just as early in the spring as a good, mellow seed bed can be prepared. The sole advantage of the smooth-seeded sorts is that they are a trifle hardier and can be planted a few days earlier; usually this is scarcely sufficient compensation for their lower quality.

When is the proper time to plant peas on the eastern shore of Maryland? Late fall or very early spring.

When is the right time to plant garden peas, also sweet peas, in this locality? (Missouri.) In the fall or as early as the ground can be prepared in the spring.

Is it possible to raise peas in the fairly well-drained, rather clayey soil of this region? (New Jersey.) Yes, if the soil is properly limed. Don't use too much nitrogen. Plant the peas before the first of April, if possible. Try 'Little Marvel' for early peas and 'Laxton's Progress' for a little later.

Can you tell me if it is possible to raise peas on light soil? Yes. Be sure that the soil has sufficient lime and humus, then use a starter solution on the seed when it is planted.

Is it possible to grow peas near salt water? (Massachusetts.) Yes, if the spray does not hit them and the ground does not contain salt.

How early can garden peas be started in my locality? Also, will peas grow in practically full shade or do they require some sunlight? (New Jersey.) Plant as early as possible. This may be April 1 or even earlier. Peas will not grow in the shade; they require full sunshine, especially in the morning.

Why are peas a poor crop in northern Virginia? This may be due to a lack of lime in the soil or to hot dry weather when the pods are ready to set. Peas must be planted in the fall or very early spring.

Is there any type of garden peas that can be planted in the fall or winter for an extra-early crop? (New Jersey.) Any variety of garden peas can be planted in the fall if they are planted late enough so that they won't germinate until spring. Drainage must be perfect; how they will come through depends largely on the winter weather.

Do dwarf peas need support? If so, what kind? While they do not need support, it is well to use it if possible in the home garden; the rows can be planted closer (24 inches or so) and the crop is more easily tended and picked than when the vines are allowed to sprawl.

What is the best support for peas and sweet peas? Cut brush, if it can be obtained; if not, use wire or string. Most seed firms sell a reusable trellis netting that pea vines can cling to. The support should be 15 to 18 inches for dwarf peas, 5 to 6 feet for tall peas and sweet peas.

What makes pea vines wither and turn brown before they mature?   Hot weather; aphids; diseases; soil in poor physical condition or with poor aeration.

What insects are most common on peas?   Plant lice or aphids. (See Section 13.)

What do I do for garden pea weevil?   Place seed in an airtight container, drop a few drops of carbon disulfide in the can, and cover tightly.

What fungus diseases attack garden peas? How can they be identified? How can they be prevented or controlled?   Powdery mildew on the leaves can be controlled with dusting sulfur. Root rots causing brown roots, caused by poor aeration of the soil, can be corrected by deeper tilling and more lime in the soil. When possible, rotate plantings each year.

What is the most effective way of protecting young peas and other succulent seedlings from slugs during wet weather in the spring?   Sprinkle some hydrated lime on the ground under the vines and even on the lower leaves on the vines. Or use slug baits sold in garden centers.

What treatment do you recommend for mildew on peas?   Dust with flowers of sulfur or a sulfur-lime dust.

How can sparrows be kept from eating the peas and beans as they come through the earth?   Some short pieces of rope should be placed where the birds will see them. (Birds fear snakes.) Or cover the row with a strip of close-mesh wire.

What is the difference between smooth-seeded and wrinkled peas?   Smooth-seeded are hardier for very early sowing, but the crop is inferior in quality. Smooth-seeded peas take two months to mature. Wrinkled-seeded are a little less hardy, the seeds being more apt to rot in cold, wet ground, but the quality and yield are superior. Treat seed with captan to prevent rot. (For varieties, see the following questions.)

What are the best edible-podded pea varieties?   The variety called 'Sugar Snap' belonging to a new class of edible-podded pea called snap peas, growing fat, edible pods and sweet, succulent peas is outstanding. (Unlike old-fashioned garden peas that need shelling, edible-podded peas can be eaten pod-and-all.) All that's needed with 'Sugar Snap' is the removal of a string along the top of the pod. This comes away automatically when the stem part of the pea is pulled off. Some of the older edible-podded pea varieties, so much used in oriental cuisine, are also easily grown in the home garden. The advantages of these varieties, such as 'Snowbird' and 'Dwarf Gray Sugar', are that they come into bearing before 'Sugar Snap', which requires about 70 days to reach harvest, and they do not grow taller than 2 to 3 feet. 'Sugar Snap' grows 6 feet tall and needs sturdy support for the heavy vines. Other snap pea varieties ('SugarBon', 'SugarMel', and 'SugarRae') grow only about 30 inches high.

What varieties of peas are best for freezing? Edible-podded or snow peas are excellent for freezing. Among standard peas 'Freezonian' is the outstanding variety for freezing. 'Little Marvel', which is one of the best home-garden varieties, is also a very good freezing variety, as are 'Lincoln' and 'Wando'.

PEPPER (CAPSICUM ANNUUM)

How can I have early sweet peppers? Buy plants from a local grower or start seeds indoors in March under lights. Set out when all danger of frost is past—just a little later than you set out tomatoes in your locality.

How do you make pepper plants bear? Mine grow beautifully but bear late and little. Grow them with little or no nitrogen. Use only lime and a 0–12–12 fertilizer.

Why do I have no success with sweet peppers? The plants have many flowers and tiny peppers but very few that can be used, yet the plants are nice and big. The plants are too vigorous. Try growing them on less fertile soil and do not put any nitrogen or manure on until the peppers are set and partially grown. Try using a liquid fertilizer sidedressing. Temperatures below 50° F. or above 90° F. cause flowers and small fruits to drop off.

What makes fruit drop off pepper plants in the summer? Too much nitrogen, a boron deficiency, or high or very low temperatures when the flowers are setting fruits. Grow them slower until the fruit is set.

Should green pepper plants be pinched back? Pinch out the growing tip of the plants at 6 inches. Later pinching will slow their harvest.

If sweet pepper plants are brought indoors in the fall, will they continue to bear during the winter? Yes, if moved carefully and with sufficient soil, but it would be difficult. Peppers need high temperatures, humidity, and sunshine.

What peppers shall I grow? *Sweet:* 'Early Pimiento', 'Better Bell', 'Big Bertha', 'Gypsy', 'Fordhook', 'Ace', and 'Sweet Banana'. *Hot:* 'Long Red Cayenne' or 'Hungarian Wax' (yellow).

POTATO (SOLANUM TUBEROSUM)

Are there any tricks about raising enough potatoes for our own use next winter? How many potatoes should we plant to get about seven bushels?   Potatoes are somewhat more difficult to grow for home use than most other vegetables. A few fundamentals must be observed. These include choosing a loamy soil, using healthy stock, and practicing a thorough program of weed control and of spraying for insects and blight. To raise about seven bushels of potatoes, plant about 30 to 50 pounds of seed stock. The former figure assumes a fifteenfold increase, which is somewhat above the average. If soil temperatures go above 85° F., tubers stop growing. A heavy mulch keeps soil cool.

Is it profitable to grow potatoes in the home garden?   It depends on whether potatoes grow well in your locality, on the size of the garden, and similar considerations. In the suburban garden of a family with a normal liking for potatoes and located near a store, the answer is probably "No." Potatoes are a big commercial crop that does not suffer too much in quality by being stored and shipped. For another opinion, see below.

Are home-grown potatoes of superior eating quality?   Definitely yes! Fresh-dug potatoes are tender, mealy, and delicious, with an especially fine flavor.

What soil do you suggest for potatoes?   Potatoes are not adapted to heavy and poorly drained soils. Farmers who do not have good potato soil grow other crops. A good potato soil is one which is loamy or friable to a depth of at least 12 inches. In choosing a soil for potatoes, it is fortunate if one can be found which is naturally quite acid in reaction. Otherwise, there will be trouble with potato scab. It is fairly easy to change, by liming, a soil which is too acid, but it is difficult to acidify a soil which is naturally within the range favorable to scab, i.e., anything above pH 5.6.

What are the best commercial fertilizers on a sandy loam for a potato crop? For clay soil?   Sandy soils are particularly deficient in soil nutrients, especially in potash. For this reason, potato growers on the sandier soils usually use large applications of such fertilizers as 5–10–10 and 4–8–12. For heavier soils, use a fertilizer relatively high in phosphoric acid, such as 4–12–4 and 5–10–5. Soil with a high clay content tends to tie up or make unavailable the phosphorous element, thereby increasing the danger of deficiency unless supplied in excess.

What is needed in fertilizer for potatoes in home gardens? My soil has a good deal of oak-leaf humus. Since such soil is well supplied with humus, the principal need for nutrients would be phosphoric acid and potash. It may be desirable to add some form of commercial nitrogen to hasten the decomposition of the humus—such as sulfate of ammonia. Whether or not this garden soil needs lime depends on its present reaction. Lime can cause trouble. A pH reading of 5.6 or lower will prevent scab. Use calcium sulfate (gypsum) if a soil test shows calcium is needed. There is probably enough acid, but you should have the soil tested.

What are certified seed potatoes? Certified seed potatoes are potatoes stored, treated, planted, and harvested under definite rules of sanitation. They are inspected for symptoms of any virus disease. There is a final bin inspection before the potatoes are bagged for shipment. If the potatoes pass inspection, they are certified by the state as being free from virus diseases.

How should seed potatoes be prepared for planting? Cut the seed potatoes into several pieces, each of which should have one strong eye, or two, and a good piece of the tuber. The "eye" is a dormant bud from which a new plant will grow, and its first food will be derived from the piece of tuber. Plant only certified, disease-free seed potatoes. Small seed potatoes need not be cut.

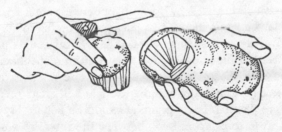

Large potatoes can be cut up into seed pieces. These should have at least two good, strong eyes.

Are seed potatoes planted immediately after cutting? They may be, but it is better practice to lay the cut pieces out in flats or shallow trays, skin side up, and leave them in a sunny but airy place for from 1 to 4 weeks until the "eyes" sprout. Or the whole potatoes may thus be sprouted before cutting. Unlike sprouts produced in the root cellar on stored potatoes, these sprouts will be dark green and closely clustered in the eyes close to the tuber. They are then planted, eyes up.

Should I use large or small seed potatoes? Small tubers of certified seed potatoes are best.

How many pounds of seed potatoes are needed for planting a half acre? (Illinois.) Most experiments show that 9 to 10 bushels of seed would be the approximate amount needed to plant a half acre of potatoes on upland soil.

How many potatoes should be planted in a hill? Place one piece of tuber every 12 inches and cover with 3 inches of soil.

When is the best time to plant early potatoes? About a month before the last spring frost is expected. By the time the young plants have come up through 3 inches of soil, any frost likely to hurt them should then be past.

When should late potatoes be planted? The word "late" as applied by gardeners means late in reaching maturity, not late in time of planting. Your seed catalog will show approximately the number of days for the variety you select; count back this number from the expected date of first frosts in the fall.

How deep should early and late potatoes be planted? Early varieties of potatoes (planted early) should be planted shallower than late potatoes. Shallower planting results in earlier emergence, which in turn tends to hasten maturity. However, most potatoes, regardless of variety, should be planted 3 to 5 inches deep, depending on the soil type.

Since July–August droughts almost regularly injure late potato plantings in the central states, would it not be well to plant the late potatoes early, along with the early potatoes? The late potatoes are varieties which take longer to mature, and the drought will affect them no matter when they are planted. Early planting would be better. Try spreading a mulch of straw 4 to 6 inches thick between the rows. This will conserve moisture and keep down weeds.

Is it practical to mulch potatoes in this area? (Southeast Kansas.) How do I do it? Yes, entirely practical. Before dry weather, spread straw to a depth of 4 to 6 inches between the rows and close up to the plants.

Should potatoes be grown under straw? The effect of a straw mulch is to maintain a lower soil temperature, to conserve moisture, and to control weeds. The straw should be applied about the time the potato plants are emerging. If applied too early, growth is retarded; if too late, the plants already started will be injured by the straw. Often as much as 12 inches of straw is used when the entire growing area is covered.

Is it possible to plant potatoes in January, February, and March? There are frosty nights but sunshine in the daytime; there is no snow. (California.) Plant the seed potatoes four or five weeks before the frosty nights are expected to end.

What is lacking in the earth that our potatoes don't grow to a normal size? They are perfect and of good flavor but remain very small. They seem to grow well and have plenty of top. There are two probable reasons. Your soil may be deficient in nitrogen, phosphoric acid, or potash. Too little fertilizer or too little organic matter in the soil may be responsible. High soil temperature (above 85° F.) stops suberization (tuber growth). If in your judgment none of these factors is involved, the most likely explanation is that the seed you have planted is infected with virus disease. The principal virus diseases are mosaic and leaf roll. Purchase certified or disease-free seed.

I grow wonderful potato vines in my garden, but the tubers are seldom larger than marbles. What can I do about it? Large potato vines and poor yields may indicate an excess of nitrogen or a deficiency of potash and phosphorus. This can be corrected by an increased application of phosphoric acid and potash. If the garden has had an abundance of organic matter, the difficulty might be corrected merely by using superphosphate, broadcasting it and working it in when preparing the plot. Another possibility is that the garden does not get enough sun. Too much shade causes an excessive ratio of top to the tuber in potatoes.

In potato growing, when should I harvest them? When the vines have completely died down. The tubers make no growth after that.

Is light harmful to potatoes after they are dug? Yes, they acquire an unpleasant flavor and should be exposed to the sun only long enough so that the adhering soil may be easily removed. (Greened potatoes are poisonous.) Then they should be taken to the cellar or some other dark storage area.

How should potatoes be stored? In a very cool cellar, and so piled or arranged that a little air can circulate around them; otherwise they are likely to sweat. Loosely woven potato sacks are satisfactory, or slat crates—much better than solid boxes or bins.

How can flea beetle and potato beetle be controlled on home-grown potato plants? When insect pests appear, use an all-purpose potato dust or spray that controls both pests and diseases. A bacterial culture containing *Bacillus thuringiensis* and sold under various trade names kills beetles as they feed. Also, look at the underside of leaves for their little clusters of orange-colored eggs and destroy these.

What causes scab on potatoes? A fungus, *Actinomyces scabies*, which thrives best in light, alkaline soils. It can be brought into the garden by infected seed potatoes; if it is already in the soil, be very wary of using lime on the potato patch. This organism does not endure acid conditions.

How often and with what should potatoes be sprayed to control late blight? The best safeguard against this disease is maneb or chlorothalonil applied as a spray. As plants increase in size, more spray is needed for thorough coverage. The spray should be applied often enough to keep all of the new growth completely covered throughout the season. Under conditions favoring rapid growth, this means an application at least every 7 to 10 days after the plants are 6 inches high.

What are early, medium, and late varieties of potatoes? First, the type of soil, climate, and other local conditions should be considered. In general, 'Irish Cobbler' is the favorite early, though many prefer 'Chippewa' or 'Early Ohio'. For midseason, 'Katahdin' and 'Kennebec'. 'Green Mountain' does well on heavier soils. For the late crop, 'Jersey Red' and 'Sebago' are among the best.

What are the best-tasting potatoes to raise? Plant 'Early Ohio' for the first crop, 'Katahdin' for the second, and if your soil, culture, and climate are good, the potatoes will be of fine flavor.

Does the 'Katahdin' potato do well in the corn belt? (Illinois.) When grown as a late potato, the 'Katahdin' does as well or better than the members of the Rural group in the northern part of the corn belt. Trials in the southern part of the corn belt have been inconclusive.

What experiments have been made with 'Sebago' potatoes and with what result? 'Sebago' has proved widely adaptable and very satisfactory as a late variety in the New England states and in New York. 'Sebago' is definitely later in maturity, white-skinned, lower in starch content, and much more resistant to scab, blight, and mosaic than is 'Green Mountain'. Experience to date would indicate that it is also more widely adapted to adverse potato soil and climate than 'Green Mountain'. Seed-spacing tests both in Maine and New York indicate larger seed pieces and more seed to the acre are desirable with 'Sebago' than with 'Green Mountain'.

Has there been any real improvement over the 'Early Rose' and 'Green Mountain' potato? No variety exists today that has a higher starch content than 'Green Mountain'. Such varieties as 'Chippewa', 'Katahdin', 'Sebago', and 'Sequoia' are lower in starch content but much more resistant to disease and more productive. However, some varieties, such as 'Houma' and 'Mohawk', have as much starch content and are as mealy as 'Green Mountain' and 'Early Rose'.

PUMPKIN (CUCURBITA PEPO)

What is the best way to grow good pumpkins?   Soil for pumpkins should be well enriched. If good garden ground is used, it is not necessary to make up special hills, but if the soil is a bit poor, work a forkful or two of compost into each hill. Plantings should be made after frost danger is past, with rows 8 feet apart and hills 4 to 8 feet apart in the row. Cover the seed about an inch deep. Dusting for striped beetle will be necessary during early growth.

Are pumpkins planted in sun or shade?   Pumpkins should have little or no shade.

What method does one follow to force or produce supersized pumpkins or squash? Does it help to cut off branch tips and keep them in a dish of milk?   The plants should be grown under favorable conditions of soil and climate. The soil should be fertile and moisture-holding. If rainfall is short, water frequently. Plants are spaced widely, about 8 to 12 feet. Allow the whole plant to grow, but remove extra fruits, leaving only 1 or 2 per plant. Sidedress the plants with a little complete fertilizer as the season goes along. Nothing is gained by cutting off the tip of the branch and keeping it in a dish of milk.

What are some good pumpkin varieties?   'Big Max' is a variety of large pumpkin, but 'Small Sugar' is considered better for cooking and pies. The 'Cushaws' (including the 'Green Striped', 'Tennessee Sweet Potato', 'Golden Cushaw', and 'Large Cheese') are favored in the South. 'Cinderella' is a bush variety for smaller gardens (6 square feet to a single plant).

RADISH (RAPHANUS SATIVUS)

What soil and plant food are necessary to produce good radishes?   Any soil that does not bake too hard will produce good radishes. Use fertilizers low in nitrogen. All organic materials such as leafmold, compost, and humus are beneficial. Sprinkle land plaster (gypsum), 3 or 4 pounds to 50 feet, along the rows and work into the soil before planting.

Why can't we raise radishes of any kind? This is hard to understand. Radishes are very easy to grow. Plant seed from April 1 to May 15, using early varieties. Thin seedlings to stand 1½ inches apart when the first set of true leaves appear. They are a cool-weather crop. Perhaps you plant them too late in the spring.

What should be done when my radishes all grow into tops instead of radishes? Probably the weather is too warm. (See the above question.)

What happened to my second crop of radishes and lettuce planted in July? They came up 2 inches and would go no farther. The first crop was fine. I have sandy soil. (Indiana.) July is a poor month to sow radishes and lettuce. Midsummer temperatures are not conducive to the production of these crops in your area. The variety 'Icicle' does better in hot weather but still must be sown earlier than July in most northern regions.

I have a small greenhouse and the radishes I planted have long, thin red stalks between the green leaves and the radish itself. What is the remedy for this? Evidently the soil is too rich in nitrogen, the night temperatures are too high, and they are not being thinned out sufficiently.

What are the names of some improved radish varieties? 'Cherry Belle', 'Champion', 'Comet', 'Sparkler' (red with a white tip); 'Giant Butter' (very large, and remains a long time in good condition); 'Long Scarlet' and 'White Icicle', both long and narrow, the latter less peppery than the former. Winter radishes: 'White' and 'Scarlet Chinese' and 'Long Black Spanish'.

RHUBARB (RHEUM RHABARBARUM)

How do you prepare the bed for rhubarb roots? Make sure that the soil is rich and well drained. If you have rotted manure or compost, it should be liberally spread and dug in. Set the roots in holes 6 inches deep and 18 to 24 inches apart, with crowns just below the surface. Firm the soil about them with your feet, applying full weight.

What yearly care is needed for established rhubarb roots? In autumn, mulch the entire surface of the bed with compost or rotted manure. In the spring, dig this into the bed lightly, being careful not to cut the roots. An application of high-nitrogen fertilizer will hasten spring growth and produce tender, juicy stalks.

How is rhubarb propagated? Rhubarb is usually propagated by dividing the older roots. This is best done in the early spring just as the first buds appear. Use a sharp spade to cut the old root into pieces, having at least 1 and preferably 2 or 3 buds at the top. Set the cut pieces in the new location immediately, with the buds just at the surface of the soil; water in well.

Do rhubarb roots ever need to be divided? Yes, about every second or third year for the best quality stalks.

When is the best time to reset pie-plant (rhubarb)—fall or early spring? Reset rhubarb in the early spring, as the first buds appear.

When is the best time to take up and move rhubarb? How many roots are placed in a hill and how do you fertilize them? I have plenty of barnyard manure. (See the above question.) Barnyard manure on a well-limed soil will grow good rhubarb. Divide old roots (free from any rot) into 2, 3, or more sections and place 1 section in a hill.

How do you cut rhubarb? Rhubarb is not cut, but *pulled,* as the whole leafstalk is usable. When young, vigorous leaves come up during the summer, rhubarb makes just as good sauce as in the spring. Pull only a few stalks for the first season, however, to give the plants a chance to get well established.

When should you divide rhubarb in California? Soon after it has stopped growing and has become dormant. If under irrigation, it should be made dormant by withholding water. After the leaves have dried, the plants can be divided and moved.

In forcing rhubarb, does it kill or injure plants for outdoor garden use? Forcing is very debilitating. Most forced plants are discarded. However, if you have space and patience, some clumps, replanted, may recover.

I have tried to grow rhubarb several times and in several locations. It always starts out well and grows part of a season, then the stalks seem to begin to rot, fall over, and the plant dies. Can you tell me what is wrong? This is due to a crown rot. If it gets into the plants and the soil, there is not much you can do except to get clean plants and set them where rhubarb has not grown before. The soil should not be acid. Rhubarb does better in the cooler parts of the country.

What is the best variety of rhubarb? 'MacDonald', 'Valentine', and 'Victoria' are considered tops.

ROQUETTE OR ROCKET SALAD (ERUCA VESICARIA SATIVA)

What is the lettucelike greens with a distinctive pungent flavor often served in salads in Italian restaurants?   You probably mean roquette or rocket salad (*arugula* in Italian), a cool-season annual member of the mustard family. It is easy to grow from seed sown early in the spring at the same time you plant radishes and lettuce. The leaves can be cut, as needed, 3 to 4 weeks after sowing. Keep flowers and seedheads cut off. In warm weather, the leaves become tough and "hot," but sometimes the plants can be cut back nearly to the ground, and the resulting leaves can still be mixed with lettuce in a salad. Generally, though, it is best to make another sowing in late summer for fall use.

SALSIFY, OYSTER-PLANT (TRAGOPOGON PORRIFOLIUS)

What information can you give on the growing of vegetable-oyster or oyster-plant?   Oyster-plant (salsify) requires 120 days of growing weather and a fertile, sandy loam soil. Sow seed early, in rows 18 to 20 inches apart, and thin plants to 4 inches. It requires a well-aerated subsoil to get long, fleshy roots. The flavor of the root is improved by freezing. It is better taken directly from the soil than if dug and placed in storage.

How hardy is salsify?   Perfectly hardy. The roots can be left in the ground during the winter and dug during a thaw or in early spring.

I planted salsify last spring but it did not come up. Why?   Salsify seed has a low germination at best and if it is several years old it will not germinate. It should be grown in well-limed soil. Obtain seed from a reliable source; sow thickly enough for the seeds to touch; if thinning is needed, do it early.

What caused my salsify to go to seed? It also rotted.   Anything that causes a dormant period or a stoppage of growth processes due to dry weather can cause it to go to seed. The decay may be due to a boron deficiency in the soil or a lack of sufficient calcium. Usually a small percentage of roots will throw seed stalks; these should be pulled out.

Why does salsify grow 3 or 4 sprawly roots instead of one good root? This is the nature of the plant. The roots can be made to grow deeper and longer by extra-thorough and deep preparation and by loosening the subsoil. Make sure that the calcium supply is adequate.

SHALLOT   (See Onion.)

SORREL (RUMEX SCUTATUS)

Recently in a restaurant I was served a soup made from sorrel which was very refreshing on a hot summer day and which had a "sour" flavor. Can I grow this plant in my vegetable garden? How else is it used in cooking?   Yes, you can grow French sorrel. It is a perennial which will last for several years if the seedheads are removed. Most seed houses offer seed. Sow early in the spring. Consult French cookbooks for recipes. Sorrel is often used with fish.

SPINACH (SPINACIA OLERACEA)

What are the soil requirements for spinach?   Any fine, friable soil that can be worked into a mellow seed bed, and which is well supplied with organic matter and nitrogen, will grow spinach. The optimum pH level is 6.0 to 6.7, mildly acid.

When should spinach be planted?   *Very* early in spring, making 2 or 3 sowings, timed so that the last will mature before hot weather comes. Sow again in late summer, 50 to 60 days before frost for the fall crop. Seed should be treated with captan or thiram to prevent damping off.

What variety of spinach is satisfactory for the home garden?   'Bloomsdale Long-standing' does not throw up seed stalks quite as readily as some others. 'Melody' is disease-resistant.

Can you expect more than one cutting from spinach? Ours usually turns yellow after one cutting.   No. The whole spinach plant is cut at the soil surface—not picked off a leaf at a time.

Can spinach be grown in midsummer? If not, please suggest substitute greens.   Spinach bolts to seed in hot weather. The best substitute—and a very good one, too—is the so-called New Zealand spinach, which resembles spinach only when cooked. It loves heat and is very easy to grow, but makes a slow start. Soak seed 2 or 3 days before planting; sow 8 to 10 seeds to the foot in rows at least 24 inches apart; thin to about 8 inches. Although it grows best in hot weather, seed of New Zealand spinach will sprout only in cool soil. Seed early.

What is summer-spinach?   New Zealand spinach (*Tetragonia tetragonioides*), which is not spinach at all but is used as such and is often called summer-spinach. Seeds planted about April 1 will yield a harvest from about July 1 until frost. The plant is a tremendous yielder and only a few feet of rows are necessary for the average family. Like beets, there are a number of seeds in each seed pod. Seedlings can be readily transplanted to fill out a row, especially as the seed pods are apt to produce quite a large group of seedlings growing close together. (See the preceding question.)

SQUASH (CUCURBITA)

How should summer squash be planted to produce abundantly? Summer squash is not difficult to raise. Start with good seed. Seed can be sown when the danger of frost is past, with rows 4 to 5 feet apart and plants thinned to about 3 feet apart in the row. The soil should be well fertilized. Plant protectors, such as Hotkaps, will permit planting 2 or 3 weeks earlier, or plants can be started indoors in peat pots and grown under fluorescent lights. Faithful dusting for a few weeks with Sevin or methoxychlor will be necessary to control the striped cucumber beetle.

Are squash grown more successfully in hills or rows? In gardens where fertility is well maintained, the practice of making hills with compost or manure has been largely abandoned. This practice may be good where soil is not rich, stirring a couple of forkfuls of well-rotted compost into the soil under each hill.

When should summer squash be picked for best table quality? When the skin of the fruit is soft. On vigorous vines, the fruit will be about 6 inches long. They should be a lemon-yellow color. When orange-yellow, they are too old and the flesh gets coarse and tasteless. Zucchini types should be picked when they are 6 inches long or smaller.

What kind of soil should I use to grow winter squash? When and how should the seed be planted? Winter squash thrives in a rather wide variety of soils. Moderately heavy soils retain moisture better, are likely to be somewhat more fertile, and give good results. Seed should be planted about the time that tomatoes are set, when the danger of frost is past. In northern climates, practically the full season is required to mature them, for they need 100 to 130 days. They must be harvested before frost in the fall. Hills should be at least 6 feet each way; or thin to single plants 4 feet apart in rows.

How are winter squash harvested and stored? Winter squash should be harvested as late as possible before a fall frost. Cut with an inch or so of vine on either side of the stem. They must have a hard rind to keep well. You should not be able to dent them with your thumbnail. If well matured, they should be kept near the furnace for several weeks to cure them. After that they can be placed on shelves in a single layer in a dry place at 45° to 60° F. Don't pile them up. *Handle like eggs!*

How can striped cucumber beetle be controlled? By dusting the plants with methoxychlor or Sevin.

What can I use on the "stink bugs" that infest the squashes? The squash bug (commonly, and not without reason, called the "stink bug") can be trapped by laying a shingle or little board on the ground near the plants. This shelters the bugs at night and they can be destroyed in the morning. Removing and destroying egg masses and young are also helpful. Dust must be applied to the underside of the leaves as well as the surface. If you have only a few hills, make cases 2 × 2 × 1 foot, covered with mosquito netting, and keep these over the hills until the vines crowd the cases. This will give the vines a good start before being subjected to insect injury.

How can I protect my vine crops from stalk borers? By mulching with aluminum foil; squash borer moths are confused so they cannot locate the base of the stalk to lay their eggs. The variety 'Butternut' is immune to borers. Vines should be examined occasionally for borers. If found, they must be removed by carefully slitting the vines and removing. Also, keep the points of vines covered with soil to encourage them to root, thus by-passing the borers. Or spray or dust the plant stems with malathion or methoxychlor weekly.

What can be done about root maggots in vine crops? Root maggots are probably the larvae of the cucumber beetle. Keep the vines covered with Sevin or methoxychlor while they are young and the beetles won't come near them.

Can acorn squash be grown in southwest Ohio? 'Table King' acorn squash grows under a wide range of conditions, matures in 60 to 75 days from seed, is prolific, and is not difficult to grow. Grow in the same way as other squash but with a somewhat closer spacing of the plants.

Can acorn squash be stored through the winter months? Acorn squash can be stored successfully for several months, using the same method as with Hubbard or other winter squash. It probably will not keep in good shape as long as 'Blue Hubbard'.

Will 'Buttercup' squash produce satisfactorily if staked up in a garden to save or conserve space? The added exposure to heat, sun, and wind might be damaging. Saving space would be offset, at least partially, by shading other crops. However, they are sometimes grown this way.

What is the best small early winter squash to grow in northern Michigan? 'Kindred', a semibush squash, is early and prolific. It matures in about 60 days from seed; an early start may be gained by starting plants indoors as with muskmelon or by using plant protectors, such as Hotkaps, in the garden. For winter use, such small varieties as 'Table King', 'Butterbush', and 'Delicata' require only 60 to 75 days to mature from seed.

What are some satisfactory summer squash? 'Seneca Butterbar' and 'Gold Rush' for yellows; 'Aristocrat', 'Elite', 'Chefini', and 'Diplomat' for green.

What is the best variety of zucchini squash? 'Aristocrat' is very dark green, a heavy bearer, and edible until quite large. Many people consider it the best of the summer squashes in flavor and quality, although some of the new yellow zucchinis such as 'Gold Rush' are becoming extremely popular.

What are the best winter squashes to grow? 'Delicious', 'Buttercup', and 'Butternut' are good for fall and early winter; 'Golden' and 'Blue Hubbard' are good for winter.

SWEET POTATO (IPOMOEA BATATUS)

Can I grow sweet potatoes? If so, how? Yes, if you have lots of room and a long, hot summer. Buy cuttings (young, rooted plants) from a reliable source to avoid transmission of diseases and set them out 18 inches apart, with 4 feet between the rows. They prefer a rather light soil.

How should soil for sweet potatoes be prepared? No other preparation than for the usual vegetable crops is required. A sandy soil is best, and it should not have a hard subsoil, which would prevent the roots from reaching down to moisture.

Should sweet potato vines be trimmed? No, injury to the vines would cause loss of nourishment to the potatoes. If the vines grow too large, it is better to loosen them from the soil, where they root at the joints.

Will sweet potatoes grow in the North, just for an experiment? (Illinois.) This is by nature a tropical plant, but it can be successfully grown where the summer is warm and free of frost for 5 months. As the vines spread extensively, their culture is more for the field than the garden.

How do you grow sweet potato plants? Growing the cuttings, or plants, to set out for sweet potatoes is rather tedious, and the home gar-

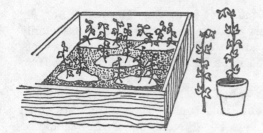

Sweet potatoes are started in a covered box or frame to supply "sets" for the garden.

dener would be better advised to buy them. They are started in hotbeds or cold frames, the sprouts or cuttings being removed with adhering roots from the old potatoes.

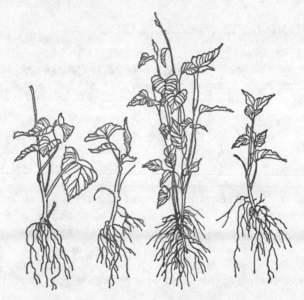

Sweet potato "sets"—young rooted sprouts started in a frame and then transplanted to the open. The "sets" or cuttings can also be bought from mail-order nurseries.

When should I start sweet potatoes in the house for sprouts? When should I plant the sprouts outside in the garden? Start 6 weeks before the date when frost is sure to be over for the season. Set out the plants only when the soil has become well warmed.

During the past season I have raised delicious, large sweet potatoes in

my garden, but my great difficulty was in digging. How can I best dig without breaking them? This problem has never been satisfactorily solved because the tubers are so very tender. There is nothing for it but to exercise great care—start digging a little way off and approach from the side instead of the top.

Do sweet potato tops die when ripe? How are sweet potatoes "cured"? The tops survive until cold comes. The potatoes are cured by storing 2 to 3 weeks at 75° to 80° F., after which they should be stored at a temperature of 50° to 60° F. until the tubers are used. Do not handle them while in storage. At all times, handle with the greatest care to avoid bruising them. Broken or injured ones should be used first.

SWISS CHARD (BETA VULGARIS CICLA)

How is Swiss chard grown? This is really a leaf beet and is grown in the same way as beets, but only the leaves and stalks are used. It is a "cut-and-come-again" crop—that is, you cut only the amount you wish at one time, rather than harvesting the entire plant. New leaves continue to appear all summer.

How is Swiss chard harvested? A leaf or two at a time may be cut from several plants. These should be outer leaves; they will be replaced as the plant grows. Or the center top is cut off, 2 inches or so above the crown, so that all new growth will be tender.

Last year my Swiss chard was covered with small brown spots. How can this be controlled? Probably this is a potash deficiency if the spots occurred along the margins; or a magnesium deficiency if in the body of the older leaves. Magnesium, lime, or wood ashes will correct the deficiencies. If the problem is serious, send a specimen to the Cooperative Extension Service in your county for diagnosis.

Swiss chard is a nourishing vegetable for summer-long harvest. Pick individual leaves with their white stalks. More will form on the plants.

What are good varieties of Swiss chard? 'Rhubarb' chard, with crimson stalks; 'Fordhook Giant', dark green leaves with white stalks; and 'Lucullus'.

TOMATO (LYCOPERSICON LYCOPERSICUM)

What is the surest way to get a crop of tomatoes? High points in tomato culture are: using the seed of a good disease-resistant variety; planting on fertile, moisture-holding soil; buying or starting strong plants; and keeping the weeds under control. Tomatoes thrive under a very wide variety of soil and climatic conditions, but will not fruit if night temperatures fall to 50° F. or lower.

Do tomatoes thrive best on alkaline or acid soils? Tomatoes seem to thrive under a fairly wide range of soil reaction. Experiments have not shown much benefit from liming when the crop is grown in acid soil. It also seems fairly tolerant up to a pH of 7.5 or so (7.0 is neutral).

Do tomatoes require much fertilizer? Tomatoes need to be well supplied with nutrients, whether this is achieved by the use of compost or phosphorus, complete fertilizer, or a combination. Phosphorus is particularly important for tomatoes, contributing to good yields and to earliness. An oversupply of nitrogen under some conditions, and with some varieties, may result in an overgrowth of vine and a poor set of fruits.

How many tomato plants will I need per person? Just for the table, 3 plants are plenty. For canning and freezing, 6 average plants are needed.

I notice some tomato varieties are described in catalogs as being "determinate." What does this mean? Determinate varieties are those with a bushy rather than a vining habit and generally require no supports. These varieties are most suitable for pot growing and for any small-space garden. Some determinate varieties are 'Patio Prize', 'Dwarf Champion', 'Stakeless', 'Patio Hybrid', and 'Pixie'. The majority of tomatoes are indeterminate and continue to grow at their stem tips, thus making support almost a necessity in a small garden.

How far apart should tomatoes be planted? The spacing of tomatoes depends on the variety as well as the size of the garden and whether the plants are to be staked or supported in wire cages or towers. Where space is ample and no support is planned, the sprawling, vining (indeterminate) plants should be set about 4 × 4 or even 4 × 6 feet apart. Most staked and caged plants can be set from 1½ to 2 feet apart in the row. Small, determinate varieties can be set even closer.

When is it safe to set out tomato plants?   They are set out when the danger of killing frost is past. This is usually 2 to 4 weeks after the average date of the last killing frost in the spring. Local experience is valuable; talk to other gardeners.

Is it best to buy tomato plants or plant seed yourself?   Growing plants require a suitable place and a little equipment, such as fluorescent lights, and the gardener must look after the plants regularly. With care, better plants can be grown at home; *and they are on hand when planting conditions are right!* It is easier to buy plants—if good ones are available at a reasonable cost—but many poor plants are offered for sale, and if more than a few plants are needed, the cost becomes significant. Growing your own seedlings usually allows wider varietal choice.

Is February too soon to start tomato seeds in the house?   In most climates, tomatoes are set out in the garden about 3 weeks after the average date of the last killing frost. For much of the Northeast, this means setting them out the last week of May. Seed may be started about 8 weeks ahead of this to get good-sized plants, although 10 weeks is preferable. Too early sowing results in ungainly plants that often outgrow their space.

How should one manage the starting of tomato plants?   Use a little box or flat, 2 to 3 inches deep, filled with good potting soil or one of the prepared mixes, such as Jiffy Mix, well firmed around the sides and corners. Sow seed in rows 2 inches apart, 8 to 12 seeds per inch. Seeds may be treated with captan or thiram. Keep the box in the window, under fluorescent lights, or in a greenhouse or hotbed at a temperature of about 70° F. Water so that the soil is moist, but not so heavily as to

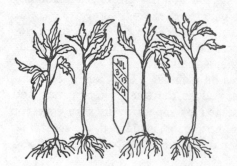

Young tomato seedlings—about 4 weeks old—at the right stage for transplanting.

result in tender, spindly growth. As soon as the seedlings come up, give them full sunshine or place under fluorescent tubes. Transplant into peat-fiber pots when the seedlings are about 2 inches high. Or sow a couple of seeds in Jiffy-7 peat pellets, pinching off the weaker seedling, in which case no further transplanting indoors should be necessary.

When should tomato seedlings be transplanted in the greenhouse? When seedlings are about 2 inches high and showing the first true or rough leaves, transplant with spacings of 2 × 2 up to 4 × 4 inches. Set the plant almost down to the seed leaves and firm the soil securely around the roots. If only a few plants are involved, they can be kept in a sunny window or under fluorescent lights in the house, or they may continue their growth in a greenhouse, hotbed, or cold frame. The temperature should be 65° to 70° F. and the plants should have the benefit of full sunshine. Water just enough to ensure steady, vigorous growth without plants becoming soft. If this is well managed, little hardening is necessary before being set out in the garden.

My staked tomatoes were high in quality but quit fruiting by late July. What did I do wrong? The mistake was in planting a determinate variety, one that sends up a single growing stem, then quits growing vegetatively and produces fruits. While determinate varieties are early and heavy fruiting, their period of production is usually short. Instead, for staked or cage-supported tomatoes, use indeterminate varieties that keep growing and throwing out new branches. They will produce until killed by frost. Staking is not essential to fruit production—both types will bear if allowed to sprawl on the ground, but few gardens can spare the space for this method.

Do you advise staking tomatoes? Does this cause sun blister? Use of wire cages (18-inch wire cylinders with 6 × 6-inch mesh) is better than staking and reduces the risk of sunscald, which can be caused when fruit are totally exposed to the sun's rays with insufficient leaf covering. With wire cages, the plant's side branches grow through the wire mesh and become self-supporting, whereas staking requires tying and pruning of side shoots. It is always better to support tomato plants than to let them sprawl on the ground, since vines on the ground take up more space and the fruit is subject to rotting and greater insect damage.

Should tomatoes be pruned? At one time pruning was recommended for tomatoes that are staked, because this made them easier to tie up, and it was thought that more fruit would result from all the plant's energy being directed into one main stem. However, this no longer is advised. As long as the soil is fertile and the plant's moisture needs are met, there is no need to prune side shoots. The side shoots also help to provide protection for the fruit against sunscald.

Can tomato plants be pruned at the top to keep them low and bushy? No. Varieties listed as determinate are usually lower than others without any pruning. Pruning tomato plants is no longer recommended.

Can new growth taken from tomato plants be rooted to make new plants? Yes, if the growth isn't too watery. Cuttings should be firm, but not too old. Cuttings made in early July often escape blight and continue to bear until frost.

My tomato plants went all to foliage. Why? This may be due to too much shade (perhaps from planting too closely) or to too much nitrogen in the soil. Use a fertilizer high in phosphorus, especially at the time of flowering, and this will encourage heavier fruit yields and early ripening.

How far away from the growing plants should tomatoes be cultivated? My tomatoes were a failure this year. Mulch rather than cultivate. This is less work and there is less chance of injuring the plants' roots.

Should you hill up the soil around tomato plants? It is now generally agreed that there is little to be gained by hilling up the soil around most vegetables. It results in damage to the roots, which spread wider than the tops.

Is mulching of tomatoes a good idea? Yes. A 2- or 3-inch layer of hay, straw, old leaves, lawn rakings, or anything of the sort serves to retain moisture in the soil, smother weeds, keep fruit clean, and the material is a good addition of organic matter for the next year. A little extra nitrogen on the soil may be necessary to balance the demand of organisms which decompose the mulch material.

Our tomatoes are finished by early fall. How can we have good ones later on in the fall? It is a good practice to set some tomato plants a bit late for fall maturity. Seed for these ('Burpee's Long-Keeper' is a good late variety) can be sown in the open May 1 to 15 in most northern climates. This also furnishes good mature green tomatoes to put away for fall use. Cuttings made from shoots on old plants are good to use in setting plants for late crops.

Our tomatoes had an acid taste. Testing indicated that the ground had too much potash. Could this account for it? It does not seem very likely that the nutrients in the soil would have very much to do with the acidity of the tomatoes. Varieties differ a good deal in this respect. Varieties of the 'Ponderosa' group and also the yellow tomatoes are milder in flavor and acidity than most varieties.

Will tomatoes do well if planted in the same location several consecutive years? Tomatoes do not seem particularly sensitive on this point, unless disease accumulates in the soil. The fusarium wilt or "yellows" is a soil disease, and long rotation helps in its control if you have the space available. It is best to use fusarium-resistant varieties, of which there are now many.

We have grown tomatoes in the same plot for several years; we find that we get a tremendous growth of vine but not very large or many tomatoes. Would you advise what to add to the soil? Probably there is too much nitrogen. Use superphosphate and wood ashes as fertilizers.

How can tomatoes be ripened in very high altitudes or in the extremely cold northern section of the Midwest where the growing season is very short? Varieties 'Starfire', 'New Yorker', 'Presto', 'Valiant', 'Coldset', and 'Springtime' have been especially developed for growing under these conditions. Get the plants to the flowering stage in 4-inch pots by the time the ground is ready to receive them. Sow seeds in flats or Jiffy-7 pellets first. Have the soil in good condition. Use a mulch. If fertilizer is needed, use it in liquid form.

What shall I use to control flea beetles on tomatoes early in the season? Dust rotenone on the plants or use Sevin or methoxychlor.

What causes tomato leaves to curl? The leaves curl for a number of reasons. Most common is a virus disease called "shoestring top." It is carried by aphids, which winter over in weeds. Spray transplants with malathion as soon as they are set out and again 10 days later. Direct-seeded plants usually escape. Spraying near tomatoes with weedkillers such as 2, 4-D can cause them to drift onto plants and curl the tips or the entire plant. Drying out of the soil (loss of spring moisture) in late June often results in curled leaves.

Should tomatoes be sprayed or dusted? If leaf diseases are prevalent on tomatoes, use an all-purpose dust specifically recommended for tomatoes.

Why do tomatoes get black spots at the blossom end? This trouble is ordinarily called blossom-end rot. It is not caused by a definite disease organism, but seems to be physiological in its nature—a failure of moisture to reach the tender tissues at the blossom end. The trouble may be due to a lack of rainfall, droughty soil, or alternating dry and wet spells. The trouble is often followed by secondary mold or fungus infection. It sometimes occurs when the soil is not particularly dry, either because the root system is defective or because there is not enough oxygen in the soil for proper moisture intake. Control is by any measure that ensures adequate water supply, such as irrigation, maintaining organic matter in soil; in some cases, improved drainage.

Can tomatoes be saved after frost?   Healthy, mature green tomatoes (that is, tomatoes that have attained full size but have not begun to show color) can be kept for 4 or 5 weeks in the fall. They will keep longer at a temperature of 45° F., but will ripen more quickly at temperatures up to 70° F. Precaution should be taken against evaporation and shriveling; that is, the storage place should be fairly humid. Tomatoes at the half-ripe and turning stage will also ripen up well in a few days. The flavor, however, will be inferior to vine-ripened fruit. Keep them away from direct sunlight. Temperature, not light, is more important for ripening tomatoes.

Are vine-ripened tomatoes more nutritive than those picked when only partially ripe?   Vine-ripened tomatoes are of better quality and flavor, and are much better for canning. It is probable that they are more nutritious, although some authorities dispute this.

Why do tomatoes grown in the northern United States lack the flavor and brightness of color of those grown 500 miles farther south? (Wisconsin.)   Tomatoes like warm weather, but with careful cultivation you can grow northern tomatoes of equal merit. Planting varieties which were specifically bred for cool climates will mean better flavor. 'Fireball', 'Springset', 'Coldset', 'Starfire', 'Valiant', and the 'Sub-Arctics' are recommended.

Is the acid and food content much different in various varieties of tomatoes, such as white, yellow, and red kinds?   Most yellow types of tomatoes are less acid than the red, while white tomatoes are almost free from acid. Food content is about the same in all types.

For late tomatoes, should one plant late varieties, or is it as well to plant early varieties at a later date?   It is better to plant late varieties for late tomatoes.

What is the earliest tomato for home or market?   'Pixie', 'Early Salad', 'Springset', 'Starfire', 'Presto', and 'Early Girl' are some good ones.

Which main-crop tomatoes are considered best for the home garden?   'Big Boy', 'Better Boy', 'Supersteak', 'Supersonic', 'Fantastic', and 'Burpee VF Hybrid' are main-crop varieties of merit. 'Sunray' is the best yellow. There are many others.

What kind of tomato plants would you recommend for a very small place, where I have room for only 4 or 5? What can be done to make the tomatoes less spindly, outside of pruning, which did not seem to make much difference? Look for determinate varieties and those suggested for pots on patios. Your spindly plants are evidently caused by lack of sun or poor soil. Add humus to the soil, if possible.

What is the best tomato variety for low, sturdy plants and early fruit? 'Pixie', 'Starfire', 'Fireball', 'Early Bird', 'Floramerica'. These should be grown on rich soil that retains moisture well. Since the vines are short, the plants may be set 30 inches apart with rows 3 feet apart. They produce a large number of fruit close to the center of the plant.

What is meant by "resistant" varieties of tomatoes? These varieties have been bred to resist the attack of the common fusarium wilt. They are attacked by the disease but do not succumb to it. There are no immune varieties. Among the resistant varieties are varieties that are identified by the initials VFN and VF. All are highly resistant. Those with an N are resistant to nematodes.

What are the best varieties of low-acid wilt-resistant tomatoes in a small garden? Most low-acid tomatoes are the yellow or orange type. Good varieties of these are 'Sunray', 'Ponderosa', 'Jubilee', and 'Golden Boy'.

In this locality, probably due to late spring and much rain, tomatoes do not mature. What would you suggest to overcome this difficulty? (Minnesota.) Grow an early variety in pots to the flower stage or early fruit stage, and set them in the ground as soon as it is ready. Put up some protection on the north and west sides of the plants. Try 'Sub-Arctic Maxi', 'Rocket', 'Scotia', and others recommended for cold climates.

What large-fruited tomato would you recommend? We have tried 'Beefsteak' but the fruits were rather late and misshapen. (New York.) Most large-fruited varieties of tomatoes are late and have a tendency to produce fruit with deep ribs. A variety called 'Supersteak VFN' is not only earlier than other 'Beefsteak'-type tomatoes, but it also produces smoother-skinned fruit and has excellent flavor.

What is the best all-around tomato for this climate? How should the seed be planted? (Missouri.) 'Supersonic' or the VF hybrids are excellent selections for all-around use. Start seeds in flats indoors under fluorescent tubes and transplant when a few inches high into peat pots. (See directions for starting tomato seeds in this section.)

Where can I get the cherry tomato varieties—those tomatoes that

grow only as large as a cherry?   Most commercial growers or seed houses have a good selection of cherry-type tomatoes.

Are so-called climbing tomatoes a success?   'Trip-L-Crop' and 'Early Cascade' are the climbing varieties of good flavor.

What is the best canning tomato?   Any solid-meated variety.

What type of tomato is best for juice?   Any of the more common types can be used. 'Big Boy', 'Moreton Hybrid', and 'Supersonic' are excellent. 'Sunray' (yellow) makes mild juice of a distinct flavor.

TURNIP (BRASSICA RAPA RAPIFERA)

How do you grow large, yet tender, rutabagas, turnips, etc.?   Plant the seed in late July in a well-limed soil that is thoroughly aerated. Don't use too much nitrogen, but plenty of potash.

When should turnips (yellow) be planted for a fall crop? (New Jersey.)   About August 1.

I was perfectly successful in raising large crops of lettuce, carrots, beans, beets, tomatoes, and mint, but my white turnips, seeded in two different places, refused to ball up and grew long like carrots. Why?   Probably due to a lack of potash. Put on some wood ashes or muriate of potash at the rate of 2 pounds per 100 square feet. Be sure that the lime content is satisfactory.

When do you dig turnips?   Turnips can be dug at any time when they are ready and one feels like eating them. For winter storage, they can be left until the first light frosts have come, then they should be lifted, topped, and stored in the root cellar.

What makes small marks on the outside of turnips?   It may be due to growth cracks or wireworms that rasp the young roots, leaving scars. Also, insufficient lime may cause this condition.

What makes turnips grow corky?   Too much nitrogen or hot weather. If they grow too fast, they get pithy. Plant late enough so that they develop during cool nights.

Our turnips, which grew fine, are hard and bitter when cooked. What is the cause?   This is probably due to hot weather when they matured or they were allowed to remain in the ground too long.

What is the best variety of turnips to grow for winter storage?   The Swede turnip, also known as rutabaga. If you prefer yellow, use 'American Purple-top', but if you think, as some do, that the white sort is milder and better flavored, try 'Purple-top White Globe'.

VEGETABLE SPAGHETTI (CUCURBITA)

How do you grow vegetable spaghetti and how do you cook it? Vegetable spaghetti is a type of vining squash that is as easy to grow as a cucumber vine. You can let it sprawl on the ground, but it is better grown up a trellis or chicken-wire fence. The fruits are ripe when they turn yellow, and they can be stored for several months without spoiling since they have a hard shell. The best method of cooking is to bake the

The vegetable spaghetti is a squash that can be boiled or baked. After it's cooked, cut it in half and remove the pasta-like pulp. The fruits can be used in the "green" stage in late summer or stored in a cool but frost-free place for use in fall or early winter.

whole fruit in an oven at 350° for 45 minutes. Then remove, slice lengthways across the middle, separate the two halves, and discard the seeds by scooping them out with a spoon. Then take a fork and scrape out the spaghetti-like strands all the way to the shell. Add butter and seasoning or a spaghetti sauce. You can also boil the fruit for about 25 minutes.

WATERCRESS (NASTURTIUM OFFICINALE)

How should watercress be started? Seeds can be germinated in a flowerpot set in a pan of water. Thin out to avoid crowding and, when large enough, transplant to a shallow stream. Or root cuttings in water; take from bunches of watercress purchased at a produce market. Plants can also be grown in moist soil if watered frequently enough to prevent the surface from becoming dry.

WATERMELON (CITRULLUS LANATUS)

How would one manage a watermelon planting in the garden? Watermelons need well-drained sandy or light soil. Use compost or rotted manure or commercial fertilizer, or a combination of all three—liberally. Seed is planted outdoors after the danger of killing frosts has passed; or plants can be started indoors in peat-fiber pots or Jiffy-7 pellets, as with muskmelons. Rows should be about 8 feet apart and plants should be thinned (or hills made) 4 to 6 feet apart, according to the variety and how well they grow under local conditions. Careful dusting to control striped cucumber beetle is usually required. Shallow cultivation is practiced as long as possible to control weeds; some pulling of weeds after that may be necessary. Mulching with black plastic will suppress weeds and warm the soil.

How do you tell when watermelons are ripe? If the sound, by snapping with your fingertip (or knocking with your knuckle), is sharp and high, the melon is immature. If there is a dull, hollow sound, it is more likely to be ripe. When the tendril or curlicue by the melon is alive and green, it is almost certainly immature. If the curlicue is dead, the melon is at least approaching maturity. Another test is to watch the change in color—a yellowing of the spot where the melon rests on the ground. A ripe melon, when pressed with a bit of weight, will usually "crackle," but this is not good for ones that are to be kept. There is a variety called 'Golden Midget' that turns yellow when ripe.

How would you raise watermelons in the North? What varieties are best here? (New Jersey.) Watermelons are very much at home in southern New Jersey, less so in northern New Jersey. However, they can be grown successfully much farther north than is ordinarily supposed. To grow watermelons successfully in northern regions, use an early variety. One of the finest is 'Sugar Baby'. This variety will mature as early as most muskmelons (in about 80 days from seeding) and thrives under northern conditions. Other early varieties are: 'New Hampshire Midget', 'Fordhook Hybrid', 'Crimson Sweet', and 'You Sweet Thing'. However, yellow-fleshed varieties such as 'Yellow Baby' and 'Honey Island' are the most cold-tolerant and earliest of all watermelons. Watermelons can be started indoors in peat-fiber pots under fluorescent lights.

Can watermelons be raised in this climate? (Massachusetts.) Yes, in the warmer parts of the state, particularly in the eastern and Cape Cod sections. The sandy soils are best suited to them. Some of the small-fruited varieties should be tried where the growing season is less than 120 days.

Please name some good new midget melons. 'Sugar Baby', 'You Sweet Thing', 'Yellow Baby', and 'Honey Island'.

Is it true that there are now seedless watermelons? Yes, but the seedless varieties need a normal watermelon to act as a pollinator since the former is not self-fertile. Several seed suppliers now list seedless varieties with precise instructions on how to grow them. Seedless watermelons are worth the trouble, since they are sweeter than the regular kinds.

II. Home-grown Fruits

NUTRITIONISTS ENCOURAGE the inclusion of fruits in the human diet. Yellow peaches, apricots, and strawberries are especially valued for their vitamin content. All fruits supply sugars of several types in easily digestible form. Minerals are found abundantly in many. Above all, the flavors and aromas that abound, while they may not add anything essential to the diet, certainly contribute something that makes eating fruits a delightful experience. Every home gardener can expect to be amply rewarded when he grows some of his own fruits.

Growing fruits in the home orchard is somewhat more difficult than growing common vegetables, but even with proper care, apples, pears, strawberries, raspberries, and others are easy to grow.

Pears produce a high proportion of usable fruits without any sprays. However, apples generally require sprays if a good portion of the fruits are to be edible when harvested. One of the most difficult problems in many regions is to control mice, which chew the trunk bark at the ground level. Also, the control of insects and diseases by sprays requires considerable vigilance and careful timing. Despite these challenging problems, mouth-watering, luscious fruits can be grown right in your own backyard if you are willing to put a little effort into it.

Before deciding what to plant, look around your state or county and see what kinds of fruits grow well in your area. Apples, for example, do not grow well in Florida or Southern California because there is insufficient winter chilling to cause the trees to break dormancy in the spring. Also, in northern districts, do not attempt to grow peaches where temperatures drop below minus 20° F. or apples where they drop below minus 40° F.

Why Grow Your Own?

Home-grown fruits, if properly cultivated and handled, are, as a rule, much superior to market fruits. Fruits for shipment must be picked in a slightly immature condition, so that they can stand packing and handling. They must often be harvested before the sugars and flavors are developed up to the point where the ripening process will continue after the fruit is removed from the tree. This is especially true of the more perishable fruits, such as the berries. One has not really had peach ice cream until he has picked from the tree a suitable variety, so fully ripe that it would squash in the hand, and used this for the making of a most delectable dessert, quite different from the supermarket product. Or, with blackberries, there is absolutely no comparison between the fruits as purchased in the market—even if you can find them—and those ripened on the canes to the point where a touch will make them fall off.

High-quality fruit varieties, not available in the markets, can be grown in the home fruit garden. Tasting these tree-ripened varieties can be a gourmet treat and a revelation to those who have only experienced the market product. Most fruits can be frozen, canned, or made into juice, jellies, and preserves. Fruit trees are attractive in bloom and contribute beauty to the landscape. Blueberry bushes, for example, would be attractive ornamentals if they never bore fruits. Children should have the opportunity of observing the marvels of fruit development—virtually impossible today unless the home garden gives them access to ripening fruit throughout the summer months.

Of course location with respect to production has a bearing. If you live in a region where fruits are harvested and delivered to a local market, the quality will more nearly approach that of home-grown fruits; but even for such local handling many sorts must be picked before fully mature.

Dwarf Fruit Trees

As home grounds become smaller, so does the available space for gardens—and standard fruit trees, such as apples and cherries. But dwarf fruit trees, which require far less space than their standard counterparts, can give home gardeners on small properties the happy experience of growing and picking their own apples, peaches, apricots, plums, and pears. (A regular-size apple tree will eventually occupy an area 20 × 20 feet or more, but nearly ten dwarf fruit trees can be planted in the same space and could include peach, plum, pear, and apricot as well as apple. However, even dwarf trees will eventually become crowded in such close spacing, so some thinning in this miniature orchard will be necessary; but before that time arrives, the harvest will have been varied and bountiful.)

Dwarfing in fruit trees is caused by the rootstock. A one-year-old fruit tree from the nursery ready for orchard planting is really made up of two different kinds of tree: the top, which will bear the fruit, and a completely different kind of tree, the rootstock. In the nursery, the rootstock of one kind was first grown, then the top fruiting variety, called the scion variety (such as 'McIntosh'), is budded onto the rootstock. There are specific varieties of rootstocks which cause the dwarfing growth of the apple tree. A 'McIntosh' apple tree can be either dwarfed or nondwarfed, depending on what rootstock is under it.

Apple varieties budded onto seedling roots grow into full-sized trees, perhaps 25 feet tall at 15 years of age. Nurserymen can grow seedling rootstocks by planting the seeds of any apple variety. However, these trees on seedling roots have no size-controlling effect on the new orchard tree. Generally, the home gardener should not purchase apple trees with seedling roots and should insist on trees having size-controlling roots.

Dwarfing rootstocks are propagated vegetatively and are removed from mother plants in the form of rooted cuttings. These are planted into the nursery and the scion variety, such as 'McIntosh', is then budded on them and allowed to grow for a year before the tree is ready for orchard planting. Dwarfing rootstocks have specific varietal designations, such as 'Malling 9', abbreviated as 'M9'.

Truly dwarfed apple trees grow to a height of about 8 feet at 15 years of age, depending on pruning practices, scion variety, and soil fertility. Trees having the dwarfing 'M9' rootstocks do not have good anchorage and tend to fall over a year or two after planting if not supported. It is necessary to drive a post or construct a trellis beside the tree and tie the tree to it.

Apple trees on 'M26' roots or interstem trees develop into semi-dwarf trees, about half the tree volume of large trees. By double budding in the nursery, interstem trees, such as 'McIntosh/M9/MM106', have a 6-inch interstem trunk section of 'M9' which causes the size control. Trees on 'Malling-Merton 106' and 'M7' roots grow to about three-fourths full size. There are many other varieties of vegetatively propagated size-controlling rootstocks, but most are not widely grown. Most of the widely used rootstocks are available as virus-free material.

Fruits borne on dwarf trees are just as large and are otherwise identical with fruits of the same variety borne on full-sized trees.

Pear trees are dwarfed by budding them onto quince rootstocks.

Sweet cherry trees have no satisfactory dwarfing rootstock. Peach trees are small enough that they do not require a dwarfing rootstock.

In addition to their space requirements, dwarf fruit trees offer other advantages for today's home gardeners. They come into bearing early, often after the second year of planting. Spraying the trees is easily accomplished with average equipment rather than high-reaching power sprayers, and, of course, harvesting the fruits from such low-growing trees is also easily accomplished. Because of their slow rate of growth, dwarf fruit trees require less pruning than standard trees. (See also Rootstocks for Fruit Trees in this introduction.)

Small Fruits

Especially suitable for home gardens of limited space are those fruits that are usually referred to as small, although there is nothing "small" about their yield. They include raspberries, blackberries, strawberries, currants, gooseberries, and blueberries. They can provide a continual supply of fruit from the first strawberry in early summer to the last autumn-fruiting raspberry. They are second only to dwarf fruit trees in their space requirements. Moreover, spraying is simpler than for all tree-borne fruits and often unnecessary.

A small strawberry bed should produce about one quart of strawberries for each foot of row. To achieve the best strawberries, space the plants adequately to prevent overcrowding, control weeds by mulches, provide water as needed, and protect the plants with additional mulching for winter before temperatures drop below 20° F. The everbearing varieties will produce lightly during late summer and fall.

Red raspberries are also excellent for the garden and are one fruit almost impossible to buy fresh because they do not keep long or withstand shipping well. Raspberries are easy to freeze—an additional attraction they offer homeowners who possess their own freezers or freezing compartments in their refrigerators. The raspberry cultivar 'Heritage' bears a summer crop and then a fall crop on the tips of the new canes, beginning in late August in central New York State (earlier southward) until a killing frost in October. While red raspberries and blackberries should be grown in rows, ideally about 7 feet apart—a luxury in space that not all home gardeners can afford—a single row of plants 20 feet long can yield enough fruit for immediate eating and freezing. Even a small "patch" of raspberries—an area about 5 × 3 feet convenient to the kitchen door and perhaps used as a screen for trash cans—will provide a sufficient harvest for a small family.

Currants and gooseberries are another example of small fruits that bear heavy crops annually. They form neat, low-growing shrubs, and only a half dozen or so plants of each are necessary to provide the makings for currant jelly and gooseberry jam.

Blueberries are attractive shrubs at all seasons, but especially so when laden with the blue fruits or when their foliage is bright red and orange in the autumn. They make a handsome boundary hedge for suburban properties and in larger gardens can border one or more sides of a vegetable garden. Or blueberry plants can be grouped among other shrubs (at least 2 varieties are needed for the most efficient cross-pollination). The major requirement of blueberries is an acid soil; if you can grow rhododendrons and azaleas successfully, your soil should also be suitable for blueberries. Otherwise you can test the soil and if necessary adjust the pH by adding sulfur. (See Section 1.)

Soil and Site

The home gardener has little choice of a site, but a consideration of its characteristics will indicate whether fruit plants can be set out with some hope of success. Soils that have been messed up in grading operations are sometimes poor places to grow plants, but they can be improved by the addition of organic matter (peat moss, compost, etc.), sand if the soil is heavy, or hauled-in topsoil (see Section 1).

The ideal soil is a deep, fertile, sandy loam at least 4 feet deep and well drained. Lighter soils can be improved by growing and then plowing under green cover crops, adding stable manure or peat moss, using more fertilizer, and watering the plants in dry weather. Heavier soils can be improved the same way, but may be in need of supplementary drainage.

Fruit soils must be well drained. In soggy situations, if tile drainage is not feasible, then the soil may be raised in wide ridges 6 inches or more in height. This will increase the chances of success in growing plants if good natural drainage is not present. Provision should be made to drain the surface water away from the planting. Peach and cherry trees are less tolerant of poorly drained soils than apples, blueberries, pears, or grapes. However, no fruit plant will grow in soil that is always wet.

A slightly acid soil is best for most fruits. Blueberries require an acid soil, preferably with a pH below 5.0. The regular use of sulfate of ammonia fertilizer on blueberry soils will tend to increase the acidity.

The best sites for orchards or home fruit gardens are on slopes so that on still, frosty nights the cold air will drain away. Frost pockets, or low spots surrounded by higher land, are less suitable for fruit plants, as frosts during bloom will injure the flowers. At the other end of the growing season, early frosts shorten the growing season.

Check with your county extension agent to find out if peach and sweet cherries bear regularly in your area. If so, the site is probably satisfactory for most Temperate Zone fruits. Also if 'Concord' grapes ripen well each year, the growing season is long enough for most fruits. All fruit plants must have full exposure to the sun for most of the day. Fruit trees will grow in partial shade, but the harvest will be very light.

On small lots the proximity of large trees should be avoided as their roots offer too much competition and their tops cast too much shade.

Planting

Fruit trees can be planted either in late fall or in early spring as soon as the soil can be worked without packing. In the northern tier of states, spring planting is usually considered to be safer. Raspberry plants set in the fall should have the soil mounded up around them or a mulch of leaves or sawdust to prevent the plants from being heaved out of the soil by frost during the winter. Strawberry plants are best set out in the spring.

One- or 2-year-old fruit trees are the preferred size for planting. Older or so-called bearing-age trees are slow to become established, if they survive the moving, and will not yield worthwhile crops as quickly as young trees properly planted and then well cared for. Dwarf apple trees and other dwarf fruit trees bear early anyway.

On arrival from the nursery, plants should be unpacked promptly and "heeled in" (roots well covered with soil) in a shady spot if they can't be promptly planted. If the bark is shriveled and the cambium is not bright green, the plants may not grow. The nursery should be notified promptly.

The plants should be set at the level or slightly deeper than they grew in the nursery in a hole large enough to hold the roots without crowding.

Dwarf apple trees on 'M9' rootstock should have the bud union about 2 inches above the soil level to prevent the scion from rooting and thus spoiling the dwarf habit of the tree. If the scion (top) is covered at the base with soil, it will develop roots and become a full-size tree.

It is helpful in getting the young tree off to a good start if the soil to be put around the roots is mixed with a pailful of wet peat moss. The soil should be packed firmly around the roots by stepping heavily on it as the hole is filled.

If the season is dry after planting, the young tree should be watered weekly until rainfall is adequate. A 3-foot-square black polyethylene mulch around the base of the young tree is helpful in getting it off to a good start. No fertilizer should be used in the planting soil during the first year. Adequate water and weed control are most important for the first 2 or 3 years.

Insects and Diseases

It is usually not possible to produce unblemished fruit without controlling the insects and diseases to which most of the fruits are susceptible. Usually, unsprayed tree fruits will not be usable because of insect or disease injuries. Some fruits and some varieties are more susceptible to injury than others, and injury varies from year to year according to weather. Plants on sites where air circulation is poor experience more injury from fungus diseases than where air circulation is good. Any insect or disease which reduces the vigor and efficiency of the leaves, even though it does not destroy them, tends to make the plant less winter-hardy and reduces the crop the following year. Pear trees produce cleaner fruit when they are neglected as to spraying than do other tree fruits.

Codling moth is the most serious insect pest of apples everywhere. Apple maggot and aphids are other apple pests. Several others can occasionally be troublesome. Scab is serious with most apple varieties, but scab-resistant varieties are being developed by breeding.

The stone fruits—peaches, plums, apricots, and cherries—are seriously damaged by brown rot, which attacks the fruit in humid weather and can destroy the entire crop if the weather is not suitable. Wormy peaches are caused by the larva of the Oriental fruit moth and the plum curculio. The latter causes wormy plums. Cherry fruit flies are the cause of wormy cherries. Aphids are also pests of these fruits.

Virus diseases, which are systemic and live in all parts of the plant, decrease plant vigor and productiveness. Some can even kill the plant.

Several viruses of different fruits are known and more than one virus in a plant can ruin it.

Techniques have been developed to eliminate viruses from plants by heat treatment and meristem culture. The resulting virus-free plants are maintained under virus-free conditions and used as sources of propagating material for nurseries. Many kinds and varieties of fruit plants are now available as virus-free plants. When ordering plants, virus-free plants should be specified, as the older virus-infected plants are still around. When possible, virus-free plants should be isolated from older plants of unknown virus content.

Spray programs for controlling insects and diseases of fruit plants are available from your State Agricultural Experiment Station or Cooperative Extension Service. The programs are revised each year as new pesticides are developed and the older materials are superseded or eliminated because of hazards to the environment.

The programs for the commercial orchardist are complicated, but simpler schedules are available for the home orchard. They will give fair control of insects and diseases and their recommended chemicals are safer for the user. These chemicals are available as mixtures or can be made up by the user. Directions for the use of pesticides should be followed exactly as to amounts and timing.

Selection of Varieties

Fruit plants should be purchased from nurseries specializing in them. Nurseries that feature ornamentals with a few fruits listed in the back of the catalog, sometimes not even by variety names, are not as good sources as the specialists.

The order should be placed early in the winter before stocks of some varieties are sold out. Varieties should be chosen carefully and ordered by name. Picking up a few fruit trees of whatever is available at the garden center at the last minute is not the best way to start a fruit garden!

Your Cooperative Extension Service (under county government in the telephone book) or State Agricultural Experiment Station issues lists of recommended fruit varieties, revised occasionally, to help you make an intelligent selection. These lists should be consulted as space does not permit a listing of varieties for all the climatic regions of the country. Some varieties are widely grown, others only in limited areas.

Older varieties that may have been superseded by newer sorts are usually just as good as when they were introduced and are often just about as satisfactory for home use as the newer varieties.

The varieties below are listed in order of ripening:

Apple: 'Julyred', 'Jerseymac', 'Viking', 'Tydeman Early', 'Burgundy', 'Jonamac', 'McIntosh', 'Macoun', 'Cortland', 'Empire', 'Jonagold', 'Golden Delicious', 'Idared', 'Melrose', 'Mutsu'.

Disease-resistant apple: 'Prima', 'Sir Prize', 'Nova Easygro', 'Macfree', 'Liberty', 'Priscilla'.

Old apple: 'Gravenstein', 'Snow' ('Fameuse'), 'Twenty Ounce', 'Cox Orange', 'Pound Sweet', 'Tolman Sweet', 'Baldwin', 'Northern Spy', 'Granny Smith'.

Crab apple: 'Hyslop', 'Dolgo', 'Young America'.

Pear: 'Clapp Favorite', 'Bartlett', 'Aurora', 'Anjou', 'Flemish Beauty' (hardiest), 'Gorham', 'Seckel', 'Bosc', 'Highland'.

Peach: 'Brighton', 'Garnet Beauty', 'Reliance' (hardiest), 'Redhaven', 'Raritan Rose', 'Harken', 'Triogem', 'Glohaven', 'Madison', 'Cresthaven', 'Redskin'.

Nectarine: 'Pocahontas', 'Morton', 'Nectared No. 4', 'Nectared No. 6', 'Nectacrest'.

Apricot: 'Alfred', 'Goldcot' (very hardy), 'Veecot', 'Hargem'.

European plum: 'Oullins', 'DeMontfort', 'Mount Royal' (very hardy), 'Mohawk', 'Seneca', 'Green Gage', 'Richards Early Italian', 'Iroquois', 'Stanley', 'Golden Transparent Gage', 'Italian Prune', 'Oneida'.

Japanese plum: 'Shiro', 'Formosa', 'Santa Rosa', 'Abundance', 'Burbank'.

Damson plum: 'French'.

Tart cherry: 'Montmorency', 'Meteor', 'North Star'.

Sweet cherry: 'Venus', 'Emperor Francis', 'Stella' (self-fruitful), 'Compact Stella' (compact tree, self-fruitful), 'Vogue', 'Ulster', 'Hedelfingen', 'Van', 'Windsor'.

Quince: 'Orange', 'Smyrna'.

Grape: 'Van Buren', 'Ontario', 'Seneca', 'McCampbell' (large-clustered sport of 'Fredonia'), 'Alwood', 'Buffalo', 'New York Muscat', 'Lakemont', 'Concord Seedless' (for grape pie), 'Glenora'.

Wine grapes: Several American grapes make good wine. These French-American and *Vitis vinifera* hybrids are excellent: 'Aurore', 'Marechel Foch', 'Seyval', 'Cayuga White', 'Baco Noir', 'DeChaunac', 'Chardonnay', 'White Riesling'. A specialist should be consulted about other French-American and *V. vinifera* hybrids.

Red raspberry: 'Jewel', 'Allen', 'Bristol', 'Huron'.

Purple raspberry: 'Brandywine' (large fruits, productive).

Blackberry: 'Darrow'. Thornless varieties for areas south of Washington, D.C.: 'Smoothstem', 'Thornfree'.

Currant: 'Red Lake', 'Wilder', 'White Grape'.

Gooseberry: 'Poorman', 'Downing'.

Strawberry: 'Sunrise', 'Holiday', 'Canoga', 'Catskill', 'Fairfax', 'Redchief', 'Midway', 'Raritan', 'Garnet', 'Fletcher', 'Sparkle', 'Geneva' (everbearing). The best-flavored strawberries are 'Suwanee', 'Fletcher', 'Fairfax', 'Holiday', 'Geneva'.

Blueberry: 'Earliblue', 'Collins', 'Blueray', 'Bluecrop', 'Berkeley', 'Herbert', 'Coville'. In the South, rabbit-eye varieties: 'Premier', 'Woodard', 'Tifblue', 'Powderblue', 'Homebell', 'Garden Blue', 'Aliceblue', 'Beckyblue', 'Centurion'.

Mulberry: 'Wellington'.

Pollination Requirements

Many fruit trees do not set fruit if the flowers are self-pollinated. Hence, at least two varieties blooming at approximately the same time should be planted to ensure cross-pollination.

All apples and pears require cross-pollination. In some areas with ideal weather during bloom, single-variety apple orchards of 'Golden Delicious', 'Rome Beauty', 'Baldwin', and others have been known to produce good crops by self-pollination without the presence of other varieties as cross-pollinators. However, in the northeastern United States, with cool, damp weather during bloom, all apple varieties should be considered self-unfruitful; that is, two different varieties having similar blooming dates must be planted within 100 feet of each other so that cross-pollination can occur between them in order for the blossoms to set fruits. Perhaps a close neighbor has a tree of a different variety that will effectively serve as a pollen source. Pollen of triploid apples is infertile, so two other varieties are needed if a triploid variety is planted.

Sweet cherries require cross-pollination, but an exception, 'Stella', is self-fruitful. The Japanese plums require cross-pollination, but some of the European types are self-fruitful and some are not. European and Japanese varieties do not pollinate each other. All the peaches, nectarines, grapes, and small fruits, except blueberries, are self-fruitful. Although blueberries are partially self-fruitful, blueberry flowers, if cross-pollinated, set much better and produce much larger berries than when self-pollinated.

Rootstocks for Fruit Trees

Clonal rootstocks are now being used generally for apple trees. The ultimate size of the tree, age of coming into bearing, and productiveness are influenced greatly by the rootstocks. The rootstocks are designated with M (for Malling) numbers. 'M9' produces the smallest tree and is most suitable for backyard trees. The trees on 'M9' grow 6 to 8 feet tall and in an orchard arrangement should be planted 6 to 8 feet apart in rows 10 to 12 feet apart. 'M7' produces trees somewhat larger than 'M9'. Trees on 'M26' are intermediate in size between 'M9' and 'M7'.

Dwarf apple trees on 'M9' and 'M26' should be staked at planting time, as the shallow root system can cause them to tip over with a load of fruit or from a high wind. Stakes are desirable for 'M7' trees during the first 5 years.

Pears are dwarfed by budding on quince roots but the trees may be short-lived. *Pyrus communis* (pear) seedlings are better rootstocks for dwarf pears. Oriental pear rootstocks should not be used, as the resulting trees are more susceptible to pear decline, a mycoplasma disease, than on *P. communis* roots.

Dwarfing stocks for peaches and plums are Nanking cherry, sand cherry, and 'St. Julien A' plum. However, trees on seedling roots are small enough for most sites and can be kept dwarf by pruning.

There are as yet no suitable dwarfing stocks for sweet cherries. The sour varieties 'Meteor' and 'North Star' are much smaller trees than 'Montmorency' and make attractive ornamentals as well as fruit producers.

Some American grape varieties are susceptible to injury by phylloxera, an insect which feeds on the roots of susceptible varieties. The rootstock 'Couderc 3309' is resistant to phylloxera and susceptible varieties or varieties that are to be planted where grapes have recently been grown will perform much better on 'Couderc 3309' rootstock.

Herbicides and Mulching

Herbicides are much used in commercial orchards, where they eliminate labor and prevent injury to the roots of the plants that result from power cultivating. They can be used in home fruit gardens, but instructions must be followed exactly to avoid plant injury. The margin of safety is narrow and unless one is exact the damage to the plants can be substantial.

Herbicides are numerous and new ones are appearing frequently, so information should be obtained each year from your county agent.

If sufficient mulching material is available, it is an excellent way to control weeds and conserve moisture and of course it is free from the hazards inherent in herbicides. A hay mulch provides nutrients as it rots. Black polyethylene is also very good for small operations. Straw should not be used where there is a fire hazard.

Why Fruit Trees Fail to Bear

The trees may not be old enough. Some apples and pears require several years to reach bearing age if on seedling roots. Dwarf apple trees (on 'M9' rootstock) fruit at 2 or 3 years. Peaches bear at 3 years as do sour cherry trees. Sweet cherries begin at 5 to 7 years and plums a year or two earlier.

Low winter temperatures, or spring frosts, when the trees are in bloom, may kill the flowers. Apricots, peaches, and sweet cherries, which are early blooming, may fail to fruit because of a frost at that time. Prolonged cold wet weather during fruit bloom prevents the bees from flying, and cross-pollination, which is essential for the flowers to set fruit, may not take place.

Some fruits are self-unfruitful. (See Pollination Requirements, this section.) If only one tree is planted and other varieties of the same species are not nearby to provide pollen, then the flowers fail to set.

Excessively vigorous trees are slower to come into bearing than trees of normal vigor. Trees low in vigor because of poor drainage, lack of nitrogen, and injury to the leaves from insects or disease can be slow to begin fruiting. Trees in shady situations will fail to fruit or bear only lightly.

The Orchard

SOIL

How can soil for orchard fruits be built up? Building up the soil is accomplished by increasing its content of organic matter to improve the physical condition. This can be done by adding large amounts, 20 tons or more per acre, of manure or peat moss; or more cheaply by seeding the land to a green-manure crop, such as grass or a legume, and fertilizing it heavily. Mow it several times a summer, leaving the clippings to rot. Turn it under after 2 or 3 years.

Does sandy soil retard the growth of apple and peach trees? Mine are 4 years old and only about 5 feet tall. Will other soil put around the trees help? Apple and peach trees will grow well in sandy soil if it is properly fertilized and provided it contains ample moisture. Adding heavy soil might help, but it would require a great deal. It would be more feasible to improve the soil by adding a 5–10–5 commercial fertilizer at the rate of about 800 pounds per acre. If the soil is dry, either irrigate with a sprinkler system or mulch with some strawlike material to conserve moisture. Heavy mulching will gradually increase the humus content of the soil. Compost, leaves, lawn clippings, or any organic materials are good mulches.

Will fruit trees grow in a scrub oak section on Long Island, New York? The soil in question is probably low in fertility and very acid, but with good care might produce enough fruit for home use. Liberal applications of stable manure or other humus-forming materials such as peat moss, annual fertilizing, and mulching to conserve moisture should make it possible to produce fruit on this soil.

Our soil is mostly sand. Would it be suitable for the raising of strawberries, red raspberries, and fruit trees? A sandy loam soil, or even a loamy sand, is suitable for these fruits if it has a reasonable supply of moisture. If it is very dry, sandy soil, you will probably have poor results unless you irrigate. Coarse sands will probably need heavy and frequent fertilization with complete fertilizers. Peaches will thrive in sandier soil than is needed for apples. Black-plastic mulches are excellent if appearance is not important.

Will fruit trees grow in muck ground? Yes, provided the muck is well drained, not too acid, and contains the necessary nutrient elements in sufficient quantities. Muck land is usually low; hence, cold air may "drain" into such an area and result in frost damage. Frost damage to the flowers may be so frequent on muck that crops will be few and far between. Winter injury may be much more serious than on upland soils. Fruit trees should have good "air drainage," so are usually set on relatively high land.

Is there any reason why fruit trees will not grow on soil adjacent to black walnut trees? Black walnut roots are known to excrete a substance that is toxic to the roots of some plants, including apples, tomatoes, and alfalfa. Grass will grow under black walnut trees, but to be on the safe side, other plants should be kept well away from the roots of the walnut.

FERTILIZER

Must fruit trees (such as apple and peach) be heavily fertilized? Fruit trees should have sufficient complete fertilizer to supply any nutrient elements which may be deficient in the soil in which they are growing. However, it is easy to overfertilize these fruits. They do not require as heavy fertilization, for instance, as is needed by most vegetable crops.

Should manure be placed on a new garden plot on which fruit trees and berries are to be planted? A good coat of manure would be about the best treatment you could give. If manure is not available, turn under a ground cover such as grass or legume sod that has been previously planted.

How is nitrate of soda applied when used for fruit trees? Nitrate of soda is usually used for fruit trees at the rate of ¼ pound for 1- to 2-year-old trees, to 5 to 10 pounds for trees 20 to 30 years old. Ammonium nitrate, which contains twice as much nitrogen, is used at one half this rate. On fertile soils, if leaves are large and dark green, omit these fertilizers.

Can you give some data on fertilizer to help fruit trees produce well and at a younger age? (Illinois.) Good production will be secured only if the trees have the proper supply of nutrients, and that in turn will depend a great deal on the natural fertility of the soil. Check with your Cooperative Extension Service for specific recommendations for your soil. No particular type of fertilizer will cause the trees to bear at a younger age. The age of bearing is influenced chiefly by the variety, the pruning, and by some rootstocks. The age of bearing can be delayed, however, by applying too much nitrogen or by heavy pruning. For the quickest-bearing fruit trees, plant only dwarf trees.

What type of fertilizer should be used for fruit trees in acid soil? Most fruit trees in the East are grown in acid soil; that is, soil which is below the neutral point of pH 7.0. If soil is very acid (below pH 5.5), lime should be added to bring the reaction to around pH 6.0, then use ordinary commercial fertilizer as required.

I have heard that fruit trees do not require lime. Is that correct? Fruit trees require lime as much as any other plants. Whether it should be used or not depends on the acidity and calcium content of the soil. The pH should be between 5.5 and 6.0. However, generally it is not necessary to add lime to garden soils for fruit plants.

PLANTING

What is the best age at which to buy apple, peach, cherry, plum, and pear trees for setting in the home garden? Apple, 1 or 2 years; peach, 1 year; cherry, 1 or 2 years; plum, 2 years; pear, 2 years. Larger trees are not recommended, and nothing is gained by planting so-called bearing-age trees.

How many fruit trees will be necessary to supply a family of 4 with an adequate amount for the year? This will vary greatly according to personal preferences. Six apple, 2 pear, 6 peach, 1 sour cherry, and 2 plum trees would provide about as much as the ordinary family would want, if varieties with a succession of ripening dates are chosen, and if the trees are on suitable soil and well cared for. Additional varieties can be grafted onto these trees to extend the season.

How early in the spring should fruit trees and berries be planted? Plant just as early as the soil can be worked. There is no danger of planting too early, provided the soil has dried out enough to be worked into good tilth.

How far apart should fruit trees be planted? I plan to plant about 10 acres. Planting distances of fruit trees depend on the kinds of fruits, their rootstocks, and, to some extent, on soil and climate. The following are average distances between trunks and rows: apple, 20 to 40 feet; pear, 24 to 30 feet; peach, 20 to 25 feet; plum, 22 to 24 feet; cherry (sour), 22 to 24 feet; cherry (sweet), 24 to 30 feet; apricot, 22 to 24 feet; quince, 18 to 20 feet.

How far apart should the trunks of dwarf fruit trees set in rows be planted and how far apart should the rows be? Dwarf apples, on 'M9' rootstock: 10 × 12 feet; on 'M7' rootstock: 6 × 12 feet; dwarf plums: 8 × 8 feet; dwarf peaches: 10 × 10 feet. Home gardeners who plant only a few trees can cheat a bit on spacing.

How should I go about planting a fruit tree? How big a hole should I dig for an apple tree? A hole 12 to 15 inches deep and 15 inches across should be large enough for the average nursery tree. If the roots are too long to fit in a hole this size, cut them back. As the soil is filled in, jiggle the tree up and down a little so that all the roots will make contact with the soil. When the hole is half full, and again when it is full, step on the soil around the trunk of the tree in order to compact it.

Finish filling the hole. If the soil is at all dry, pour in a pail of water before the hole is quite full.

How deep should fruit trees be planted? If the nursery tree has been budded onto size-controlling rootstocks, such as apple on dwarfing 'Malling 9' or pear on quince roots, it is essential, at planting time, to identify the height of the rootstock-scion bud union. Generally, there is a slight crook in the tree trunk at the bud union. The tree must be planted as deep as it was growing in the nursery or at a depth so that this bud union will be about 2 inches above the soil level. If the bud union is planted below the soil level, the base of the top scion variety will be in the soil and it will send out roots. This is known as scion rooting. Roots produced by the scion portion of the tree have no dwarfing effect; they will cause the tree to grow to full size. The dwarfing benefits of the 'Malling 9' will be completely lost. If the tree has been budded onto seedling rootstocks which have no dwarfing effect, the depth of planting is much less important, but having the bud union at ground level is still a good depth.

How should nursery-grown trees be treated upon receipt? Remove from packing at once and plant immediately or heel in. Examine carefully. If the plants are dried out, soak in water, completely immersed, if possible, for 24 hours. If they do not plump up, return them. The bark when cut into should be bright green.

I received nursery fruit trees in the fall. What is the best way to hold them until spring? If they cannot be planted at once, heel them in, in a shaded place. Dig a trench wide enough and deep enough so that the root systems will almost go in them. Place the plants in the trench, packed close together, at any angle of about 45°. Place loose soil around the roots, work down and pack tight, then mound. No grass or weeds should be against the roots. The object is to keep the roots moist during the winter.

How large does a body of water have to be to cause conditions to be favorable for fruit growing? The moderating effect of the body of water is caused by the changes in temperature occurring in air masses as they move across the water toward the fruit-growing section. If prevailing winds do not blow across unfrozen water long enough to have their temperature raised, then there will be no effect on temperatures in the orchard. This means a body of water will have to be several miles wide and remain unfrozen in order to have very much effect.

Is locality taken into consideration in regard to the types of trees that should be planted? Yes. Fruits that thrive in Louisiana would not survive the winters in New England, and New England varieties would not do well in Louisiana. Cultural methods also vary greatly in different localities. The length of the growing season and summer heat are also important factors.

SPRAYING

We have a new orchard of fruit trees. What should they be sprayed with, and when? The damage likely to be caused by certain pests varies a great deal in different localities; hence, spraying recommendations vary from one producing region to another. Unless the trees are sprayed regularly and intelligently, the fruit will be worthless and the trees severely injured by diseases and insects. Each Agricultural Experiment Station has developed spraying directions to fit conditions within the state. These directions may change from year to year as chemicals are changed. Get directions each year from your Cooperative Extension Service or your state university.

How and how often should orchard trees be sprayed? The number of sprayings varies according to the locality, the insects and diseases, and whether one wants perfect fruit or will be satisfied with fair control. They should have a minimum of 4 sprayings, with a good pressure sprayer. One dormant spray should be given, and at least 3 before and while fruit is forming. Commercial growers use as many as 11 sprayings in one season.

Does the Japanese beetle do much harm to fruit trees? What spray can be used against it? Carbaryl (Sevin) is quite effective. Check the label for precautions to observe on ripening fruits.

MULCHES AND COVER CROPS

How does a mulch of straw provide more water to young trees? No more water is provided, but what is already there is conserved. The mulch prevents wind and sun from striking the ground and evaporating moisture from the surface. It also prevents the growth of weeds and grass which would compete for water with the trees. During a very hard rain, the mulch prevents or lessens surface runoff.

How should fruit trees be mulched? They were 3-year-old trees when planted, and have been growing in a yard for 3 years. By mulching is meant the placing of enough strawlike material around the tree to keep down weeds and grass and thus conserve moisture. The mulch is usually applied from the trunk to a point under the tips of the branches; hence, the area mulched increases as the tree increases in size. Straw, spoiled hay, lawn clippings, or leaves can be used. Black plastic is good, but must be anchored and covered with additional mulch for the sake of appearance if trees are included in the landscape scheme. If leaves are used, place some hay or brush over them to prevent their blowing away. Mice often injure mulched trees, so it is best to rake the mulch away from the trunk in the fall (a distance of 3 or 4 feet) and spread it again in the spring.

Is the growing of fruit trees in grass sod satisfactory in a small orchard? Peach trees are better with cultivation or a mulch, but the other fruit trees may be grown in sod if it is mowed as frequently as a lawn so that the competition for moisture is reduced. Thick vigorous sods may need occasional partial breaking up with a disk-harrow or a rototiller to reduce competition. Herbicides are very useful if properly applied.

What is the best ground cover for a young orchard of 2-year-old trees? Cultivate near young trees. Maintain closely clipped sod elsewhere.

What are the advantages of mulching trees? Moisture is conserved, weeds are controlled, plant food is added by the decaying mulch, and drop fruits do not bruise much when they fall on the mulch. Root injury from tillage is eliminated.

What are the disadvantages of a mulch? It creates a fire hazard and should not be used if there is danger of fire. Mice are much worse under a mulch and they should be poisoned and the tree trunks protected by a wire collar or a mound of gravel around the trunk.

If I grow my trees in sod, how should I manage it? Mow it frequently, several times a summer, to reduce competition with the trees. Leave the mown grass to rot under the trees.

PRUNING AND TRAINING

How and how often should fruit trees be pruned? Trees are pruned during the dormant season, preferably toward spring in severe climates. The object of pruning is to produce a structurally sound tree that will not experience limb breakage from a heavy crop or ice storm. The scaffold branches should be about 6 to 12 inches apart and pointing in different directions. Crotches with each member of equal size should have one member cut back a little each year until it becomes a branch of the other. Interfering and broken branches should be removed as well as those with disease. Pruning should be a little each year rather than a lot at longer intervals. It is better to err on the side of too little rather than too much pruning.

When and how much should I cut back fruit trees planted this fall? The tops should be reduced about one half, leaving 4 or 5 branches 6 to 12 inches apart and pointing in different directions. It is better to wait until spring to cut back the newly planted trees, especially in the northern states.

Is it advisable to cut the heart or center limb out of a fruit tree to prevent its growing too tall? Peach trees are usually trained to an open center, so the central leader is cut out. Apple trees are well adapted to the modified leader system, in which the leader is allowed to grow to a height of 8 to 10 feet before it is cut out.

How should fruit trees be pruned so that branches will not bend down or break off when fruit gets large? We would like to make the branches stronger and not lose more fruit than necessary. The branches are bound to bend down if a crop is being produced. However, heading back the long, leggy branches will reduce their length in relation to their diameter. Such branches will not bend or break so badly because the leverage exerted by the load of fruit is not so great. Breakage can also be prevented by propping with poles and by thinning off excess fruit.

Is root pruning the proper way to reduce wood and leaf growth on a fruit tree? Root pruning is seldom justified unless the tree is growing in a greenhouse or is used as an ornamental where its size must be strictly limited. If a tree is making too much wood growth, it can usually be checked satisfactorily by withholding nitrogen from the fertilizer application or by growing it in a grass sod.

What is meant by the "ringing" of fruit trees? Taking out a ring of bark around the trunk or one or more main limbs of a tree—usually an apple tree. This causes carbohydrates synthesized in the leaves to stay in the top of the tree, above the ring. The result usually is a heavy set of fruit buds followed by a large crop, but the roots are starved for carbohydrates, so the tree is weakened. It will die if the ring is too wide to heal over in one season; therefore, scoring by cutting through the bark in one or more places, all around the trunk, but without actually removing any bark, is a safer method. Ringing or scoring is usually used only on filler trees which are to be removed in 2 or 3 years anyway. Dwarf apple trees (on 'M9' and 'M7' rootstock) bear much earlier than do regular-size trees.

PROTECTION

Is whitewash beneficial to fruit trees? How should it be applied? Whitewash was once considered of some benefit in preventing sunscald of fruit trees, but it is rarely used by fruit growers now and is probably of doubtful value.

Would it be advisable to use a good white-lead and oil paint on fruit trees? No paint should be used on fruit trees except possibly on pruning wounds. Most commercial growers do not paint wounds unless they are much larger than that. The paint does not cause the wound to heal faster but may help to keep the exposed wood from decaying before the new bark grows over the wound and seals out decay organisms. Small wounds, 2 inches in diameter or less, do not need painting. Larger wounds may be painted with an asphalt emulsion in water.

Cylinders of hardware cloth protect young fruit trees from winter injury by rabbits and rodents.

How are young fruit trees best protected from mice in the winter? Remove the mulch and loosen the plant material from around the trunk for a foot or more. Use strychnine-poisoned oats in the runways under matted grass. The county Cooperative Extension Service can advise as to the best poison baits and where they may be obtained. Cylinders of hardware cloth placed around the trunks with their bases embedded in the soil are good protection.

What is the best protection against rabbits, for young fruit trees, other than using wire netting? Guards of wire-mesh cylinders are the best protection. County agents can supply information about chemical repellents, but these may be short-lived and must be replaced frequently.

POLLINATION AND FRUITING

What is cross-pollination? Cross-pollination is the transfer of the pollen of one variety to the pistil in the blossom of another variety.

What is meant when you say that a plant is self-sterile or self-unfruitful? The two terms are commonly used synonymously, but there is a slight difference. Self-sterile means that a variety will not form seeds with its own pollen. Self-unfruitful means that it will not form fruits with its own pollen.

Is there any explanation as to why a variety may be self-unfruitful? It is based on genetic factors. Sometimes the pollen may be sterile, i.e., not capable of germinating. In other cases, it will be able to germinate but will fail to function on its own pistil, functioning on the pistils of other varieties.

Which fruit trees are not self-fruitful? Fruits that are not self-fruitful are most apples; all varieties of the European pear and its hybrids; a few varieties of peaches; all sweet cherries (except 'Stella') and 'Duke' cherries; many of the European plums, most of the Japanese plums, and many of the hybrids arising from American plum species.

Will any variety of apple cross-pollinate another? No. There are certain varieties that definitely will not pollinate themselves, nor will they act as pollinators, because of a weakness in the pollen. These are called triploids because of the chromosome number. Varieties that bear a close relationship, as 'Delicious', 'Starking', and 'Richard' (the last two being bud sports of 'Delicious'), will not cross-pollinate each other.

Do crab apples require cross-pollination? Like the large-fruited apple varieties, crab apples are also self-unfruitful, i.e., they fail to set fruits by their own pollen. They must be pollinated by another variety. Large-fruited apple varieties, such as 'Liberty', will effectively pollinate crab apples, and vice versa, crab apples will pollinate large-fruited apples. However, they must bloom at approximately the same date. Like large-fruited apple varieties, some crab apple varieties bloom very early, some midseason, and some late.

Are there some varieties of apples and cherries that will act as pollinators for one variety and not for another? 'Delicious' forms good pollen but will not cross-pollinate its bud sports, 'Starking', 'Richard', and several others. Among sweet cherries, there are a number of varieties that are cross-unfruitful.

Why do seedlings of fruit trees differ so much from the parents in fruit quality? Nearly all of our fruits are of complicated parentage, so that when seeds are sown all sorts of variations may be expected to occur. Often the weakest qualities of the genus show up, or susceptibility to disease. Some do come relatively alike; 'Elberta' peach seedlings, for instance, may all resemble 'Elberta' in shape and color, but many will be clingstones and many will be of poor quality. Very few seedlings are superior to their parents.

For how many years can the following fruit trees be expected to bear heavily: apple, pear, peach, sour cherry, sweet cherry, plum, quince? It will depend somewhat upon variety, and definitely upon climate, site, soil, culture, and control of insects and diseases. Apple, 50 to 75 years; pear, 35 to 50 years; quince, 25 to 30 years; peach, 15 years; plum, 30 years; sour cherry, 30 to 40 years; sweet cherry, 50 to 60 years. Profitable commercial production may be less. Virus diseases often shorten the productive lives of stone-fruit trees.

Can I have young transplanted fruit trees bearing in a year or two? The age at which a young tree begins to bear fruit depends on the kind and variety (some are early bearing, some may take a number of years), the rootstock and the care, especially pruning. Many fruit trees should begin bearing at 4 to 6 years of age. Peach trees bear at 3 to 4 years. Dwarf apple trees may bear at 2 or 3 years of age. Frosts and disease or insect troubles may cause delays.

My fruit trees were set out 2 years ago but seem to show small progress. What should I do to get more rapid growth? (Tennessee.) Give them good growing conditions by cultivating and applying fertilizer. It may be necessary to spray to control pests. Dry weather may have been a factor; if so, mulching will help. As they become well established and older, they will grow faster.

How can I develop fruit trees quickly? I set out 15 trees 2 years ago and have had poor results. Fruit trees normally develop rather slowly —apple trees, for instance, take 4 to 12 years, depending on the variety, to come into bearing. Give them good growing conditions, full sun, sufficient moisture, weed control, and the fertilizer needed by your particular soil.

I have a few fruit trees: peach, pear, and plum. None bear any fruit. Why? There might be several reasons: too young; weak, because of faulty nutrition; overvegetative, because of too heavy pruning or too much nitrogen in the fertilizer; injury to buds or blossoms by low temperatures; injury by pests; and possibly, if they blossom, because cross-pollination is not provided.

I have a home fruit orchard: apples, peaches, pears, plums, and cherries. The fruit seems small. How can the size be increased? The size will depend on the variety, planting distance, natural fertility of the soil, fertilizer treatment, moisture supply, and the amount of pruning and thinning. Overbearing is a common cause of small size. Severe thinning of plums, peaches, and apples is necessary for good fruit size. Try to determine which factors were responsible, then improve conditions with respect to those factors. The system under which they are grown is a factor, whether on sod, cultivated, or mulched. Build up the humus content of the soil by the use of cover crops if the trees are on cultivated soil. If the soil is light and tends to dry out, use the mulch system and apply fertilizer early in the spring. Trees in their first years should be well grown to eventually make vigorous trees.

Can I get quick returns from berries and grapes? This is the second season for berries, the third season for grapes. Strawberries fruit the second year and raspberries a little the second year and nearly a full crop the third year. Everbearing strawberries will fruit the first fall. Autumn-fruiting raspberries fruit the first fall if well grown. Grapes bear some the third year and nearly a full crop the fourth year.

Does covering berry bushes with cheesecloth to keep birds away retard growth and ripening of fruit? Cheesecloth to keep birds away from berry bushes should be put on just as the fruit starts to ripen, and at this stage it will not appreciably retard the growth or date of ripening. However, the special netting, usually of plastic, sold by seed and nursery firms, is easier to use than cheesecloth.

How can heavily laden branches of fruit trees be prevented from breaking? Proper thinning of the fruits should be done after the so-called June drop; if still heavy, prop with stout, crotched stakes.

HARVESTING AND STORING

What is the right time to pick apples, cherries, and pears? For home use, summer and fall apples may be left on the tree until ripe enough to use or until they start to drop. Summer apples keep only a few days unless stored cold. Winter apples are picked before eating-ripe and stored until they are ready in late fall or early winter. Most varieties of pears should be picked when fully grown but still relatively hard—when the first few specimens begin to acquire a yellowish tinge and start to drop. Cherries should be picked when fully ripe.

How should fruit be harvested that is to be stored for the winter? Each apple or pear should be picked from the tree, by hand or with a picker, before it is dead ripe. Avoid bruises, scratches, and cuts. Store only perfect fruits.

Where apples are stored in a fruit cellar and the temperature is controlled only by opening windows to outside air, but where humidity can be controlled, what degree of humidity should be maintained? Give as much ventilation as possible, and a relative humidity of 85 per cent. To prevent shriveling, store in polyethylene bags.

Should the door of a fruit house (built into a bank, with stone sides, wooden roof, ventilating opening in roof, concrete floor) be kept closed in early fall for apple storage? Close on warm days and open at night on cold days to bring the temperature down close to 32° F.

Should apples in storage be kept dry or moist? The air should circulate and the room should be ventilated. The air should, if possible, have a relative humidity of around 85 per cent.

Should apples in storage be sprayed with water? The floor of the storage area, rather than the apples, should be sprayed to maintain the humidity.

Will apples keep longer if waxed? Commercial-wax emulsions will reduce shriveling in storage but may increase "scald" if not properly used. Moistureproof polyethylene wraps will also reduce shriveling. The best assurance of good keeping is to store a long-keeping variety where the air is moist and as near 32° F. as possible.

Should apples be wrapped when stored? Wrapping will help to prevent shriveling and will keep decay from spreading if a few bad apples are mixed with the good ones. Special oil-treated wraps will prevent scald. Most apples stored commercially for any length of time are wrapped in oiled paper or have oil-impregnated paper strips scattered through the package.

Some apples placed in a cold storage room looked fine when they came out, but 2 days later they looked as if they had been dipped in hot water. Why? This is a storage trouble known as apple scald. It is worse if the fruit is picked before it is fully matured and colored. Some varieties are much more susceptible than others. Good ventilation in the storage area will help to some extent. Wrapping the apples in thin paper impregnated with oil will prevent scald almost entirely. The immediate cause seems to be certain gases given off by the apples themselves, and the oil in the wraps will absorb these gases.

I have had some very fine apples but no place to store them; my cellar is too warm; the attic and garage are too cold. How can they be stored inexpensively somewhere outdoors? You could build an insulated storage room in the cellar near a window. Or they can be stored in a barrel pit. (See Storage.)

Can I successfully store fruit in a cellar with a central heating sys-

tem? The cellar is much too warm. You should construct an insulated room which can be ventilated through an outside window. Try to keep this room as close to 32° F. as possible. A bulletin from the United States Department of Agriculture describes several simple types of home fruit and vegetable storage.

EXHIBITING

How are tree fruits selected for shows? They are usually shown as plates of 5. Select fruits that are typical in form, size, coloring for the variety and vicinity; that are uniform in form, size, and color; and free from insect and disease injury. Do not wash or polish: soil may be wiped off, but even this may mar the natural appearance.

PROPAGATION

What are Malling rootstocks? Apple rootstocks were formerly mixed in the trade so that variety names were meaningless. The East Malling Research Station in England collected all the types and classified them according to their effect on tree growth. They are now being used by many nurseries for propagating apple trees. Some produce dwarf or semidwarf trees; others produce large trees. 'Malling 9' produces the smallest tree, 6 to 8 feet tall and generally considered best for home garden use. 'Malling 7' produces semidwarf trees 8 to 10 feet tall.

Can grapes, peaches, cherries, and apples be grown from seeds obtained when you get them from the fruit you buy? All fruits are originally grown from seeds. They seldom resemble their parents and more often than not are decidedly inferior. This is why superior types are propagated vegetatively.

Would it be practical for me to attempt budding or grafting named varieties of apples on some young wild apple trees growing on my property? Yes; neither process is very difficult, although in this, as in most things, "practice makes perfect."

How and when should seeds of cherry, peach, plum, apple, and pear be planted? Mix with sand in the fall and place outdoors, where they will be kept moist. Freezing is not essential; however, the temperature should not rise above 51° F. The optimum temperature is about 36° to 40° F.

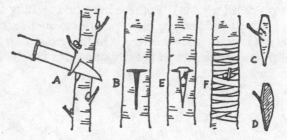

BUDDING

Budding is the simplest method of propagating a desired variety upon another of the same (or a closely related) species. (A) Bud stick; (C and D) different views of bud, after being cut from bud stick; (B) T-shaped cut in bark on stock (stem or branch that is to be budded); (E) bud inserted; (F) bud bound in tight with raffia or rubber band.

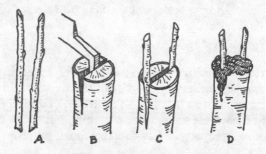

BARK (CLEFT) GRAFTING

A simple method of grafting. (A) Scions, or sections of small branches of the variety it is desired to obtain. (B) Heel of grafting tool holding open the split or cleft in the end of the branch on which the graft is to be grown. (C) Scions cut to wedge shape and inserted so that the bark layers of the branch and scions come into direct contact. (D) Grafting wax applied to protect wound and prevent drying out.

What is the difference between "budding" an apple tree and "grafting" one? Both budding and grafting are used by nurseries in growing young fruit trees. In the former case, a bud (with a sliver of bark attached) is used; in grafting, a small section of a branch or shoot, with several eyes (called a scion). Both budding and grafting are also used when it is desired to add one or more varieties to an older tree. Budding is done in midsummer when the tree is in full growth. Grafting is usually done in the spring just as growth starts, but can be done later if dormant scions are used.

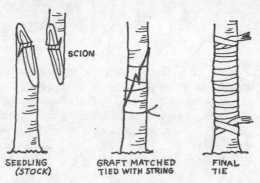

SCION

SEEDLING (STOCK)   GRAFT MATCHED TIED WITH STRING   FINAL TIE

Steps in grafting a young fruit tree.

WHAT TO GROW

Can I grow orchard fruits on a small place? Yes, if you are willing to do the spraying necessary to protect the trees from insects and diseases. Dwarf apples (on 'Malling 9' rootstock) require very little space. Plums and peaches are small trees naturally, but sweet cherries are too large for a small property. Pears are kept small by propagating them on quince stocks.

Which are the best kinds of tree fruits for home gardens in northern New Jersey? This will depend somewhat on the personal preferences of the gardener. If there is room for only 1 or 2 trees, the apple would probably be most generally satisfactory: it makes a fair shade tree and can stand neglect better than the peach. Most pear varieties blight badly, except 'Seckel', 'Kieffer', 'Magness', and 'Moonglow'. The sour cherry 'Montmorency' is fairly easy to grow, but birds are likely to get a good share of the fruit.

What kinds of fruit trees shall I plant in a space 75 × 150 feet to give our family of 5 the best selection of fruit and assure fertilization of the blossoms? (New York.) The varieties, and to some extent the kinds of fruit to plant, will depend on how cold it gets during the winter. If you are in a part of the state where peaches can be grown, try the following plan: Row 1 (4 feet from the fence), strawberries. Row 2 (8 feet from the first row), raspberries, currants, or other bush fruits. Row 3 (10 feet from the second row), grapes. Row 4 (20 feet), 4 peach, 2 sour cherry, 2 pear. Row 5 (23 feet), 6 dwarf apple trees. This will make the apple row 10 feet from the edge of the plot, which may be too close or not, depending on who owns the adjoining land and the purpose for which it is used. There will be no pollination problem with the small fruits or sour cherries. With peaches and pears, planting of more than one variety will practically ensure a satisfactory supply of pollen. 'McIntosh', 'Delicious', 'Cortland', 'Grimes', and many others are good pollinizers for other varieties of apples.

We plan to put in a few fruit trees. Our soil is fairly good but somewhat shady. Choose dwarf fruit trees if your space is limited. However, they require open sunny situations.

In planting a new orchard (of as few as 6 trees) on a property having no fruit at present, what would you advise? Your choice of fruits should be governed by your soil and climatic conditions. Plant what is already growing well in your community or consult your Cooperative Extension Service. Unless you plan to spray, stick to the small fruits, such as blueberries and raspberries.

What fruits can be grown in a cold region with a short growing season? Elevation, 5,700 feet. (Montana.) Only the hardiest varieties, such as some of the new fruits produced by breeding at the Minnesota and South Dakota Experiment Stations. Write to your own Experiment Station for a list of recommended varieties.

What fruits are best for the home garden? The small fruits require less space, bear early, have less trouble from insects and diseases than tree fruits, and need less equipment for their care. Strawberries are the first choice, with red raspberries, currants, gooseberries, blackberries, and blueberries nearly as good.

Specific Tree Fruits

APPLE (MALUS)

What are spur-type apple trees? For several apple varieties, genetic mutations have occurred in nature or by artificial irradiation resulting in new sports that have smaller tree size. For example, 'Oregon Spur Delicious', 'Starkcrimson Delicious', 'Redchief Delicious', and a score of others are spur mutations from the original, larger tree, 'Red Delicious'.

Similarly, 'McIntosh', 'Golden Delicious', and other apple varieties have spur types, but no spur types have yet been discovered for many varieties. 'Compact Stella' is a spur type of the 'Stella' sweet cherry. Because spur types grow into trees that are about two thirds normal size, they are preferred for planting in the home garden as well as in commercial orchards. They bear more fruit per unit volume of tree.

FRUIT TREE SPURS
(*Left*) *Spur-type branch showing how productive spur varieties can be.* (*Right*) *Spurs of regular fruit tree branch.*

Are genetic dwarf fruit trees the same as spur-type dwarfs? Do they tend to be more dwarf? I have a nursery catalog that lists several genetic dwarfs among cherries (including a self-fruitful 'Garden Bing'), apricots, almonds, apples that are on standard-size rootstocks rather than the usual dwarfing stocks. The degree of dwarfing among different varieties of the various fruits is a relative thing. Some varieties are much more dwarfing than others. In today's commercial apple orchards, a large portion of the new plantings of 'Red Delicious' are spur types. Spur-type apple varieties could be referred to as mild genetic dwarfing.

The term "genetic dwarf" is usually reserved for varieties that are truly dwarfed, perhaps only one fourth as large as most standard varieties. The 'Bonanza' peach is a genetic dwarf. Genetic dwarfs are usually characterized by short internodes (lengths of twig between leaves). Thus, the several genetic dwarfs you asked about are true dwarfs. These genetic dwarfs grow small even when they are propagated onto vigorous standard-size rootstocks.

A word of caution, however: Dwarf nectarine trees of such commonly grown varieties as 'Pocahontas', 'Cherokee', 'Nectared No. 4', or 'Nectared No. 5' are dwarfed, not because they are genetic dwarfs, but because they have been budded onto seedlings of dwarfing rootstocks, *Prunus tomentosa* or *P. besseyi*. Nectarine or peach varieties budded onto seedlings of these two *Prunus* species will produce trees that are dwarfed, but the rate of mortality at 3 or 4 years or younger is generally excessive. This is not a good type of tree to buy if longevity is your aim.

When is the proper time to plant apple trees? Some say fall; others say spring. Either spring or fall. If you can get the plants and you live in a region where the autumn is long, fall will perhaps be better, as the soil can be handled and the trees planted when there is not much pressing work.

Can an apple tree be transplanted without injury to it if it has borne its first crop of fruit? Transplanting any tree is a shock, and if a tree has been bearing, transplanting (unless the entire root system is taken with it) may result in rapid vegetative growth that will retard fruiting. If the tree is 4 or 5 years old, it will be better to set a new young tree.

How should a 13-year-old apple tree be fertilized? Apple trees require a complete fertilizer treatment containing the important nutrient elements. The amount of each element needed is determined by the natural fertility of the soil and its past treatment. Therefore, the requirements of a 13-year-old tree might vary from nothing in a very fertile soil to 20 pounds of a 5–10–10 formula on light sand. (See Fertilizer.) Most soils will need nitrogen in the form of ammonium nitrate or nitrate of soda. A few soils are deficient in potash.

What is the best time to plant apple and pear trees in the state of Connecticut? What is the best time of year to prune such trees? Prune and plant in very early spring before the buds begin to swell.

Should an apple tree be fertilized at planting time? No, it is too easy to burn the limited root system with chemical fertilizers. During the first growing season, water is most important.

How can I improve a heavy soil at planting time? Mix the soil removed when digging the hole with a pail of wet peat moss and work this mixture around the roots as the hole is filled. Firm the soil by stepping on it as the hole is filled.

When is the best time to prune apple trees? Any time during the dormant season is satisfactory. Actually the best pruning weather is likely to be in late fall, just after the leaves have dropped and before the weather becomes too cold. In regions where unusually severe cold (25° to 30° F. below zero or lower) may occur, pruning should be delayed until the severe cold of winter is past, as winter-injured trees may experience much more damage if pruned than if not pruned.

What are the main points to keep in mind when pruning a bearing apple tree? Do not remove a branch unless there is a good reason why it should come off. Some varieties will require very little pruning. Take out limbs that are dead, broken, or badly diseased, too low or too high; remove water sprouts (sucker growth, usually whiplike and nonfruiting) from the trunk and main limbs; thin out a little in the top, if necessary, to admit light to the lower limbs; remove slender, obviously weak twigs.

How can I prune so there will not be a lot of water sprouts? If large branches are to be removed, take them out gradually, over 2 or 3 years. This will result in fewer water sprouts, and these can be detected and rubbed off before they become large.

Is it true that fall pruning of fruit trees cuts down sucker growth? Fruit trees react the same to dormant pruning regardless of whether it is done soon after the leaves fall in the autumn or just before growth starts in the spring.

What happens when apple spurs are pruned off? Most of the fruit in certain varieties is borne on short, crooked growths known as spurs. These spurs start to form on 2-year-old wood and grow very slowly. If spurs are pruned off a particular section of a limb, they will not be replaced and that part of the tree cannot produce any fruit.

Is summer pruning of trees advisable to make them bear fruit earlier? Most experiments have indicated that dormant pruning is preferable. The reduction in leaf area from summer pruning may be a disadvantage to the tree by preventing normal ripening of the fruit. Certainly summer pruning is not of any practical value as a means of hastening fruit production by young trees. Some summer pruning, really pinching back of succulent growth, is recommended for dwarf fruit trees to keep them compact and to improve their shape.

How often should apple trees, just planted, be pruned? Prune at planting time and early each spring thereafter.

Should bearing-age apple trees, which were pruned when shipped from the nursery, be further pruned when planted? It may be necessary if the trees are shipped bare-root. If there appears to be any drying out, more pruning may be necessary—back to live wood. The top should be reduced proportionately to the size of the root system. Heavily pruned large trees are really no better than young trees.

How should I prune apple trees that are in their second or third season? Apple trees of this age should receive only corrective pruning. In other words, do not remove any branches except those that especially need to come off. This would include branches that are broken, too low on the trunk, crowding other branches, or that make a narrow angle with the trunk. Crotches with narrow angles (less than 45°) are more likely to split apart than are wide-angled crotches. If two members of a crotch are of equal size, cut one back each year until it is a branch from a larger limb or remove it entirely. Keep the central leader dominant at this stage by shortening branches that may be competing with it

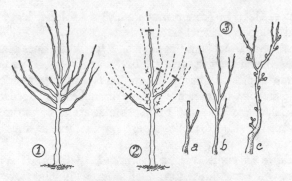

APPLE TREE PRUNING

(1) A 2-year-old nursery-grown tree, as received and planted. (2) The same tree after being pruned. The "X" signs indicate branches removed entirely. (3) Effects of cutting back compared with thinning. (a) Twig severely cut back. (b) Growth from cutback twig is all vegetative (no flowers). (c) Growth from tree with thinning pruning only; good balance of twig growth and flowering spurs is clearly evident.

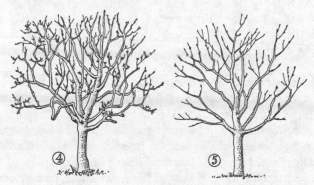

(4) Neglect of early training results in poor framework. A 'Stayman' apple about 6 years old with three leaders (very undesirable), polelike growths, and bad crotch. To correct these faults now means a high head. (5) Early training results in good form. 'Stayman' apple about 6 years old; good spacing of scaffold branches. Central leader still present. Note development of secondary branches.

for dominance. Head in (prune moderately) very long, leggy limbs to make them develop side branches.

After planting a 'Dolgo' crab apple tree 3 feet high, does one prune it the first year, and how much? What care does it need in the winter? Crab apples are hardy. They don't require winter care. The only pruning needed is to remove those branches not needed for the framework. Select the 3, 4, or 5 branches that are to form the frame so they are spaced 8 to 12 inches apart on the trunk, thus avoiding crotches. Remove the rest.

Can mulching an apple tree be overdone? Seldom. If a mulching material that will pack down too much is used, it might prevent root aeration. Loose material to a depth of 4 to 12 inches is good. Heavy mulching for several years with a hay mulch relatively high in nitrogen, or a legume mulch, may make the tree overvegetative. The apples may color poorly, drop prematurely, and lack keeping quality. Susceptibility to injury from low winter temperatures is another possibility.

What special care do apple trees need in the spring? Proper pruning and spraying, and then attention to the fertilization of the soil. (See Fertilizer.)

How should the fruit of an apple tree be thinned? What is the best method and time? Thin when the young apples are about the size of hulled walnuts. Leave at least 6 or 7 inches between fruits. The small apples can be removed by snapping the stem with your thumb and finger, being careful not to injure the spur. Special thinning shears are available and very useful.

Can bearing-size fruit trees, such as apple, cherry, or peach, be purchased at a nursery? "Bearing age" trees may be nursery scrubs that were not large enough to sell at 1 or 2 years of age. They experience such a shock from moving that they are not likely to bear much fruit any earlier than the 1- or 2-year-old trees customarily planted. They should not be planted in spite of claims of early bearing.

I have just purchased a 6-foot 'McIntosh' apple tree. How many years, approximately, until it bears fruit? With good care it should bear in the sixth year.

How much should a 'Red Delicious' apple tree grow a year if planted at 2 years of age? The first year it should increase its height about 2½ feet; the next year, 2 feet. Ordinarily, 3 to 6 shoots, 30 to 48 inches long, may be produced in the first year.

My apple tree bears fruit by halves—that is, first one side bears apples and the next year the other side. How do you explain this? (New York.) Some varieties bear a full crop in alternate years. In the case of your tree, something happened to upset the periodicity on one side. This is a desirable condition.

We have an 'Astrachan' apple tree that bore no fruit last year. It is about 12 years old and bore abundantly the previous year. Would you have any explanation? 'Red Astrachan' is generally an alternate-year bearer.

I have two early apple trees bearing only every other year, but together. Can I change the bearing years of one of them? Thinning sprays applied during the bloom of early apples will make alternate bearers into annual bearers.

What can be done to an apple tree (about 5 years old) to get it to blossom and bear fruit? It is now about 10 to 11 feet high. Any variety of apple must reach a particular state of internal development before it will set fruits. Do only corrective or formative pruning, and do not fertilize too heavily with nitrogen. When the proper balance is reached, the tree will fruit; to use means to hasten this might prove dangerous. Some varieties bear in 3 or 4 years; some take 10 to 12 years.

What causes a young medium-size apple tree to have only one large flawless apple? Probably it is a self-unfruitful variety and needs to be pollinated by a compatible variety.

We have a 'Wealthy' apple tree about 8 years old that seems to produce a lot of foliage but few apples. What is the reason? 'Wealthy' is one of the earliest varieties to bear. Your tree probably had too much nitrogen or too heavy pruning. Inexperienced persons have been known to prune off the fruiting spurs. Lack of cross-pollination, if the tree blossoms, could be the answer if there are no other apple varieties nearby.

I have a 'Grimes Golden' apple tree in my yard that is 8 years old. It has been pruned by people from an experienced nursery for 2 successive years, yet it will not bloom; hence, no fruit. Why? 'Grimes Golden' should bear in about 5 or 6 years in the orchard. Probably the pruning was too heavy and encouraged vegetative growth.

I have a 'Golden Delicious' apple tree, 10 years old, that has had only 5 apples on it. The tree looks fine and is 12 feet high. Why are there no apples? Although 'Golden Delicious' is capable of some self-pollination, much better results can be expected with another compatible variety nearby.

I have a small orchard of 10 apple trees, 16 years old, which do not bear any fruit. Can anything be done to make them bear? (Wisconsin.) This may be due to winter injury; if so, there is little chance of correcting the condition. If a tree is making very vigorous growth and does not form fruit buds, the lack may be caused by pruning too heavily, or by using too much nitrogenous fertilizer, in which case the remedy is evident. If the trees are all of one variety and do blossom, then lack of cross-pollination is a possible reason. Severe injury to the foliage from disease (apple scab) or insects is another possibility.

How can immature apples be prevented from dropping? Nearly all species of fruiting trees lose some fruits by dropping them when the fruits are small; this is called the June drop. The reason is that more fruits are formed than the tree can support, but sometimes the drop is because of imperfect fertilization by pollen. And sometimes it is caused by codling moth or curculio, which can be prevented by spraying.

What spray is used to prevent premature dropping of apples? Various commercial brands of hormone sprays or preharvest sprays can be obtained. These are for prevention of premature dropping of nearly mature fruits.

My 2 apple trees have full bloom, but when the apples form they fall off. Spraying helps very little. Can you offer a solution? If the fruits attain a size of ½ to ¾ inch, the spraying may be with the wrong material, or applied at the wrong time, or otherwise inadequate. If they drop at a smaller size, it may be a question of incompatible pollination or too rapid growth.

How old must a 'Northern Spy' apple tree be to produce fruit? What is the matter if an apparently healthy tree does not yield? A 'Northern Spy' apple requires the longest period of any variety to reach the stage of fruitfulness. This can be as much as 15 or 20 years in some instances. Try to reduce its vigor by growing it in sod. Do not prune the tree. They will fruit much earlier on 'M9' rootstock, which then makes them a dwarf fruit tree.

What is the best method to make apple and pear trees 50 to 60 years old profitable? Pruning, spraying, soil enrichment, etc. If they have been long neglected, it might be better to start anew. They may be too tall for profitable handling, and then many new and better varieties have come along since these were planted. If in fair condition, a renovation pruning, together with fertilizer and spraying, may bring them back.

How about apple trees that have been neglected for several years and no longer bear fruit fit to eat? Can these trees be brought back to a normal condition? If so, how? Renovation pruning, fertilization, and proper spraying are indicated. These measures will gradually restore the trees to vigor, provided, of course, that they are not too old.

How can I preserve an old apple tree that is beginning to de-

cay? Remove all dead wood. If space is available, plant replacements, since old, declining trees are not good producers, although they can be picturesque in the landscape.

How can I tell flower buds from leaf buds on apple trees in late summer? Apples form most of their flower buds at the ends of short spurs. Some varieties may form them laterally, on longer twigs of the current season's growth. Flower buds are plump and more rounded than the narrow-pointed leaf buds.

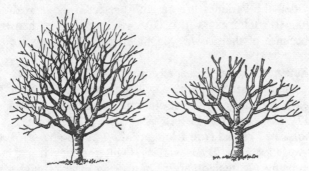

Old, neglected fruit trees can be cut back severely to form new, lower heads to make them easier to care for and eventually productive.

Is there any way to keep apple trees from blooming too early? Frost always gets our blossoms. There is no practical way to delay the blooming date. Certain varieties, such as 'Rome Beauty', 'Northern Spy', and 'Macoun' bloom later than most. Consult your State Experiment Station as to hardy varieties for your locality. Trees in a frost pocket experience much more injury to flowers from spring frosts than trees well up on a slope. You may be in a place where the climate does not permit apples to be grown successfully.

Is it possible to determine the variety of apples by the appearance of the leaf on a "5-in-1" apple tree? Probably only a few people in the country are qualified to determine, negatively or positively, some varieties of apples by their foliage. It would require an unusual knowledge in this field.

What varieties should I look for on a "5-in-1" apple tree? Whatever the nursery chooses to put on. (Usually the varieties are stated.) However, as far as possible, they should be uniform in growth, because there is great variation in the growth of various varieties. There must be at least one good pollinator in the lot.

What special care do dwarf apple trees require? Apple trees on 'Malling 9', the most dwarfing rootstock, should be planted with the bud union (indicated by a swelling) about 2 inches above the ground. The soil must not be allowed to get above this point or the top may develop roots and soon become a full-sized tree. Dwarf trees should be tied to a stout stake since the roots are brittle and the tree may topple over with a heavy crop. (See also Dwarf and Espalier Fruit Trees.)

Is an apple tree that bears several kinds of apples good to grow? If there is space for only one apple tree, one with several varieties may be used, provided the varieties are carefully selected. Several dwarf trees (on 'Malling 9' rootstock) will occupy no more space than one large tree and because of their lower height, 6 to 8 feet, they are easier to manage.

About how much room is needed for a "5-in-1" apple tree? If these are grafted on standard roots, they will require a space about 35 × 45 feet. For ease in management, get one on a dwarfing rootstock, such as 'M9' or 'M7'. 'M9' needs 6 × 12 feet; 'M7', 12 × 20 feet.

How soon can I expect fruit from a "5-in-1" apple tree? It depends upon the varieties used. Some varieties will produce fruits in 3 to 5 years after being planted; others require 5 to 8 years, and sometimes more. Growth conditions, as governed by site, soil, fertilization, and disease and insect control, will also have an effect. A dwarf tree will bear sooner.

Will a "5-in-1" apple tree continue to bear heavily over a long period of years? If properly cared for, it should bear as long as if the same varieties were planted individually.

What precautions should be taken in pruning a nonbearing "5-in-1" apple tree? Try to secure as uniform a development of each variety as possible. If one is weaker than the others, prune it more lightly than the more vigorous kinds. Prune only in the winter, but pinch back rapid growths in the summer to act as a stopper.

My "5-in-1" apple tree is lopsided. Why? The varieties are such that they do not grow at a uniform rate, or the union on one may not be as good as with the others. The exposure as related to shading may affect one more than another. (See also Section 13 for more on plant problems.)

My apple tree is turning green around the trunk. What is the cause? What is the remedy? The green color is probably caused by moss or lichens growing on the dead outer bark. It will do no harm, but could indicate poor circulation of air or too much shade. Possibly pruning has been neglected. This condition usually does not occur on sprayed trees.

What causes hard brown spots in apples? The trees appear healthy, but the apples are not fit to use. Probably "bitter pit," usually associated with excessive tree growth late in the season. Some varieties are especially susceptible, such as 'Baldwin' or 'Northern Spy'. In some localities, lack of boron in the soil can cause brown spots in the flesh of the apple.

Is it the same kind of aphids that we have on other plants that curl up apple leaves? These are "green" and "rosy" apple aphids. A summer infestation can be controlled with malathion.

Are there borers that attack apple trees? There are 3: round-headed apple tree borer, flat-headed apple tree borer, and leopard moth borer. The round-headed usually attacks young trees, and the laying of eggs may be prevented by means of repellent paint or by covering the trunks with fine-meshed wire or with paper. The flat-headed borer usually works in old, neglected trees. The leopard moth attacks young trees or branches. Examine the trees frequently, and if sawdust is seen near the trunk, look for the hole. Sometimes the larvae can be killed in the hole with a fairly stiff wire. There are commercial preparations such as Borerkil. If you have many trees, consult your Cooperative Extension Service.

My apples all have worms in them. What shall I do? The worms are codling moth, the most serious insect pest of apples. Consult your Cooperative Extension Service, since the spray program is rather complicated and new insecticides vary from year to year.

What causes young apples to fall off? They have crescent-shaped marks on them. This is the egg-laying mark of curculio. Methoxychlor is effective in controlling the curculio. Pink-bud and petal-fall sprays are important, but others may be necessary in different localities. Consult your county extension agent for a spray schedule.

In July, when I approach my apple trees, myriads of little flies come out. What are they? They may be leafhoppers. Keep watch just after the trees bloom. The nymphs cannot fly then, but are very shy and sidle away. This is the time to kill them with malathion. They are not as easy to kill as adults.

What is San Jose scale? A sucking insect which forms a hard circular covering that attacks orchard fruits and related plants, especially apple, peach, and pear. It may kill young trees in 2 or 3 years. It is indicated by a scurfy appearance when the scales are thickly clustered on young twigs. There may be a reddish discoloration along the veins of the leaves or small circular red spots on the fruits. Control is miscible oil as a dormant spray.

How can I get rid of tent caterpillars? Apple tree tent caterpillars east of the Rockies, and a similar species west, infest wild cherries, apples, etc. In regularly sprayed orchards they are usually no problem, but in home fruit gardens they may be. Do not burn them, as this will injure the tree. Spray with malathion when the nests are about the size of a silver dollar. Better still, follow the regular spray schedule for your state, which will control them.

What are the brown and somewhat star-shaped spots on my apples? This is apple blotch, prevalent in the South and Southeast. Consult the spray schedule from your county extension agent.

Why should red-cedar trees be cut down near apple orchards? The red-cedar and the apple are alternate hosts for the so-called cedar rust, which is indicated by light-yellow spots changing to orange on apple leaves and fruits in the spring and summer; cedar rust galls on cedar in winter, developing to release spores in early spring. If there are only a few red-cedar trees, destroy all within half a mile to protect the apples. If too numerous to destroy, ferbam sprays on the apple will give good control.

What makes the leaves on some of the twigs of my apple trees turn black and dry up, just as if they had been burned? This is fire blight, a bacterial disease. Cut these off well back from the dead part. Use a solution of zinc chloride to sterilize tools after each cut. Look for cankers on the trunk or limbs and clean these out. Regulate the growth of the trees so that it is not too vigorous. Spraying with Bordeaux mixture while the trees are in full bloom will often prevent infection through this means. Antibiotic sprays have also proved effective in controlling fire blight in some areas.

What is apple scab? Apple scab is the most serious fungus disease of apples in the North. It partially, or sometimes nearly completely, defoliates apple trees, thereby greatly reducing them in vigor and productiveness as well as making them susceptible to winter injury. The scab lesions, if numerous, also disfigure and spoil the fruit. Ferbam, captan, and other materials are used in controlling scab. Because of the importance of this disease, the county Cooperative Extension Service issues special bulletins on the latest control measures. These should be followed for best results, since careful timing is important in securing good control.

What is the best and quickest-growing apple tree? If you want apples in a hurry, plant dwarf trees that are propagated on the 'Malling 9' rootstock. Most varieties will start bearing on this root in 2 or 3 years. 'Golden Delicious', 'Jonathan', 'Tydeman Early', and 'Jerseymac' are good varieties.

Which varieties of apples have proved suitable in New York? 'Jerseymac' ripens in August, 'Tydeman Early' in September, 'McIntosh', 'Cortland', and 'Macoun' in early winter. 'Mutsu' is a good winter variety.

For a family that likes crisp, hard, slightly tart, and very juicy, old-fashioned apples, and which has room for only 2 or 3 trees, which varieties would you recommend for central New Jersey? You might try 'Tydeman Early' for medium early, 'Jonathan' for early winter, and 'Stayman' or 'Mutsu' for a late variety.

What is the best all-round or all-purpose apple tree to plant in New England? 'Mutsu'.

APRICOT (PRUNUS ARMENIACA)

Can apricots be grown in central Massachusetts? Yes. If peach trees are hardy, 'Alfred' and 'Farmingdale' are good. 'Sungold' is one of the hardiest varieties.

We have 2 apricot trees, 8 to 10 years old. What can I do to prevent fruit rotting just before it becomes ripe? (California.) Get the current spray schedule from Agricultural Experiment Station, Davis, California.

CHERRY (PRUNUS)

Under what conditions of soil and climate can sweet cherries be grown successfully? They need a sandy loam, deep and well drained. Climate is even more important. The shores of the Great Lakes, the Hudson Valley of New York, and the Pacific coast are the areas where sweet cherries are grown commercially. They are susceptible to winter injury and late frosts and do not like extremely hot summers.

Are sour cherries fussy as to soil and climate? These can be grown over most of the Atlantic coast and in the Mississippi Valley. Commercially, they are grown in New York, Wisconsin, and Michigan. They are hardier than the sweet varieties. They can be grown on sandy or heavy soils, if well drained, and can stand drought better than sweet cherries.

When should young cherry trees be fertilized to bring them most quickly into bearing? If young cherry trees need fertilizing, do it in early spring. As a general rule, they would start bearing at an earlier age if they were grown a bit slowly. It is desirable to grow good-sized trees as quickly as possible, in order to get a large crop; hence, the trees are usually forced while young, thus sacrificing very early bearing for the larger size of the tree.

What is a good fertilizer for cherries and how should it be applied?   On young trees, apply 10–10–10 at a rate of ½ to 3 pounds per tree. On older trees, use ammonium nitrate at a rate of 1 to 3 pounds per tree, depending on its vigor. Broadcast complete fertilizer in early spring and the ammonium nitrate later as needed.

What is the best age to buy cherry trees and when should the trees be planted?   One- or 2-year-old trees. Plant in early spring in the North; farther south, in late autumn.

What rootstock is best for cherries?   Cherries are propagated on two rootstocks, mahaleb and mazzard. Sweet cherry trees on the mazzard root are longer lived than trees on the mahaleb root and generally more satisfactory, especially on heavy soils. Mahaleb roots are used generally for sour cherries. To get cherries on mazzard roots, you must specify them and pay more as they are more expensive to produce.

Are there dwarfing rootstocks for cherries similar to apples?   No suitable dwarfing stock for cherries has been found. Tart cherry varieties, such as 'Montmorency', are generally budded onto mahaleb cherry rootstocks, and sweet cherry varieties, such as 'Stella', onto mazzard (wild sweet cherry) rootstocks. 'Colt', introduced in 1974 in England as a dwarfing cherry rootstock, has proven not to have any significant dwarfing effect.

Should cherry trees be pruned and at what age?   Cherry trees should be pruned lightly each year, but removal of a few undesirable twigs may be all the pruning needed. They require less pruning than the apple or peach.

When is the best time to prune cherry trees?   The best time is in early spring—during the latter part of March. They may, however, be pruned at any time during the dormant season. Do not prune after unusually cold winters.

How should cherry trees be pruned?   With sweet cherries, little need be done except to remove dead or injured branches and twigs that are growing in an undesirable position and that are too high or tending to make a weak crotch. Sour cherries should be started as delayed open-center trees with a short trunk about 6 feet high and several well-spaced scaffold limbs. Besides the "corrective" pruning, as recommended for sweet cherries, some thinning of tops will be needed to keep the trees from becoming too dense and so shading out fruit-bearing wood in the lower part. If trees are pruned every year, not a great deal of cutting will be needed at any other time.

I have been told a 'Bing' sweet cherry will not produce fruit when planted by itself. What variety will? I don't want more than one tree. 'Compact Stella', a spur-type sweet cherry, will produce fruit on its own pollen. Nearly all sweet varieties will pollinate others. In your case, you might top-work (graft) 'Windsor' or 'Black Tartarian' on a branch of the 'Bing'. This will provide enough pollination for one tree. 'Bing', 'Lambert', and 'Napoleon' are cross-incompatible and do not pollinate each other successfully.

I have a 'Black Tartarian' cherry tree surrounded with plums, peaches, Rocky Mountain cherry, and apples. Does it need any other cherry for fertilization? None of these is an effective pollinator. You could use 'Bing', 'Windsor', 'Napoleon', and other good varieties.

What do you recommend doing for a white cherry tree when very small green cherries fall off before maturing? Plant another variety to act as a pollinator.

What causes the small green cherries (sour cherry) to drop off the tree? It may be due to a lack of pollination, attacks by curculio, or frost injury during bloom or shortly after.

I planted 3 cherry trees and 2 days later we had frost. How should I protect these trees from frost? If the trees were dormant, as they should have been for transplanting, frost a few days after planting would not hurt them.

I have a 15-year-old sweet cherry tree. Why does it bear only a few large fruits? This tree is located in a strip 4 feet wide separating two cement driveways. This is a very poor location for a tree. And probably there is no other sweet cherry variety in the near neighborhood to act as a pollinator.

How long does it take for a cherry tree to blossom? A sour cherry should produce its first blossoms 3 or 4 years after being planted. A sweet cherry tree may take 1 to 3 years longer.

How can I retard the blooming of cherry, peach, plum, and apricot trees? There is no practical method of retarding blooming dates of fruit trees in order to avoid frost injury. Some varieties naturally bloom a little later than others.

We raised a cherry tree from a pit; it is 3 years old. Will it bear fruit? It will bear eventually but is not likely to resemble the parent.

A sour cherry tree bore fruit one year and none the next. Why? The blossoms or buds were probably injured by cold weather.

I have 4 cherry trees which bloom but have only a dozen or so cherries. Why? Probably because of imperfect pollination. If your trees are all of one variety, plant some other. There are 7 distinct groups which will not pollinate each other, so the variety must be selected with care and also as to the possibility of frost injury.

I accidentally broke a branch in the lower part of a cherry tree that left a groove in the bark; the sap keeps running out at the foot of the tree. What must I do to correct this? Sap will run from any kind of an injury on a cherry tree. There is no practical method of repairing an injury such as the one described. If the tree is growing vigorously, the wound may heal over eventually.

How can I keep my cherries free of insects and diseases? Plum curculio, cherry maggot, and brown rot are the worst enemies of cherry trees. Cherry leaf spot appears first as yellow spots in the leaves. These turn brown and fall out. They look like shot holes. The leaves themselves turn yellow and then fall. Sometimes the tree is completely defoliated. Follow the spray schedule obtainable from the Cooperative Extension Service in your county or from the state university.

How can I keep birds from eating my cherries and other fruits? This is a hard question to answer. The enclosure of the tree or its branches is the only sure method. Covering the branches with large cheesecloth bags will save a few of the fruits for you and rarely can the birds eat the entire crop!

I have heard of virus diseases of cherries. What can I do to avoid them? As the result of an extensive search for virus-free trees of the important cherry varieties, nurseries are now propagating virus-free trees. These should be specified when ordering trees. They are superior to stock of uncertain virus status.

PEACH (PRUNUS PERSICA)

What kind of soil is needed for peach trees? Any good soil that is well drained. They prefer sandy loam, however.

Should I mix fertilizer with the soil when I plant a peach tree? Do not mix fertilizer with soil used to fill in around the roots, as it might cause some injury. Dig it under before the tree is planted or work into the soil around the newly planted tree but outside the limits of the hole in which it was planted.

Should I plant a peach orchard in the spring or fall? In general, except where winters are quite mild, spring planting is best.

Is it wise to plant new peach trees in the same places from which the old ones have just been removed? It is not. Peaches so planted often fail. The trouble is not well understood, but it may be nematodes, root aphids, or possibly something else from the roots of the old trees.

I have a bearing peach tree. When can I move it? Moving a bearing-age peach tree is hazardous. It must be pruned heavily and might be as long coming into bearing again as a new tree. It can be moved in the fall, but very early spring would be better.

How does one care for a peach tree in a suburban backyard? The ideal treatment would include preventing weed or other growth around the tree; use of a complete fertilizer; adequate pruning; some spraying and thinning of fruit whenever a heavy crop is set. Control of the peach borer, which works in the trunk just above the level of the soil, is very important.

My peach tree has 3 main trunks at the ground level, forming a sort of cup which is filled with gum. How shall I treat it? This is probably the result of killing the leading shoot when the tree was a year or two old. Cut away 2 of the trunks as close as possible and arrange drainage so the water will not stand in a "cup," if one is left. Paint the wounds.

I have a 'Halehaven' peach tree which has had only a half-dozen peaches. Could you explain why and what to do to improve the fruit? The tree may be too young to bear a full crop. It should have a full crop by the fourth year if it is making good growth and has not been injured by cold weather. Low winter temperatures or spring frosts at blooming can prevent fruit from forming.

Do peach varieties have spur types like apples? 'Compact Redhaven' is identical with 'Redhaven', except that it develops into a smaller, more compact tree. Unlike the enhanced productivity of spur types in apples, this compact peach variety is less fruitful than the normal, noncompact 'Redhaven'. 'Bonanza' is another very dwarfed, dark-green peach tree with very dense leaves; but again, it is not sufficiently fruitful to be recommended except as a novelty. It can be grown in a tub.

Why do some peach trees fail to bear? (California.) This might be due to any one or more of these factors: lack of enough winter cold to complete the rest period; frost injury to buds or flowers; lack of pollination (if a self-sterile variety); or faulty nutrition.

I have a 3-year-old peach tree about 8 feet high which has not blossomed. It grew from a 'Halehaven' pit. When will it bear fruit, or must I graft it? Peaches usually bear at 3 or 4 years of age. Whether a seedling will bear good fruit is a matter of chance. Some seedling peaches are good enough for home use.

What is the approximate life of a peach tree? With good care, peaches can be made to produce for about 20 to 25 years. However, severe winter temperatures or borers can shorten the life of peach trees.

I have a young peach tree about 12 feet away from a large oak tree.

Will it grow and produce fruit there as well as it would in the open or should it be moved?   You have two handicaps: competition of roots, and shade. Better move it. Peaches need full sun.

Will a peach tree that came up from seed ever bear good peaches?   It may or may not. If it is a seedling of 'Elberta', it will resemble that variety. Keep it until it fruits and decide then whether you want to keep it.

My peach tree is simply loaded with fruit but it never gets large enough to amount to anything.   The fruit should be thinned when it is a little larger than a robin's egg. Take off all small or stunted peaches, leaving at least 6 inches between the fruits that remain on the tree. Thinning will result in larger size, better color, and less breakage of limbs.

What is the best method of "domesticating" wild-grown or neglected 2- to 3-year-old peach trees?   It is probably better to start anew if they were badly neglected. If not too bad, plow, fertilize soil, prune, and give good spraying. Take out very bad trees and replace.

How can a peach tree, 4 years old, be changed to another variety?   Peaches can be top-worked (see Grafting), but cleft grafting used for apples or pears is not successful with peaches. The way to proceed is to cut off branches 2 or 3 inches in diameter in late winter. During the summer, shoots will appear, and these can be budded in July, August, or early September, just as seedling peaches are budded.

Will peach tree roots block up a drain or sewer?   Peach roots will not seek out a drain or sewer; but roots of any tree planted above or very close to a loose-joint sewer will enter it.

When and how should I prune newly planted peach trees?   Prune just before the trees are planted or just after. Small nursery trees, 3 to 4 feet high, should be pruned to a "whip" (a single stem) and cut back to a height of 24 to 30 inches. Larger trees, 5 to 6 feet, should be cut back to about 30 to 36 inches, but instead of cutting off all side branches, leave 3, suitably spaced to be used as scaffold limbs, and cut them to stubs 4 to 6 inches long.

What is the proper way to prune a young peach tree?   Develop an open center, bowl-shaped type of tree with its lowest scaffold limb at least a foot from the ground. Remove limbs that are too low, that head in and tend to fill up the center, or that crowd other limbs and make any part of the tree too dense. The tallest limbs should be headed to side branches pointing outward in order to get maximum spread and keep the center open.

What time and method should be used in pruning old peach

trees? Pruning is best done in late winter or early spring after the time when dangerously low temperatures may occur. Pruning should be more severe than for younger trees. Cut out weak twigs and limbs, thin out year-old shoots by taking out weaker ones. Cut back shoots that are longer than 12 inches. As the tree gets older, severe pruning needed to maintain vigor may cause it to be smaller than it was as a younger tree.

When is the best time to remove a limb from a peach tree? Any time it seems necessary, although it is usually done during the dormant season.

What is the best way to fix a peach tree limb that was broken because of the heavy crop? If the branch can be spared, cut it off. If it is split in the middle, prop it up and put in a few small bolts with washers. Early thinning prevents limb breakage from overbearing of fruits.

Should one cut all dead limbs from peach trees? All dead limbs should be removed from all trees, as they present a disease and insect hazard. You should have no dead limbs if you prune peach trees properly.

How do you prune a nectarine tree? The fruit of a nectarine is essentially a peach without fuzz, and so the tree is pruned in the same way as a peach.

Must peach trees be cross-pollinated? Only varieties that have poor pollen need other varieties near to provide good pollen. 'J. H. Hale', an old variety, has poor pollen, but all satisfactory recent varieties have good pollen.

When I cut open peaches that appear to be sound, why are there little pink worms in them? These are the larvae of the Oriental fruit moth. Spray trees according to the Cooperative Extension Service directions obtainable from your county agent.

Do peach trees need a mulch for winter? Mulching the soil around peach trees will have no appreciable effect on their susceptibility to injury by cold weather.

What is the best method to protect young peach trees from freezing in the winter and from rabbits? There isn't much that can be done in a practical way to protect peach trees from freezing. If they are of a hardy variety and in good growth condition, they will be as resistant to cold as it is possible to make them. Rabbits usually are not as likely to bother peach trees as apple trees. Mechanical protection, by use of wire cloth, building paper, or even newspapers wrapped around the trunk, is probably the most satisfactory method.

What is the best method of propagation for peaches? Peaches are usually budded on seedlings grown from wild peach seeds. (See Budding.)

What are the main insects and diseases that trouble peaches? See Section 13, and consult bulletins from your state Cooperative Extension Service.

What are the best varieties of peach trees to plant? See the introduction to this chapter.

PEAR (PYRUS)

When does one fertilize young pear trees to bring them into early bearing? The trees will bear earlier if making a moderate growth than if growing too vigorously. Overfertilization is also conducive to fire blight. If the soil is poor, make a light application of a complete fertilizer in early spring. Otherwise, if the tree is making good growth, do not use fertilizers.

What soil is best for pear trees? Heavy sandy loam or clay loam with plenty of humus, which will hold moisture, yet assure good drainage.

When is the best time to plant pears? Plant trees as early in the spring as the soil can be prepared. Planting should be completed by the time fruit-tree buds begin to expand.

How do I plant, care for, and prune 'Bartlett' pear trees? I am setting out 100 trees this spring. A hundred trees of 'Bartlett' pears will involve considerable care and expense. It would be advisable, therefore, to get rather complete information from your Cooperative Extension Service as to fertilizing, spraying, etc., under your particular local conditions. When making planting plans, some provision should be made for cross-pollination by planting at least 5 or 6 trees of another variety which should be something other than 'Seckel', as 'Bartlett' and 'Seckel' do not pollinate each other.

Our 5-year-old 'Bartlett' pear has twice borne fruit sparingly. It is of good size and its leaves look healthy, but they are very small and few. This tree is doing well to have borne fruit twice the first 5 years. 'Bartlett' leaves are normally rather small, so perhaps the tree has nothing wrong with it. If you stimulate its growth too much, you may have trouble with the disease known as fire blight.

Are there dwarf pear trees? Are they worth planting? Pear trees are dwarfed by propagating them on quince roots. They are suitable for the home garden.

Will one pear tree alone in a garden bear fruit? Most varieties of pears will bear a much better crop if cross-pollinized, so in making a new planting it would be highly desirable to include at least 2 varieties unless there are other varieties growing in the immediate neighborhood. However, single trees sometimes prove to be fairly reliable croppers.

Is the 'Bartlett' pear self-fertile? If not, what variety should I plant near it? 'Bartlett' will set a much better crop if cross-pollinated. Any of the common varieties, such as 'Sheldon', 'Bosc', or 'Anjou', would be satisfactory pollinizers.

Does a 'Duchess' pear need cross-pollination? Experiments in New York and in California indicate that this variety can bear a fair crop if self-pollinized but a better crop if cross-pollinated.

How should mature pear trees be pruned? Mature pear trees of most varieties require very little pruning and are likely to be injured by fire blight if pruned too heavily. Simply remove dead and broken branches. If the trees become too high, leaders can be cut back a little to a side branch.

How do you prune pear trees at planting time? One-year trees will be unbranched whips. Head a 5-foot tree back to 3½ or 4 feet. Two-year nursery trees will have 2 to 6 side branches; remove all side branches below 30 inches, except 2 to 4 of the stronger ones well distributed around the trunk and spaced at least 4 inches apart. Remove the rest; head the leader back by about one third.

Our pear and plum trees have not had very much fruit for several years. They have never been pruned. How and when should this be done? The lack of fruit is probably due to other factors than lack of pruning, such as frost injury, insects, or diseases. Pruning would probably result in larger fruit. Remove dead, very weak, or broken branches, limbs that are too low or that rub and crowd other branches. If the trees are getting too high, the tallest limbs should be cut back to side branches. Avoid overpruning. The pear can be injured by fire blight if cut too hard. If there is a great deal of cutting needed, spread it over 2 or 3 years. If the soil is fairly fertile, withhold fertilizers during the years when heavy pruning is done.

How should I prune a young 'Seckel' pear tree? The 'Seckel' pear makes a rather dwarfish, compact tree which requires very little pruning. Remove only dead or broken twigs and those branches which are definitely out of place.

When pruning pear trees, is it harmful to remove some of the branches which had borne fruit during the past summer? It is claimed that this helps the growth of trees. No effort should be made to remove those branches which have borne fruit, as they should continue to bear for many years.

The trunk of our 20-year-old pear tree has produced 3 offshoots this year. If I cut them off and set them in a container of mud and water, will roots develop?   No.

Is there anything to be done for fire blight on pears?   Not much. Prune off the afflicted limbs. 'Bartlett' is reputed to be less subject to blight when not overstimulated by fertilizers or pruning. The varieties 'Moonglow', 'Maxine', and 'Magness' are considered to be blight-resistant.

Is it necessary to spray pears to secure good fruits?   Pears are attacked by San Jose scale, codling moth, and fire blight. (See Apple.) Fire blight is serious. Pear psylla is sometimes called a jumping plant louse. A black fungus grows in the excreta on the leaves. Pear trees produce better fruit without spraying than other fruit trees. Consult your Cooperative Extension Service for instructions.

What pear varieties are suitable for home-garden planting?   See the list in the introduction to this chapter.

Can you give some information on the 'Comice' pear?   The 'Comice' pear has excellent fruit but the tree is a poor grower, subject to blight, and not very hardy. It is a valuable commercial variety on the Pacific coast but likely to prove disappointing elsewhere.

What is the best pear for the Lake George region? (New York.)   'Flemish Beauty' and 'Clapp Favorite', both of which are more winter-hardy than most other varieties, are suggested for the Lake George region. Two varieties are necessary to provide cross-pollination.

PLUM (PRUNUS)

Do plums require a special type of soil?   Heavy soils are preferred for the European types and lighter soils for the Japanese varieties; but they will all do well enough for home use on a fairly wide range of well-drained soils if the site is otherwise suitable.

How should young plum trees be fertilized to bring them into early bearing?   Young fruit trees usually make a rather vigorous growth if the soil is reasonably fertile. The addition of fertilizer, if not carefully regulated, may make growth too vigorous and delay bearing instead of hastening it. Fertilize only enough to maintain good growth and trees will bear early. On sandy soils, of course, fertilizer will be needed every year if good growth is to be secured. The fertilizer program must be adapted to local soil conditions.

What is the proper way to plant plum trees? Order 1- or 2-year-old trees and plant in early spring 20 feet apart (or a little less for Damsons). Dwarf plum trees can be planted 8 feet apart.

Can a single plum tree bear fruit? A few varieties such as 'Stanley', 'Italian Prune', 'Reine Claude', and the Damsons will set fruit if self-pollinated. Most varieties of plums, however, will set a very poor crop, or none at all, unless their blossoms are fertilized by pollen from another variety of the same species of plum. All Japanese plums are self-unfruitful. Bees will carry the pollen for some distance, but it is better to have trees close together to ensure cross-pollination.

I have a young plum tree which bloomed last spring but no fruit followed. Can you tell me the reason? There are various possible reasons for the failure to produce fruit. The variety may be self-unfruitful and require another variety to pollinize it. Frost may have injured its blossoms and prevented them from setting fruit. A young tree may sometimes be overvegetative and fail to set on that account. Pruning would make the tree more vegetative and would not induce fruiting.

We have a plum tree that blooms but never sets fruit. What causes this and what can be done to set fruit on this tree? It is probably a self-unfruitful variety requiring pollen from a tree of another variety. If this is a Japanese plum, plant another Japanese variety nearby and let the bees do the rest. If it is a European variety, plant another European, as the European and Japanese plums are not satisfactory pollinizers for each other.

Does the purple-leaf plum bear fruit? Yes, if pollinized by another variety of the same species.

I have a plum tree and think it needs pruning. Should I cut the branches short or just thin them out? Some cutting back may be needed to prevent the tree from getting too tall and "leggy." Most of the pruning should be a thinning out to remove undesirable branches and keep the top from becoming too dense.

How should a Japanese plum tree be pruned? This type of plum grows and bears much like the peach and should be pruned a good deal like it. Train the young tree to an open center and practice fairly heavy annual pruning to keep the top from becoming too dense. This will help maintain the vigor of the tree and the size of the fruit.

I have several year-old plum trees grown from pits. Can I expect these to bear eventually, or should I have planted only grafted trees? As the seedlings may not bear fruits worth having, it is much better to plant trees of a known variety. However, you might get a tree or two worth keeping.

When and how should sand (or cherry) plum seed be planted? If you want named varieties of plum, they must be budded onto seedlings, as seedlings do not "come true." To produce seedlings for budding purposes, plant seed in the fall in furrows about 2 inches deep. If only a few seeds are to be handled, it will be better to stratify (that is, mix the seed with sand and bury in a well-drained place). It can be protected against rodents by hardware cloth. Take up the seed in early spring and plant in shallow furrows.

What causes my plums to rot and fall off? This is the brown rot of stone fruits. It is more difficult to control on plums than on peaches because of their smooth skins. Follow the spray schedules obtainable from your Cooperative Extension Service.

Why are my plums wormy? The plum curculio is probably responsible. Follow spray schedules obtainable from your Cooperative Extension Service.

What caused all my plums to drop off? The tree is 6 years old. The trouble may be frost injury to the young fruits, and plum curculio if they are wormy. A virus disease may also be responsible. If the trouble continues, the tree should be replaced with one that is free from virus troubles.

Dwarf and Espalier Fruit Trees

How many dwarf fruit trees can I plant in my backyard? There are no trees of any kind there now. Probably several, but this of course depends on the size of your property, the dimensions of which you didn't give. Dwarf fruit trees (apples on 'M9' rootstock) can be planted as close as 6 × 6 feet (between trunks), but 8 × 8 feet, or 10 × 10 feet, or 10 × 12 feet in the case of an orchard (when the trees are set in rows), is better. The so-called dwarf cherry trees, varieties such as 'North Star' and 'Meteor', soon reach the proportions of a small tree, such as a flowering dogwood, and require more space than other dwarf trees. Write to your State Agricultural Experiment Station or Cooperative Extension Service for bulletins on dwarf fruit trees.

Do dwarf fruit trees require any special care? Yes. They must be looked after in the same way as are standard fruit trees: spraying to control pests and diseases, fertilizing, and some pruning. In addition, they may require staking when their fruit load is heavy. Plant with the bud union at least 2 to 4 inches above the ground.

When should I prune my dwarf fruit trees? Late winter through early spring are the best times.

Do dwarf fruit trees require as much pruning as standard fruit trees? No, because they are grafted on stocks that limit their growth to maintain a dwarf habit. The major pruning of dwarf trees is for special training, such as when the plants are grown against a fence or wall (see espaliers below) or when they are planted too close to one another. Some initial pruning may be necessary to prevent bad crotches and to help make the tree structurally strong.

Are dwarf fruit trees generally as long-lived as standard trees? Probably not, because of problems that can arise between the understock and scion.

I have had 2 dwarf apple trees for several years. In the past year or so, one plant has grown very fast, the new shoot growth considerably exceeding its former growth rate and making it much taller and wider than the other tree. What should I do? It would appear that you have become the victim of a fairly common occurrence among home gardeners who grow dwarf fruit trees! What may have happened is that your tree has lost its "dwarfness" because the scion—the variety grafted onto the dwarf understock—has formed roots and is outgrowing the dwarf understock. If you want to retain a dwarf fruit tree, the only course you can follow now is to cut down the tree and buy another dwarf plant. When planting, be sure that the graft is 2 to 4 inches above the soil level to avoid scion rooting.

What are some good apple varieties available as dwarf trees? Most nurseries specializing in dwarf fruit trees offer the following: 'McIntosh', 'Beacon', 'Lodi', 'Red Delicious', 'Golden Delicious', 'Spartan', 'Cortland', among many others.

Is it true that dwarf apple trees start to bear fruit sooner than standard apple trees? Yes, much sooner. For example, a 'Red Delicious' dwarf apple tree, planted on 'M26' rootstock, at 4 years of age, can produce between 40 and 50 fruits. The tree could be barely 4 feet tall. It will eventually reach a height of about 8 feet, about 2 feet more than the ultimate height of a tree dwarfed by 'M9' rootstock.

What is an espalier fruit tree? It is a tree trained in formal shape to a given number of branches, usually in a vertical plane. The tree is planted against a wall, building, or trellis where it takes up little space and provides decoration as well as fruit. It can be trained to a single shoot or to 2 shoots opposite each other, or in a fan or other shape. The training is begun when the tree is very young. Espalier fruit trees have always been popular in Europe, where the protection afforded by wall training makes it possible to grow orchard fruits in climates less favorable than those in this country.

Are espalier trees practical for the average home garden? If you want fruit trees on a small property, they may do, but since most of them are on dwarfing rootstocks anyway, you might find it easier to grow dwarf fruit trees and give them only moderate training rather than trying to follow the intricate practices and patterns of formal espaliers. The yields, while often of high quality, are never plentiful on true espaliers.

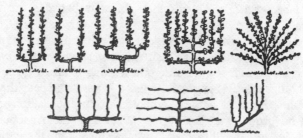

*Various forms of espalier (or trained) fruit trees.
They are usually grown against walls or fences, or
secured to very strong wires or trellises.*

What is the place of espalier fruit trees in the garden picture? Where there is limited space or if novelty design is wanted or in climates where severe weather changes prevail, this type of tree has its place. Training espalier fruits in traditional shapes is a garden art and can be time-consuming.

What part of the season is fertilizer applied to dwarf fruit trees? Two to 4 weeks before the trees come into bloom, when ½ pound of ammonium nitrate can be applied.

What fertilizer materials are used to feed dwarf fruit trees? Nitrogen has been found to be the main element in the growing of tree fruits but a complete fertilizer such as a 5–10–5 is usually satisfactory. (See also the above question.)

How is fertilizer applied to dwarf fruit trees under the mulch system? Broadcast the material on top of the mulch. Water in if dry weather is encountered.

How should espalier trees be pruned? The object is to maintain the skeleton form into which the tree has been trained. This means frequent pruning at an early stage to prevent undesired branches and suckers from getting a start.

Will dwarf fruit trees continue to bear as many years as standard-size fruit trees? With proper attention to pruning, training, fertilization, and spraying, they might. However, the general expectation is that they will not.

In training one's own trees, which are the most suitable varieties of apple, pear, peach, and apricot to use? Any varieties can be used. The fruits mentioned should be on dwarfing roots. The standard tree grows too vigorously to permit the intensive pruning an espalier is subject to.

Where may dwarf fruit trees be obtained? Any first-class mail-order nursery should be able to supply them.

Can fruits be grown in pots as indoor plants? Fruit trees in pots are very practical for persons who have very small garden areas or for those who wish to see fruit blossoms in the very early spring while the snow is still blowing. Peach, cherry, and apple trees have been grown continuously in pots for 20 years, with good results. Potted crab apple trees make beautiful displays of bloom.

In early March, purchase 1-year-old, not 2-year-old, dormant nursery trees of your preferred variety. The trees must be budded on dwarfing rootstocks: apples on 'M9' or 'M26'; pear on quince; cherry on mahaleb; peach on peach. Plant into 9- to 14-inch pots. Hold in a cool cellar for 2 weeks after potting, then move to a cool, sunlit area of the living room. Trees may not bloom the first year after potting, but in the second or third year, blossoms should open 2 or 3 weeks after the trees are brought into the warmth. If fruits are to be set, hand-pollination, using pollen of another variety, must be done as blossoms open.

In May, when the fruits are one third grown, they should be thinned if there are too many. Early shoot pruning should also begin in May by pinching back the tips of shoots. Keep strong upright growth in check. Shape the trees into pyramids.

In June, move the potted trees out-of-doors; keep watered. Most fruit plants require winter chilling of three months below 45° F. before they are ready to break leaf again in the spring. Potted fruit trees must be kept outside or in a cold cellar for 3 months, during which time the pots must be insulated by deep mulching to prevent root freezing and pot breakage. Protect from rodents.

Every other year, just before the trees are brought into a warm atmosphere in March, they should be removed from the pots, one third of the roots pruned off, and the trees repotted. Root pruning reduces excess shoot growth and promotes fruit bud formation.

I plan to grow a few dwarf fruit trees in containers on my terrace as ornamentals and (I hope) for some fruit. Will these survive the winter

in their tubs? Is any special winter attention needed? The roots of fruit trees are much less tolerant of severe winter temperatures than are the tops. In midwinter in the orchard, apple tree tops may withstand a temperature as low as 40° F., but roots are killed at plus 10° F. Roots of peach and cherry trees are even less hardy than those of apple. Thus, fruit trees grown in tubs require special care to protect the roots. During the winter, the tubs must be kept in a cool cellar or a hole can be dug in the garden and the pot put into it and covered with heavy insulating material such as a thick layer of leaves or several layers of a heavy fabric.

Small Fruits

BLUEBERRY (VACCINIUM)

What is an ideal blueberry soil? A well-aerated mixture of sand and peat moss, with the water table 14 to 22 inches below the surface. In such a soil, there is excellent drainage near the surface, but water is always available within the reach of roots. A plentiful supply of peat moss means plenty of organic matter and usually the required acid reaction of pH 4.5 to 5.5. Such soil conditions are seldom available in the home garden, so they have to be approximated by spading in peat moss or leafmold, by mulching, or irrigation, or all three.

How can I make my soil sufficiently acid for successful blueberry culture? The soil should be moist, full of peat or other organic material, and with a reaction of about pH 5.0. The soil may be made acid through the use of acid peat moss, oak leafmold, and sulfur. The quantities of sulfur necessary have to be calculated in relation to the composition of the soil and its pH reaction. Have your soil tested and get recommendations from your Cooperative Extension Service.

How can hybrid blueberries be grown on neutral soil? Limestone soils vary. Sometimes, if the underlying rock is limestone, the topsoil can be acid. If the soil is deep and of limestone origin, the conditions are different. Investigate. Why try something that may be troublesome in later years? For instance, you might make the soil acid enough originally, but if it is necessary to irrigate, and the water is hard, trouble will develop. However, if you must have blueberries, try this: Excavate a bed 4 feet wide and 2 feet deep, and put in a layer of 6 or 8 inches of peat moss or acid leafmold. Fill with soil that has been acidified chemically or by being composted with acid peat or leafmold. Use water that does not contain lime. Line the hole with a polyethylene sheet with drainage holes in the bottom.

How is ordinary soil prepared for growing blueberries? Is there any way to test it? Most State Agricultural Experiment Stations or Cooperative Extension Services will test the soil for residents of the state. Methods of acidifying the soil are discussed elsewhere. In many cases, it will not be necessary to acidify artificially, and then the main requirement is assurance of a uniformly plentiful supply of moisture. If the soil is dry, it may be necessary to irrigate. If it is fairly moist, a permanent mulch of straw, rotted sawdust, or peat moss will give the best results by conserving what moisture there is.

Our soil is too rich for blueberries. What can we do about it? It probably isn't too "rich," as blueberries will grow in very fertile soil provided other conditions are right. Your soil may be alkaline, deficient in one or more elements, or too wet or too dry.

Would you recommend blueberries for an acid garden? Blueberries will do excellently in an acid garden and will usually be an asset to it. They require the same cultural conditions as azaleas and rhododendrons. Full sun most of the day is essential, although some berries are produced in partial shade.

Is the soil in Cleveland satisfactory for blueberries? The ground is quite clayey. (Ohio.) Blueberries probably will not grow successfully in unmodified Ohio clays. They are lowland plants that like acid soils stuffed with humus and with a strong acid reaction.

We are much interested in trying to raise blueberries in an ashy soil in a dry climate; we have plenty of water to irrigate, but the atmosphere is very dry. Can it be done? (Idaho.) Your main difficulty would be in getting your soil acid enough. It would be best to start in a small way first. See the suggestions above.

How should blueberries, already planted, be fed and cared for? Assuming that the soil is acid, apply a mulch to a depth of 2 to 4 inches, and renew as needed to control weeds. Rotted sawdust, peat moss mixed with rich compost, pine needles, strawy manure, etc., are suitable mulches. Fertilize with sulfate of ammonia at the rate of 1 ounce for each year of age of the plants up to 8 years. During the first years of the mulch, double this amount may be necessary.

What is the best fertilizer for blueberries? I have a field of very fine native lowbush berries in Maine, which I wish to improve for marketing. Experiments at the Maine Agricultural Experiment Station have indicated the value of a complete fertilizer for lowbush blueberries provided that weeds are kept under control. Since this is to be a commercial venture, write for the latest recommendations from the Maine Station at Orono, Maine 04473.

How and when should blueberry shrubs 3 years of age be pruned? Prune during late fall, winter, or early spring. Three-year-old bushes will need comparatively little pruning. Remove small, rather weak lateral twigs to prevent their fruiting. Long shoots, well covered with fruit buds, may need to be cut back to leave only 2 or 3 fruit buds. Remember that 1 fruit bud will produce a cluster of flowers and of fruit. If the fruit buds are not thinned by pruning, too many berries will be set, the fruit will be small and late in maturing, and the bush will be weakened.

When is the best time to make blueberry cuttings, and how are they cared for? Make hardwood cuttings in late winter or early spring and place them in peat moss, or ½ sand and ½ peat moss, in ground beds under a lath house, or in a special raised propagating frame. Cuttings should be about 6 inches long, of good 1-year-old twigs, preferably without fruit buds. Place them at an angle in the moss, with at least ⅔ of the cutting covered. Great care must be taken in watering and ventilating, especially in raised frames which are covered with a hotbed sash and kept closed in the early stages of rooting.

Are 2 blueberry bushes sufficient to assure fruit, or is it necessary to have more than that number? If so, how many? Two bushes are enough if they are different varieties that bloom at the same time. If only 1 variety is planted, a fair set might be obtained, but the berries would probably be a little smaller than if they had been cross-pollinated.

Is any progress being made in adapting blueberries to dry land? The only way this can be accomplished is by crossing those which require moist soil with one of the dry-land types. The cultivated blueberry has been crossed with the lowbush blueberry of Maine, a dry-land type, and also with 2 or 3 dry-land species of the South. Suitable varieties have been developed for the South. Mulching and irrigation are helpful if the soil is dry.

What are the requirements of hybrid blueberries? The so-called hybrid blueberries are essentially like other plants with respect to most of their requirements, the two principal exceptions being that they require a rather acid soil and an ample and uniform moisture supply.

Where should blueberries be planted in the home garden? Blueberries require acid soil, good drainage, full sun, and aeration. They need a space of 6 to 8 feet between bushes.

Can blueberries be cultivated in a limited space under favorable conditions? Yes. Favorable conditions, however, include full exposure to sunlight, which is not always possible in a very limited area.

How can I promote faster growth of blueberry bushes? Be sure that growing conditions are favorable with respect to weed control, soil fertility, and moisture supply. Some varieties grow more rapidly than others, but all are rather slow-growing compared, for instance, with a peach tree.

Will blueberries grow under tall, large oaks in semishade? They may survive in this environment, but the yield of fruit will not be equal to that of plants grown in the open.

How are weeds controlled in the blueberry regions of Maine where cultivation isn't practical? By burning over the blueberry fields every other year or every third year. Straw is spread thinly over the area and burned when conditions are right for a quick fire that will not injure the blueberry roots.

I have 2 acres of well-drained swampland; how and when should I plant highbush blueberries? Be sure that the swampland is well drained but not too dry; blueberries are very sensitive to moisture conditions. Plant as early in the spring as the soil can be put into condition. Set the plants carefully, slightly deeper than they were in the nursery row, about 5 feet apart in rows 10 feet apart.

We have very large blueberries in a pasture. Can they be moved to a garden with good results? Very large bushes would be difficult to move, but you could move smaller ones. Some would need to be split up to make several plants. The size, color, and quality of the fruit are not likely to be as satisfactory as that from the named varieties, plants of which you can buy. Be sure your soil is properly prepared with humus-rich materials before digging the wild bushes.

My cultivated blueberry plants have been neglected for approximately 3 years. Will transplanting and proper care revive these plants? Prune them to thin out the probably too dense bush, control weeds with shallow cultivation or a mulch, and fertilize with sulfate of ammonia.

How often should a planting of blueberries be renewed? Blueberries, with good care, should be as permanent as tree fruits, that is, 15 to 25 years or more.

Under ideal conditions, are the leaves of blueberries light or dark green? Could a yellowish-green color be due to any factor other than incorrect soil reaction? The leaves of blueberries that are doing well are large and dark green, although the intensity of the green may vary somewhat in the different varieties. The yellowish-green color might be due to nitrogen deficiency; a too wet, poorly aerated soil; a too alkaline soil with which might be associated iron deficiency; or a virus disease known as stunt.

I have blueberries which are not doing well. What can be done? Check the following, which may be responsible: soil that is not acid enough; soil lacking in fertility, especially nitrogen; too dry; too wet; injury by low temperatures or by some pest.

How can I grow blueberries successfully in Ohio? For soil requirements, see the previous questions. Plant 5 feet apart in a row, using balled and burlapped stock, either in the fall or spring. Always plant 2 or more varieties to ensure good pollination. Water once a week if rain does not fall for the first season. Cultivate shallowly or mulch the plants with rotted sawdust, compost, or oak leaves. In the spring, apply 1 ounce of sulfate of ammonia for each year of the age of the plants. After the plants are in full bearing, remove old, unfruitful branches during the winter.

Will the large blueberries grown in south Jersey do as well in northern New Jersey? Yes, if proper growing conditions are provided. However, there is not nearly as much good blueberry soil in the northern part of the state as in the southern part.

Does the blueberry make a good ornamental shrub? Yes, it is attractive in bloom when the fruit is ripe and when the leaves turn red in the fall. The twigs in winter are also striking. Results will be disappointing, however, if the growing conditions are not right. If they are favorable, it may be possible to raise an adequate crop of fruit in a border of ornamental shrubs. The fruits are attractive to birds, so unless you want to share the harvest, cover the bushes.

What are the advantages of mulching blueberries? Blueberries are shallow-rooted, so that the advantages of mulching are very substantial and greater than with many other plants. The mulch conserves moisture, eliminates most of the weeds, keeps soil temperatures lower, and prevents injury to the roots from too deep cultivation.

How hardy are highbush blueberries? They will stand temperatures down to 20° to 25° F. below zero and sometimes even lower. When in bloom, they will stand more frost than other fruit blossoms. Injury may be expected in bloom when temperatures drop below 22° F.

How are blueberries protected from birds? The plants should be covered with plastic netting sold for this purpose or a cage made of poultry netting small enough to keep out birds or to keep the birds from strangling themselves. Scaring devices (except the family cat) are of little value as the birds soon become used to them. Birds rarely can clean up all the fruits on established bushes.

What is meant by hybrid blueberries? The term is commonly used to designate the named varieties of the type known as the highbush, swamp, or cultivated blueberry. The first varieties to be cultivated were merely wild highbush blueberries that were somewhat superior to the general run of wild blueberries. All of the good cultivated varieties now are several generations of breeding removed from their wild ancestors.

What is the difference between blueberries and huckleberries? The term huckleberry is often erroneously applied to blueberries outside of New England. Blueberries (*Vaccinium*) have many small seeds, 60 or 70, that are not noticeable, while huckleberries (*Gaylussacia*) have 10 comparatively large seeds that are very noticeable and crackle between the teeth. Huckleberries have small yellowish dots on the underside of the leaves; blueberries have none.

What are the best blueberry varieties for the home garden? Ripening from early to late, the best varieties are 'Earliblue', 'Bluetta', 'Collins', 'Blueray', 'Bluecrop', 'Berkeley', 'Herbert', 'Darrow', 'Coville', 'Late Blue'. 'Jersey' is still a good variety and one of the hardiest.

I have seen blueberries growing in western Florida. What kind are they? These are a different species than grows in the North. It is known as *Vaccinium ashei,* the rabbit-eye blueberry. It is suited to the Deep South and makes a much larger bush than the northern types. Improved varieties now being grown are, in order of ripening: 'Woodard', 'Coastal', 'Garden Blue', 'Callaway', 'Tifblue', 'Homebell', 'Menditoo'.

What is the difference between the cultivated blueberries and the ones that grow in Maine? The species usually meant when the term "cultivated blueberries" is used is *Vaccinium corymbosum,* otherwise known as the highbush or swamp blueberry. The ones commonly seen in Maine belong to the species *V. angustifolium,* the lowbush type, which grows in dry upland in both sun and shade.

What are the important blueberry-producing states? New Jersey, North Carolina, and Michigan produce the most cultivated blueberries. There are some commercial plantings in Massachusetts, New York, and Maryland. Maine is in the lead in the production from wild lowbush blueberries. Nurseries in New Jersey, Michigan, Massachusetts, Maryland, and North Carolina are propagating blueberry varieties.

CRANBERRY (VACCINIUM MACROCARPUM)

Is the highbush-cranberry worth planting for jelly? The highbush-cranberry, *Viburnum trilobum,* is not a true cranberry, but is a red-fruited viburnum with fruit of about the same size and color as the true cranberry. It makes a fair jelly, but is not equal to jellies made from currants, grapes, quince, and several other fruits. It is most useful in regions too cold for these other fruits.

Where is the creeping cranberry native? *Vaccinium macrocarpum* is native to Newfoundland, south to North Carolina, Michigan, and Minnesota.

What are the soil requirements of the cranberry? Cranberries are grown in acid peat bogs that can be flooded. A level peat bog with a clay subbase is selected. The growth of weeds is killed by flooding for a year. Clear sand is added to a depth of 2 or 3 inches, and cuttings are thrust through this into the peaty soil beneath, 12 to 18 inches apart. They fruit in about 3 years. Bogs are flooded from December to April or May, and at other times to control insects, to prevent frost, and to harvest loose berries. Bogs are fertilized every year or two and are sanded at intervals to prevent too rapid, tangled growth.

Can cranberries be grown from seeds? Cranberries can be grown from seeds stratified in the fall, but the plants grow well only in very acid wet soil, as described above.

Is it safe to collect and eat wild cranberries that grow in a swamp near our summer place? (Long Island, New York.) Yes, quite safe! You will want to wear boots, as the bogs are usually full of water in late fall when the berries are ripe.

CURRANT AND GOOSEBERRY (RIBES)

Are currants and gooseberries particular as to soil? They can be grown successfully on an average garden soil that will grow vegetables and flowers.

How should currants and gooseberries be fertilized? Ammonium nitrate at the rate of about 4 ounces per plant, or nitrate of soda at the rate of 8 ounces per plant is most likely to be profitable. On light soils, sulfate of potash, at about 3 to 4 ounces per plant, may be useful, but it will not be needed every year. A hay or straw mulch is also useful.

Where should bush fruits such as currants and gooseberries be planted? They are somewhat tolerant of shade and may be planted on the north side of buildings or fences and between young fruit trees and grapevines if space is limited. In such a case, beware of spray residues on the currant and gooseberry fruits from sprays used on the trees.

When should currant and gooseberry bushes be planted? These plants start growth very early in the spring, so they should be set either in the fall or by the latter part of March.

How far apart are currants and gooseberries planted? In the garden,

3 to 4 feet in the row and ideally 5 to 6 feet between rows, but less if space is limited.

Can gooseberries and currants be planted near pine trees? In regions where white-pine blister rust is serious, and white pines are important, the planting of gooseberries and currants may be forbidden. Consult your county agent.

How many currant and gooseberry bushes should be planted per person in the home garden? Currants—2 plants. Gooseberries—2 plants.

What care do currants need? Annual pruning, fertilization, and cultivation or mulching to control weeds. A dormant spray to destroy aphid eggs and summer sprays for anthracnose may be necessary.

Do red currants need to be cultivated? Currant bushes sometimes struggle along in sod and produce some fruit, but they will do much better if weeds and grass are suppressed by shallow cultivation or mulching.

Should I purchase bearing-size currant bushes? Good 1- or 2-year plants are much superior to bearing-age transplants. They are cheaper and more likely to survive.

How often should currants and gooseberries be picked? For jelly, currants are all picked at once, as soon as ripe, but for dessert, they can be picked as needed for 3 or 4 weeks, since they remain in good condition for some time. Gooseberries may be picked when they are half grown to make green gooseberry pie or sauce, delicious desserts known to very few these days. This early picking of part of the crop amounts to a thinning which makes the late berries much larger. Gooseberries are sometimes scalded by unusually hot weather (90° F. and above) so they should be harvested promptly.

Can gooseberries be successfully grown in the small home garden? Gooseberries are easy to grow and have few pests. The plants are very compact, so that the few needed by an average family will not require much room.

Why are gooseberry bushes not grown more in Massachusetts? Currants and gooseberries are alternate hosts for white-pine blister rust, a serious disease in New England as well as other parts of the country. Various state and federal laws provide for eradication of these plants in certain areas, and in Massachusetts, state authorities have the right to remove them when deemed necessary, thus aiding in the control of this disease.

At what time of the year should currant bushes be pruned? Late fall, winter, or very early spring. Since so many things have to be done in the spring, autumn is the most practical time.

What is the best method of pruning red currant bushes? Remove canes 4 years old or older; low-growing canes that droop to the ground when heavy with fruit; broken or diseased canes; the weaker 1-year shoots. After pruning, an ideal bush might consist of about five 1-year shoots, four 2-year canes, three 3-year canes, and possibly two or three 4-year canes, if they are vigorous.

Do red currant bushes that have borne heavily for 3 years have to be trimmed? They don't seem to have any dead wood. When the canes get to be about 4 years old, they usually weaken and become unproductive. Such canes should be taken out, down to the ground, before they actually die.

Do gooseberry bushes need pruning? They may continue to produce for a long time without being pruned, but the bushes will be more vigorous and the fruit larger if they are pruned.

When should gooseberries be pruned? At any time during the dormant season; that is, after the leaves fall and before growth starts in the spring.

How does one prune gooseberry bushes? Remove any dead or broken canes, then those branches that are borne around the lower part of the bush, low enough to touch the ground when loaded with fruit. Canes more than 4 years old usually are too weak to be productive, so they should be cut out. This will usually be all the pruning needed, although it may be desirable to remove a few twigs here and there to shape up the bush or open up a crowded part of it.

Are currants raised from cuttings? That is the usual method—hardwood cuttings taken in late winter. Cuttings are made of 1-year canes and are usually 6 to 8 inches long. Currants can also be propagated by layers; that is, low-growing branches covered with soil except for the tips. After roots have formed, cut the branches from the plant and set where desired.

Will gooseberry bushes root from cuttings? Hardwood cuttings are usually used, but they will also root from half-ripe cuttings in the summer. They are easily layered—often branches resting on the ground will root.

What causes currants to have distorted, crinkly leaves? Aphids feeding on the leaves cause them to become distorted. These are best controlled by spraying the bushes with malathion at the first sign of leaf distortion. Use at the rate of 8 tablespoonfuls in 5 gallons of water, being sure to hit the underside of the leaves.

We have found our currant bushes stripped entirely bare of leaves. What causes this? This is undoubtedly the work of the imported currant worm, which usually works in large numbers and can strip a bush in a very few days. Watch your bushes carefully in early summer. When the greenish worms appear, spray with malathion, 6 tablespoonfuls to 5 gallons of water. Or dust with rotenone or pyrethrum. Bordeaux sprays used for disease control may kill many of the worms.

Do early browning and dropping of leaves from currant bushes mean that the bushes have died? Or will they come out again next spring? The leaf-spot disease and injury by the currant aphids may make leaves turn brown and drop prematurely. If the twigs are still plump and the bark, when scraped, is bright green, you can expect the leaves to come out again next spring. However, premature defoliation weakens the plants so that they are less productive the next year.

We have been told that currant and gooseberry bushes and pines do not mix. Must one or the other necessarily be the host of the attacking disease? Currants and gooseberries are the winter host for the white-pine blister rust, which attacks only those species of pines that have 5 needles in a bundle. The disease is limited in areas, and where not present, the fruits may be grown. Black currant is the worst, gooseberry next, and the red currant is permitted except in seriously infested areas. Your county extension agent should be consulted if you have doubts.

What varieties of currants are recommended for the home garden? Try 'Red Lake', one of the newer varieties.

What is a good gooseberry variety? (Pennsylvania.) 'Poorman' is a good red-fruited variety. 'Chautauqua' is very large-fruited and yellowish green when ripe.

ELDERBERRY (SAMBUCUS)

Is the elderberry worth planting for fruit for pies and canning? Yes, if you have the space. Elderberries are ornamental, and many people like the blossoms for wine and the fruits for pies and jelly. They are of easy culture, growing almost anywhere. Elders need cross-pollination, so more than one variety should be planted. Good varieties are 'York' and 'Nova'.

Does the 'Adams' elderberry spread and become a nuisance? All elderberries spread by means of suckers from the roots. With watchful care, these can be eliminated.

FIG (FICUS CARICA)

What is the best fertilizer for a fig tree in acid soil? A good garden fertilizer, such as 5–10–5, used at the rate of 1 pound per 50 square feet, will probably supply sufficient nutrients.

What is the best time to prune a fig tree growing in a tub? If it's in a greenhouse, at any season when it is not maturing fruits. If out-of-doors, prune in early spring.

How are fig trees pruned? (Maryland.) Figs require very little pruning. Most of this is done in training the tree while it is young. It is especially desirable in regions where winter injury is probable and the trees must be protected. If trained to 3 or 4 branches, it is easy to lay these down and cover them with soil, mounding up over the center point, for protection from the cold.

How can one keep a fig tree from freezing in the winter? (New York.) Many methods are used, depending upon the protection afforded by buildings. One way is to tie up the branches and wrap them with several layers of burlap. Or heavy waterproof paper may be used. The surest way is to train the plant so that it branches close to the ground. These branches may then be pressed to the ground, fastened, and covered with a foot or more of soil, with the soil mounded over the central point.

Should a fig tree on Long Island, New York, on the side of a house, be covered for winter? Fig trees will need good winter protection on Long Island. (See previous questions.)

What is the method of propagating a fig tree by layering? (Pennsylvania.) Bend a branch over in the early spring until a portion that is 2 years old may be fastened down and covered with soil. A notch in the underside of the covered portion, held open by a sliver of stone, may help. Keep this covering of soil moist. Roots should form by the middle of summer, when the new plant may be detached and planted.

In what parts of the country will figs bear successfully for the home garden? In the southeastern Atlantic and Gulf states, in parts of California, much of Arizona, and New Mexico. In northern states, figs need winter protection and usually bear little fruit.

What is the treatment for fig trees in a greenhouse? The soil should be rich in humus, and it is advisable to keep the trees mulched with well-rotted manure or compost. Winter temperature, 50° F. night, 65° F. day. In spring, increase to 65° F. night and 70° F. day. Figs must have plenty of air and moisture until the fruit is set.

I have a fig tree that is covered every winter, but only a few of the figs ripen before frost. Is there any way of forcing them to ripen earlier? (Ohio.) The variety factor enters here. Some varieties, such as 'Brown Turkey', mature fruits earlier than others.

How can I learn the variety of fig trees I have? (California.) Your county agent might be able to identify the variety.

GRAPE (VITIS)

What soil is most suitable for the cultivation of grapes? A good loam or sandy loam is probably ideal, but grapes will grow satisfactorily on a wide range of soil types, provided the moisture supply is adequate. Extremely dry or extremely wet soils should be avoided.

Do grapes like alkaline or acid soil? Grapes thrive on soils showing rather wide ranges of soil reaction. On the whole, acid soils seem preferable to alkaline soils.

Will grapes grow on muck soil? Grapes are never grown commercially on muck soil. Grapevines are usually planted on slopes because they will not tolerate poor drainage, and most muck soils offer drainage problems at some seasons of the year. Also, grapes should have good air drainage, and the level surfaces of muck soils do not favor air drainage. Frosts are worse on muck soil sites than on elevated land.

What is a good fertilizer for grapes? Grapes on the average soil are most apt to respond profitably to nitrogen at the rate of 60 or more pounds to the acre. Apply 200 pounds of ammonium nitrate or 400 pounds of nitrate of soda. Per vine, this would be ¼ pound of ammonium nitrate or ½ pound of nitrate of soda. On light soils, a need for potassium may be indicated by a marginal browning of the leaves. Here, sulfate of potash may be used. A hay or straw mulch will supply potassium, too.

What is the best way to apply fertilizer to grapes? Broadcast the fertilizer, covering an area a foot from the trunk out to 4 or 5 feet away from the trunk.

My 'Caco' grapevine is 5 years old, has made wonderful growth, but it bears no grapes. What fertilizer should I use on it? The fact that your grapevine is making wonderful growth indicates that it does not need more fertilizer, but, on the contrary, needs to have all such materials withheld from it. It is possible that you have been pruning it too closely. Leave at least 40 buds on it the next time you prune it. If it is still too vigorous and nonfruitful, leave 60 buds a year later.

What location is best suited for grapes? Do they grow well near trees? The ideal location for a vineyard is gently sloping land. Air and water drainage must be good to avoid the danger of late spring frosts and "wet feet." Steep slopes should be avoided because they favor erosion unless rows are planted on the contour. Southern exposures favor earlier starting of growth in the spring and earlier ripening of fruit, but are more susceptible to late-spring frost injury and to summer drought. Northern slopes are less susceptible to injury from late-spring frosts and summer droughts, but ripen their crops later than southern slopes. Deep, sandy soils that contain a good amount of organic matter will give best results for grapes. Soils too poor for other crops are not good grape soils. Planting grapes close to trees is usually not a good practice because the trees compete with the vines for water and soil nutrients as well as furnish cover for insects which may attack grapes. Shade from trees may favor diseases, delay ripening of the fruit, and reduce productiveness of the vine.

Where should grapes be planted?   On fences, trellises that mark boundaries, or on arbors especially constructed for the purpose.

Do grapevines need much sun?   Grapes are sun-loving plants, as is shown by their tendency to climb over the tops of tall trees. The outstanding grape regions of the world are in areas that have much clear, sunny weather and few fogs. Lack of sunlight favors the spread of mildew and black rot and retards the ripening of fruit. However, grapevines will do fairly well if they receive direct sunlight at least half of the day. Though grapevines will grow fairly well in partial shade, they will not produce well under such conditions.

How far apart should grapes be planted?   A suitable spacing for most varieties is 8 feet between rows and 8 feet between vines in the row.

How should grapevines be planted?   After the ground has been prepared and the rows have been marked, dig holes of sufficient size to accommodate the roots of the vines after they have been cut back to within 8 inches of the trunk. The top should be cut back to a single strong cane of 2 buds' length. The vine is then placed in the hole and the roots spread out evenly. A few shovels of soil are then thrown in on roots while the stem is shaken gently to sift fine soil in around the fine roots. More topsoil is then thrown into the hole and thoroughly tamped into place with the feet. Holes should then be well filled.

My 'Concord' grapevines, now 5 years old, should be moved to a better location. When is the best time? Will it destroy them if their root systems are cut?   Any time in the fall after the vines are fully dormant. A good-sized ball of earth should be moved with the vine, so that as many roots are kept intact as possible. The tops should be cut back severely so that the top growth is kept in balance with the greatly reduced root system. Vines should not be allowed to bear fruit the first year after being moved, and only a light crop the following year. It is really much better to set a new vine than to move a 5-year-old vine.

How many grapevines will a family of 4 need? This will depend on how you use the fruit. For table use, include 2 plants of very early varieties, 2 early, 6 to 10 midseason for jelly and juice, and 2 to 4 late to very late.

Is it necessary to dig around grapevines? Cultivation is only to control weeds and should be shallow. Mulching is a good substitute for cultivation.

What treatment should I give my grapes? They are fruiting poorly on clay soil. The fact that grapes are not fruiting well on clay soil indicates that the vines are probably not making enough growth to permit heavy fruiting. As a rule, grapes prefer lighter and sandier soils, but many good vineyards are found on clay soils. Fertilize vines with ⅓ pound of nitrate of soda or sulfate of ammonia per vine. Apply when the shoots are starting their growth in the spring. Frequent cultivation to keep down weeds and close pruning will encourage more vine growth and eventually result in heavier fruiting. Be sure that insects and diseases are not responsible for the poor cropping.

What can I do to make my grapevines bear heavily? An application of proper fertilizers, plus cover cropping and cultivation, should result in vigorous vines capable of bearing good crops of fruit. Pruning vines properly to not more than 40 buds per vine should enable them to set good crops. Spraying to control mildews, black rot, and leafhoppers favors ripening of such heavy crops. If vines overbear, the grapes do not ripen well and vines may winter-kill.

How soon and how much will grapes bear? Grapevines should not be allowed to bear any fruit until their third season, and then only a small crop. The fourth season may be expected to give a good crop of fruit, and by the fifth season, if vines are well grown, they may be expected to have reached full production. This may be from 10 to 20 pounds per vine, and vigorous vines, properly pruned, should produce twice that amount. An average of 10 pounds per vine would give about 3 tons per acre for vines spaced 8 to 10 feet apart.

Why do my grapes grow all to vines and bear no fruit? How often and at what season should they be trimmed? The vines have probably been thrown into an overvegetative stage by being grown on too rich a soil, by overfertilization, or by being pruned too closely. Very vigorous vines should have from 40 to 60 or more buds left to fruit. Grapevines require pruning only once each year, when the vines are fully dormant.

Dense shading encourages excessive vine growth and tends to discourage fruiting.

My 'Concord' grapevines, 15 years old, in recent years have ripened fruit very unevenly, with green and ripe berries of uneven sizes on each bunch. What is the cause and remedy?   The primary cause of uneven ripening is high night temperatures, as in coastal plain areas south of Washington, D.C., or in portions of Oklahoma and similar climatic areas.

What is necessary to have grapes grow in nice bunches and have all the grapes ripen at about the same time?   Uniform ripening of fruit is more likely to occur when the vine does not bear too heavy a crop. This

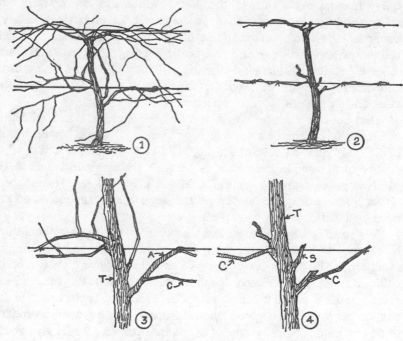

GRAPE PRUNING

(1) 'Concord' grapevine (several years old) before pruning.
(2) Same vine, pruned back during winter (Kniffin system).
(3) Detail, before pruning. T—main stem or trunk; A—arm, or lateral, 2-year-old wood; C—cane, 1-year-old wood. (4) Detail, after pruning. T—trunk; C—renewal cane, 1-year-old wood, tied to wire; S—spur, 1-year-old wood, cut back to 2 buds.

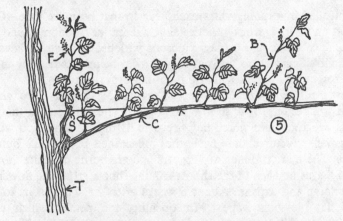

(5) *Vine is early summer growth, showing fruiting habit. T—trunk; C—renewal cane; B—shoot, current year's growth; F—flower cluster; S—spur, producing new shoot, which may be used as a renewal arm the following year.*

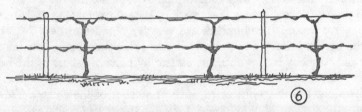

(6) *Trellis for Kniffin system; wires 3 feet and 6 feet above ground; posts are placed 15 to 20 feet apart.*

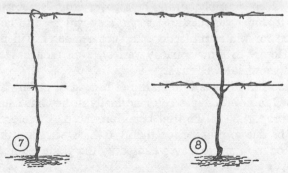

(7) *One-year-old grapevine after being pruned, tied in 3 places to top wire. (8) Two-year-old vine after being pruned; 5 buds left on each lateral cane on top wire; 4 buds on each at bottom wire.*

is controlled by pruning vines each year so that no more than 40 buds are left on such vigorous varieties as 'Concord' or 'Fredonia', and about 30 buds, or fewer, are on less vigorous varieties such as 'Delaware' or 'Diamond'. Spraying to prevent leaves from being attacked by mildew, black rot, or leafhoppers will also favor uniform ripening.

How can I recognize the flowers of grapes? My 3-year 'Caco' vine has shown wonderful growth but no grapes. If you will look at the young shoots on grapevines when they are 6 to 10 inches long, you will find tiny green structures that have the appearance of a small bunch of grapes. These are rudimentary flowers and are borne opposite the lower 3 or 4 leaves on each of the shoots. As the shoots grow, the flower clusters enlarge and expand. About 6 weeks after the shoots start to grow, individual blossoms appear. In opening, the petals, which remain greenish in color, are shed, leaving only pistil and anthers. The reason for nonfruiting may be overfertilization or underpruning, which produces lush, soft growth at the expense of fruit. Perhaps your vine is not 'Caco' but is another variety that may produce poor pollen and hence require another variety with good pollen to pollinate it.

We have 'Tokay' grapes that crack open before ripening and are sour; also, some dry up. The bunches are very large and crowded. Cracking of the berries followed by souring is due to clusters being too compact. The only remedy is to reduce the cluster by pinching some of the berries from each cluster soon after they are set in the spring. A good plan is to remove one fourth to one third of the branches of the cluster. This will reduce the size and should loosen it enough to prevent cracking.

What prewinter care should be given to grapevines? In regions where grapes are not injured by winter temperatures, no special fall treatment, except possibly sowing of a cover crop, is necessary. In the far North, if tender varieties are grown, they will need to be laid down and covered for winter protection. In such regions it will probably be more satisfactory to grow a hardy variety, even though such varieties may be of somewhat lower quality.

What causes my grapes to remain red instead of getting blue as they are supposed to do? Grapes color normally if they have sufficient leaf surface in proportion to the fruit being produced. Therefore, failure to ripen may be due to pruning too lightly (which will result in an excessive crop) or to injury to leaves caused by the grape leafhopper, Japanese beetle, or mildew.

Can good fruit be grown on an arbor or must there be more sun available? It is the sunlight on the leaves, not on the fruit, that determines whether grapes can be grown. The shade of nearby trees and buildings should be avoided. An arbor can produce heavy crops of fruit if the vines are sprayed and pruned regularly.

When is the best time of the year to prune grapevines? Grapevines should be pruned when the vines are fully dormant, in late fall, winter, or early spring. Pruning in late winter means the canes that have suffered from winter injury can easily be detected and cut out, thus leaving only sound canes on the vine. Spring pruning is not recommended because as buds begin to swell they become brittle and break off easily, thus reducing the size of the crop.

What is the difference between grape training and pruning? Training is the arrangement of the trunk and canes to facilitate care of the vines. Pruning is the removal of excess wood growth to adjust the number of buds to produce a crop that the vine is capable of maturing.

How are grapevines trained? The single stem 4-cane Kniffin system is a good method. A vine trained this way consists of a trunk 6 feet tall with two arms 3 feet from the ground and two at the top of the vine. A two-wire trellis with the lower wire 3 feet from the ground and the top wire 6 feet from the ground is used.

How are young vines pruned after the first year? The second year, the best cane is cut off at 6 feet and tied to the top of the trellis. All blossom clusters are removed to prevent fruiting. The third year, a vigorous vine should have two 10-bud canes left at the top wire and 2 spurs at the lower wire. A light crop is allowed to be produced. If the vine is weak, prune it the same way but remove all blossom clusters.

What is the umbrella Kniffin? A single stem reaches to the top wire and all canes arise near the top of the trunk and are twisted slightly over the top wire with their ends tied to the lower wire. This is a good system.

How are grapevines pruned the year that they are planted? The vine is cut back to 2 buds. Several shoots will grow. The strongest is saved and tied to a stake so that it will make a straight trunk. The others are removed. Vines over 3 years old are pruned as bearing vines.

How should bearing grapevines be pruned? Pruning is the removal of excess wood growth to adjust the crop to the vigor of the vine. To take this operation out of the realm of guesswork, a method has been devised. The pruner first selects 6- to 10-bud canes to fruit and cuts off all the rest of last year's growth. This is weighed. If the prunings weigh 1 pound, reduce the number of buds to 30 by leaving three 10-bud canes. For each additional pound of wood, leave another 10 buds. Thus, 2 pounds of wood would require that 40 buds be left. This is for the 'Concord' variety. For 'Fredonia', leave 40 for the first pound and for

'Catawba' leave 25 for the first pound. Two budspurs should be left near the trunk for canes for the following year.

I have been told to prune my grapes in the summer to let the light in to the fruit. Is that necessary? It is not only unnecessary but undesirable. The fruit will color normally even if no light at all gets to it—quite different from the apple in this respect. Furthermore, removal of leaf surface at this time of year will delay or prevent normal ripening; hence, it will defeat the very purpose for which it is done.

Would you recommend thinning foliage on grapevines in the fall to hasten the ripening of fruit before frost? Thinning the foliage would not hasten the ripening of the fruit but would delay ripening, inasmuch as leaves are the food-manufacturing organs of the plant. Nothing can be done at this stage of the season to hasten the ripening of fruit. Thinning the crop shortly after blossoming might have speeded up the ripening of the remaining fruit if the vine had set too heavy a crop.

How do you trim grapevines that have been neglected for years? Neglected grapevines should be renewed by cutting the old trunk back to the ground. New shoots will start from the roots. Only 3 of these should be allowed to grow, and at the end of the first season the strongest one should be selected for a new trunk and the others should be removed. The new trunk should be cut back to the desired length and 4 side branches, of about 10 buds' length each, are then selected.

How can I best revitalize an old, neglected grapevine? Cut back the old vine severely. If the old trunk is in bad shape, cut it back to the ground and start a new trunk from one of the new shoots. If you do not care to cut it back that severely, and if the trunk and old arms are still in fair condition, cut the vine back to the point from which most vigorous shoots, closest to the trunk, are arising. Leave a few, preferably 4, spurs of 2 buds each when the vine is cut back to provide new growth. It will be necessary to sacrifice a year's crop in order to get the vine back to a desirable form and fruiting condition.

Can I cut an old grapevine stem that has grown too long? Renew the trunk of the old vine (see above) by cutting it back to the ground. Many new shoots will start, but only about 3 should be allowed to grow the first season. The next winter, remove 2 of these.

Will you please advise me as when and how to trim 'Scuppernong' grapevines? 'Scuppernong' grapevines are usually trained on overhead trellises or arbors in home plantings. This system calls for a single trunk running to an overhead trellis. At that height, 8 arms, radiating from the trunk like the spokes of a wheel from a hub, are selected and trained to grow out over the trellis. After the arms have been established, they are pruned by cutting back all side branches on them to short spurs 2 or 3 buds long. As the arms become older, it may be desirable to renew some of them by cutting them back to a strong lateral cane near the trunk. It is a good plan to renew 1 arm each year in this way. The best time to prune is in late winter, after the danger of severe freezing has passed. At that time, one can easily tell which wood is alive. Avoid leaving injured wood. Pruning after the buds begin to swell is not desirable because the buds break off easily.

How do you construct the standard grape trellis? The standard grape trellis in the East is the Kniffin trellis. This is simply 2 wires, one 3 feet from the ground and the other 3 feet above the first, supported by posts every 18 to 20 feet. No. 9 wire is the best size for this purpose.

Do grapes cross-pollinate? If so, how close can different varieties be planted? Yes, grapes frequently cross-pollinate when several vines are planted near each other. This is true in spite of the fact that most commercially important varieties are self-fruitful. Grape pollen is very light and fluffy, is easily scattered about by winds, and is carried about by many small insects. However, you need not fear that the pollen of one variety will in any way influence the fruit of another variety. It has been shown many times that there is no immediate effect produced by pollen of one variety being placed on pistils of another variety. Only the seedlings produced from such cross-pollination will show any effect.

Should all grapevines be grafted? In some areas of the country, grapes should be grafted on rootstocks that are resistant to the grape phylloxera or root louse. Where this insect is not prevalent, vines can be grown from cuttings. Grafted vines of some varieties often perform much better than own-root vines. Consult your State Experiment Station concerning your own locality.

How can I get another vine started from the one I have? The easiest way is to lay a cane on the ground, peg it down if necessary, and cover a portion of it with soil. Roots will form at the joints that are covered, and the cane can be cut loose from the old vine and used as a new plant. Most vines are propagated commercially by means of cuttings.

What is the best way to get grape cuttings started and set out so that they will grow? Should grafting wax be used? Select straight, vigorous, well-matured 1-year-old wood of pencil size. Cut into sections 3 buds long, making a lower cut through the node opposite the lowest bud and an upper cut about an inch above the third bud. Tie the cuttings in bundles of 50 and bury them in a trench, butt ends up, and cover with 6 inches of soil during the winter. After the ground has warmed in the spring, set the cuttings in well-prepared soil so that they are about 3 inches apart and with only the upper buds above the soil. Hoe, cultivate, and water them during the summer as needed. On good soil they should make enough growth in one season to permit transplanting them to the vineyard the next spring. No grafting wax or other materials need be used on cuttings handled in the manner described.

My grapes have begun to look like raisins on the vine but don't taste like them. Your grapes have been affected by black rot disease, which is caused by a fungus. It can be controlled by spraying with Bordeaux mixture. The most important times to spray are when new shoots are about 1 inch long, when they are 12 inches long, right after blooming, and again 10 days later. (See Grapes, Section 13.)

How can I protect my grapes from birds? Cover the clusters with 2-pound white paper bags such as are used in bakery stores. Do not use the brown bags as they give the grapes an unpleasant flavor. The bags are put on as the grapes begin to color and are folded around the cluster stem and fastened with a stout pin.

How can I keep bees and wasps from destroying my grapes? The bees and wasps are secondary; the birds puncture the skins and the insects move in. Sprays that will poison them will poison the grapes and spoil them for food. Bag the clusters as described above.

Is there a seedless 'Concord' grape on the market? There is a variety of grape available to growers which is known as 'Concord Seedless'. It is thought that it originated as a sport or mutation of 'Concord' grape. The berries are much smaller than those of 'Concord' and have only very rudimentary seeds which are hardly noticeable.

How does 'Sheridan' grape compare with 'Concord' grape? Where it can be grown properly the 'Sheridan' grape is an improvement over 'Concord'. It has a larger berry and cluster, a more compact bunch, is more attractive, has a finer flavor, tougher skin, and will keep in fine condition in storage until January. It requires a long season to mature, however, ripening about 2 weeks after 'Concord' in central New York.

Are there any varieties of grapes which will keep better than 'Concord', either on the vine or after picking? Long-keeping grapes are 'Seneca', 'Buffalo', 'Yates', 'Sheridan', and 'Steuben'.

What grape variety is usually made into grape juice? The most common sweet grape-juice variety throughout the East is the 'Concord'.

What varieties of grapes should I plant for a long season of harvesting? In order of ripening, from earliest to latest, the following are good varieties: 'Van Buren', 'Fredonia', 'Seneca', 'Buffalo', 'Delaware', 'Concord', 'Yates', 'Steuben', 'Sheridan', 'Golden Muscat', and 'Catawba'. Unless you have a long season, you may not be able to grow those ripening after 'Concord'.

What are some good varieties of hardy seedless grapes? The new seedless grapes—'Canadice', 'Glenora', 'Himrod', 'Lakemont'—originated at Geneva, New York, will endure winter temperatures down to about −15° F. These four varieties are much like the 'Thompson Seedless' of California. 'Concord Seedless' is like 'Concord' in flavor, but the berries are much smaller. The vine is as hardy as 'Concord'.

I would like to grow some of the California varieties of grapes in New Jersey. Do they require special culture? Yes. If disease control is very good and overbearing is prevented by proper pruning, some of the earlier ripening north European varieties are worth trying on an experimental basis where winter temperatures are not lower than −5° to −10° F.

Will 'Scuppernong' grapes grow in Pennsylvania? You are too far north for this type, which is widely grown in the South. The northern limit of the 'Scuppernong' or 'Muscadine' type is southern Virginia.

Do ordinary table grapes make good wine? Some varieties that are good table grapes—'Delaware', 'Iona', and 'Catawba'—make excellent wine. Generally speaking, the best wines are made from grapes suitable only for wines. Recently, French hybrids have been planted considerably in New York for wine and several have considerable promise.

Can the California grapes like 'Tokay', 'Malaga', etc., be grown in the eastern United States? Some California grapes may be grown in the East where winter temperatures are not lower than −5° to −10° F. and disease and insect control is excellent. They should be grafted on phylloxera-resistant roots. 'Seneca' and the seedless varieties listed above are much like California varieties.

Are there any grape varieties hardy enough to be grown in northern Minnesota? 'Beta' is one of the hardiest of all grapes. The Minnesota Agricultural Experiment Station at University Farm, St. Paul, Minn. 55101, can supply information as to the best grapes for northern Minnesota.

JUJUBE, CHINESE (OR DATE)

What is the Chinese-date fruit like? How old are the trees before they fruit? (Kentucky.) Fruit of the Chinese-date, more commonly called the Chinese jujube, is a drupe (stone fruit), oblong, up to 2 inches long, brown, with a sweet, whitish flesh of applelike flavor. The trees bear when young, usually in their second or third year where growing conditions are favorable. Several jujube seedling trees have survived at Geneva, New York, for many years, but produce very few fruits because of high humidity.

JUNEBERRY (AMELANCHIER)

Is the Juneberry worth planting? The dwarf Juneberry or serviceberry bears heavy crops of bluish-black fruits about the size of wild blueberries. The flavor is insipid, but if they are cooked with lemon juice they make fair pies. The bushes grow 3 to 4 feet in height, are covered with white flowers in early spring, and are very hardy, which makes them useful in the cold Great Plains region. Birds are very fond of the berries and, in most cases, this is a major reason for growing them. There are several species with similar characteristics.

MULBERRY (MORUS)

What are the chief uses of the mulberry? The fruit is good to eat and quite sweet. The trees grow fast and bear large quantities of fruit ripening over several weeks, which makes it a fine tree to attract birds. Since the fruit is messy, the mulberry should not be planted near the house or a sidewalk.

Are mulberries easy trees to grow? Yes, they like almost any soil and thrive under varying conditions.

Did the so-called Russian mulberry actually come from Russia or is it just a name? Yes, it really came from Russia. It was brought to the western states by Russian Mennonites in 1875 to 1877.

Is it true that there are male and female mulberry trees? Must you have both to have berries? Also, is there a difference in the foliage? Yes, the sexes are separate, but usually both are present on one tree. There is little difference in the foliage. Both should be present to ensure fruiting.

We have 2 mulberry trees planted about 30 feet apart. They are over 15 years old. Why are they full of blossoms every spring but never set fruit? Mulberries are often dioecious, that is, staminate (male) and pistillate (female) flowers on separate trees, although generally both sexes are borne on the same tree. The failure to set fruit is undoubtedly due to lack of pollination. Both your trees may either have all flowers of one sex or the male and female flowers do not mature at the same time. If you cannot judge, cut a small branch of each tree just before the flowers open and submit them to a botanist for examination.

How can a mulberry tree that has sprouted from the bottom (top dead) be cultivated to grow right? It is about 2 years old. Cut off all but the strongest sprout. If the stub of the original stem remains, cut this (with a sloping cut) close to the shoot that was selected to carry on.

What are the best varieties of mulberry for fruit production? Mulberry varieties true to name are hard to get. 'Wellington', an old unknown variety renamed, is good.

PERSIMMON (DIOSPYROS)

Are persimmons reliably hardy in the North? The native American persimmon, *Diospyros virginiana,* is native from Connecticut to the Gulf of Mexico. Selected varieties are hardy at Geneva, New York, and some mature early enough to ripen fruits nearly every year. The Oriental persimmon (*D. kaki*) is grown in the South and on the West Coast.

Is the native persimmon worth growing for its fruit? Most of the wild trees produce fruits that are small and very astringent. However, there are a number of selected varieties that produce large, sweet persimmons that are well worth growing.

Do persimmons need frost to make the fruit edible? Frost does not hasten the ripening of the persimmon or make it edible. On the contrary, a hard frost before the persimmons are ripe will spoil them. After they are ripe, the frost will not spoil the fruit. Probably many persimmons ripen about the time of the first frost, hence the idea that frost is needed to ripen them.

Is the persimmon tree fussy about soil? No, they often grow on very poor soils. In the South, on abandoned eroded farmland, the persimmon is one of the first plants to come in. They respond to good soils and care, however.

How should a persimmon tree be transplanted? With a burlapped ball of earth, even if the tree is of small size, in early spring.

How should persimmons be cared for in order to ensure fruits? Very little care is needed. Reduce competition from competing trees, shrubs, grass, and weeds. Be sure that a male tree is nearby to pollinate the flowers or there may be no fruit.

Do persimmon trees have staminate and pistillate varieties? Persimmons are usually dioecious; that is, staminate and pistillate flowers are on different trees. Some pistillate trees produce parthenocarpic (seedless) fruits without having been pollinated.

I have some persimmon seeds. How should I start them? Plant the seeds about 1 inch deep as soon as they are ripe.

QUINCE (CYDONIA OBLONGA)

Does the quince make a good home-garden fruit? If it is sprayed thoroughly to control the Oriental fruit moth, to which it is very susceptible, and if it is not allowed to grow vigorously, thereby making it subject to fire blight, it is a good garden fruit. It can be used to make very fine jelly, quince honey, etc.

What soil does the quince require? How are the trees planted? Quince needs somewhat heavy, moist soil. Set 1- or 2-year specimens, in early spring, 8 to 10 feet apart.

Are the quinces of an ornamental flowering quince bush edible? Are they useful for jelly or quince honey? They can be used in any way the ordinary quince is used, but their jelly is not equal to other jellies in flavor. In addition, they can be dried and used among linen for their aroma.

How and when are quince trees pruned? Pruning should be very light to avoid stimulating vigorous growth that may be attacked by fire blight. Remove dead twigs and those which are growing "out of bounds"—too low, too high, etc. The bush form is probably preferable to the tree form. Prune in early spring.

I wish to cut back a tall quince tree. How many branches should I leave? It is difficult to spray as is. Remove a few of the tallest branches one year and a few more the next in order to reduce the height gradually. Too severe pruning all at once will probably result in an outbreak of fire blight.

It seems to me that the books I have consulted give contradictory advice regarding pruning a quince. My tree is suffering from fire blight. The instructions are to cut back the diseased wood, but won't this compound the problem since heavy pruning helps induce fire blight? Fire blight on quince, pear, or apple does, indeed, present a paradoxical situation. It is important to prune off infected shoots during the summer, making the cuts 4 to 5 inches below the last visible signs of dying. This heavy pruning causes more vigorous growth on the other shoots, and it is the most vigorously growing shoots that are most susceptible to new infections by fire blight.

However, do not feel that the situation is hopeless. A general recommendation is to convert the tree into a lower state of vigor. This may mean withholding fertilizer applications completely for 3 or 4 years. Eventually, the tree may lose all of its blight infection and grow normally.

How do you graft a quince bush? It is not necessary to graft quinces, as they can be propagated by cuttings—a much easier method of getting new plants.

STRAWBERRY (FRAGARIA X ANANASSA)

In what sort of soil should strawberries be planted? What advance fertilization is necessary? A sandy loam soil is good, but any well-drained soil that is fairly retentive of moisture can be made to produce good strawberries. Turn under manure or compost combined with commercial fertilizer (see below) before the plants are set.

Do strawberries require an acid soil? I have a patch that does not do very well. My soil has a tendency to be alkaline. The alkalinity of the soil probably has very little to do with the failure of your strawberry bed to do well. (See below.) Various diseases and insects are more likely to be causing the trouble.

Is lime needed for strawberries? There is a popular belief that lime may be injurious to strawberries, but actually they will respond to lime about as well as other crops. If the soil is alkaline or only mildly acid (pH 5.6 or above), then lime won't be needed and might even be harmful. But if the pH is down around 4.0 to 5.6, then by all means use lime.

Should you use fertilizer on strawberry plants? What is the best kind to use? A complete fertilizer, such as 5–10–5, at the rate of 2 to 4 pounds per 100 square feet should be broadcast and worked into the soil before planting.

Is animal manure too alkaline for applying to strawberries for the winter? A straw mulch applied before temperatures drop below 20° F. is better for the winter. Manure is best used in adding humus to the soil before planting the strawberries.

How can a strawberry planting be tied in with a vegetable garden? A good plan is to have it adjacent to the vegetable garden. When an old row of strawberries is removed, vegetables can take their place, as it is not desirable to keep strawberries in one place too long. If space permits, strawberries should not be grown on land that has grown tomatoes, peppers, eggplants, and potatoes during the previous 2 or 3 years. A few feet between them is enough.

How much space should be planted in strawberries for each person in the family? Twenty-five feet of row per person in fruit, and another 25 feet of young plants coming along for the following year.

I have a slope in the back of my yard that I wish to have covered with strawberries. If I plant them at the bottom, will they climb? Do the leaves stay green in the winter? Better to plant in rows 2 feet apart across the slope. As runners form, you can place them where needed to cover the soil. The leaves remain more or less green during the winter, depending upon the site. In cold regions, where winter temperatures drop below 20° F., they will need to be covered.

I plan to start a strawberry patch for a family of 2. I want some for freezing. How many plants do I need? One hundred feet of row would take 40 plants, set 30 inches apart, and would yield 30 to 40 quarts if all goes well. Decide how many quarts you want and compute the number of plants needed.

How far apart are strawberry plants set? Varieties that do not make runners freely (especially the everbearers), about 18 inches apart; a fair plant takes 24 inches; a good plant takes 30 inches. The rows should be 36 to 48 inches apart.

When should strawberry plants be set? Strawberry plants are usually set in the spring as soon as the ground can be worked. If dormant plants from cold storage are used, then later planting is all right. Late October and early November is also a good time to plant. Fall-set

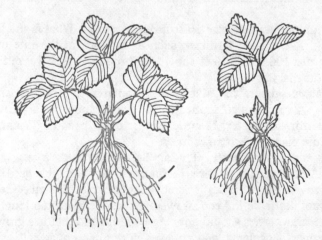

SETTING OUT STRAWBERRY PLANTS
Old leaves removed and roots trimmed back.

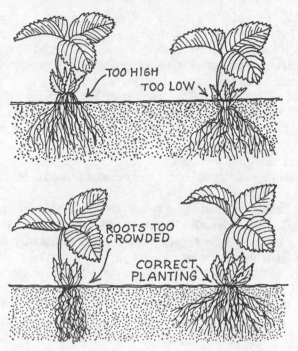

SETTING OUT STRAWBERRY PLANTS

plants should be mulched the first winter, the mulch removed in the spring, and the blossoms removed to prevent fruiting the first summer. Care is then the same as for a spring-set bed. Midsummer is not a good time to plant strawberries.

How should strawberries be planted?   Have the soil in good tilth. Scoop out a hole with a garden trowel to a depth of 4 or 5 inches; plant firmly, being sure that the roots are well spread and extend down into the hole and are well covered. The plants should be set as deeply as possible without covering the crown. If set too deeply, the plants will be smothered; if not deeply enough, part of their roots will be exposed and will dry out.

What is the hill method of strawberry growing?   The plants are set a foot apart and all runners removed as they appear. Single rows are often used, but much higher yields will be obtained if 2 to 4 rows are set a foot apart with an alley between each set of rows.

What is the matted-row method of strawberry growing?   The plants are set 18 to 30 inches apart, in rows 30 to 48 inches apart. The runners are allowed to develop and take root, forming a "matted row,"

18 to 30 inches wide, of plants which will produce fruit the following season. Matted rows are often overcrowded, with a consequent reduction in yield. Runner plants as they develop should be spaced about 6 inches apart until the row is 18 inches wide. Thereafter, the runner plants should be considered weeds and removed.

How long is a strawberry bed good for when using the hill method of planting? If properly cared for, a bed will be productive for 3 or 4 years; the first crop will be the best, and later crops will be successively poorer. It is best to set new plants each spring, let them fruit the following spring, and then spade them under.

How often should strawberries be renewed to maintain an abundant yield? At least every 2 years; better, every year.

Should strawberry runners be removed to prevent them from sapping the strength of the plants? The production of runners by strawberry plants is a perfectly natural process and is not necessarily devitalizing. The severe competition from overcrowding in a matted row is the reason for removing runner plants in excess of those needed to form a fruiting row. In the hill system of growing, all runners should be removed in order to keep the plants properly spaced. In the common matted-row system, the only runners removed are those in excess of the number required to produce a matted row, with plants spaced at least 7 to 8 inches apart. Each runner soon produces leaves and roots of its own and becomes a "self-supporting," individual plant.

How many runners should be allowed to develop from each mother plant in the matted-row system? Allow at least 7 or 8 inches (in all directions) between runner plants. If the plants are 30 inches apart in rows, allow 12 to 14 runner plants to develop from each mother plant. The excess runners should be cut off, preferably before they take root.

What shall I do when my strawberries grow too thick? Keep the runners spaced and thinned so the plants will stand at least 7 or 8 inches apart in the matted row. Usually the beds are replanted every year or two, setting runner plants in a new location.

We have been advised to cut strawberry leaves off in the fall. Is this correct? The leaves definitely should not be cut off in the fall. They are the organs in which those foods which feed the plant are manufactured. Cutting off the leaves "starves" the rest of the plant.

Can strawberries be weeded in the spring? Most strawberry beds need weeding in the spring unless the ground is unusually free from weed seeds. Some weed seeds come in the mulch. Many of the weeds should be pulled by hand to prevent damaging the strawberry plants. Herbicides, properly used, can reduce the amount of weeding needed.

Why did my strawberry plants bloom so profusely but set no berries?   The blossoms may have been injured by frost, which, without injuring the petals, often kills the part which will develop into fruit.

My strawberry plants blossom and set berries, but they do not develop after being half grown. Why?   Misshapen and knotty berries are often caused by the feeding of the tarnished plant bug, an insect which feeds on the blossoms. It is easily controlled by spraying the plants, following current instructions from the Cooperative Extension Service.

I seem to have no luck with strawberries. They do not bear very heavily.   First, be sure that you have a productive variety and one suited to your soil and climate; set a new bed frequently and keep the soil well, but not too heavily, fertilized. Do not let the plants crowd in the matted row. Do not fertilize in the spring of the bearing year.

How are strawberries propagated?   In the summer strawberry plants produce long, stringlike growths called "runners," at the tips of which grow new plants. These send roots into the soil. They are allowed to develop until the following spring, when they are dug up and set out in new beds. Some varieties make many runners; others make only a few.

How should strawberry runners be cared for before they are set out in a new bed?   If using runners from your own beds, dig only when ready to plant. Remove old ragged or dead leaves, leaving the small leaves at the tip of the crown. If you purchase plants, try to plant them as soon as you receive them. If this cannot be done, "heel in" in a shallow trench in a cool place and keep them well watered until planting time.

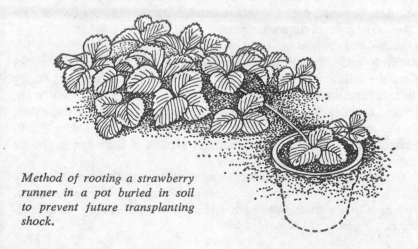

Method of rooting a strawberry runner in a pot buried in soil to prevent future transplanting shock.

How can runners be rooted in pots? Fill 2½- or 3-inch pots with a good humus-rich soil and sink them in the ground around the mother plants. Place a runner tip over each pot and hold in place by putting a stone or clod on the runner near the tip, or bend or twist wires into hairpin shape and peg the runners down, or use clothespins. When the new plant is well developed, the runner can be severed from the old plant.

Are potted strawberry plants any better than those runner plants which have been allowed to become well established in the garden before transplanting? For starting a new bed in late summer or early fall, only potted plants will stand transplanting satisfactorily. However, spring planting of ordinary runner plants is preferred.

Pot-grown strawberry plants for late-summer planting.

Can strawberry seeds or plants be started in the spring and produce worthwhile results the same year? There are certain small-fruited European varieties which "come true" from seed and will fruit the same year the seed is planted. The common garden strawberry of North America, however, does not "come true" from seed. Plants do not produce full crops until the second year.

Should strawberries be mulched during the winter? Mulching is advisable to prevent winter injury, conserve moisture, and keep the berries clean the following spring. Plants are more likely to heave out during alternate freezing and thawing on heavy soils than on sandy soils; hence, mulching is more essential on heavier soils. Apply the mulch after 2 or 3 sharp freezes, but before temperatures drop below 20° F. Temperatures lower than this when the ground is bare can injure the strawberry plants.

What is the best material to use as a winter mulch on a strawberry bed? Wheat, oat and rye straws, and marsh hay are all good mulches. Pine needles are good. Sawdust has been used satisfactorily but supplementary nitrogen will be needed with it.

How is mulching material applied to a strawberry bed? The straw is scattered over the bed with a fork to a depth of 3 or 4 inches. In windy situations, weight it down with brush.

What are the advantages of mulching strawberries with marsh hay, and when should it be applied? This hay is freer from weed seeds than wheat, oat, and rye straws, and is easy to get in coastal areas.

Is it all right to mulch strawberry plants with tree leaves? Tree leaves are a fair mulch, but if too thick they can mat down and make it difficult for the strawberry plants to push through in the spring.

How soon is the mulch removed from the strawberry bed? The mulch is removed in early April when inspection of the plants shows that the new leaves are beginning to grow from the crown. Part of the mulch is pulled off the plants into the space between the rows and part is left over the plants. The leaves and flower clusters push through the mulch and the berries rest on the straw, which keeps them clean.

What are "everbearing" strawberries? These are varieties that form a crop of fruit in the spring and another in late summer. The total yield is smaller than that of one-season berries.

Are everbearing strawberries successful? They do not live up to the descriptions in some of the catalogs, but if you like strawberries well enough to put up with the faults of everbearing varieties, then they can be termed "successful." One of the faults is that the crop is produced over such a long period that only a very small picking can be made on any one day.

Are everbearing strawberries as prolific as the ordinary kind? If the plants are grown in hills and mulched with sawdust and the blossoms removed until the middle of July, most varieties will produce a fairly large crop per plant. The soil should be fertile and watering is essential in dry weather. An inch of water per week from rain or a hose is desirable. The fruit will then ripen over a period of 2 to 3 months, but the picking on any one day will be rather small. If the blossoms are not removed, the plants will exhaust themselves by producing heavily during the hot midsummer months. The fruit produced in cooler fall weather will be of better quality than that produced in midsummer.

Should the runners be removed from everbearing strawberry plants? A maximum fall crop will be produced if the plants are set close together, about 12 to 15 inches apart, in rows 2 feet apart, and all runners removed as they form. This is known as the hill system.

How and when are everbearing strawberries thinned? Most varieties will need no thinning unless grown in hills, in which case all the runners should be kept off. Set a new bed each spring rather than try to rejuvenate the old one.

Should the first blossoms be removed from everbearing strawberry plants? When should they be allowed to bear? Best results will be secured if all blossoms are removed up to the latter part of June. The first fruit would then ripen about the middle of August.

If I transplant everbearing strawberry plants in the spring, will they bear the same season? Yes, they should bear their maximum crop in the fall of the year in which they are planted.

My everbearing strawberries do not have the flavor of standard strawberries. Are there any that compare with usual spring berries? 'Geneva' is of highest quality. 'Ozark Beauty' is another popular variety.

What care should be given to everbearing strawberries to keep them bearing from year to year? It can't be done. You could get some fruit for 2 or even 3 years, but many plants would die and the others would get progressively weaker. Don't count on one planting to produce more than one fall crop, followed by a spring crop.

What care should be given everbearing strawberries through the winter? Do they thrive better in moist ground or dry? They should be winter-mulched like any other strawberries. Everbearers are getting ready during the hot, dry weather of midsummer to produce a fall crop; hence, they must have ample moisture or the results will be disappointing.

I have a 50-gallon oak barrel in which I want to grow strawberries. How should I prepare the soil and set the plants? How far apart should the holes be? Beginning 1 foot from the bottom, bore holes at irregular intervals, 9 inches apart and large enough to hold a plant without cramping. Bore a number of smaller holes in the bottom for drainage and set the barrel on flat bricks. Put in 6 inches of drainage material—coarse gravel or cinders, topped with finer material. Mix good garden soil with ⅓ its bulk of rotted manure or rich compost and ⅓ screened cinders. To every bushel, add 1 pound of a complete fertilizer. It is not necessary to fill the whole interior with this soil. Maintain a 6-inch thickness around the inside and fill the center with any gravelly material available. Planting and filling are done at the same time. Begin by covering the drainage with soil to the level of the first holes. Push the plants through from the inside, spread their roots, and cover with soil. Repeat to within 12 inches of the top; fill this with good soil and plant the entire top. See that the moisture conditions are uniform.

What variety of plant should be used in a strawberry barrel? How should the plants be wintered over? Select a variety of high quality adapted to your climatic conditions. It is desirable to use potted plants if you can get them. Mulch with straw over the top; protect the side plants, if possible, with straw or burlap after the first heavy freeze. Unless well protected in cold regions, the plants will be injured or killed by winter cold. Check moisture conditions occasionally to prevent drying out.

What is the proper way to handle strawberry plants in a strawberry jar (barrel) after they are through bearing? Remove the old plants and replace a little later with newly formed runner plants that have been rooted in small pots.

Do strawberries need to be sprayed? Probably not—only if certain pests (such as leaf roller, tarnished plant bug, or weevil) are bad. Most strawberries in the home garden do quite well without being sprayed.

What causes the purplish spots on the leaves of my strawberry plants? One of two diseases—either leaf spot or leaf scorch. During most seasons, the modern varieties will not be injured enough to make it worthwhile to spray.

What causes the buds to drop from my strawberry plants before they bloom? The strawberry weevil, a tiny insect, lays an egg in the bud and then cuts the stem just in back of the bud. Follow the current spray program from your Cooperative Extension Service.

Are any strawberry varieties resistant to the red stele root rot? 'Sparkle', 'Redglow', 'Surecrop', 'Midway', 'Redchief', 'Sunrise', and 'Guardian' are resistant.

What are "virus-free" strawberries? They are plants which tests have shown are free of virus diseases. They are much superior to the old stock, most of which was infected with a virus disease that reduced the vigor and productiveness of the plants. Most good strawberry plant nurseries are selling them. Plants that are obtained from sources that are not attempting to produce virus-free plants should be avoided.

What are the best strawberries for freezing? 'Sparkle' and 'Midland' are two good ones.

What are "runnerless" strawberries? These are a strain of the alpine or European strawberry, *Fragaria vesca,* that produces no runners so they must be raised from seeds. The berries are small, pointed, and have a distinctive flavor. The plants fruit throughout the summer.

Can wild strawberries be transplanted in a regular bed? If so, do they give a good crop? Wild strawberries in cultivation (that is, fertilized and weeded) will give better yields than in the wild, but it requires a good many to fill a quart basket. Berry size is improved very little under cultivation. But they *are* flavorful!

Cane Fruits

What is meant by the term "bramble or cane fruits"? This group includes the fruits belonging to the genus *Rubus:* the red, black, and purple raspberries, the dewberry, and the bush and trailing blackberries. The loganberry, boysenberry, etc., can be classified as dewberries.

Have the "brambles" any preference as to soil? Raspberries and bush blackberries do best in heavier soils; dewberries like sandy soils and will not thrive on heavy soils. If the soil is well drained and in good physical condition, the brambles will grow satisfactorily on a fairly wide range of soil types.

Can cane fruits be grown successfully in a sandy soil? A sandy loam soil is satisfactory, but coarse sands are too subject to drought and are low in fertility. Irrigation and mulching are helpful here as well as the incorporation of peat moss, compost, and/or rotted manure at planting time.

What fertilizer should be used for brambles? Use a nitrogenous material such as ammonium nitrate or nitrate of soda. If marginal burning of the foliage is present, sulfate of potash should be used.

Where should cane fruits be planted? They should be planted on fertile well-drained soils that are well supplied with organic matter. The black and purple raspberries should not be planted on land that has grown tomatoes, peppers, eggplants, and potatoes within the past 3 years or near wild raspberries or runout cultivated raspberries, which often harbor diseases and insects that can ruin the new planting.

Can you plant berry bushes during the winter when the ground is soft? It could be done, but if the soil has much clay in it, it will be too sticky to do a good job. If there is much freezing and thawing afterward, the plants might heave out of the ground unless mulched and mounded up with soil. Fall or early-spring planting would be preferable.

How much space should be planted with cane fruits for a family of 4? Personal tastes must be considered, of course, but here is one suggested assortment: plants 3 feet apart in a row, in rows 6 to 8 feet apart. Red raspberries, 50 feet of row; black raspberries, 24 feet of row; blackberries, 50 feet of row.

Can raspberries be planted near pine trees? If there is distance enough between them so that there is no root competition or shade.

What berry bushes thrive in the shade? No plants that bear fruit will thrive in much shade. The more sun they receive, the better the crops.

When do you plant everbearing raspberries? Everbearing raspberries can be set either in the fall or spring and should have the same care that the ordinary one-crop varieties receive.

Can bramble or cane fruits be grown in a very small city garden? They may be grown if sunlight is adequate (most of the day). Keep them in bounds by hoeing off unwanted suckers.

Do cane fruits need support? Cane fruits do not require support, but most growers use some means of training to keep them from growing too "ragged" and occupying too much space in the garden.

How would you construct a trellis for dewberry vines? A 5-foot stake driven 1 foot into the ground beside each plant will be quite satisfactory. Cut out old, dead canes and tie up new, vigorous canes in early spring, cutting them off at the top of the stake.

How should I care for the 'Heritage' raspberries that I set out last spring? How should they be pruned and sprayed? (Vermont.) In the same manner as the one-crop varieties. (See the question on pruning raspberries below.) Spraying is not necessary.

What is the correct yearly cultural care of established cane fruits? Constant shallow cultivation to control weeds is important. Mulching is a good plan, using well-rotted manure or rich compost. Prune living canes only where necessary for the training of plants. Prune out all dead canes after the fruiting season. Apply nitrate of soda (or a similar high-nitrogen fertilizer) in the spring, 1 to 2 pounds per 100 feet of row.

How often should berries be picked? Pick red raspberries every day; blackcaps and blackberries, every third day.

How can I increase my stock of raspberries? Black and purple raspberries are propagated by tip-layering. The tips of the new canes are inserted vertically in the soil in late August to a depth of 4 inches. Roots form on the tip in late fall, and in the spring the tip is dug, severed from the mother plant, and planted where desired. Red raspberries send up many sucker plants, which can be dug in late fall and early spring for planting elsewhere.

How often should the brambles be planted? Usually in 5 to 10 years, but if weeds are not bad and diseases are kept under control, the plantings last longer.

What kind of fruit bushes can I grow on a strip 3 × 40 feet? (New York.) If the area is exposed to full sunlight, you could grow any of the small fruits, such as grapes, strawberries, raspberries, currants, or gooseberries, or combinations of the ones you like best. For instance, 3 currant bushes would take up about 10 feet, leaving 30 feet for strawberries if you particularly like these two fruits; or all the area may be planted with raspberries or blackberries.

Our garden is in Maine, rather far east on the coast. Can you give some information on varieties of small fruits we can plant? 'Sparkle', 'Catskill', and 'Fairfax' are good home-garden strawberries; others are 'Fletcher' and 'Raritan'. 'Latham', 'Newburgh', 'Heritage' (fall-bearing), and 'Taylor' are good red raspberries. 'Bristol' and 'Dundee' are the best black raspberries. 'Brandywine' is the best purple variety.

What would be a profitable fruit planting, producing in about 3 or 4 years, that could be tended on weekends and will produce for at least 10 years without being replanted? There are 2 acres, a half mile from the ocean, and full sun. Red raspberries are rarely grown commercially now so there is no competition for a crop that can be very profitable. Or you might make a miscellaneous fruit planting for your own use and sell the surplus. In that case, choose the fruits you like and take a part of your "profit" in personal satisfaction. If profit is the main objective, secure enough land to make an economic farm unit. Be sure that the land is a good farm soil. Consult your Cooperative Extension Service.

What different kinds of berries should be planted in order to have a continuous supply from late spring until frost? Start off with strawberries, then raspberries, currants, gooseberries, and blueberries. These will cover the season until late August. Everbearing strawberries and raspberries will fill out the rest of the season.

What kind of everbearing raspberries are suggested for south of Boston? The best variety is 'Heritage'. This is really fall-bearing. The fall crop is produced at the tips of the new canes and next summer the same canes bear another crop.

Can we grow the 'Oregon Evergreen' blackberry in this state? (Massachusetts.) Grow the 'Darrow' variety instead.

What is the best variety of blackberry for Maine? 'Darrow'.

BLACKBERRY (RUBUS)

Will blackberries grow on any soil? They do best on good sandy loam soil containing plenty of humus but well drained.

Can manure be used on blackberries? Yes, manure or complete fertilizer can be used to improve poor soils on which blackberries are grown. A yearly cover crop, turned under in the spring, or the turning under of summer mulch, adds needed humus to the soil.

When is the best time to transplant blackberry or raspberry bushes? Early spring, although fall planting can be successful if the plants are set rather deeply and mounded somewhat to prevent heaving during the winter. This applies to red raspberries; black raspberries should be set in the spring.

How far apart should raspberries and bush blackberries be planted? Three feet apart in the row and rows 7 to 8 feet apart are standard distances, but when space is limited in the home garden, you can plant them much closer.

How far apart should blackberries of the trailing type be planted? Trailing blackberries such as 'Black Diamond' (called 'Oregon Evergreen' in the West) need plenty of room. Set the plants at least 6 feet apart in rows 6 to 8 feet apart.

When and how should blackberries be pruned? In June the tips of new shoots are pinched off at a height of 3 feet to make them branch. The following spring the branches are cut back to a length of about 15 inches. After the crop is harvested, canes that have borne fruit are removed.

Why do some blackberries blossom and not have any berries? There are two possible causes. A sterile blackberry has been widely distributed by nurseries. It produces no fruit although it blooms. Another cause is the feeding of the tarnished plant bug on the flowers, causing them to develop into sterile or partially sterile fruits. The plant bug is easily controlled by spraying the plants with malathion at the rate of 6 tablespoonfuls of the 25 per cent Wettable Powder in 5 gallons of water. This is applied just before the plants bloom. Make a second application immediately after the petals fall.

Are the trailing blackberries (that is, dewberry, boysenberry) propagated the same way as regular blackberries? These are usually propagated by tip-layering.

Can the suckers that come up from the roots of blackberries be used to make plants of the same variety? Yes. Usually nurseries use root cuttings 3 to 4 inches long and the thickness of a lead pencil.

Why do blackberry leaves get a bright orange color and then seem to die? The orange color is made up of spores of a disease known as orange rust. Infected plants will die. The only control is to dig out diseased plants before spores have been discharged to infect other plants. Be sure to dig out the roots, since shoots coming up from these would be diseased.

Is it satisfactory to transplant wild blackberry bushes for home use? This is all right if you can find really superior wild bushes; otherwise, you will have much better results by planting named varieties. Wild blackberries sometimes do not do as well under cultivation as they do in the wild. Try the 'Darrow' variety.

Is the thornless 'Thornfree' blackberry as good as the thorny type? Yes. Thornlessness is a very valuable asset, as can be attested by anyone who has picked from or pruned the thorny type.

Would raspberry and blackberry plants make a good ground cover for a steep embankment? Raspberries and blackberries will grow satisfactorily on a steep bank if the soil is fertile and the ground is mulched to prevent its being washed away. Steep banks, however, can be badly eroded, in which case the soil is not suitable for the brambles. Also, caring for the plants and harvesting under such conditions would be a chore.

BOYSENBERRY (RUBUS)

Are boysenberries worth growing in the East? Boysenberries are not winter-hardy north of Washington, D.C., and even though protected, the crops are very light. The other small fruits will produce much more fruit with less effort. Boysenberries are an excellent fruit in California and Oregon.

How should boysenberries be fed? Boysenberries can be fertilized with nitrate of soda or sulfate of ammonia at the rate of 1 pound per 100 square feet.

I have some boysenberries that I set out last spring which I would like to move. When can this be done? (Washington.) Boysenberries can be moved in late fall or early spring before their growth starts. In mild sections of your state, they can be moved any time during the winter.

How are boysenberries pruned and trained? Boysenberries are a trailing vine. The canes grow one year, bear fruit the second, and then die, other canes taking their place. To facilitate the harvesting of fruit and tillage operations, fruiting canes are tied up to a trellis at the beginning of the second season. A suitable trellis consists of a wire 3 or 4 feet above the ground. Canes are gathered together and tied at the top of this wire. The ends are cut off or tied along the wire. Canes can also be tied up to 5-foot posts, their ends cut off at the top of the post. After the crop is harvested, the fruiting canes are removed and new canes, which will fruit the following year, are tied in.

I have 6-year-old boysenberry bushes that were planted close to young shade trees and now are shaded too much. Can I transplant them this coming spring? The plants are very large and strong. Can I divide them and make more plants? (Oregon.) Old berry plants are not transplanted and reestablished readily. Either buy new plants or cover the tips of new canes with soil in late summer. Roots will form at the tips. New plants may be severed from the parent plant the following spring and moved to their permanent location. Dividing old plants is hardly practical.

RASPBERRY (RUBUS)

When is the best time to plant red raspberry bushes? Red raspberries can be set in late fall if the soil is mounded around the plants to a height of several inches to prevent heaving from frost. In the spring the soil is worked down level. Raspberries can also be set in early spring.

Is it wise to plant virus-free raspberry plants back onto ground formerly occupied by virus-infected plants? No. Many viruses of fruit plants are carried in the soil by certain species of nematodes, which are very small eelworms about $\frac{1}{16}$ inch long. As long as weeds or other plants are growing in the soil, nematodes can feed on the roots and remain alive in the soil year after year. If a virus-infected raspberry planting is removed in the fall with the intent of replanting with new, virus-free plants the next spring, these new plants will soon become virus-infected if planted on the same ground. They will become infected by virus-carrying nematodes, which will chew on the roots.

Commercial raspberry growers fumigate the soil with a poisonous gas in the fall. This kills the nematodes and virus-free raspberry plants can then be safely planted. Fumigating the soil is probably impractical for most home gardeners. Viruses, of course, are not always the cause of poor growth and low yields. The home gardener should not allow these potential virus problems to deter his enthusiasm. In most cases you will be delighted with the delicious raspberries you are able to produce.

When is the best time to transplant black raspberries? Tip plants are set in the spring, but "transplants" can be set either in the spring or in the late fall.

How far apart should raspberries be planted? Plant suckering varieties 3 feet apart, in rows 5 or 6 feet apart; blackcaps, 4 or 5 feet apart, in rows 6 or 7 feet apart.

Can raspberry bushes which were not planted in the fall be held over until spring without heeling them in? They must be heeled in (that is, their roots covered with soil) or packed in moist material such as sphagnum moss and stored in a cellar where the temperature stays 32° F. The roots must not be allowed to dry out and the temperature must be low enough to prevent the canes from sprouting. Surely you have space to heel them in during the winter.

Is it possible to plant between the rows of raspberries? It seems as if there is space going to waste. Small vegetables, but not tomatoes, pepper, eggplants, or potatoes, may be planted between the rows the first season, but not close enough to the raspberries to compete with them. After the first year, the raspberries will need all the ground.

Should raspberries and blackberries be pruned in the summer? Red raspberries should not be summer pruned except for old canes of everbearers which can be cut out at the base after harvesting ends in early summer. Blackcaps and bush blackberries should have their canes pinched back when they reach the height at which branching is desired. This would usually be at 24 to 30 inches for black raspberries and 30 to 36 inches for bush blackberries. If pinching is done at the proper time, it will consist of merely nipping out the growing tip of the cane with your fingers.

How should red raspberries be pruned and trained? Red raspberries are commonly tied to stakes or a wire trellis in the garden, but support is not necessary. Plants should be grown in hedgerows not over 1 foot in width. In early spring, canes that grew during the previous season are cut back about one fourth of their height. Weaker canes should be removed so that the remaining canes are spaced about 6 inches apart in rows 1 foot in width. Canes that fruited the previous summer should be removed if this was not done after the crop was harvested. Red raspberry plants send up a multitude of suckers between the rows and unless these are subdued by vigorous use of a hoe, a veritable thicket will result.

How should black raspberries be pruned? Remove canes that are dead, broken, obviously diseased, or that grow at such an angle that they will bend to the ground when in fruit. Cut back good canes to about 24 to 30 inches and then shorten the lateral branches to about 6 inches.

Do red raspberries need a trellis? Not necessarily. If they are pruned rather short (cut back about one half, if 5 to 6 feet tall), they will hold themselves up. However, a trellis of one wire on each side of the row, supported by posts and crosspieces, will hold the canes up during storms, prevent breakage, and keep the berries from getting into the mud. Mulching protects lower berries from being splashed with mud.

Last summer I planted some 'Sodus' purple raspberries. They have grown to a length of 9 to 12 feet. How far and when should they be cut back? In early spring, the canes should be cut back to a length of 4 or 5 feet and tied up to a stake or wire trellis. To eliminate the need for support, pinch off the tips of new shoots when they reach a height of 30 inches. This makes the canes branch and they are sturdier and self-supporting. The following spring, cut the branches back to a length of 10 or 12 inches and no support will be needed.

What, if any, winter protection should be given 1-year-old black raspberry bushes? (New York.) Black raspberries are hardy without winter protection except in the coldest parts of the country like northern New York.

How can I protect raspberries during the winter? (Massachusetts.) Hardy raspberry varieties should not need protection in Massachusetts. If protection is desired, bend the canes down and cover the tips with soil. In this position, snow will provide protection. Where snow blows off, straw or earth can be used to cover the canes.

What materials are suitable as a mulch for raspberry bushes? Compost, rotted manure, straw, old hay, and decayed leaves are good mulching materials for raspberries.

Do everbearing raspberries bear continuously? Two crops are borne, the first in June or July on canes which grew during the previous season, and the second or fall crop in September and October on the tips of the new or current season's canes.

My red raspberry patch has grown so profusely. Would it be wise to take out every other row and start a new patch? It is rather difficult to subdue and restore order in a raspberry patch that has run wild. It will be easier and more satisfactory to take up healthy sucker plants and set a new patch, resolving to take care of it and keep suckers in bounds. Have the rows in the new patch 6 or 7 feet apart and keep the rows of plants about 1 foot in width.

Can shoots of red raspberry be cut away from their parent plant and transplanted in the spring? If so, how and when? New shoots of red raspberries can be taken up in June after they have reached a height of 6 or 8 inches. Care should be taken to get part of the old root. Cloudy, moist weather is essential and the plants should be watered in. This method of starting raspberries is not successful in hot, dry weather.

When is the best time to propagate "wild" red raspberries? Red raspberry sucker plants can be taken up and set either in late fall or early spring. They are usually not worth growing as the berries are too small and the crops are too light, unless they happen to be a good variety that has escaped cultivation.

How can I get new plants to renew my raspberry planting? Red raspberries are propagated from suckers from the roots of old plants. These are dug up, the large root severed, and new plants set in place. Black and purple cane raspberries are propagated by tip layers.

Will red and black raspberries mix if planted close to each other? No. Not at all.

How can I keep birds from devouring my red raspberries? Cover the plants with netting or cheesecloth. Usually the birds can't catch all the crop on established plantings.

How can I keep rabbits from gnawing raspberry bushes during the winter? Fence them out with poultry netting, 30 inches high.

What causes the mosaic disease of raspberries? This is a virus disease spread from one plant to another by aphids. The only remedy is to keep digging out and destroying diseased plants. Be sure to take out the roots, as all the shoots coming up from the roots of a diseased plant will also be diseased. Nurseries now sell virus-free plants, but if exposed to diseased plants they will soon become infected.

What are the symptoms of viruses in raspberries? Unlike the mosaic virus, which is visible, several viruses which infect raspberries are referred to as being latent. This means that they do not exhibit distinctly visible external symptoms on the raspberry plant; the infection will, nevertheless, cause reduced plant vigor and yield. Several cultural factors, such as wet soil or too much shade, can also reduce plant vigor and yield. Therefore, it may not be possible for a home gardener to know whether virus is present. Scientists can detect the presence of latent viruses in raspberry plants by transferring leaf sap to virus-sensitive indicator plants such as the lamb's-quarters weed, which does show distinct symptoms.

Some of the latent viruses in raspberries are tomato ring spot virus (crumbly berry), mosaic virus, tobacco streak, black raspberry latent and raspberry bush dwarf virus. Latent viruses are widely distributed in raspberries. In some varieties, all plants are infected. Extensive testing of plants from many sources has located some that are free of all known viruses. Heat treatments of many varieties can remove viruses. The most that the home gardener can do is to buy virus-tested raspberry plants from a reliable nursery so that he or she can start out with healthy material.

What causes a hard, woody knot to grow at the ground level on my raspberry bushes? This is caused by the disease known as crown gall.

There is no cure for a diseased plant, and the disease will live in the soil for some time. Set clean, inspected plants in soil that has not recently grown any of the bramble fruits.

What causes the tips of my 'Latham' raspberry plants to wilt over? The raspberry cane borer, a beetle, lays an egg near the tip of the cane, then cuts a girdle just above and below the egg, which usually causes the tip to wilt and die. The most practical control consists of breaking off the wilted tips and burning them. Break or cut a couple of inches below the girdle in order to get the larva, which will start to bore down through the pith of the cane as soon as it hatches.

My black raspberries have gray spots on the canes and on the fruit. What can I do? This is the disease known as anthracnose. A delayed dormant spray of 1 part lime sulfur to 20 parts water, when the buds are out about ½ inch in the spring, will usually give control. In seasons favorable for anthracnose (prolonged wet spells), ferbam at the rate of 12½ tablespoonfuls to 5 gallons of water should be applied when the new shoots are 12 to 15 inches high and again just before they bloom.

Why aren't red and black raspberries supposed to be grown together? Because of certain diseases, mosaic in particular, which are carried by the reds and readily transmitted to the blacks. Mosaic infection may not injure a red variety very rapidly but will kill a blackcap in a much shorter time (that is, the reds act as carriers of the disease). The blacks would be much safer a couple of hundred yards away, far enough so that aphids will not get from one to the other.

Why aren't purple raspberries more widely grown? They are susceptible to the mosaic disease. They are not very attractive in the box and do not sell well. But those who know them frequently prefer them to the reds and blacks. The plants are very productive and the tart berries are useful in the kitchen.

Are everbearing raspberries more desirable than standard sorts? For the home gardener, everbearing sorts are desirable to extend the season. 'Heritage' is the best everbearing variety. It bears two good crops in one season.

What black raspberries are the best producers for home use? 'Bristol' and 'Dundee' are both productive, high-quality varieties.

What red raspberry do you consider best for home garden and market garden? (Wisconsin.) For Wisconsin, 'Latham' is a standard variety. 'Taylor', 'Newburgh', and 'Heritage' should also be tried.

What are good early and late red raspberries? 'Newburgh' for early and 'Latham' for late would make a good combination.

Nut Trees

GENERAL

What is the best soil for nut trees? I have an open field. Any well-drained soil that will produce good farm crops is suitable for nut trees. The native walnut especially prefers fertile bottom-land soil, while the Persian (English walnut) is thought to need limestone soils. Poor, eroded soils are not suitable for nut trees.

What is the general care for nut trees? The principal care required is to eliminate weed competition by cultivation or mulching. If the soil is not fertile, an annual application of nitrate of soda or sulfate of ammonia, at the rate of ¼ pound (or ½ that rate of ammonium nitrate) for each inch of trunk diameter, should keep the trees growing.

Will the planting of nut trees in a fruit orchard react against either the fruit or nut trees in the presence of each other? Nut trees are too vigorous and grow too large to be grown in the same orchard with fruit trees.

Can nut trees be grown as far north as Brunswick, Maine? Those best suited are the native hazelnuts, the shagbark hickory, and butternuts. The growing season in Maine is too short and too cool for many nut trees. Also, the winters are too cold.

How can nut trees be grafted? Several methods of grafting are used in nut-tree propagation. Splice grafting or whip grafting is used when propagating young Persian walnuts in nurseries in the West and for young pecans in the South. Scions are grafted onto a 1-year-old seedling understock. In the Persian walnut, the union is waxed but not tied; in the pecan, the union is tied with raffia. Soil that was removed from around the seedlings before grafting is pushed back and the scions completely covered to a depth of 2 inches. When trees are being top-worked to another variety, the cleft graft method is used. This method, however, has been largely supplanted by that known as bark grafting. (See Grafting.)

Is there a miniature nut tree? No dwarfing stock for nut trees has as yet been introduced.

What kind of nut trees will grow in the East? (New Jersey.) Black walnuts, butternuts, and Chinese chestnuts are probably the most satisfactory. Hickories are slow-growing and the trees take up a lot of space.

What kinds of nuts can be successfully grown in the southern Pennsylvania climate? How do I start such an orchard? Is it necessary to purchase trees from nurseries or can they be grown successfully from nuts? Southern Pennsylvania has suitable soils and climate for all of the nut trees of the eastern states such as black and Persian walnuts, shagbark hickories, Chinese chestnuts, and filberts. Heartnuts and Japanese walnuts grow well, but the nuts are not of high quality. The practicability of commercial nut culture in this region has not been demonstrated, and plantings should be experimental or for pleasure. The named varieties available from nurseries as grafted trees are much superior to seedlings. Seedlings should be used only for reforestation or as food for game.

What are several quick-producing nut trees that can stand cold and strong wind? (New York.) Filberts will bear nuts in 4 or 5 years and are about as hardy as peaches. Grafted black walnuts also bear young, but will not produce many nuts until the trees develop sufficient bearing surface, which takes 8 or 10 years. Some Chinese chestnuts, most of which are seedlings, also bear fairly early.

ALMOND (PRUNUS DULCIS VAR. DULCIS)

Can almond trees be grown in this country? Commercially, only in California. They are almost as hardy as the peach, but because they bloom earlier, they are especially susceptible to damage by late spring frost. Their care and culture are the same as for peach trees.

Will almonds come true from seeds? (Oregon.) No. Named varieties are increased by budding them onto seedling almonds or seedling peaches.

BUTTERNUT (JUGLANS CINEREA)

Would you advise the home gardener to plant butternut trees? Butternut belongs to the walnut family but is hardier than our native black walnut, growing from New Brunswick to Arkansas. It is a good choice for an extensive property in the North, but grows too large for small gardens. The oblong nuts have a rich but delicate flavor, preferred by many to the stronger-flavored black walnut. Butternut trees reach 50 to 75 feet in height.

CHESTNUT (CASTANEA)

What kind of soil do chestnuts need?   Well-drained, acid soil, preferably sandy. They will also grow fairly well in neutral soils.

Are the blight-resistant Chinese chestnuts hardy?   Less so than our native chestnut. They may suffer injury in severe winters in the northern United States. Nuts of the Chinese chestnuts are usually larger than those of the American chestnut and of equally good flavor. The trees branch like apple trees.

Have the Chinese chestnuts which I see advertised been definitely proven to be blight-resistant?   Chinese chestnuts are generally sufficiently resistant to blight to permit their culture in regions where the blight has destroyed the native American chestnut. Many of the Chinese chestnuts in the trade are seedlings instead of grafted trees and exhibit considerable variation in blight resistance. Several named varieties are available from nut-tree nurseries, among which are 'Abundance', 'Nanking', 'Kuling', and 'Meiling'. Because of the incompatibility between the scion and rootstock, the grafted trees often die young. Seedlings, in spite of their variability, are preferable. Chestnut flowers require cross-pollination to produce nuts; hence, two or more seedlings should be planted.

Where can I get Chinese chestnuts and the thin-shelled black walnuts and pecans?   A list of nurseries specializing in those named varieties of nut trees may be had from the New York Experiment Station, Geneva, N.Y. 14456.

Will any chestnut stand the climate of Montreal, Canada?   It is doubtful if any chestnut trees are hardy enough for Montreal.

I have in my garden a chestnut tree severely afflicted with blight. Is there any effective treatment which might be applied to save this tree?   If this is an American chestnut, it is hopeless to attempt to save it.

We have an American chestnut tree which bears many false (empty) burs. If a Chinese chestnut was planted, would it fertilize the American? This tree has died down several times, but sent up a few shoots which would live about 3 years and then die.   No treatments will save the American chestnut. It will send up shoots for many years, but these will die as they become infected with blight. Planting another tree alongside this one would have no effect whatever on it.

FILBERT, HAZELNUT (CORYLUS)

Will filberts grow in this country? What are the best varieties? The European filbert (*C. avellana*) is grown commercially in Oregon and Washington. In the northeastern states near the Great Lakes where peaches are hardy, filberts may be expected to grow well. They will grow as far south as southern Pennsylvania at least. Hybrids between the native American hazels (*C. americana* and *C. cornuta*) and the European filbert grow well in the North.

Where should filberts be planted? Any good well-drained soil is suitable. A north slope or the north side of buildings and a site protected from cold winds are desirable.

Should filbert (hazelnut) trees be trimmed to the tree shape or allowed to grow as bushes? They may be grown either as trees or bushes; but as suckers are freely produced by many varieties, a bush is much easier to grow than a tree with a single stem.

How should filberts be pruned? Prune them like peaches, only not as severely. Severe pruning may result in winter injury. A moderate thinning is sufficient.

HICKORY (CARYA)

Are hickories worth growing? The shagbark hickory (*C. ovata*) nut is of very fine flavor, excelled only by the best pecans. 'Wilcox', 'Fox', and a few others propagated by nut nurseries are worth growing and they are much superior to seedling hickories. Hickory trees are difficult to transplant and establish because of the long taproot. They are suitable only for extensive rural properties.

Where should one report good nut trees, when found, so that they may be preserved (for instance, hickory and black walnut)? The New York Experiment Station, Geneva, N.Y. 14456.

MACADAMIA (MACADAMIA INTEGRIFOLIA)

What is the macadamia nut? This is an edible nut of a species of Australian tree. It is commonly called the Queensland nut.

Is the macadamia nut tree grown in this country? Yes, these nut trees are cultivated in California and in parts of Florida. They are a commercial crop in Hawaii. They thrive in rich, loamy soil with plenty of moisture, although they have been reported growing in dry sections. The tree is an evergreen and is ornamental as well.

PECAN (CARYA ILLINOINENSIS)

Are pecans successfully grown in the North?   Pecan trees are hardy in the North, but the growing season is too short and too cool to mature the nuts. Several northern pecans, as they are called, will mature nuts as far north as Washington, D.C., and the Ohio River Valley. The nuts are not as large as the southern varieties.

Of several small pecan trees I planted, all have died but one. Is there some special way to dig holes or set them out to make them live and grow well? (Georgia.)   Vigorous pecan trees that have been carefully dug and not allowed to dry out should not be difficult to establish. Set the trees in the fall; firm the soil tightly against the roots; keep down weeds; and water and mulch the trees when drought threatens during the first year or two.

What should be done for pecan trees when the nuts do not fill properly? They hull themselves as they should, but do not fill out. (Virginia.)   Control diseases and insects that attack the foliage. Varieties suitable in the Deep South may not fill well in Virginia. Grow northern varieties there.

How old does a soft-shell pecan tree have to be before bearing nuts?   The age of bearing depends on the variety of the tree, but not many nuts will be had until the trees are 6 to 8 years of age.

How should pecans be grafted? (Alabama.)   Varieties of pecan are propagated almost entirely upon seedling stocks of pecan species. Stocks of certain varieties are said to have some influence upon the growth of the grafted tree. Various pecan stocks are used in Texas. In Louisiana some use is made of the water hickory as a stock. Study local conditions as to the stock used.

PISTACHIO (PISTACIA VERA)

In what part of the country can the pistachio nut tree be grown?   Only in California and Mexico. It needs a climate like that required by olive trees.

WALNUT, BLACK (JUGLANS NIGRA)

Is the black walnut a good tree for the home garden?   If you live where winter temperatures do not drop too low and want a handsome specimen tree which will produce nuts, the black walnut is a good choice. The tree requires lots of room and is hardly suitable for most suburban properties. Some plants will not grow within the reach of its roots as these produce a substance toxic to these plants. Grass will grow all right under a black walnut. Although individual specimens live for years in New York State and similar sections, black walnuts are not considered reliably hardy where winter temperatures drop below −20° F. Butternut is hardier.

What special requirements has the black walnut? Wild specimens are often found growing in dry, rocky upland pastures as well as in woodlands. To produce nuts, this tree needs good, well-drained soil with regular supplies of moisture. A wild tree in a dry, unfertile location, if subjected for a few years to fertilization and sufficient moisture, will increase its yield tremendously. If caterpillars, such as canker or inch worms or gypsy moth caterpillars, defoliate the tree, they should be destroyed. They gather in clusters on the trunk at night, at which time they can be destroyed by rubbing out the colony with a broom. If the leaves are destroyed prematurely by caterpillars, anthracnose, or early fall frost, the nuts may not fill properly. Spraying the foliage with malathion or any stomach poison is also effective.

What are the dirty-white worms all through the outer husks of my black walnuts? What can I do to get rid of them? (New York.) These are the maggots of the walnut-husk fly, distributed throughout the East to the Kansas–Nebraska line on black walnuts and butternuts. A closely related species attacks the central and western black and English walnuts. Flies, a little smaller than house flies, with transparent, black-banded wings, lay their eggs in the husks in August. The maggots tunnel through the husks for several weeks, drop to the ground before or with the nuts, and pupate several inches down in the soil. They emerge as flies the next summer, or wait until the second or third summer. They do little injury to kernels, but they stain the surface of the nut. This insect is difficult to control, and hardly worth the trouble for most home gardens.

How can I grow native walnut seedlings from walnuts? So far I have had no luck. (Missouri.) Plant the seeds in the fall about 2 inches deep. If squirrels are troublesome, store the nuts in a box of moist sand outdoors and cover with wire netting to keep out rodents. Plant the nuts in the spring.

WALNUT, JAPANESE (JUGLANS AILANTHIFOLIA)

Can you give some information about a Japanese walnut? The Japanese walnut is a rapid-growing, very handsome tree. The nut is elongated, smooth, cracks poorly, and is inferior in quality to other walnuts. The heartnut, a supposed sport of the Japanese walnut, is much superior in cracking quality.

WALNUT, PERSIAN (ENGLISH) (JUGLANS REGIA)

Is the Persian walnut hardy in the East? Many seedling trees have been grown for years in the fruit-growing regions of the Great Lakes and on the eastern end of Long Island, New York, but occasionally a severe winter that injures peach trees may kill or seriously injure many of these trees. Several superior varieties, supposedly of greater than average hardiness, are now being propagated by nut-tree nurseries. Among them are 'Metcalfe', 'McKinster', 'Broadview', 'Littlepage', and 'Hansen'.

What are the soil and cultural requirements of the Persian walnut? Good, deep loam, well drained but with plenty of moisture to produce large crops of nuts. Where peaches are hardy in the North, the walnuts are worth trying. Farther south, many of them start their growth too early and are injured by frost.

Are Persian walnut trees harmful near shrubs? The Persian walnut is not considered to be harmful to shrubs, but of course it will compete with them for plant food and moisture.

I have a Persian walnut tree that is 14 years old. It never bore until the last 2 years. All its nuts fell off both years when they were quite small, but nuts inside were formed. Why does this happen? The nuts may not have been pollinated. If no other Persian walnut is near this tree, another should be planted to provide pollination.

What can I do to have more walnut nuts mature? The tree sets plenty of fruit, but nearly all drop off when they reach the size of large cherries. Lack of cross-pollination may be the cause of the trouble. Another variety of the same species should be set nearby. The tree may need fertilizing to increase its vigor. Nitrate of soda or sulfate of ammonia at the rate of ¼ pound for each inch of trunk diameter may be tried.

Is the Persian walnut self-pollinating? Persian (English) walnut varieties usually require cross-pollination by another variety, since its own pollen often is not shed at the time when the pistils are receptive.

How are Persian walnuts washed and dried to be stored for the winter? Remove the husks promptly and wash the nuts immediately. Lay the nuts out one layer deep in an airy room until they are thoroughly dried. Keep them in a cool, dry place.

We have a Persian walnut tree. Is there some way to treat the nuts to prevent mold while drying and to keep nut meats white? The nuts should not mold if they are husked promptly, washed, and thoroughly dried in an airy place.

Do you know a good soft-shelled walnut—better than 'Manchurian'— that will stand 10° or 20° F. below zero if need be? Our average winter temperature is 10° F. (Washington State.) The 'Hansen' variety of the Persian walnut and the Carpathian strain of the same species are thought to be somewhat hardier than the usual varieties and may be worth trying.

12. House Plants

HOUSE PLANTS HAVE two delightful functions—they make charming decorations for our rooms and they are fun to care for. The degree of satisfaction they give depends first on the conditions you can offer in which they can thrive. If your house is flooded with winter sunlight, you can grow almost any plant you wish; if it is well lighted, you also have a wide selection; but if it is quite dim, the light cut off by nearby walls or heavy evergreens, your selection must be very limited unless you install fluorescent lights. With these, a great variety of plants will flourish in previously dark corners or even in basements.

Although plants suitable for indoor culture have to a degree different individual requirements, there are certain basic needs of light, heat and humidity, moisture, food, and rest common to all. Keep them in mind as you become familiar with the individual nature of each indoor plant. Thus, African-violets, begonias, and ferns are kept barely moist all the time, but the sansevieria and aspidistra are allowed to dry out a little in between waterings.

Today in modern houses and office buildings floor-to-ceiling windows offer a handsome setting for tree-form lantanas or geraniums if there is sun, and for great foliage specimens in fully lighted locations—bamboos, ferns, philodendrons, Norfolk-Island-pines, aralias, and the schefflera. Attractive containers of brass, china, earthenware, or basketry add to the charm of house plants individually or in groups; for vining plants, there are, besides ceramic and brass baskets on chains, wicker cages, brackets that are copies of kerosene lamps, and wrought-iron pedestals to set off graceful cascades.

The great thing is to have only healthy plants. Sickly specimens are better discarded than pampered, and if you have had less success than you wish, try the easy ones—spider-plant, grape-ivy, Swedish-ivy, tradescantia, philodendron, asparagus-fern, pick-a-back plant, and ever-blooming wax begonia, all nearly foolproof but offering possibilities for attractive displays.

Light, Natural and Fluorescent

Most plants require a fully lighted location. Fresh-from-the-greenhouse specimens hung on a bracket in a dark hall or set at the mantel ends of a dim living room are destined, no matter what their original condition, for a short life—and not a very merry one. Light permits the plant organism to turn certain substances into usable foods. There are, of course, a number of excellent foliage plants which need no direct sun. The wax begonia and the patience-plant will bloom to some extent in a fully lighted location, without direct sunshine, but for most flowering plants sunshine is required—not an occasional hour or so, but every bit a southern or eastern window (from 4 to 6 hours) can offer. Without a maximum of sunshine, the geranium will fail to bud, and the jasmines and wax plants will remain an enduring green.

Fluorescent lights make it possible to grow plants in otherwise dark areas. Tubes can be fastened under kitchen cabinets and bookcase shelves and above counters. Table fixtures with hoods can be purchased and set over pebble-filled plastic trays. Carts fitted with fluorescent tubes are available by mail order, as are various special growth lamps. However, it has been found that standard tubes, available locally, are perfectly satisfactory, especially in a combination of one warm white and one cool white tube.

It is important to allow 15 to 20 watts of fluorescent light per square foot of growing area: for instance, two 48-inch 40-watt tubes for a 1 × 4-foot plant shelf. The center of the tubes gives the strongest light. Most plants thrive with tops 8 to 10 inches from the lights, which are kept on 12 to 14 hours a day. African-violets, other gesneriads, small begonias, and many miniature plants are a delight under fluorescents.

Temperature

Grown at 60° to 65° F., almost every house plant is better off than at 70° or 75° F. (indoor temperatures once normal in most northern winter interiors but virtually obsolete because of higher heating costs), while a night drop to 55° F., similar to nature's outdoor falling of temperature after sunset, is a further cultural benefit. Many of the most decorative plants can be grown in a really cool house window where the average is 50° to 60° F. For this reason a plant room, today's version of yesterday's sun porch, makes an ideal location for indoor gardening, since temperatures are usually lower there than in the house itself.

On record, for example, is one where night temperatures dropped to 35° and 40° F., and where only a small amount of electric radiation supplemented the effects of the sun during the day. Here begonias and geraniums bloomed incessantly. The cyclamen, with never a yellow leaf, opened bud after bud for a full 3 months. Primroses and paper-white narcissus kept fresh for extra weeks, while ivies, wax plants, *Asparagus* 'Sprengeri', many ferns (even maidenhairs), and strawberry-begonias maintained marvelous health. Of course these plants were all set back somewhat from the glass and, if outdoor temperatures threatened to go below 20° F., they were covered at night with newspapers.

When plants develop weak, soft, spindly growth, foliage color is light, and buds blast or fall prematurely, it is very often because they are suffering from too warm an atmosphere.

Air conditioning is not generally harmful. In areas of high humidity in summer, it is beneficial, a safeguard against leaf rot. However, air conditioning can have a drying effect, decreasing the atmospheric humidity so that plants require extra water.

Humidity

The greatest foe to successful indoor gardening, however, is lack of humidity. Outdoors the air is moist. Inside it is usually much too dry. This results in parched foliage, especially on English ivy, even when the owner has never neglected moistening the soil.

Now how can humidity be increased? A humidifying device can be added to the furnace or a room humidifier, cool-vapor not hot-steam type, placed in the room where plants are growing. Supplying the window garden with metal or plastic trays filled with 2 to 3 inches of pebbles is probably the easiest means of increasing humidity. Excess water from the pots runs through to the trays, and more water is added as needed to keep the level just below the surface pebbles. (Plants must never stand in water.) Water beneath the pebbles serves as a source of evaporation for constantly moistening the air circulating about the plants.

An occasional cleansing of the foliage with water from a sprayer during the day keeps house plants in good condition and free from insect pests.

Extra-large, pebble-filled saucers with water can be set under each plant or, better yet, large trays that will hold several plants can be used. Furthermore, humidity as well as cleanliness is increased if plants are frequently sprayed from a bulb syringe or set under a shower or faucet. Usually this can be managed only monthly or weekly, while a light syringing may be a daily matter. But again there must be interpretation according to individuals. The hairy-leaved African-violet, gloxinia, and rex begonia, and the tightly crowned cyclamen or pandanus, may be harmed by heavy showering, but light misting also benefits these. Always use room-temperature water.

Watering

The question most often asked by house-plant growers is, "How often should I water my house plants?" or, "Is there a rule, so much water for so much soil?"

Only in a very general way can a rule be offered. *When the topsoil feels dry to the touch, then it is time to water*. Then water so thoroughly that the entire root system is saturated and in a little while excess seeps out into the pot saucer. Empty this excess from the saucer; roots rot if pots stand in water.

The most important "Beware" in connection with watering applies to the little-and-often method. Pouring water on plants just for the fun of it does them no good. Often it results in a too-wet upper half of soil and a too-dry lower. Especially is this true of thick-rooted plants such as palms or very large specimens of almost any plant, particularly those of the shrubby type—gardenia, azalea, and the like. All such are wisely set,

Use a mister with a fine spray to increase the humidity temporarily. Several mistings a day can be very beneficial.

about once a week, in a pail filled with water to within an inch of the pot rim. Here they remain until enough moisture has been drawn up to make the surface feel moist. Then they are removed in a thoroughly refreshed condition, especially if tops are syringed at the time.

Most plants are safely moistened by applying water at the edge of the pot rim. Some with thick crowns, like the cyclamen or bird's-nest fern, are better moistened from below by pouring water into the saucer and letting the plant draw it up according to its need. Saved rainwater is better than faucet water, especially in places where the local supply has been treated with chemicals, the residue from which often collects on the soil and discolors the containers. Room-temperature water also is better than cold, which may have a retarding effect on growth. Most plants, however, are fairly tolerant and given regular care will not be too fussy about the type of water supplied, only the amount. Actually, most beginners tend to overwater rather than to neglect. Experience reveals which plants, like the African-violet, begonia, cyclamen, and ferns, want a "just-moist" soil at all times; while others, notably the jade plant, many of the cacti, and the sansevieria, thrive only when allowed to become quite dry between drinks.

In addition to the drinking habits of the plant itself, other factors influencing the amount of water required are: the size of pot (little ones dry out faster); the type of pot (plastic ones permit less evaporation); the stage of plant growth, whether active or resting; and the temperature of the room. The weather is also a factor: on sunny days more water is required than during dull ones. All these conditions are to be taken into consideration. Complicated as all this may sound, however, it soon becomes second nature to water the poinsettia twice a day and the big jade plant only once in 10 days, when the feel of the soil is made the actual guide.

Ventilation

A close atmosphere is very hard on house plants. Even when the weather is definitely cold, they require a fresh atmosphere. The best plan then is to admit fresh air indirectly through a window or door in an adjoining room, or through a window ventilator in the same room, but not directly beside the plants. It is most important to provide an abundance of fresh air for several weeks after plants are brought in in autumn; and again in spring, as the midday hours become increasingly warm.

Where manufactured gas is used for heating and cooking, plenty of fresh air is especially necessary; but even this will not counteract the effects of escaping gas, the fumes of which spell ultimate death to most plants. Some of them are extremely allergic to gas. The Jerusalem-cherry, for instance, is one of these. First it drops all the fruit, then the leaves shrivel, and finally the plant dies. Natural gas, however, is not harmful to plants.

Air is essential to the roots as well as to the tops of plants. A constant loose condition of the surface soil, and hence aeration of the roots, is readily obtained by an occasional stirring with a fork.

Pruning and Training

Plants are kept shapely by being turned frequently so that all sides receive an equal amount of light, and by the cutting back of overlong growth, which tends to make ungainly specimens. Sometimes, too, a drastic pruning back is necessary to promote health. Thus in autumn the summer geraniums are cut back to stubs 3 to 6 inches long, while the dormant poinsettia in summer is started all over again by hard pruning.

Fertilizing

Extra fertilizer is not nearly so important as good texture and structure of soil and proper potting. Sickly plants especially are more likely to be suffering from too much heat and water, or from some insect pest, than from starvation. Usually a plant from the grower requires no extra nutrients for a month or more. If a plant is at a standstill when, by all the rules of its own nature and the time of year, it should be growing, or when its buds are not maturing, or its foliage color is poor—although a proper system of culture is maintained—then extra feeding definitely is to be considered. Generally speaking, flowering plants require more nutrients than foliage ones, at least up to the time the buds show color. Plants growing under fluorescent lights require more food than those at windows. For slow-growing plants, occasional light top dustings of complete fertilizer are good. Any one of the "complete" fertilizers especially prepared for house plants is excellent, provided directions are followed and it is not assumed that because a little is good for a plant a lot will be better. Nor should a resting plant be "pushed" with a quick-acting fertilizer when the need is for quiet and not for action. Thus the summer-weary geranium or wax plant in fall requires not fertilizer but coolness and time to resuscitate itself.

Certain items are *not* suitable fertilizers—notably tea, coffee, cigar ashes, castor oil, and leftover alcoholic beverages!

Repotting

When a plant has actually outgrown its living quarters (when, after the pot is removed, a fine web of roots is seen on the outside of the earth ball), that plant needs another container, but probably one only a size larger. Usually established plants need shifting only once a year; some only once in 2 years. Often, worn-out soil can be carefully washed from the roots of a large plant and the plant then repotted in the same size pot.

Repotting is not a panacea. A too-large pot with unneeded amounts of soil and moisture more often kills an ailing plant than cures it. The best general policy is to keep plants in as small pots as possible. Overlarge antique specimens of plants, dear as they may be sentimentally, are rarely, when dispassionately viewed, very attractive in themselves or as part of the general window-garden arrangement. Institutional-size plants do not belong in people's houses, nor do sickly plants which, outside a greenhouse, will be unlikely to regain health under the trying conditions of most houses in winter.

The best time for repotting is in spring; then the resulting shock is offset by months of ideal outdoor life. In the spring, when the weather is settled, a practical plan is to take all the plants outdoors, discard some, divide others (repotting the divisions into smaller pots), and then shift the remainder into larger pots.

Arranged in a row, small to large, with a few pots on hand larger than any already in use, plants are easily repotted—the largest plants going into the new pots, which if of clay have first been soaked in a pail of water for 24 hours, and the others, successively, to the outgrown pots, which are thoroughly scrubbed out before receiving new occupants.

Plants are readily depotted for examination or repotting if they are first watered and then inverted on the gardener's left hand, with the main stem placed between the index and middle fingers. The pot rim is then knocked sharply against a table or step. So loosened, the pot is lifted off by the right hand and the root condition examined.

When needed, a larger pot is fitted with an arching piece of broken flowerpot above the drainage hole and, if it is above a 3-inch size, a few more pieces of broken crock are fitted over this. In large pots a handful of gravel or pebbles is placed above the "crocking" and a drainage layer of coarse compost or sphagnum moss (saved from mail-order packing) is spread over this. (When pots have no hole, the drainage layer of this coarse material is especially necessary; also a bit of charcoal mixed in the soil to ensure "sweetness.")

When the drainage layer is in place, a sifting of soil is added. Then the plant is centered in the pot and extra soil firmly pressed around it with a potting stick—a piece of lath or an old ruler. The soil is kept ½ inch or so below the rim of the pot, this space being needed to receive water.

Potting Soils

Although there are almost as many soil formulas as there are types of house plants, it is a matter of experience that plants try to accustom themselves to any soil that is of proper texture or friability and well drained. A generally good formula (which may be altered in its proportions according to the type of plant to be grown) consists of 1 part loam from vegetable or flower garden, 1 part compost or other humus such as leafmold, commercial humus, or peat moss, and 1 part sand (builder's, not seashore) or perlite. For enrichment, a 4-inch pot of a complete fertilizer is added to a wheelbarrowload, or its close equivalent, of soil or 1 teaspoonful to an 8-inch pot of soil.

The loam contains nutrients, sand facilitates drainage and aeration of roots, while humus materials increase the water-holding capacity and thus prevent too-rapid evaporation of moisture and caking of soil. Humus also helps to produce a light, mellow mixture which roots can easily penetrate. To these essentials may be added, when convenient, a little charcoal to "sweeten" the soil (especially in pots lacking a drainage hole).

Apartment gardeners as well as others who value convenience can procure ready-made soil mixtures from florists or hardware stores or artificial soil mixes compiled according to the famous Cornell and other universities' formulas. Versions of these are available under such trade names as Jiffy Mix, Readi-Earth, etc. These mixes usually include vermiculite, sphagnum peat, superphosphate, limestone, and a complete fertilizer. Using prepackaged potting mixes is an easy way to avoid soil pests and disease organisms frequently found in garden soils.

If the plants have heavy roots—such as those of pandanus, sansevieria, or palm—less sand and more loam is used, because such roots have force enough to penetrate a firm mixture, and the plants prefer it. The fibrous-rooted ferns, begonias, and fuchsias thrive in a lighter medium—about ½ leafmold or peat moss, ½ loam, and plenty of sand.

Summer Quarters

Summer is the ideal time for all plants with future possibilities to be resuscitated after the trying months indoors. Summer quarters can be established outdoors on porches, terraces, breezeways, or in garden beds. (Even a cool, light window indoors will do, if plenty of fresh air is available.) Wherever placed, the plants should be out of the way of strong winds and grouped to facilitate watering and syringing. Pots are not removed because house plants, freed of their containers, develop in an open garden bed such extensive root systems that autumn repotting becomes almost impossible.

It is a healthful procedure to place your plants in a garden bed that offers suitable gradations of light for the varying needs of sun-loving geraniums and shade-requiring ferns. A location under some open-leaved tree, like an apple or a honey locust or an oak, with branches not too low, is ideal. Nearest to the trunk, where the shade is deepest, go the ferns; below the open branches in light shade are set resting geraniums and heliotrope, vines, foliage plants, and most of the flowering subjects: gardenias, azaleas, fuchsias, and shade-loving begonias; near the edge, but not under the overhang, where sun daily penetrates, are placed the young geraniums, wax begonias, and poinsettias.

A bed is dug deep enough to contain the largest pot, plus a 3-inch layer of stones or other worm-deterring drainage material. Here the plants are arranged according to their light requirements, and around them is packed light soil containing plenty of water-holding humus, preferably peat moss. When placing is completed, pot rims remain slightly above the soil surface. About once a week each plant is turned. This prevents anchoring roots from taking hold through the drainage hole, and also facilitates the development of shapely tops.

The watering of house plants should not be forgotten in summer. Even when placed outside, they require, because of their restricted root systems and location under tree branches, more frequent watering than average summer rainfall supplies.

The best procedure is to let a hose with its nozzle removed trickle slowly into the bed for a period long enough to moisten it completely to a depth of 6 inches. This will suffice for a week or 10 days even in hot weather. During long, hot, dry spells, an oscillating sprinkler played on the bed through the late afternoon hours will give the plants a lift. The cool night hours to follow should revive them completely.

An ordinary rotary sprinkler should not be used unless it produces a fine spray, for heavy drops falling successively in the same spot or on the same leaf or flower over a long period may do more harm than good.

Some pruning may be required to promote shapely growth, and insect pests must always be watched for. Usually frequent hose syringing deters them, but sometimes, as in winter, aphids or mealybugs must be sprayed with an insecticide.

Plants in Autumn

Plants are prepared for winter well before frost. It is a good precaution to remove the pot from each specimen and, if necessary, to renew the drainage arrangements. At this season, however, roots should be disturbed as little as possible.

Plants should be brought inside before the first touch of frost, for many are from the tropics, and hence are easily harmed by cool fall weather. Pots should be scrubbed and tops sprayed with an insecticide. Then set plants on a sheltered porch or terrace for a week or so, when another spraying is given. During the first weeks indoors much attention to ventilation and syringing is necessary. Now more than at other times plants are particularly inclined to resent the dry, close air of the house. Falling leaves and blossoms are signs of unfavorable reaction. A thorough drenching under a faucet will often immediately check leaf dropping. This is also the time for insect pests to attack. A sharp eye should be kept out for these and an all-purpose house-plant aerosol bomb used if any pests are discovered.

If a systemic is mixed in the potting soil, many pests are unlikely to appear. The material, drawn up through all parts of the plant, is lethal to insects that suck and particularly efficacious against whitefly. The systemic must be used exactly according to the manufacturer's directions.

Rest Period

All plants have growth cycles that include periods of rest. As trees lose their leaves in fall and enter into a dormant period, so do house plants at some time rest in greater or lesser degree. In winter, ferns and palms are less active and produce fewer new leaves than in spring. In early fall many of the cacti remain utterly quiet. After flowering, some plants, such as cyclamens, appear on the point of death, when really they are only going to sleep.

All plants that are resting require less water and warmth than when they are in a period of active growth. None should be fed at this time. The resting condition of plants is not always an easy one to identify, but constant observation of each kind eventually reveals it, and the indoor gardener is accordingly guided in the treatment given them.

General Culture

SOIL

Are all house plants potted in the same soil mixture?   No, there are variations in soil mixtures for different types of plants, although most house plants do very well in general-purpose mixtures. (See the following questions.)

What is a good standard or general-purpose potting mixture for house plants?   Two parts garden loam, 1 part leafmold or peat moss, 1 part sharp sand. For general use, add 1 pint of a complete fertilizer and 2 quarts of a commercial cow manure, or well-rotted cow manure if available, to each bushel of mixture.

An alternate (although more expensive) approach is to purchase ready-to-use commercially packaged potting mixtures, which are free from weed seeds and pests. Common garden soil often contains organisms that are harmful to house plants. Some of these mixtures contain soil and some, such as Jiffy Mix and Readi-Earth, are soilless. They can save time and trouble and can be modified to fit specific plant requirements. For example, sand and fine gravel can be added for desert cactus or fine fir-bark chips for jungle cactus and columneas, extra-coarse peat moss for azaleas and gardenias.

What are the proportions of a typical soilless growing medium? I would like to mix my own to save money. One bushel of vermiculite; 1 bushel of peat moss; 1¼ cup of ground limestone (preferably dolomitic); ½ cup of 20 per cent superphosphate; 1 cup of 5–10–5 fertilizer. Mix thoroughly before using.

What mixture of soil is best for azaleas and other acid-loving plants? Add to a standard potting mixture (see the previous question) 25 per cent in bulk acid (hardwood) leafmold or peat moss, and to each bushel, add 2 quarts of a commercial (dehydrated) cow manure and 1 pint of a complete fertilizer.

What mixture of soil do I need for ferns grown indoors? A fibrous mixture. Add to the standard potting mixture 25 per cent in bulk leafmold, compost, or peat moss, 2 quarts of a commercial manure, and 1 pint of a complete fertilizer.

How shall I prepare the potting mixture for house plants which need an alkaline soil—some herbs, for instance? To each bushel of standard mixture, add 1 quart raw ground limestone, 1 pint bone meal, and 2 quarts well-rotted or commercial cow manure. Some potted herbs, such as rosemary or lavender, benefit from an occasional dusting of wood ashes from the fireplace, which should immediately be watered into the soil.

What potting soil shall I use for desert cacti and other succulents? A sandy mixture. Add 25 per cent in bulk sharp sand or crushed soft stone (or crushed flowerpots) to a standard potting mixture (see the previous question). Add to each bushel 1 quart raw ground limestone and 1 pint complete fertilizer or bone meal. Make up the mixture 2 weeks or more before its use. (See Cacti.)

Do tender bulbs, such as amaryllis, tuberous-rooted begonias, etc., need a special potting soil? Yes. Place 1 to 2 inches of manure or rich compost in the bottom of the pot, and for potting soil use well-rotted compost. If compost and cow manure are not available, use 1 part garden loam, 1 part peat moss or leafmold, and add to each bushel 3 quarts of a commercial (dehydrated) cow manure and 1 part complete fertilizer.

Which house plants prefer peat moss in the soil? Please add information concerning its use. Most house plants can tolerate peat moss in the potting soil, as it is a source of humus. Azaleas and gardenias thrive with up to 50 per cent coarse peat in a potting mix.

What do you think of the prepared potting soils sold by garden cen-

ters and stores? Most of these are well-balanced mixtures suitable for African-violets, begonias, ferns, etc. Although they do differ in quality and usefulness, there is little way of judging them until you try them and see the plant's performance. More reliable are the soilless mixes, which consist of formulas devised by Cornell University and the University of California.

How should the soil surrounding house plants be prevented from getting solid? Is there any danger of cutting rootlets if the soil is dug in to loosen it? Stir the shallow, surface soil frequently. Use the soil mixtures recommended in the previous questions. Then spread a little fresh soil on top if the soil appears "watered down."

POTTING AND REPOTTING

Which are better: clay or plastic pots? Most plants grow well in both, as long as cultural care is satisfactory. As a rule, those in plastic pots need less water than those in clay. Plastic is easy to keep clean. Some modern plastic pots look like wood or ceramic, come with snap-on saucers, and are available in different colors. But top-heavy plants in small plastic pots often tip over, especially when the lightweight soilless mixes are used.

What size pots are best for winter-blooming plants? It depends on the plant and its stage of growth; 3½-, 4-, and 4½-inch pots suit most of them. As a rule, flowering plants give more bloom if grown in pots just big enough to hold the roots.

Should the soil on a potted plant be changed? If so, how often? See the introduction to this section.

When should house plants be repotted? This varies with the kind of plant. A good general rule is to repot each year in the spring when plants are taken outdoors. Some, such as agapanthus, need attention only every few years. It is best to examine the roots in the spring when the plants are first taken out.

How can I tell when my plants need repotting? When the plants are knocked gently from their pots (see the introduction to this section) the root system shows whether repotting is necessary. If roots have formed a thick, dry web on the outside of the root ball, repot. If visible roots are few and appear succulent and healthy, return to the same pot; if a rotted condition is seen, knock off as much soil as possible, cut back any soft roots, and plant in a smaller pot with fresh soil.

When repotting house plants, how much larger should the new pot be? Usually one size larger is adequate. Overpotting does not produce healthy plants. (See the introduction.) For most plants, use one size larger in the spring for plants that are to be sunk in garden beds in their pots. For fast-growing wax begonias and impatiens, use two sizes larger. Even so, these may need fall repotting in spite of this precaution.

How should tender bulbs be potted for indoor bloom? Most of these bulbs, such as amaryllis, calla-lily, and tuberous-rooted begonia, are planted with the top third of the bulb exposed.

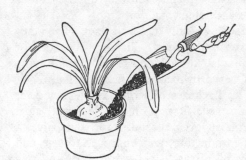

With some bulbs (such as amaryllis) and other plants in large pots, the soil is renewed (usually yearly), without repotting, by removing as much as possible of the old soil and then refilling with new soil.

How can I provide good drainage in the pots of my house plants? Place a bit of broken flowerpot, curved side up, over the drainage hole of small pots before adding soil. For 4-inch or larger pots, use several pieces of this "crocking"; for large bulb pans and large pots, cover the entire bottom with broken bits of pot, always being sure that the piece which covers the drainage hole is placed so as to allow the free outflow of water. Then spread a thin layer of roughage, such as gravel, small driveway stones, unmilled sphagnum moss, or very coarse compost.

FEEDING

When shall I feed my house plants? See the introduction to this section.

What fertilizers are best for house plants? In the questions on Soil in this section and in the introduction, recommendations are made for fertilizing the soil mixtures. In addition to this, complete fertilizers may be given in liquid or tablet form according to package directions. Instant liquid cow manure is easily prepared from a commercial mix. An organic fish-emulsion fertilizer is useful for many plants and available from garden centers and house-plant specialists. Special foods are sold for some plants, such as African-violets. (See Culture of Specific Plants.)

Do you think liquid manure is a good fertilizer for house plants? Yes. It gives excellent results. You can use it sparingly about once a week on plants in active growth that prefer a pot-bound condition (amaryllis, pandanus, palms, nerines, etc.) and on plants that bloom steadily with every watering if you apply a very weak mixture.

Several of my house plants look very sick indeed. Shall I give them fertilizer? It is wise to discard such plants, for they rarely can be brought back to health under average home conditions.

What is the proper means of feeding plants that were grown from cuttings as house plants to carry over until spring? Plants propagated for carrying over to spring, or old plants cut back and potted for the same purpose, don't need feeding until new growth shows toward spring.

What do the numbers mean on packages of fertilizers? They refer to the three basic elements—nitrogen, first, promotes leaf and stem strength and stimulates growth; phosphorus, second, is for roots, gives a steady push to flower and seed production, and improves foliage and flower color; potash, third, wards off disease, stabilizes growth, and also intensifies color. (See Section 1.)

Is black tea of any value to ferns? No.

WATERING

What is a good general rule for watering house plants? Water only when the plants *need* water, not whenever it seems that they may stand watering. Whenever water is supplied, give enough to saturate thoroughly the whole ball of soil. Never merely sprinkle the surface.

How often should one water house plants—namely, ferns, wax begonias, and geraniums? Watering is governed by the temperature and humidity of a room. Keep geraniums barely on the dry side if they are not actively growing; begonias and ferns in a room of 60° to 70° F. will need water almost every day. The feel of the soil is the best guide.

Can you tell me why growing house plants rot or decay from the roots up? This sounds like overwatering. Do not permit the plants to stand with their roots soaking in water. Surplus water should be poured from the saucer after each watering, and water should be given only when the surface of the soil feels dry—or almost dry.

What can be done to counteract the effect of watering house plants with the hard water we have in this locality? If the hardness of the water is merely due to lime, use an acid fertilizer such as sulfate of ammonia.

Do plants kept in the cellar in winter need much water? If the cellar is poorly lighted and not warm, the plants should be kept fairly dry. Most modern basements are too hot.

How can I give enough water to azaleas, hydrangeas, and other house plants which seem to dry out completely? Once a week, when the topsoil is a little dry, set the potted plant in a pail or dishpan of water so that the water is absorbed from the opening in the bottom of the pot and the soil is thoroughly soaked.

How can I keep my house plants from having "wet feet"? Pot them properly and place a handful of large pebbles or gravel in the saucer under each pot or in the tray or on the shelf on which the pots are set. If there is surplus water, the pebbles will provide good drainage.

Must all flower pots have drainage? Plants can be grown in pots without drainage and no outlet for surplus water, but care must be taken not to overwater. During the winter and spring, narcissus and some other bulbs can be grown in pebbles in pots without a hole at the bottom.

How often should house plants in glazed pots be watered? More sparingly than those in clay pots since evaporation does not occur through the walls as with clay pots. A quart of charcoal bits added to each bushel of potting soil helps keep the mixture "sweet."

How often should plants in plastic pots be watered? Usually less often than those in clay pots because of slower evaporation, but let the feel of the soil guide you. As a rule, a plant in a clay pot may need water every day; one in plastic, only every second or third day.

TEMPERATURE

What temperature is best for most house plants? Many flowering house plants are happiest at 55° F. or lower. Cineraria and calceolaria prefer 45° F. That's why so many people fail with house plants in hot rooms. It also explains why cyclamen, Jerusalem-cherry, ornamental pepper, etc., last such a short time after coming from the florist. If your home is kept at 70° F. or above, day and night, grow semitropical foliage plants, cacti and succulents, African-violets, some orchids, and poinsettias. If a low night temperature can be maintained, many plants preferring a cool temperature will do quite well.

Why do my house plants die within a short time—all except a Chinese-evergreen and some ivy, both in water? I tried different soil and fertilizers. I put them in the sun and in the shade with no result. They grow nicely outside in the summer but die in the house even in the sum-

mertime. Probably too high temperature, too low humidity, poor drainage, or too much water or a combination of these factors.

I am determined to keep my house temperature at 65° F. during the day and 60° F. at night to cut down on my oil bill. How will this affect my vast and varied house-plant collection that has formerly done quite well at winter temperatures about 70° F.? Your house plants should do very well. The majority of house plants prefer cooler temperatures. African-violets and some of the other strictly tropical plants prefer warmer temperatures, but they should adjust and continue to bloom well, especially if you grow them under fluorescent lights where the temperature will be a few degrees higher.

What plants can be grown in an unheated but enclosed breezeway? I am trying geraniums, sweet marjoram, parsley, sage, winter savory, and ivies. Your suggestions will be appreciated. (New Jersey.) Such a room in winter is difficult, since in severe weather everything will freeze. However, if you can protect the plants when the temperature dips below freezing and remains there, you may have success. Other plants to try are azaleas, chrysanthemums, camellias, Norfolk-Island-pine, and French lavender.

Will house plants survive in a home that has a temperature of 75° F.? They may survive or even do well if the temperature drops to 60° F. at night. When high temperatures are the rule, house plants are apt to develop many difficulties such as falling leaves and buds, pests and diseases, and general unthriftiness. Tropicals such as African-violets, poinsettias, semitropical foliage plants, etc., are exceptions to the rule when humidity can be kept above 40 per cent.

Why do house plants do well in country farmhouses? Because the temperature is low, especially at night, and the humidity high, due to a lack of central heating. The steaming kettle on the farm kitchen range is a first-class humidifier. Although most farmhouses today have central heating, their rooms are generally cooler and better lighted than those of most city apartments and suburban houses.

Is a very cool sun porch suitable for house plants in the winter? If the night temperature is safely above freezing, house plants such as camellia, azalea, gardenia, and cymbidium orchids, which prefer coolness (see individual plants), will be far happier there than in the warmer living room.

VENTILATION

Do my house plants need fresh air in the winter? Yes, decidedly.

See that fresh air is admitted daily to the room where they are kept, but avoid direct drafts. A window or door opened for half an hour each day in an adjoining room will provide the needed ventilation. (See the introduction to this section.)

SUMMER CARE

What shall I do with my house plants in the summer? See the introduction to this section.

How can I arrange my house plants outdoors in a garden bed so that they will receive the right amount of sunshine and shade? Choose a location near a water supply where part of the bed receives morning sun and partial shade. Place geraniums and other flowering, sun-loving plants in the sunniest location. Ferns, foliage plants, and other shade lovers go in the shade.

What house plants suffer from being sunk in a garden bed in the summer? African-violets and other gesneriads, calla-lily, most begonias, and other delicate-leaved plants cannot endure beating rains and winds. Place these on a sheltered terrace or at an open window.

Will house plants take care of themselves if sunk in garden beds in the summer? Rarely, and only if there is adequate rainfall. In a drought, they must be watered slowly and deeply by letting the hose run into the ground around them with the nozzle removed. Keep weeds down and cultivate the soil occasionally.

AUTUMN CARE

When should house plants be brought indoors in autumn? At least 2 to 3 weeks before you plan to turn on the heat, and of course before frost. This permits plants to acclimate gradually to the more difficult winter environment of the house. A few kinds of cold-hardy plants should not be rushed indoors. They include Thanksgiving and Christmas cacti, citrus plants, and azaleas.

How shall I prepare my house plants for the autumn move to the house? Two weeks before they come in, loosen the pots in the ground. Prune back long, unsightly branches. If the plants tend to wither, prune more severely. At the end of a week, lift the pots and place the plants on a sheltered patio or against a retaining wall where they will have outdoor light and air. At the end of a 2-week period from first loosening the pots in the ground, scrub the pots, spray for pests, and remove them to the house.

Do house plants need special care when they first come indoors in autumn? Yes, the leaves of glossy-foliaged plants should be frequently syringed. Water moderately. Ventilation should be good. Pests are apt to appear now. Keep a close watch and have an aerosol spray handy.

Is it possible to leave coleus, geraniums, and begonias in the ground during the winter (covering them for protection) or should they be taken into the house? (New Jersey.) They positively will die however well you protect them. Take cuttings of those you want. There is only one begonia that is hardy with protection, the tuberous *Begonia grandis*.

What shall I do with fuchsias, lantanas, and other summer bloomers when they come indoors in the fall? Place in a cool cellar window or a cold (but never freezing) sun or plant room. Water very sparingly until new growth appears in late winter. Then cut them back and give them light and more water.

What shall I do for house plants that turn brown when brought in the house during the winter? I am losing all of my plants. Grow them cooler. Do not overwater. See that they get fresh air. Cut back withered portions. Check your humidity.

VACATION CARE

How can I safely leave my plants when I go away in the winter for two to three weeks? One way is to get a "plant sitter" who knows plants and will follow your written instructions for their care. Or leave them untended and turn down the thermostat to 60° F. Water the plants (to the moist, not soggy, stage), remove buds, open flowers, and any old leaves. Place each plant in a light, not sunny, place. Cover with a plastic bag held by a long enough stake to keep the plastic from

There are various means available to ensure house-plant survival while the gardener is on vacation. One of the most simple, good for 2 to 3 weeks, is encasing the plant's pot in a plastic bag that is closed around the stem. Some gardeners prefer to enclose the pot and the entire plant in a plastic bag.

touching the foliage. Cut a small hole in each bag to allow for more ventilation.

When I go away in the summer, how can I leave my plants untended? I have a great many. Two New Jersey indoor gardeners give these directions for a two-week summer absence. One gardener says, "Take one, or more, large cartons. Put on cellar floor. Fill with sphagnum moss. Wet down until thoroughly soaked. Allow plants to go without watering until leaves are limp enough to pack pots closely. Remove blossoms, water well from the top, and pack. Be sure to leave a window slightly open. The plants will do all right without much light in the cellar for a couple of weeks, but they *must* have fresh air." The other gardener tells how she sets her plants on a well-soaked 2-inch layer of builder's sand in a big washtub in which she rigs up a wick system. A canvas ironing board cover serves as a wick. One end is pushed well down in the sand under the plants; the other rests in a big pail of water placed beside the tub. This system works for a week or more, depending on the rate of evaporation.

EXPOSURE

What flowers and vines are suitable for a mostly sunny (full west exposure) window? Most flowering plants including amaryllis, geranium, abutilon, shrimp-plant, miniature roses, kalanchoe, oxalis, cacti and other succulents, forced spring bulbs, chrysanthemums, veltheimia, citrus plants, herbs, azaleas, most begonias, and many orchids, such as miniature cymbidiums. *Vines:* tradescantia, Kenilworth-ivy, *Campanula isophylla,* nasturtium, and morning glories.

Which house plants will grow in a window in the winter? It has all of the morning sun. Flowering plants that will keep blooming if the temperature is not high (55° F. at night) are primroses, bouvardia, begonia, impatiens, and all kinds of bulbs which potted in the fall will keep up a succession, including paper-white and other narcissus (daffodils), amaryllis, veltheimia, and the other plants listed above.

What house plants will blossom with only 2 or 3 hours of sunshine during the winter months? The small-flowered begonias are dependable; also, various bulbs potted in the fall will help out. African-violets and bromeliads will sometimes bloom without direct sunshine. Four to six hours of sun will give more and better-colored flowers.

What house plants would you suggest for east windows partially shaded most of the time, and in a steam-heated room which is consistently overheated? Why expect the impossible? Plants will not tolerate extreme heat unless they are tropical subjects that require high humidity, which almost never prevails in overheated rooms. About the only things we can suggest are sansevieria (snake plant) and the kangaroo-vine (*Cissus antarctica*). Both can stand dryness and warmth to an unusual degree.

What house plants are suitable for rooms having little sunshine? Much depends upon the temperature maintained. Dry, hot rooms will kill anything, but if the temperature is moderate and you maintain a fair amount of humidity, you can grow small palms, ferns, ivies, philodendrons, many large-leaved begonias, bromeliads, and tropical-foliage plants.

What plants can be grown in a sun porch without southern exposure? Almost anything you fancy if there is sufficient heat during winter to keep the night temperature around 45° F. Both blooming and foliage plants from the florists will get along in such a porch.

What flowers and vines are suitable for a shaded window? Begonias, lobelia, English ivy, German-ivy, variegated panicum, strawberry-geranium, trailing fuchsia, creeping fig, grape-ivy, Kenilworth-ivy, ceropegia, chlorophytum, palms, Chinese-evergreen, dracaena, dieffenbachia, nephthytis, rubber plants, and ferns. Keep the night temperature down to 55° F. if possible.

What flowering house plants can be grown successfully without a great amount of sunshine? Other than wax begonias and bromeliads, you won't find many that will bloom in poor light. The room temperature counts for a lot, and if about 65° F. in the day and about 50° F. at night, you can expect all kinds of ferns, palms, and ivies to get along well. Better install fluorescent tubes if your plants receive less than 4 hours of sunshine daily.

Can I keep house plants in a west window? Yes, plants that do not need full sunlight, such as African-violets, large-leaved begonias, foliage plants, ivies, etc.

What plants other than Chinese-evergreen and nephthytis will grow in water in a northern exposure? Philodendron, tradescantia, English ivy, grape-ivy, redwood burls, and umbrella-plant (*Cyperus alternifolius*).

What can I grow in a north window? All kinds of ferns, ivies, philodendron, and other foliage plants; African-violets; large-leaved begonias; pick-a-back plant; bromeliads; strawberry-begonia.

ENVIRONMENT

What are the conditions under which my house plants will flourish in the winter? See the introduction to this section.

The atmosphere in my house in the winter is very dry and I have difficulty getting house plants to live. Place humidifiers on your radiators or stand your house plants on pebbles in water-filled trays to increase humidity. See that they get fresh air daily, without direct drafts.

Does coal gas injure house plants? Yes, it is deadly, even in very small amounts.

Does cooking gas affect house plants? Manufactured gas is harmful only if there is a leak. Natural gas does no harm.

How does a plant room differ from a greenhouse? A plant room, usually opening off a living room, dining room, or hall, makes it possible to enjoy and care for plants easily, as part of the room is used for everyday living. If there is sun, and humidity is maintained with pebble-filled trays of water, most plants do almost as well as in a greenhouse; tending them is a more incidental and personal procedure. Also, the plant room can be a very decorative addition to your house. Usually light comes only from windows and doors, not through the roof. A greenhouse of glass or plastic offers a more businesslike, less decorative way of raising plants with greater control of heat and humidity.

What is a lath house? This is a structure made of laths or slats that admits a good circulation of air but only about half the usual amount of light. Slats are usually set about an inch apart.

Is it possible in Connecticut to grow plants in a lath house like those you see in California? It can serve in the summer as protection for tender foliage from strong sun but it is not for year-round use in cold areas, as it is for tropical and subtropical regions. There, the lath house is much used for growing orchids and ferns.

Is the cold from windows injurious to plants? Definitely so, if the plants are tender kinds; take them out of the window at night or place thick paper between the glass and plants. Cold drafts are very bad. Various kinds of plastic sheeting are useful to put between the plants and the glass in freezing weather.

What house plants can be easily kept in a hot, dry room with only a small amount of diffused sunlight? No plant can thrive in a hot, dry room, but some of the cacti and other succulents can put up with a lot if kept mostly dry during the winter.

Do plants grow under incandescent light? Yes, incandescent light can be used as a substitute for sunlight, although plants do better under natural conditions or under fluorescent light. Incandescent light is very hot and can harm plants too close to it.

How do you grow house plants under artificial light? Install fluorescent light fixtures over the bench or table on which the plants are to be grown. The tubes should be 8 to 10 inches above the tops of growing

Many house plants thrive under fluorescent lights, such as this tabletop model, which contains 2 tubes.

plants and long enough to illuminate the entire growing area. Leave the lights on 12 to 14 hours a day for optimum results. Use daylight or white fluorescent tubes, or a combination of the two. Plants require more water and food than under natural conditions. Keep cacti and other succulents very close to the tubes. Orchids will do best with fixtures that hold at least 4 lamps, but they will also thrive with a mixture of sun and fluorescent light. Using lamps over a greenhouse bench and under the bench is an excellent way to supplement sunlight for a too shady greenhouse. You may want to experiment with the special lamps developed for plant growth.

What house plants grow best under artificial light?   African-violets and all their relatives seem particularly happy under these conditions, also many other flowering plants. Among orchids, *Paphiopedilum* and *Miltonia* are some of the orchids that thrive under fluorescents. Planters and carts are available commercially with built-in light fixtures above them, but more reasonable are the general-purpose "shop" lights. For more information, write the Indoor Light Gardening Society of America, 128 West 58th Street, New York, N.Y. 10019.

Why do my house plants have luxuriant foliage but the buds dry up and fall off before opening?   This may be due to high temperatures and low humidity and irregular or too heavy watering. (See Watering, Temperature, and Sanitation.)

What causes the lower leaves on a small palm plant to turn brown and then die? What is the remedy?   Unsuitable soil. Dryness at the root. Dry atmosphere.

How can I prevent plants, grown indoors from seeds or cuttings, from growing spindly?   This is caused by too much warmth and not enough light and humidity. Direct sunshine is needed by most seedlings. Pinch out the tops to make the plants branch. Or grow them under fluorescent lights, about 4 inches from the tubes.

INSECTS AND DISEASES

How can I prevent pests from getting a start on my house plants? Spray all house plants before bringing them inside in the fall. If any specimens from the garden or purchased from a florist are infested with pests of any sort, segregate them and get them entirely clean before letting them join your healthy plants. Make it a habit to look all plants over weekly for possible pests. Sponging with soap and water at intervals checks such pests as scale, mealybugs, and red spider. Keep all dead leaves picked off. Use a pressure-bottle all-purpose house-plant spray as soon as pests are discovered and keep infested plants segregated until clean. Frequent "fogging" or spraying is a good preventative.

What shall I use to get rid of aphids on house plants? Give a strong water spray at the sink for a mild infestation; for a heavy attack, spray with a weak malathion solution or dip the top of the inverted plant in it. A granular insecticide, such as 2 per cent Di-Syston Dexol Systemic House Plant Insecticide, added to the soil according to directions, will control aphids without your having to spray.

What is the best method to clean mealybugs off plants? Place the plants in a bathtub and wash off the bugs by directing a spray of water at them forcibly. Go over hairy-leaved subjects like African-violets with an alcohol-dipped swab.

Kill mealybugs by dabbing them with a cotton swab dipped in alcohol.

How can I get rid of red spider mites on my house plants? Forcibly syringe with clear, cold water, particularly the underside of the foliage.

For heavy infestation, spray with a miticide such as Kelthane or discard the plant.

An occasional cleansing of the foliage with a stream from the hose on plants summering outdoors is recommended. This is especially important just before the plants are brought indoors for the winter.

What is the scalelike pest which adheres closely to the leaves and stems of ivy, and which seems to attract ants? What will kill this pest? It is probably brown scale. Hand-pick a light infestation; for a heavy attack, spray with a weak malathion solution or dip inverted tops of the plant in a basin filled with the solution.

What can be done about white jumping insects in the soil of house plants? These are probably springtails, which usually breed in the organic matter in the soil. Try standing the pots in a vessel of water kept at 110° F. for a few minutes. This temperature is fatal to many insects, and most plants are unaffected by it even when completely immersed. The springtails, however, are harmless.

How can one kill whiteflies? Do these flies hatch in the earth or on the leaves of plants? They are difficult to control on house plants. Repeated sprayings with resmethrin, found in formulas such as Dexol Whitefly Spray and Pratt's Whitefly Spray, have proved to be very efficient. The eggs are small translucent bodies laid on the undersides of the leaves.

SANITATION

How often should house plants be syringed or washed under a spigot? Glossy-leaved plants profit from a monthly syringing or sponging. Fuzzy-leaved plants should be dusted with a camel's-hair brush or very lightly with warm water.

In washing the leaves of house plants, should soap be added to the water? Many green-fingered gardeners do use soapy water in sponging off the foliage of glossy-leaved foliage plants. Plain water is just as good if all dust is removed, unless the plant is infested with red spider, scale, or other pests, when soapy water helps to destroy them.

What causes the white and brownish moldlike substance on the outside of clay flower pots? The white film is the lime or alkali in the clay. Wipe the pots occasionally; scrub with a wire brush dipped in hot soapy water.

Why does the soil of house plants get moldy? It is not mold, but algae, the spores of which are in the air and perhaps in the water. Loosen the surface of the soil occasionally with a fork. Wipe off the pots occasionally.

Why does the soil in my house-plant pots smell sour and musty, and sometimes have a green, mosslike coating on the top? See the introduction to this section on Potting Soils. Bits of charcoal mixed through the soil will help keep it "sweet." Do not overwater; try to admit fresh air daily, without direct drafts. Check the drainage in the pot.

PROPAGATION

How should I take cuttings from house plants and make them grow? Take shoots or tops of the plants, 4 to 6 inches long with firm, but not hard, stem growth. Fill a pot with sandy soil, vermiculite, or other rooting medium, dip the lower ends in a hormone rooting powder, and insert the cuttings around the edge. Make the holes with a stick and press the soil around the cutting firmly. Sink about 1 inch. Shade from the sun and keep only just moist. When growth starts, pot singly. (See also Section 3, Propagation.)

Is there any way of dividing very large house plants so they will not take up so much room in the house? It is usually better to root cuttings, discarding the unwieldy parent plants. Geraniums and many others can be pruned back very severely. Large tropical foliage plants such as dieffenbachia, monstera, and rubber plant can be air-layered.

What can I feed house plants that will encourage blooms? I have a fairly cool room and southern exposure. My geraniums and fuchsias refuse to bloom during the dreary winter months. I have taken my rosemary indoors, but it will not grow in spite of all my efforts. If your geraniums and fuchsias have been in bloom outdoors in summer, they are now resting. Start cuttings in the summer for late-winter bloom. Rosemary can also be readily rooted by cuttings and the young plants will grow more thriftily than the old, sometimes even coming into bloom. Use low-nitrogen fertilizer to encourage bloom. Are they receiving sufficient light?

Which blooming house plants can be started in March? If you have ample light, a temperature not above 68° F., and understand the rudiments of plant raising, you can have success with begonias, African-violets, gloxinias, and other gesneriads. For lower temperatures, cinerarias, primroses, and calceolarias can be grown for temporary color effects.

What is the procedure for starting house plants from seeds, rather than from the usual cuttings? Use milled sphagnum moss. Sow each kind thinly in a pot, making moss fairly firm and level beforehand. Use hot water to moisten the moss. After sowing, cover with glass held several inches above the seed or put the pot inside a clear plastic bag. Give shade and a temperature of 60° to 70° F. Always water from the bottom. Transplant into other pots or window boxes when true leaves show. (Seeds can also be sown in prepackaged soilless mixes and the seedlings can be transplanted into the same mixes. Using these mixes, which are sterile, eliminates disease problems.) The best time for sowing such seeds is between January and March; but some, like primroses, can be sown in June, and cinerarias and calceolarias can be sown in August or September. Miniature plastic greenhouses and casserole dishes with covers that can be lifted for ventilating can be used instead of pots. Seedlings will thrive under fluorescent lights.

What is "damping off" and how can it be prevented? This is a fungus disease prevented by using soilless mixes or by sterilizing the soil or treating the seed with a disinfectant such as benomyl.

How can one start bougainvillea cuttings in the house? Take short side growths or tips 6 inches long. Insert in sandy soil in a small pot or insert several around the edge of the pot. After watering, stand them in a big pot and cover with a plastic bag, giving them a warm place. Don't overwater but never allow to dry.

How can one take cuttings from a rubber tree? *Ficus elastica* can best be propagated by air layering. Make a slanting cut halfway through the stem with a sharp knife, insert a toothpick to keep it open, bind around with a ball of damp sphagnum moss, then wrap tightly with a sheet of plastic film, fastening near each end with wire fasteners. While rooting, stake the branch to avoid breakage. When the moss is filled with roots (3 months or more), cut it from the parent plant and pot the cutting in soil.

Can I start seeds under fluorescent lights? Yes, lights make it possible to get good plants in short order for outdoor planting. Sow seeds on milled sphagnum moss or packaged seed-sowing mixes mentioned above, all of which are available at garden centers or from mail-order seed houses. Set the trays close to the lights, about 3 to 4 inches. If you can't regulate distances by moving the light canopy up and down, then set the tray on inverted flowerpots, big ones at first, then smaller ones as the seedlings grow and have to be placed farther from the lights, about 6 to 8 inches. Give no fertilizer until the seedlings are well advanced, then quarter-strength fertilizer once a week will be about right.

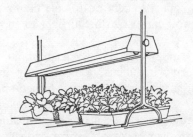

Wax begonias, impatiens, African-violets, and other gesneriads can be started from seed under fluorescent lights.

How can I propagate pick-a-back plant? The small plants on the leaves will quickly root if the leaf is taken off the plant and pegged on the surface of the soil in a pot. This is about the easiest of plants to propagate.

Decorating with House Plants

How can I make a window garden? Have a 12- to 15-inch shelf built to fit a sunny bay, deep-silled window, or in front of one or more windows. Support the shelf with brackets. Buy plastic plant trays in sizes to fit your shelf, available by mail order or from local hardware or garden centers. Trays are green or gray, in 4 × 8-inch to 11 × 22-inch sizes. Fill the trays with pebbles and set the plants on them. Keep the trays filled with water to humidify the atmosphere around the plants, but don't push the pots down into the pebbles where the roots would be kept constantly wet.

What sort of indoor window box do you recommend? A box with a waterproof metal lining will work, but plastic window boxes are less expensive. Some plastic window boxes are made very narrow to fit on small windowsills and other models have clip-on drainage trays. You can plant directly in drained window boxes. Undrained boxes can be used to hold individually potted plants. The pots can be hidden under sheet moss or set on wet gravel or coarse perlite inside the window box. Or the box can be filled with peat moss, into which the pots can be sunk.

Which flowers can be grown in the house throughout the year? I have a planter about 8 × 4 feet; the earth is about 3 feet deep with drainage. A box of this size needs to be in a glassed porch or greenhouse. If your room isn't especially well provided with windows, don't expect all plants to be a success, unless you expect to rely on foliage plants that get along on less light. Of course, you can use artificial light to supplement natural light.

What are sure-to-bloom winter window flowers? Wax begonia, jasmine, many orchids, crown-of-thorns, impatiens, azalea, many bulbs such as paper-white narcissus, veltheimia, amaryllis, and forced spring bulbs.

What are ten good plants for providing a long succession of blooms during the winter? Wax begonia, Rieger begonia, African-violets, and shrimp-plant give constant bloom; paper-white narcissus and hyacinths can be started for succession and are very fragrant; scented geraniums, veltheimia, amaryllis, and jasmines strengthen the picture. Also, you can pick up azaleas and chrysanthemums in flower at your local florist's. Laelia, miniature cymbidiums, and slipper (*Paphiopedilum*) orchids have very long-lasting flowers.

What blooming flowers may I put in my fernery to keep in the house during the winter? I have it in front of south windows, but I have venetian blinds which I keep tilted just a trifle—the sun is not there all day because of the next house. Better give up the idea of much flowering in a fernery that gets no sun, but you might try the African-violet, impatiens, or some of the winter-blooming begonias.

What flowers and other plants can be grown in a window box in the heart of the city? Begonias, geraniums, lobelias, chlorophytum, English ivy, sansevieria, German-ivy, and Kenilworth-ivy. Some dwarf orchids, such as *Epidendrum* and *Oncidium,* will thrive if the light is bright.

What house plants will survive in a city apartment with little or no sunshine? Snake-plant, aspidistra, Chinese-evergreen, English ivy, pothos, tradescantia, bromeliads, palms, fatsia, dieffenbachia, grape-ivy, dracaena, rubber plant (*Ficus elastica* and *F. lyrata*), pandanus, monstera, and peperomia.

What house plants require a great deal of moisture? Calla-lily, Chinese-evergreen, ferns, hydrangea, primula, cineraria, cyclamen, Jerusalem-cherry, baby's-tears.

Which house plants do well if kept on the dry side at the roots? Aloe, bromeliads, agave, crassula, sedum, sansevieria, and other succulents including most cacti (except the orchid cactus).

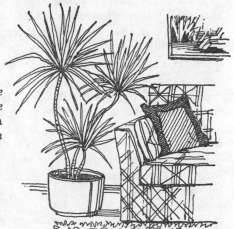

Modern interiors require the presence of large foliage plants, such as this Dracaena marginata, *which is treelike in its growth habit.*

How can I supply needed humidity in the room where I keep my house plants? By fitting humidifiers to the radiators or to the heater; by placing shallow trays or wide saucers filled with pebbles or sand (which must be kept moist) beneath the pots; by spraying the plants more than once a day with a fine atomizer.

Is there any way of safely leaving house plants during a vacation of a week to 10 days without care? Would it be harmful to leave them standing in saucers of water so that they do not dry out? Standing house plants in water is rarely a good idea. An alternative is to water the plants well and then stand the pots in a box packed around with wet paper or peat moss. Set in a cool, not sunny, place and cover with plastic supported by stakes to hold it above the foliage. (See Vacation Care.)

What are the names of some house plants that are easy to raise? Wax and other begonias, most ferns, English ivy, grape-ivy, Swedish-ivy, philodendrons, jasmines, carissa (Natal-plum), sweet-olive, and spider-plant respond well to regular care.

Which low-growing plants would be suitable for house use in small containers without drainage holes? (Michigan.) Containers without drainage or a vent at the bottom will soon sour the soil. If not carefully watered, air is driven from the soil and no plants can stand that. With care you may, for a time, keep ivies, African-violet, cacti, and succulent plants in variety in good shape. Succulents and most cacti need very little water until spring. Mix finely broken bits of charcoal in your potting soil and place a layer of pebbles in the bottom of each container.

What dwarf plants are best suited for growing in small containers to keep on glass window shelves? (Maine.) Small-leaved ivies, Kenilworth-ivy, wax begonias, various ferns, small crotons and other tropical foliage plants, cacti, and succulents in variety; African-violet, *Hoya lacunosa,* miniature orchids, and many others according to fancy, room conditions, light, etc.

How shall I place house plants in a window garden with a southern exposure? Put the flowering plants that need full sun close to the glass. On the edge of the shelf, facing the room, use small-leaved ivies or ferns that do not need sun. Against the walls on each side can go foliage plants with colored leaves to give a variety of color. When the forced bulbs are ready for bloom, these can be placed just behind the ivy, away from the full heat of the sun. Such flowers as amaryllis, primula, and fuchsia can also occupy this less sunny space when they are in bloom.

The only place I have for a window garden gets little sun. Is there any special way to arrange the plants? If plants are used that do not need sun, like the ferns (but which nevertheless require light to perform well), these can be placed next to the glass to give the best effect. Use foliage plants with variegated and colored leaves, like the spider-plant, purple velvet-plant, coleus, and fittonia.

Miniature Gardens

TERRARIUMS

What type of soil should I use in planting a terrarium? Use a packaged terrarium mix or make your own with a third good garden soil, a third humus, and a third sand or perlite with bits of charcoal added to keep the soil "sweet."

How can one make a terrarium? Use any large glass container, like an aquarium; cover the top with a sheet of glass. (A glass or hardware store will cut it for you.) Other possibilities are candy and pickle jars, clear glass wine jugs, covered glass casseroles, Victorian domes, and bubble bowls. Spread a layer of coarse gravel or small stones over the bottom. Add ½ inch of granulated charcoal, then the soil mixture above or whatever mixture is appropriate for the kind of plants you plan to grow.

How should the interior of a terrarium be arranged? After the drainage layer and soil have been placed in the bowl, a grade may be

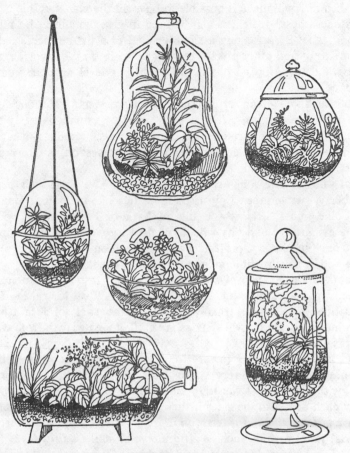

BOTTLE GARDENS AND TERRARIUMS

To the traditional fish bowls and discarded aquariums, long used for terrariums, can be added new or used bottles, ginger jars, and the imaginative hanging "egg" container shown above. Terrariums can be satisfying and successful if a few rules are followed: Don't overwater—once watered, it is unlikely that additional moisture will be required for months unless the container is kept open. Don't keep the container in direct sunshine for more than a few hours. Don't use containers of colored glass or plastic that will shut out light. Choose the correct plants that will thrive in a humid atmosphere. Good ones are small terrestrial orchids, ferns, fittonia, baby's-tears, and Sinningia pusilla and varieties.

established that will make it possible to have all the plants visible at one time. Stones, moss, or lichens can be used to give the effect of a miniature landscape. By arranging a slope instead of a flat surface, seedling trees of shrubs and other erect growers can go in on the low side, with creeping and low-growing plants on the higher level and between the taller ones.

What cultivated plants are suitable for terrariums?   Various ferns, small palms, pellionias, selaginellas, begonias, small ivies, pileas, fittonia, maranta, small crotons, peperomia, and saintpaulias—whatever plants appreciate humid conditions. Some plants soon outgrow their quarters, so replanting at intervals is necessary.

What wild plants can be used in a terrarium?   Wildings such as partridge-berry, wintergreen, pipsissewa, rattlesnake-plantain, hepatica, ground-pine, moss, lichens (on bits of bark or half-decayed wood), seedling evergreens, and tiny wild ferns do very well in a glass garden. Collect only species not protected by conservation laws or save plants endangered by construction on land soon to be developed.

What seed can I sow in a woodsy terrarium?   It is not customary to sow seeds in a terrarium, but such a container is ideal for raising ferns from spores. The spores usually found on the back of fern fronds, shaken into a terrarium, will start as green, flattened growth from which tiny ferns will duly emerge.

What is the proper way to care for a terrarium?   Keep it in a light, not sunny place. Water very sparingly, especially if the container is topped with glass. Don't wet the foliage when watering. Wipe the glass top dry each day, also the sides if there is a great deal of condensation.

Can I grow orchids in a terrarium?   Yes. Those best suited are the terrestrial jewel orchids such as *Anoectochilus* and *Ludisia* (syn. *Haemaria*). Some dwarf lady's-slipper (*Paphiopedilum*) species and their primary hybrids thrive in large terrariums under fluorescent lights. Miniature epiphytic orchids such as *Ornithocephalus* and *Pleurothallis* will also do well in larger terrariums under fluorescent lights.

What flowering plants thrive in a terrarium?   Miniature African-violets grow well, also related gesneriads such as the tiny gloxinia species *Sinningia pusilla* and the almost white *S.* 'Wood Nymph' and lavender *S.* 'Bright Eyes'. 'Cupid's Doll', 'Dollbaby', and 'Cindy' are a pretty trio of small gloxinias, all treated about the same as African-violets, with the terrarium top left open a little all the time and completely removed for an hour or so each day to ensure adequate circulation of air.

TRAY AND DISH GARDENS

What plants are suitable for dish or tray gardens? Cacti and other succulents such as small specimens of crassulas, gasterias, echeverias, kalanchoes, and sedums. *Saxifraga stolonifera*, cryptanthus, ferns, myrtle, seedling evergreens, pileas, small *Begonia semperflorens*, peperomias. Go to a garden center and select any very small potted plants that will fit in your dish or tray. Or try small plants from your own garden or window garden.

How is a dish or tray garden arranged? A shallow dish or tray is lined with coarse gravel or small pebbles, over which is placed a thin layer of light garden loam, sandy for cacti and other succulents, mixed with peat moss or leafmold for woodland plants. The plants are set in to simulate a miniature landscape and earth is packed firmly about their roots. Moss can be used to cover the bare soil of the surface.

How should a tray or dish garden be watered? When the garden is made, enough water should be given to moisten thoroughly the roots of the newly set plants, but not enough to leave them soggy and waterlogged. After first watering, give water sparingly when the soil feels dry to the touch. Pour water directly to the roots with a small pitcher or long-spouted watering can.

How can I keep the soil "sweet" in my dish garden? Mix small pieces of charcoal through the soil mixture that you are using.

How long will plants survive in a dish garden? That depends on the plants used and the care given. Cacti or other succulents often live for months or even for years if planted in sandy loam and watered sparingly. Foliage plants do not last quite as long, but if given proper care they will remain fresh and green for weeks or longer.

What is bonsai? This is the Japanese art of dwarfing plants by restricting roots and pruning tops so that even a century-old plant may thrive in a pot or on a tray.

Is a miniature garden the same as a dish garden? Not exactly. The dish garden, more often than not, is a collection of small plants in a "dish" that have not been given any studied arrangement or consideration as to their appropriateness with each other. A miniature garden is more likely to be what its name implies—with the creator of the garden trying to reproduce a landscape in miniature—whether house plant or hardy plant material is used.

What is saikei? Saikei is another garden art from Japan, the creation of miniature landscapes in shallow ceramic pots or clay trays. It is akin to bonsai but the emphasis is on reproducing a part of a landscape —trees, mountains, or islands (suggested by rock), sand and moss (to serve as water and grass), etc. Usually hardy dwarf evergreens or trees are used, but variations of saikei can be made by the house-plant enthusiast with tender material. (See *Saikei: Living Landscapes in Miniature,* by Toshio Kawamoto, and other books on Japanese tray gardening.)

I have been given a potted juniper which has been trained as bonsai. What should I do with the plant in the winter?   Do you have a plant room, enclosed breezeway, sun porch, or the like that remains protected and above freezing but very cool in the winter? If so, this would be a good place to keep your bonsai, which should receive some sun and ample light during the day and water as it dries out. A second choice would be a cool window ledge where the temperature remains several degrees cooler than in the rest of the house. A third choice is to winter the plant outdoors, in a cold frame, or in the open ground where the container must be protected by soil and a mulch. Or the plant can be carefully removed from the pot and planted. It can be repotted in the spring. Hardy plants grown in bonsai style just do not thrive indoors in the winter in warm dry rooms.

What plants make good bonsai subjects?   A great many, especially dwarf evergreens and shrubs. Fake bonsai subjects can be achieved by selecting certain house plants that resemble trees and potting them in special bonsai containers. A common house plant used this way is the jade plant (crassula), but many others are suitable. They, of course, are much easier to take care of in heated rooms than hardy trees and shrubs that need to rest during the winter. There are many books on bonsai that explain the technique and also suggest ways to adapt it to house plants and indoor gardening.

THE KITCHEN-WINDOW HERB GARDEN

What herbs can I grow in my sunny kitchen window?   *Annuals:* parsley, sweet marjoram, basil, anise, coriander. *Perennials:* mint, chives, thyme, sage, lemon balm, tarragon. *Tender perennial shrubs:* scented geraniums, lemon-verbena, rosemary, French lavender.

What kitchen-window herbs can be grown from seed?   Sweet marjoram, parsley, basil, anise, coriander. Sow seeds in late summer or fall for winter use.

What kitchen-window herbs do better if purchased as plants?   Rosemary, lemon-verbena (tender shrubs), tarragon, mint, chives, thyme, sage, and lemon balm are perennials and give quicker results when purchased as plants.

Where can I purchase herb plants and seed for growing indoors in the winter? Most leading seed houses now carry lists of herbs. Some firms offer herb-growing kits with seed, soil, pots, and instruction book.

What kind of soil is necessary for herbs grown indoors? Three parts of good garden soil and two parts of sand or perlite make a good mixture with a teaspoon of lime added to a 5-inch potful. Or use one of the soilless mixes.

Can chives be grown indoors in the winter? If so, how? Yes, chives do well for a while in a kitchen herb garden. Bring in a clump of bulbs from the garden, setting it in a bulb pan of light, "sweet" soil. Cut back the foliage and let new growth start. Grow in a sunny window or under lights at a low temperature, preferably 55° F. Keep on the dry side.

Can I grow scented geraniums in a kitchen herb garden? Yes. (See Geranium.)

Do you think one should bring in lemon-verbena during the winter? I did, potted it, and kept it in my basement near a window and watered it once a week. Am I doing the correct thing? (Michigan.) Being a native of Argentina and Chile, the lemon-verbena would not winter over out-of-doors in Michigan. You are doing the right thing with it, if it stays alive all winter in the basement. It can be cut back when brought in from the garden and grown through the cold weather in a sunny window. It can stand a higher temperature than that preferred by most herbs.

Can I leave my rosemary plant outdoors the year round? I have seen plants as big as shrubs in gardens on Cape Cod but my friends tell me to bring it indoors here in the vicinity of New York City. Rosemary is unreliably hardy in the North but where humidity is high and temperatures not too frigid, as along the seacoast, it survives outdoors surprisingly far north. However, you were well advised to take it in. When pruning it back in the fall, preparatory to bringing it indoors, root some of the cuttings in moist sand or vermiculite. They are easy to propagate.

How can parsley plants be grown in a house during the cold months? Cut back, lift, and pot strong plants in the fall and give them a well-lighted window with a temperature never above 55° F. Don't overwater and don't fertilize.

Why does house-grown parsley become very pale, with long, weak stems? I give fertilizer every 2 or 3 weeks. It probably lacks sun and is grown too warm. Parsley grown indoors is almost always weaker and less thrifty than that grown in the garden. It wants plenty of sun, a temperature of not more than 55° F., and enough but not too much water (keep it rather on the dry side). Try growing it under fluorescents.

Should parsley and chives be kept very moist when growing in a kitchen window?   No. Be careful with watering; with a little practice, you can tell by the weight of the container or the feel of the soil if it needs water or not.

Does it injure tarragon, rosemary, and marjoram to pot them every winter for use indoors?   It does not injure them if they get the proper care and the plants are not too large. They should be set into the garden again in the spring to recuperate. Eventually they will get too big to pot up. Cuttings should be propagated to produce young plants, leaving the parents in the herb garden out-of-doors. If the young plants are left in their pots and placed in the garden through the summer, they will sustain less shock when brought indoors in autumn.

What is the truth about growing herbs indoors?   The truth is that few herbs do well indoors unless they have the conditions which they prefer; namely, no soaring day heat—70° F. is acceptable but 60° is better. They need a night temperature of about 55° F.; plenty of light and sunshine (grow under fluorescent tubes if natural light is inadequate); sufficient humidity, as from pebble trays; good air circulation; and regular care with adequate water (no drying out of the soil but no sogginess, either). These conditions are hard to provide in the average heated home. A plant room, cool window, or lean-to greenhouse offer good possibilities.

Specific Flowering House Plants

ABUTILON (FLOWERING-MAPLE)

Does abutilon make a good house plant?   Abutilon used to be a favorite house plant and was also a good garden subject, growing tall and bushy and blooming freely in sunny, open beds. It deserves a comeback. It will thrive in a cool window but needs several hours of sun to flower abundantly. The foliage and bell-shaped flowers are most attractive. Cuttings root readily. If an old plant is brought indoors in fall, cut it back severely to prevent wilting and to encourage new growth. It rapidly becomes pot-bound and therefore needs a lot of water. It is subject to whitefly. Repot in a standard potting mixture. (See Soil, this section.)

I have a small plant with leaves almost exactly like a maple. After I set it outdoors in July, it thrived, producing orange-colored flowers like "Japanese lanterns" on long, fine, drooping stems. What is it? What winter protection does it need? (Pennsylvania.) The plant is abutilon or flowering-maple. It is not hardy and must be grown as a pot plant indoors in your part of the country. If possible, grow cool, at 50° to 60° F., and it will flower freely in the winter. Root cuttings to make new plants. It grows quite large.

How can abutilon or flowering-maple be raised from seed as a house plant? Sow the seed in a pot in February or March in sandy soil, barely covering the seed. Place a sheet of glass on the pot and keep in a warm room. Give some light when germination starts, but use care in watering, as the seedlings are tiny. Transplant into another pot, 1 inch apart when in rough leaf, and grow on like any other tender plant. Variegated *A. pictum* 'Thompsonii' is propagated by cuttings.

AFRICAN-VIOLET (SAINTPAULIA)

Please suggest the best soil mixture in which to grow African-violets. A light mixture easily penetrated by the fine roots is best, such as 1 part peat moss, 1 part perlite, and 1 part vermiculite. Add fertilizer according to the directions on the container. If there are no nematodes in the soil in your area and you have well-decayed compost, which is all humus, sift this through a half-inch screen and add sand or perlite until the texture feels light and open.

Packaged soil from hardware stores, garden centers, or by mail order are available. Some are fine right from the bag; other mixes may need lightening with sand or perlite (or added fertilizer). Here is one well-tried formula that contains fertilizer:

Mix 2 parts (by bulk) good garden loam, sterilized (see below)
    1 part vermiculite or sterilized sand
    1 part peat moss
Add 1 quart broken bits charcoal per bushel
    2 quarts commercial cow manure or rich compost per bushel
    1 quart fine bone meal or superphosphate per bushel

Is it necessary to pasteurize African-violet soil? If so, describe the method. Yes, it is usually advisable, since African-violets are susceptible to a number of soil-borne pests and diseases. Only loam, sand, and pots need be sterilized, as vermiculite and packaged peat moss are free from harmful organisms. In a roaster that has a cover, moisten the soil, etc., with hot water and bake at 180 degrees for 1 hour. (The odor produced is offensive to some people.) Let stand uncovered in a cool place for about 2 weeks. Stir occasionally.

What is the best temperature for African-violets? The minimum night temperature in the winter should be 60° to 65° F. At 50° to 55° F., saintpaulias only struggle along. The day temperature can reach 75° F. or a little above, but 70° F. is preferred. Plants seem to adjust to cooler daytime temperatures as low as 65° F.

Will an African-violet thrive without sunshine? Frequently these plants bloom even at north windows, but better results are obtained in the winter with plants grown in a sunny (4 or more hours of sun) exposure, with pots set back a little from the glass. Under fluorescent lights, African-violets bloom prolifically. (See the discussion of fluorescent lights under Light, Natural and Fluorescent, in the introduction.)

How should African-violets be watered? Because of its thick crown and velvety leaves, moisture is avoided around the heart of the plant, and water is supplied from the saucer or around the edge of the pot. Pour excess water from the saucer after about half an hour, when the plant will have drawn up all it needs. Let the soil approach dryness but not really dry out between waterings: the soil should never be sopping wet or be dry for long.

Is cold water bad for African-violets? Yes. Lukewarm water is essential.

My African-violet has white rings and spots on the leaves. Is this a disease or fertilizer deficiency? Neither. It is the result of applying cold water to the soil or letting it fall on the leaves. Warm water sprayed on the leaves is not harmful.

Please tell me how to get African-violets to bloom. My plants remain green and healthy, but shortly after they leave the florist's they cease flowering. Shall I repot them? The difference in humidity between a greenhouse and an ordinary living room is probably the reason for their not blooming. For best flowering, plants should be kept standing on moist pebbles, which afford a constant "aura" of humidity. Faded flowers must also be promptly snipped to prevent seed formation, which is always a deterrent to further bud development. Plenty of fresh air indirectly admitted in cold weather is likewise important. Repotting may be necessary but usually is not in the case of a newly purchased plant, so other factors in culture are first considered. Perhaps your plants are not receiving enough light! An African-violet plant food or one of the several reliable house-plant foods may be applied according to the directions on the package when buds begin to appear. *Do not* feed during the short periods when plants are resting and producing no new growth, usually during the summer in the North.

How often should I feed my African-violets? You can feed them very lightly at every watering except in prolonged periods of overcast weather or when the plants are taking a brief rest after heavy bloom.

Should African-violets be grown in small pots? Yes, the root system is small and plants do not thrive if overpotted and then overwatered. "Squatty" 2¼-inch plastic pots will do for quite large plants, and 3-inch pots are as large as you should get.

Does keeping an African-violet plant in a glazed flower pot prevent it from blooming? In such a pot, even if it has a drainage hole, the plant will not dry out as readily; but it does not do as well in glazed pots as in porous clay pots because air circulation in the soil is poorer. Wick-fed plastic pots are satisfactory.

What is the best location for African-violets in the summer? They are either set in a light north window in a well-ventilated room or else on a sheltered porch or patio except when heat and humidity are high; then they are better indoors, and air conditioning is not harmful. They should never be grown in a garden because hard rains and wind can injure the brittle leaves.

How are plants kept free of dust, if spraying is harmful to the hairy leaves? Dust is removed with a soft brush. A flat camel's-hair paintbrush is ideal. Leaves may be sprayed occasionally with a fine mist of room-temperature water. Until completely dry, plants must remain in complete shade, away from drafts, and out of direct sun.

What makes the blossoms of an African-violet fall off while they are still fresh? It is natural for them to do so. They fertilize or pollinate readily, and after that happens they slide off.

Why do African-violets drop their blooms before they open? Probably the temperature or the humidity is too low. They prefer 70° F. by day, not less than 60° at night, and humidity around 60 per cent.

Will gas heat cause the buds to fall from African-violets? Leaking manufactured (not natural) gas, however slight, will make any plant drop its leaves or buds.

How can one keep the leaves of African-violets from drooping onto the edge of the pot and thereby rotting away where contact is made? This condition, due to deposits of fertilizer salts, occurs more often on clay than plastic pots, especially if the plants are overwatered or grown too cold. Cut the center from a small paper plate, slit one side, and fit like a collar under the foliage. This prevents contact and encourages the plant to grow up, not down. Because of this problem, most growers prefer plastic pots for African-violets.

What can I do to prevent my African-violets from developing long bare "necks"? Probably you can't prevent this. As the plant grows, old leaves are discarded. But you can conceal the stem by repotting the plant, cutting off or spreading out the lowest roots, and setting the plant low enough, often in the same pot, to cover the bare stem. If you can't fit it again in the pot, use a deeper one.

How can I keep my African-violets from growing lopsided? These plants grow so readily toward the light that giving a quarter turn once a week is necessary to keep the plants shapely. Plants grown under fluorescent lamps are the most uniform.

What causes a gnarly condition on African-violets? New leaves and blossoms have no stems; they just grow out from the base of the plant. Need of division might be the explanation, but more likely the invisible cyclamen mite is at work. Use an aerosol spray recommended for mites or apply a miticide like Kelthane. Discard badly infested plants.

How can I clean up mildew on the leaves and mold on the stems of African-violets? What causes these? These thick-leaved velvety plants are often a prey to mildew and mold without any apparent cause, although poor ventilation and insufficient sunlight seem to be contributing factors. Badly affected sections are sharply cut away and the leaves, both upper- and undersides, dusted with fine sulfur, or one of the dusts with sulfur as an active ingredient. The "mold" on stems may be mealybug.

How can mealybugs be cleaned up on African-violets? The end of a skewer or matchstick is wrapped with cotton and dipped in wood alcohol (or in a little cologne). This is applied to all affected sections of the plant. Repeat as needed.

I have 7 African-violets which had blossoms steadily for 3 years, but now are infested with a webby substance on the underside of the foliage. The leaves are spotted yellow. What causes this? This sounds like red spider, a minute insect forming colonies of red dots on the underside of the foliage where webs are formed for protection. Increase the humidity in the room. Forceful syringing with clear, lukewarm water to break the web and wash away the insects is somewhat effective, but you will probably also have to spray regularly with a miticide like Kelthane.

My African-violets have developed pale, limp leaves and the flowers collapse before they fully develop. What causes this? Probably nematodes. Remove the plant from the pot and examine its roots. If swellings are present and decayed areas visible, destroy the plant and pour boiling water through the potting soil before discarding it. Next time, pasteurize the soil.

Can African-violets be successfully divided? Readily. Indeed, as soon as the crown gets overthick, flowering usually wanes. Carefully pull apart and reset; each fair-sized repotted section usually begins to flower soon afterward. It is also easy to maintain your stock by rooting leaf cuttings. But you usually get more shapely plants if you prevent thick multiple crowns by removing with tweezers the little side growths that push out from the main stem, and grow only single-crown specimens.

Which is the better time to divide African-violets—in the spring or the fall? The spring is better. The divisions then grow on into good plants by the following winter.

What is the best method of propagating a large number of African-violets? The leaves may be sharply cut with 1½-inch stems from the base of the plant at any time (although commercial growers prefer October and November). These are inserted in small separate pots, which are placed in a large bulb pan of light soil or in a plastic bread or shoe box with a lid. Half sand and half peat moss or vermiculite seems to give the quickest results. Leaves are inserted the length of the stem. The soil is kept warm, in a light place, and moist while roots are forming. Keeping the pots or flats in a propagating case helps to maintain ideal, quick, humid rooting conditions; or the pots may all be set in a box containing a layer of sand always kept moist and covered with plastic. When roots are formed, new leaves will begin to appear at the base of the old ones. The cover is then removed and new "plants" are separated from the parent leaves and potted up separately in an African-violet

PROPAGATION OF AFRICAN-VIOLET
(*Top*) *Leaf cutting inserted in pot of sandy compost.* (*Below*) *Potted young plant, with saucer for watering from beneath. Plant (right), repotted, has reached flowering size.*

potting mixture in 2-inch pots. Generally speaking, it takes 4½ to 5 months for young plants to be ready for separate potting. The first blossom by this method will show at 6 to 12 months.

How can African-violets be rooted in water?   Mature leaves cut with plenty of petiole or leaf stem will root if placed in a glass with just enough water to cover the end of the stem but not up to the leaf. As soon as roots develop, the "plant" is moved to a small pot of sandy soil. It helps if foil is crimped over the glass and the leaves inserted through holes punched in the foil. This method is slower than inserting leaves in a rooting medium such as vermiculite or sand.

Where did the African-violet originate?   *Saintpaulia ionantha* was first discovered in East Africa in 1893 by Baron Walter von Saint Paul. Forms of it introduced at that time were *purpurea*, dark purple; *grandiflora violacea*, large flowered; and *albescens*, white tinted pink. These forms seemingly were all lost, as up to the time 'Blue Boy' was originated in California the only saintpaulias available were forms of the species *S. ionantha*, usually grown from seed on a limited scale.

ANTHURIUM

What are the requirements of an anthurium plant to make it bloom?   Anthuriums are tropical and demand high humidity and heat while in active growth but accept cooler conditions while in flower. The pot must be well drained and a mixture of sphagnum, peat moss, fibrous loam, and sand should be used. The crown must be above the soil, and as the base rises, it should be wrapped with moss. Most adaptable are selections of *A. scherzerianum*, such as brilliant red 'Flamenco'.

AZALEA   (See Gift Plants.)

BEGONIA

What is the best soil mixture for begonias?   A loose, humus-rich mixture suits most begonias best. One part good loam, 2 parts leafmold, 1 part sand, ¼ part small lump charcoal, ¼ part dehydrated cow manure, plus bone meal at the rate of 1 pint to the bushel is satisfactory. Packaged potting soils like Jiffy Mix and Readi-Earth are also satisfactory, with a third part of sand or perlite added for drainage.

What type of soil and amount of moisture do fibrous-rooted begonias need; what room temperature and humidity? Should they be kept in a

sunny window or shaded? They need a light, humus-rich, well drained soil. Never permit the soil to become really dry, but avoid a saturated condition and grow them at 55° to 70° F. Provide them with sun or fluorescent lights in the winter, partial shade in the summer. Increase humidity by using pebble-filled saucers or trays under the plants.

How should I feed begonias growing in pots? They respond best to organic fertilizers, one of the best of which is diluted fish emulsion, but any complete house-plant fertilizer that will dissolve in water may be used. Never feed plants that have not filled their pots with healthy roots, unless they are in soil-free mixes.

What are the best winter-blooming begonias? Nothing equals the wax begonia (*Begonia semperflorens*). Even plants lifted from the summer garden bud again quite quickly and never completely stop through the winter and then continue through the summer, too. Wax begonias are one of the most dependable of all house plants and are available in many floriferous hybrids. The trick in their culture is not to overwater.

What are some good smaller-growing begonias? I have very little space for the plants. Six-inch miniatures that bloom during the winter and spring include 'Baby Perfectifolia', 'Bow Joe', 'China Doll', and 'Robert Shatzer'. 'Dew Drop', 'Robin', and 'Wood Nymph' are rex types. Dwarfs up to 10 inches include 'Black Falcon', 'Silver Jewel', and 'It', a silver-spotted rex type. Some small begonias perform best in terrariums and include *Begonia prismatocarpa* and *B. quadrilata*. Consult specialists for additional kinds, as there are many.

What are the rules for repotting a healthy, fibrous-rooted begonia that has filled its pot with roots? (1) Water thoroughly a few hours before repotting; (2) the new pot should be only an inch or two wider than the old pot; (3) put crocks (drainage material) in the new pot; (4) avoid damaging roots; (5) moderately firm the soil around the root ball; (6) water thoroughly. Shade from bright sun for a few days. Do not overwater!

What is the proper care for begonias? They grow well but hardly ever blossom. About once a year they bud and then the buds drop off. Bud dropping suggests lack of light or too low humidity (45 to 70 per cent is desirable). Try fluorescent lights.

Can begonias in the house be pinched back severely to prevent them from growing leggy, or does this condition indicate some cultural defect? Pruning back can be done. Some varieties (the *coccineas,* for example) send up long, canelike growths. Lack of light and too high temperatures may also be responsible for legginess.

Where in the house do begonias do best? A sunny window during the winter where the night temperature is not below 50° F. and the day temperature is not above 65° F.

How should fibrous-rooted begonias be watered?   The soil should be kept moist but not waterlogged. When water is given, thoroughly saturate the whole ball of soil (preferably by immersing a big pot in a pail), then give no more water until the soil begins to show signs of dryness. Use water at room temperature.

How do you take care of begonias? My plants are withering.   Begonias that have tuberous roots die down and rest for a period each year. Most others thrive in 55° to 70° F., provided the atmosphere is not too dry and the light is reasonably good. The soil should be light, humus-rich, and moderately moist. Begonias with thick rhizomes should be allowed to dry out slightly between waterings.

Should begonias have a rest; if so, when, and what care should follow?   It is impossible to generalize. The tuberous kinds need a complete rest through the winter. *Begonia socotrana* and some South African kinds rest during the summer. Many benefit from a partial rest (but are not dried off), while others continue their growth year-round.

What is your method for growing a calla-lily begonia? One person's directions contradict another's. (New Jersey.)   Place the plant in the window of a country home and see how it grows! This prima donna seems to do best under cool and well-lighted conditions. Professional gardeners often fail. A west window in a room with a night temperature of about 60° F., reasonable humidity and fresh air, with moderate watering from below (or without wetting the heart of the plant), may keep it alive. It should be grown quite dry during the winter, with just enough water to keep its leaves from drooping, and not overwatered in summer, which is their time of active growth.

Why is it so difficult to grow the calla begonia south of New England?   This seems to be due to the extremes of summer weather. Like sweet peas, delphiniums, and some other garden plants, this house plant abhors spells of weather when both days and nights are hot and humid.

How can I keep a Christmas begonia over summer so it will bloom next winter?   Rest it for a few weeks after it blooms; cut back and repot in light soil in the spring; grow in a humid atmosphere (minimum temperature, 60° F.). Shade from bright sunshine; repot as necessary during the summer. Control pests. You can scarcely expect success without a warm greenhouse.

How do you care for 'Gloire de Lorraine' (Christmas) begonias after they are through blooming?   They are usually discarded because young plants develop into better specimens for the following year. If you wish to continue growing old plants, rest awhile by reducing the water supply somewhat. In the spring, cut partly back, repot, and start into growth again.

How can I make my angel-wing begonia bloom? Provided that the plant is growing well, it should bloom after it attains a reasonable size if it is kept in a fully lighted or sunny place and fertilized regularly.

Why do my angel-wing begonias, after a few days' growth, dry up and lose the leaves? I keep them well watered and cool. The common causes of leaf dropping are too much or too little water, low temperatures, exposure to drafts, too dry an atmosphere, and careless repotting. The minimum temperature should be 55° F.

What disease causes begonia leaves to turn yellow? This is usually not due to any organic disease but to the plants receiving a check to their growth due to dryness, too strong sunshine, an arid atmosphere, or too low temperature.

Why do begonias bloom in greenhouses and not after I get them home? I have one now, it grows just fine, but has no flowers. Possibly there is too little light. Begonias need light shade from intense summer sun, but sunlight is necessary for flower production, especially during the winter. Also, humidity of 45 to 70 per cent is needed.

Most begonias grown for their foliage effect rather than flower display require a fairly moist atmosphere and do not thrive in hot, dry rooms.

The begonias kept on my terrace during the summer, and brought into the house in the fall, dropped all their leaves. What can be the cause or causes? We use bottled gas in the house. Leaking gas may be the cause, but much more probably the dry air inside (especially after heat is turned on) is responsible. Install humidifiers. Stand the plants on trays in moist gravel.

My potted, wax begonia blooms on one side branch only. What can I do with it? It is about 9 inches tall and has 4 stalks full of foliage so it should be bushy. The plant needs good light to bloom well. It will stand more sunlight than most other begonias.

When a rex begonia droops, is it going into a rest period? It has just finished blossoming. Should I water it less often? When grown in the house, this often happens at the approach of winter. Reduce the water supply (but keep the soil somewhat moist). Repot and water more when signs of new growth show in the spring.

My rex begonia never seems to increase in size. As soon as a new leaf appears, another leaf turns yellow and dies. What is wrong? The wrong soil, too low temperature, or too dry an atmosphere. The soil should be humus-rich but porous; the temperature should not be below 55° F. A humid atmosphere suits these plants best.

Why do my begonia cuttings rot instead of root when I try to start them in water? While some people report success with *some* varieties of begonias in water, a generally preferable method is to use moist sand (not sea sand) or vermiculite as a rooting medium. If water is used, add a few lumps of charcoal.

Can calla begonias be made to grow from cuttings, and how? (New York.) Yes. You must be careful to select the greenest shoots for cuttings. The white ones are devoid of chlorophyll and will not grow. The green ones produce white tips later. Root in a covered plastic dish.

When is the best time to take cuttings of double-flowered begonias? At the same time that cuttings of single-flowered varieties, belonging to the same section, would be taken; thus, of most fibrous-rooted and tuberous-rooted kinds, in the spring; of most winter-flowering hybrids, in early winter.

How can rex begonias be propagated? They can be increased by seed, division, or from leaf cuttings. Cuttings are best made from mature leaves in the spring. Insert them in sand, or sand and peat moss. Keep moist and shaded from direct sunlight. Young plants should develop in a few weeks.

How do you start the new plants of a Christmas begonia? Most commonly from single leaves treated as cuttings and inserted in a bed of moist sand in December. They need 70° F. temperature and moist atmospheric conditions to succeed. They can also be grown from ordinary stem cuttings inserted in the spring.

My Begonia sutherlandii has developed swellings or lumps on its stems. Can these be used to start new plants? Yes. If planted in the spring, these bulbous growths will develop into new plants.

Which is the best way to propagate the hardy Begonia grandis? Collect the small bulblets that form so freely on the stems in late summer. Store them in a cool place for the winter and plant them in boxes of light soil in the spring. Also by division of old plants.

What precaution should be observed in sowing begonia seed? Use soilless mixes or milled sphagnum moss (sold in bags in garden centers or by mail-order seed firms). Water well *before* sowing. Scatter the dustlike seed evenly and press in lightly. Do not cover with soil. Cover the pot with glass or clear plastic and set in a dim place—temperature, 60° to 70° F.—until seed germinates. Then place under fluorescent lights, 3 to 4 inches beneath tubes. Never allow the soil to become dry. Water by standing the pot in a dish so that moisture seeps up from below.

How can begonias be grown from seed? I have difficulties; they always damp off. Damping off is caused by a fungus that thrives when conditions for the seedlings are unfavorable. Avoid overwatering, too heavy shade, extreme fluctuation of temperature. Sow seed on milled sphagnum moss, not on soil or on soilless mixes. Be sure that the mix is well drained. Water only on sunny days.

How should seedling begonias be transplanted? They are such tiny things. Prepare shallow boxes or pans by placing drainage material in the bottom and filling with a mixture of pasteurized house-plant mixture or any soilless mix, much preferred over garden soils. Top the mix with ½ inch of moist milled sphagnum moss. Loosen the seedlings and lift them with their roots intact (use a wooden label with a V notch) and plant with leaves on the surface, roots covered. Water with a fine spray or from below. Keep warm and shaded. Grow under lights.

What causes the younger leaves on begonias to crinkle and get a crumbly, webbed, grayish look? Mites (microscopic insects), which suck the juices from the plant. Spray forcibly at the sink to break webs and spray with Kelthane.

My begonias fail to grow. I have been told that they have root knot. What shall I use? Root-knot nematode causes swellings on roots and, finally, decay. The only control is to repropagate from tip cuttings, throw out old plants, and keep new ones growing in sterilized soil.

Little green plant lice are on my begonia plants. What shall I do? Use malathion as a spray or dip. When using as a dip, cover the soil with foil, invert the plant, and dip the foliage and stems so that they are thoroughly wetted.

What kinds of begonias are best in the house? A good selection of easy-growing kinds includes: *B.* x *feastii* (beefsteak), *B. semperflorens* (wax), *B.* x *argenteo-guttata* (trout), *B. coccinea* (angel-wing), *B. heracleifolia* (star), *B. scharffii*, 'President Carnot', and *B. foliosa miniata*. *B.* 'Tom Ment' is a graceful, arching angel-wing with dwarf habit, pink flowers, and spotted foliage.

What are 'Lorraine' begonias? Commonly known as Christmas begonias, they are the result of hybridizing *B. socotrana* and *B. dregei*. The first hybrid produced was named 'Gloire de Lorraine'. More adaptable are recent *B.* x *hiemalis* hybrids such as 'Aphrodite Red' or 'Aphrodite Pink'.

What is the name of the begonia with green and white, and some all-white, leaves and small red and deep pink flowers? It is often called calla begonia or calla-lily begonia. These are varieties of *Begonia semperflorens*.

Can you tell me the name of a hardy begonia? *Begonia grandis,* a native of China, is the hardiest species. In a sheltered position, it will live outdoors in New York. It comes in both pink- and white-flowered varieties.

BROMELIADS

What is the correct care for bromeliads? Bromeliads, of which there are many species, are relatives of the pineapple. A few, such as *Dyckia,* are considered succulents. They like a winter temperature of 55° to 60° F. Most popular are nonsucculent epiphytic sorts. The common name is air-plant because they derive most of their nourishment from air and water, being tree perchers in their native habitats. A number make fine house plants and include *Billbergia, Vriesia,* and *Aechmea.* The leaves of many species are vaselike, rising from a tight base, and the exotic, colorful, long-lasting flowers on stiff stems are borne in winter. Vaselike bromeliads should be watered in the "vase," which holds moisture well. They are excellent for city conditions.

What are the best bromeliads for beginners to grow? You could hardly go wrong with varieties and species of *Aechmea* and *Billbergia. Vriesia* and *Tillandsia* are a little more temperamental and need more care.

Can you give me some information about watering bromeliads? The majority of bromeliads—*Aechmea, Billbergia, Guzmania*—need their growing medium just slightly moist, but they absolutely require that the "vases" be filled with water all through the growing season. Those without water reservoirs—*Cryptanthus,* silvery *Tillandsia* species—need an evenly moist growing medium through spring, summer, and fall, with a slight drying out in winter. Small, silvery *Tillandsia ionantha* and similar species thrive when mounted on chunks of tree fern or cork bark. Mist them with room-temperature water on bright mornings.

What is the best potting medium for bromeliads? A half-and-half mixture of shredded osmunda or tree-fern fiber with soil. Also, a handful of pebbles suits most bromeliads. Exceptions would be the terrestrial species—*Cryptanthus,* for example—which can be grown in a standard house-plant soil.

Do bromeliads need sunlight to bloom indoors? Any flowering plant, bromeliads included, will do better with some sunlight, not only to encourage bloom, but also for good leaf color. This is especially true for bromeliads. Much of their beauty is in their colorful foliage.

Is it true that putting an apple in the "vase" of a bromeliad will make it bloom? Yes, the gas given off by the apple apparently stimulates flowering. Cover the plant and apple securely with plastic.

CALCEOLARIA

How can I grow calceolarias from seed? If you propose to do this in an ordinary window, you have chosen a tough subject. Like cineraria, the spotted and other hybrid calceolaria varieties need coolness. Sow the fine seeds on the surface of a level soilless mix in a pot in July or August; provide full shade and never leave dry; transplant the tiny seedlings to a flat and keep in a shaded cold frame. Pot later and keep in the frame until late fall, then move to a light place with a temperature around 40° to 45° F. at night. If the temperature runs above 50° any time during the winter, failure is almost certain. Beware of aphids and whiteflies.

CAMPANULA ISOPHYLLA (LIGURIAN HAREBELL)

There is a plant common in Cape Cod homes which is generally called star-of-Bethlehem. This is not the same as the hardy plant that grows in our garden from a bulb. It is a larger plant with beautiful blue or white flowers. Can you give me some idea of the right name? This is *Campanula isophylla,* a native of Italy. It is a trailing plant with beautiful gray-green foliage, a summer to late-winter bloomer. It can be purchased by mail order from house-plant specialists.

How can star-of-Bethlehem, or Ligurian harebell, be grown in the house? Grow in sandy soil that has humus added. Provide a sunny window in the winter, light shade in the summer. Supplement short winter days with fluorescent light for maximum bloom or grow the plants under lights for 16 hours in the winter if a sunny window is not available. Keep moderately moist in the winter; water freely in the summer. Feed with diluted fertilizer when in growth. Propagate by cuttings in the spring.

CINERARIA (SENECIO X HYBRIDUS)

Can cinerarias be grown in a south window? Can they be carried through the summer for flowering again the next season? Cinerarias are short-lived plants in a warm room. They are grown at 40° to 45° F. and never above 50° F. When they are through blooming, discard them, as they don't like summer weather.

How can I raise cinerarias from seeds? I used moist sand and covered them with a glass, but one by one they died. As cinerarias have to be sown in July or August to get sizable plants for winter or early spring, damping off in hot weather is always a menace. Use soilless mix and don't cover. Stand the pan where it is shaded, and keep as cool as possible. Sow late in August or early September to escape the hot days and nights. Cinerarias must at all times be grown cool, 40° to 45° F.

What causes cineraria leaves to curl and dry at their edges? Probably too hot and dry an atmosphere; possibly the plants are dry at the roots. Cinerarias don't last long in a hot, dry temperature; 45° F. at night is plenty. Aphids are prone to attack them. They are greenhouse subjects that rarely last more than 2 to 3 weeks in the average house. It is best to discard them when their bloom is finished.

FUCHSIA

How are fuchsias handled as house plants? Cuttings are rooted in the spring, taken from old plants that have been started after a winter rest. If you keep them growing all year in a warm room, without a rest and subsequent new growth, you won't get flowers. Most are spring and summer bloomers. They like full light but not full sun, and rich soil, plenty of water and humidity when in growth. Feed liberally when in growth with one of the "complete" house-plant fertilizers.

What fuchsias will bloom indoors in the winter? *F. magellanica macrostema* is a winter bloomer. It will look well in a hanging basket, as it is a drooping, almost vinelike variety. The small flowers are ruby red. Variety 'Variegata' has white markings on the leaves. The winter-blooming hybrids of *F. triphylla,* including 'Gartenmeister Bohnstedt' with pink and orange-toned flowers, are adaptable to intermediate temperatures, even to growing under fluorescent lights. Most fuchsias are summer bloomers. By taking slips from larger plants in the summer and having them well rooted by early winter, you may get bloom in late winter or very early spring. Or buy young, blooming plants from a grower who has forced them.

I have a fuchsia that blossomed in May and June. What should I do so it will bloom during the winter months? Fuchsias are not naturally winter bloomers. The winter is their resting season.

Should fuchsias be given a rest period or can they be kept in bloom all through the year? Fuchsias are not everblooming, and in the winter old plants are best kept dry and cool until early spring. They should be potted and rested in a cool cellar or room and watered very little. Cut back in February or March and give warmer quarters, watering more when new shoots begin to appear. If you can't accommodate growing plants so early, keep practically dry and cool until April, then place them outdoors on warm days, indoors at night. Don't plant outside until all danger of frost is past.

What is the cause of buds and blossoms falling off a fuchsia plant on a window shelf indoors? Too hot and/or dry an atmosphere, resulting in red spider or whitefly attack. Possibly they are either too wet or too dry at the root. Root injury always causes leaf drop. Spring and summer are the blooming seasons. Don't expect flowers in the winter. The plants should be resting unless they are young plants. Daily misting of growing plants is a good deterrent to pests.

Can fuchsias be kept during the winter in a cold frame? If the frame is absolutely frostproof and the fuchsias are kept dry and dark until March, they might survive. The so-called hardy variety *Fuchsia magellanica* is the only sort that will stand real frost.

GERANIUM (PELARGONIUM)

Which kind of soil should be used for geraniums to get good flowers? A half-and-half mixture of good garden loam and sand or perlite will grow good flowering plants. Apply a liquid fertilizer when the plants are growing, not when they are resting. The old idea of poor soil kept dry is no longer acceptable.

What is the best fertilizer for geraniums? A low-nitrogen fertilizer is best. Nitrogen is the first number in the fertilizer formulas. It encourages growth rather than bloom.

What do you suggest feeding geraniums for Christmas blooming? Provided you have a good winter-blooming variety, and have grown it especially for winter bloom, any good complete fertilizer that is moderately quick-acting may be used after the final pots are well filled with roots.

What must I do to start geraniums left to hang in a cellar (root upward) when spring arrives?   Take them down, prune them back somewhat (cut back roots as well), and pot in a sandy soil in pots just large enough to hold the roots. Give one good soaking and put in a light, cool place. Unless you have a cellar that is really cool and not a warm basement, hanging plants through the winter is rarely satisfactory. Avoid watering frequently until new growth is well started.

When is it safe to plant geraniums from a window into an open garden?   After all danger of frost has passed and the ground has warmed up (about the time beans are planted). Harden the plants gradually before planting by standing them for a few days in a cold frame, on a porch, or in a sheltered place outdoors.

Should I break the soil and spread out the roots of potted geraniums when I plant them in a garden?   No, leave the root ball intact. Thoroughly soak it an hour before planting it. Make a hole big enough, press soil firmly around the root ball; water well. The top of the root ball should be a half inch below the surface.

What window is best for geraniums?   The sunniest one. They like it cool, somewhat below 68° F. and about 10 degrees less at night.

Should geraniums always be kept toward windows, one side always facing the window, or can they be moved? (Maryland.)   They can be moved if desired, but it is advisable to turn them frequently only at the same window so that all parts get the light and the growth is shapely.

How should one care for geraniums in the house? What about using milk on them? What size pots should be used?   Do *not* use milk. Pots must be adjusted to the size of the plants. Avoid pots that are too large. When the pot is well filled with healthy roots, transfer the plant to a pot a size or two larger, using the soil mixture suggested in the first question on geraniums. A 4-inch pot is a good average size.

How shall I water my potted geraniums?   Watering must be adjusted to the individual plant and environment. Your aim is to keep the soil moist (but not wet and boglike) throughout. When water is given, saturate the whole ball of soil. Let the soil approach dryness between waterings. Sunshine, high temperature, breezy weather, and vigorous growth all make more frequent watering necessary.

I have potted my garden geraniums. What procedure do I follow to keep them blooming in the house? Please give directions for watering, sunlight, clipping tops, and temperature.   See other questions. Cut tops about halfway back at potting time. Give all available sunlight, and fresh air, without drafts. Plants potted from the garden are unlikely to bloom again until late February or March.

Can anything be done to correct the growth habit of a pink-colored geranium which is growing too tall and not sending out any side shoots below a distance of about 10 inches from the flowerpot? Yes. You may "stop" the plant by pinching out the tips of the growing shoots, or, if necessary, you may prune the stems back to force new growth nearer the pot.

Is it true that if geraniums bloom continuously outdoors during the summer they seldom bloom freely in the winter? Garden geraniums are unlikely to be good winter-blooming types. Furthermore, potting them from garden beds causes considerable root disturbance and adjustment must be made before the plants set buds again.

How can I make my geraniums bloom through the winter? To get good winter bloom, take cuttings from May to June. Repot until roots fill 4-inch pots. Young plants should be blooming size by October. August-to-September cuttings probably won't bloom before February. Mail-order specialists can supply geraniums of many types (not just the familiar zonals) that will give you a variety of winter bloomers.

Should geraniums be repotted and how often? Mine are scrawny and do not blossom since being brought in from outdoors. Plants that have given a good display all summer can scarcely be expected to continue throughout the winter. Prune back severely when you bring them indoors. Rest them somewhat by keeping them drier, but not completely dry, until new growth begins in late winter.

How do you treat and store geranium plants through the winter? The best procedure is to cut the plants back partway and pot them a couple of weeks before a killing frost may occur. Winter in a cool plant room or window where the temperature does not drop below 55° F. Water sparingly during the winter.

I have geraniums in flower boxes in my basement. Last summer they developed rather long stems and I want to cut them back this year. How shall I do it? I had these boxes in an unheated porch, but when the weather got too cold I put them in the basement for protection against frost. They lost all their leaves while in the porch (which I wanted to happen, to give them a rest during the winter), but now in the basement they are producing small buds all over and it will not be long until they have new leaves. What shall I do? Prune away ½ to ⅔ the length of each shoot. Repot into new soil, put in a light place, and they will develop nicely by summer.

Can geraniums planted outside be successfully wintered by storing

plants in peat moss or similar material, or must they be potted? They probably could be planted in peat moss and sand, but potting would undoubtedly be surer and better.

Will geraniums keep all winter if pulled up by the root and kept in a cool fruit cellar? I have some beauties I would like to keep. Yes, under the conditions you mention. Hang them up by the roots from the ceiling and pick off all leaves that decay.

What is the best care for ivy-leaved geranium? Mine becomes straggly and root-bound in spite of being cut back and continuously changed to larger pots. Perhaps your plant is so old that it would be wisest to start afresh from a cutting. When plants are well rooted, feed with liquid fertilizer at weekly or biweekly intervals. Pinch the tips out of growing shoots occasionally to induce branching.

What is the proper treatment of ivy geranium—soil, exposure, watering, etc.? Pot in a rich, mellow soil that is well drained. Grow in full winter sun; light shade is desirable during the hottest part of the day in the summer. Water to keep the soil always evenly moist, but not wet and stagnant. Good ventilation and plenty of room are essential.

Why do ivy geraniums always have some dead leaves during their blossoming season? This seems a common complaint except with plants grown in a comparatively humid (and perhaps lightly shaded) greenhouse.

What are conditions favorable to growth of the Lady Washington geranium? Soil and moisture required? Cool, airy, sunny conditions (minimum night temperature 45° F.). Porous, fertile soil with some lime added. Plenty of moisture when growing rapidly; little or none when resting.

How do I care for my Lady Washington geranium that bloomed this summer? These are difficult to care for in a house; it is better to treat them as disposable pot plants after their 4- to 6-week spring display is over. Obtain new plants each year from a mail-order house in a 2½-inch size.

Why do the leaves on my normally blooming geraniums turn brown and drop off? There are many possible causes: too dry an atmosphere; lack of water; too much water; damage to roots when repotting; or too strong fertilizer or spray.

What causes brown edges on geranium leaves? Probably too low humidity. Try standing the plants on pebble-filled trays of water and syringing their tops about once a week.

What causes my geranium leaves to turn pale green and not thrive? They have been recently repotted, but long enough ago to be growing

and thriving. Probably you are growing them with too little light. Low temperature could also be a factor. Try full sunshine and a minimum temperature of 55° F.

Will geraniums thrive inside in a window box when the house is heated by gas? Unless artificial gas is escaping into the room atmosphere, the method of heating will make no difference. Good light, reasonable temperatures, proper soil, and good care are the factors that count.

What makes our geranium house plants thin and spindly instead of short, stocky plants as they are outside? Too high temperature coupled with too little light. Pinching tips out of plants occasionally will help. (Read other questions and answers on this subject.)

My geraniums won't blossom. They are in a southeast window, and the room temperature is between 75° to 80° F. most of the time. What is wrong? The temperature is much too high for them, and most other plants. The ideal temperature for geraniums is 50° to 60° F.

What causes the buds of a geranium to turn brown and dry up? Low humidity is the most likely cause of trouble.

What causes a geranium to have flowers of different colors—first red, then pink? Plants sometimes "sport" or mutate. A red-flower geranium may produce a branch that bears pink flowers, and vice versa. Temperature and fertilizer also influence flower color.

When I cut off pieces of my rose geranium and put them in a bunch of flowers, they start wilting almost at once. What can be done to prevent this? Very little. It will help to cut the geranium ahead of time and put it in cold water in a dark cool place for a few hours.

What is a good method for propagating geraniums? By cuttings (terminal pieces of stem 4 or 5 inches long with lower leaves removed and bases cut cleanly across just beneath a joint). Plant firmly in clean sand; keep shaded from direct sunshine and in a fairly moist atmosphere at about 60° F.

What is the best way to start geraniums from cuttings? What kind of soil should be used, and how much water? Start with good, clean cuttings made of shoots that are neither hard and woody nor yet very vigorous and watery. Plant in sand. Keep just moist (not sopping wet). When roots have formed, pot singly in small pots, using for this first potting a very sandy soil.

What is the recommended time for taking cuttings of rose geraniums? Cuttings will root any time, but the most favorable months are May, August, and September.

When is the right time to take cuttings of geraniums so they will

flower for Memorial Day? August or September. Many of the hybrids flower in 4 months from seed.

When should geraniums be started for planting in outdoor planters? From August to February, depending on the size of the plants needed. Early cuttings will finish in 5-inch pots; late cuttings, in 3½- or 4-inch pots.

Why don't my geraniums bloom in the house before February? I usually start them from cuttings in August. They are very beautiful otherwise, with very large, thick, glossy leaves. The flowers are large and beautiful when they do bloom. For early bloom, propagate in May.

Is it better to root geraniums in water or in sand? What is the best time to root them for early blossoming? Moist sand is best. Take cuttings early in September for late spring blooming; in May, for winter blooming.

Before frost in October, I take geranium cuttings and plant them in sand in a pot indoors for rooting. About 90 per cent eventually rot at the soil line. What is wrong? You will stand a greater chance of success if you take your cuttings in late August or early September. Let the cut ends form a dry callus for a day, then dust the cut end with a hormone powder, available in garden centers. Set the cuttings no more than 1 inch below the sand. Shallow placement encourages sturdy new roots and discourages rot. Keep the sand moist but not wet. You are probably keeping the rooting medium too wet. (See also diseases of Geranium.)

My geranium cuttings looked very healthy at first, but now the leaves are turning yellow and dying. The plants are in a south window. What is the trouble? The cuttings are losing water faster than they can take it up. Reduce the transpiration by shading from bright sun, syringe plants lightly every day, and increase ventilation.

When and how do I pot geranium cuttings rooted in sand? As soon as the roots are ½ to 1 inch long, plant singly in small pots, using very sandy soil without fertilizer added. Do not press soil too firmly. Water well immediately; syringe for a few days.

I have a rose-scented geranium and can never start a new cutting. When and how should I try? In May or August. Make the cutting 4 or 5 joints long; cut with a sharp knife below the joint; remove lower leaves; plant firmly in moist sand; keep moist, shaded from strong sun, in a moist atmosphere at 60° F. or more.

How does one take cuttings from Lady Washington geraniums? Very much as any other geranium. The shoots that root with greatest ease are young ones produced after plants have been started into growth in late summer, but tips of older shoots can also be used.

How can geraniums be grown from seeds? Sow seeds in the spring in pots of soilless mix. Cover very lightly, keep moist (and shaded until seedlings appear) in a temperature of 60° F. If the seed is good, it will soon germinate, and under favorable conditions the transplanted seedlings will make rapid growth. 'Carefree' geraniums grow easily from seed and make fine pot plants.

Why don't my seedling geraniums bloom? Possibly they are growing too vigorously because of the too-rich soil. Too much shade also reduces blooming. Try keeping some plants in pots.

How long after geranium seed is planted may blooms be expected? From 4 to 6 months for standard types, slightly faster for 'Carefree' and 'Firecracker'.

How can a large geranium plant be divided into smaller plants? What fertilizer is recommended? Geranium (*Pelargonium zonale*) plants do not lend themselves to this method of propagation. Increase stock by means of cuttings. Any commercial fertilizer can be used advantageously.

Can geraniums be grown under fluorescent lights? Yes, the miniatures and dwarfs. Taller types require too much space and equipment. Place plants with their tops about 3 inches below the lights; raise tiny growers on inverted flowerpots. Pinch tops to make the plants bushy and give 14 to 18 hours of light. More water and fertilizer will be needed than for window plants.

I have an ivy geranium that is almost 3 feet tall. It was a cutting last spring; now the leaves are starting to curl down. What is the cause of this? It may be due to a severe attack of aphids. Examine young shoots and the undersides of leaves; if plant lice are found, spray with any good contact insecticide.

I have a pelargonium, 6 years old; it bloomed once with gorgeous red and brown blooms. It has never blossomed since. I've changed soil and pots, and started new cuttings, but none will bloom. Whiteflies bother it all the time. What shall I do for it? This is a Lady Washington (*Pelargonium x domesticum*) variety. To control whiteflies, spray at weekly intervals (until the trouble is cleared up) with malathion used according to the manufacturer's directions, or with an aerosol resmethrin spray recommended for the purpose. For cultural details, read answers to other questions. Lady Washington geraniums are difficult as house plants.

Why do geranium cuttings rot while in the sand and turn black and die without rooting? The fungus disease known as black leg causes these symptoms. The rot begins at the base and works upward to the leaves. It is wise to discard rotted cuttings and start over. Use clean flats and sand that has been thoroughly baked or use sterile vermiculite. Propagate from healthy plants only.

There is a small-leaved geranium similar to rose geranium, with a most unusual and delightful scent from the leaves. What is its name? Perhaps you mean *Pelargonium crispum* (lemon-scented), *P. denticulatum* (pine-scented), *P. x fragrans* (nutmeg), *P. odoratissimum* (apple- or nutmeg-scented), or one of the numerous other scented-leaved geraniums with small leaves.

I have seen a geranium on the market in both red and light pink. The green leaves have a white border. What is the name of this geranium? There are many geraniums that can fit this description: 'Mme. Salleroi', 'Hills of Snow', 'Madame Languth' (pink).

What are some good small geraniums that are easy to grow? The tiny miniatures are difficult, but the larger dwarfs, smaller than the standard zonals, will give you continuous color and are of easy culture. These include: 'Bumblebee', 'Dancer', 'Dopey', 'Emma Hossler', 'Gypsy Gem', 'More Mischief', 'Mr. Everaarts', 'Pride', 'Prince Valiant', 'Robin Hood', and 'Sparkle'.

GERBERA

Does gerbera, or African-daisy, when brought indoors from the garden, get a rest period; or should the plants continue to show leaves? Gerberas do best when kept growing during the winter at 55° F., as that is their real flowering season. They are not likely to prove good window plants at ordinary room temperatures.

GESNERIADS

I hear that there are plants similar to the African-violet that require the same culture but will give variety to my window garden. What are they? These are the fibrous-rooted gesneriads; among them, *Aeschynanthus* (the lipstick-plant), *Columnea* (the goldfish-plant), *Episcia* (peacock-plant), *Nematanthus,* and *Streptocarpus* are all excellent flowering subjects.

Are there any trailing gesneriads I could arrange with my African-violets? Episcias make delightful trailing plants, as do *Aeschynanthus,* especially 'Black Pagoda', and the various kinds of *Nematanthus*. However, you will not find them as free-flowering as their African-violet relatives.

What is the best temperature for gesneriads, and how should I water and fertilize them? Like the African-violet, the other gesneriads thrive in a daytime temperature of 65° to 72° F. with a drop of some 10 degrees at night. Keep the soil just evenly moist while plants are in active growth and feed them at every watering with a diluted solution of a water-soluble house-plant fertilizer according to the directions on the container.

Do other gesneriads require as much humidity as African-violets? About the same and not less than 50 per cent. Mist the tops frequently with warm water. This misting, plus the regular fertilizing, promotes bloom.

What is a good soil mix for gesneriads? An open porous soil that drains perfectly, about the same as for your African-violets—good garden loam (pasteurized) plus sand or perlite, or use one of the soilless mixes available at garden centers.

HELIOTROPE (HELIOTROPIUM)

Is heliotrope a satisfactory house plant for winter bloom? Heliotrope can be made to bloom in the winter only by purchasing plants forced by the grower (its normal flowering time is summer) or by starting cuttings in the summer that are ready to bloom by late winter. To force winter bloom on mature plants, they must be kept pinched back and disbudded through the summer. Heliotrope must have a very sunny position in a cool window garden. Water moderately. Cut back long, sprawling branches occasionally. Watch for whitefly.

Can a heliotrope potted from the garden be kept during the winter and set out again in the summer? Yes. Cut back a bit and keep cool—not above 55° F. Cuttings can be rooted in February to make more plants to set out in late May.

Can heliotrope and lavender be treated in the same manner? It depends on which lavender you mean. The French (*Lavandula dentata*) and Spanish (*L. stoechas*) lavenders are not hardy and can be treated as heliotrope is (see above).

IMPATIENS (PATIENCE-PLANT)

How do I care for impatiens indoors? Impatiens plants make excellent everblooming house plants provided they can be grown fairly cool, not above 65° F., and with the humidity above 40 per cent. Setting pots on pebble-filled saucers of water and syringing the tops once or twice a day promote humidity. If long bare stems develop, cut these all the way back. Patience-plants established in clay pots need a lot of water and will drop or show yellow leaves if allowed to dry out for even a few hours. They require a position in good light and do well under fluorescent tubes.

Do patience-plants come in other colors than pink?   Yes, hybridizers have extended the color range and you can grow from seed or find in the spring at your garden center dwarf or standard-size plants in shades of coral, red, orange, scarlet, lavender, and purple as well as white (also some that are variegated red and white, such as 'Go-Go'). Hybrids bred from New Guinea species have both colorful flowers and variegated foliage. Garden centers and several mail-order sources offer New Guinea hybrids suitable for indoor growing in bright light.

Can I dig up impatiens plants from my garden and expect them to bloom indoors in the winter?   Yes, pot them carefully early in September; set in a somewhat shaded, sheltered place outdoors for a couple of weeks; spray to clean up any pests; then bring indoors and provide good air circulation and bright light, including at least 4 hours of sunshine. Given proper care (as above), they will produce a wealth of bloom. Don't overlook seedlings in the garden. In small pots, they will also begin to bloom soon. You can also take cuttings of especially good seedlings.

MARGUERITE DAISY or BOSTON DAISY (CHRYSANTHEMUM FRUTESCENS)

Are marguerites satisfactory as house plants?   Yes. Purchase blooming plants from a florist. They will do well in a sunny window. Sink pots in a garden bed in the summer where they will do almost equally well. For winter bloom, keep plants disbudded through the summer. New plants root readily from cuttings. Marguerites need ample water. Watch for aphids. Use a standard potting mixture. (See Soil, this section.)

NEOMARICA

Is the neomarica sometimes called "twelve apostles"? Does it make a good house plant?   Yes, the neomaricas are sometimes given this nickname because of the number of their irislike leaves, which sometimes reaches twelve. *Neomarica gracilis* is the smaller-leaved of the two generally grown and has white and violet, irislike fleeting blossoms which appear at the tips of leaflike peduncles in late winter. *N. northiana* has larger leaves and blooms about the same time, having larger violet and white fragrant blossoms. It blooms less freely than *N. gracilis*. New plants can be started from the peduncles, which produce young plants after bloom. These plants need sunshine and warmth for early bloom. Sponge the glossy leaves to keep them free from dust. Use a standard potting mixture. (See Soil, this section.)

I have a Neomarica gracilis which grew lustily and increased greatly in size. Why didn't it bloom? Perhaps you kept it too cool. At 50° to 60° F., bloom is considerably delayed. The flowers should appear in late winter if the plants are kept at a day temperature of about 70° F. Pot-bound specimens seldom bloom well. Yours may need division; or discard the old plant and start new stock.

Is it safe to divide old plants of neomarica? Yes, they can be easily divided. Or start new plants from those which develop on blooming stalks.

How old does the "twelve apostles" have to be before it blooms? This plant (*Neomarica,* formally classified as *Marica*), if grown from a small offshoot, can take 2 to 3 years to reach blooming size. Put the plant outdoors in partial shade during the summer. Bring in before frost.

Does the "twelve apostles" require much sun and water? It can take its full share of sun and light in a window, but do not overwater; placing it outside in partial shade during the summer is desirable. It blooms in late winter or early spring, depending on the species.

What makes the tips of my neomarica leaves turn brown? Probably they were watered too much. This plant is related to the iris, and, while evergreen, it has its resting season. When the leaves go bad, repot it in fresh soil (after cutting away dead roots) and give only enough water to prevent wilting until it becomes active again. Too low humidity also causes leaf-tip browning.

ORCHID

I would like to try growing a few orchids but I am confused by the many kinds available. How do I begin? First of all, see the questions and answers that follow. Obtain a good book on orchids, such as the books listed in Section 16. Then survey your growing conditions. Orchids are divided into warm (day temperatures of 70° to 80° F.; nights, 65° to 70° F.), intermediate (days, 65° to 70° F.; nights, 60° to 65° F.), and cool (days, 60° to 65° F.; nights, 55° to 60° F.) groups. There is obviously some overlapping between the last two groups. Orchids also require several hours of sun (or fluorescent lights) and humidity—the same requirements of most flowering house plants.

Is it true that orchids can be grown successfully indoors at a window instead of in a greenhouse? If so, which ones? In recent years much has been learned about orchids as house plants. Excellent results have been obtained at windows with varieties of *Cattleya* (corsage), *Paphiopedilum* (lady-slipper type), *Epidendrum, Oncidium* (butterfly type), and *Phalaenopsis* (moth orchids) as well as many others. These are mostly intermediate to warm growers that bloom from winter to late spring. The monthly bulletins of the American Orchid Society (84 Sherman Street, Cambridge, Mass. 02140) usually contain one or more articles on orchids as house plants.

What is the culture for orchids at windows? This is a complex business (see the above question). The epiphytes (tree-grown), which represent the majority, thrive in coconut fiber, a fir-bark mixture, or chopped tree fern. Those with moisture-holding pseudobulbs (cattleyas are an example) are allowed to dry between waterings; those without pseudobulbs (paphiopedilums, phalaenopsis) are kept evenly moist, not soaked; orchids potted in a humus-rich soil, such as paphiopedilums, are watered like other house plants. Frequent fogging benefits all of them and they do very well under fluorescent lights. Advances in meristem propagation (cloning by tissue culture) have made prices of superior clones more reasonable (although orchids are still more expensive than most house plants). See color catalogs for mericlone orchid selections, especially dwarf clones well suited for window ledges or gardens under fluorescent lights.

I have an east-facing large window that is too cool in the winter for most house plants (as low as 50° F. on some winter nights). I was surprised when a neighbor (who has a greenhouse) suggested cymbidiums, as I thought orchids liked warmth. Not all orchids require warm temperatures and cymbidiums are a prize example of this exception. They should do very well in your window but you will want to grow miniature hybrids only, as the standard kinds grow much too large. Even the miniatures in some varieties can reach 18 to 24 inches or more *above* their 6- to 8-inch pots. Most of the hybrids are terrestrial and thrive in a peat moss-bark mixture or something similar that is humus-rich but drains well. The plants can be summered outdoors in partial shade and toward the end of summer moved into a sunnier spot and watered less. The cool autumn nights will force flower spike initiation for many varieties. (Others should form buds during winter and spring.) Bring the plants indoors before heavy frosts begin. To maintain humidity indoors, place the pots on pebbles in water-filled trays in an east, south, or west window.

PRIMROSE (PRIMULA)

What primroses can I grow indoors in winter? *Primula sinensis* (Chinese primrose), single or double, bears pink, magenta, or white blooms. It has a long blooming period. *P. malacoides*, fairy primrose, has small, frothy violet blossoms throughout the winter. *P. obconica* (poison primrose), with vigorous hairy leaves, has larger flowers. Water daily, in the saucer. Keep in a cool east window, standing the pots on pebbles in water-filled trays.

What can I do to make a primrose bloom? It is about 3 years old. Not knowing the kind of primrose, we can't advise. There are several types grown in pots for winter and spring flowers in greenhouses, and dozens of hardy kinds that bloom outdoors in the spring and early summer if conditions are right. The greenhouse kinds are usually discarded after one season.

What conditions are best for primroses as house plants? How much water? How much light and sun? How much heat and how cool at night? For *Primula malacoides* and *P. sinensis,* not above 50° F. at night; even less is better. *P. obconica,* 50° to 55° F. at night. All like partial shade, ample water, but plenty of drainage in the pots.

What care does the Christmas-blooming primrose require? If you mean *Primula obconica,* this is raised from seed sown in February or March, grown in pots in moderate shade through the summer, and from fall on kept at 55° F. or so. Don't give it too much water, yet never allow it to wilt for lack of moisture at the roots. Discard the plant after it blooms. This is the species that can cause a painful dermatitis on allergic people who handle the plants.

How can I propagate a Chinese primrose? The Chinese primrose (*Primula sinensis*) is raised from seed each year. Choice double sorts that do not form seed usually produce side growths that can be cut off with a knife and rooted.

SHRIMP-PLANT (JUSTICIA BRANDEGEANA)

What exposure does a shrimp-plant like? Shrimp-plants like plenty of sun and plenty of water. This is a fine house plant, untroubled by any insect pests.

What will I do with my shrimp-plant when it gets tall and leggy? Cut the plants back each spring and root cuttings for new plants to bring indoors in the fall. Cuttings will root easily, either in pots of sand or in a cold frame. Of course, you can keep the big plant, simply cutting it back enough to promote bushy growth rather than letting it achieve a 3- to 4-foot height.

Can a shrimp-plant be wintered in a cold frame? No, it is too soft and will die, even with protection. Even at a temperature of 45°, the shrimp-plant is unhappy. It grows best at 55° to 60° F.

Can you tell me the native habitat of the shrimp-plant and any legend or general information about the plant and its care? It comes from tropical America. There are no legends, as it was practically unknown except to botanists up to 1905.

SPATHIPHYLLUM

What is the correct growing medium for Spathiphyllum? Pot in terrestrial orchid mix or 50 per cent coconut fiber with 50 per cent houseplant soil, all over good drainage of gravel and a few chunks of hardwood charcoal.

Which spathe flower varieties are best as house plants? Choose the compact, adaptable sorts such as hybrid 'Mauna Loa' and the dwarf species *S. quindiuense.* Both of these have shiny strap-shaped leaves and long-lasting white spathes. Spathiphyllums thrive in intermediate to warm temperatures (65° to 70° F. nights), 50 to 60 per cent relative humidity, and diffuse light. *S. quindiuense* is mature at 6 to 8 inches, so it is suitable for many fluorescent light gardens.

STRELITZIA

How is bird-of-paradise (Strelitzia) handled in the winter? Should I take it out of its pots and plant it in the ground in the summer? The strelitzia is a big subject for a house plant, needing a tub—since it won't bloom until of some size. In the winter, give it only a moderate amount of water; good rich soil with plenty of drainage; full light but no feeding while semidormant. Don't take it out of its pot or tub in the summer; sink it in the ground to the rim and feed it regularly. Strelitzia generally blooms in late summer and fall. In the winter it should have a temperature of 45° to 50° F.

Whenever my bird-of-paradise makes a new leaf, an old leaf dies. Why doesn't it bloom? You won't get blooms until the plant has 10 or more healthy leaves. The dying leaves indicate something wrong at the roots. The cause may be either insufficient size pot, poor drainage, not enough water while in active growth during the summer, or too much water in the winter when it should be semidormant.

SWEET-OLIVE (OSMANTHUS FRAGRANS)

How shall I care for a sweet-olive as a house plant? Sweet-olive does well in an east or west window if you can give it a day temperature of 60° to 65° F. It needs plenty of water and a humid atmosphere. Syringe the leaves daily and feed occasionally with a "complete" plant food after the pot is filled with roots.

Annuals and Biennials as House Plants

Is it possible to raise annuals indoors in the winter without the plants becoming stalky? Yes, if you choose varieties that are dwarf and use fluorescent lights (a combination of cool-white and warm-white tubes will be satisfactory unless you want to experiment with the special plant tubes, which will be more expensive), either solely or as a supplement to sunshine on cloudy days. The lights should be on from 14 to 16 hours.

ALYSSUM, SWEET- (LOBULARIA MARITIMA)

Can I make sweet-alyssum bloom indoors? Yes, if you have enough sun or fluorescent lights and a really cool window or plant room. Sow the seed in late summer and fall for winter bloom, in early winter for spring bloom.

BROWALLIA

Is the browallia an annual? I potted mine in the fall and about January the leaves withered and it died. *Browallia americana* is an annual for outdoor use. *B. speciosa* is a biennial or perennial, but not hardy. It is sown in the fall, carried along in a greenhouse through the winter, and planted out in the spring; or sown in the spring to flower indoors in the winter.

Are browallias suited to a window garden? Yes, *Browallia speciosa* makes a most satisfactory house plant. The tubular flowers, rather like small petunias, are blue, violet, or white, and literally cover the plants through a long blooming season. They are easily grown biennials that form shrubby, compact plants. Purchase them in bloom from a grower or grow them yourself from early spring-sown seed.

FORGET-ME-NOT (MYOSOTIS SYLVATICA)

Can forget-me-not be made to bloom indoors? Yes. It needs a cool but humid atmosphere and, unlike most other annuals and biennials, can stand some shade, though not much indoors. Plant the seed in the spring for the following winter's bloom. This is really a greenhouse subject for winter bloom, but with the right conditions, such as fluorescent lights, you may have flowers.

LOBELIA

Is lobelia a plant which can be made to bloom indoors in the winter? Yes, you can grow lobelia from seeds or cuttings to produce winter bloom. It does not need as much sun as many other flowering plants but will require artificial light for best results. You will have a good chance of success if the window or location under lights is cool.

MORNING-GLORY (IPOMOEA)

Can I grow morning-glory in my window garden? Yes, if you have a cool, sunny window. Plant seeds in individual pots in August. Transplant to larger pots as needed. Have strings ready near the glass to encourage the vines to climb.

NASTURTIUM (TROPAEOLUM)

How can nasturtiums be grown indoors in the winter? They must have a cool, sunny window or plant room. Plant seeds in late summer in pots of soil without too much fertilizer. Or take cuttings of some of the summer bloomers in the garden, keeping them cut back to prevent bloom until winter. Of course, black aphids will attack them indoors as well as out. Use some of the double fragrant varieties. Long, budded sprays cut early in the fall and placed in a vase of water will bloom for weeks indoors.

PETUNIA

How can I grow petunias in the house during the winter? I took a few in this fall and they wouldn't grow. Petunias make fine blooming house plants, especially under fluorescent lights. Lift in September, cut back tops, and set in quite small pots, for the root systems are not large. Give a clean-up spray, and after a week or so in a sheltered place outdoors, take to a sunny window. New shoots will appear and buds will develop about January. Syringe frequently at the sink to ward off aphids. Take cuttings from established plants to maintain a succession of bloom.

My petunia plants potted from the garden are growing well but the foliage feels sticky and there are a number of yellow leaves. Although petunia foliage is naturally a little sticky, this sounds like an attack of aphids. Examine the underside of the leaves; if you see tiny white dots and if water spraying (see above) doesn't clean up the infestation, try a house-plant bomb, or for a bad attack, a *weak* malathion spray.

SNAPDRAGON (ANTIRRHINUM)

Are snapdragons practical house plants? If you have a very cool sun porch or bay window (40° to 50° F. night temperature), you may be able to have blooming snapdragons (*Antirrhinum*) through the winter. Though these are perennial in the South, they are grown as annuals in the North. Buy budded plants or grow your own from seed planted the previous spring. Select dwarf, rust-resistant varieties. Or you can start plants in the summer for winter bloom by propagating by cuttings those growing in the summer garden. Whether plants are started from seeds or cuttings, they should be kept pinched back to encourage winter bloom.

Foliage Plants

GENERAL

What temperature is best for foliage plants indoors? No one temperature is best for all. The majority grow well in a night temperature of 55° to 60° F. with a rise of 10° in the daytime permitted. For cooler rooms, try English ivy, leopard-plant, Australian silk-oak, aspidistra, baby's-tears, pick-a-back plant, strawberry-geranium, spider-plant, and Norfolk-Island-pine.

Does it help to spray water on the leaves of foliage plants grown in the home? Daily sprinklings with mist benefit all plants having leathery leaves, such as rubber plants, palms, and pandanus. On the mornings of bright, sunny days, syringe plants with thin or hairy leaves, such as coleus or pilea.

Some people tell me to wash my foliage plants with milk; others say to wipe the leaves with olive oil. Which is better? Both are harmful. They merely result in an artificial gloss due to the oil or to the fat of the milk. When you sponge leaves, use lukewarm, soapy water.

My foliage plants indoors do well in the summer, but in the fall their leaves turn yellow and drop off. What is the cause? When artificial heating is used the air becomes too dry for the plants. Lack of atmospheric moisture is one cause of failure with house plants. Install humidifiers. Stand the plants on shallow trays of sand or gravel, kept moist.

Can you give a list of foliage house plants that can easily be raised from seed? *Eucalyptus globulus* (blue gum), *Eucalyptus citriodora* (lemon-scented eucalyptus), *Grevillea robusta* (Australian silk-oak), coleus, *Asparagus densiflorus* 'Sprengeri' and *Asparagus setaceus* (syn. *plumosus*) (asparagus-ferns), and *Cordyline indivisa* (*Dracaena indivisa*).

ARALIA   (See *Fatsia japonica*.)

ASPARAGUS

What kind of soil does Asparagus setaceus like—acid or alkaline? More on the acid than the alkaline side. It likes a garden soil that has both peat moss and sand in it (2 parts soil, 1 part peat moss, 1 part sand); this should be enriched by ⅛ part (in bulk) of dried cow manure mixed with a sprinkling of superphosphate.

What are asparagus "ferns"? Three are commonly grown: *Asparagus setaceus*, with flat sprays of fine foliage; *A. densiflorus* 'Sprengeri', with coarser and less regular leaves; and *A. densiflorus* 'Myers', with tightly clustered foliage. These foliage plants are not true ferns and are in the same genus as the vegetable. They are subject to red spider, so spray once a week with cool water. Transplant once a year, or whenever the pots become filled with roots. They like plenty of light and air. Water regularly and feed once a month. (See the next question.)

What are the water requirements of Asparagus 'Sprengeri'? Is it the moisture or temperature conditions that turn the foliage yellow? *Asparagus densiflorus* 'Sprengeri' likes adequate and regular watering. Once or twice a month, give liquid plant food. Leaves turn yellow from a lack of food, if the plant is pot-bound, or if the temperature is above or below 55° to 65° F.

How do I raise asparagus "ferns" from seed? Very easily. Soak the seed in tepid water for 24 hours before sowing, then plant 1 inch apart and cover to a depth of ¼ inch in light, sandy soil in a pot or pan. Keep moist, dark, and in a temperature of 65° to 70° F.

ASPIDISTRA ELATIOR (CAST-IRON PLANT)

Why do the leaves of my aspidistra turn yellow? Yellowing leaves mean either red spider mites are sucking the life out of them, that you have watered too much, or have exposed the plant to extreme drought. If red spider is the trouble, spray or sponge the leaves with any good contact insecticide.

Does the aspidistra plant ever bloom? Old, well-established plants sometimes do. The flowers are relatively inconspicuous, are reddish-brown, and are borne at soil level.

Can aspidistra be increased in any other way than by division? No. In nature it may propagate by seed, but seeds do not seem to form in cultivation. Divide in the spring and keep newly potted divisions in a warm room and a moist atmosphere until new roots become established.

AUSTRALIAN SILK-OAK (GREVILLEA ROBUSTA)

What kind of soil does Australian silk-oak (Grevillea robusta) like? A sandy and rather peaty mixture that does not tend to become waterlogged. Very heavy soil is unsuited to this plant, particularly in its young stages.

AVOCADO (PERSEA AMERICANA)

How can I raise an avocado plant from a seed? Select a seed from a ripe fruit. The seed should show signs of cracking and not appear hard

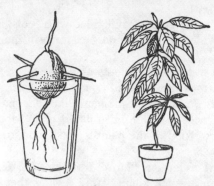

*An avocado pit (seed) will develop
into an attractive foliage plant. Insert toothpicks into the sides of the
pit so it can be suspended in water.
After it has sprouted and roots have
formed, it can be potted.*

and dry. Insert 3 toothpicks into the sides just deep enough to support
the seed on the edge of a tumbler of water. Keep the water level just up
to and touching the bottom of the seed; don't float or submerge the entire seed in water. In a few weeks, roots and shoot growth appear, and
then the rooted seed can be placed in a 4-inch pot. Several pinchings of
top growth will be necessary if you wish a bushy plant. When potting
the seed, put about three fourths of it in the pot; the remainder can pro-
trude above the surface.

BABY'S-TEARS (SOLEIROLIA SOLEIROLII)

**What is the plant called baby's-tears and how can I grow it in the
house?** Baby's-tears, or creeping-nettle, formerly known as *Helxine
soleirolii,* is a native of Corsica and Sardinia. It looks like a fine green
moss and grows well in sandy soil, kept moist, in morning sun or very
light shade, but it resents a hot, dry room. It is excellent for a terrarium.
Baby's-tears is easily propagated by pulling it apart and setting the
pieces in soil.

BAMBOO

Can bamboo be grown indoors as a house plant? Yes, some genera
make handsome specimens in tubs in fully lighted, cool interiors. Keep
the plants in relatively small containers and do not repot unless really

pot-bound. They will need plenty of water and benefit from summering outdoors in light shade. The Chinese goddess (*Bambusa glaucescens riviereorum*) is often used indoors but may reach 6 feet in height. Other cultivars of *B. glaucescens* are worth considering and searching out, as some do not grow as tall.

BAY TREE (LAURUS NOBILIS)

Are there several varieties of bay trees, and how should they be treated? Mine were given me as a gift. I am at a loss as to how to keep them growing. You must be talking about sweet bay or laurel (*Laurus nobilis*), whose leaves are used as a flavoring. It is not hardy in cold climates. It eventually grows to large size. Tubbed specimens are best wintered in a cool, light situation with reduced watering.

BEAUCARNEA (BOTTLE-PALM)

What is the odd but intriguing plant with the swollen base and stem topped by a cascade of ribbon foliage? The elephant-foot plant or bottle ponytail or bottle-palm (*Beaucarnea recurvata*), an oddity that becomes handsome as it ages. It is a long-lived plant that enlarges slowly, tolerating a wide range of indoor temperatures and low humidity. The swollen part of the stem holds moisture. Allow soil to dry out between waterings and water sparingly during the winter.

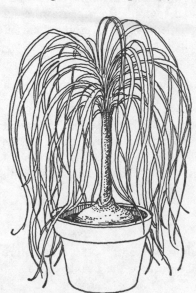

Ponytail or bottle-palm are two names for Beaucarnea recurvata. *This foliage plant has a gray trunk swollen at its base. The plant grows slowly and, though tolerant of neglect, speeds up its growth and improves in appearance when given daily sun and water as the soil dries.*

CHINESE-EVERGREEN (AGLAONEMA MODESTUM)

What are the requirements of Chinese-evergreen, so often grown indoors in water? *Aglaonema modestum* is a very satisfactory house plant for rooms with little sun. Grown in water to which a few small pieces of charcoal have been added to keep the water "sweet," it behaves well in average living-room conditions. A ¼-strength solution of water-soluble house-plant fertilizer can be used instead of water, once the stems have roots.

COLEUS

Can I dig up coleus plants from the garden and put them into pots for winter decoration indoors? If plants are cut back at the time of potting, they may grow into decorative specimens by late winter; but a much better plan is to take cuttings from outdoor plants in August, root them in sand, and pot them up to provide young new plants for your indoor garden.

How can coleus be raised as house plants? Mine always become sickly. Coleus are raised from seed or cuttings. They like full light, temperatures not above 65° F. in the winter, and protection from mealybugs.

Mealybugs on my coleus are a constant source of trouble. What shall I do? Mealybugs on coleus are difficult to eradicate because forceful syringing with water is apt to damage the leaves. Try brushing them off with a soft camel's-hair brush dipped in soapy water or denatured alcohol.

CROTON (CODIAEUM)

I have a croton, potted in fibrous loam, but while the plant in general does well, sometimes leaves wilt and drop. What causes this? If the plant is growing outdoors, cool spells may be the cause. This plant loves lots of heat. It is not a good house plant unless high humidity with heat is provided.

CRYPTANTHUS (EARTH STAR)

What is a cryptanthus and how should it be grown? It is a miniature bromeliad (pineapple relative) that is grown for the beauty of its stiff little leaves. For best foliage color, give some exposure to the sun or grow under lights. It grows best in a terrarium or in a warm room where the air is not too dry. Pot in a sandy, humus-rich soil with charcoal added, or in a mixture of bark and leafmold.

DIZYGOTHECA (FALSE-ARALIA)

How can I grow dizygotheca? This treelike false-aralia is not demanding and thrives at 55° to 75° F. Give it good light and keep the soil evenly moist. A 5-inch pot is usually about right.

DUMB-CANE (DIEFFENBACHIA)

I have a dumb-cane (dieffenbachia) in the house and the lower leaves turn yellow. What shall I do? Too low a temperature or lack of moisture in the air are the most common causes of yellowing. Excessive dryness at the roots may be a contributing cause. This plant likes warmth, a moist atmosphere, shade from strong sunshine, and a fair amount of soil moisture.

Why is dieffenbachia called dumb-cane? Is it poisonous? It is not poisonous, but, like its relative the Jack-in-the-pulpit, it contains sharp crystals of oxalate of lime. If the stem is chewed, these pierce the tongue, causing it to swell with intense pain. Speech may be impossible for several days—hence the common name.

Can a "leggy" dieffenbachia be successfully air-layered? The plant is 30 inches high. Cut halfway through, diagonally and upward. Insert a toothpick and bind with a large ball of sphagnum moss. Then wrap tightly in plastic, binding at each end with wire fasteners. A thick stem may take a year before it is rooted enough for you to cut below the moss and place it in a pot. Set leftover cane section on moist unmilled sphagnum moss if you want sprouts from the dormant buds.

FALSE-ARALIA   (See Dizygotheca.)

FATSIA JAPONICA

Is Fatsia japonica a house plant? It is an easy subject to grow in a light window where the temperature ranges between 55° and 65° F. Shade from bright summer sunshine is desirable. Water to keep the soil always evenly moist but not waterlogged.

How can Fatsia japonica be raised from seed? Sow seed in pots of light, sandy soil in the spring; cover seeds with sifted soil. Keep moist and at a temperature of 65° F. When an inch or two high, transplant to small pots of sandy soil. Grow in a light window.

FERNS (See under separate headings, this section.)

FIG, WEEPING (FICUS BENJAMINA)

Can I propagate the weeping fig from cuttings? Yes. Use tip cuttings and insert them in a soilless mix. Enclose the pot or flat in polyethylene.

HOLLY (ILEX)

I have a dwarf holly plant in a pot. Can it be made to fruit indoors? Holly is not a house plant, but some species are not hardy except in the South and can be grown for a time indoors in a cool location. Most hollies are unisexual and fruit is not possible unless both types (a male plant and a female plant) are grown near each other.

LEOPARD-PLANT (LIGULARIA)

Is the leopard-plant classed as a foliage or a flowering plant? Like most "foliage plants," *Ligularia kaempferi* 'Aureo-maculata' blooms (and the yellow flowers are quite attractive) but it is grown primarily for the beauty of its large, rounded leaves, which are conspicuously spotted with yellow markings.

Under what conditions does the leopard-plant grow best? How is it propagated? It likes a rather cool room with full sun or partial shade. Provide a freely drained soil, but enough water to keep it always moist. In the summer, plunge the pot to its rim outdoors in a partially shaded position in the garden. Propagate by dividing the old plant in the spring.

MANGO (MANGIFERA INDICA)

I am raising a mango tree from seed. Do you think it will bear? Not indoors. The mango is a large tropical tree that sometimes attains a height of nearly 100 feet. It is hardy only in the most tropical parts of the United States. Fruits of seedling mangoes are very inferior to named varieties but they make very attractive foliage plants for a well-lighted, rather cool situation indoors.

MARANTA (PRAYER-PLANT)

How should Maranta leuconeura and its variety kerchoviana be cared for? Marantas, grown chiefly for their unusual foliage, are tropical plants which flourish in the winter at a north window with evenly moist soil and 40 to 50 per cent humidity. They rest in late fall. When some leaves turn brown, especially around the edges, cut them off. Then keep the plant quite dry until about February. Then water freely again and fertilize regularly. It is often called prayer-plant because it folds its leaves at night.

MONSTERA (SWISS-CHEESE PLANT)

What is the foliage plant, of climbing habit, with large, heart-shaped cut leaves? You are probably referring to *Monstera deliciosa,* a very showy foliage plant which looks well in modern rooms and which can be grown in good light without direct sun. Though a climber, it grows rather slowly and is usually treated as a foliage plant, trained on cork bark. It has many other common names, including Mexican breadfruit.

NEPHTHYTIS (SYNGONIUM PODOPHYLLUM)

What are the requirements of nephthytis? Nephthytis is a tropical vinelike foliage plant which usually comes from the grower trained on cork bark. It does not need full sunlight and stands ordinary living-room conditions well. Trailing portions cut from the main plant do well grown in water.

NORFOLK-ISLAND-PINE (ARAUCARIA HETEROPHYLLA)

How do we take care of Norfolk-Island-pine during the summer? This evergreen tree makes a good but slow-growing pot plant. During the summer, sink the pot outside in soil up to the pot's rim in light shade and syringe and water regularly. In the winter, it prefers a temperature of 55° to 60° F., and even light to keep it shapely. Spray regularly to prevent red spider mite and mealybug attacks.

I have had an araucaria for the past 4 years. It is now 40 inches high. The branches are starting to droop. Can you suggest the reason? It is natural for lower branches eventually to droop. If the plant is really wilting, you have either overwatered or given too much fertilizer with perhaps not enough light and too much heat. Stimulants are not called for when plants droop. Keep cool and water less in the winter.

The Norfolk-Island-pine is a beautiful evergreen that can eventually reach 5 to 6 feet. It grows best in cool indoor temperatures, 50° to 55° F. at night and 60° to 65° F. during the day.

PALM

How shall I take care of a date palm? (1) Temperature from 55° to 65° F.; (2) soil—loam, peat moss, and sand, proportions 5–3–1; also, a 5-inch pot for a 6-foot specimen; (3) watering—never completely dry but not too wet; deep occasional soaking in a pail or tub; (4) exposure —bright light.

Is there any special fertilizer or treatment to give palm trees and how often must they be watered? Palms need full shade and must never be dry, yet not constantly soaking wet. No feeding is needed until the pots are full of root.

What possibility is there of growing palms? Many palms are good house plants if given full light but not direct sun and are not subjected to dry, hot rooms in winter. The dwarf *Chamaedorea elegans* adapts well to indoor pot culture.

PANDANUS (SCREW-PINE)

How should I care for a pandanus plant? Keep out of bright sunshine and use care in watering. It is easy to kill this plant with overwatering.

My pandanus leaves are turning yellow, especially at the tips. What is the cause? This is a sure sign of root trouble; you probably have overwatered. Keep it on the dry side and don't use too large a pot. Don't expose it to bright sunshine.

How and when should shoots from pandanus be rooted? Cut off the suckers at the base and insert them in sandy soil. If you can place the pot in a box and cover it with a sheet of glass or plastic, all the better. Do this in the spring, when growth is active.

PEPEROMIA

How can I grow the striped peperomia (P. argyreia) successfully? Peperomias require fairly warm, humid conditions and protection from direct sunshine. A humus-rich soil (well-drained), kept uniformly moist, is desirable.

Rooted leaf cutting of peperomia.

What causes small brown spots on the underside of peperomia leaves? Spots on the underside suggest injury from thrips or other insects. Poor foliage generally is due either to sunburn, lack of moisture in the atmosphere, or too much water on the leaves.

My peperomia gets large, irregular brown spots on the back of the leaves. Can you tell me why and what to do? Such spots or patches are usually an indication of disease brought about by atmospheric conditions. Try to increase the humidity.

PICK-A-BACK (TOLMIEA)

What is the pick-a-back plant? *Tolmiea menziesii,* a native of our Pacific Northwest. It has the curious habit of producing young plantlets on its leaves from which new plants can be grown. It is an interesting, worthwhile house plant.

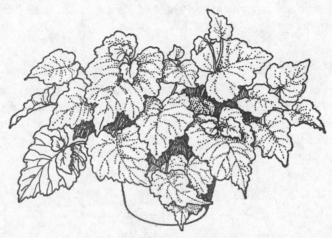

The pick-a-back plant (Tolmiea menziesii) *is an oddity among foliage plants. It forms plantlets on its growing leaves.*

How shall I care for the pick-a-back plant? Grow in pots of light, rich soil. Keep quite moist at all times. It thrives in full sun or partial shade. Although a hardy plant, it seems not to object to ordinary room temperatures as long as its potting soil does not dry out. Propagate by planting well-developed plantlets that are borne on mature leaves.

PINEAPPLE (ANANAS)

How can I start a pineapple plant? Cut off most of the leafy top, leaving a little attached to a small section of the fruit. Scoop out the pulp and let the cut surface dry for a few days. Then plant the top in a pot of sandy soil. (Do not keep sopping wet or rot will occur—and no roots.) New shoots will soon push out from the old top.

What can I do with a pineapple plant that is nearly 2 years old and does not seem to grow any more? It stands nearly 8 inches high now.

Doesn't it flower? If a true pineapple (*Ananas comosus*), grown from the tuft of the fruit, it needs full sun to bloom. Perhaps you have a different species. Flowers are not showy but dwarf *Ananas nanus* is interesting for the miniature pineapple fruit it eventually bears. Variegated-leaf pineapples (*A. comosus 'Variegatus'*) are also attractive in a sunny window. To encourage bloom and fruiting on a mature pineapple, place the plant in a warm room in a clear plastic bag with a ripe apple for a week. The ethylene gas from the apple forces flowering. Although the pineapple is an interesting plant, there are other members of the bromeliad family that make better house plants, take less space, and have more attractive foliage. For example, *Aechmea fasciata*, *Billbergia zebrina*, and the various dwarf terrestrial *Cryptanthus* cultivars.

The pineapple is a bromeliad. It can become a house plant by rooting the top saved from a fruit.

What care is needed for the pineapple plant? The true pineapple needs plenty of warmth, light, and sun, and very careful watering, as it quickly resents very wet conditions at the root. Frequent feedings (2 a week) with a balanced fertilizer are of great help to a healthy plant.

POMEGRANATE (PUNICA GRANATUM)

Can pomegranates be grown from seed? Yes, they can, and if wanted merely as house plants they are quite satisfactory. For fruit production (when they can be grown outdoors), named varieties are used, and these will not come true from seed.

How are pomegranates propagated? By hardwood cuttings planted in open nursery beds in February; by taking rooted shoots directly from the base of the plant; by layering; by green cuttings taken in the summer.

REDWOOD BURL (SEQUOIA SEMPERVIRENS)

How long will a redwood burl last? Also, can a sprout of it be rooted and grown as a pot plant?   A burl kept with its base in a shallow container of water lived and thrived for many years at the New York Botanical Garden. Sprouts sometimes form roots when the atmosphere is humid. If you wish to encourage rooting, put damp sphagnum moss around the base of active green sprouts and keep the plant in a bright location at a moderate temperature, 50° to 60° F., at night.

RUBBER PLANT (FICUS)

What care is needed in watering and feeding rubber trees grown as house plants?   *Ficus elastica,* the recognized rubber plant of early days, and *F. lyrata* like good light and lots of room, as they eventually become very tall, rarely branching. Give plenty of water except in winter when growth is less active. Occasionally wipe its leaves with a damp cloth. A more compact selection which often has small yellow "figlets" is *F. deltoidea,* the mistletoe fig. It makes a good indoor bonsai subject.

How does one encourage the rubber plant to branch out rather than grow as a single upright stem?   *Ficus elastica* is not very responsive to being cut back, but if done after the plant has 6 or 8 leaves, removal of the point will induce 2 or 3 breaks. The natural habit is to grow single stemmed for many years before branching.

Can I cut back a large rubber plant when the trunk is thick?   *Ficus elastica,* if cut back, may die from the shock if it is treelike and has no lower leaves. The regular method of propagation is to slit the stem partly through, wrap with moss, and keep constantly moist. If your plant has a branch with a ½-inch stem, you can so treat the branch, but if there are no branches and the trunk is really heavy, 1 inch or more, it's too large for this air-layering method.

What is the name of the rubber plant with leaves that widen out toward the tips? What culture does it need?   This is the fiddle-leaved fig (or rubber plant), *Ficus lyrata.* It requires the same general care as the common rubber plant, *F. elastica.*

SAGO-PALM (CYCAS REVOLUTA)

I have a sago-palm in a pot. It is about 20 years old, but I've had it only 5 months. It hasn't done well since I brought it inside. Can you

give its proper care? *Cycas revoluta* likes bright light and a sandy soil. Avoid overwatering, especially in the winter when the plants are inactive, but never allow them to dry out completely. In the fall, don't be alarmed if the lower leaves turn brown and drop. It's natural for them to drop as new ones are produced.

SCHEFFLERA (BRASSAIA ACTINOPHYLLA)

Is the schefflera a good house plant? Yes, if you have plenty of room for a tub specimen. It is easy to grow, producing decorative leaves and sometimes red flowers (but only on aged plants), even under less than ideal conditions of 55° to 75° F. It requires full light, not sun, and water only when somewhat dry, about once or twice a week. It is decorative in front of a long window of a modern house, or for a well-lighted public room.

SENSITIVE-PLANT (MIMOSA PUDICA)

How can I grow a sensitive-plant in my sunny window? Sow seeds of *Mimosa pudica* in a pot of light soil in March. Transplant seedlings into a 2½-inch pot when the second set of leaves is well grown. Later, pot into a 4-inch pot. Use special care to keep as many roots as possible since *M. pudica* resents being transplanted. Grow in well-drained soil with a minimum temperature of 60° F. Never permit it to suffer from dryness.

SNAKE-PLANT (SANSEVIERIA)

Under what conditions will sansevieria do best? In dry, moderately warm rooms with full light. Water carefully once a week. This is enough under ordinary conditions, as it is easily killed by overwatering.

I can never get sansevieria to grow and do well. Why? Too much water and not enough light. This plant, when well rooted, does not require frequent watering. Shade is also detrimental.

My sansevieria plant had flowers on it this summer. Is this unusual? Not as unusual as is sometimes thought. Old, well-established specimens are apt to bloom, and once they begin, they repeat the performance year after year. The flowers are light greenish, on feathery spikes, and are very fragrant.

How does one increase sansevierias? These are grown from divisions of roots or rhizomes. Pieces of leaf planted in moist sand will root and make plants, but if you so treat the variegated sort, the young plants will be green-leaved rather than variegated.

SPIDER-PLANT (CHLOROPHYTUM COMOSUM)

Please describe the spider-plant. The form 'Variegatum' has green-and white-striped leaves and sends out long, slender stems which bear young plants at their extremities. It is very easy to grow and also most decorative. Grow in a light place and take care not to overwater. Cut off the plantlets and pot them if you want more plants, but it does not harm the parent plant to let offsets stay. They are an added interest. Another name is airplane plant.

STRAWBERRY-GERANIUM (SAXIFRAGA STOLONIFERA)

What will encourage the growth of strawberry-geranium? Should it be kept on the dry side? In the sun or shade? *Saxifraga stolonifera,* also known as mother of thousands, is usually winter hardy in the North if protected by a cover of leaves. Don't try to grow it in a hot, dry room, or it will become infested with red spider. Sun or bright light is good. Provide moderate supplies of water. If you want runners bearing young plants to develop, grow it in a hanging basket.

UMBRELLA-PLANT (CYPERUS ALTERNIFOLIUS)

What conditions does the feathery green plant called umbrella-plant require? This is really a bog plant and needs a moist or wet soil. It is one of the few house plants that does well if the pot is kept standing in a saucer of water; it prefers plenty of sunshine.

How are young plants of the umbrella-plant raised? *Cyperus alternifolius* is easily raised from seeds sown in soil kept constantly moist. Another method of increase is to cut off the leafy top with about an inch of stem attached and submerge the stem in a pot of sandy soil.

VARIEGATED PLANTS

What plants with colorful leaves can be grown among green plants at well-lighted windows? These make pleasing accents with green plants: purple-tinted velvet-plant; prayer-plant (*Maranta*) with maroon or silver markings; also aucuba, aphelandra, columnea, sansevieria, episcia, fittonia, various kinds of dracena, *Cissus discolor,* and many kinds of begonia. In the summer, a few pots of caladiums will enliven collections of house plants sojourning on the terrace, as will New Guinea impatiens, which have brightly variegated foliage, too.

VELVET-PLANT (GYNURA AURANTIACA)

I have a foliage plant with velvety purple leaves. What is it and how shall I care for it? This is *Gynura aurantiaca* or velvet-plant. Place it in an east window and water freely. It is of easy culture.

Gift Plants

AZALEA (RHODODENDRON)

What is the proper soil for azaleas and other ericaceous plants? Acid, well-drained, and humus-rich soil. The addition of liberal amounts of oak leafmold or peat moss to the mixture is recommended. (See Soil, Acid Potting Mixture, this section.)

How shall I care for a tender azalea after it blooms? Keep it well watered, in full light, in a room at 50° F. If it is overlarge for the pot, shift to a pot 1 inch larger, soaking the soil well after repotting. Use an acid potting mixture. Pot firmly but do not ram the earth down hard.

Should I cut back my indoor azaleas, and when? No, merely pinch back any extra-long shoots, but don't prune in the usual way for shrubs or the plants may die. Azaleas make only short growths each year.

What care is needed for an azalea plant grown indoors? Pot azaleas should be indoors only during the winter and while in bloom. From mid-May on the pot should be sunk in the ground, with light shade, regular watering and spraying, and pinching back of overlong growths. Use a general or liquid fish fertilizer occasionally. Bring indoors to a cool room before severe frost.

How should I treat my tender azalea plants after bringing them indoors in autumn? Keep just moist, in a light, cool room at 40° F. until 4 weeks before you want full bloom, then bring into a warmer, sunny room, water plentifully, and mist foliage daily. Give a complete fertilizer until color shows on the buds.

Should an azalea plant have a rest period during the winter? Yes. After being brought indoors before severe frost, a potted azalea must be kept cool (40° to 60° F.) and just moist until after Christmas. In January or February, bring to a sunny but cool window, fertilize as new growth develops, and syringe the tops frequently to ward off red spider.

How can I tell whether my tender azalea is going to bloom? The buds should be well set when brought indoors in the fall.

An Easter azalea plant was put aside and forgotten after blooming until it was discovered in November in a dry, warm cellar. Is this plant dormant or really dead? An azalea so treated is dead—or it ought to be! Don't waste time on it. Azaleas after flowering need a cool place, moderate water, and good light before being sunk outdoors. The plants that flower in pots are practically evergreen and should never be bare of all leaves.

How are evergreen azaleas propagated? These are easily rooted from cuttings, using the short shoots that come after blooming. Root in sand and peat moss in a propagating box or in a pot enclosed in a plastic bag.

I was presented with a fine azalea plant. Why has it shed all its leaves? You either let it get dry at the roots or the foliage became infested with red spider. Both will cause defoliation, and, if complete, the plant cannot be revived.

I have an azalea which I purchased 2 years ago. Last year it bloomed beautifully. Now it is dying. Can you give me any help in the care of the plant? Your rooms are probably too hot and dry. Keep the plant in as cool a place as possible. Once a week, submerge the pot up to the rim and let it stay until the topsoil feels moist.

Should I plant outdoors a pink-flowered azalea purchased in a florist's shop? (Vermont.) If your azalea is small-flowered, it is a Kurume, and there's little chance of its surviving a winter outdoors in your state. If large-flowered, it positively will winter-kill. If you want garden azaleas, plant sorts listed as such. (For correct care of your azalea, see previous questions.)

I have a small-flowered and a large-flowered house azalea. Can you tell me what they are? There are many named varieties of azaleas grown as potted plants.

CHRYSANTHEMUM

How long can chrysanthemums be kept flowering indoors? Two weeks is average. Spraying daily with cool water will help to keep foliage fresh-looking and prevent its turning brown and dry before the flowers fade. Keep in a cool location.

Are any of the potted chrysanthemums used for gift plants hardy

enough to be transferred to a garden? Yes, but the kind of chrysanthemum as well as your climate must be considered. And, of course, the time of year you receive the plant determines when it can be planted in the garden.

Is there any way to save chrysanthemum plants sent in the fall from the florist? They don't winter over outside. After they bloom, cut their stems down, store the pot in a cool, light cellar or shed, and water occasionally. Sink in the garden in April. Lift in September and bring into a very cool plant room, water and fertilize, and hope for bloom.

How can one best grow chrysanthemums to bloom during the months of November, December, and January? We have the severe cold of Lake Erie and a long winter. Could they be brought into the house when winter comes and so bloom during these months? Pinch plants well early in the season. Pot from the garden in early October. Use late varieties. Give a sunny location in a cool room.

CYCLAMEN (CYCLAMEN PERSICUM)

Why does cyclamen always die a few days after it comes from the florist? The commercial grower grew the plant in a moist atmosphere and a temperature of 40° to 50° F. Living-room conditions are too warm and dry; however, you should be able to keep the plant for a few weeks if you can find a window where its ideal requirements are more nearly met.

The leaves on the cyclamen I received for Christmas are turning yellow. What caused this? The sudden change from a greenhouse to the dry, hot atmosphere of a house is responsible. Cyclamen should be kept cool, well watered, and away from too much sunlight. An east or west window is best. Syringe their tops daily, water more than once a day from the edge of the pot, and move to cold, not freezing, quarters at night—perhaps the garage floor.

How cold is it safe to have cyclamen when flowering, and when not flowering? At 40° to 45° F. a plant in flower will be far happier and last much longer than in a room of 60° to 70° F. After it blooms, gradually dry the plant off and rest it in the cellar or in a cold frame outdoors. Repot in July, and with luck you may get the corm to start again. Or try a newer system. Set on the porch or terrace in the summer and don't dry off the plant at all, just water less after bloom is over and until new growth appears.

How shall I water cyclamen plants during their flowering period? If cyclamens are kept cool enough—40° to 50° F.—they will not dry out quickly. If kept in a hot room, watering freely and frequently may prolong their lives for a week or two, although it will not take the place of a low temperature. Water from below or at the top around the edge of the pot, keeping the soil moist but not soggy.

How long must you let a pot of cyclamen soak in a pan of water to wet it thoroughly? If the water in the pan is halfway up the pot and the soil is moderately dry, allow to soak 10 to 15 minutes, then stand in the sink to drain off the surplus. You can tell from the feel of the topsoil whether the whole soil mass has been moistened.

Are cyclamens difficult as window-garden plants? Cyclamens are among the most difficult of all plants for the overheated living room. Old corms that have blossomed can be dried off and kept dormant in a cool place until July, but it's a 50–50 chance to get them to start up strongly again.

How long should a cyclamen bloom? Cyclamen should flower either in a greenhouse or under favorable home conditions from Christmastime until April, depending on the number of buds. Remove faded blooms.

Should faded blooms be removed from cyclamen with a knife or scissors? Neither. Get a firm grip on the stem of a dead flower or yellowed leaf and give a sharp pull. It comes out cleanly.

Can one grow cyclamens from seed? What soil should I use and how long is it before blooming? Seedlings are easy to start if seed is sown thinly in a soilless mix in July or August; but after that, troubles begin. If you can simulate greenhouse conditions for 18 months and can keep the plants free of mites and other pests, you might succeed. Plants like a compost of good loam, sand, rotted manure or rich compost, and peat moss; shade during the summer, yet full light; careful watering; high humidity and frequent spraying; and in the fall and winter, a temperature not above 55° F. More adaptable and long-blooming are recently developed dwarf strains that can be grown from seed.

GENISTA (CYTISUS CANARIENSIS)

Can anything be done with a genista after it has stopped blooming? (New York.) Genistas (the greenhouse kinds) are strictly gift plants, not even good house plants for any length of time. They are not hardy outdoors in the vicinity of New York. Keep in a sunny window, water well, and see that there is circulation of air around them. Don't crowd genistas in with a lot of other plants.

HYDRANGEA (HYDRANGEA MACROPHYLLA)

Why did my hydrangea die the day after I received it as a gift? The hydrangea does not die that quickly. If the leaves and flowers wilt, it is suffering from a lack of water. Immerse the whole pot in a pail of water for 20 minutes. It will revive immediately.

How long should a hydrangea flower in the house? It should flower not less than 3 weeks. Keep it away from a hot, sunny window and heat outlets. Water thoroughly twice a day.

What care and treatment should be given pot hydrangeas? Florists' hydrangeas are propagated from cuttings in early spring, grown in 4-inch pots that are sunk in the open ground during the summer, and well fed. Put into larger pots in September and place in a cold frame with a sash, but keep well ventilated. Bring inside before hard freezing and keep in a cool cellar at 40° F. until late December or January. Give just enough water to prevent drying, although leaves will fall off. Start in full light at 50° F.—never above 60° F. Give plenty of water at all times and lots of light. After blooming, cut back well and carry outside during the summer if a large specimen is wanted the next season.

What must I do to make a pot hydrangea bloom in March or April? If you have only living-room facilities, don't expect to do what commercial growers can't always manage. A hydrangea has to rest in a cold place until late December. Start into growth at 50° F. and never above 60° F. Grow it cool, or you'll have a flowerless plant.

Can my hydrangea be planted in the garden after it has stopped flowering? Yes. After it has finished blooming, cut back its stems about half their length, remove the plant from the pot, and plant in a garden where it will have plenty of room. It will grow into a big, shrubby plant. Water well.

I would like to know something about hydrangeas. Are they hardy? The florists' hydrangeas are hardy, but in areas where hard freezing occurs, the wood is killed to the ground. If you have a variety that will bloom on the new wood, well and good. If not, and the wood is killed back, you'll never see any flowers. Such kinds have to be kept in pots and brought indoors and rested during the winter.

Twice I have purchased plants of hydrangea 'Bluebird', and after potting, new shoots appeared, but in a week or two the plants died. The potting mixture had a pH of about 4.5. Temperature, watering, and light conditions apparently perfect. What was wrong? If you bought actively growing young plants, why not in pots? Why did you use such extremely acid soil? Unless your soil is naturally alkaline, forget the pH and use a good rich compost with waterings as suggested below.

What element is it that makes the hydrangea flowers blue or pink? Acidity of the soil causes blue flowers, but some varieties become blue more readily than others. Repeated watering with alum solution or aluminum sulfate (1 level teaspoon to 1 gallon of water) will cause blueness. Add 1 tablespoon of alum to the potting mixture to get pink flowers.

JERUSALEM-CHERRY (SOLANUM PSEUDOCAPSICUM)

Why do leaves and berries fall off a Jerusalem-cherry soon after I receive it? If your house is hot, Jerusalem-cherry will not survive. It likes a cool room (about 50° F.), plenty of water, and a location away from chills or drafts. Spraying the leaves daily may help. It is a poor house plant.

Are the fruits of Jerusalem-cherry edible? No. They are poisonous.

How shall I treat a Jerusalem-cherry after it has fruited? Unless you want to grow a big specimen, throw the plant away. Old plants can be cut back a little, kept on the dry side until spring, then shifted into a larger pot and put outdoors with slight shade during the summer. Give plenty of water and feed; bring indoors in September.

When should the seed of Jerusalem-cherries be sown for Christmas fruiting? Sow the seed in January or February. Grow in pots and plant outdoors in late May. Lift carefully with the root ball in September, pot, and shade until established, then place in a bright window or greenhouse. Selected types can be raised from cuttings taken early in the year.

KALANCHOE

What care does this holiday plant require? Cut off the faded flower stems above the foliage; more will push up and probably continue to appear until May. This succulent will thrive in a 72° F. living room and does not require high humidity. Take care not to overwater—every third day is usually enough. Be on the watch for mealybugs among the tight leaves.

How should I handle my kalanchoe to make it bloom again next Christmas? In the spring, repot it in a gritty soil—half humus and half perlite—and place in semishade for the summer. Bring indoors before frost. Since this is a "short day" plant, requiring 12 to 14 hours of darkness for 3 weeks before Christmas to produce buds, move it to a dark closet about 6 P.M. every night and let it stay until 8 A.M. from Thanksgiving on. Bring it to full sunshine during the day.

Are there kalanchoes in other colors besides red, which doesn't look nice with the color scheme of my living room?   Yes, there are yellow, cream, coral, and pink varieties you can grow from seed or buy as plants from florists and garden centers.

ORNAMENTAL PEPPER (CAPSICUM ANNUUM)

How can ornamental peppers be kept small and full of bloom as you see them in the markets?   Try the compact 'Holiday Time' and 'Holiday Cheer' and other varieties you will find in seed catalogs. Raise from seed annually in the spring and grow in full light. You can't expect the plants grown in a window to equal those grown in a greenhouse, but growing under fluorescent lights will result in well-shaped, bushy plants. Or plant outside for the summer and pot up in August indoors in 5-inch pots at temperatures of 50° to 60° F.

Are the fruits of the Christmas pepper poisonous?   No, but they are hot and should be used as a condiment with discretion. You can dry the fruits as you would hot peppers grown in the vegetable garden. The fruits of Jerusalem-cherry, a pot plant also available around the holidays, are poisonous.

POINSETTIA (EUPHORBIA PULCHERRIMA)

Are the pink and white poinsettias harder to grow than the red ones?   The Mikkelsen, Ecke, and other pink hybrids do beautifully, often holding their color until June, as do the newer red varieties. The greenish whites may not hold longer than two months and are difficult to make bloom a second year.

Will my poinsettia bloom again? How should it be treated?   Care for it as you do your house plants, keeping it growing as long as possible. Flowers, really bracts, often last until June; if they drop sooner, set the plants in a 50° to 60° F. place and water just enough to prevent complete dryness. After frost danger is over, take your plant outside, cut its stems back to 2 to 3 inches, repot in fresh soil mixture, keep in a light open place, and water and feed weekly with a liquid fertilizer. As new leaves form, pinch back to keep growth low. Bring in about mid-September and make certain the plant gets complete darkness, as in a closet or cardboard carton, for at least 12 hours for 70 days. Water as necessary.

I carried over a poinsettia last year and it made good growth but never bloomed. What was wrong?   One cause is keeping it near a light at night. The poinsettia is a "short-day" plant, and if placed in a room where the lights are on several hours every evening, it won't bloom.

I raised a poinsettia this summer in a pot in the yard and brought it in the house in October. Just as the buds for the blooms started, they dried up and fell off. I saw some fine web. Has some minute insect done the damage?   Bring indoors earlier if in your part of the country it gets cool at night after August. The web suggests red spider. Regular spraying is needed to prevent this and mealybug attack.

After bringing in poinsettias from a summer in the garden (in September), how can one "hold them back" from blooming until about Christmastime?   Yours is an exceptional case. The trouble with most people is to get them to flower. Temperature should not be above 60° F. at night. Too high a temperature will cause premature, poorly developed blooms.

I brought some dormant poinsettias from California in May, planted them, and they grew; when cold weather came, I carefully potted them. Why did they wither and die?   Poinsettias in growth won't tolerate root disturbance.

If you cut poinsettias close to the soil, will they sprout again?   Poinsettias may be cut back two thirds while quite dormant, but when actively growing, no cutting back should be practiced unless the young shoots are to be rooted as cuttings.

When and how does one make cuttings from poinsettias and grow them into blooming plants?   The cuttings are taken off when they are 4 to 6 inches long and rooted in sand between June and August—the latter date for small plants. They need a greenhouse to grow successfully.

Should poinsettia cuttings be started in part sand? What temperature is needed?   Short 4- to 6-inch cuttings will root either in plain sand or a sandy soil. Successful growers use a bottom heat at 70° F. with high humidity. They can be rooted outdoors in June or July in a shady place.

Is it safe to remove the ferns that are sometimes planted around the base of a gift poinsettia?   Yes. These are probably *Pteris tremula* and make excellent house plants. When you take your poinsettia outdoors in June and repot it, remove the ferns and pot them separately.

ROSE (ROSA)

Are roses good house plants? As a general rule, no. However, miniature roses thrive in a bright window or under fluorescent lights. Several nurseries specialize in these small roses. The large-flowered gift plants received at Eastertime will flower for about 2 weeks and then should go into the garden. While indoors, spray the foliage daily with tepid water and give the soil plenty of moisture. Placing the plant on a pebble-filled saucer of water increases humidity.

Can miniature or baby roses in small pots be grown indoors and if so how? Miniature roses do well in the window garden or under lights if properly cared for. Give them a sunny spot in a cool room or window (not above 60° to 65° F. daytime temperature and 10° lower at night). Water daily or whenever the soil is dry, but do not let the water stand in the saucers. Frequent syringing of foliage is helpful. Turn the pots frequently to receive maximum sunshine. After their bloom is over, prune as you would garden roses and decrease watering to encourage a resting period of 2 to 3 months. In the spring, when outdoor roses are starting, repot and sink them in their pots in a sunny place. Or, if you prefer to grow them as outdoor plants, remove them from their pots and plant in a well-enriched bed. They are perfectly hardy.

Shrubs

AZALEA   (See Gift Plants.)

CAMELLIA

How should a camellia plant be grown? Place a pot or tub in light shade outdoors in the summer. Bring inside in September. Its night temperature should be 50° F. It requires sun. Keep the soil always moist, but not waterlogged. In the spring, after the plant blooms, repot it or topdress as necessary. Feed once a week when good growth is being made.

When should I pot my camellia and in what soil mixture? Never repot unless the soil is obviously unsuitable or unless the pots are crowded with roots. Do this as soon as flower buds have set. The soil should be acid and consist of good loam, leafmold and/or peat moss, sharp sand, with some superphosphate and dried cow manure added. After potting, spray frequently with clear water. Avoid overwatering.

What about pruning camellias? Prune only sufficiently to keep the plant shapely. Thin crowded plants by removing weak growths. Cut back any long, straggly shoots. Do this immediately after they flower. Remember, flowering shoots for the following year arise from the base of the flower; cutting back flowering shoots destroys the following year's bloom.

How can buds be kept from falling off a camellia plant? It was just loaded with buds when I took it in this fall and all but 3 fell off. Indoor camellias ordinarily lose buds: (1) because the indoor temperature is too high and the atmosphere too dry; (2) lack of sufficient moisture; (3) lack of light.

Can a camellia be grown in the house? How old must it be to bloom? Camellias are not satisfactory house plants unless, perhaps, you can keep them in a cool window or plant room. In the wintertime, they are harmed by temperatures higher than 50° to 60° F. Plants often bloom when quite young—3 or 4 years old.

The indoor camellia plant has conditions in my home similar to gardenias. Is this right? Is it a sun-loving plant? (New York.) Camellias need cooler growing conditions than the florists' gardenia. They enjoy sunshine and a free circulation of air. It is important that the soil be kept reasonably moist.

Can one start camellias from a bud in the winter? Not from a flower bud. Camellias are propagated by cuttings, grafting, and layering. July is a good time to take cuttings.

What shall I do to prevent scale on my camellia plants indoors? Frequent syringing of the leaves with cool water is helpful. You can pick off a few or rub them off with a soapy sponge. If the attack is severe, use an aerosol spray containing malathion.

CITRUS FRUITS

What sort of potting soil shall I use for citrus fruit trees grown as house plants? A general-purpose potting mixture.

I have a grapefruit tree grown from seed, now 10 years old, 8 to 10 feet tall, in good condition. I plant it out-of-doors during the summer and in a wooden tub in the winter. Why has it never bloomed? You should not be shifting your grapefruit plant from open ground and back into a tub. Keep it in the tub. But seedling grapefruits are capricious as to time of blooming, particularly when grown as house plants. In the winter, they should be grown in cool temperatures, 40° to 50° F., and light, airy conditions.

Can you give me information about the indoor culture of dwarf ponderosa lemon trees—type of soil, exposure, room temperature? The soil should be rich, rather coarse, and well drained. Expose to maximum sunshine. Night temperatures should be 45° to 50° F. with a 5° to 15° rise permitted in the daytime. Place the plant (pot and all) in an outdoor garden bed in the summer.

Will a lemon tree planted from seed ever bloom without being grafted? It is about 5 feet tall; its trunk diameter is 1½ inches. It may bloom with age. Seedlings often take many years from the time of seed sowing until they bear flowers.

What fertilizer could I use to feed a lemon tree? Any complete commercial fertilizer will be satisfactory. It is not necessary to select one having a particular analysis.

What is the correct care for orange trees—temperature and fertilizer? Can they be grown as other house plants with success? Essentially the same as for grapefruits and lemons. (See replies to inquiries on these subjects.) The plants grow well as house plants, but often they fail to bloom or develop fruits.

How can I treat an orange tree, as a house plant, to always have oranges on it? Don't expect the impossible. Oranges of all kinds, including the dwarf Otaheite (*Citrus* x *limonia*), need lots of light and to be kept free of insect pests such as scales, mealybugs, and spider mites. Plant the pot outdoors in the summer, as this may induce flowers to set fruit.

Why do the blossoms on dwarf orange and lemon trees drop and bear no fruit? Lack of light or improper water relations within the plant (due to unsatisfactory environment) are probably responsible. Or indoors, lack of pollination may be at fault. Pollinate the flowers by hand. Rub powdery pollen on the sticky stigma with a paintbrush. Take care that the plant is not kept too dry when flowers and fruits are developing.

What varieties of citrus fruits can be grown as pot plants? Plant the dwarfs such as 'Ponderosa' lemon, Otaheite orange, 'Meyer' lemon, Satsuma orange, and calamondin orange (x *Citrofortunella mitis*).

CRAPE-MYRTLE (LAGERSTROEMIA INDICA)

Could a crape-myrtle be grown in a tub like an oleander—outdoors in summer, indoors during the cold months? Yes, very easily. Store it in the wintertime in a frostproof place and at that season keep the soil very nearly dry.

GARDENIA

Can gardenias be grown as house plants? Yes, if you can supply sufficient atmospheric humidity.

What type of soil do gardenias thrive best in—acid or alkaline? Acid. A pH of 5 to 5.5 is generally considered best. Chlorosis (yellowing of the foliage) results from alkaline soil conditions.

Can you recommend a good soil mixture for gardenias? Two parts mellow loam, 1 part coarse sphagnum peat moss, ½ dried cow manure, ½ sharp sand. To this, add a 4-inch pot of superphosphate and a heaping tablespoonful of iron sulfate (copperas) to each bushel, the last to prevent chlorosis (yellowing of the foliage). Or use Sequestrene, according to directions on the container.

What kind of food should be given to gardenias? A 4–12–4 fertilizer is recommended. Particularly suitable are fertilizers that provide nitrogen in the form of ammonia, such as sulfate of ammonia.

The gardenia that I received for Christmas has developed yellow leaves at the tips of the shoots. What is the trouble? This may be a deficiency of iron. To prevent as well as cure, apply ½ teaspoon of iron sulfate to the soil and water thoroughly. To keep the plant growing, apply ½ teaspoon of 4–12–4 or 5–10–5 every 6 weeks. Never apply lime. Acidity is promoted by watering with a vinegar solution—½ teaspoon to 1 quart of water. If high heat and low humidity are causing difficulty, try a cooler location and promote humidity by covering the plant for a time with a plastic bag.

When is the best time to repot my gardenia house plant? It appears pot-bound to me. Any time from April to August that the plants show evident need of this attention. The final pots should be filled with roots before winter begins.

When and how should gardenias be pruned? Pruning consists of "stopping" (pinching out the tips) growing shoots each time they attain a length of 6 inches or so from spring to mid-August. You can also shorten branches by picking flowers with long twigs rather than cutting only the bloom.

What causes gardenias to dry up? The leaves become brittle and drop off and the plant seems to be dead. I've had 3 plants do the same. Gardenias need high atmospheric humidity. This is difficult to provide in the house and is one of the major causes of failure. Try covering with a plastic bag such as those used by cleaners to protect clothing.

What is the correct application of water to the gardenia? Because of varying environmental factors, no exact answer is possible to your question. In general, keep the soil evenly moist and once a week let it dry out just a little. Then set the pot in a pail filled with water up to the rim. Let it stay until the topsoil feels moist.

How would I treat a gardenia plant that was hit by frost or cold air in the house? If severely damaged, it probably won't recover. If the damage consists only of moderate injury to leaves, keep in a warm place. Water with great care, so that the soil is not kept in a saturated condition, and lightly mist the branches 2 or 3 times daily.

My year-old gardenia plant has never bloomed. Would sinking the pot in the ground outdoors in the summer help? Placing it outdoors in partial shade and in a deep peat moss mulch should help.

How do you make gardenias bloom? No simple method can be given. You must provide conditions that are to the plant's liking, so it grows vigorously. Flower buds appear on new growth at temperatures of 60° to 65° F. at night and 70° to 75° in the day.

Can limbs be cut off a gardenia plant and rooted, and, if so, when is the best time? Large branches that have become woody are not suitable material for propagation. Cuttings of the young terminal shoots that are firm, but not hard and woody, are started in the winter and spring.

What is the most successful way to root gardenia cuttings? Cuttings 3 or 4 nodes long are dusted with a rooting hormone powder, then inserted in sand or sand and peat moss from December to March and enclosed under polyethylene. The sand is maintained at a temperature of 75° to 80° F. and the surrounding atmosphere is 70°. A humid atmosphere is necessary and is easily maintained in an enclosed plastic container.

What are the white, woolly insects that cluster on my gardenia? How can I kill them? They are mealybugs, one of the worst pests of this plant. Wash them off with a forceful stream of water or spray with malathion and repeat in 10 days. You can clean up a few by touching with a Q-tip dipped in rubbing alcohol.

HIBISCUS (HIBISCUS ROSA-SINENSIS)

How shall I care for hibiscus as a house plant? Presumably you have the Chinese hibiscus. If so, prune the plant back hard in the spring and repot in any good, well-drained soil. Spray lightly with water each sunny day. Keep the soil moist but not waterlogged. Give full sunshine. In the winter, keep the soil just moist in a temperature about 50° F.

I have a Chinese hibiscus growing in a pot, as the cold here would kill it if I planted it outside. What is the best plan for keeping it safe all winter?   Keep it in a light cellar or plant room where the temperature is not less than 40° F. or more than 50° F. Give only sufficient water to prevent the soil from drying out completely.

HYDRANGEA   (See Gift Plants.)

LANTANA (LANTANA CAMARA)

How are lantanas handled to bloom in the winter?   Buy small plants in the summer and sink the pots in soil out-of-doors until autumn. Bring in before frost. Do not repot at this time. Keep in a cool, sunny window or plant room at not more than 60° F. Give water sparingly at first, then more water and liquid plant food. They should start into fresh bloom in December or January. In the spring, repot in a standard potting mixture (see Soil, this section) and sink outdoors in a garden bed. If winter bloom is desired a second year, keep the summer bloom pinched back. It would be better, however, to buy new small plants for winter bloom.

I have a weeping lantana. When does it bloom?   Lantanas are naturally summer-to-fall bloomers. They must be brought indoors after September. Keep them moderately dry and cool throughout the winter. Cut back and give more water and warmth from March on; plant out in late May.

LEMON-VERBENA   (See Kitchen Herb Garden, this section.)

OLEANDER (NERIUM OLEANDER)

How can oleanders be grown successfully in tubs?   Prune back old growths, topdress in the spring, and increase the temperature and water supply. Feed occasionally during the growing season. Give full sun. After midsummer, keep somewhat drier. Store in the winter in a light, cool, frostproof place and keep nearly dry. Spray to keep clean of scale and mealybugs.

My oleanders look perfectly healthy, but never bloom. I keep them on a glass-enclosed porch in the winter and around an outdoor birdbath

in the summer. **What else do they need?** This is often due to insufficient ripening of the wood. To induce ripening, make sure that the plant has ample light and air and rather dry conditions at the root after the season's growth is completed.

ROSEMARY (See Kitchen Herb Garden, this section.)

SWEET-OLIVE (See Flowering Plants, this section.)

Ferns

CULTURE

What soil is recommended for indoor ferns? Mix together 2 parts good loam, 2 parts leafmold, 1 part sand, ¼ part dried cow manure or rich compost, ¼ part broken charcoal, and add ¾ of a pint of superphosphate to each bushel. Or take it easy and mix pasteurized garden soil with plenty of humus from the compost pile and some perlite or sand. The aim is a soil that feels light and porous.

What is the best fertilizer for ferns? There are many good commercial preparations. Plant tablets, dry commercial fertilizers, or liquid fertilizers are all satisfactory if used according to the manufacturer's directions. Fish emulsion is excellent, but don't feed ferns unless they are in active growth. Many are in a somewhat resting state from November to February.

Should house ferns have large, roomy pots or do they prefer to be pot-bound? How deep should the plant be set in the soil? Most plants thrive in pots just large enough. Too-big containers allow an overabundance of food and water, resulting in plant "indigestion." Let the crown of the plant be level or just a little above the soil level. Allow a 1-inch space above the soil in order to receive water.

Is good soil enough or is it necessary to provide additional drainage for ferns? Although moist soil conditions are appreciated, drainage must be perfect for ferns. The soil should be porous, there should be an inch or more of small stones or coarse sphagnum over the broken crock in the bottom of the pot, and ferns should not stand in a saucer or jardiniere in which water has been allowed to collect. Some epiphytic ferns such as *Polypodium aureum,* platyceriums, and davallias thrive in tree-fern pots or grow well in coconut-husk fiber.

How often should ferns be repotted?   Usually not more than once a year. Divide, if necessary, and always give them fresh soil. Young ferns that have filled their pots with roots by July may need a second potting but should not be divided. With a large specimen, knock it out of its pot in the spring and crumble off as much old soil, top and bottom, as possible, replacing it with a fresh mixture.

When is the best time to divide and replant an old Boston fern?   In the spring, just as new growth is beginning. Select younger and stronger crowns from outside the plant for replanting rather than old woody interior parts, which can be discarded.

Are there any tricks to watering ferns?   The soil should never be allowed to "bake out" or be kept constantly soggy. Keep it medium-moist, and when water is given, soak the ball of roots and soil thoroughly. Never apply water in a stream heavy enough to settle in the heart of the plant. The best way is to immerse the pot in a pail or tub of water, then allow it to drain before replacing it in a saucer.

Do ferns like plenty of sunlight?   Ferns prefer light but not direct sunlight. In fact, too much sun may be the cause of a sickly, light-green appearance, but winter sunshine or fluorescent lights are rarely too strong.

What window is best for ferns?   An east, west, or north window, or any place within a room where they receive plenty of light.

Is there a general routine for keeping ferns looking bright and crisp? Dry leaves form on my ferns right away.   Probably a lack of moisture, either in the soil or air. Water regularly and keep away from a radiator or heat source; keep in a temperature above 55° F. When buying a new fern, look for a young one that has not been growing in a greenhouse too long.

How should ferns be cared for in a city apartment?   Use the same procedure as for the care of ferns in a house. They do not like direct sun and want plenty of light, moisture in the air and soil, warmth, and to be kept away from drafts. Choose only the thriftiest ferns for apartment conditions, such as rabbit's-foot, holly, and bird's-nest. Set plants on large saucers or in a plant tray filled with pebbles and water.

Will it help my fern if I cut off fronds that have turned brown at the tip or have been broken off?   Cut off brown or damaged fronds. Ferns must have plenty of room, for fronds are easily damaged either from close contact with other plants or people brushing past them.

Should one cut the runners on ferns grown in a house? A friend told

me to cut them off my fern, and it doesn't seem to be growing as well since I did it. By all means, cut the runners off house ferns. They never develop into fronds and only take the strength from the rest of the plant. Perhaps your fern needs repotting in fresh soil.

What special care should be given a house fern to produce luxuriant foliage? Mine has a tendency to turn yellow frequently. Is it possible the pot is too small? Yes, it is possible that the pot is too small, but even more likely, the humidity is too low.

Will ferns do well in a Wardian case or terrarium? Yes, many of them do better there than in the average living room. Pteris ferns are especially good for terrariums, as are the small rock ferns or polypodiums, small holly ferns, and possibly the maidenhair.

Should ferns (house plants) be put outside during the summer? Many ferns benefit from being plunged (planted nearly to the rims of the pots) in an outdoor bed of peat moss or humus-rich soil that retains moisture around the pots in a shady spot during the hottest months. They will also thrive in the summer on a sheltered porch or terrace.

What causes the fronds of ferns to turn brown and fall off? This may be due to people passing by and injuring their tips. It may also be due to growing conditions: too small a pot, too low temperature, too hot or too dry atmosphere, lack of water in the soil, poor drainage. Check up on conditions. However, it is normal for some of the oldest fronds to die after a season of growth.

How can I save my fern, just an ordinary house fern, after an overdose of fertilizer? Obviously, the roots were burned from the overdose of fertilizer. Better start over with a new fern.

I left a fern in an unheated room and it froze. What can I do for it? If only the tops and not the roots were frozen, the tops should be cut off and the roots repotted in fresh soil to encourage new top growth. If the roots as well as the tops were frozen, the plant is a total loss.

What is the proper care for a Boston fern? Provide well-drained soil, plenty of water, air, light (but not direct sunlight), and humidity in the atmosphere (most rooms are likely to be too dry). They should never be where the temperature drops below 55° F.

My Boston fern does not send out sprouts, only long stems, and very few leaves. Should it get fertilizer in the form of cow manure? Cut off long stems, or runners, which do not turn into fronds and only take strength away from the plant. If the plants are otherwise healthy, liquid fertilizer, such as fish emulsion, can be given when the plants are in active growth. (For other cultural directions, see previous questions.)

How should lace ferns be grown? Probably you mean one of the sports of the Boston fern. It needs essentially the same care as the common Boston fern, but special care must be taken to keep any dead leaflets off and to prevent water lodging in the centers of the plants.

Mold is beginning to show around the topsoil of my indoor planter in which are several plants of the common Boston fern. What does the soil need? Mold seems to indicate that the drainage is poor or that you are not providing sufficient ventilation. Are there drainage holes in the bottom and an inch of broken crock or small stones under the soil? Better change the soil and pay attention to drainage when repotting.

Why does an unusual type (ostrich-Boston) fern revert back to the Boston type? Your fern is a somewhat unstable sport from the Boston fern. Such mutants often tend to revert to type. Unless the typical Boston fern fronds are cut out, they will eventually displace the weaker-growing type.

Is there such a plant as a holly fern? The holly fern is a cyrtomium. Its fronds are divided into small leaflets, each one resembling a holly leaf in outline. It is one of the best ferns for the house and grows steadily. In the summer, put it outdoors in a shady spot.

What are the best growing conditions in the house for the maidenhair fern? Maidenhair fern is one of the most difficult to grow in the house. It likes a porous soil that contains plenty of humus and more moisture in the air than is usually found in any house. The Australian maidenhair fern (*Adiantum hispidulum*) is one of the most adaptable in the genus. A temperature of about 65° F. and shade from direct sunlight are necessary. A large terrarium is most likely to provide the requisite conditions.

What is the best time to pot and what is the best fertilizer for pteris? Several species and forms are available, all generally known as "table ferns." They grow rapidly under favorable conditions and should be repotted into the next size pot whenever their containers become filled with roots. Liquid plant food such as fish emulsion, applied once a month to well-rooted specimens, is sufficient.

How should rabbit's-foot fern be cared for? Rabbit's-foot fern (*Davallia*) can stand higher temperatures and drier air than any of the other house ferns. It should do well in the average living room. Keep it out of direct sunlight but see that it has plenty of light. Davallias will grow in well-drained porous soil, but they look best when grown in a tree-fern basket or tree-fern planter so the attractive fuzzy rhizomes can creep about in the open. Maintain a minimum relative humidity of 40 per cent. Let the roots dry slightly between waterings to prevent rhizome rot, but the fronds can be misted with room-temperature water any morning.

How are ferns propagated from the spores on the back of the leaves? The average person may find it difficult to do. Take a piece of soft brick and a clay saucer. Sterilize these by baking. Stand the brick in a saucer and wet thoroughly. Scatter the spores over the surface of the brick. Keep a little water in the saucer and cover with glass, leaving a slight opening at the bottom for ventilation. Keep in diffused light at a temperature of 60° to 70° F. The first growth of the fern looks like green scales.

Is it safe to divide fern plants? Yes, but not more than once a year. New crowns or heads which have sprung up around the original crown can be pulled or cut off gently and each piece potted in a pot of suitable size. Probably the original plant can go back into the same pot with fresh soil.

When ferns have black specks on the underside, is that fungi? If these black or brown specks appear in even lines or a regular pattern on the undersides of the leaves, they are sori, which contain the spores by which ferns reproduce themselves. They are not harmful to the plant.

My sword fern has little black spots on its stems. Is it a disease? If these black spots are on the stems, not on the back of the leaves, they are a scale insect. If there are only a few scales, hand-pick them with a toothpick or try to wash them off with a soapy sponge. For a bad attack, try a *very weak* malathion solution or discard the plant.

What are the best ferns for indoor culture? Boston fern (and its several variations), holly fern, bird's-nest fern, pteris (table) ferns, and rabbit's-foot. All of these will thrive in the average home if given reasonable attention.

Is ostrich-plume fern all right for the house? The native woods ostrich fern is hardy and not suitable for indoor culture. If by ostrich-plume fern you mean one of the feathery Boston fern types, it is a suitable house plant.

Vines for Indoors

WHAT TO GROW

Will most vines do better in a greenhouse than in the house? Yes, if ideal conditions and care are given; yet remarkably good results are obtainable in the house with vines that are adapted to such conditions. This group is by no means a small one.

What kind of house plants grow long and trailing, in addition to ivy and philodendron? *Cissus antarctica* (kangaroo vine) is one of the best and longest growing; grape-ivy, pothos, tradescantia, zebrina, *Setcreasea purpurea, Jasminium rex,* lipstick vine, waxplant (*Hoya*), and sweet potato.

What vines grow best in a light window? Can they be grown in water? Ivy, philodendron, and tradescantia are stand-bys to grow in water. They do not need sun. Pothos and nephthytis will grow in either water or soil. Grape-ivy, Kenilworth-ivy, German-ivy, passion vine, creeping fig, and kangaroo vine do well in soil.

What are the names of vines that will grow in water in the house? In a light place: English ivy, philodendron, tradescantia, pothos, nephthytis, passion vine, sweet potato. In sun: trailing coleus and *Zebrina pendula,* whose leaves are purple on the underside and silver-striped on the upper.

What vines are best for a city apartment? The thriftiest vines are philodendron, pothos, kangaroo vine, with grape-ivy a close runner-up.

What about growing vines indoors in water? Should the water be plain or are there solutions that should be added? Many vines grow satisfactorily in water—plain water plus a small piece of charcoal to keep the water "sweet." Don't disturb the roots by changing the water; simply add more as needed. Water-soluble fertilizers can be used at one fourth strength for sturdy plants.

Is it safe to use foliage vines to frame the sides of a sunny south window used for other house plants? Yes, if the foliage vines are not kept in the direct sunlight of the window but are fastened or trained to the window frame facing in toward the room.

How should the leaves of vines be kept clean? Spray vigorously once a week with cool water on both the upper- and the undersides of the leaves. This not only prevents insects but keeps the foliage fresh-looking. Or sponge leaves with soapy water occasionally.

Can any vines be grown from seed for use indoors? Morning-glory, especially the Japanese ones and 'Heavenly Blue'; black-eyed-Susan vine (*Thunbergia alata*), cup-and-saucer vine (*Cobaea scandens*), canary-bird vine (*Tropaeolum peregrinum*).

What are the names of some perennial flowering vines to grow in a light window? The passion-flower, *Hoya,* and also such gesneriads as the lipstick vine *Aeschynanthus* 'Black Pagoda'; the goldfish-plant *Columnea* 'Yellow Dragon'; the peacock-plant *Episcia* 'Yellow Topaz';

and hybrid *Nematanthus* with pouch-shaped flowers in red or orange tones and waxy green foliage. *N. wettsteinii* is an adaptable trailer with small green leaves, orange and yellow flowers, and restrained growth. Specialists also offer trailing African-violet hybrids, which are graceful and long-blooming when conditions are to their liking.

How should Boston-ivy be cared for in the house? True Boston-ivy is *Parthenocissus tricuspidata*. This is a large-leaved vine that drops its leaves every autumn. It is an outdoor, not an indoor, vine. Perhaps you are thinking of grape-ivy or kangaroo vine in the genus *Cissus*.

CREEPING FIG (FICUS PUMILA)

Can you suggest a creeping vine that will cling to a masonry wall behind a small pool in a plant room? The creeping fig will suit your purpose. It is small-leaved, intensely green, and makes a flat mat against the wall up which it creeps. A variegated variety is also available.

ENGLISH IVY (HEDERA HELIX)

How can hardy ivy be grown in the house? Keep in a cool, light place, away from radiators and direct sunlight. Spray foliage once a week with cold water to keep clean and free from dust and red spider. Keep its soil moist; feed monthly with a pinch of complete fertilizer. It also grows well in water and even better in ¼-strength water-soluble house-plant fertilizer.

Does ivy require sunshine when grown indoors? No. Ivy should not be in direct sun. It does need good light—a north window is preferable.

We have been unsuccessful in keeping ivy cuttings alive during the winter in the house in water. What is the proper method? A glass container is best; be sure to have a piece of charcoal in the water so that it will stay "sweet" and not have to be changed; add water as needed. A light but not sunny place is preferred.

My ivy, grown in water in the light, dries up and dies. How can this be remedied? The location is either too sunny and hot and/or the plant has red spider. Spray both sides of the leaves vigorously with cool water once a week. Keep in a light but not sunny place.

What is the best method of starting indoor ivy? By cuttings rooted in water. Take the tip ends of ivy, having at least 4 mature leaves. Remove 2 lower leaves and stand in water. Longer stems may be used but leaves must be removed from as much stem as is under water.

Why do the leaves of ivy turn yellow? Too much sunshine perhaps, a too-hot and dry atmosphere, or a soil too dry.

My ivy (indoor) has a brown scale on its leaves. What causes this? Brown scale is an insect. The most effective control is to dip the plants in water and malathion, mixed according to directions. If necessary, use a soft toothbrush to remove scale from the stems.

How can variegated ivy be grown successfully? Variegated ivies should be grown in north windows only, or in eastern exposures if shaded by larger plants. Good soil, moderate watering, and spraying of the foliage once a week to keep it clean are of basic importance.

I have a green and white variegated ivy. As the new leaves come out, the old ones turn brown and die, beginning on one side of the leaf. Why? Probably due to too much sun. Keep in a north window. Check other general factors—soil, watering, and cleanliness of foliage—for additional causes.

What are the best kinds of English ivy for indoor culture? The standard English ivy (*Hedera helix*) and the 'Pittsburgh' cultivar are the two thriftiest kinds. Many variations have been developed and can be obtained by mail order from house-plant nurseries or at local garden centers.

GERMAN-IVY (SENECIO MIKANIOIDES)

I have seen German-ivy grown indoors in ferneries. Is this a difficult house plant? No, *Senecio mikanioides* does well in window boxes or fern stands in full diffused light and without direct sun. Plant in a standard potting mixture to which charcoal has been added to keep the soil "sweet." When German-ivy is growing well, water it weekly with liquid fertilizer. Cuttings root easily in moist sand.

GRAPE-IVY (CISSUS)

I have a trailing house plant that looks like poison-ivy. What is its name and of what country is it a native? *Cissus rhombifolia*. Its common name is grape-ivy and it is a native of northern South America.

Is the grape-ivy a satisfactory house plant? Yes, it is splendid and will thrive with any reasonable care in a warm room. It appreciates sunshine except for shade from intense summer sunshine, a good rich soil, free drainage, adequate supplies of water, and feeding when pot-bound.

Is grape-ivy a form of English ivy? No. Grape-ivy is *Cissus rhombifolia,* which is quite different in appearance from English ivy (*Hedera* *helix*). Its leaves are made of three leaflets while those of the English ivy are merely lobed. It is less subject to insect pests than English ivy and usually looks well longer.

HOYA (See Waxplant.)

KANGAROO VINE (CISSUS ANTARCTICA)

Does kangaroo vine make a good house plant? Yes, this is one of the toughest and least temperamental of house vines. It does not object to living-room temperatures. New plants can be propagated from cuttings.

KENILWORTH-IVY (CYMBALARIA MURALIS)

Can I grow Kenilworth-ivy as an indoor vine? Yes, this dainty little vine, with its violet flowers and leaves tinted with red beneath, grows well in a sunny window if the atmosphere is not too dry. It requires a standard potting soil and about a 4-inch pot. Often it will seed itself in the soil around the base of other pot plants. In the summer, it grows riotously in a wall or rock garden out-of-doors and seeds itself freely (in the vicinity of New York City). The main indoor pest, especially under dry conditions, is red spider mite. Wash gently with lukewarm water every few weeks to discourage mites.

MYRTLE (VINCA MAJOR)

Will myrtle grow indoors? Yes, it will, but it must be sprayed, without fail, once a week with cool water to ward off red spider, its greatest handicap to growing well indoors. It does not like too warm a location. Myrtle will root and grow in water or larger plants can be potted in soil.

PASSION-FLOWER (PASSIFLORA CAERULEA)

Would passion-flower grow in the house during the winter months? Should it be cut back before being brought in? Passion-flower makes an excellent winter house plant. It grows luxuriantly outdoors during the summer and it may have to be cut back before being brought indoors. Train to a bamboo stake and put strings against the window up which it can climb. To encourage the growth of the vine, it *must* be provided with something on which to climb. Its growth depends on the height of the trellis or string provided.

My passion-vine, kept in a south window, grows well during the winter but does not flower. Will anything encourage blossoms?   Early winter should be a season of comparative rest (temperature 55° F.; soil on the dry side). In late winter, increase the temperature 15° to 20°; give more water. Repot if necessary, or, if not, feed every 2 or 3 weeks. A rest season is important.

How can you propagate the passion-flower?   By tip cuttings rooted in sand kept constantly moist or in water in a glass container. Keep in a light but not sunny window. When well rooted, pot up in a humus-rich soil.

PHILODENDRON

What are the cultural directions for philodendron?   The philodendrons used as house plants are tolerant of warm rooms and some shade, although they appreciate atmospheric moisture and sunlight. Give well-drained, humus-rich soil, and avoid potting too frequently.

What is the proper method for growing philodendron—in water or soil?   Philodendron grows well in either. If in water, keep a piece of charcoal in the container to keep the water "sweet." Do not change the water but add to it as needed. If soil is more convenient, any good garden soil that is porous is all right. See that it is watered regularly.

How does one obtain a cutting of philodendron?   By cutting off the tip ends or any side shoot. The piece cut off should have at least 4 leaves. Remove the 2 bottom leaves so that the nodes from which the leaves grew can go under water. New roots will appear from these nodes. Sometimes cuttings can be selected with aerial roots already formed at the nodes.

What can be done to make a philodendron branch and to prevent it from becoming stringy?   As soon as the distances between leaves start to get longer than normal, pinch off the ends of the vine. The plant will branch out and the several pieces, if long enough, may be rooted in water to make new plants.

What should be done with philodendron when the leaves become too small?   It is probably growing in too dark or too cool a place. It does not need sun, but plenty of light and a temperature of 60° to 70° F. If the roots are healthy, give it a plant tablet or feed with liquid manure or a good complete fertilizer once a month. Overwatering also results in small leaves.

How should philodendron vine be taken care of? The leaves seem to die off. Do I water too much? Dying leaves are evidence of root injury or too dry atmospheric conditions. Never water a plant if the soil is really moist. Shake out your plant, and if the roots are decayed, cut back soft growth, repot, and water carefully. Don't use much fertilizer. Perhaps you have been overfeeding.

POTHOS (SCINDAPSUS PICTUS)

What kind of exposure does pothos like? Pothos is very adaptable. It will grow in either sunlight or good diffused light. It is good for a south window as well as for an east or west one.

SWEET POTATO (IPOMOEA BATATAS)

How do I start a sweet-potato vine in water? Select a good-sized sweet potato and a glass container about 8 inches deep and suitably wide. Wash, but don't scrub, the tuber to remove any chemical applied to retard sprouting. Thrust a toothpick in the middle of either side of the potato and let the toothpicks rest on the rim of the container. Keep water at a level so that the lower end of the potato is always covered. Remember to add water as evaporation occurs. Dryness would be fatal.

How long does it take a sweet-potato tuber to grow into a plant? After about 10 days in a cool dark place, a sweet potato, properly planted with the *root end* down in the water, will begin to develop roots. Move then to a light or sunny window and sprouts will show in 3 to 4 weeks after you put it in water. As growth develops, pinch out all but two or three strands and train these on a cord where you wish them to grow.

WANDERING JEW

What is the botanical name of the trailing indoor plant called wandering Jew? Two plants of very similar appearance go by this name. One, *Tradescantia fluminensis,* produces white flowers; its leaves are often variegated. The other, *Zebrina pendula,* flowers pink or red-purple; its foliage is striped above, purple beneath. Both are of the very simplest culture and will grow under similar conditions.

What is the best time to root cuttings of wandering Jew? They root readily at any time if planted about 2 inches apart in pots of sandy soil. Stand the pots in a box with 1 inch of sand or cinders in the bottom.

Water well, cover with a sheet of glass, and shade lightly from bright sunshine. Cuttings also root well when cut ends are ½ inch under water.

WAXPLANT (HOYA)

Please tell me about the house plant known as "parlor plant". It has thick waxy leaves and clusters of small, star-shaped waxy flowers. From your description, this must be *Hoya carnosa,* or waxplant. It is a native of southern China and Australia and is an old-time favorite. Botanically it is related to the milkweeds (*Asclepias*).

What kind of soil should be used for waxplant? A soil rich in humus. One part good garden soil, 1 part coarse sand, 2 parts leafmold or peat moss, with the addition of ⅛ part of bulk of dry cow manure or rich compost and a pint of superphosphate to each bushel.

Should waxplant have sunshine or shade, plenty of moisture, or kept on the dry side? It appreciates sunshine, good drainage, and plenty of moisture in the spring, summer, and fall, but should be kept drier and cooler (50° F. night, 60° to 65° F. day) in the winter.

Why doesn't my waxplant (5 feet long and 5 years old) bloom? Although slow to flower, your plant is large enough to do so. Does it get plenty of sun and has it filled its pot with roots? Plant must be pot-bound to bloom well; hence, avoid overpotting. A partial rest in wintertime is very beneficial.

Are there other waxplants suitable for growing indoors? Yes, several attractive varieties are available from mail-order firms. Some of the most beautiful are cultivars of *Hoya carnosa* but have red and cream markings on the foliage. Other species with larger leaves than *H. carnosa* are *H. kerrii,* with very thick, heart-shaped leaves, and *H. purpurea-fusca* 'Silver Pink', with long silver-spotted waxy leaves and red and white flowers in big clusters. Miniature types include *H. bella* and *H. lacunosa,* which has fine twining stems, small glossy dark-green leaves, and clusters of fuzzy fragrant flowers.

Cacti

SOIL AND FERTILIZER

Are cacti in the house grown in all sand? Cactus plants can be kept alive and will grow in sand for long periods but thrive better and are more permanent if planted in a loose, porous soil mixture.

What is the proportion of sand to soil for cacti grown in the house? From ¼ to ½, depending upon how sandy the soil is.

What soil do cacti require? Cacti form a large group and there are some differences in the soil requirements of individual kinds. In general, a loose, porous soil, fertile but not overrich in nitrogen, is desirable. Many species benefit from the addition of lime. (See Sandy Potting Mixture.)

When should we start feeding cacti, and what month? Never feed cacti unless they are strong, vigorous plants that have filled their pots with healthy roots. Feed only during their growing season (usually spring and summer), and then sparingly.

CULTURE

When should cacti be repotted? The repotting of healthy cacti that have filled their containers with roots should be done at the beginning of their growing season (in most cases, from spring to early summer). A plant that is planted in unsuitable soil and is consequently unhealthy may be carefully repotted at any time.

How can a cactus be made to bloom? The cactus group is a large one. Some kinds flower regularly and with ease while others are much more capricious. Study the individual plant, provide it with the best possible environment, and see that it has a period of rest immediately before its season of active growth in spring.

What temperature must be held to keep cactus plants healthy? A minimum of 50° F. for plants grown indoors. A few kinds are hardy outdoors even in the North.

What is the best method of watering cactus plants? Submerge pots nearly to their rims and leave in that position until water entering drainage holes in the bottom of the pots seeps through and wets the surface of the soil.

Can you tell me something of the care of cacti so they will blossom? I have one that blossoms about July; last year the buds formed and then dried up. You probably kept the plant too dry. Pot-grown cacti require moderate amounts of water over the greater part of the year. Supply quite a generous quantity when growth or flowers are developing.

How often should cactus plants in small flowerpots be watered? This depends largely upon the prevailing weather and other environmental factors. In general, water often enough to prevent the plants from shriveling. The soil should be allowed to become nearly dry before each watering.

How often should cacti in small pots be watered when they are in the house during the winter? In the winter, most cacti are resting and the soil should be permitted to dry out completely before water is applied. The frequency with which this occurs varies with the individual plant and its environment.

How can succulents and cacti be kept thriving in an apartment with not much sun? Grow them in a window where they will receive the maximum amount of light possible (even though this is not direct sunlight) or under fluorescent lights. Attend carefully to watering, potting, cleaning, and other details.

Will cacti grow and bloom better if set outside in the summer? Should they be left in pots or set directly in the ground? If their indoor position is a sunny one and otherwise satisfactory, it makes little difference whether they are left indoors or are set outside. If set outside, they should remain in their pots.

How can cacti be carried successfully through the summer out-of-doors? We have a lath house. Would that be better than the rock garden? A lath house is probably too shady for most kinds of cacti. It is better to bury the pots to their rims in a sunny open position.

Why do my miniature cacti fail to grow? Because the soil or other environmental factors are not to their liking. Read with care the answers given to other inquiries and be guided accordingly.

I have 2 cacti, 6 feet tall, that have never bloomed. Why? Some cacti do not bloom until they are several years old. Resting plants by keeping them decidedly on the dry side and cool (50° to 60° F. at night) during the winter often helps blooming, as does exposure to sunshine or fluorescent lights.

Will the peanut cactus plant blossom? The peanut cactus (*Chamaecereus silvestri*) normally blooms from May to July. Its flowers are tubular, nearly 3 inches long, and orange-scarlet.

How should cactus cuttings be made? Most cacti root readily from cuttings. Make cuttings in the spring or early summer. Leave them lying in the sun for a few days to dry the cut surface, then insert them in a sand bed. Keep the sand just moist and the atmosphere *not* close and humid as recommended for cuttings of most plants.

How should seedling cacti be grafted on larger or stronger stock? I have raised many from seeds. Seedling cacti are not usually grafted. Grafting is reserved for varieties that do not do well on their own roots.

While a simple process, this can scarcely be adequately described in a brief reply. (See Grafting, Section 3.)

How can I start cactus seed? Plant the seeds in pots filled ⅓ with crocks and ⅔ with very sandy soil that has had no fertilizer added to it and that has been passed through a ¼-inch screen. Sow in the spring. Cover the seed to their own depth. Keep the soil moderately moist at all times. The temperature should be 60° to 70° F.

How long does it take cactus seeds to come up? From 1 to 2 weeks under favorable conditions.

How can I remove mealybugs and scale insects from my cactus plant? Mealybugs are easily washed off with a forceful stream of water. Scale can be removed by scrubbing gently with a soft toothbrush dipped in soapsuds or in a pyrethrum, rotenone, or malathion insecticide.

ORCHID AND NIGHT-BLOOMING (JUNGLE) CACTI

What kind of soil is needed for night-blooming cactus? The soil must be very porous, so that water drains through quickly, even when packed together. Mix good garden soil, sand, and broken brick until you get this result, then add ¹⁄₁₀ part in bulk dried cow manure and a pint of superphosphate to each bushel. Or use a packaged mix that is porous; or try 4 parts leafmold, 1 part sand, 1 part perlite (or vermiculite), and 1 part charcoal.

What will make a night-blooming cereus-type cactus bloom and not lose its buds? Good light, suitable soil; proper temperature; plenty of water and feeding when growing (during spring and summer); little water during resting period (winter); freedom from scale and mealybugs.

How should a large night-blooming cactus be cared for during the winter? Would it do all right in a dark cellar? It should be kept in a light place at all times. Providing the soil is kept nearly dry during the winter, it may be kept in a temperature of 40° to 45° F. At warmer temperatures, more water is needed.

Could a jungle cactus be cut back? I had one given to me and it had been broken in many places, but this past summer it put out new growth. When is its blooming time? Yes, it can be cut back. Dust the cuts with finely powdered sulfur. Summer is its blooming time.

A night-blooming cactus started from a cutting bloomed once when it was 2 years old but hasn't had a flower since. It seems healthy enough and is growing well. What is wrong? Young plants bloom either irregularly or not at all, especially when growing vigorously. Your plant will probably bloom when it is older. Avoid overfeeding or overpotting.

How long does it take for a night-blooming cereus-type cactus rooted from a cutting to bloom? This cannot be stated with any degree of precision. Usually several years or when the plant becomes pot-bound.

When should a large night-blooming cactus be transplanted? In April or May.

I have two cactus plants that are night-blooming, with a cream-yellow waxlike flower about 5 inches in diameter. Can you tell me the correct way of increasing these to make more plants? Cuttings of the stems, each a foot or so long, taken in the summer and set in clean sand that is kept moist will soon form new roots.

What is a good potting mixture for an orchid cactus or epiphyllum? This needs a moister and richer soil than desert types of cacti. Two parts loam, 2 parts leafmold, 1 part sharp sand, plus a pint of bone meal to each bushel should be about right.

What is the best fertilizer for epiphyllums? Liquid fertilizer low in nitrogen.

What time of year do the orchid cacti bloom? Will they freeze in the winter? The epiphyllums and other orchid cacti bloom from April to July ordinarily. They are natives of the warmer parts of North, Central, and South America and are not adapted for outdoor culture where freezing weather is experienced.

What is the trouble when a night-blooming orchid cactus sets many buds which turn brown and wither when they are no larger than peas? The plant is well watered and sprayed with water after the buds appear. Lack of potash in the soil is said to cause buds to drop. Overwatering will also bring this about. Probably too low humidity is a factor.

What is the reason my epiphyllums grow but seldom bloom? To bloom satisfactorily they must be given a rest each year. This is done by keeping them as dry as possible (without permitting the leaflike stems to shrivel) for a period of 8 to 10 weeks during the winter.

CHRISTMAS, THANKSGIVING, AND EASTER CACTI

Are the Christmas and Thanksgiving cacti the same? No. The Thanksgiving cactus, also known as the crab-claw or claw cactus, is *Schlumbergera truncata* and usually blooms in late November. Its flat joints are decidedly "clawlike" and its flowers less symmetrical than those of the Christmas cactus, *Schlumbergera* x *buckleyi*, which is supposed to bloom around Christmas but is often late. Both kinds are often called Christmas cactus. Their generic name was formerly *Zygocactus*.

THREE KINDS OF HOLIDAY CACTI

*Christmas cactus (left) blooms around Christmas or
later and has leaf margins that are less indented than
those of the Thanksgiving cactus (center). The Thanksgiving cactus blooms close to that holiday and is also
called the crab-claw cactus because of its pronounced
leaf indentations. The Easter cactus (right) blooms in
the spring and has pretty star-shaped flowers.*

**I have a beautiful white-flowered Christmas cactus that always
blooms around Thanksgiving. Why doesn't it bloom at Christmas?** You probably have 'White Christmas', a hybrid probably more
closely related to the Thanksgiving cactus (*Schlumbergera truncata*)
than the Christmas cactus (*S.* x *buckleyi*).

**I have been given a plant called an Easter cactus but to me it looks
just like my Christmas cactus. Does it really bloom at Easter?** The
Easter cactus out of flower does resemble the Christmas cactus
(*Schlumbergera* x *buckleyi*), but its flowers are definitely star-shaped
and rose-red. They appear in late March or early April and usually coincide to some degree with the Easter season. Its botanical name is
Rhipsalidopsis gaertneri.

**What kind of soil is best suited to Christmas and Thanksgiving
cacti?** Equal parts of loam, leafmold or compost, and coarse sand
(not seashore sand) together with a pint of superphosphate and a quart
of wood ashes to each bushel is a good mixture. Or packaged mixtures,
including soilless mixes, can be used.

How often should a Christmas cactus be repotted? Ordinarily every
2 or 3 years, or whenever the pot is filled with roots and the soil appears to be worn out. However, plants can exist many years without
being repotted.

When should a Christmas cactus be transplanted? In the spring, if
the plant is healthy. A plant that is unhealthy because of poor root condition may be carefully repotted at any time and is usually transferred
to a smaller pot.

**Must the Christmas and Thanksgiving cacti have sunshine to
bloom?** Both need exposure to sunshine, except from May to Septem-

ber; during this period, shade from the full intensity of strong sunlight.

How do I care for my holiday cactus after it blooms?   Rest the plant by keeping it nearly dry for 6 to 8 weeks. When new growth appears, repot or topdress with fresh soil and water so that the soil is kept fairly moist.

Why do Christmas cactus leaves turn yellow and fall off indoors each winter and come out again on the porch in the summer?   Because the indoor atmosphere is too arid for these epiphytic plants. Use humidifiers. Stand your pots on trays of moist gravel or sand.

What makes Christmas cactus leaves turn yellow and grow very small? They do not grow as broad as they should. They are planted in sandy soil.   The soil is probably too poor. Try repotting into a richer (but still porous) mixture.

What care must I give to my Thanksgiving cactus so that the buds will not drop off? Out of 25 buds appearing on the plant, about 7 or 8 develop into full-blooming flowers.   Common causes of bud dropping are overwatering, exposure to cold drafts, a position too close to a heat source, and low humidity. Syringe foliage frequently in autumn. Water the plant sparingly. Feed a little liquid fertilizer weekly after buds appear. Some bud drop is normal when a great many buds form.

I have a Christmas cactus plant several years old, and it hasn't bloomed. Someone told me it must be a male plant. Are there male and female plants? How can you tell?   No, there are not separate male and female plants. Both the Thanksgiving and Christmas cacti bear male and female parts in the same flower, not on separate plants.

What can I do to have my Christmas cactus bloom at Christmastime instead of in March?   Leave the plant outdoors as late as possible in the fall and not near artificial light. It can be kept outside until frost danger approaches and temperatures fall below 40° F. Buds will have formed when the plant is brought indoors.

Why does Christmas cactus send out tiny hair roots at each leaf joint?   This is quite a natural phenomenon and occurs particularly if the plants are grown in a moist atmosphere. This phenomenon is especially typical of the Easter cactus (*Rhipsalidopsis gaertneri*).

How can a claw cactus be started from an old plant?   By stem cuttings planted firmly in moist sand in the spring. By grafting onto pereskia, cereus, or other suitable stock in early summer. (See Grafting, Section 3.)

Succulents

GENERAL

What is the difference between cacti and succulents? A cactus is any plant of a fleshy character adapted to conserve water and store it in its tissues. Nearly all cacti are succulents, but not all succulents are cacti. Century-plant, aloe, air-plant, stapelia, and many others are succulents that belong to families other than Cactaceae.

Do succulents need the same kind of soil as cacti? Generally, yes, but succulents that are not cacti form a much more diverse group than those that are, and, in consequence, their specific needs tend to vary more. However, they also need good, sharp, soil drainage.

In what kind of soil should succulents be planted? This varies to some extent with the individual needs of the large number of species that comprise this group. It *must* be porous but should not, as beginners often think, be nearly all sand. Many species appreciate lime.

Do succulents need a resting season? Yes, all do. As they come from many different parts of the world, their seasons of rest vary. Thus, most South African succulents grow in our winter and should be rested in the summer, while species that are native to lands north of the equator commonly rest in our winter. When resting, keep cooler and drier than when growing.

What are some of the most interesting succulents, other than cacti, for the window garden? The list is vast. You might try euphorbia, echeveria, stapelia, haworthia, gasteria, senecio, cotyledon, crassula, kalanchoe, and some of the South African rock plants (lithops).

CRASSULA (JADE PLANT)

What could cause a crassula (jade plant) to drop most of its leaves? Too much water or possibly very extreme drought. This succulent plant should be treated like a cactus—plenty of drainage in the pot but water enough to prevent shriveling. The exact frequency of watering depends upon the size and condition of the plant as well as upon the weather and its position in the house.

What can be done to encourage a jade plant to bloom? It has been kept in good health for 10 or 15 years. The jade plant does not normally bloom until it is many years old. Younger specimens sometimes bloom if pot-bound.

I have a so-called rubber plant about 10 years old; it bloomed 2 years in succession, the last time 3 years ago, and not since. Why? Your plant is probably the so-called Japanese rubber, *Crassula argentea;* its failure to flower regularly is probably due to giving it too much water, so that it never rests. This plant is a succulent and needs to be kept on the dry side in late summer and early fall.

How can I propagate my jade plant? It is now so large I can no longer handle it. You can scarcely help doing so! Branches and leaves of *Crassula argentea* or jade plant, which makes a showy, treelike house plant, root so easily that if a piece is accidentally broken off and falls in the pot, roots soon form in the surface of the potting soil. The thick, glossy, rounded leaves will also produce roots if the bases are inserted in damp, sandy soil.

CROWN-OF-THORNS (EUPHORBIA)

How can I keep my crown-of-thorns (Euphorbia milii var. splendens) green? The leaves come on and drop off. It just refuses to bloom in the house. Probably you are keeping the plant too dry. It cannot produce leaves and flowers without a constant supply of moisture during its growing season.

Does crown-of-thorns require a dry soil? The soil should be exceedingly porous and well drained but should be kept moist whenever leaves are present on the stems. When the leaves fall off, keep the soil nearly dry until new growth begins.

Which plant food is best for crown-of-thorns? Avoid the excessive use of fertilizer. A vigorous plant with a strong, healthy root system will respond to small amounts of any complete fertilizer applied during its active growing season.

What window should a crown-of-thorns stand in? Why do the buds blast? The sunniest possible window. Bud blasting (failure to develop properly) may be due to extreme dryness, gross overwatering, or low temperature. Ordinarily temperature should not go below 45° F. Increase humidity by placing the plant on a saucer of wet pebbles or gravel.

Is the crown-of-thorns a constant bloomer? Yes, if kept in good growing condition, it will bloom much of the year. (See previous questions for culture.) *Euphorbia fulgens* (sometimes listed as *E.* x *keysii*) has pink flowers throughout the year when given good light. Other interesting selections have yellow flowers.

ECHEVERIA

I have a tender succulent which resembles the common hardy hen-and-chicks. What is it? Probably an echeveria. The handsome rosettes of these succulents are often silver-gray, gray-green, or almost white, touched with pink. Plant them in the rock garden in the summer and bring them indoors in the winter, before the first frost.

KALANCHOE

What is the proper soil and care for successful blooming of the Kalanchoe blossfeldiana? The soil should be moderately rich and quite porous. Grow in full sun. Propagate by cuttings in the spring. Repot the plants as roots fill the pots. Water fairly freely when in active growth and feed gently when the final pots are root-filled. (See also under Gift Plants.)

How can I make an air-plant (Kalanchoe pinnata) bloom? Give good culture that has as its object the rapid production of a large, vigorous plant. It needs a rather warm temperature (60° to 70° F.), plenty of sun, rich but quite porous soil, rather ample supplies of water, and feeding when it has filled a 6-inch pot full of roots. Low temperatures, too dry soil, and lack of light prevent blooming.

What is the name of the house plant that produces many little plants along the edges of its fleshy leaves? Several species of kalanchoe possess this habit. They are easily propagated from the plantlets.

LIVING STONES (LITHOPS)

How should living stones be treated? Plant closely together in shallow pans filled with exceedingly porous soil. The tops of the plants should be well above the soil level. Cover the surface of the pans with gravel or small stones. Water freely from October to May but let the soil dry out between waterings. Keep nearly dry at other times. Shade lightly from bright summer sun. Grow in a temperature of 50° to 60° F.

SEDUM

How can healthy, small, potted sedums be kept growing? Grow them in the sunniest window in a room where the temperature is not excessive. Pot them in a porous, well-drained soil and keep moderately moist at all times. Sedums are easy to grow.

STAPELIA

I can never get stapelia to grow and do well. Why? They are sometimes rather tricky. They need an open, porous soil and regular watering in spring and summer. Give light shade during the summer when they should bloom. They should be kept nearly dormant in the winter by giving less water. (See below.)

Concerning stapelias: mine are rested, kept fairly dry in the summer, and form buds in late August or early September. The buds wilt, however, without maturing. How should they be treated? Perhaps you keep them too dry in the summer. A usual practice is to rest them by keeping them nearly dry in the winter and to water them moderately and encourage growth in the summer.

Hardy Bulbs for Forcing

IRIS

Can 'Wedgwood' iris be grown successfully in the house in the winter? If you have a cool room (50° to 55° F.), plant the largest size bulbs in 6- or 8-inch pots; give full light and sun; keep free of aphids and don't disturb the roots. This iris may flower, but it really needs greenhouse or outdoor culture. Don't use small bulbs for indoors, as they won't bloom.

LILY (LILIUM)

Will regular garden lilies bloom indoors? The regal lily is a good pot plant but rather tall. Potted in late fall and given a temperature of 55° to 60° F., with full light, it will flower in April or early May. Other hardy lilies recommended for forcing include the Mid-Century Hybrids, such as 'Enchantment'. For others, see catalogs of bulb specialists.

How can Easter lilies be made to bloom in time for Easter? The starting temperature should be 50° to 60° F. After rooting, provide a minimum night temperature of 65° to 70° F.; day temperature, 75° F.

When the plants are 3 to 4 inches high, move them to a lower temperature (60°) for 14 days, then to high temperatures. Water frequently.

What lilies will succeed in a bright window or greenhouse? The new dwarf lilies such as fragrant 'Little Rascal' and 'Connecticut Lemonglow' will succeed in pots with temperatures of 55° F. at night, 65° to 70° F. during the day in bright light. Plant the bulbs in containers with 2 to 3 inches of soil over the top of each bulb.

LILY-OF-THE-VALLEY (CONVALLARIA MAJALIS)

Can I make lily-of-the-valley bloom indoors? Yes. Order large, cold-storage pips sold for forcing. Plant in moist fiber or mix, leaving the tops exposed. Place at once in a sunny window and give plenty of water. These are especially treated—your own roots won't work.

Hardy Spring Bulbs for Indoors
(*See also Section 5.*)

What spring-flowering bulbs can be forced in pots of soil for winter bloom? Follow recommendations for best forcing varieties in bulb mail-order catalogs. These include hyacinths, daffodils, tulips, and crocus.

How are hardy (spring-flowering) bulbs forced for winter bloom? In late October, pot the bulbs in a standard potting mixture or any garden soil that drains well. Allow 6 to 7 crocus bulbs, 3 to 5 daffodil bulbs, 5 to 9 tulip bulbs, and 3 to 6 hyacinth bulbs to each pot (bulbs are set much closer for forcing than they are in the open ground). The tips of the bulbs should be level with the surface of the soil in the pot. The bulbs require a cold period of 8 to 14 weeks to form roots, best accomplished by burying the pots in a trench so the tops of the pots are about 4 inches below the ground surface.

After watering the pots well, pack peat moss and/or leaves or straw around and on top of the pots about 4 inches deep. You can also place inverted flowerpots on the top of each pot before applying the mulch, which will keep out rodents. Or use a sheet of hardware cloth.

An alternative to the trench method, which makes it difficult to lift the pots when the ground freezes solid, even with the 4-inch mulch, is to put the pots in a cold frame—if you have one and there is space for the pots. Another alternative is to keep the pots in a cellar or basement

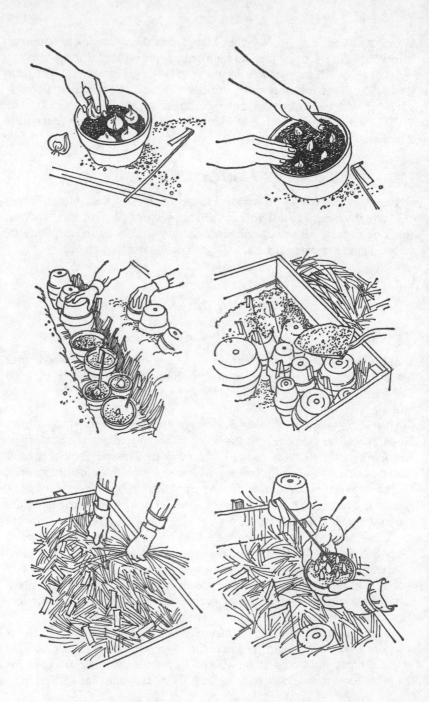

where the temperature does not go above 40° to 50° F. Do not let the soil dry out during this cold-storage period indoors.

As the pots develop shoots about 2 inches long, bring indoors to a cool, partially light place for about 10 days, then to a sunny window. Water as necessary. When blooms open, remove from full sun (but keep cool) to prolong the display.

Do you water daffodils or tulips that are potted and kept in a cold cellar for later forcing? After the bulbs are potted, they should be thoroughly soaked. If conditions are right (i.e., if there is proper humidity in the cellar), they will not require additional watering. However, if pots dry out, they must be watered.

In how many days will tulips bloom after they are taken out of the cold-storage pit? They will bloom in 4 to 8 weeks, depending on the earliness of the variety, the temperature, and how close the blooming period is to spring.

Can we plant tulip bulbs in indoor pots to bloom at Easter? Yes. Bring pots into 60° F. about 3 to 4 weeks before Easter.

What care is given to spring-flowering bulbs forced for winter bloom after they have bloomed? Foliage is ripened as in a garden, being kept green as long as possible. When leaves turn yellow and dry off, plant outdoors for garden bloom. Forced bulbs are unlikely to bloom again indoors and can take several seasons before recovering sufficiently to bloom again in the garden.

FORCING SPRING BULBS FOR INDOOR BLOOM
(Top row) Bulbs are planted close together, but not touching, in a pot or special bulb pan (a squat pot) so that the tips of the bulbs are at or just below the surface. (Second row) After covering the bulbs with soil, water thoroughly, then place the pots in a trench or cold frame. Inverted flowerpots protect the bulbs from rodents (or use a length of hardware cloth). Pots are covered with soil. Straw or leaves can be added to prevent the soil from freezing solid. (Bottom row) After several weeks, pots with sprouted bulbs can be brought indoors, but avoid very hot, dry rooms. Put the pots in your coolest rooms, especially when they are first brought indoors.

Tender Bulbs for Indoors

In what sort of soil should tender bulbs be grown? Light, well-drained, and fertile soil. Avoid the use of *fresh* manure.

ACHIMENES   (See Section 5—Bulbs, Tubers and Corms.)

AGAPANTHUS

What is the proper care for an agapanthus in both the winter and summer? In the winter, rest it. Keep nearly dry in a temperature of 45° F. In the spring, increase its water supply and temperature. In the summer, stand it outside in a sunny position; water and feed it freely. Repot in the spring only when growths become crowded. Expect bloom in April and May, water freely, and feed then. If you have space, dwarf varieties in small tubs will be most attractive.

How deep should lily-of-the-Nile (agapanthus) be planted in pots to take into a basement for the winter? The tuberous roots should be planted just beneath the soil surface, so that the crown of the plant is practically at the surface.

AMARYLLIS (HIPPEASTRUM)

Are amaryllis bulbs planted inside or out? If outside, should they be lifted for the winter? When do they bloom? (Ohio.) Plant in pots indoors, leaving the upper half of the bulb sticking out of the soil. They bloom from January to April, but the same bulb does not produce bloom over this entire period.

What soil should be used for amaryllis? Garden soil enriched with superphosphate (1 pint per bushel) and commercial cow manure or compost (2 quarts per bushel).

How shall I plant an amaryllis bulb? Select a pot just large enough to hold the bulb, comfortably surrounded by soil. Pot in the potting mixture described in the previous question, with the top half of the bulb exposed. Water well from below after potting.

When should I plant an amaryllis bulb? I planted one last year and there are no blooms. Plant new bulbs from December to March.

Two satisfactory house plants to grow from bulbs: the quick-growing, fragrant paper-white narcissus (left) and the flamboyant amaryllis (right).

Should amaryllis bulbs be kept in the dark until rooted? This is not necessary. A temperature of 60° to 70° F. and just sufficient moisture to keep the soil damp (all the way through) is all that is needed.

How can amaryllis bulbs be kept from year to year? Keep the plant growing by watering and feeding it during the season when leaves are developing or present—usually in the spring and summer. When the leaves die down, keep the plant dry. Repot every third or fourth year; topdress at the beginning of the growing period during other years. (See answers to other inquiries.)

How shall I topdress a potted amaryllis? By scraping off the top inch of soil in the pot without disturbing the bulb and substituting good garden loam containing a complete fertilizer.

Is there some fertilizer that I can feed an amaryllis to produce better and more blooms? When the plant is growing, and provided that the pot is well filled with roots, use any complete house-plant or garden fertilizer.

What is the trick of raising amaryllis indoors? Make sure that it is rested in the fall and early winter. Water freely, feed and otherwise encourage growth when the leaves are growing. Plunge (bury pot to its rim in soil) outdoors in a partially shaded spot during the summer. When potting, do not bury the bulb more than halfway in the soil.

How long do you leave an amaryllis bulb in dry soil before applying water? From the time the leaves are yellow and die away in late summer to fall, until the first signs of new growth can be seen sprouting out of the top of the bulb.

How long should amaryllis bulbs be dried off? I want mine to bloom in March. Individuals vary greatly. Some are nearly evergreen; others die down quite early in the fall. Six or 8 weeks would perhaps be a minimum.

When should I start to water amaryllis bulbs to have them bloom in January or February? They are now in a cool, dark room in pots. Pick out bulbs that went to rest early. Examine carefully in December, and if you can find any that show tips of flower buds out of the top of the bulb, start these by watering them and placing them in a temperature of 70° to 75° F.

Last Easter I bought an amaryllis. I left it outdoors without watering it until September, when I brought it indoors and started to water it again. To date there is no sign of any growth. What is wrong with it? You dried it off too soon. It should be encouraged to grow as vigorously as possible through the summer to build up the bulb and the following year's bloom.

In what window should amaryllis be kept—south or east? Either exposure should be satisfactory. They need as much sunlight as possible during the winter and spring, and light shade during the summer.

I have some fine hybrid amaryllis bulbs which bloomed the first year; now—in spite of following directions for resting, feeding, etc.—I get no more blooms, though the bulbs are growing well with big leaves. I have had bulbs 2 years. What is the trouble? Amaryllis bought and flowered the first year often fail to bloom the second year. Their energy is used to establish a new root system. As good foliage has developed, your plants should bloom from the third year on. Usually 2 to 3 leaves guarantee that the bulb will form buds.

Why don't hybrid amaryllis bulbs brought home from Florida bloom? I have about 3 dozen bulbs and all bloomed before we got them. It may be that they have not established themselves yet. This may take a year. (Read other replies on this subject.)

What is the best way to grow amaryllis bulbs to a really large size? Mine seldom reach 3 inches in diameter. Good cultivation over a period of years is the answer. This implies potting, watering, feeding, resting when required, suitable soil, temperature, and light conditions, as well as maintaining the plants free from pests. (See previous questions.)

Is bulb fiber as good as soil for growing an amaryllis bulb? No. To grow these successfully so that they will last from year to year, nourishment is needed, and this is not contained in most kinds of bulb fiber.

Is it unusual for an amaryllis to bloom in December? No, it is not particularly unusual, although most bulbs produce their flowers later in the winter.

Do amaryllis often bloom more than once a year? Mine bloomed 3 times this year. The amaryllis (*Hippeastrum*) does not bloom more than once a season. Strong bulbs will sometimes produce more than one flower scape, however. If your plant blooms every 3 or 4 months, it is something other than *Hippeastrum*. There are many bulbs of the amaryllis family (*Amaryllidaceae*) with varying characteristics.

How can a fine hybrid amaryllis (Hippeastrum) be propagated vegetatively to make a rapid increase in the stock of bulbs? By cutting the bulb into segments, each containing a small part of the basal ring. These pieces are planted in sand and peat moss and placed where a bottom heat of 70° F. is available. Keep just moist and shaded and new bulblets should arise in a few weeks.

I have amaryllis hybrids, from seed, already as big as marbles, but they have stopped growing. Should the bulb be nearly out of the soil? What fertilizer should be used and how often? What soil is needed? Bulbs of young amaryllis naturally grow out of the soil. They will cease growing for a period in late summer. Use superphosphate in the soil, which should be a medium porous loam. Feed when in active growth with liquid fertilizer.

AMAZON-LILY (EUCHARIS GRANDIFLORA)

Can I grow the beautiful Amazon-lily outside a greenhouse? Yes, this very fragrant member of the amaryllis family will thrive in a light, rather than a sunny, location.

How should I plant bulbs of Eucharis-lily? This makes a big plant with 18-inch stems and glossy evergreen leaves. Allow a 5-inch pot for each bulb and provide a fairly warm place, 70° to 75° F., until buds appear. Then cooler growing, about 65° F., is better. Water well after potting and fertilize until the bloom is developed; then stop feeding until a new set of buds appears. After each period of bloom, induce a 4- to 5-week rest with the soil somewhat dry, but not to the point that the plants' leaves wilt.

AMORPHOPHALLUS (See Hydrosme.)

ARUM PALAESTINUM (BLACK-CALLA)

What is the history of the black-lily-of-the-Nile? *Arum palaestinum,*
also called the black-calla, is a native of Palestine, a relative of our
common skunk-cabbage, of the tropical anthurium, and of the white
calla-lily. It was first discovered by the Genevan botanist M. Boissier
near Jerusalem.

**What can I do to make a black-calla come into bloom? I have tried
but to no avail.** Perhaps your tuber is too small and will bloom when
older. Grow it in rich soil, keeping it moist and in a light place during
the summer. Dry it off completely during the winter.

BOWIEA VOLUBILIS (CLIMBING-ONION)

How can bowiea be grown? The climbing-onion is a South African
plant with large onionlike bulbs from which are formed tall, delicate,
green vinelike growths. Pot in a porous soil with only the base of the
bulb buried. Give it a sunny window. Keep the soil moist when green
growth is in evidence, dry at other times. It goes many years without
needing to be repotted.

CALADIUM

What is the proper culture for caladium tubers? Set each tuber in a
5-inch pot of humus-rich soil. Their growing time is April until October
so they are more useful as terrace rather than house plants. At the start,
give shade and heat, 70° to 80° F., and keep well watered. Gradually
dry off toward fall. *Caladium humboldtii* is a dainty miniature useful in
large terrariums and gardens under fluorescent lights.

**After getting caladium bulbs to start, I find that the leaves are small,
but the stems of the leaves are abnormally long. What causes this? The
bulbs are growing in a window which gets some sun during the
day.** This is usually true of the first few leaves. If the condition persists, it is probably because of a lack of light or humidity, which should
be 60 per cent or higher.

**How should a caladium that has finished blooming in the house be
treated?** As soon as the plant begins to lose foliage in the fall, gradually reduce watering. When all leaves have gone, withhold water completely and store the pots containing the bulbs in a dry place, at 60° F.,

or remove the tubers, dry them off, and store each one in a heavy paper bag for 2 to 3 months of rest.

CALLA-LILY (ZANTEDESCHIA)

When should calla-lilies be planted for Christmas bloom? Pot tubers in August, each in a 4- or 5-inch pot of humus-rich soil; water and set in a dim place at 55° to 60° F. until growth is well started; then move to light and warmth, but below 70°, and fertilize. As flower stalk develops, move to a sunny place. Water moderately at first but keep almost wet as the plant develops.

How should calla-lily tubers be cared for after blooming? Keep feeding the plants (good organic fertilizer) and encourage strong growth until June, then gradually dry them off, turn the pots on their sides, and rest until September. Repot and start into growth at this time.

I have a white calla-lily 5 years old which never has blossomed. What is the reason? This plant needs rich soil, ample moisture during the growing season, at a temperature of 50° to 60° F., feeding when in active growth, and a definite rest period during late summer.

CLIVIA

Can clivias be grown as window plants? Yes. Stand potted plants outdoors in the summer; feed and water them regularly. Bring indoors before frost and give them a light window. Water enough to prevent shriveling, as the plant is evergreen. When buds push up, give the plants more water.

I have had a clivia 6 years which bloomed only when I bought it. Are there any secrets of how to make it bloom? Clivias need cool growing conditions and full sunlight, except during summer months, when light shade is appreciated. They resent disturbance at their roots. The soil should always be moist but not waterlogged. During the summer, feed at weekly intervals with liquid plant food.

CRINUM

Can you give me information on crinum-lilies? When grown in large pots or tubs, they need good drainage and rich soil. Plant them half out of the soil. Store them in the winter in a light place, at a temperature of 50° F., and water only a little. In the spring, increase the temperature and water more freely. In the summer, water freely; feed generously; place outdoors in a sunny location. These are summer-blooming.

What is the proper culture for crinum (milk-and-wine-lily)? Mine does not bloom but develops many bulblets. Plant in a very rich but well-drained soil in large pots or tubs. Set the bulbs with their top half protruding above the soil. Water and feed established plants generously in the summer and grow in a sunny position (outside in hot weather). Keep in a cool, frostproof place and nearly dry in the winter. Repot only every 3 to 4 years.

EUCHARIS   (See Amazon-lily, this section.)

FREESIA

When is the best time to start freesias in the house and how should they be taken care of?   Plant bulbs in September in fertile, porous soil. Space them 1½ inches apart. Put in a cool place. Give only a little water at first, more as growth develops. Place in a cool, sunny window, 50° to 60° F., when the tops are 1 to 2 inches high. Avoid overwatering. Feed lightly when flower buds appear.

How can I have a succession of freesia blooms in my window garden?   Plant bulbs at 2-week intervals from September to November; 3 months are needed from planting to flowering.

My freesias planted in pots grew well but did not bloom. Why?   After being planted, freesias need a period in a cool, frostproof, light place to develop root growth. When growth starts, the temperature should be 40° to 50° F. at night, with a 5° or 10° rise in the daytime.

My freesias last year were more beautiful than all expectations, exceeding those at the Philadelphia Flower Show. This year I took care of them but they are spindly and small-leaved; I used fertilizer this year but not last. This has happened before. Why? I bought giant-sized bulbs.   It is advisable to buy new bulbs each year. The quality of bloom depends largely upon the cultivation the bulbs received the *previous* year. In a house or small greenhouse, it is difficult to provide ideal conditions for bulb development.

Why are my freesia leaves turning yellow? They are 8 to 9 inches high.   Overwatering will quickly cause freesia leaves to turn yellow. Lack of sufficient light, low humidity, or extreme dryness of the soil will cause a similar condition.

My freesias are growing spindly without blossoming and are drying

up. Why? The temperature may be too high, the atmosphere too dry, and possibly there is a lack of sufficient sunlight.

How should freesias that bloom in the house be cared for to have bulbs for another year? Mine will bloom about Christmastime. If brought into bloom as early as Christmas, it may be difficult to provide conditions that will ensure good bulbs for the following year. Water, feed, and keep them growing in a sunny, cool position until the foliage fades, then gradually dry them off. It is more satisfactory to start with new bulbs each year.

I've grown freesias from bulbs and have lots of little bulblets. Will they bloom? They are planted now. They will not bloom while very small, but if grown under good conditions they should soon make blooming-size stock.

GLORY-LILY (GLORIOSA)

What is the proper culture for this climbing lily? This is *Gloriosa superba* or *G. rothschildiana,* two excellent plants for a warm, sunny window. Plant in February in a 6-inch pot half full of house-plant soil. Lay the flat tuber on this and cover with more soil to within an inch of the top. (Insert three equidistant 2-foot stakes unless you plan to train the plant on strings around a window.) Growth will start in about 2 weeks. Apply liquid plant food every other week from then on. Buds will appear in about 12 weeks, the yellow or yellow-marked scarlet blooms continuing through spring and summer.

Does the glory-lily require a rest period? Yes, gradually reduce watering and withhold by October. Leave the tuber in the pot. If possible, do not repot when growth is started again in February; try to scrape away the topsoil and add a fresh mixture.

My gloriosa tuber looks healthy but it will not sprout. What could be wrong? Most gloriosa tubers have only one live bud or "eye." If something happens to this primary growing point, the tuber may remain sound (like a potato) for several years without sprouting. If your tuber does not have a plump live bud, it would be better to start with a new tuber. When selecting tubers at garden centers, be sure to pick sound tubers with an obvious bud.

GLOXINIA (SINNINGIA)

What soil mixture should gloxinia tubers have for best growth? Should gloxinias be watered from the top or bottom? A loose, humus-rich soil. Adding flaky leafmold, compost, sharp sand, and broken charcoal to the mixture is helpful. They can be watered from top to bottom, provided that the soil is thoroughly wetted and no water is splashed on the leaves.

What are the cultural requirements for the gloxinia (Sinningia speciosa), from tuber planting to maturity and back to rest again? Put tubers in pots just large enough to hold them, in light, humus-rich soil, February or March. Keep just moist in a temperature of 70° F., increasing the water supply as growth develops. Pot into 5- or 6-inch pots when the first pots are filled with roots. Feed a complete fertilizer biweekly when in full growth. Shade from the sun. Dry off gradually after flowering.

Will you please tell me if gloxinias grow best in a shady or sunny place? Shade from anything but weak early-morning and late-afternoon sunlight is necessary. They thrive under fluorescent tubes.

What is the correct temperature for gloxinias? How should watering be done? During the growing season, a minimum temperature of 60° F. (rising to 70° in the daytime) is satisfactory. Watering should be done with caution until a good growth of leaves has developed, then it may be given more freely.

Why do my gloxinia buds turn brown and die? This may be due to an infestation of mites, but more probably the air is too dry. A moist, but not stagnant, atmosphere and freedom from draft provide congenial conditions.

Why do my gloxinias grow tall and lanky? Those I have seen at florist shops are bushy. This can be due to too little light. They need shade from bright sun, but good light otherwise. Grow your gloxinias 6 to 8 inches below three or four 40-watt broad-spectrum fluorescent lamps.

Why do gloxinia leaves curl and look limp? I drop no water on the leaves. You probably are keeping the soil too dry or you have watered it so much that the roots have rotted off. Gloxinia leaves normally die down after flowering.

What is the proper care for gloxinias after they bloom? Shortly after their blooming is over, begin to reduce the moisture supply by increasing the intervals between applications. As the leaves die down, intensify this drying-off process; finally store the plants (leaving the tubers in the soil) in a dry place at a temperature of 45° to 50° F.

When can I take my gloxinia out of storage and start it growing? From mid-February to the end of March. If it shows signs of activity (new leaves appearing), it should be potted and started without delay.

What is the proper blooming season for gloxinias? Under green-house conditions, with skilled cultivation, they may be brought to bloom at almost any time. However, they are naturally summer and early-fall bloomers, and it is easiest to have them in flower at those seasons.

Are there any compact or dwarf gloxinias suitable for small gardens under fluorescent lights? Yes, hybridizers have developed dwarf gloxinias with 4- to 8-inch mature height although the flowers are large and showy. The red and white 'Tom Thumb' is a popular dwarf gloxinia. Then there are the miniature sinningias, which vary in spread and height from a few inches to about 6 inches. They have small tubers and tend to be nearly everblooming, especially in the humid atmosphere of a terrarium or brandy snifter. *Sinningia pusilla,* one of several small species, has tiny lilac flowers; 'Dollbaby' has larger lavender-blue flowers.

Which gives the better result in starting a new gloxinia: to plant a leaf after it has rooted in water or to plant the unrooted leaf in soil immediately? The best plan is to root the leaf cuttings in moist sand or sand mixed with leafmold or peat moss.

How and when does one start new gloxinia plants from their leaves? Leaf cuttings consist of partly matured, medium-sized leaves with some of the apex portion cut away. They are taken in early summer and planted in sand and leafmold, or sand and peat moss, in a warm propagating bed. Keep only just moist until new tubers form.

In starting gloxinias from leaf cuttings, what is done after a tuber and roots have formed? Mine don't seem to start. If cuttings are started late in the season, the young tubers are rested through the winter and started up in the spring. Even with early summer-rooted cuttings, a period often elapses between the formation of the roots and tuber and development of leaves.

What is the best method of starting gloxinia from seed? Sow in January or February on milled sphagnum moss. The seeds are exceedingly small and should not be covered with soil but firmly pressed into the surface. Sow sparsely or you will be inundated! Keep evenly moist at all times in a temperature of 70° F. Shade seedlings; feed with ¼-strength water-soluble fertilizer when fully germinated. Transplant as soon as they are large enough to handle.

HAEMANTHUS (BLOOD-LILY)

Can the blood-lily, a native of South Africa, be started in the house in the winter and set out in the spring, then taken in the house again and

the same culture repeated?   Haemanthuses should not be taken out of their pots and set in the garden. If desired, pots could be plunged to their rims in soil outdoors (in light shade) during the hottest months.

HYACINTH (HYACINTHUS)

I have seen hyacinths forced in the winter in dishes of fiber or pebbles. What kind are they, and how should they be handled?   These are the delicate, fragrant Roman hyacinths. For Christmas bloom, plant in mid-October and grow cold for 5 to 6 weeks while roots form. Then bring first to a cool, light window, then to a sunny place as buds form.

(Left) Bulb pan removed from prerooting storage, ready to be brought indoors. (Right) Paper cone with a small opening at the top is used during early growth of hyacinth (center) to draw flower stem from foliage.

HYDROSME

What is the sacred lily-of-India?   This plant has been known as *Hydrosme* but is now called *Amorphophallus rivieri*—a relative of the calla-lily and a native of China. In the spring, large tubers produce a tall, dark-colored, fetid, callalike bloom; in the summer, a single, stout leaf of umbrella shape finely divided into many leaflets.

I have been given a sacred lily-of-India which is supposed to bloom black. It looks like a large potato. How do I care for it?   Grow it in a pot of loose, humus-rich soil or plant it out in a garden in the summer. A leaf is produced in the summer, a flower in the spring. In the fall, dig up (if in the garden) and keep dry until the following spring. The flower is exceedingly interesting, but it has an offensive odor. However, the flower doesn't last long and the leaf that follows is very ornamental.

IXIA

How can ixias be grown? I cannot make them live. Bulbs start, then die off. Treat exactly like freesias. Pot in early fall, spacing the bulbs about 2 inches apart. Water carefully at first, more freely afterward. Grow in a cool, well-lighted position (night temperature, 45° F.). Dry off gradually after flowering. Avoid overwatering and high temperatures.

NARCISSUS (DAFFODIL)

Which tender narcissus bulbs are grown as house plants in water and pebbles for winter bloom? Is the culture the same for all? Paperwhites, pure white, fragrant; 'Soleil d'Or', golden yellow, fragrant; Chinese sacred-lily, two shades of yellow, fragrant. Yes, all are forced in the same way.

How can I grow tender narcissus as house plants? Buy bulbs from a reliable source so that you will know that they have been well grown. Plant in a soilless mix or soil, or put in dishes of water and pebbles to which bits of charcoal have been added. Place for 2 weeks in a cool dark closet or cellar until growth starts. As roots develop, bring to more light. Keep cool. When foliage growth begins to develop, place in a cool, sunny window.

I started some paper-white narcissus the first of November; now they are about 3 inches high. How long before I should bring them into the light and a warmer temperature? They should be brought into the growing temperature immediately.

When narcissus bulbs are planted in the house, is there any way to keep them from getting so tall? My present ones are now 30 inches high. These are undoubtedly being grown at too high a temperature. The best daytime temperature is 65° to 70° F. The lower the temperature, the shorter and more satisfactory the plants will be. Moving plantings to a cool garage at night helps to keep growth lower and to prolong bloom after the flowers open.

Why do my narcissus bulbs have only leaves and not flowers (bulbs grown indoors in water)? If the bulbs are of good quality, failure is most often caused by excessively high temperatures.

My paper-white narcissus, growing in pebbles in a cool cellar, grow tall and fall over before blooming. Why? They must have been planted too early and kept in a dark place too long. They must have full light to mature. If planted about September 5 to 10, they should bloom by Thanksgiving, a matter of 10 weeks. Later plantings take less time; plant in mid-November for Christmas.

What procedure should be used in keeping paper-white narcissus bulbs for next season? It is impractical to keep paper-white narcissus over from year to year. Discard after flowering unless you live in a mild climate. Then the bulbs can be planted in the open ground.

ORNITHOGALUM (STAR-OF-BETHLEHEM)

What is the proper culture for Ornithogalum arabicum? Is it a good house plant? Excellent. You can plant 6 or 7 bulbs, 1 inch deep, in a low flowerpot (bulb pan) in a mixture of half-and-half leafmold and sand. Plant from September to February. Grow cool, about 60° F., in a light place, particularly until the foliage is well advanced. Then move to a sunny place and keep the soil just moist. Let the foliage go on growing until it begins to die down naturally. Store the pots in a cool, dark place until fall. Then repot in a fresh soil mixture.

I have carefully followed the directions for Ornithogalum miniatum, with poor results. Only 1 bulb out of 4 in the same pot has started and that has blossomed low. What is the trouble? This species needs considerably more warmth and more moist conditions than most ornithogalums. A temperature of 60° F. at night and 65° to 70° F. in the daytime is not too much.

OXALIS

How should I care for oxalis? I have several different kinds. Tender oxalis are potted in September, 3 or 4 bulbs in a 4-inch pot or bulb pan in porous, fertile soil. Water carefully at first; more freely as growth develops. Repot into a 5-inch pot when the 4-inch pot is filled with roots. When blooming is over, gradually reduce water and keep quite dry through the summer. Grow in a temperature of 60° F.

Why can't I grow oxalis successfully in the house? Because the environment is likely not suitable. They need plenty of sunlight, ample water during their growing season, none during the dormant period, a loose, porous soil, and a temperature of 55° to 65° F.

How do you store, and where is the best place to plant, oxalis bulbs? During their dormant season, leave the bulbs in soil in the pots, keep dry, and store in a cellar or shed. They may be grown in pots or in hanging baskets in a greenhouse, sun-room, or sunny window.

Why do my oxalis bloom for only a short time in my window garden? Oxalis have a definite season of bloom. Unlike some geraniums, begonias, and fuchsias, they do not produce flowers over a period of months.

Why don't my oxalis bloom? I have one in an east window and one in a west window. Possibly lack of sufficient light. These plants need full exposure to sunshine for good results. Overcrowding or an unsuitable soil may be contributory causes, or too low humidity.

RANUNCULUS

My ranunculus is dying leaf by leaf; it's in a north window. What is the cause? Probably it is too warm and dry. This bulbous plant must be grown indoors in cool (night temperature, 45° F.) moist conditions for best results. A cool sun or plant room would afford the right conditions.

VALLOTA SPECIOSA

What can you tell me about Vallota speciosa? The Scarborough-lily is a tender evergreen bulb. It needs rich, porous soil. Repotting is resented and should be resorted to only when absolutely necessary. Never let its soil become dry. Grow in full sun and feed the plants vigorously.

VELTHEIMIA VIRIDIFOLIA

How shall I plant and care for my veltheimia bulb? Pot in a standard soil mixture in a 6- or 8-inch pot with the upper half of the bulb exposed. Give regular water and sunshine through autumn. The bloom should begin to develop around Thanksgiving and be open for Christmas or soon after. It lasts several weeks. After flowers fade, cut off the blooming stem but continue to give water and light while the handsome foliage remains green. As it dies back, toward spring, gradually reduce its water. Store in its pot turned on its side on the damp floor of a potting shed or outdoors during the summer. When new growth starts in the fall, increase its water, feed it with a complete plant food, and give it full sunlight in a cool window.

Veltheimia is a winter-flowering bulb native to South Africa. In a cool, well-lighted window garden the bloom remains in good condition for 5 to 6 weeks.

What shall I do with the small bulb which has appeared on the side of my veltheimia?   When its leaves die back, gently remove the offset from the parent bulb and pot it separately.

13. Plant Troubles and Their Control

PLANT PESTS ARE probably as old as the plants themselves. We know that insects antedated man by millions of years and we know that plant diseases plagued the ancient Romans. Some diseases, like the potato blight that caused the Irish famine of 1846, have changed the course of history. The application of pesticides is likewise not new, sulfur being recommended as early as 1000 B.C., but our modern concept of protecting plants with chemicals starts with the discovery of Bordeaux mixture in 1882.

For many years gardeners took care of their problems with a limited number of pesticides. The plant medicine chest usually included nicotine sulfate and soap for sucking insects, lead arsenate for chewers, or sometimes pyrethrum and rotenone, lime-sulfur or oil for dormant spraying, and sulfur or copper for plant diseases.

The development of DDT during World War II brought spectacular success in control of plant as well as human pests and encouraged a flood of synthetic organic chemicals. In 1947, the Federal Insecticide, Fungicide and Rodenticide Act (known as FIFRA) provided for the registration of all pesticides with the U. S. Department of Agriculture. A further requirement of this act was that complete information concerning the chemical be carried on the label of the container. Soon, more than 60,000 formulations were registered under trade names and it became difficult to select the right product for a particular problem.

In 1961, it was one woman, Rachel Carson, and the publication of her *Silent Spring* that focused attention on the effect of all these pesticides on the environment. Since then the flood of new chemicals has been reduced markedly and registration has been shifted from the U. S. Department of Agriculture to the Environmental Protection Agency, formed in 1970.

In 1972, the Federal Environmental Pest Control Act, which drasti-oally amended the Federal Insecticide, Fungicide and Rodenticide Act, was signed into law to become fully effective by 1976. This legislation regulated, for the first time, actual uses of each pesticide by making it illegal to apply a chemical inconsistent with the directions on the label. Thus, an insecticide or fungicide could be used legally only for those pests and plants specifically named on the label. In 1978, amendments were passed to permit the use of a pesticide for a pest or pests not on the label, *if* the chemical is labeled for use against another pest on the same plant and if the label does not say for use *only* against those pests listed. Also allowed under the amendments are application methods other than those outlined on the label unless expressly prohibited, and dilution rates *less* than specified.

The amended FIFRA also provides for the classification of pesticides into two categories—*general use,* for home gardeners, and *restricted use,* for certified applicators, either private or commercial.

A process has been devised to evaluate the registration of pesticide uses by the EPA, including the reregistration of uses on existing labels. It is based on the known and probable disadvantages and advantages or risks and benefits of pesticide usage. The EPA is responsible for determining the risks of pesticide use and the USDA, the benefits. The process is referred to by the acronym RPAR (Rebuttable Presumption Against Registration). In applying this process, when a potential risk is identified by the EPA it becomes the basis for a presumption against registering specific, or, in some cases, all, uses or restricting certain uses. That presumption can be rebutted, followed by a benefit-risk evaluation, and a decision by EPA to register, not to register, to restrict, or to ban existing or newly developed pesticides. This is and will be a continuing effort for the foreseeable future, making it essential that you keep in close contact with your local and state Cooperative Extension Service for current, legal recommendations.

The quality of the environment is the main concern, and under the amended FIFRA legislation, penalties may be incurred by anyone who uses a pesticide in a manner inconsistent with instructions on the label. States can legislate further restrictions, and many have already done so. At the present time, a number of pesticides are either under or being considered for RPAR review, including carbaryl (Sevin), lindane, benomyl (Benlate), and others.

The pesticides that the home gardener can now purchase without restrictions are relatively safe for plants, the environment, and the user but they should still be applied with caution. Carbaryl, for instance, is widely recommended for performance and for safety, but it does kill bees and some other beneficial insects. Rotenone, long used on vegetables, kills fish. Pesticides should be applied only as necessary, at the proper dilution rate and at the *right time,* after proper diagnosis of the problem. In some cases, protection of the environment may mean less-than-perfect control of a pest.

Importance of Diagnosis

In plant medicine, as in human medicine, accurate diagnosis is nine tenths of the cure. You must know what is wrong with your plant before you can select the right control measure. The wrong medicine, or even unnecessary medicine, can do more harm than good.

Some diseases and pests are readily recognized by home gardeners; others are extraordinarily difficult even for a specialist to identify. If you are in doubt, do nothing until you get advice from some competent person. (Your neighbor is usually not qualified, even though his advice is profuse and free!) The most reliable source of advice is your county agent or your State Extension Service. It is helpful to send a specimen and a description. Send a whole plant if feasible, for the trouble you think is in the leaf may originate in the stem or roots. Diseased material travels best flattened out between layers of newspaper. Don't send live insects about the country, for they can escape and establish themselves in some hitherto-uninfested area. Insects may be quickly killed by dropping them into a small jar or vial of 70 per cent rubbing alcohol.

In making your own diagnosis, check the obvious things first. *The name of the plant is of primary importance.* Some insects and diseases are promiscuous, attacking a wide variety of plants; but others are highly selective, attacking only the members of a certain family, or even genus, so that the name of the host plant can mean almost immediate identification.

Consider also the time of year. A webby mass in a tree in the spring probably means tent caterpillars; in late summer it indicates fall webworms. An elm leaf perforated in May is probably chewed by a cankerworm; in June, by the elm-leaf beetle; in July, by the Japanese beetle. These dates are for New Jersey. If you live in Florida, or California, or Maine, your dates, as well as your pests, may be quite different. That is one reason for you to keep in close touch with the information put out by your own local Cooperative Extension Service.

Diagnosis is a process of elimination. After knowing the plant that is being attacked and the time of year, look at the foliage. Holes in leaves are probably the work of some chewing insect, although there are one or two diseases that cause shotlike holes.

Disease is the term applied to the abnormal condition that comes from the work of bacteria, fungi, nematodes, viruses, one or two higher forms of plants, or unfavorable environmental conditions.

Injury is the term applied to havoc caused by insects. The different chewing insects make their own patterns in the leaves. When all the leaves of a single twig or branch are chewed off down to the midrib, or, as in the case of pine, the needles are chewed down to the fascicles, then sawfly larvae may be responsible. Flea beetles make tiny round perforations, so familiar in newly set tomato plants unless they have been coated with a protective dust; weevils produce rather typical angular openings; beetle larvae (grubs) and certain caterpillars often "skeletonize" leaves, chewing everything but the epidermis and veins.

If the leaf is yellowish, or stippled white, or gray, the loss of color may be due to sucking insects. You may see them or their cast-off skins, eggs, or excrement on the underside of the foliage. Yellowed or finely stippled leaves that are cobwebby underneath indicate red spider mites, while whitish streaks mean thrips. If there is no sign of insects, the yellowed leaf may be a symptom of malnutrition, perhaps lack of nitrogen or unavailable iron. Leaves curled up or cupped down may harbor aphids; deformed leaves may be due to the cyclamen mite or to sucking insects on buds or developing new growth; blotches or tunnels, to leafminers; round or conical protrusions, to mites, aphids, midges, or gall wasps.

Leaf spots with definite outlines and filled with numerous minute dark pimples are of fungus origin; smooth spots are usually symptoms of a bacterial disease. Fungi may produce irregular blotches on a leaf, but if the black specks or pimples are missing, the blotches may be sunscald or windburn—the result of cells collapsing when water could not get up from the roots fast enough to replace that evaporated from the leaves. Spray injury also produces leaf spots. When phlox leaves die progressively up the stem, it very likely is due to some unbalanced water relation; but if chrysanthemum leaves die in the same fashion, it may be due to drought, leafspot fungus, a wilt fungus in the soil, or to leaf nematodes, the latter being more probable with Korean varieties. Reddish pustules on a leaf indicate rust, very common on hollyhocks; a white felty growth, mildew; and dark soot, a mold living on aphis honeydew.

A dark lesion, or canker, on a stem indicates a fungus disease; a sawdustlike protrusion is the sign of a borer; but a gummy substance exuding on a peach tree may be caused either by the peach-tree borer or the brown-rot fungus.

Wilt—the partial collapse and dying back of a plant—can result from any one of many causes: high temperature, lack of moisture, root injury from too-close cultivation, too-strong fertilizer, a soil fungus that invades the vascular system, or one that causes a crown or stem rot, large grubs, or microscopic nematodes working on the roots. Rots may follow physiological disturbances, and then millipedes and other small animals feast on the disintegrating tissues. *Determine, if you can, the primary cause, and don't worry about the secondary effects.*

It all sounds enormously complicated, but with a little practice you learn to recognize at a glance the signs and symptoms of common pests and diseases, just as you recognize your acquaintances when you pass them on the street. You don't stop to analyze why that is Mrs. Smith; you just know that it is. With a little more training you'll be noticing signs in spite of yourself and walking along the street muttering, "The lacebugs have certainly made Mrs. Smith's azalea look sick; I wonder why Mrs. Jones never sprays her junipers for scale; Mr. Brown's corn smut is a public menace. If the Board of Health makes me cut down my ragweed they ought to make him clean up his smut boils."

Types of Control

Having, as far as possible, diagnosed your plant trouble, how are you going to control it? There are four main avenues of approach: immunization, exclusion, suppression, and protection—and sometimes it takes all four.

1—Immunization means the development, by hybridization or selection, of varieties which are resistant to certain pests. One hundred per cent resistance, or total immunity, is impossible, but if you can buy varieties reasonably resistant to the pests most prevalent in your locality, that is the first, and easiest, control method to attempt. Most seed catalogs list resistant varieties, and your Cooperative Extension Service will help you out with suggestions.

There is a theory, widely held by gardeners, that vigorous plants are more resistant to diseases and pests. This is more often due to coincidence rather than to any true relationship between lack of vigor and susceptibility. The same cultural practices which produce a vigorous plant often check the spread of pests. Spider mites flourish and plants languish in close quarters where there is little air circulation. Proper pruning and feeding of elm trees check the spread of Dutch elm disease only indirectly by reducing weak or dead wood in which the bark beetle, disseminator of the fungus, lays its eggs. Some fungi, weak parasites, can enter plants only through wounds, and thrive on decaying tissue; but other parasites, such as rusts, smuts, and mildews, can operate only on a vigorous plant. In corn-breeding experiments it has been found that hybrids of high vigor are more susceptible to smut than those of low vigor; but since vigor is more important than smut resistance, we must continue to control this fungus by eradication methods. Vigorous plants can better withstand many pests, which may make them appear to be more resistant.

Japanese beetles definitely prefer young, succulent leaves to old and wilting ones, and you never find Mexican bean beetles waiting until plants are weakened before they move in!

There are some rather hazy theories about plant nutrition as a factor in disease resistance, but we have not yet gone very far along this line. No matter how well plants are cultivated and fed, one still cannot ignore their insects and diseases. The sooner this fact is recognized, the sooner the gardener will get over having nightmares about pests and learn to take them in his stride. He cannot have a garden without planting seeds; he cannot continue to have a healthy garden, year after year, unless pest control becomes a routine operation.

2—*Exclusion* is practiced by counties, states, and countries by means of quarantine laws and regulations, backed up by careful inspections. You can apply the same principle to your garden by looking at every plant, whether acquired by gift or purchase, with a suspicious eye before allowing entry. If you insist on acquiring a diseased plant, either disinfect it or put it in isolation, far removed from your healthy plants.

Buy certified seed when you can. That means that government inspectors looked at the seed plants in the field and certified them as being free from specific diseases. Treating seed with hot water or a disinfectant is another exclusion measure. Farmers, through their cooperatives, have been able to obtain treated seed more readily than the home gardener, but many seed dealers do disinfect seeds sold in small packets.

3—*Suppression,* of course, means the destruction of a pest after it gets established in an area. It includes soil sterilization to kill soil fungi or nematodes, or treating the soil with an insecticide to kill grubs—or eliminating an ant nest, or breaking off a tent caterpillar egg mass or hand-picking bagworms. It means picking Japanese beetles and dropping them into a can of kerosene, or putting milky-disease bacteria into the soil where their grubs develop. It may mean taking up an entire plant and its surrounding soil (as in crown rot), or cutting off a branch of apple or pear that has fire blight. It means removing rose leaves infected with black spot; cleaning up peach or plum "mummies" (wizened, dried-up fruits) or maggot-riddled apples; or spading under all vegetable refuse after harvest. Burning is now restricted in an effort to decrease local air pollution.

Suppression may mean crop rotation to starve out the insect or disease, or cleaning up additional weed hosts, or eliminating some plant that is an "alternate host" and so a necessary factor in the life cycle of a certain disease. Pest-control measures were applied long before people understood the nature of the plant disease. The first barberry eradication law was passed in France in 1660, when it was noticed that wheat rust flourished when barberries grew nearby. Nowadays we sometimes try to isolate red-cedars to prevent the apple rust fungus from completing its cycle, and take out black currants to save nearby pines from blister rust.

To sum it up, suppression is really garden sanitation, the removal of all factors injurious to plant health. *It is probably the most important control method available to the home gardener.*

4—*Protection* involves the spraying and dusting of plants to prevent or to keep away insects or diseases. (Some dormant spraying, however, is more properly a suppression measure.) When chemicals are applied in a wet mist, we call it "spraying"; and when they are applied as a dry powder, the operation is known as "dusting." There are many arguments as to the relative advantages of dusting and spraying; but each has its place, even in the small garden. The lazy gardener will use an aerosol can or his small dust gun more often than his sprayer, which should be—though it seldom is—thoroughly cleaned after each use.

A spray or dust used against insects is called an "insecticide," and one against bacteria and fungi a "fungicide." In addition there are "fumigants" and "disinfectants," "attractants" and "repellents," as well as materials called adjuvants to make the sprays spread and stick.

Sometimes one chemical serves two purposes. A dormant lime sulfur is used both as a fungicide and a dormant spray for scale insects and aphid eggs. Sulfur dust is effective against mildew and red spider mites. Bordeaux mixture—a copper fungicide—sometimes serves as a repellent for insects.

Insecticides can control insects by being swallowed; by hitting their bodies or touching their feet; when their vapors enter the insects' breathing organs; and when they repel them because of odor or taste.

Just how any given insecticide affects insects may depend on its characteristics, when it is applied, how it is applied, and the nature of the pests involved. Most of our newer insecticides will destroy insects in more than one of the above ways.

Insecticides and fungicides are sold under hundreds of different brand names, all variations in one way or another, based on a relatively small number of chemicals. The brand name is unimportant except as it indicates a reliable manufacturer; *it is important to read the label on each package and know you are using the right chemical at the right dilution for your particular purpose.* Most pesticides have both a trade name, such as Sevin, with its first letter capitalized, and an accepted common name, carbaryl, with a small letter. Both names, unlike the brand name, do indicate the pesticidal ingredients. Other examples are: benomyl (Benlate), folpet (Phaltan), maneb (Manzate D, Dithane M-22), mancozeb (Manzate 200, Dithane, Fore), malathion (Cythion), diazinon (Spectracide, Gardentox), dicofol (Kelthane), chlorpyrifos (Dursbar), and dimethoate (Cygon, DeFend).

The possibility of spray injury is ever present. Some plants are at all times sensitive to certain chemicals; others can stand them if it is not too warm or too cold. There is grave danger of injury when two incompatible chemicals are mixed together.

It is not possible to cure all garden troubles with one general spray any more than one kind of pill will cure all human ills, from a sprained ankle to cancer. Sometimes, however, sprays or dusts can be combined to take care of both insects and diseases of certain kinds. Such combination sprays or dusts can be purchased under brand names or, occasionally, mixed at home.

The timeliness of the application is most important. Fungicides should be applied *before* rains, so that a protective coating will be present when the fungus spore or the bacterium starts to grow in the presence of moisture. For fungus diseases, spraying should start *well before the disease is expected,* and should be continued, at whatever intervals are needed, to keep it in check. For rose black spot, in New Jersey, that means weekly treatments from early May until the end of October; but July 1 to September 1 usually covers the spraying period for late blight of potatoes. The adult Japanese beetle is with us from mid-June to mid-September, but for the pine needle scale there is only a two-week period in May, during which the crawlers are active, when spraying will have any effect.

Know your insects and know your diseases, and don't waste your money and your patience by spraying too early or too late, or with any material but the right one.

Biological Control

Biological control is defined as the suppression of the reproductive potential of organisms through the action of other organisms. Natural enemies include lady beetles, lacewings, syrphid fly larvae, praying mantises and other predators, and various parasitic wasps. Lady beetles can be purchased by the gallon but they frequently fly away to other gardens when released. It may be just as helpful to encourage the lady beetles already present in a garden by leaving some plants unsprayed to harbor their food, mostly aphids. Praying mantises will eat some beneficial insects as well as plant pests.

There are some fungus and viral diseases that attack injurious insects. A very useful microbial insecticide, prepared from the bacterium *Bacillus thuringiensis,* has been widely used as a spray against gypsy moth caterpillars and cankerworms. Spores of the bacterium *B. popillia,* causing milky disease, are applied to sod for the control of Japanese beetle grubs.

A relatively recent development in biological control is the release of male insects, sterilized by irradiation, to mate with normal females and so render the eggs infertile. Chemical sterilants have been developed but these have proved to be quite toxic. Sex attractants have been made synthetically to be used as bait in traps. As gardeners, we can only practice an integrated program, using chemicals with discretion and in ways that will least affect our insect friends.

 Insects, Diseases, and Their Controls

ACEPHATE   (See Orthene.)

AEROSOLS

Please explain how an aerosol insecticide works.   Aerosols are pesticides dispersed in the form of a fog or mist by means of a liquefied gas or superheated stream ejected through an open valve; or in the form of a smoke by igniting a combustible material in which they are dispersed. Practically all pesticides (insecticides, fungicides, weedkillers) that can be dissolved in sufficient concentration in organic solvents can be applied in aerosol form. Generally, insecticides are much more quickly applied and more potent when used in this form, but how aerosols act on insects is determined by the nature of the insecticide and the amount deposited on the plants.

How do I go about selecting a suitable aerosol? It all depends on the pests involved and the area to be covered. Sprays in aerosol form are now available as combinations of insecticides, and insecticides and fungicides. They are purchased in small to large hand-borne metal containers (aerosol bombs) with a valve release for home, garden, or greenhouse use; in cans for combustion in the greenhouse. The small pressurized cans sold for house and garden use are very useful for spot treatment of aphids and some other pests. Remember to hold the can 18 inches away from the plant to avoid injury.

ANTS

What can be done about ants in the garden? Ants are undesirable in the garden not so much because of their feeding but because they loosen the soil around the roots, causing the plants to wilt and die, and they cart around and nurse aphids and mealybugs for their honeydew. They may be fought either by applying carbaryl, diazinon, or malathion to the nests.

How can you exterminate the large red ant leaf eater which strips the bushes clean? (Texas.) The leaf-cutting ant does not eat the leaves but carries them to its nest where it chops them up in pieces as a medium on which to grow fungi it uses for food. Spraying the foliage with carbaryl might have some deterrent effect. Ordinarily the injury by this ant is more interesting than serious.

How can I get rid of half-inch-long black ants that live inside the trunk of my English walnut tree? The entrance is a narrow fissure 18 inches long. I have tried filling it with cement but they burrow around it. This is the black carpenter ant, which does not chew through healthy bark or wood but enters through wounds to construct a nest inside the tree. Ants do not eat wood as do termites, but chew large excavations in dead and decaying heartwood to make room for a nest. Piles of "jawdust" often can be seen expelled from areas where carpenter ants are constructing a nest. If the nest site can be located, soak the entrance and the bark of the tree where the ants crawl with a residual aerosol or garden sprayer from an approved insecticide for ants.

APHIDS (PLANT LICE)

What year-round program would you suggest for aphids? Aphids are soft-bodied sucking insects controlled by contact or systemic insecticides; in general, spray for them when you see the first few individuals. They are more numerous at certain seasons of the year, the time varying with the host plant, so that spraying is generally spasmodic rather than regular. Often an aphicide may be included in a spray put on for other purposes. Or spot treat with an aerosol.

What should I use to destroy plant lice? Nicotine sulfate, 1 to 1½ teaspoons, and 1 cubic inch of laundry soap, not detergent, or 2 level tablespoons of flakes to 1 gallon of water is an old and successful spray for aphids, but now seldom available.

Malathion or diazinon is at present the most effective spray material for use on aphids, but pyrethrum, rotenone, dimethoate, or Meta-Systox-R can also be used. Acephate (Orthene) is excellent on ornamentals, but should not be used on food plants.

Can anything be done to destroy the white aphids which feed on the roots of plants? Malathion, when used at 1 tablespoon a gallon and poured into a depression around the plant stem, is helpful. Root aphids are usually tended by ants, so that ant-control operations should also be started.

How do I control aphids on trees? A dormant oil spray applied to fruit trees kills aphid eggs. The same spray will also kill aphid eggs on shade trees but should not be used unless needed for scale insects. The spray is not safe on all evergreens. The fluffy white bark aphids on pine and the spruce gall aphid are best controlled with malathion applied on a warm day in the late winter or early spring.

ARMADILLOS

How do I get rid of the armadillos that root up my garden at night? (Florida.) Armadillos are as difficult as rabbits to control. The best method is a fence of 2-foot chicken wire around the garden, otherwise shooting, if permitted, or trapping in rabbit traps put across their paths. They cannot be easily poisoned.

ARMILLARIA ROOT ROT

What is the fungus disease, especially prevalent in California, which

kills trees, shrubs, and other woody plants, being most destructive on lands recently cleared of oak? It may be recognized by the white mycelial threads or fans, black shoestring strands extending through the soil, and honey-colored toadstools that grow near the base of the trunk. Remove dead trees and shrubs, taking out all roots. Rhododendrons and azaleas may sometimes be saved by exposing crowns and main roots for a season. Avoid planting in areas of high-moisture content. The soil where diseased plants have been taken out can be disinfected with methyl bromide. However, its use is restricted to a commercial applicator.

ARMYWORMS

What is the dark-green, white-striped worm, similar to a cutworm, which attacks grasses, corn, and grain crops, feeding at night and hiding under clods, stones, or leaves during the day? Armyworm. Controlled by scattering poison bait in late afternoon or by spraying with malathion or methoxychlor. (See Cutworms.)

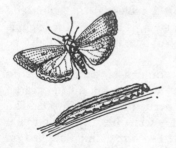

Armyworm with female moth. The worm is dark green with white stripes or is light tan and resembles a cutworm. It feeds at night on corn, grain, and grass.

ASIATIC BEETLES

How do you identify the Asiatic beetle? (New York.) There are two: the Asiatic or Oriental beetle (*Anomala orientalis*) and the Asiatic garden beetle (*Maladera castanea*). As grubs, they both are the size and shape of Japanese beetles and feed on grass roots. The adult Oriental beetle varies in color from light brown to black, with or without mottled marking. It is sometimes found feeding on roses and other flowers but does not do much damage there. The Asiatic garden beetle is a smooth copper brown, and has been described as an animated coffee bean. It stays in the ground during the day and feeds on foliage, bangs against windows, and flies into cars at night. The larvae injure grass roots and some vegetables. The adults injure leaves of asters, zinnias, and other low ornamentals and carrots, parsnips, turnips, beets, and pepper tops.

How do you combat the Oriental beetle? (New Jersey.) Treat lawns with diazinon or Dursban and spray foliage of ornamentals with carbaryl (Sevin). Rotenone may act as a deterrent on food plants. (See Japanese Beetles.)

Are castor bean plants a protection from Oriental beetles? (Connecticut.) Their efficacy has been greatly overrated. Entomologists claim that tests in cages show that the foliage is practically nontoxic and they cannot be used as trap plants in the field because beetles do not go to the castor bean before their favorite food plants have been exhausted.

Last summer I found hundreds of young Oriental beetles in a semi-dormant state around my garden plants. How do they hibernate? Will my garden be eaten up next summer? (Massachusetts.) They will hibernate as grubs in the soil under grass roots, and the beetles may fly to feed on your plants late next summer. However, treating your lawn with diazinon or Dursban in early September should reduce the infestation. Adults can be killed with Sevin.

Is it possible that Oriental beetles came from the roses and destroyed the bent grass in large spots? (Iowa.) The Oriental beetle is not prevalent in Iowa. The lawn may have been injured by white grubs or chinch bugs or the fungus disease called brown patch, and your rose pest is probably the rose chafer. (See Rose.)

What should I do to prevent the Oriental beetle? (California.) Nothing. According to statistics, the Oriental beetle is not a problem in California.

BACILLUS THURINGIENSIS

What are biological insecticides? They are naturally occurring diseases of insects that can be produced commercially and formulated for application as sprays or dusts as are chemical insecticides. They include two spore-forming bacteria, *Bacillus popillia* (milky disease), for Japanese beetle, and *Bacillus thuringiensis* (Dipel, Thuricide, Baktur), effective against various caterpillars, such as cabbage loopers, gypsy moth, bagworm, and others. The specificity of toxic action to the limited insect hosts make them safe to use around food, water, and animals. When susceptible insects feed on the host plant, spores are consumed that cause fatal disease in the pests.

BAGWORMS

How do you destroy bagworms? (Georgia.) This pest, generally distributed in the East, is more severe in the South. Hibernation is in the egg state in the female bags, made from interwoven twigs and leaves. The young hatch late in the spring, spin their own bags, and immediately start feeding on evergreen and deciduous trees. Control by picking off bags by late winter and by spraying with Sevin or Kelthane, malathion, dimethoate, acephate (Orthene), *B. thuringiensis,* or diazinon when feeding starts in late May to mid-June.

BEETLES

What are real "beetles"? Members of the insect order Coleoptera, with chewing mouth parts and hardened front wings forming convex shields. Except for a few beneficial types, such as ground and lady beetles, they are injurious both in their grub or larval stage and as adults. They are controlled by stomach or contact poisons used in the ground or on the foliage.

Do beetles ever come through closed windows into the house in the winter? No. In the fall, lady beetles and elm leaf beetles (and box-elder bugs, too) get in through very small cracks and crevices around windows, eaves, and siding to spend the winter. They may become active during warm spells in the winter and crawl on windows as they go toward the light. In the spring, they are more active and conspicuous as they try to get back out of the house.

BENEFICIAL INSECTS

What bugs are harmful and which are harmless in the garden? (Ohio.) The harmful bugs are discussed under the different host plants. Of the harmless or helpful ones, lady beetles, ground beetles, and praying mantises are most often seen in the home garden, although sometimes, if you look closely at a group of aphids, you will see a sluglike creature, larva of the syrphid fly, preying among them.

BENLATE

What is Benlate? Benomyl, sold as Benlate, is a systemic fungicide. It is excellent for control of powdery mildew on roses and other plants,

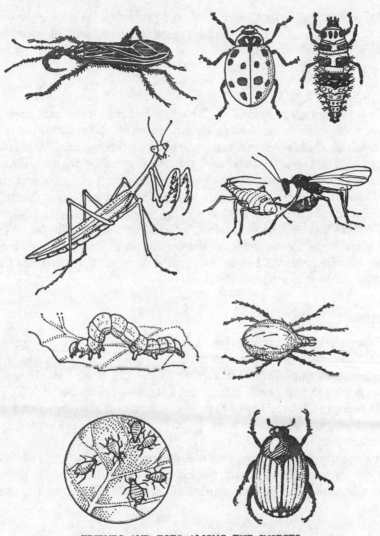

FRIENDS AND FOES AMONG THE INSECTS

(Top row, left to right) The friends: assassin bug; lady beetle, adult and larva. (Second row, left to right) Praying mantis; tiny wasp depositing egg in an aphid. (Third row, left to right) Some foes: cabbage looper; a spider mite, much enlarged. (Bottom row, left to right) Aphids on underside of leaf; Japanese beetle.

usually effective for rose black spot, and promising for a wide range of fruit, nut, turf, ornamentals and vegetable crops, and of some use against the Dutch elm disease.

BIOLOGICAL CONTROL

What is biological control?   The control of plant or animal pests by other living organisms. Notable examples include the work of the Australian lady beetle on the cottony cushion scale, ground beetles on gypsy moths, parasitic wasps, and the bacterial milky disease on Japanese beetles. Biological control can never completely exterminate a pest and usually must be supplemented by mechanical measures. (See also *Bacillus thuringiensis,* this section.)

Is there any biological control for codling moth? (Illinois.)   Yes, birds and many insects work on the codling moth, but they have never been able to reduce it below the point of commercial damage. Other control methods usually must be used.

BIRDS

What is the best way to keep birds from eating vegetable seeds?   Farmers' supply stores sometimes sell a crow repellent for treating seeds, but some say that crows often work down a whole row of corn, hoping to find a kernel that is not treated and palatable.

Is there any known object besides old-fashioned scarecrows that will keep birds out of a strawberry patch?   Cover the strawberries with coarse cheesecloth or netting.

Can you tell me anything that will poison sparrows?   The baits used for cutworms and slugs sometimes kill birds by mistake, but do not put it out for sparrows; you may kill desirable birds, also. Use a sparrow trap.

BLISTER BEETLES

What are those long bugs that attack potatoes and other plants? (North Dakota.)   Blister beetles. They are common in most states, feeding on vegetables and many ornamentals, especially China-asters and Japanese anemones. They are as much as ¾ inch long, plain black, or black with gray margins, or yellow or gray stripes, or brown or gray. When crushed on the skin, they can cause blisters.

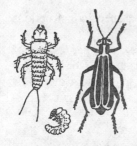

Adult blister beetle (right) feeds on asters, anemones, potatoes, and many other plants. Yet in its triungulin form (left) it eats eggs of certain grasshoppers.

What is the best insecticide for blister beetles? They are hard to kill. Sevin should do a good job. Knocking the beetles off into a jar of kerosene or chlorine bleach is a helpful measure.

BORDEAUX MIXTURE

What is Bordeaux mixture? An old fungicide still of some value in the control of plant diseases. The regulation formula is 4–4–50, meaning 4 pounds of copper sulfate and 4 pounds of hydrated lime to 50 gallons of water, but for many ornamental plants a weaker solution is used. Bordeaux mixture may be purchased in dry powder form to be mixed with water at the time of spraying or it may be made at home by preparing 2 stock solutions, 1 made by dissolving 1 pound fine copper sulfate crystals in 1 gallon of water and the other by dissolving 1 pound of lime in 1 gallon of water. Dilute only at the time of use, the amount of water determining the strength of Bordeaux; never put 2 stock solutions together, but add the water to the lime solution and then stir in the copper sulfate solution. For a 4–4–50 mixture, use 1 part of each stock solution to 10½ parts water; 3–3–50, 1 part to 14⅔ parts water; 2–2–50, 1 part to 23 parts water.

Please define 3–5–50 Bordeaux mixture or any such combination of figures. What do they stand for? They are a kind of shorthand to describe the strength of the spray. The first figure is for the copper, the second for the lime, and the last for water; in this case it means 3 pounds of copper sulfate and 5 pounds of lime to 50 gallons of water. Ordinarily lime and copper are used in equal amounts, as 4–4–50 or 3–3–50, but sometimes lime is increased to avoid injury to specific crops.

What can you substitute for Bordeaux mixture when you do not have an agitating sprayer? Will tribasic copper act the same? (Oregon.) There are several metallic copper sprays that may be used to replace Bordeaux mixture and they are safer when lime is undesirable.

Tribasic copper is one of these, but you should get specific instructions from your county extension agent.

What amount of Bordeaux mixture should be used per gallon of water? The directions come on the package, usually 8 to 12 tablespoons of prepared dry Bordeaux powder to 1 gallon of water. For most ornamental spraying, about half this amount is safer, less conspicuous, and equally effective.

BORERS

How can borers be prevented from doing their deadly work? Borers are caterpillars or grubs, larvae of moths or beetles, that work in woody or herbaceous stems. Some, like the European corn borer or common stalk borer, are best prevented by cutting down weed hosts and burning old stalks at the end of the season. Twigs infested with borers should be cut out and destroyed. Once the borer is in a woody trunk, such as rhododendron or lilac, little can be done to control it. Newly set trees should be protected from borers by wrapping trunks with Kraft crepe paper wound spirally from the crown to the first branch. Three or four applications at 3- to 4-week intervals of lindane or methoxychlor to the trunks and branches of trees and shrubs beginning in mid-May will help to protect them from borers.

BOX-ELDER BUGS

What will destroy the bugs that infest my trees and eat the fruits and flowers? The young are red and the adults are dark gray, with a red border. (Arizona.) These are box-elder bugs. Spray with carbaryl to prevent their swarming into the house. Avoid planting the pistillate tree nearby, for the eggs are laid on the fruits.

BUGS

What is a bug, horticulturally speaking? A term used by the layman to denote any insect, but by the scientist to mean a sucking insect of the order Hemiptera, which means half-winged. The basal half of the fore wing is thickened and the other half is membranous. They often have an offensive odor. True bugs include stink bugs, lacebugs, plant bugs, and chinch bugs.

What can I do to kill sucking bugs? Use a contact or systemic insecticide. (See also Insects.)

CANKERWORMS

What should be done about inchworms? There are two species of these inchworms or measuring worms. Both have green- and brown-striped caterpillars and wingless female moths. The fall cankerworm female crawls up trees to lay her eggs in autumn; the spring cankerworm deposits her eggs in the spring. A sticky band of Tanglefoot (available from garden centers or garden-supply firms) has sometimes been suggested to prevent egg laying but spraying is far more effective. In seasons when a heavy infestation is forecast, have your trees sprayed with carbaryl (Sevin), methoxychlor, or the bacterium *Bacillus thuringiensis*. Oaks and elms are most seriously affected. These pests are cyclical and most years they are not a serious problem in the home garden.

CAPTAN

Is captan really as wonderful as some writers would indicate? It is an excellent general fungicide sold as a 50 per cent Wettable Powder or a 7 to 8 per cent dust for foliage and fruit diseases but it is not a "cure-all." Many general-purpose spray mixtures contain captan. It will not control powdery mildew or rust diseases. Captan is widely used as a seed protectant; in drenches, it controls damping off of seedlings and cuttings; and in dips for corms and tubers, it prevents storage rots. Its toxicity to warm-blooded animals is quite low. Dogwoods, apples, and crab apples have had their foliage injured by early season captan sprays.

CARBARYL

Is Sevin safe to use? Carbaryl, sold under the brand name of Sevin, is a very useful broad-spectrum insecticide comparatively safe for plants and the user. It does kill bees and some other beneficial insects and can increase the spider-mite problem. Sprays should usually include a miticide. However, carbaryl will suppress or control some rust and gall mites.

CATS

How can cats be kept out of the garden? (Massachusetts.) They can't very well. Aside from a small city garden, where numerous cats may congregate, they do little damage to the garden itself, but of course they are destructive to birds. Automobiles kill more birds than cats do and cats can be a great help to the gardener in the control of rabbits, mice, and moles.

CENTIPEDES

When digging, I see quite a few slender, orange and brown insects, about 2 inches long, that run fast, seek the dark, and look like thousand-legged brown or tan miniature snakes. Are they injurious to plants? (Kentucky.) These are probably centipedes, meaning hundred-legged, although literally they have about 15 pairs of legs. They are usually beneficial in the garden, preying on other insects, but the larger ones may inflict painful bites on people.

What is the color of a centipede in infancy? (New York.) The true centipede is yellow to brown, like the adult. The garden centipede, so-called, but really a symphyllid, is small and white. This creature injures plants and has become an important pest in greenhouses and truck-garden fields in some states. Lindane is effective but may be restricted in some states. Try malathion.

CHINCH BUGS

How do you guard against chinch bugs? (Ohio.) Chinch bugs are very small, black and white sucking insects, red when young, which injure corn and small grains of the farmer and lawns of the homeowner. In hot, dry seasons, large brown patches in lawns are very commonly chinch-bug injury. Treat lawns with granular Sevin or with diazinon. Growing soybeans between the corn rows will shade the base so that the chinch bugs will avoid the corn (they do not touch soybeans or any plant outside the grass family).

The chinch bug is a very small black and white sucking insect that is destructive to lawns.

CHIPMUNKS   (See Squirrels.)

CHLOROTHALONIL

What is a good fungicide to use for leaf spots and blight on vegetables?   Chlorothalonil is marketed by the trade name Bravo, Exotherm, or Daconil 2787. It is a broad-spectrum fungicide recommended for leaf spots, leaf blights, anthracnose, powdery mildew, and several other leaf diseases of tomato, potato, celery, cucurbits, onions, watermelons, and some ornamentals.

COMPOST

Is there a way of combating insects and diseases by treating the compost heap and using it where plants are to be grown?   The compost itself may be treated to ensure against its being pest-ridden, but it will confer no immunity to the plants in the garden bed.

What is the danger of carrying over fungi and insect pests in compost?   There is some danger, and that is why we recommend disposing of plant material known to be diseased or likely to harbor insects.

CONTACT INSECTICIDES

What is meant by a contact insecticide?   A chemical that kills insects by direct contact in contrast to some older materials such as lead arsenate, a stomach poison, or *Bacillus,* effective only if eaten. Most modern contact insecticides act as stomach poisons also, when ingested with plant material. Contact action occurs when insects are hit directly by sprays or dusts, when they simply walk on insecticide deposits, eat the foliage, or chew through the bark. There is considerable variation in the toxicity of different insecticides to different pests; some insects may be killed by one insecticide but not another. Those that are effective against many kinds of pests are called broad-spectrum insecticides. Generally, most insecticides do not control mites, and miticides do not control insects.

CRAWFISH

I am having considerable trouble with crawfish digging up my lawn. How do you exterminate them? (North Carolina.) Mix 8 tablespoons of Sevin in 1 gallon of water. Pour 1 ounce into each hole. Or dig them for food. They are a delicacy, like lobster.

CROWN GALL

I noticed swellings on the roots of my roses when transplanting them. What shall I do about this condition? This is crown gall, a bacterial disease that is soil-borne as well as plant-borne and gradually weakens and kills the plants. Take up the plants and burn them, if possible, or place them in plastic bags in a trash disposal. Then plant in a new area or in sterilized soil. Refuse new plants with galls.

CROWN ROT

What will prevent crown rot? Crown rot is a disease causing sudden wilting of plants from a rotting at the crown or soil line. *Sclerotium rolfsii* is the causative fungus. The best prevention is to put healthy plants in a new location. The fungus may live for several years in the soil in the form of reddish-tan sclerotia, which resemble mustard seeds. Therefore, it is important to take out all surrounding soil when the diseased plant is removed. Unless the soil can be dug out for 1 foot deep and 2 feet or more in the area and replaced with fresh soil, Terrachlor (PCNB) should be poured over the earth and the crowns of nearby plants.

CUTWORMS

How can I prevent cutworms from nipping off new seedlings or transplants? One way for newly set bedding or vegetable transplants is a heavy paper on a thin cardboard collar around each stem, 1 inch into the ground and 2 inches above the ground. Another way is to apply diazinon granules to the soil prior to planting or using diazinon spray or dust applied to the plants and soil immediately after planting. It is best to treat in the late afternoon or evening.

Do cutworms stay in the soil in some form during the winter? Usually cutworms overwinter as larvae in cells in the soil, or under trash, mulch, or in clumps of grass. Sometimes they overwinter as pupae or adults. The larvae are active in the spring, cutting off seedlings at the soil level or nipping off young tender leaves at the petiole. They pupate to adult moths that give rise to one new generation in the North and several in the South. Both adults and larvae are nocturnal and hide during the day.

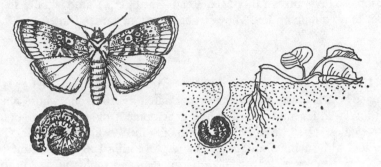

Cutworms attack young cabbage and tomato plants and other seedling vegetables and flowers. (Left) Greasy cutworm; (right) dark-sided cutworm.

In midsummer, many annuals had their foliage devastated, but no insects could be found. What caused this? (Virginia.) If there were no slime trails to indicate slugs, it most likely was climbing cutworms, such as the variegated cutworm. The larvae hide in the soil or under debris during the day and feed voraciously on the foliage at night. In small patio gardens, hand-picking at night while searching with a flashlight will reduce populations. Spraying the plants and soaking the soil with diazinon is effective.

DAMPING OFF

What would cause seedlings in flats to rot at the stems just at the top of the soil? This is known as damping off, a disease caused by any one of several soil fungi. There are two types: pre-emergence damping off, when the sprouted seeds rot in the soil; and post-emergence damping off, when the young seedlings wilt and fall over. For growing in flats, either soil or seeds may be treated, but seed treatment is more practical for sowing directly in the garden. That is why most seed is now treated prior to sale. It pays to buy treated seeds.

What is the safest preparation for soil treatment to prevent damping off in seed flats? Formaldehyde, perhaps. Dilute 2½ tablespoons of commercial formaldehyde with 6 times as much water and sprinkle over a bushel of soil, mixing thoroughly. Place in flats. Wait 24 hours before planting, and water well immediately after planting.

When starting seeds in the house in boxes, what is the safest thing to use to prevent damping off? See the above question. However, the various soilless mixes (Jiffy Mix, Readi-Earth, etc.) are virtually sterile since they contain no soil. They can be bought at garden centers.

DDT

DDT was once acclaimed as a miracle insecticide. Why is it banned? DDT was the original chlorinated hydrocarbon whose amazing insect-killing powers led to the development of many other potent insecticides. Used as a public-health aid in World War II, DDT is credited with saving 5 million lives and preventing 100 million illnesses. It is, however, persistent in the environment and builds up in the food chain, an example being birds killed by eating earthworms that had ingested DDT. It may be related to the thin eggshells that may have caused the decline of bald eagles and some other endangered species. Some insects became resistant to DDT and it increased the mite problem by killing certain beneficial insects. DDT was probably safer for man than some of the highly toxic phosphates that are replacing it on some commercial crops and we do not yet have an adequate substitute for the control of some pests.

DERRIS

What is derris? One of the plants used as a source of rotenone. It is imported from the Far East.

DIABROTICA BEETLES

What do you do about the 12-spotted beetles? They ruin all the late blooms—roses, gerbera, carnation, chrysanthemum. (California.) These are the 12-spotted cucumber beetles, Diabroticas, very common in your state. They are hard to kill, but dusting or spraying with methoxychlor or carbaryl would be helpful.

DICOFOL

I often see the name dicofol suggested for mites. What is it? Dicofol is the accepted common name for Kelthane, a very effective and widely available miticide for spider mites on ornamentals.

DIMETHOATE

Is dimethoate a systemic insecticide? Yes. Sold as Cygon or De-Fend, this reasonably safe phosphate is used as a foliage spray and sometimes for soil treatment to control insects and mites. It is injurious to some plants; apply only to those listed on the label.

DOGS

What are your views and advice on the dog-nuisance question? Owners should be willing to keep their dogs restrained and, when walking them on a leash, should keep them curbed rather than allowing them to ruin lawns and shrubs near the sidewalk. Moth balls around shrubs and various chemicals sold as dog repellents in garden centers or through mail-order houses may help. Also, a barberry hedge and a few chopped twigs of barberry scattered about is one idea that might work. Wire shrub guards are usually quite successful.

DORMANT SPRAYING

What is a dormant spray? A spray applied while plants are dormant, which means sleeping; that is, while deciduous trees are bare and before evergreens have started into new life. At this time, the plant can stand a stronger spray than during the growing season, and a strong spray is needed to get hard-shelled insects like scales.

When and how should the dormant spray be applied to trees and bushes? (Illinois.) The safest time is toward the end of their dormant season, just before new growth starts. In Illinois, that might mean the end of March for lilacs and early April for evergreens. For dormant spraying, the home gardener usually has a choice of lime-sulfur or an oil spray, or a commercial mixture of both. The liquid lime-sulfur should be diluted with 7 to 9 parts of water. It is safe, but unpleasant to use, impossible near painted surfaces because of the indelible stain, and leaves an objectionable residue on evergreens. Miscible oils—colorless oils which mix readily with water to form a white liquid—are sold under many trade names. Most manufacturers suggest a 2 to 3 per cent dilution for deciduous trees and 1 to 2 per cent for evergreens. Oil sprays may be injurious unless they are used on a bright, clear day with the temperature well above 45° F. Do not use on beech, black walnut, butternut, Japanese or sugar maple, or magnolia. Do not use on such evergreens as false-cypress, cryptomeria, Douglas-fir, true firs, hemlock, Japanese umbrella, pine, or yew. Oil sprays will remove the "bloom" from evergreens, especially blue spruces.

DURSBAN

What is Dursban and what is it for?   Dursban is an insecticide, also called chlorpyrifos, that is recommended for some ornamental pests and chinch bugs, cutworms, and sod webworms in lawns. It has a warning label and most of its uses are restricted to commercial applicators. For many of those uses it is sold under the trade name Lorsban.

DUSTER, GARDEN

What is a garden duster?   A machine for applying insecticides or fungicides in dry dust form. For the small garden, choose a hand rotary duster, or a dust gun, ranging in size from 1-pint to 2-quart capacity. Choose one with an extension rod and a flange, which will allow you to stand up while using the duster and yet drive the dust from the bottom of the plant up through it. For the larger garden, a knapsack bellows or a rotary duster will save much energy in operation.

DUSTING

How do you know how much garden dust to use? I tried a dust gun which didn't cover the leaves sufficiently without extreme labor and the dust when tossed out by hand seemed too much. Many plants wilted. I used sulfur and rotenone. (Virginia.)   Apply only as much dust as will cover the plants with a thin, even coating. This can be done only with some sort of duster. If yours was too hard to work, it either was the wrong type for the number of plants or else needed adjusting. Coverage of the underside of the leaves is most important and can be done only with the right apparatus, never by throwing it on. Your method of application together with the sulfur in your dust would account for the plants wilting. Sulfur may be injurious to any plant in hot weather, but vegetables are particularly sensitive. Beans occasionally require sulfur, but cucurbits should never have it.

Do you dust plants when they are wet with dew or when they are dry?   There is always an argument on this question, but if ornamental plants are dusted when they are wet, they are left with a too conspicuous residue.

EARTHWORMS

Do earthworms or angleworms feed on and destroy peony, iris, and other tubers? I have dug them up and found worms imbedded in them and nothing left but the outer shell.   Your peony probably succumbed to botrytis blight and the iris to borer and rot. Earthworms do not feed on living plant tissue.

When garden worms are found in flowerpots, do they feed on the roots of the plant?   No. Worms in pots are chiefly a nuisance because they clog up the drainage holes. Watering with lime water will get rid of them.

EARWIGS

Is there anything possible on this earth to exterminate earwigs? Earwigs resemble beetles and have two claspers on the hind end that look like large "jaws." They hide under debris, crawl into picnic baskets and other household belongings used out in the yard during the summer. There is little that can be done to exterminate them, since they may be scattered all around the yard. Spraying with diazinon, carbaryl, chlorpyrifos, or malathion will kill those that come in contact with the spray.

Earwigs

FALL WEBWORMS

What is the difference, if any, between the fall webworm and the fall cankerworm?   The fall webworm makes increasingly large silk webs or tents from June to September on the outer ends of branches of many trees, unlike the eastern tent caterpillar that constructs its nest in branch crotches only on wild cherry and flowering fruits. The caterpillars are hairy, white to orange, about 1 inch long, and gregarious, feeding in broods on foliage within the webs. Fall cankerworms, prevalent only in the spring (usually May) on many tree hosts, are light green or dark gray, hairless, and "inch" along, resulting in such names as inchworms, loopers, or measuring worms. (See Cankerworms.) All of these defoliators can be controlled with carbaryl or methoxychlor.

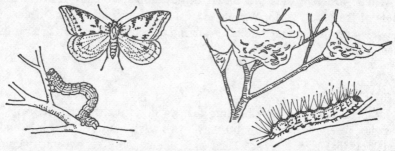

Fall cankerworm (left) and fall webworm (right).

FERBAM

Can you give me some trade names under which ferbam is sold?   Trade products containing ferbam are Fermate, Carbamate, and Karbam Black. It is a good general fungicide, especially for rust diseases of plants. The usual dosage is 2 tablespoonfuls per gallon of water.

FLEA BEETLES

What about flea beetles? (Florida.)   Flea beetles, which get their name from their habit of quickly springing several inches when disturbed, are small, black, oval beetles that chew tiny shot holes in the foliage of most garden crops. Two species in Florida are most troublesome on beets, cabbage, and tomatoes. In the North, potatoes and seedling tomatoes, peppers, eggplants, and crucifers are almost sure to be riddled by flea beetles early in the season. Dusting or spraying with carbaryl, diazinon, or methoxychlor will control flea beetles.

FOLPET

What is folpet? An excellent fungicide, sold as Phaltan, used on fruits, vegetables, and ornamentals and very safe for the operator. It is recommended for apple scab, cherry leafspot, rose black spot, and many other diseases.

FORMALDEHYDE (FORMALIN)

What is formaldehyde? A useful soil disinfectant. (See also Soil Sterilization.)

Is it safe to use a weak solution of formaldehyde (1 to 50) on a seed bed that has been planted, but seed not germinated, to curb damping-off fungus? (West Virginia.) This is not a weak solution of formaldehyde; it is the standard strength for drenching *fallow* soil, which will probably have to air out at least a week before planting. It would not be safe to use after the seed is planted. (See Damping Off for the formaldehyde method of treating soil for flats, and see Seed Treatment for ways to prevent damping off in garden soil.)

What concentration of formaldehyde will kill insects and larvae without destroying the foliage on seedlings? None. Formaldehyde is never to be used around living plants. If you must disinfect the soil, the plants will have to be moved out for a couple of weeks, and since you do not want to set infested or infected plants back in treated soil, you have to start a new batch of seedlings. So try some other method of controlling your insects.

FUNGI

What are fungi? Members of the Thallophytes or lowest plant group. Lacking the power of manufacturing their own plant food, they live as saprophytes on decaying plant tissue or as parasites on living higher plants. They are characterized by a vegetative stage, consisting of fungus threads or mycelium and fruiting bodies which contain the reproductive organs. Some fungi are readily recognized at a glance: mildew with its white weft of mycelium growing over a leaf; rust, which produces reddish dusty spore pustules; and smut, with its masses of black spores. Some can be differentiated only by microscopic examination.

What do you do for white fungus? (California.)   Such a question is too indefinite. A white fungus may be the coating of mildew on a leaf; it may be the white weft of mycelium at the base of plants in crown rot or southern blight; or it may be the fans of white mycelium peculiar to the armillaria root rot, prevalent on woody shrubs in California. Then there is downy mildew and many other possibilities.

What do you recommend as treatment for mustard-seed fungus? (Missouri.)   This question is almost as brief as the one above, but it can be answered definitely because there is only one fungus, *Sclerotium rolfsii,* that would be present in Missouri, known as the mustard-seed fungus. It causes the disease known as southern rot or blight or crown rot and gets its name from the reddish sclerotia which look like mustard seed. It is fairly common as crown rot of delphinium. (For control, see Crown Rot.)

FUNGICIDE

What is a fungicide?   A material used to eradicate bacteria and fungi in the soil or on seeds. It is more commonly used as a protectant to cover susceptible plant parts before the disease organisms arrive. Most of the older fungicides are compounds of either copper or sulfur. The most common newer ones are dithio-carbamic acid derivatives (ferbam, zineb, mancozeb, maneb, etc.) and captan, folpet, and benomyl.

GOPHERS

What is the best way to poison California pocket gophers?   There are many species of pocket gophers (ground rats) found in California, Oregon, and Washington. There are special gopher traps on the market. Consult your county extension agent for regional restrictions and recommendations for available baits.

GROUND BEETLES

I have found several June bugs in the ground this fall. Are they harmful? (New York.)   You would not be apt to find June beetles in the ground. You probably found ground beetles, black or brown or iridescent large beetles with very prominent jaws that live in the ground or under stones. These are beneficial insects, feeding on cankerworms and other pests, and should not be disturbed.

GRUBWORMS   (See White Grubs.)

GYPSY MOTHS

What is the history of gypsy moths?   The gypsy moth, *Lymantria dispar,* is an example of an introduced pest that has wreaked havoc in a new country. In 1868 a few moths were brought to Massachusetts from France by a professor who thought he could make a hybrid to produce silk. Their cage was broken open by a windstorm and the caterpillars, brown, hairy, with red and blue tubercles, escaped, prospered, and now feed on many deciduous and evergreen trees, with a particular preference for oaks. They are so voracious that a single caterpillar can eat a square foot of leaf surface in 24 hours. Evergreens, eaten only after deciduous foliage is gone, may be killed by a single season's defoliation; other trees may die after 3 or more successive defoliations. Massachusetts has spent millions of dollars trying to cope with this pest and for many years a barrier zone confined it east of the Hudson River. Now, however, the gypsy moth is a menace in New England, New Jersey, New York, Pennsylvania, and Maryland, and has been spotted in Virginia, Michigan, and other states.

In 1957 a large-scale aerial spray program, using DDT, was launched

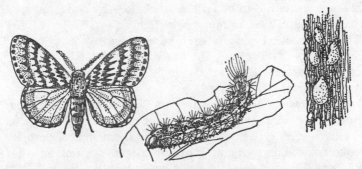

Gypsy moth caterpillars attack tree foliage and, occasionally, vegetables and other plants. Caterpillars are 2 inches long with conspicuous blue and red markings. (Right) Egg cases on tree trunk.

but had to be given up because of public outcry against the environmental effects. To prevent further spread, it is vitally important that individuals cooperate in observing quarantine regulations. The tan egg clusters, with a feltlike texture, about an inch long, may be attached to almost any object, but are especially conspicuous on tree trunks and limbs. Don't try to bring Christmas trees or other plants out of the regulated area without inspection. Check your automobile or trailer if you have vacationed in gypsy moth country and your home is in an uninfested area. If you expect a heavy infestation in your area, trees can be sprayed with carbaryl (Sevin) or *Bacillus thuringiensis*. The U. S. Department of Agriculture is releasing parasites for control of gypsy moths, experimenting with sex attractants in traps, and utilizing insect growth regulators as sprays.

Most of our property (about 2 acres) is a woodland, mostly of oak trees. Last summer, for the first time in this area, we had a severe infestation of gypsy moth caterpillars and most of the tree foliage suffered accordingly, although I can't report that there was total defoliation in all cases. My neighbors predict that a second and third year of devastation by these caterpillars will result in the death of the trees. Is this true? Predicting when a tree will die, short of chopping it down, is not easily done, as many factors must be considered. Certainly successive defoliations weaken trees, especially old ones and those that are sick or diseased, but usually it is a combination of factors rather than a single cause, such as the gypsy moth, that finally kills the tree. Oaks are most susceptible to gypsy moth infestation and repeated defoliation may contribute to the death of some. In your case, it is doubtful that all or even any of your trees will die, and the caterpillars will probably move on after a few years. But to be on the safe side, why don't you spray with the bacterial agent *Bacillus thuringiensis?*

What is the safest spray to use against the gypsy moth caterpillar in the home garden? Probably the bacterial agent *Bacillus thuringiensis,* or carbaryl (Sevin). However, Sevin is highly toxic to bees if they are active in the areas being sprayed.

Do you believe in aerial spraying with Sevin to control the gypsy moth caterpillar? First, aerial spraying permits much more thorough and uniform coverage of large tracts with very small amounts of pesticide compared to conventional ground spray equipment. The time span for effective spraying in good weather conditions is very limited and large areas can be treated quickly and economically. Second, Sevin is highly efficacious against gypsy moth, does not persist in the environment, and is very low in toxicity to warm-blooded animals. However, it kills shellfish and fish, as well as bees, and should not be used over bodies of water or in coastal areas.

Sevin may destroy many parasites and predators of the gypsy moth, so it should not be used where those natural enemies have developed moderate to high population densities. Where Sevin cannot or should not be used, Bt (*Bacillus thuringiensis*) can be applied to reduce gypsy moth infestations without harming bees, fish, or natural enemies. Where trees or woodlands are of low value in generally infested areas, it is best not to use insecticides and let natural enemies function. Control strategies depend on whether the location in question is within the generally infested gypsy moth range, within the fringe or leading edge of its spread west and south, or in a previously uninfested area.

What are methods the home gardener can use to control a gypsy moth infestation? You can have your trees and shrubs sprayed with Sevin or *Bacillus thuringiensis* in midspring just after the eggs hatch. (If the spray chemical is mixed with molasses, usually only one treatment is necessary.) Consult your State Extension Service for other recommended methods. In the fall and winter, when the tan egg clusters are most conspicuous, you can coat them with creosote. A sponge or rag fastened to a long pole will reach some of the higher-up clusters. Or you can scrape the clusters into a can and then burn them in the fireplace, where they will pop like little firecrackers. In early summer, when the large caterpillars are crawling down tree trunks, they can be trapped by wide bands of overlapping burlap wrapped around the trunks. The caterpillars, which are most active at night, hide in the burlap during the day when it is quite easy to collect and drop them into containers of liquid bleach.

Most home gardeners prefer the first method—spraying, which is not a serious environmental hazard when done by competent, careful professionals. For tall shrubs and trees, power sprayers are essential. The majority of home gardens are artificial situations composed of ornamental plantings designed to give enjoyment and comfort to the owners, quite different from the complex environmental factors referred to in the preceding question on aerial spraying.

HARLEQUIN BUGS

How do you get rid of harlequin bugs? (Kansas.) These brilliantly colored red or yellow and black or blue bugs cause the leaves of horseradish, mustard, cabbage, and related crops to curl and turn brown. They lay clusters of black-banded eggs that look like barrels. Hand-picking before egg laying and removal of eggs are the best control. Destroy all old plant parts and dust with rotenone.

HYDROXYQUINOLINE SULFATE

How is hydroxyquinoline sulfate used for the prevention of soil rots? For cuttings of succulent plants, use a 25 per cent material at the rate of 1 teaspoon per gallon of water, and soak cuttings for 5 minutes. Use the same strength for a seed-bed drench and apply at the rate of 1 gallon to 10 square feet. This compound acts as a chemotherapeutic or systemic fungicide. It is now sold as Chinosol.

INFORMATION

What we need is plenty of information on pests. We find some that are different from those of eastern states. Are they harmful or beneficial? (California.) Your own State Extension Service is set up to give you exactly that knowledge. Not many gardeners realize what a wealth of information, applicable directly to their own state, may be obtained by a phone call or visit to your local county agent. In your particular case, you can write to the College of Agriculture, Berkeley, Calif. 94720, and ask for a list of publications. Practically every state's land-grant university has concise information ready for the home gardener as well as the farmer. Ask for it.

INSECTICIDES

What is an insecticide? Chemical compounds that are used in the control of insects are generally called insecticides. Any given insecticide may act on insects in one or more ways. However, it is generally grouped according to its main mode of action: a *stomach poison* attacks the internal organs after being swallowed; a *systemic insecticide* is a stomach poison absorbed and translocated in the sap of plants, destroying sap-sucking pests mainly; a *contact insecticide* kills upon contact with some external portion of the insect's body; a *residual contact insecticide* kills insects by foot contact for long periods after application; a *fumigant* is a chemical that produces a killing vapor in the air; and a *repellent* is a substance that is distasteful or malodorous enough to keep insects away. Of the older insecticides, the arsenicals are stomach poisons; nicotine sulfate, pyrethrum, and dormant oils are contact poisons; rotenone kills in both ways; and chloropicrin and methyl bromide are typical fumigants. The newer organic insecticides are generally effective for a variety of pests regardless of the way they feed. Many chewing and sucking insects are readily destroyed by either malathion or carbaryl.

INSECTS

Just what are insects? Members of the animal group Arthropoda, meaning jointed legs. True insects, of the class Hexapoda, meaning 6-legged, are characterized by always having 3 pairs of legs and 2 pairs of wings in the adult form, except for flies, which have only 1 pair. The body is composed of a head, thorax, and abdomen. Along the abdomen are small holes, spiracles, which form the breathing apparatus. Contact poisons work through their action on the spiracles or directly through the chitin. Chewing insects have jaws and bite holes in plant tissue; hence, they can be controlled by spreading a stomach poison in advance of the insect. Sucking insects cannot bite but obtain their food through a beak that pierces the plant epidermis to get at the sap. Since they cannot be injured by stomach poisons unless they are systemics, contact sprays are necessary.

JAPANESE BEETLES

What are effective ways to suppress Japanese beetles? (New York.) Chemical treatment of soil in lawn areas; biological control by distribution of a natural parasite, the milky-spore disease dust; spraying foliage during the flying season; hand-picking; trapping in special beetle traps.

How and when do you fight the Japanese beetle? (Pennsylvania.) Lawn treatment is done either in late August or early September. Summer spraying for adults normally starts at the very end of June and may have to be continued until the end of September on plants like roses, although beetles often stop feeding on vines in late August. If shade trees are sprayed with carbaryl at the end of June, one or two sprayings will normally give protection for the season. With shrubs, vines, and flowering plants, the number of applications depends on the rapidity with which new growth is formed. Roses and ampelopsis require a spray weekly to keep the new growth covered.

Is there any control, other than chemical, for Japanese beetle grubs in lawns? Yes. The spore dust of milky disease—a natural enemy of the beetles—is another means of controlling and eliminating this pest, and it is available commercially as Doom. Directions for use are printed on the packages. Do not apply to areas treated with insecticide.

Is there anything I can do to the soil in flower beds? The beetles destroy hollyhocks, cannas, petunias, roses, and geraniums. Soil treatment for flowers is ineffective. Beetles lay their eggs primarily in turf grass. For flowers, the most effective control is picking off the beetles; for roses, cutting the buds when they show color and enjoying them in the house. Aerosol bombs for use on flowers will paralyze or kill beetles without disfiguring blooms, but in general you have to rely on carbaryl (Sevin) or methoxychlor in a spray or dust to take care of the foliage and hand-picking the beetles into a jar or can of kerosene.

Can you tell me something to get rid of Japanese beetles? I have tried traps and they seem to attract them. That is exactly the purpose of a trap: it is painted bright yellow and baited with geraniol just to attract the beetles. Unfortunately, the trap attracts more beetles than get caught in it, so that the nearby plants serve as beetle food and suffer proportionately.

What is the best method of exterminating Japanese beetles before they are hatched? Spraying for the adults before they can lay their eggs in the grass. Otherwise, eggs will hatch into grubs. If the soil has been treated, the poison in the soil will kill the grubs as they feed on grass roots.

Is it possible to recognize the Japanese beetle in the daytime? How can you fight the Japanese beetle on rose bushes? (Louisiana.) In Louisiana, you probably will not have to fight Japanese beetles on rose bushes. If and when you do, carbaryl or methoxychlor or a combination spray will keep the foliage reasonably whole; but to save the flowers, you should cut the buds and let them open indoors. The beetle is readily recognized. It works in the daytime and prefers hot sunshine. It is about ½ inch long, shiny metallic green, with bronze wing covers and tufts of white hairs protruding from under the wing covers. It is a very handsome beetle, one of the scarab beetles.

What do you do about Japanese beetles? (California.) Nothing in California. It's not your problem yet. (But see preceding questions.)

What is the most effective repellent of the Japanese beetle? (Connecticut.) Hydrated lime will serve as a repellent on grapes. Grape foliage is a favorite target of the beetles.

Can I check Japanese beetles with castor-oil beans? Probably not. (See Asiatic Beetles.)

Does fall spading help exterminate the Japanese beetle? No. But it helps for other white grubs in the garden, if you take the trouble to destroy or throw out to the birds the grubs you turn up. Birds, by the way, are great allies. The holes you see in the lawn in late summer are where the robins, starlings, and other birds have gone in after the grubs. The starlings are given the most credit for eating the hard beetles, but some other birds work at them. Brown thrashers will pick a beetle off a rose bush and then whack it down onto a cement path to soften it up for eating. Skunks will mutilate turf with a lot of grubs.

Is the Japanese beetle nuisance likely to abate soon? Does severe cold tend to kill them? (Connecticut.) The menace has abated, due to natural enemies and man-made control methods. Any newly introduced insect does more damage initially than after it is a long-established pest. Beetles, as with tent caterpillars and cankerworms, are nuisances to be expected each season but not to be unduly excited about.

Do Japanese beetles bother geraniums? They are attracted to them; indeed it is a derivative of geranium that is used as bait in traps, but there is some evidence that beetles are killed by eating certain varieties of geraniums.

Which plant is easy to cultivate, a free bloomer until frost, and free as possible from Japanese beetles? (Connecticut.) Phlox and the 'Heavenly Blue' morning-glory answer your requirements. Roses, marigolds, and zinnias are favored food plants; delphiniums are not much bothered by beetles, but they are not easy to grow. Blue eupatorium will contrast with your phlox and give you color until frost. It has few insect enemies. To replace marigolds, try 'Goldcrest' cosmos. It has almost no pests or diseases and grows with no effort at all. Scatter the seeds in any odd corner; rake them in lightly. With no more attention, they bloom from early July to November.

Japanese beetles devouring a ripening apple. The beetles attack many ornamental plants as well as fruits and vegetables.

Which vegetables would be least affected by Japanese beetles? Most vegetables are little affected by Japanese beetles. However, they are extremely fond of soybeans, pole beans, and sometimes appear on snap and lima beans; they injure the silk of corn; they are numerous on, but seldom injurious to, asparagus foliage; and they often play havoc with rhubarb leaves.

I have a pet cat. What spray is safe on garden flowers and vines? I have Japanese beetles. Sevin will not harm the cat. It is one of the treatments applied for fleas. Dogs and cats like to follow around when you are spraying and kittens want to play with the nozzle, but if you shut them in the house during the actual mixing and application of the spray, there is no problem with the residue on the plants. Of course, you do not want to leave the pail of any pesticide standing where a dog or cat might try to take a drink. Mix up your spray and dispose safely of what is left in your spray tank and you will have no trouble.

JUNE BEETLES

What is a June beetle? It is the adult of any of a number of scarab beetles in the genus *Phyllophaga*.

KARATHANE

How often is it necessary to apply Karathane to plants to control powdery mildew? Karathane should be applied about 3 times at weekly or 10-day intervals to stop the progress of this disease. The normal dosage is 2 level teaspoons in 3 gallons of water plus a spreader. It may also be obtained as a ½ to 1 per cent dust. Mixtures with the common summer insecticides and fungicides are safe on foliage.

LACEBUGS

How do you kill lacebugs? (Iowa.) Lacebugs, small bugs with lace-like wings that work on the underside of leaves, sucking out the sap so that the upper surface becomes a stippled white, gray, or yellow, are killed by any contact or systemic insecticide applied with a good spreader and sufficient pressure. Malathion, Orthene, or carbaryl is effective.

LEAD ARSENATE

What is lead arsenate? A formerly widely used stomach poison, valuable for spraying ornamentals and for some food plants like apples. Because of the residue problem, lead arsenate being the most poisonous of the arsenicals, and because it burns some tender foliage, it was of little value in the control of vegetable pests. Arsenicals are now restricted or banned.

LEMON OIL

Is it harmful to put lemon oil on plants? If you mean the furniture polish that goes by that name, yes; but there is a tried-and-true insecticide called lemon oil sold for years for use on house plants and perfectly safe when used according to directions.

LIME-SULFUR

What is lime-sulfur? A fungicide, often acting as an insecticide also. Formerly valuable in dormant spraying for the control of fungus diseases and scale insects, but also useful as a summer spray to control apple scab and other diseases, boxwood canker, red mites on fruit trees, spider mites on evergreens. Liquid lime-sulfur is used at a 1 to 7 or 1 to 9 dilution as a dormant spray and 1 to 40 or 1 to 50 as a summer spray. It stains paint and leaves an objectionable residue, but is relatively safe. Do not use it within one month of using oil. It is not as available in stores as it once was.

LINDANE

Is lindane safe to use on my vegetables? Lindane is no longer recommended for home use on vegetables. It had been used widely for many types of insects both because of its residual effectiveness and vaporizing activity. It is now used primarily for borers, bark beetles, white pine weevil, and leafminers on deciduous trees. It is an excellent aphicide, but may not presently be registered for that use.

MAGGOTS

What causes ground maggots and how can you get rid of them?

(Maryland.) Maggots are legless white larvae of flies that lay their eggs in plants near where the stem meets the ground or in crevices in the soil. The cabbage maggot is the one most bothersome to the home gardener. (For control, see Cabbage.) Maggots are also pests of radishes, turnips, onions, beans, and corn. Diazinon is effective for control.

MALATHION

I have a cat and dog which roam around in my gardens. Will malathion sprays applied to the plants harm them? Very unlikely. Malathion is one of the least toxic insecticides to warm-blooded animals and in addition loses its toxic properties rapidly on exposure to air moisture, so that in two days no toxic residue is left. The only precaution I would suggest is to keep pets and children away from freshly sprayed plants.

MANCOZEB

Is mancozeb another name for maneb? No, it is a coordination product of zinc iron and maneb plus zinc sulfate. Maneb is sold under trade names Manzate 200 and Dithane M-22. It is effective against rusts, potato seed-piece decay, scab on cucurbits, and blights and leaf spots on many ornamentals.

MANEB

What is maneb? It is the "coined" name for the manganese salt of dithiocarbamic acid. This is another valuable general fungicide safe to use in combinations for fruits, vegetables, and ornamentals, but like captan it will not control powdery mildews or rusts. Delay applying to cucurbits until they are beginning to branch out. Trade names are Manzate and Dithane M-22.

MEALYBUGS

What are the fuzzy white bugs on my house plants? Mealybugs, sucking insects closely related to scales; flattened, oval, with short, white, waxy projections from the body, and often looking like bits of cotton fluff because of the eggs carried by the females in a cottony sac. Mealybugs are serious pests of house and greenhouse plants, and in the South on such outdoor plants as gardenia, azalea, and citrus fruits. In the

North, yew is often heavily infested, and the Comstock mealybug is an apple pest.

What is the life history of the mealybug? How does it travel? The female mealybug deposits her eggs in a cottony waxy sac attached to the rear end of her body. When she has laid 400 to 600 eggs, the sac is left at the axils of branching stems or leaves and the female dies. The eggs hatch in about 10 days, and the flattened, oval, yellow young crawl over the plants, sucking the sap, and soon a waxy covering is exuded from their bodies. They are sluggish and do not move much. The males transform into small, active 2-winged flies to mate with the females and then die. Mealybugs are disseminated by ants, and by moving about infested plants.

Mealybugs are small, soft bugs covered with a cottonlike fluff. They attack many house plants.

How can I rid a small greenhouse of mealybugs? Plants can be sprayed with or dipped into a solution of 1 pound of soap to 3 gallons of water, but this must be washed off within 2 hours to prevent burning. Spraying with malathion or Orthene is probably the easiest solution, provided that the manufacturer's directions are rigidly followed.

What is the best method of getting rid of mealybugs and how long does it take? (California.) First, wash off your plants with a strong spray from the hose, then use malathion or Orthene. It may be necessary to spray malathion 2 or 3 times at weekly intervals to clean up an infestation. For a few small plants, an aerosol plant bomb is very effective.

What will destroy mealybugs in the soil? (Ohio.) Remove the soil from around the roots and pour in some of the spray described above as in a light watering.

Can window boxes once infested with mealybugs be used again? (Connecticut.) There is no reason why not, if the soil is cleaned out and the box thoroughly washed with strong soap and water.

We are plagued with mealybugs on our flower and vegetable plants. Can you recommend a safe spray so as not to harm the plant or poison the vegetables? (Pennsylvania.) I cannot believe that mealybugs in an outdoor garden would be that much of a pest in Pennsylvania, although I have occasionally seen coral-bells and yew with bad cases of mealybugs in this region. Perhaps you have root aphids. (See Aphids.)

METHOXYCHLOR

What advantages has methoxychlor? It is very safe to use around warm-blooded animals; its residual toxicity lasts only about a week; it does not injure cucurbits; and it controls the plum curculio and the Mexican bean beetle. It does not adversely accumulate in the environment.

MICE AND RATS

How can you keep rats from eating plants in a city garden where, because of lack of cooperation from neighbors, it is impossible to get rid of all of them? (Maryland.) Poison put out for the rats would probably harm a pet cat or dog, and even traps would have to be used cautiously to avoid maiming a pet. When the house plants on my window were mysteriously chewed, I could not believe it was a rat until I caught it in the act one night. It was killed in a trap baited with sunflower seed. A pival-cornmeal or warfarin-cornmeal poison bait placed in a protected feeding station so that larger animals cannot get to it is a most effective and relatively safe way of killing rats and mice by internal hemorrhage. Rats and mice must be allowed to feed on this bait daily for at least a week for it to take effect. Constant rat and mouse protection will be obtained by leaving the bait and replenishing it when necessary.

Is there any practical way to get rid of mice in the garden? Not really, and what little can be done is only moderately helpful at best. The experts on rodents tell me that persistently using snap traps is the best, and certainly the safest method. Having cats around that are good mousers will help, although winter snows as well as mulches provide mice with protection. Wire screen around the base of trees, as for rabbits, helps. The poisons available in years gone by are not available generally and were extremely toxic to use around yards and pets. Chlorphacinone (Rozol) and diphacinone (Ramik-brown) are used commercially but may not be available to the home gardener in most states. They are also very poisonous to cats and dogs, if not used properly. You should consult your local extension agent for recommendations and currently available products.

MILDEW

What makes mildew on plants? (Texas.) A fungus, of the type they call an obligate parasite, because it must get its food from living plants. When the wind carries a spore (little seed) to a leaf and the moisture conditions are right, the spore sends out a germ tube that grows into white threads, mycelium, which branch over the leaf in a soft, white, felty coating. This fungus does not grow inside the plant but sends little suckers, haustoria, into the sap. In a few days, chains or spores are built up from the mycelium which gives the powdery effect. Later, black fruiting bodies with the sexual or overwintering spores are formed. Because it is on the surface, mildew is more readily controlled than many other fungi and may even be eradicated after the first signs of it appear.

How can one control mildew? (Minnesota.) Sulfur is a specific for mildew and the easiest way to apply it is in dust form, but sulfur or copper sprays may be used. Karathane and Actidione PM are used specifically for mildew control. Benlate is also very effective.

MILLIPEDES

What is the best way to rid a garden of the dark-brown, hard-shelled, spiral variety of worm which eats root vegetables? (Massachusetts.) This is a millipede. The name literally means thousand-legged, but the number falls far short of that, although this animal comes in many segments and there are 2 pairs of legs on each segment (the centipede has only 1 pair to each segment). Ordinarily, millipedes in the garden act more as scavengers than as a direct cause of injury, but they do some feeding on potatoes and other root vegetables. For control, use malathion, carbaryl, or diazinon. (See Wireworms; Sowbugs.)

MITES

What can be done to avoid or control mites? There are 3 kinds of mites apt to be troublesome in the home yard: spider mites, gall and rust mites, and cyclamen mites. Mites are relatives of spiders since they have 8 legs rather than 6, like insects. They are microscopic in size, so a hand magnifier is necessary to identify mites as the problem. Spider mites have silk glands and make webbing on the undersides of leaves or between needles. Their sucking of plant sap stipples foliage and needles, resulting in yellow foliage or rusty brown needles. Spruce mite and southern red mite should be controlled in the spring (May) or fall (September); honey locust mite in mid-June to early July; and two-spotted mites throughout the growing season whenever they occur. Spider mites are encouraged by the use of carbaryl (Sevin), but can be controlled with Kelthane, tetradifon, chlorobenzilate, or Omite. Gall mites are common on trees but seldom injurious. Rust mites can bronze or yellow the foliage of hemlock, privet, elm, and honey locust. Sevin suppresses these mites (*Eriophyidae*), but use Kelthane to control them. The cyclamen mite is most common on African violets and cyclamens as house plants, but stunts and deforms some outdoor flowers, especially delphiniums, causing blackened buds that never develop. Destroy severely infested plants and spray others every week or two with Kelthane.

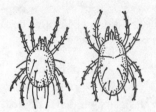

Red spiders are very tiny. They make fine webbing on the undersides of foliage.

What is the best material to use for spider mites on my garden and greenhouse plants?   There are several specific miticides on the market. (See the above question.) Spider mites can be partially checked by washing the foliage with strong jets of water.

MOLE CRICKETS

How do you get rid of mole crickets? (Florida.)   Mole crickets are dark-brown burrowing insects, about 1¼ inch long, with their front legs enlarged for tunneling. They come out at night to feed and are destructive because they eat the vegetative parts of seedlings as well as disturb the roots. Diazinon or Dursban will control mole crickets.

MOLES

How do I get rid of moles?   This is a very common problem. It was sent in by 91 gardeners in 32 different states. It is unfortunate that moles, which really do a lot of good in the world by eating white grubs and other insects, should also have the bad habit of making unsightly ridges and mounds in lawns and of disturbing the roots of flowers and vegetables by their tunnels. Actual feeding on plants is done by mice that use the mole runs. (See the following questions.)

Do moles eat bulbs?   No. They are carnivorous. Mice eat bulbs.

How do you get rid of moles without traps or poison? (Pennsylvania.)   There is not much left except patrolling the ridges and watching for movements indicating that the mole is at work and then killing it with a spade or a fork. A dog after a mole is disastrous, but cats may catch moles without any extra damage to the garden. One cat of an acquaintance had an unbroken record of a mole a day. Flooding the mole runs with water in the spring will drown young moles and mice in some soils.

What is the best method of controlling moles? (Oregon.)   Trapping. The Fish and Wildlife Service in Oregon and Washington report negative results with poison baits and cyanide dust but success with traps correctly set. Traps should not be set in the shallow runways but in the deeper main highways. Two types of traps may be used: the scissors and the diamond-jaw. Both depend on a trigger, sprung when the mole follows its natural instinct of burrowing through an obstruction of loose earth placed in the runway. Use a strong trowel to set the trap in the runway, aligning it so that the jaws of the scissors trap straddle the course or so that the choker trap encircles it. Pack the earth firmly under the trigger so the mole cannot work through without springing it. In gravelly soil, the choker works best.

What will eradicate Townsend moles? (California.)   These are Oregon moles. (See the previous question.)

Can one ever get rid of moles? (Iowa.)   Maybe, with persistence, but you don't want to get rid of those that are not actually injuring your garden. Think of your white-grub problem in Iowa. The loop or choker trap has been found to be very effective in Iowa soil.

How do you combat moles? (New York.)   New York State has 3 different moles. The naked-tail mole does much of the damage to lawns and golf courses on Long Island and in the lower Hudson Valley. In central and western New York, the star-nosed and the hairy-tail moles are present. The star-nosed mole throws up earth in a mound similar to a gopher mound, but the other two make the familiar ridges. Use mole traps for these, but snap-back mousetraps for the star-nosed variety. Treating the lawn for white grubs is often helpful in discouraging moles.

MOTHS

What is the difference between moths and butterflies?   Both are adults of caterpillars, often called worms. Moths are night fliers and their antennae are never clubbed.

I have small golden moths infesting my shrubs and grass and when I use the hose they fly up in great numbers. No one seems to know what they are or have not noticed them. They last from June or July to September. What are they? (New York.) They are probably the crambid moth, adults of sod webworms. Webworms are not a major lawn pest in New York, as they are in California and some other states, but sometimes the larva, a fat caterpillar which lives in a silklined nest, injures the grass roots. Spray your lawn with chlordane, carbaryl, or diazinon. In your particular case, the larvae of your moths may not be doing enough damage to bother about.

NEMATODES

What are nematodes and in what manner does soil become infested? (Georgia.) Nematodes are roundworms or eelworms, too small to see with the naked eye, that live in moist soil, in decaying organic matter, or as parasites in living plant tissues. They can travel only a short distance in the soil by themselves but are spread by surface water, by moving infested soil from place to place, and, very commonly, by local transfer and shipment of infested plants. Nematodes are more serious in sandy soils in southern states and in California. In the North, they may live during the winter in perennials and can also survive free in the soil.

How do you recognize the presence of nematodes? (Texas.) Injury to plants is slow to show up and not at all dramatic. Usually conspicuous above-ground symptoms do not appear until a heavy population of nematodes has built up. Nematodes should be suspected when plants show a slow decline in vigor and growth, when they become stunted and unthrifty, when water does not help them much in drought, or when the foliage becomes discolored yellow or bronze, as from a nutritional deficiency. You may or may not find swellings on the roots. The feeder roots may be lacking and the root system stunted and sparse or matted and shallow. Washed roots may disclose abundant small reddish-brown lesions in the epidermis. A hairy root condition occurs in some plants. Often roots are partially to wholly decayed because of secondary fungus or bacterial infections starting in lesions made by the nematodes. Foliar nematodes, common in chrysanthemums, produce angular brown lesions in the leaves; and bulb and stem nematodes produce discolored streaks or rings in narcissus bulbs, thickened stems, and crinkled leaves. The root-knot nematode, most common in southern areas, infests more than 1,700 species of plants. The nodules formed by beneficial nitrogen-fixing bacteria on legumes should not be confused with the root galls produced by this nematode.

How can root-knot nematodes be destroyed without killing shrubbery and perennials in infested beds? (California.) Nematocides are now available that destroy nematodes without killing plants; however, not all plants are tolerant to them, so read directions carefully and use on the specified plants only. You may use either V–C 13, a complex phosphorous compound, or Nemagon, 1, 2–dibromo 3–chloropropone. Both may be watered directly into the lawn or under plants with a watering can or hose proportioner. Granulated formulations can be applied by hand or with a fertilizer spreader and then watered in.

What is the latest information on combating nematodes in the southern garden? (Texas.) Either of the above nematocides may be used some 2 weeks previous to planting on prepared soil for susceptible plants or after planting on tolerant plants. An excellent preplanting treatment that may be used in any garden area after the soil has been prepared, but some 2 weeks before planting, consists of applying sodium methyl dithiocarbamate (Vapam or VPM). Just apply it with a watering can or with your hose and hose spray proportioner. This treatment destroys disease-producing fungi and most weed seeds, as well as nematodes.

Is there a quick, economical method of ridding garden soil of root-knot nematode? (Georgia.) The chemical methods discussed above are quick but not economical for large areas. Both ethylene dibromide and methyl bromide are more economical but not as easily applied. Ethylene dibromide may be applied as an undiluted liquid with special equipment on a field basis or in furrows 6 inches deep and 10 inches apart by pouring a stream along the trenches at the rate of ½ cup for every 75 feet. A quart container with 2 nail holes in opposite sides of the lid will facilitate application. As the application is made, another person should follow, filling the trench with soil and tamping it down. Wait two weeks before planting. Methyl bromide (Dowfume MC–2, Bromo-Gas) is a volatile liquid that must be kept under pressure at ordinary temperatures. Small amounts of soil for use in flowerpots, flats, and greenhouse benches can be treated in a large garbage can with a tight cover. Use ½ ounce per cubic foot of soil for 24 hours and allow 3 days for aeration before using. This treatment destroys soil fungi, weed seeds, and insects, as well as nematodes. For larger prepared-soil areas such as cold frames, gardens, and seed beds, a plastic tarpaulin is essential to confine the fumes for 24 to 48 hours. The rate is 1 pound per 100 square feet, and allow at least 2 days for aeration. The soil temperature should be above 60° F. to make treatments effective. Avoid treating the soil under trees and shrubs, and the soil to be used for carnation growing. This is highly toxic; get a professional applicator.

Two other soil fumigants, D-D and chloropicrin (Larvacide), are used chiefly in commercial enterprises: the first, for nematodes and insects; the second, for all soil organisms including weed seeds. They are applied with special hand applicators or tractor-borne applicators attached to plows or cultivatorlike devices. A water seal is necessary, along with a 2- to 3-week wait before planting.

I have heard that growing marigolds in gardens with other plants controls nematodes. Is this true? Marigolds grown with or in advance of other plants produce a toxin that will reduce the number of root-lesion (meadow) nematodes, but *not* root-knot and other types. Best results come from growing a crop of marigolds one season, spading it under, and putting in susceptible plants the next.

NICOTINE SULFATE

What is nicotine sulfate? Formerly widely available as Black Leaf 40, it is now hard to obtain. It is a useful contact insecticide. It is poisonous, but not as hazardous in diluted form, to people. It is readily washed off, and so can be safely used on vegetables and fruits to within a short time of harvest. It is used ordinarily in a soapy solution but it can be added to fungicides and some other insecticides. The dosage varies according to the insect to be controlled. A normal solution (1 to 800 dilution) is made with 1 teaspoon of nicotine sulfate and 1 ounce of soap (1 cubic inch of laundry soap) per gallon of water. For more resistant insects, the dosage is increased to 1½ to 2 teaspoons per gallon. Ordinarily, nicotine sulfate can be used without injury to plants, but caution is needed on a very hot day in the garden or in an enclosed greenhouse that is too warm.

OIL SPRAYS

Where and when can oils be used on plants? Normally called "dormant oils" (see Dormant Spraying), petroleum oil is an effective insecticide against mites, aphid eggs, and scale insects, while being nontoxic to animals. At recommended dosage rates, it is not injurious to most plants, even when used as a summer oil spray. The spray oils of recent years are more highly refined and thus more insecticidal and safer to use on plants than those of 20 to 30 years ago. Be sure to follow label uses and directions carefully.

ORTHENE

My extension agent suggested that I use Orthene for aphids in my garden and for mealybugs on some house plants. Is it the same as acephate? Acephate is the accepted common name for Orthene (trade name). It is used against a wide range of insect pests and has systemic properties. It is very effective for aphids, leafminers, mealybugs, scales, some caterpillars, and other common pests. It is registered for use on ornamentals in the garden and many house plants, but not the vegetable garden or fruit trees. Some plants are sensitive to it, so be sure to read the label for precautions.

PESTICIDES AND PUBLIC HEALTH

Federal, state, and even local laws regulate the sale and use of pesticides and at the same time help to protect the public from dangerous residues and the environment from deleterious hazards. All pesticides must be label-approved by the Environmental Protection Agency for specific crops and pests. Any use inconsistent with label directions is illegal under federal and state laws. Residue tolerances on food crops and quarantine periods to control reuse of treated areas have been established by law. Pesticides have been and are still in the process of being designated for general use, or for restricted use only by certified private and commercial applicators. For large-scale or area-wide spray programs, environmental impact statements by the applicators are required and must be approved by local, state, or federal agencies before control operations begin. The home gardener often has misused pesticides by using more than the recommended rate given on the label (it does *not* improve results!), treating too often, treating when or where pests are not a problem, or by dumping excess spray material into sewage systems, storm drains, or sites where runoff ends up in streams or other bodies of water. It is very important to read and follow *all* of the label directions and precautions carefully with regard to uses for specific pests and crops or plants, safe intervals between last spray and harvest, and precautions for the applicator, pets, children, and wildlife.

PRAYING MANTIS

Can you tell me about the praying mantis? I am planning to purchase an egg case next spring. (Illinois.)   If the praying mantis is not naturally present in your neighborhood, it might not pay to purchase egg cases, for these ferocious-looking beneficial insects are not commonly found much north of 40° latitude. The mantis belongs to the grasshopper family. It is very long and thin, with prominent eyes and enormous front legs used for catching other insects (aphids, mites, caterpillars) but often held up in a praying attitude. The baby mantis looks just like the adult, except for lack of wings. Their cannibalistic instincts are so well developed that they often eat one another. Do not let the egg masses hatch in the house, for heat brings them out in the winter and there is no way to feed the young mantises until they can survive out-of-doors. The praying mantis is generally a good predator, but will not control all garden pests.

I have hundreds of praying mantises in my garden. What do the egg cases look like? I find so many tentlike formations. (Kansas.)   The egg cases are a sort of dingy cream or yellow, shaped something like an oblong hatbox, but not especially regular, about 1 inch across, and made of a frothy gummy substance which hardens in that same frothy texture. They are usually attached to twigs of trees or shrubs. Egg masses are produced in late summer and hatch the following spring.

PYRETHRUM

What is pyrethrum?   A contact insecticide obtained from the pyrethrum plant, mostly grown in Africa. It is especially effective against aphids and soft-bodied insects, but it will kill whatever chewing insects it hits. It is useful for spraying flowers where a stain would be objectionable. For use on the Mexican bean beetle, impregnated pyrethrum dusts are more efficient.

RABBITS

Other than by fencing, how can rabbits be kept out of the garden? (Pennsylvania.)   Some sort of fence is still the best solution. If you cannot get the poultry wire ordinarily recommended, a picket fence can be substituted, or a low concrete wall built. The expense of either of these would be justified if the vegetable garden is to be permanent, and would look better than a wire fence (although green wire fencing is inconspicuous). There are reports that a row of child's windmills, or glass bottles stuck in the ground (neck down) will act as a fence in scaring rabbits away. A few cats will greatly diminish the rabbit population.

Will dried blood sprinkled around the roots of beans or other vegetables prevent rabbits from eating them? (New Jersey.) Dried blood has long been listed as an effective rabbit repellent, as well as being good for the garden. Some gardeners report that it is not always effective.

What is a good rabbit repellent? (Illinois.) The New Jersey Fish and Game Commission has listed 9 repellents for harassed gardeners: (1) dust plants, when damp, with powdered lime; (2) dust liberally with dusting sulfur (some vegetables do not take kindly to sulfur); (3) sprinkle plants with red pepper; (4) spray with a solution of 3 ounces of Epsom salts in 1 gallon of water; (5) spray with 1 teaspoon of Lysol in 1 gallon of water; (6) spray with 2 teaspoons of Black Leaf 40 in 1 gallon of soapy water; (7) spray with a solution of common brown laundry soap; (8) spray with 1 ounce of tartar emetic and 3 ounces of sugar in 1 gallon of water; (9) sprinkle naphthalene flakes between the rows of plants. One of the easiest methods is the family's pet cat! (The more cats, the fewer rabbits.)

How can you keep rabbits from eating young soybeans? Soybeans are often used to keep rabbits away from other plants. They worked that way in my garden, and I still get a lusty crop of soybeans. Formerly I credited moth balls with repelling the rabbits just enough to give the soybeans a fighting chance, but I visited a garden one summer where the rabbits had not allowed one soybean plant out of hundreds to get above 6 inches high and moth balls were so thick that the garden looked white. Now I have come to the conclusion that it is my neighbor's cats, hunting young rabbits, that keep the population down to reasonable proportions.

Rabbits have chewed the bark completely from the trunk of a young flowering crab planted this spring. Can anything be done to save the tree? (New Jersey.) You might try bridge grafting, which has worked successfully for apple trees girdled by rabbits and mice. Unless you are acquainted with this art, it would be better to have the work done by a tree expert, and that might cost as much as a new tree. Next time, protect your tree with a cylinder of close-mesh woven wire, 24 inches wide, sunk into the ground a few inches, and held away from the trunk with stakes. Sometimes prunings left on the ground around the trees and bushes will feed the rabbits enough to keep them from injuring the trunks. (See the answer to the previous question.)

RACCOONS   (See Squirrels.)

RED SPIDER MITES   (See Mites.)

RESMETHRIN

I have read that resmethrin is good for whiteflies. What is it?   It is the common name for one of several man-made chemicals similar to natural pyrethrins that are derived from the chrysanthemum. These synthetic pyrethroids have become available in the 1970s, primarily for greenhouse and house-plant use, but not as yet for food crops or vegetable gardens, although they appear to be effective against many kinds of insects. For the first time, they provide for the kill of whitefly nymphs as well as adults. Other pyrethroids include permethrin (Ambush, Pounce) and tetramethrin. The aerosols available to the home gardener may have only the long chemical name on the label, but will also prominently display the designation "Whitefly Spray."

ROTENONE

What is rotenone?   The principal insecticidal constituent in roots of plants such as *Derris* or *Lonchocarpus*. It acts as a stomach and contact poison for insects, kills fish and other cold-blooded animals, but is not injurious to man except as a throat irritant. It leaves no poisonous residue on the plant. Rotenone formerly was obtained from the Far East and is now coming from South America. *Lonchocarpus* has been established there to provide a new source of rotenone. Rotenone dust is available in a 1 per cent dilution. *Derris,* with an analysis of 4 to 5 per cent rotenone, is used for spraying.

RUST

What is a good spray for rust on plants? (California.)   That depends on whether or not you have true rust, a fungus that manifests itself in erumpent reddish-brown or reddish-orange pustules of spores, or, in the case of red-cedar and apple rust, in long, gelatinous spore horns, for which there is no chemical control. Zineb, mancozeb, or sulfur and ferbam are the best fungicides for the control of rust. For ornamental plants, they can be applied as a dust. Very often gardeners speak of "rust" when they merely mean a reddish discoloration of the tissue, which might be due to a variety of causes but never to the true rust fungus.

SCALE INSECTS

What is the life history of scale? What plants are attacked? What are the treatments? Do you mean indoors or out? There are many different scale insects, but 2 general types. Those found in gardens in New York would be mostly of the armored-scale type, that is, after they finish the young, crawling stage, a hard, separable shell is formed on their bodies and they stop moving around. In this group is the oyster-shell scale on lilacs, scurfy scale on apples, rose scale on roses, euonymus scale on euonymus and bittersweet, juniper scale, pine-needle scale, and many others. This group is controlled by oil spray before growth starts in the spring (see Dormant Spraying) and malathion for the young scales or "crawlers" in midsummer. The second group includes the soft or tortoise scales, represented in a northern garden by maple, tulip tree, lecanium, and magnolia scales. More often seen on house plants are soft brown scales that have to be scrubbed off or sprayed with an aerosol plant bomb, Orthene or malathion. (See House Plants.)

How do you get rid of cottony cushion scale on trees? (Texas.) Ask your State Extension Service where you can get a colony of Australian lady beetles. A malathion spray can also be helpful.

SEED TREATMENT

Should seeds be treated before being planted? Yes, the application of a chemical protectant is insurance against damping off, either in the seed flat or the garden row, and in addition can prevent some diseases due to organisms carried on the outside of the seed. Nowadays, most seeds available to the gardener have been treated. It pays to buy seeds already treated. Also helpful is sowing the seeds in soilless mixes, such as Jiffy Mix, which are sterile.

What about the organisms carried inside the seeds? They cannot be killed with external dusts. The seeds must be soaked in hot water—a treatment usually not given unless the disease organism is presumably present. Tie seeds loosely in cheesecloth bags and keep the temperature of the water constant: 122° F., 25 minutes for cabbage, 15 minutes for other crucifers; tomato seed, 25 minutes; 118° F., 30 minutes for celery.

SLUGS AND SNAILS

Is there any way to rid my garden of slugs? (California.) No, but they can be suppressed or minimized by a combination of good sanitation practices and proper use of slug baits. Slugs and snails live where it is very moist and hide in the dark in daytime beneath stones, boards, and trash on the ground and in the soil. By keeping the garden well tilled, free of weeds, and uncluttered by stones, stakes, and plant refuse, slugs will have few places to thrive. Two slug baits that may be sold under various trade names are metaldehyde and mesurol. Mesurol is not labeled for use around food plants, but metaldehyde is. Be sure to follow label directions carefully when treating the soil. Do not treat the plants directly. Supplementary measures for small gardens include trapping. Boards placed in the garden in the evening provide ready places for them to hide when daylight comes. Slugs can then be killed. Beer will attract slugs if placed in shallow dishes with the rim at soil level. Slugs crawl into the dish and drown. Salt or lime will kill slugs when sprinkled on them.

What is the best method for combating slugs? We use lime but it whitens our shrubs. The slugs attack cherry trees, purple-leaf plum, and flowering quince. (Utah.) Put your lime on the ground in a circle, enclosing the tree trunk. Try spraying the slugs at night with a spray of ¼ to ½ pound of alum per gallon of water. Try metaldehyde baits or beer in deep saucers. If "slugs" are seen on the leaves during the day, they may be sawfly larvae. (See Rose.)

Will a boardwalk in a garden be the cause of an exceptionally large number of slugs? It would provide the protected hiding place favored by slugs, but it should also prove a help in getting rid of them, for poison baits put under the boardwalk would not endanger children, pets, or birds.

What is the best way to destroy slugs and snails without the risk of poisoning birds or pets? (Ohio.) If poison baits are put out under little jar covers or pieces of board, there is little danger to pets, but to play it absolutely safe, resort to lime on the ground, cleaning up plant debris, hand-picking, and probably spraying or dusting plants with an insecticide. There is practically no danger to pets when a poison is used on plants.

Are hard-shell snails or big, fat, soft ones harmful or beneficial in the garden? I have roses, iris, lilies, etc. (Pennsylvania.) They are not exactly beneficial. Roses will be little bothered by true slugs in Pennsylvania, but they have their special brand of false slugs or sawfly larvae. (See Rose.) Any plant with leaves close to the ground like iris or lily will be apt to be eaten by slugs.

SOIL STERILIZATION

Isn't there some way to get the soil in such a healthy condition that insects and diseases will not bother a plant? Disease organisms in the soil can be killed by soil sterilization, but there is no known way to render plants immune to attacks by fungi or insects. There are a few instances where fertilizing is somewhat linked up with resistance, but there is little exact knowledge along this line.

How do you sterilize soil? The usual aim is not a complete destruction of all living organisms but a partial sterilization which will control harmful organisms. Heat is one of the best means, but there are difficulties. Steam is excellent but practical only for the commercial greenhouse operator; hot water can be used, but it is apt to puddle the soil; baking is used for small quantities, but toxic materials can be liberated; this can be true also when electricity is used. Formaldehyde is most useful for treating small lots of soil to prevent damping off of seedlings. Formaldehyde dust is used, but the liquid sprinkle method seems more generally satisfactory. For each 20 × 14 × 2 and ¾-inch flat of soil, use 1 tablespoon of Formalin diluted with 6 tablespoons water. Sprinkle it over the soil and mix thoroughly. Let stand 12 to 24 hours; after the seeds are sown, water immediately.

How do you treat the soil in a garden? It is rather an expensive procedure recommended only for the control of specific organisms when crop rotation is not feasible. Formaldehyde is usually used for root-rot fungi. Dilute 1 part commercial Formalin with 50 parts water and apply ½ gallon to each square foot of soil. Cover for 1 to 2 days with burlap, paper, or boards. Spade to air out the gas and wait about 2 weeks before planting. Vapam is registered and available for treating home gardens as a preplant treatment. It is effective against nematodes and other soil-borne plant pathogens. Soil preparation and temperature are very important. After applying either 1 pint per 50 square feet with a sprinkling can or 1 quart to 3 quarts of water per 100 square feet with a hose proportioner, immediately cover the area with a plastic film. Post-treatment cultivation during a waiting period is essential. Be sure to follow all directions carefully from Cooperative Extension recommendations and on the label.

SOOTY MOLD

I have had trouble in my greenhouse with a black sooty substance forming on the leaves. It is hard to wash off. What is it and how do I prevent it from forming? (Wisconsin.)   This is a black fungus growth called sooty mold, but the fungus is not parasitic on the plant; it is merely growing in insect honeydew that drops on the leaves—in your case, very likely from aphids, scales, or mostly whiteflies, but on outdoor shrubs mostly from aphids or scale insects. There is not much hope of washing it off. You can prevent it by spraying to control your insect population.

SOWBUGS

How do you destroy sowbugs? The bug is flat and fairly round, and has hard legs along the side. (Virginia.)   Sowbugs, probably named for female hogs because of their shape, are sometimes called pill bugs because of their tendency to roll up into little balls. Sowbugs are not true insects but crustacea, related to crayfish. They are grayish, segmented, with 7 pairs of legs about ½ inch long. They hide at the base of plants under clods of earth or manure. Dust the soil with malathion, carbaryl, or diazinon to control them.

Do sowbugs eat seed in flats?   I am not certain about the seed itself, but they injure the seedlings by feeding on the stems and tender growth at the soil line.

SPITTLEBUGS

What causes the white frothy substance that looks like white foam to come on plants?   This is the spittlebug, so named because the young nymphs have the habit of secreting a quantity of frothy material between molts. The adults leave the "spit" protection and look something like leafhoppers, but because of their bulging eyes, they are often called froghoppers. In Michigan, the pine spittlebug can be injurious to pines and other conifers by sucking the sap. Occasionally young trees are killed. Spray with methoxychlor or malathion, and apply the spray with great pressure.

What can I do to rid my plants of an insect in a sort of "bubble"? I have heard it called spitbug.   Various species of spittlebugs occasionally injure garden plants. In New Jersey a while back, a devastating attack on strawberries was repulsed with *Derris* dust. Any fairly potent contact insecticide applied with enough pressure to penetrate the protective froth should be satisfactory. Spittlebugs do get around. They have been several times reported from penthouse gardens high over New York City.

SPRAY MATERIALS

Spraying charts are usually given for the large farmer, not the back-yard gardener. Will you furnish a simplified spraying chart where a gardener needs to mix only a pint or a quart at the most? Label directions are usually given for 1 gallon. One pint, or even a quart, will not go very far, even in a backyard garden. Moreover, anyone capable of filling out income-tax blanks should be able to do a little arithmetic on garden sprays. Remember that there are 3 teaspoons in 1 tablespoon, 16 tablespoons in 1 cup, or 8 liquid ounces, 4 cups in a quart, and 4 quarts in a gallon. Buy a set of kitchen measuring spoons and a glass cup marked off in ounces. When the directions call for 1 teaspoon per gallon and you need only a quart, use the tiny ¼ teaspoon measure. When 1 tablespoon per gallon is needed, mix ¾ teaspoon in 1 quart.

What can I use on vegetables that is harmless to people or dogs and will kill the chewing bugs? Rotenone. Methoxychlor is also relatively safe and may be used within a week of harvest.

What are the main spray materials to have on hand? I understand some of these sprays are the same, only they are under different names. You understand correctly. Insecticides and fungicides are sold under hundreds of different trade names, but basically they now depend on malathion, carbaryl, methoxychlor, diazinon, acephate, *Bacillus thuringiensis,* pyrethrum, rotenone, and oils for action against insects; and copper, sulfur, and the new organic fungicides captan, ferbam, benomyl, folpet, maneb, zineb, mancozeb, and chlorothalonil for diseases. Miticides include Kelthane, Tedion, Omite, and chlorobenzilate. Always read the label on your proprietary mixture and know what you are buying. Only the plants you grow and the diseases and pests you have can determine how many different materials are required in your garden. Theoretically, 1 fungicide, 1 stomach poison, 1 contact insecticide, and a miticide would see you through, but not all fungi react to copper or to sulfur, and not all insects can be controlled by rule.

Isn't there some one spray I could use for all the garden ills to which the Deep South is heir? (Louisiana.) Unfortunately, no, but a general-purpose garden spray comes close to taking care of some of the most important southern pests. Write the Department of Entomology, State Agricultural Experiment Station, Baton Rouge, La. 70803 for help.

Would you suggest how to plan a spray schedule for a perennial border? It depends on the plants you have. Check through the alphabetical list of ornamentals in this section and see which problems apply to your garden. Consult the books listed in Section 16 under Pests and Diseases for further information.

What ingredients would you advise in a general-purpose spray mixture for use on fruits, vegetables, and ornamentals? A good general-purpose spray or dust may have malathion for sucking pests and mites; methoxychlor or carbaryl for chewing insects; captan, folpet, or zineb for diseases; and Kelthane as a miticide. Karathane or benomyl may be needed for powdery mildew control. General-purpose sprays applied periodically eliminate the necessity for knowing what foliage or fruit insects or diseases to worry about on your plants.

SPRAYERS

What are garden sprayers? Equipment to apply liquid insecticides or fungicides to plants in a fine mist. Sprayers vary from aerosol bombs and pint- or quart-size atomizers useful for house plants to huge power apparatus that will spray tall trees with 500 pounds of pressure. For the average garden, a cylindrical compressed-air sprayer or a knapsack sprayer of 1½- to 3-gallon capacity, which fits on the back, will be sufficient. For small trees and shrubs, a bucket or barrel sprayer mounted on wheels to move around the garden will be most convenient. Small motor-driven sprayers are also available. If a copper or stainless steel sprayer rather than a galvanized one can be procured, it will be worth the extra price in longer life. No sprayer is better than the care given it. Rinse thoroughly immediately after use and occasionally take it apart for cleaning. Strain all spray mixtures into the tank through cheesecloth to prevent clogging. Extra parts can often be obtained from manufacturers or distributors to keep old sprayers in operation.

Is any single sprayer, such as the hose proportioner type, sufficient for all average conditions? Hose sprayers of the proportioner type are very convenient and easy to use and are suitable for shrubs and small trees as well as flowers and vegetables. They handle solutions and emulsions readily, but you may run into trouble with suspensions because of clogging. Not all types give a suitable dispersion of the active chemical in the spray. Those with a shut-off near the nozzle are much preferable to those that have no shut-off and require you to place your finger over a hole to start the chemical mixing with the water spray. The 1- to 3-gallon compressed-air sprayers will handle all chemicals and will do a good job in most gardens. In addition, gardeners should have a few aerosol plant bombs on hand for spot treatments of pests.

SQUIRRELS, RACCOONS, AND CHIPMUNKS

How do I get rid of chipmunks? (Massachusetts.) It has been said, although I cannot prove it personally, that chipmunks are unsuspicious creatures readily caught in live-animal or snap-back traps baited with a nut, pumpkin seed, or peanut butter, and placed near their burrows. These ground squirrels eat some slugs and insects and should not be destroyed without reason. Bulbs can be planted in wire baskets to protect them. Cats will also discourage chipmunks.

Our corn patch was neatly devastated, a dozen ears per night, by some animal that shucked as it ate. Is it likely to have been squirrels? How can we combat such an unseen adversary? (Connecticut.) It may have been woodchucks or squirrels, but more likely raccoons if the ears were husked. There is not much solution except to trap or shoot them or to plant enough for you and the animals, too. In my garden, they are satisfied with the outside row. Creatures have their rights, too, and their place in the environment. (See Corn.)

How do you get rid of gray squirrels? (Virginia.) Get permission to trap them or to shoot them, which is easier said than done in many communities.

How do you prevent squirrels from monopolizing feeding stations? (New York.) If the feeding station is hung from a horizontal wire, metal guards can be placed on either side; or if the feeding station is on top of a post, a guard can be placed underneath; but if the station is anywhere within leaping distance of a tree, the guard is useless. Put out enough food for the squirrels—and the birds.

STREPTOMYCIN

Do any of the antibiotic drugs for people work on plant diseases? Yes, streptomycin has been used to control a number of bacterial plant diseases such as fire blight of apples and pears, bacterial spot of tomato and pepper, and bacterial wilt of chrysanthemum. The formulations are sold under the names Agrimycin, Agri-Strep, and Phytomycin. Effective dilutions range from 50 to 100 parts per million.

SULFUR

How is sulfur used in the garden? Sulfur is a valuable fungicide with many uses, but especially in the control of rust and mildew, and also of some value as a miticide in the control of spider and other mites. In the home garden, sulfur is usually used in dust form, and it can be safely combined with insecticides. Wettable sulfurs are available to use as liquid sprays. In very hot weather, sulfur should be used cautiously, for it is apt to burn the plants. It is incompatible with oil and should not be used within 30 days of an oil spray. It will injure viburnums.

SYSTEMIC OR CHEMOTHERAPEUTIC AGENTS

I have heard that some pesticides can be absorbed by plants to kill the pests and fungi that attack them. Which chemicals are they and how do they work? There are a number of systemic insecticides and at least one fungicide. Since this type of chemical tends to be relatively more toxic to animals also, most are restricted to use by professional applicators. Those that are available to the home gardener include the insecticides acephate (Orthene), dimethoate (DeFend and Cygon), and oxydemeton methyl (Meta-Systox-R or MSR), and the fungicide benomyl (Benlate). Whereas warm-blooded animals must be injected or eat chemicals (drugs) for medication, plants can take up chemicals through the roots, through the foliage, or be injected. Injection techniques are registered for use by professional applicators. Although it might seem that a toxicant within the plant would protect against any insect or disease, that is not the case. Systemic insecticides are effective primarily for sucking insects and mites that feed on the foliage, some caterpillars that feed on foliage and new growth, but seldom those feeding on or in the bark or wood. Extreme caution should be used when systemics are used, since the dosage rate that renders plants toxic to insects approaches the dilution rate that may be injurious to the plants. Granular formulations of disulfoton (Di-Syston) are available for mites and sucking insects on roses and some floral crops and leafminers on birch and holly trees.

TENT CATERPILLAR

How can I control the tent caterpillar, which attacks wild cherry and apple trees in the spring? As soon as the webs form, while worms are still very small, wipe them out of the crotches of branches with a pointed stick or a swab dipped in kerosene or spray them with carbaryl. If webs must be destroyed after the caterpillars are well developed, do so in the early morning or after sunset when the caterpillars have returned to the web for warmth. A preventive control is to cut off and burn the twigs bearing egg masses, which can be seen after the leaves have dropped in autumn or winter.

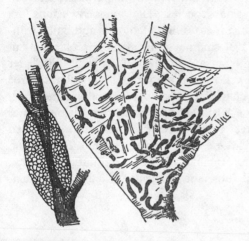

Tent caterpillars form large gray-white webs in the crotches of branches. (Left) Egg mass on a winter twig.

TERMITES

Where termites are in cordwood, 50 feet from a brick house, is there danger that they will get started in the house itself? (Maryland.)   Not unless there is any woodwork on the building in direct contact with the ground. If there is, a metal shield can be inserted. It is wise to get rid of the termites in the woodpile by burning the wood and treating the termite nest with chlordane.

TERRACHLOR

My dealer does not have Terrachlor—where can he get it?   Terrachlor, or PCNB, is manufactured by the Olin Chemical Corporation, Little Rock, Arkansas, as a 75 per cent Wettable Powder or a 20 per cent dust. It is very promising for some soil-borne diseases such as club root of crucifers and crown rot of iris and many other plants. Use Wettable Powder at the rate of 1½ pounds per 12 gallons of water per 1,000 square feet, or the dust at the rate of 5 pounds per 1,000 square feet. Work the dust into the upper soil before planting.

TEXAS ROOT ROT

Has there been anything found to control root rot? (Texas.) Texas root rot, also called cotton or Phymatotrichum root rot, is probably the chief problem in gardening in certain parts of Texas, Arizona, and New Mexico. The fungus *Phymatotrichum omnivorum* is a native soil inhabitant in semiarid regions of low humidity, high temperature, and soil alkalinity. It attacks 1,700 plant species. The monocotyledons are immune, so you can grow palms, irises, lilies, gladiolus, and bulbs without trouble. During the period of summer rains, dense circular mats of fungus mycelium appear on the surface of the soil, at first white, later tan and powdery. Plants turn yellow and die rapidly. Sometimes a tree can be saved at the first sign of wilting by applying ammonium sulfate, 1 pound to 10 square feet, in a basin around the tree and letting water run in until the soil is wet 4 feet deep. Garden soil may also be treated with ammonium sulfate, but if there are no shrubs within 20 feet, the fallow soil may be treated with formaldehyde (1 to 70 dilution, 1 gallon applied per foot) or with soil fumigant fungicides. (See under Nematodes.)

THRIPS   (See Gladiolus.)

WHITE GRUBS

This spring I plowed and planted land that had not been farmed for 25 years; grubworms killed the potatoes, cabbage, etc. What was the reason? (Illinois.) Grubworms are white grubs in your area, soft-bodied white worms with brown heads and curved bodies ½ to 1 inch long. They look like Japanese beetle grubs but are a little larger. They

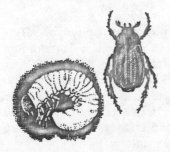

White grub, a large, soft, white grub with a brown head, is the larva of the June beetle (right) and eats roots of grass and other plants.

damage lawns in the same way and are much more injurious to root vegetables than are the grubs in the East. As you continue to garden your land, the injury should get less. It is most serious in areas neglected for a long time. White grubs are larvae of June beetles. There is a 3-year cycle, the grubs staying in the ground 2 years and the large brown beetles flying the third year and eating tree foliage. Injury from the worms is greatest the year after beetle flight.

How shall I rid my soil of grubworms? (Texas.) Prevent trouble, if possible, by not planting garden crops on sod land or land covered with weeds and grass the preceding year. If such land must be used, till or spade in the fall. Legume crops will suffer less than corn or potatoes.

WHITEFLIES

Is there a really good control for those clouds of little white flies among my house plants? Yes. Use an aerosol, according to container directions, that contains resmethrin. (See Resmethrin.)

WIREWORMS

I have a pest in the soil about the thickness of a darning needle, light brown, very tough. I have to cut off the head to kill it; it is ¾ to 1½ inches long and seems to live in the roots. Is it harmful to plants? (Indiana.) You have described a wireworm, a chewing insect that feeds underground on germinating seeds and underground roots, stems, and tubers. Potatoes, beets, beans, cabbage, carrots, corn, lettuce, onions, turnips, and other vegetables may be injured. Damage is worse on poorly drained soil or on land that has been in grass sod. The adult stage of the wireworm is a gray, brown, or black click beetle, an amusing creature that clicks itself right-side-up when it falls on its back.

What is the best method for exterminating wireworms? (New Jersey.) If newly broken sod must be used, till it thoroughly and then apply diazinon as a broadcast treatment prior to planting and thoroughly mix the top 4 to 8 inches of soil.

WITCHES'-BROOMS

What are witches'-brooms and their cause? (Massachusetts.) They are broomlike excessive development of twigs in response to an irritation caused by insects, fungi, or some virus. Hackberry is a notable example, with often hundreds of brooms, each a mass of stubby twigs, arising from a swelling at the base of a branch, on a single tree. A gall mite and a powdery mildew fungus seem to be jointly responsible for this deformation. There is no control in this case, but cutting out the brooms improves appearance.

WOODCHUCKS

How do you get rid of woodchucks?   The United States Fish and Wildlife Service has developed a special woodchuck cartridge, which can be obtained through county agents or at farm-supply stores. When lighted according to directions and placed in a den mouth, this will diffuse a lethal gas through the den.

How can I prevent woodchucks from eating strawberries?   A fence is the only sure protection, except a dog.

What can I do about woodchucks that eat my garden plants?   Watch for them in early morning and late afternoon and shoot them, if it is allowed in your area. Consult your county extension agent for local recommendations and restrictions.

Ornamentals and Their Pests

ACONITUM

Why do monkshood leaves and stems die? What is the cure? The roots look healthy. (Connecticut.)   If the vessels are black when you cut across the stem, dying leaves are probably due to verticillium wilt, the result of a soil fungus affecting the vascular system. There is no cure. Plant healthy roots in new or sterilized soil.

Can one prevent yellowing of leaves or complete defoliation of aconitum before blooming? (Ohio.)   Since this is presumably the same verticillium wilt, nothing will prevent the disease except starting over with new roots in fresh soil.

Is there any other cause of blight of aconitum except verticillium? (New Jersey.)   Yes, sometimes the crown-rot fungus so destructive to delphinium attacks aconitum. In this case, you usually see white threads or seedlike bodies on the soil, and the plant may topple over at the crown. Remove the plant and the surrounding soil. Disinfect the area with bichloride of mercury or Terrachlor.

Why do the flower buds of my aconitum turn black and not open?

(New Jersey.)   The cyclamen mite affects aconitum as it does delphinium. Remove infested portions and spray weekly with Kelthane throughout the growing season.

AFRICAN-VIOLET (SAINTPAULIA)

My African-violets are stunted—they have twisted stems, misshapen foliage, and few and imperfect flowers. What is the trouble?   The trouble is a cyclamen mite and bad news. It is too small to see with the naked eye and can spread from pot to pot of African-violets. Keep new plants isolated until you are sure they are healthy. Badly infested (deformed) plants are best destroyed. Kelthane is recommended as a dip (1 teaspoon to a gallon of water) and a spray (follow directions on the label).

How can I get rid of the mealybugs on my African-violet?   It is difficult because spraying injures the foliage. Watch for the first signs of these white, woolly sucking insects and remove them with a small brush dipped in alcohol. Touch only the bug, not the leaf. Avoid a too hot, dry atmosphere. A house-plant aerosol bomb is also effective. Try Orthene; it is excellent for aphids.

How do I rid my African-violet of a small insect that leaves white cotton all over it?   It is probably a mealybug, and if the infestation is that bad, you'd better destroy the plant and start with a healthy one.

Is there a remedy for lice on African-violet plants?   You probably refer to mealybugs, for ordinary aphids are not as common on this plant. Constant vigilance is the remedy; pick off the first bit of cotton fluff you see, or touch each insect with a small swab of cotton on a matchstick (or a very small paintbrush) dipped in alcohol. A malathion or Orthene spray will also control mealybugs.

What causes a moldlike covering over the topsoil of houseplants, particularly African-violets?   Insufficient aeration. Cultivate the soil occasionally with the tines of an old fork. Too much water compacts the soil and encourages the moldy surface growth. You may need to repot with a fresh mixture.

AGERATUM

What do you do for whiteflies on ageratum?   The whiteflies, which usually come along when you get your plants from the greenhouse in the spring, cause minute white spotting on the foliage all summer, getting worse toward fall. Use a whitefly spray (resmethrin) or aerosol.

How can I keep "mooly" aphids or milk cows from my blue ageratum? I lose the plants each year. (Missouri.)   "Mooly" is evidently
mistyped for woolly, but the pun is too good to lose. Ants keep root
aphids herded together so they can feed on the honeydew (milk) excreted. Make a shallow depression around each plant and pour in malathion solution. (See also Ants, for their control.)

ALYSSUM (AURINIA SAXATILIS)

Why does basket of gold alyssum die?   Possibly because of wet feet.
Good soil drainage is necessary; the foliage should be kept dry. This
plant thrives on walls and other dry locations. The plants are not long-
lived where summers are hot and humid, as they are alpines. Keep a
fresh supply of seedlings to take the place of older plants.

AMARCRINUM

How do I get rid of thrips on x Amarcrinum memoria-corsii and Urginea maritima (sea-onion)?   Spray or dust weekly with malathion.

AMARYLLIS (HIPPEASTRUM)

Can mealybugs be removed from the scales of an amaryllis bulb? I
have tried alcohol sprays but there are still mealybugs.   Be wary of alcohol sprays. You can remove bugs with a tiny cotton swab on a toothpick dipped in alcohol. Or try dipping in a malathion solution.

What is the grub that gets into amaryllis bulbs?   Probably the larval
form of greater or lesser narcissus bulb flies. Grub of the greater fly may
be up to ¾ inch long; the lesser, up to ½ inch. Commercial growers
often treat bulbs with hot water, but there is nothing for the home
grower to do after the injury is noted.

Why do amaryllis leaves turn yellow and die? They do not dry up but
have something like wet rot.   If the rot is wet, it may be bacterial soft
rot following the work of bulb-fly larvae. If the bulb is not sound, do
not save it for another year. Destroy it.

ANEMONE

How can one protect Japanese anemones (windflowers) from the
blister beetle?   Only by constant vigilance when the beetles appear in

midsummer. Dust or spray with carbaryl or methoxychlor. Pyrethrum-rotenone sprays are also helpful, as is hand-picking of the beetles. (See Blister Beetles.)

ARBORVITAE (THUJA)

What is the best chemical to use on arborvitae when the branches become a rusty color? (Illinois.) The rusty color is often due to spruce mite. The most potent spray is a miscible oil, applied before new growth starts in the spring. (See Dormant Spraying.) During the growing season, spraying with Kelthane, Tedion, or chlorobenzilate is effective in early May and late September. Treat when seen at other times in the season.

What might be the cause of arborvitae turning brown and dying? (Mississippi.) If the whole tree dies, it may be from prolonged injury from spruce mites, but the browning and dying of inner leaves are a natural shedding. Dying of the tips of the branches, twig blight, is a fungus disease, calling for cutting off the infected portions. Tiny tan patches in the foliage may be from arborvitae leafminer. (See the questions below.)

How do you destroy little red bugs that suck the sap from arborvitae? (Arkansas.) You may mean the arborvitae aphid, a very small, hairy, amber-brown plant louse. Apply a good contact spray, such as malathion, with as much pressure as possible, since these aphids are covered with a powdery film, which makes them hard to kill.

Why do the tips of arborvitae twigs turn white? (Connecticut.) This is the work of a leafminer, which winters in the leaves and emerges as a moth to lay eggs in June. Spraying with diazinon or dimethoate in late June and early July helps to kill larvae as they enter the base of the leaves.

ASPIDISTRA (CAST-IRON PLANT)

What causes the white-looking fungus or scale or whatever it can be called on aspidistra leaves? How can it be cured? (Louisiana.) There is a fungus disease, anthracnose, characterized by white spots with brown margins. Spraying is seldom necessary or profitable. Fern scale is also found on aspidistra. Perhaps you refer to mealybugs. (See House and Greenhouse Plants in this section, for control.)

ASTER, CHINA- (CALLISTEPHUS)

Will paper collars adequately protect transplanted seedlings, China-aster particularly, from grubworms? (Oregon.) Collars will protect against cutworms (fat caterpillars that cut off plant stems near the surface). Collars offer no protection against the white grubs, larvae of June beetles, which stay in the soil and feed on roots of garden plants.

After reaching full growth and flowering size, my China-asters dried up and died. What was the cause? (New York.) Aster wilt, a disease caused by a soil fungus, a species of fusarium, which grows into the roots and affects the vascular or water-conducting system of the plant. Young plants may be infected and not show symptoms until flowering, as in this case.

Why do some China-asters thrive until they are 7 to 8 inches tall, then turn brown, rusty, and die? I can't find anything at the roots or on the tops. (Idaho.) This is an earlier manifestation of the same aster wilt. Infection often takes place at transplanting time, with the leaves drying and dying somewhat later. Plant wilt-resistant seed, many varieties of which are now on the market.

When China-asters have blighted, how long a time must elapse before they can be safely grown in the same ground? (Illinois.) No one knows exactly how long the fusarium wilt fungus lives in the soil, but it is several years.

What can I do to prevent root rot in my China-aster bed? I plant wilt-resistant seed, disinfected with Semesan, without the desired results. (Illinois.) Certain soils are so infected with the wilt fungus that a certain percentage of "wilt-resistant" plants will succumb, the situation being worse in wet seasons. Try sterilizing the soil in the seed bed and transplanting seedlings to a fresh location. (See Soil Sterilization.)

Is there anything to sterilize the ground for infected China-aster plants? It is a large space. (Wisconsin.) It will scarcely pay to treat a large space. For a small area, try a formaldehyde drench, spading the soil, and then saturating with a solution of 1 gallon of commercial Formalin diluted with 50 gallons of water. Apply ½ to 1 gallon per square foot of soil, cover with paper or canvas for 24 hours, and then air out for 2 weeks before planting. (For other methods, see Soil Sterilization.)

What causes some China-aster flowers to open greenish-white instead of coloring? (California.) Aster yellows, a virus disease transmitted from diseased to healthy plants by leafhoppers. The leaves lose their chlorophyll and turn yellow, while the blossoms turn green. Plants are usually stunted. This is the most serious aster disease and occurs throughout the United States.

How can I prevent China-aster yellows? Only by preventing insect transmission. Remove diseased plants immediately, so there will be no source of infection. Spray frequently with contact insecticides to kill leafhoppers. Commercial growers protect China-asters by growing them in cloth houses made of cheesecloth or tobacco cloth with 22 meshes to the inch.

How can I get rid of the small root lice that suck life out of China-asters and other annuals? (Illinois.) Make a shallow depression around each plant and pour in the same malathion solution used for spraying above-ground aphids.

What treatment will reduce damage to China-asters by the tarnished plant bug? (Kansas.) This small, light and dark brown sucking insect is hard to control. It is very active, occurs on many kinds of plants, stinging the flower buds and spotting the leaves, and has several generations a season. Spray with carbaryl or malathion. Rotenone dust is also effective. Cleaning up all trash and weeds will make hibernation difficult for the bug.

What is the control of the common black beetle on China-asters? (Michigan.) You probably mean the long, slim blister beetle, which is very destructive to these asters. Dust or spray with carbaryl or methoxychlor. (See Blister Beetles.)

AZALEA (RHODODENDRON)

What is azalea flower-spot disease? (Louisiana.) A fungus disease that has spread from South Carolina through the Gulf states since 1931 and has been reported from California and as far north as Connecticut, New Jersey, and Pennsylvania. Pinhead spots on the flowers enlarge to brownish blotches and the flowers collapse in about 3 days. Black resting bodies form in the petals and winter in the fallen leaves. The indica varieties are especially susceptible.

How do you control azalea flower-spot? Spray with zineb 2 or 3 times a week starting when midseason varieties come into flower. Treating the soil with Terrachlor and a barrier mulch has been recommended but has little effect because spores are readily spread from untreated azaleas. Never purchase azalea plants in flower from an infected area.

What are the cause and treatment of moldlike white threads, resulting in a general decline of azalea plants? (California.) Azaleas in California are subject to attack by the oak-root rot fungus (*Armillaria mellea*). Besides the white threads (mycelium), the fungus has shoestringlike black strands which go through the soil and produce honey-colored toadstools. Increase the vigor of plants by feeding; remove some of the soil from the crowns and roots; avoid a too high soil moisture content. Soil known to be infected should be sterilized. (See also under Nematodes.)

My azalea buds blight before they open. Why? (Ohio.) There is a fungus that blasts terminal flower buds in the summer so they do not bloom the following year and sometimes kills leaf buds and twigs. Prune out and destroy all diseased material. Spray with Bordeaux mixture after blossoming.

What bores holes in my mollis azalea? It goes in near the ground and comes out at the top of the branches. Probably the azalea stem borer, but this starts at the top and works down. The beetle lays its eggs near the tip and the young larvae enter near the leaf node and bore down through the twig into the crown. Cut off dead and dying tips; inject borer paste into holes showing sawdust.

My azalea plants (outdoors) have been attacked by lacebugs. How can I get rid of them? (New Jersey.) Spray with malathion, Orthene, or carbaryl when the young nymphs hatch, usually in early June. There are 2 or 3 broods of the azalea lacebug, and it may be necessary to spray at 3-week intervals. Cover the undersurface of the leaves very thoroughly. The sucking of lacebugs turns the leaves of evergreen azaleas coffee-colored and those of deciduous varieties whitish.

What kills black aphids on azaleas? (New Jersey.) Aphids are not ordinarily as common on azaleas as on other hosts, but they may be killed with the usual malathion spray or any other contact insecticide.

When and with what do I spray azaleas for spider mite and other pests? (West Virginia.) Spray with Kelthane for spider mites. (See above for other pests.)

What causes the leaves to drop on a webby string from an azalea house plant? Is dry sulfur good for this? This is probably the work of spider mites. Water is more important than sulfur. If the plants are bathed frequently, or treated with a fine mist spray from an atomizer, and kept under sufficiently humid and cool conditions, mites will never have a chance to cause this much damage. After the plant has been thoroughly washed and dried, spray with Kelthane.

In late August or early September, I found large caterpillars that seemed to defoliate my azaleas overnight. What were they and how can I prevent it next time? (Virginia.) Caterpillars about 1½ inches long that feed voraciously like that must be azalea caterpillars. The apparent onslaught is because they are nearly full grown and consume large quantities of food. As young larvae, the caterpillars are inconspicuous and consume less foliage over a period of time. Sevin will control them most effectively when small. Careful surveillance during early and mid-August is necessary to detect this pest early. It is not possible to predict if and on which plants it might occur next year.

BEGONIA

What makes the leaves of begonia turn brown on the edge and get lifeless? Perhaps unfavorable environment and perhaps injury from leaf nematodes, which cause irregular brown blotches, enlarging until the leaf curls up and drops. Prune off and burn infested portions; do not let the leaves of two plants touch; water from below instead of wetting the foliage. The nematodes will be killed if potted plants are submerged in hot water held at 115° to 118° F. for 3 minutes, but this may cause injury and is more for the commercial grower than the home grower.

Dry spots form on the leaves of my begonias until they are almost eaten up. What is the cause and the treatment? Possibly sunscald, possibly the leaf nematode just discussed, and possibly lack of humidity.

I have a calla begonia, healthy a month ago, now with leaves withering and tops of new branches falling off. Why? (Wisconsin.) This is probably due to unfavorable environmental conditions rather than any specific organism. The calla-lily begonia is conceded to be difficult. Cool, moist air, fairly dry soil, and watering only from the saucer are recommended. Allow the soil to dry out between waterings.

When my tuberous begonia was budded to bloom, the leaves, then the stalk, turned brown and dropped. What was the trouble? (Nebraska.) It is hard to be sure without personal inspection, but there is a soil fungus, pythium, which causes a stem rot and may produce a soft rot and collapse of the crown and stalk. Avoid crowding the plants. Do not replant in infected soil without sterilizing.

A tuberous begonia rotted after a promising start. It wasn't overwatered. What could we have done wrong? (Ohio.) Tuberous begonias are sometimes attacked by larvae of the black vine weevil, which destroy the roots, so that the plants wilt and die. If the white grubs are found in the soil and if a good root system exists, knock the soil off the roots and repot. No insecticide is labeled for this pest.

What blight or insect attacks tuberous begonias to keep them from developing properly? (New York.) Insufficient light may be responsible, even though these are shade-tolerant plants. The cyclamen mite or possibly thrips may cause deformation. Frequent spraying with Kelthane before blooming may be of some benefit.

What spray shall I use for plant lice on a Lorraine begonia? Malathion before flowering; pyrethrum while in bloom.

What is the tiny white or transparent worm that gets in the stalks and roots of begonias? It is probably only a scavenger worm feeding on tissues rotting from some other cause, possibly a fungus stem rot. If the plant is this far decayed, you should start over with a healthy plant in fresh soil.

What causes a sticky sediment on my begonia? It is honeydew, secreted by sucking insects, aphids, mealybugs, or whiteflies.

BIRCH (BETULA)

How can white birches be protected against a small worm that gets between the layers of the leaves? (New York.) This is the birch leafminer, which causes a brown blotch on the outer half of the leaf. The worm is the larval stage of a black sawfly. Spray with carbaryl, Orthene, or malathion as soon as leaves are fully out. Or apply a systemic chemical to the soil, following the directions on the container.

How can I stop insects from eating the leaves of a cut-leaf birch? (New York.) The birch aphid sucks the sap from the leaves of a cutleaved birch and may be controlled with malathion or Orthene spray. Cankerworms chew holes in birch leaves in May. Spray with carbaryl or methoxychlor.

How can I eliminate bronze birch borer from a weeping birch? (New York.) The flat-headed, light-colored grubs, ½ to 1 inch long, make winding galleries underneath the bark; the adult beetles feed on the foliage. Trees growing under adverse conditions may die. Treat the bark of larger upper branches with lindane. See that trees are well fed and watered.

BITTERSWEET (CELASTRUS)

What is the treatment for scale on Oriental bittersweet? The euonymus scale often covers bittersweet vines with a heavy infestation of slim white male scales and darker, rounder females. Spray before growth starts with a dormant oil, at a 1 to 25 dilution. Spray again in the summer, when your scales hatch, with malathion.

BOXWOOD (BUXUS)

What is good for boxwood with white scale? The leaves are dying on most of the bush and spreading to others. (D.C.) Oystershell scale may infest boxwood, but it is dark brown or gray in color. You may refer to nectria canker, a serious fungus disease that kills the leaves and twigs and produces pinkish-white spore pustules on the backs of the leaves and on the stems. Your area has been invaded by wax scale. It is white, ¼ inch across, and round. Spray with Sevin the second week in June.

How do you control boxwood canker? (New Jersey.) Chiefly by sanitary measures: cleaning out old leaves and dead twigs twice a year and getting rid of all material that can hold moisture. Never water boxwood so that the foliage is wet for long periods. Try a spray of Bordeaux mixture in the spring or summer. Direct the spray into the interior of the bush.

What should I do for my young boxwood, which is dying by degrees? (North Carolina.) Probably the canker disease just discussed is responsible, or possibly nematodes. This is somewhat more prevalent farther north, but it is sometimes serious in your state. Clean it out; avoid prolonged wetting of the foliage. Spray with Bordeaux 3 to 4 times during the spring and summer.

What treatment will keep boxwood leaves from turning brown? (Delaware.) Winter injury, nectria canker, serious infestations of scale, nematodes, or leafminers will all cause brown, unhealthy foliage. Winter protection and sanitary measures are most important.

What about the orange flies that come on boxwood in May? (Connecticut.) These are the adults of the boxwood leafminer. Spray with diazinon when the flies first begin to emerge or with dimethoate or diazinon in mid-June after the eggs have hatched.

What shall I do for red spider on boxwood bushes? (Tennessee.) Spider mites turn the leaves a light, unhealthy color. Spraying with a miticide, as recommended under azaleas, should be effective.

BROWALLIA

How do you treat the black spotty disease that infects the foliage of browallia? (Mississippi.) Smut has been reported on this host and would make black sooty masses over the leaves. The best thing to do would be to remove the smutted leaves. However, you may merely be having sooty mold growing in insect honeydew, in which case you use contact sprays for the insects.

BULBS

What formulas have been used with known success in combating fungus diseases of newly planted bulbs? The most successful formula is to plant clean, healthy bulbs. Look them over carefully and discard any that show signs of black sclerotia, small, flat, hard bodies under the outer scales. Discard diseased bulbs. Plant in a new location or in treated soil if you have been previously troubled with much disease.

How can ants be destroyed that occur in clumps of bulbs? (Alabama.) Soak a malathion, diazinon, or Dursban solution around the bulbs. (See also Ants.)

What are the minute white worms found in and around rotting bulbs? Do they cause the decay or are they scavengers that are cleaning up? (Minnesota.) They are scavengers, doing their appointed job. Don't worry about them, but do hunt for the primary cause of the rotting.

CACTI

What shall I do for white furry web spots on small spiny cactus? The spots are probably mealybugs, which can be removed with a toothpick or small brush; by washing off with water applied as a fine spray; by spraying with an aerosol bomb, Orthene, or with malathion, using caution. (See House Plants.)

How do you control mealybugs on cacti too spiny to use a brush on? Use an aerosol bomb or spray as recommended above.

How do you cure cactus scab? Maybe you refer to a corky spot due to unfavorable conditions, often prevented by increasing light and decreasing humidity, but perhaps you are describing scale. Remove scale with a brush dipped in a malathion solution or scrape off with a small piece of wood.

What causes prickly-pear cactus to get a white fungus or mold on it, and what can be done to prevent it? (Texas.) A white mold is rather improbable on cactus. You may be describing mealybugs; or possibly one of the scale insects common on prickly-pear cactus. (See previous questions for control.)

My Christmas cactus is covered with a web and large pieces drop off. How can I prevent this? The web is probably produced by red spider mites, which flourish in a dry atmosphere. The Christmas cactus does not need to be kept as dry as other cacti and should be frequently syringed with water to keep spider mites in check. Try also spraying with an aerosol plant bomb containing a miticide.

How can I use sulfur on cactus with mildew?   True mildew, a white powdery coating, would not be common on cactus. Perhaps you have a rot encouraged by overwatering. Cut out the diseased portions and dust the cut surfaces with captan. Reduce watering.

What is the cause of cactus plants dying off at the base?   Probably too much water. Cacti are very subject to rot caused by fungi that flourish in the presence of moisture. Infection often starts through wounds, which should be avoided as much as possible. Water the plants sparingly.

How do you overcome silver and brown rust on cactus?   This "rust" is more likely due to unfavorable light conditions than to a fungus. Increasing the light and decreasing the humidity may help.

CALADIUM

Worms have appeared in my caladium plant and all the brightly colored leaves have withered and died. What can be done?   Probably nothing at this stage. Worms in the soil can be flushed out with lime water, but they do no damage except to clog the drainage holes. It sounds as if the plants had either been drowned, with the roots in too soggy soil, or else had dried out.

CALENDULA

Is there something that will kill black bugs on calendula? (Minnesota.)   Malathion, Orthene, or diazinon spray applied thoroughly and often should clear up the black aphids, which are practically inevitable on calendula.

CALLA (ZANTEDESCHIA)

Why didn't the bud on my calla-lily open?   There are only two diseases of calla-lilies: a root rot that may prevent flowering and a slimy, soft rot that starts in the rhizome and spreads up into the flower stalk. Your plant may have been infected with the root-rot fungus or some physiological condition may have prevented blooming. In either case, it would pay to start over with a fresh rhizome.

CAMELLIA

What do you do when camellias have root lice? (North Carolina.) If you are sure the trouble is root aphids and not the root-knot nematode, a weevil grub, or other pest, scoop the soil away from the trunk somewhat and pour in a solution of malathion. There are also root mealybugs. If they or root lice get too serious, you have to take up the plant, wash off the roots carefully, and replant in fresh soil.

I have a camellia that has small spots on its leaves, pinhead size. The leaves are light green and sick-looking. It is growing in a tub in a greenhouse. What can I do for it? (Texas.) The soil may be wrong or the plant may be in too strong sun or improperly watered, but the light spots indicate that the tea scale is working on the underside of the leaves. This is the most serious pest of camellias. Spray with malathion or dimethoate. Two treatments may be necessary to clean up a heavily infested plant.

CANDYTUFT (IBERIS)

What is the cause of candytuft turning white? It looks like mildew and is dying. (North Carolina.) A white rust is common on candytuft and other members of the crucifer family. White pustules appear on the underside of the leaves, which turn pale. Destroy diseased plants or plant parts and clean up cruciferous weeds, such as wild mustard. Spraying with Bordeaux mixture may help.

CANTERBURY-BELLS (CAMPANULA MEDIUM)

What can be done to prevent canterbury-bells from rotting just before blooming? (Ohio.) Possibly growing plants in a new location or disinfecting the soil with formaldehyde, perhaps merely by improving the soil texture. It might be due to winter injury.

Why don't I have success with Campanula medium? They rot away. They have a dry soil. (Delaware.) There are two soil fungi which may cause crown or stem rot under moist conditions, but your trouble may be physiological and due to insufficient water. Try another location and improve the soil with organic matter such as leafmold or peat moss.

CARNATION (DIANTHUS CARYOPHYLLUS)

What causes me to lose my clove pink? Foliage turns brown in the center of the clump and spreads until the entire bed is dead. (Tennessee.) It may be a fungus stem rot, partially controlled by spraying with captan. Try healthy cuttings or plant in a new location. They need a very well-drained soil.

Is there any pest that will cut carnations off at the joints? (Montana.) Cutworms, possibly. Try diazinon dust around the plants. A fungus, called branch rot, may girdle the nodes or joints and cause death of the branch. Remove infected parts.

What do you recommend for baby snails that feed on carnation buds? (California.) Hand-picking or a poison bait. Consult your Cooperative Extension agent for local recommendations. (See Slugs and Snails.)

My greenhouse carnations wilt and dry up. What shall I do to produce strong, healthy plants? (Rhode Island.) Several soil fungi cause wilts or stem rot, being more prevalent at high temperatures and in wet soils. Steam sterilize your greenhouse soil and bring in only healthy plants. (See also Soil Sterilization.)

What is wrong with my hardy carnations? I get them started and they bloom until August, then droop and die. (Iowa.) Are there rusty pustules on the underside of the leaves and do the leaves turn pale? If so, try zineb spray or dust to control rust. More likely, soil fungi are to blame. Try a new location. Perhaps your carnations merely dry out and require more organic matter in the soil. Or the weather may be too hot and humid.

CEDAR, RED- (See Juniper.)

CHINESE-LANTERN (PHYSALIS ALKEKENGI)

What type of insecticide will kill the striped beetles that ruin our Chinese-lanterns? They resemble cucumber bugs but are much hardier. (Minnesota.) They probably are striped cucumber beetles, which are certainly hardy but should be killed by spraying the plants with methoxychlor or carbaryl. If you want to grow cucumbers, you'd better get rid of the Chinese-lanterns entirely, because the beetles carry a virus disease, mosaic, from one host to the other.

A yellow and black bug lays eggs, hatching a slimy, sucking bug.

What will destroy these? (Michigan.) If your "bug" is spotted, it is the tortoise beetle; if striped, it is the cucumber beetle. (See above.) The "slimy" bugs are the larvae, or immature beetles. Those of the tortoise beetle carry their excreta in a pack upon their backs. Spray with methoxychlor or carbaryl.

CHRYSANTHEMUM

What causes the leaves of an outdoor chrysanthemum to curl up and turn brown? This question, in one form or another, was asked most frequently of all the pest questions. Verticillium, or fusarium wilts, septoria leafspot, or improper watering will all turn foliage brown, but in 9 cases out of 10, leaf nematodes are to blame.

What are leaf nematodes and how do they work? They are eelworms—microscopic animals that live in the soil and in wet weather swim up the stems of chrysanthemums and enter the leaves through the stomata—small mouthlike openings in the leaves. Infection begins with a yellowish-brown discoloration bounded by the larger veins, so that the discolored area is usually pie-shaped. Later the entire leaf turns brown and brittle, and may fall.

How can leaf nematodes be controlled? First, by removing seriously infested plants; next, by cutting off all chrysanthemum tops after blooming. Make cuttings or divisions only from healthy plants or clumps, and either plant in a new location or sterilize the soil with a nematocide. (See Nematodes.) Propagate only by tip cuttings if plants are possibly infested.

How do nematodes spread from one plant to another? If the leaves touch, they can swim across in wet weather. They can also be carried by the gardener on hands, tools, or clothing. Do not cultivate or handle the plants when they are wet with rain or dew.

Early in the summer my chrysanthemum plants start turning yellow on their lower leaves. The leaves turn brown and crisp. This moves up the stem until the entire plant is dead. The roots show no growth since planting. What should I do? (Utah.) This may be nematode injury, but in your state it is likely to be verticillium wilt. Start fresh with healthy plants in a new location or in sterilized soil.

How do you prevent the lower leaves on tender chrysanthemums from spotting and shriveling? (Ohio.) If your trouble starts as definite black spots, rather than brown wedges, you probably are dealing with a fungus disease, septoria leafspot, which is controlled by spraying with folpet and picking off infected leaves. If the spotting is white and powdery, it is due to the mildew fungus, and you should dust with sulfur or spray with Karathane or Benlate.

What causes my chrysanthemum plants to get black and wilted at the lower part of the plants? (New Jersey.) If you are sure it is a black wilting, it may be due to a leafspot fungus or a soil fungus. If the color is brown, it is probably the work of leaf nematodes. (See answers to the above questions.)

Will the fungus Sclerotium delphinii, which caused crown rot among hybrid delphiniums, be likely to affect chrysanthemums planted in that bed next spring? Infection is possible, since this fungus is known to occur on almost every garden plant, but the disease is far more prevalent on delphiniums. Play it safe and treat the soil with Terrachlor or Vapam this fall or very early next spring. (See Soil Sterilization.)

What do you advocate for exterminating dodder on chrysanthemum plants? (Pennsylvania.) This charming parasite seems to be increasing as a garden pest. Once a plant is entwined with the orange tendrils, there is no remedy except breaking off the parasitized plant parts before the white dodder flowers set and drop their seed for another year.

What insect causes chrysanthemums to open only partially? (Illinois.) If the foliage is not brown and crisp, suggesting leaf nematode injury, it may be the gall midge, which lives in little conical projections of the leaves and flowers. Pick off and destroy infested plant parts. A fungus disease, ray blight, also deforms flowers.

What shall I spray with to kill those little black bugs that get on chrysanthemums? (Missouri.) These are aphids, almost inevitable on chrysanthemum tips in late summer, and sometimes all summer. They are readily killed with any contact insecticide, such as diazinon, Orthene, or malathion. Spray often enough to protect the new growth.

I have a chrysanthemum plant with black insects creeping on it. If I cut the branches down, will it be all right to put it out in the garden in the spring? (D.C.) Yes, you may safely move your infested plant to the garden. Aphids are readily killed with any contact insecticide. (See the previous question.)

Each year my indoor chrysanthemum gets covered with little green bugs. How can I get rid of these pests? The green bugs are undoubtedly aphids, or plant lice. Spray with diazinon, Orthene, or malathion if they get numerous, but pure water will help in prevention. Wash the foliage frequently or apply a fine mist from an atomizer.

What can I do to prevent root aphids? (New Jersey.) Scoop out the soil from a shallow depression around each stem and pour in about a cupful of malathion, 1 tablespoon per gallon of water. Control ants.

What poison can be used in a cold frame for a small green caterpillar that eats young leaves? (New Jersey.) Spray with carbaryl or methoxychlor; keep the glass sash off until the spray has thoroughly dried.

What is the little bug like a ladybug that eats the flowers of chrysanthemums every fall? (Texas.) If the "bug" is green with black spots, it is the spotted cucumber beetle, known in your section as the diabolical diabrotica because it is so fond of so many garden flowers.

How do you eliminate diabrotica beetles? Control is difficult because sprays discolor the flowers. Pyrethrum or rotenone would be best. As a last resort, spray or dust with carbaryl or methoxychlor.

What treatment shall I use for insects that eat the centers of chrysanthemums? (Missouri.) Probably these are the 12-spotted cucumber (diabrotica) beetles discussed above.

What are the flying, hard-shelled, rather beetlelike bugs that attack some chrysanthemums during the blooming season? (Indiana.) Black-spotted green beetles are diabroticas; long, black beetles are blister beetles. For the latter, try spraying or dusting with Sevin. (See Blister Beetles.)

What do you do for a small beetle, yellow with black spots, that eats beans and chrysanthemum flowers? (New York.) The Mexican bean beetle is not ordinarily a chrysanthemum pest, but when it has devoured all the bean foliage in sight, it may seek other fields. Try spraying or dusting the chrysanthemums with rotenone or methoxychlor.

What can one use to keep grasshoppers from eating buds? (Kentucky.) Spray the chrysanthemums with diazinon or malathion after the buds form but before they flower.

What is the treatment for gall on garden chrysanthemums and the disposition of infected plants? (New York.) Assuming this is the bacterial crown gall that appears at the base of the plant, and not the gall midge, there is nothing to do for infected plants except to remove them.

Is the soil liable to harbor crown gall infection the succeeding year? Yes, the bacteria may live for some time in the soil. Plant in a new location or sterilize the soil.

What is the gall midge? A fly that lays its eggs on foliage and buds, where the larvae stimulate the formation of small conical galls. This is primarily a greenhouse pest (controlled with restricted pesticides by commercial growers only) that sometimes attacks outdoor plants. It is usually easier to remove infested chrysanthemums.

About July something attacked my chrysanthemums; they broke off about 3 inches from the ground, leaving piles of what looked like white ant eggs. What caused this? (Ohio.) The stalk borer was probably responsible, the "ant eggs" being frass excreted by the caterpillar inside the stem. When you see borer injury, it is usually too late to help the plant. Cleaning up weeds, especially in the fall, is the best prevention.

What is the round black worm around the roots of Shasta daisies? (New Jersey.)   Likely a millipede feeding on roots rotting from some other cause, perhaps a fungus stem rot. Remove the diseased plant if the roots are destroyed.

How shall I exterminate termites in beds? (Texas.)   Water with a chlordane solution into the soil around the plants.

CITRUS

How shall I control scale on dwarf citrus fruits in the house?   Spray with malathion, Orthene, or a house-plant aerosol bomb. (See House Plants and Greenhouse Plants for special precautions.)

My grapefruit tree has become infested since being taken in from the garden. Same pest is on cacti. What is it?   The infestation is probably mealybugs, which flourish on cacti. Use the same treatment as for scale.

What is the cause and cure of syrup substance on the leaves of dwarf lemon and orange?   The sticky material is a honeydew secreted by sucking insects, probably mealybugs in this case, although possibly scale insects, whiteflies, or aphids. (For control, see the previous two questions; see also House Plants and Greenhouse Plants.)

CLEMATIS

In late fall, what attacks Clematis paniculata, which has flourished like a green bay tree? Hordes of beetles practically denude the vines overnight. (Georgia.)   These are probably blister beetles. Spray with Sevin or malathion. (See also Blister Beetles.)

How can I kill blister bugs that eat my vines in the summer? (Louisiana.)   Blister beetles are more prevalent on clematis in the South than in the North. They are hard to kill, but spraying or dusting with malathion or carbaryl may be effective. Knock off the beetles into a can of bleach.

My Clematis x jackmanii climbers, after getting several feet high, wilt unexpectedly. If dry stem rot causes this, what can be done? (Wisconsin.)   It sounds like stem rot. After the fungus has girdled the stem so that the vine wilts suddenly, nothing can be done. Spraying or dusting with sulfur through the season may aid in prevention. Start cuttings from healthy plants.

COLEUS

Are mealybugs on coleus caused by too much or too little watering? Mealybugs, like most sucking insects, thrive in a dry atmosphere, but too little water cannot "cause" them. Also, if the plants are unhealthy from a waterlogged soil, they may succumb more readily to mealybug injury. Spray at the first sign of bugs with malathion, diazinon, or Orthene.

What is one to do to get rid of the soft white fungus scale on coleus? I scrape it off, but this is not drastic enough. It is neither a fungus nor a scale that you describe, but mealybugs. (See above.) Spray house plants with a house-plant aerosol bomb.

What causes blistered or puckered leaves? It sounds like the work of the cyclamen mite, which attacks so many indoor plants. (See Cyclamen.)

What can I do to stop a white moldy rot on coleus, kept as a house plant? There is no white mold on coleus, but you may have a combination of white woolly mealybugs, very common on this plant, and a black rot called "black leg" because it rots the stalks at the base. For the mealybugs, spray with Orthene or malathion; for the rot, destroy infected plants and pot new ones with fresh soil.

What causes white fungus growth? I changed the plants from glazed to clay pots, but the white growth persists. Changing the pot won't affect mealybugs on the foliage. Spray and spray again until you clean them up. (See answers to the previous questions.)

COLUMBINE (AQUILEGIA)

How can one keep the roots of aquilegia from becoming infested with worms? (Minnesota.) The worms are probably millipedes, and usually they swarm around when a plant is weakened or dead from other causes, either disease or unfavorable cultural conditions. They cause little injury, but can be controlled with a diazinon drench.

What makes hybrid columbines pass out in a perennial bed where everything else is happy? (Pennsylvania.) Hybrid columbines, like hybrid delphiniums, are usually short-lived, but sudden passing out may be due to crown rot, a fungus disease, or to the columbine borer.

What remedy will prevent crown rot? (Alabama.) Crown rot in Alabama is caused by *Sclerotium rolfsii,* a fungus that is generally prevalent in the soil and kept viable because it can attack so many different plants. Soil sterilization is difficult and not too satisfactory. Remove infected plants as soon as noticed and pour a Terrachlor solution over the area.

What about the columbine borer? This is a salmon-colored caterpillar that works in the crown of the plant. All you can do is pull up the victim and in the fall destroy all weeds and other debris that might harbor borer eggs during the winter. Protect other columbines with carbaryl or methoxychlor.

The leaves of our columbine have little silvery-white lines all over them. Could you tell me the cause? (Rhode Island.) These are the serpentine tunnels of the columbine leafminer. The larvae work inside the leaf and a small fly emerges to lay eggs for the next generation.

What is the cure for white line discolorations in leaves? (Illinois.) There is no cure, but picking off and burning all infested leaves as soon as they are noticed and cultivating the ground around the plants in the fall and early spring will help prevent further infestations. Spraying with Orthene or malathion may help.

What shall I do for plants turning brown because of a certain type of spider that gets on them? (Florida.) If this is spider mite (the tiny mite that makes webs on the underside of the leaves), try sulfur dust, but not when the temperature is so high (above 90° F.) that the sulfur will burn the foliage. Kelthane or another miticide is more effective.

COSMOS

What is the cause of cosmos turning brown and dying? (Nebraska.) It may be a bacterial wilt, but more likely a fungus stem blight. A grayish lesion girdles the stem and all parts above die. Spraying is of little value. Remove infected plants when they are noticed and pull up and destroy all tops after blooming.

CRAB APPLE (MALUS)

Why do the leaves of a Bechtel's crab curl up and drop in the summer? Bechtel's crab is peculiarly susceptible to red-cedar and apple rust, a disease prevalent over much of the country. Spores are carried from the red-cedar galls in the spring and the resulting infection of orange spots on the crab apple leaves shows up in midsummer. Defoliation follows heavy infection.

How do you prevent rust? Never plant red-cedars (*Juniperus virginiana*) and crab apples together. It is preferable not to have them on the same property, but at least get a windbreaker such as a house or trees between the two as a barrier to windborne spores. Remove red-cedar galls in the winter and early spring. Spray crab apples with sulfur and ferbam, zineb, or maneb when the leaves come out and every 10 days until July.

I have sprayed my Malus floribunda but it is always full of aphids. What can I do? (Michigan.)   Try spraying with a dormant oil spray just before the buds break. (See Dormant Spraying.) If aphids appear during the growing season, spray with malathion.

What treatment shall I give a small flowering crab? There is no new growth, the leaves shrivel, and there is a fuzzy white substance that appears at crotches and twig intersections. (Rhode Island.)   The fuzzy white substances are woolly aphids, controlled by spraying thoroughly with malathion. The tree is apparently dying from other causes—improper planting or some soil trouble.

What solution should be painted on the trunks of young flowering crab trees in March to prevent green worms from climbing up and depositing their eggs? (Illinois.)   None. No chemical should be applied directly to the trunk. If you have time and money to burn, apply a band of balsam wood and cover with Tanglefoot. This will prevent canker-worm moths from climbing the crab apples but will not stop young worms from dropping onto crab apples from nearby shade trees. Spray with carbaryl (Sevin) or methoxychlor in May in any case, for the trunk treatment reduces infection not more than 10 per cent.

CRAPE-MYRTLE (LAGERSTROEMIA INDICA)

How is mildew on crape-myrtle controlled? (Alabama.)   Either by a dormant spray of 1 to 8 lime-sulfur when the buds start swelling or by spraying with wettable sulfur, Karathane, or Benlate after growth starts. It is important to spray early; otherwise the white fungus will stunt the buds.

What spray formula will destroy the whiteflies covering my crape-myrtles, causing smut? (Louisiana.)   The smut is a fungus, sooty mold growing in the honeydew secreted by aphids. Spray after blooming with Orthene or diazinon. If whiteflies are there, use Orthene.

Every year, without fail, my crape-myrtle are beset by plant lice. Isn't there a simple cure?   Crape-myrtle has very few insect pests. However, wherever they grow, aphids are a common problem. Since aphids are winged and active, they may infest new succulent growth as it develops.

Apply aphid controls at 1- to 2-week intervals while the plants are actively growing. (See Aphids.)

CROCUS

Is there any method of preventing squirrels from eating crocus bulbs? (Massachusetts.)   Plant the bulbs in wire baskets, which can be made at home from ½-inch wire mesh. A few naphthalene flakes may act as a repellent, but too many will injure the bulbs with their fumes. Plant a lot of crocus bulbs each fall; the squirrels won't destroy all of them.

CYCLAMEN (C. PERSICUM)

What causes a cyclamen to become soft and die? I watered mine carefully through the bottom of the pot, but it died within 2 weeks.   It sounds like bacterial soft rot, usually serious only when plants are too wet, or shaded, or not well ventilated. Your plant may have been infected when it came from the greenhouse.

What would cause a cyclamen to wilt suddenly and the bulb to rot?   Probably the bacterial soft rot suggested in the previous question. Possibly a fungus disease called stunt, although here the dying is usually gradual.

What is cyclamen mite, and how does it affect the plants?   This mite is a microscopic relative of the spider mite, white to pale brown in color, that infests many varieties of ornamental plants, causing puckering, curling, or other deformation of the leaves; flower buds become blackened and distorted. If plants are kept close together, the mites can crawl from one to another. They can also be spread by hands, tools, clothing. Spraying with Kelthane will help.

DAFFODILS   (See Narcissus.)

DAHLIA

What causes dahlia roots to rot? (Florida.)   Any one of several fungus or bacterial diseases. With verticillium wilt, the lower leaves gradually lose their color, the roots are decayed, and the stem shows black streaks when cut across. With stem rot and soft bacterial rot, wilting is rather sudden.

How are the wilt diseases of dahlias cured?   There is no cure. All you can do is remove infected plants immediately and plant healthy tubers in a new location, or sterilize the soil with chloropicrin or methyl bromide.

When the tubers rot, is the soil too damp? (New York.) A heavy, wet soil encourages stem rot and bacterial wilt, but the organisms have to be present. Improving drainage and lightening the soil with sand or coal ashes will help.

There is a little brown worm about ½ inch long that eats my dahlia roots. How should I treat the ground before I plant? (Ohio.) It is probably a millipede feasting on tissues rotting from one of the wilt diseases just discussed. (See the previous questions.)

When I dig my dahlias in the fall, the tubers are almost always rotted away. Why are gray-blackish insects present? (New York.) They are probably millipedes. They look brown to some, grayish to others. They are hard, with many legs, usually coiled into a circle, and almost always scavengers feeding on rotting tissue.

My dahlia tubers are drying up and some show rot all through. How do you prevent this? (New York.) Botrytis, fusarium, and other fungi and bacteria may cause storage rots. Use care in digging to avoid wounds, store only well-matured tubers, avoid any frost damage, and keep at 40° F. in sand that is only very slightly moist. Too much moisture will increase rotting. Dusting tubers with captan before storage may help.

Some dahlia leaves have bright yellow mottling; is that mosaic, and what can be done? (Montana.) The mottling is a typical symptom of mosaic, a virus disease carried from one plant to another by aphids. There is usually dwarfing or stunting. Control aphids with contact sprays, and remove and burn infected plants.

What are the chief causes for dahlia "stunt"? (Illinois.) Either mosaic or the feeding of sucking insects, often leafhoppers, but sometimes thrips or plant bugs. Stunted dahlias are short and bushy with an excessive number of side branches. Leafhoppers cause the margins of the leaves to turn yellow, then brown and brittle—a condition known as hopper burn.

How do you control stunt caused by insects? Spray once a week with malathion, beginning early in the season and covering the underside of leaves thoroughly.

After plants are stunted, are the tubers good the following year? (New Jersey.) Yes, if the stunting was due to leafhoppers and the tubers appear sound. But if the stunting was due to mosaic, a virus disease, the tubers should be destroyed.

My miniature dahlia is full of buds, but they rot. What is the matter? (Ohio.) It may be gray mold, the same type of botrytis blight that affects peony buds. Remove all diseased buds and spray with captan. Burn all plant tops in the fall.

How can I prevent mildew? (Pennsylvania.) Dust foliage with sulfur or spray with Karathane or Benlate, especially in late summer.

If dahlias mildew badly at the end of the season, will the tubers be injured? (California.) Probably not, but mildew is a serious disease on the West Coast, and dahlias should be sprayed or dusted with one of the above fungicides.

Is the borer which attacks dahlia stalks the corn borer? (New Jersey.) Yes, if the borers are flesh-colored when young, later turning smoky or reddish. If the caterpillar is brown, striped with white, it is the common stalk borer, also a pest of corn.

What can I do to prevent borers? (Illinois.) Clean up stalks of all herbaceous plants in the fall. Include the weeds, for many of these harbor borers during the winter. Spray or dust stalks with malathion plus methoxychlor.

How do you prevent the little black flies from biting or stinging buds so that they only partially open? (Vermont.) The tarnished plant bug is brownish rather than black, but it stings and blackens the buds. Control is difficult. Keep down weeds and spray frequently with carbaryl or malathion.

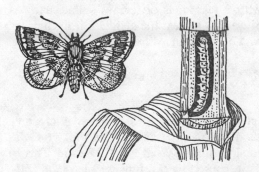

The pink larva of the European corn borer frequently attacks dahlias. The adult moth is yellowish brown.

Last summer I found a lot of black bugs and some ladybugs on my blooms. The petals had holes in them. Were the little black bugs to blame? (Texas.) The black bugs were probably aphids or plant lice, controllable by spraying with malathion. If the "ladybugs" were green instead of red, they were diabrotica or cucumber beetles and responsible for the holes. (See Chrysanthemum.)

What can I do about aphids on roots? I have tried ground tobacco. (Wisconsin.) Tobacco dust in the ground should help, but pouring a solution of malathion in a shallow depression made around each dahlia stem will be a more potent remedy.

This year grasshoppers ate our dahlia blooms. Is there any way to prevent this? (Mississippi.) Spray or dust the flowers with diazinon. Keep down weeds. (See also Grasshoppers.)

How do you rid dahlias of snails? (Michigan.) Try one of the metaldehyde or mesurol slug baits, obtainable under a commercial trade name such as Bug-geta or Slug-geta. (See also Slugs.)

Do spider mites attack dahlia plants? Yes. Spray with a miticide, such as Kelthane, being sure to cover the undersides of the leaves.

Do thrips ever attack dahlias? How may they be controlled? (Iowa.) They may infest the flowers, turning the petals whitish. Regular spraying with malathion for the control of leafhoppers may discourage infestation by thrips. (See Gladiolus.)

How do I prevent earwigs from destroying my dahlia flowers? Dust or spray your plants and the surrounding soil with diazinon, carbaryl, or malathion.

DAPHNE

The leaves of my daphne are turning yellow. Why? (California.) This may be chlorosis, due to an alkaline soil, which makes iron unavailable. Spray the leaves with 2 teaspoons of ferrous sulfate and ¼ teaspoon of glue in a quart of water. Or treat the soil with iron chelates available under trade names. Your *Daphne odora* may also be dying from armillaria root rot.

DELPHINIUM

Last summer I lost a great number of my delphiniums. A creamy, seedy substance formed around the plants, making the roots rot off. Later it spread to the phlox and buddleia. What is it? (Ohio.) This is a good description of crown rot, caused by the fungus *Sclerotium rolfsii*. White fungus threads, mycelia, form at the base of the stalk and spread over the ground. Seedlike bodies are attacked so that the plant is readily pulled up. This fungus attacks more than 100 species of ornamentals and readily spreads to the other plants in wet weather. A common name for this rot is the mustard-seed fungus.

How shall I grow delphiniums when the plants rot off at the ground

and the earth turns white and rust color? (Kansas.)   This is another
phase of crown rot. The sclerotia, which are at first cream-colored, turn
reddish or rusty as they mature, and there may be so many crowded together at the base of the plant that it seems as if the earth itself has
changed color.

How shall I keep delphiniums from getting crown rot? How can I
stop its spread to other plants? (Illinois.)   Stopping the spread immediately is very important. Dig up an infected plant as soon as noticed,
using a shovel so as to get all the surrounding soil harboring the sclerotia. If you pull up the plant and leave the sclerotia behind, they may
live for months or years, ready to infect other plants. Wrap the diseased
specimen and soil in several thicknesses of newspaper and hurry it to
the garbage pail. Treat the diseased area with Terrachlor, but don't
plant delphiniums in the same area again.

Is there any other chemical to prevent crown rot? I have tried naphthalene flakes. (Iowa.)   Naphthalene is somewhat effective in stopping
the spread of the white mycelia, but it cannot be relied on to kill the
sclerotia. Sulfur dust will likewise check the mycelial growth, and Terrachlor as a crown drench may be effective. The permanent remedy is
to sterilize the soil, when all plants have been removed, with formaldehyde. (See Soil Sterilization.)

Can delphiniums be replanted after sterilizing the soil in a bed where
others died of sclerotium rot? (New Jersey.)   Yes, if you use soil
sterilizers according to directions and wait until all the odor has disappeared from the soil before replanting—usually about 2 weeks. Naturally, put back only healthy plants. The treatment is not guaranteed; a
new location is preferable.

What makes delphiniums get a mildewed appearance and what can be
done to prevent it? (New York.)   This is powdery mildew, a fungus
appearing as a white coating on the leaves. In the East, it is seldom serious before late summer. Dust with sulfur, or spray with Benlate or
Karathane.

Is it possible to prevent mildew? (Illinois, Minnesota, Colorado.)   The mildew problem seems to increase in importance as one
goes west, until a climax is reached in California. However, many of the
new hybrid strains are fairly resistant to mildew, and spraying gives reasonable control. (See the above question.) There is no "prevention" except cleaning up all old plant material.

Why do delphiniums mildew so badly? (California.)   It's the famous
California climate, which seems to encourage mildew on delphiniums,

roses, and other plants. Try to get California strains of delphinium more or less resistant to mildew and treat as above.

How do I prevent rust and white mold? (Wisconsin.) The white mold is mildew. (See the answers to previous questions.) True rust is not very common on delphinium. Discolored patches on the leaves can be due to the broad mite or the leafminer.

How do you control black spot? This bacterial disease appears as tarlike black spots on the leaves. It is not serious except in wet seasons, when it may be controlled by spraying with Bordeaux mixture or possibly streptomycin. In a normal season, picking off infected leaves and cleaning up old stalks in autumn are sufficient.

How should dry Bordeaux mixture be diluted for spraying delphiniums when they come up in the spring? (Pennsylvania.) Use about half the strength recommended on the package, which usually gives directions for a potato spray. If your brand calls for 8 to 12 tablespoons per gallon, use 4 to 6, adding 2 tablespoons of flour to the dry powder before stirring the water in very slowly. Strain through cheesecloth into the sprayer and use *immediately*.

Is there a remedy when leaves curl and the plants fail to bloom? Those that do bloom have green blossoms. (Utah.) This is a virus disease, probably aster yellows. There is no cure except taking out infected plants as soon as noticed and spraying with contact insecticides to control the leafhoppers, the insect carriers of the virus. Such diseases are common in the Northwest.

Why do my delphiniums grow large and thrifty, have one blooming period, and then get a black rot? (Ohio.) There are various delphinium rots besides sclerotium crown rot, caused by at least 2 bacteria and several fungi. Rotting is usually worse in wet weather and with succulent tissue. Some growers feel that the act of cutting down the old stalks after blooming spreads the rot organisms.

What causes the yellowing of leaves on hybrids? When the plants were treated with nitrate of soda every 10 days, they took on a healthy green again. (Illinois.) You answered your own question: evidently your plants lacked nitrogen. But be careful about applying too much. Getting too succulent a growth will mean more rot diseases.

Why do my delphiniums turn yellow? (Indiana.) Possibly due to fusarium wilt, this fungus being common in soils in the Middle West. There is usually a progressive yellowing of leaves from the base upward. But the yellowing may also be due to crown rot, lack of nitrogen, lack of water, or intense heat. Try a new location.

What causes delphinium buds to become black and wadded up? (In-

diana.) The cyclamen mite, a light-colored relative of the spider mite too small to see with the naked eye, and a very serious pest on delphiniums. It deforms the leaves, blackens the flower buds, usually preventing bloom, and stunts the plant.

What can be done to overcome cyclamen mite on delphiniums? (Wisconsin.) Spray weekly with Kelthane. Start spraying very early in the spring. Pick off deformed parts; discard severely infested plants.

What should be done for brown spots on the underside of leaves of delphiniums? (Illinois.) If these spots are rather glassy in appearance, they are due to the broad mite, which is not as harmful as the cyclamen mite and more readily controlled with sulfur dust.

What causes blighted areas in the leaves? The larvae of leafminers feed inside the leaves, which collapse and turn brown over rather large areas, usually near the points. Remove infested leaves. Spraying with malathion may help.

Why are there red lice during blooming time? (Michigan.) Why any calamity? These are the same aphids so prevalent on annual larkspur. Spray thoroughly and frequently with malathion.

I have tried sulfur dust for the little red lice. How can I prevent them? (Michigan.) Sulfur dust will be of little benefit. You need a malathion spray.

My delphiniums always get orange lice on the underside of the leaves. When shall I start watching for them and what shall I do? (Michigan.) These aphids usually get serious toward midsummer, but sometimes appear in the spring. When the leaves start cupping downward, looking like umbrellas, you always know red aphids are underneath. Use a spray rod with an angle nozzle so you can cover the underside of the leaves.

My delphinium leaves get infested with tiny red insects. Are they red spiders? (New York.) Probably they are red aphids. Red spiders are almost too small to see with the naked eye and form a mealy cobweb on the underside of the leaves. Use malathion for aphids, Kelthane for mites.

DOGWOOD (CORNUS FLORIDA)

What can be done for bark borers on flowering dogwood trees? (New Jersey.) Twig borers can be taken care of by cutting below the infested portion, but bark borers are best prevented by wrapping newly transplanted trees in Kraft crepe paper, extending from the crown up to the first branches. Leave on for 2 years. After infestation, borers can be surgically removed, but it is not always possible to save the tree. Lindane sprayed on trunks twice in the spring and early summer will also help prevent borers, but lindane is a restricted chemical which in many states can be applied only by a professional.

I planted 2 flowering dogwoods. One died; its bark blistered, chipping off easily. Can the other tree be saved? (Ohio.)   A crown canker disease might have that effect but I do not know of it occurring in Ohio. It may have been bark borers. (See the previous question.) If you cut out all borers in the remaining tree, wrap the trunk and feed and water it, it may live.

Dogwood, pussy willow, other shrubs, and roses have some disease; they are covered with scales of a shell-like nature. The trees finally die. What is the remedy? (Maryland.)   All these and other plants are subject to attack by scale insects. There are many different types with various host preferences. Dogwood can have round scurfy scale, lecanium scale, or cottony maple scale. Oystershell scale occurs on willow and also on dogwood, as well as other shrubs and trees. Rose scale can be destructive to roses. Dormant oil sprays are effective for most scale insects, followed by a contact spray during the growing season when crawlers are active. Each species of scale insect has its own crawler period. Get a positive identification and information on crawler periods from your local Cooperative Extension Service.

ELM (ULMUS)

What is best to use for yellow striped bugs on Chinese elms in July? (Ohio.)   This is the elm leaf beetle, a chewing insect little affected by a contact insecticide. Have your trees sprayed with methoxychlor or carbaryl early in June.

What spring care can be given to an elm that gets covered with small worms, causing the leaves to turn brown and fall in midsummer? (New Jersey.)   Cankerworms chew foliage in May, but in June the dark, dragon-shaped larvae of the elm leaf beetle skeletonize the leaves, causing the browning and defoliation. Two carbaryl sprays are best: the first for cankerworms after the leaves come out in May; the second for elm leaf beetle in early June. Power spraying by a tree expert is required.

What is a practical insecticide for Siberian elms? The affliction is a black caterpillar worm that attacks the foliage. (New Jersey.)   This is the larval stage of the mourning-cloak butterfly, but it can be controlled by power spraying with carbaryl.

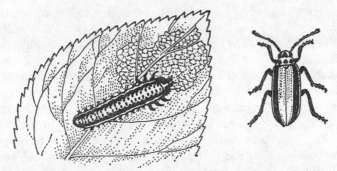

Black larva of the elm leaf beetle. The beetle has distinct yellow stripes.

What is the scale infecting the bark of my Siberian elms? (New York.)   Elm scurfy scale and 2 or 3 other scale insects may appear on elm bark, causing the death of branches and occasionally of young trees. Use a dormant oil spray before growth starts. (See also Dormant Spraying.)

Why did my elm tree give off a black secretion so that the lily bed under it looks like a city garden? (New Hampshire.)   The secretion was colorless honeydew from aphids on the elm, but when it dropped onto the lily leaves, a black fungus grew in it. (See Sooty Mold.) There is no control except spraying the elm for aphids, and the expense may not be warranted.

The leaves of our 5-year-old elm turn yellow and fall off in August. (Ohio.)   The elm leaf beetle may be the cause, or the Dutch elm disease, or cephalosporium wilt, or a virus disease common in Ohio called phloem necrosis. Call in a tree expert for diagnosis, or send specimens of twigs to your county agent at your Cooperative Extension Service or to the Agricultural Experiment Station at Wooster.

What is the Dutch elm disease?   A wilt disease, first reported in Ohio in 1930 and in New Jersey in 1933. It is transmitted by bark beetles, which came in from Europe on elm burls imported for furniture veneer, wood for dish crates, etc. Wilting is followed by yellowing, curling, and dropping of leaves. When the twigs are cut across, the vessels are black, but this is also true of cephalosporium and verticillium wilts, so that laboratory cultures are needed for a true diagnosis.

Area-wide integrated control programs are most effective in keeping Dutch elm disease at a low level. Demand for and support of sound municipal control programs are essential to reduce the probability of infection for privately owned trees. The prompt removal of infected trees, pruning of dying wood in healthy trees, and spraying of healthy trees with methoxychlor will keep disease incidence low by minimizing bark beetle populations. The beetles transmit the fungus to healthy trees after breeding in dying and recently cut or killed wood. Do not keep elm for firewood unless the bark has been removed. In numerous cases, the removal of an entire large limb within a week of the first sign of wilting will prevent the fungus from systemically infecting the entire tree. The systemic fungicide benomyl (Benlate) in some cases provides preventive control and suppresses infections if treatment is timely enough. Large specimen elms can be worth thousands of dollars and well worth a professional arborist's services. Keeping trees healthy and vigorous by feeding, watering, pruning, and spraying is essential.

What causes Siberian elm trees to bleed so long after pruning? Mine have been discharging for two years. (Illinois.)   Elms are subject to a condition known as slime flux, which means a continuous exudation from wounds due to positive pressure in the sap. Often this bleeding flux has an alcoholic odor and attracts insects.

What will dry up sap flowing from a borer hole wound? (Oklahoma.)   It is slime flux. Sometimes it helps to drill a hole below the bleeding wound into the heartwood and insert a drainpipe. This carries the flux out beyond the tree trunk and gives the wound a chance to heal.

EUONYMUS

Why do the stems of my Euonymus fortunei radicans variety, 15 years old, growing against a cement garage, become white? (Massachusetts.)   Your vine is completely covered with the euonymus scale. Look closely and you will see thin white male scales, mostly on the leaves, and brownish or gray oval females on the stems. When the young scales hatch, they are yellowish and crawl slowly about, but the adults are motionless. Scale is always worse on a vine attached to a wall.

How shall I check or prevent euonymus scale?   Use a dormant oil spray in the spring before growth starts; in the summer, when young scales hatch, spray with dimethoate or carbaryl. The temperature must be above 45° F. for spring spraying. If your plant is against a wall, try to get the spray in back of the vine, close to the wall.

What is a satisfactory treatment for blight of the evergreen shrub euonymus? (Virginia.)   You probably have euonymus scale, treatment for which is given in the previous question. Sometimes, in the South and West, euonymus foliage is covered with the white coating of

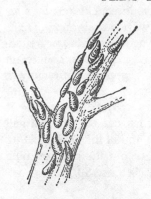

Oystershell scale, one of the most common pests on fruit trees, is controlled by spraying with a miscible oil spray (a spray that will readily mix with water).

the mildew fungus. A sulfur spray or dust will control this, but it must not be used within 30 days of an oil spray.

EVERGREEN

Is there any spray with an odor that will keep the dogs off my evergreens? (Tennessee.) There are on the market many dog repellents that may give some measure of protection.

Is there anything I can do to keep dogs off evergreens? The repellent sprays have only a fleeting effect. (Wisconsin.) Lasting and inconspicuous are the wire shrubbery guards, placed 3 or 4 around each shrub. If they are unavailable and you can spare some wire coat hangers, borrow some wire cutters and make your own guards. File one end to a point, make a right-angle bend so that the point sticks out from the tree, and put the other end in the ground.

Is it advisable to use a dormant oil spray for pines and junipers? Yes, if you have a serious infestation of scale insects. Spray only on a bright day, before new growth starts, with the temperature above 45° F., and follow manufacturer's directions for the dilution for evergreens. Oil sprays should not be used every year, but only when definitely needed. A dormant lime-sulfur spray is safer for evergreens but can be messy.

Should evergreens have a dormant spray in early spring for spider mites? (New York.) It is better to rely on Kelthane and syringing with a hose during the growing season. If you use a dormant oil spray, wait 30 days before applying any form of sulfur.

What is the most effective control measure for bagworms on evergreens? (Illinois.) If an infestation is small on one or a few shrubs, pick off and destroy the bags between fall and early spring. The easiest way is to spray plants with one of many effective insecticides or *Bacillus thuringiensis* in early to mid-June, when the worms are young. Treatments when bags become large in July and August are not very effective. (See Bagworms.) If carbaryl is used, add a miticide to counteract any mite buildup. Control is easy and effective if applied thoroughly at the proper time.

What is the best treatment for gall on evergreens? (**New York.**) It depends on the evergreen. If it is red-cedar, then cut out the rust gall before the spore horns develop; if spruce, spray to kill the aphids before new growth starts, using a malathion spray. Cut out the galls on blue spruce before they turn brown in early summer. (See also Spruce.)

Stages in the development of rust galls on red-cedar (Juniperus virginiana) *in the spring.*

What can I use to prevent grasshoppers? They are destroying the evergreens around my new home. (**Ohio.**) Grasshoppers occasionally are destructive to evergreens. Try a methoxychlor or diazinon spray.

The inside of my evergreens are brown, with their needles fallen off, but the outside looks all right. Could this be caused by grasshoppers in them all the time? (**Maryland.**) Possibly this is due to spider mite injury. If the browning occurs in late summer and fall, it is merely the natural maturing of the needles. The individual leaves of evergreens do not stay on forever, but ripen and drop off as they do on any other tree. The new outer leaves stay green while the older inside foliage is lost each year.

What feeding procedure should be followed to revive dying evergreens? (**Illinois.**) Feeding may kill them off more quickly, just like giving a large meal to a person with high fever. Have the cause of the dying evergreen diagnosed by an expert before you try to revive it by feeding.

FERN

What is wrong with a fern when it gets minute white specks all over it, and brown ones which are slightly larger? The white ones can be moved, but the brown ones are tight. This is a perfect description of the fern scale. The white bodies are male scales; the brown pear-shaped objects are female scales, which stay put. A severe infestation ruins the fern. Try spraying with malathion using ⅓ the usual dosage; repeat 3 times at 10-day intervals and wash off with a pure water spray several hours later, as malathion injures ferns. Remove badly infested fronds.

My fern is covered with brown spots and a sticky substance on the backs of leaves. A friend insists that these are not spores but living creatures. However, the spots don't move. What are they? Probably the brown soft scale or the brown hemispherical scale common on ferns. The sticky substance is honeydew. If you can't get rid of them with a brush dipped in soapsuds, try a house-plant aerosol bomb. Malathion, often used to control scales, may injure delicate ferns such as maidenhair and even Boston types. An alternative is to drench the soil with Cygon. Or spray weekly with rotenone or pyrethrum.

What is the most effective treatment for white lice on ferns? Do you mean whiteflies, those tiny mothlike creatures? See scale control in the above question.

My maidenhair fern gets brown areas on the leaves; what are the cause and cure? Nematode injury is a possibility; this may cause brownish areas in leaves, although more often they are black bands. Remove infested leaves.

I have a staghorn fern that is attacked by worms each year; they eat foliage at night and hide in the ground during the day. What will kill the worm and not affect the fern? (Florida.) This is the Florida fern caterpillar, pale green changing to black, which feeds at night, and may strip a fern in a day or two. Dusting with methoxychlor will probably be effective.

What "laces" fern leaves? We can find no insect that causes it. (Kansas.) Possibly the Florida fern caterpillar, with its nocturnal habits, has come to Kansas. (See the previous question.)

Will Bordeaux hurt Boston ferns? A weak solution of Bordeaux mixture should be fairly safe. It is sometimes recommended to control the rhizoctonia damping-off disease, which may rot the lower fronds of Boston ferns.

What causes rust on sword fern? (Washington.) Rust is a fungus disease somewhat common on outdoor ferns. In the Northwest, there are 8 fern rusts that have fir as an alternate host, causing white blisters on the fir needles. Ferns and firs should not be grown close together.

FIR (ABIES)

The lower branches of several fir trees are dying. Is this usual in this type of evergreen? (New Jersey.) There is usually a definite reason when branches die, even though it may be unfavorable location, crowding, or injury from spider mites. Lower branches of firs are occasionally infected with a fungus needle-and-twig blight. Prune out and burn infected parts.

Four beautiful Douglas-firs (Pseudotsuga menziesii) have died on our property this past year. Is it caused by an insect between the bark and wood and will it spread to more trees? (Washington.) Firs in the Northwest may succumb to various rust diseases and to the dwarf mistletoe. Bark beetles are also a possibility. The latter will spread to other trees if infested dead wood is left untreated. Call in a tree expert for exact diagnosis.

FUCHSIA

How can small whiteflies infesting fuchsias be controlled? (California.) Whiteflies seem to be inevitable on fuchsia, whether it be a greenhouse plant or grown outdoors. Spray with resmethrin or an aerosol whitefly bomb.

Black spots appear on the underside of fuchsia leaves, which turn yellow. What are the cause and remedy? There is a rust that comes in brown spots on the underside of leaves, but yellowing of leaves is probably due to sucking by whiteflies, and the black spots may be parasitized whitefly nymphs or whitefly pupae. (For control, see the previous question.)

What causes root rot in fuchsia? (Kansas.) Probably a waterlogged soil, although a verticillium wilt has been reported from fuchsias growing outdoors in California.

GAILLARDIA

How can I keep grubs out of the stems of gaillardias? Your grubs may be larvae of the common stalk borer, with the best control depending on cleaning up all weeds and woody stems in autumn. Frequent spraying with methoxychlor plus malathion may partly repel borers. (See also Dahlia.)

GARDENIA

What is the best insecticide for mealybugs on gardenias?   Probably Orthene, but malathion and diazinon are effective. (See Mealybugs.)

My gardenia has a little white speck that looks like mold, but when you mash it, it is alive. What is it?   The specks are mealybugs. Clean up the first you see, before the infestation gets serious.

How do you get rid of lice on gardenias?   You probably mean mealybugs. If you refer to aphids, the same sprays will do.

My cape-jasmine, which grows outdoors, had some sort of insect eat a fringe around the leaves, but I never can find the insect. What can I spray with? (North Carolina.)   It may have been some sort of weevil with nocturnal habits. Spray the foliage with methoxychlor.

How should I rid my gardenia plant of beetles? (New Jersey.)   It depends on the kind of beetles. Fuller's rose beetle, a gray-brown snout beetle, is sometimes reported on gardenias. It feeds at night. Spray with methoxychlor.

GERANIUM (PELARGONIUM)

Is there any way to prevent geranium stalk rot? Some of mine rot each winter, but I do not think they are too wet.   Stem rot is usually associated with poor drainage or excessive watering. Start with cuttings from healthy plants placed in fresh or sterilized sand or a growing medium.

About a third of my geranium cuttings have shriveled at the ground, turned black, and died. What is the cause?   Either a fungus or a bacterial stem rot. Take cuttings from healthy plants and place them in clean new sand. Keep them on the dry side.

What spray should be used to kill the tiny white insects on the under part of the leaves of a rose geranium?   These are whiteflies. Spray with resmethrin whitefly spray or Orthene.

My choicest pelargoniums have green bugs. How can I get rid of these pests?   Spray with malathion, diazinon, or Orthene for aphids.

After pruning geraniums and using a 45 per cent angle, the stems turn black and rot back for 4 or 5 inches. What can be done? (California.)   Try frequent pinching back instead of occasional heavy pruning. When you prune, do it close to a node and disinfect your knife between cuts in 5 per cent Formalin or denatured alcohol.

GLADIOLUS

How do I recognize thrips on my gladioli? (Wisconsin.)   The gladiolus thrips is a small slender insect, $\frac{1}{16}$ inch long and only as wide as a small needle. When young, it is yellow, but changes to black as an adult. It feeds by rasping petals and the leaf surface. It is hard to find because it hides under the leaf sheaths and inside the flowers.

What causes gladioli to fleck or get speckled and the foliage to turn whitish? (Wisconsin.)   These are typical results of thrips injury. Infested spikes may fail to bloom, or the flowers may be spotted, or they may dry and shrivel.

Does the planting of onions near the gladioli increase the possibility of thrips on the gladioli? (Illinois.)   No, the onion thrips is a different species.

What is the best spray for gladioli to avoid the difficulty caused by thrips? (New York.)   Spray or dust plants every 10 days with methoxychlor, malathion, or Orthene.

How high should gladiolus plants be before you start spraying and how often after the first time? (Wisconsin.)   Start when the plants are not more than 6 inches high and repeat weekly for about 6 weeks, or until flowering.

Why do my gladioli bloom only partially? Only 2 or 3 of the lower flowers open. Should the corms be left in the ground all winter? (Oklahoma.)   Thrips are probably to blame. Take up the corms and treat them with malathion dust. Make sure that all old tops and debris are cleaned up in the fall, since thrips may live through an Oklahoma winter. Plant in a new location if possible.

Is it harmful to next year's plants to leave thrips-infested gladiolus corms in the ground during the winter? (New York.)   In New York thrips would presumably be killed over the winter, but the corms might harbor various fungus diseases. Why not clean up?

Will it be safe to plant new gladiolus corms in the same ground affected by thrips this past summer? (Minnesota.)   I think you can rely on a Minnesota winter being cold enough to kill the thrips.

If in storing my gladiolus corms I keep the temperature near 40° F. from December 1 to March 1, will I be free of thrips?   No, you will need to treat the bulbs in storage, or else dip them before planting, or both.

I am using naphthalene flakes on my gladiolus corms this winter to check thrips. Will you tell me when, how long, and how much to use? Use malathion dust on the corms for greater safety, or soak in Lysol (1½ teaspoons to 1 gallon) for 3 hours before planting.

I lost almost 1,000 gladioli this last season. My husband refuses to use naphthalene flakes, as he says they injure the corms. How about this? They may. See the above question.

I have to store my gladioli, tigridia, and zephyranthes, side by side. Should they all be treated? (Michigan.) The gladiolus thrips does infest tigridia, its near relative. As far as I know, the gladiolus thrips has not been reported on zephyranthes.

Is Semesan good for treating gladiolus corms in the spring before planting? It has been used to control scab, a bacterial disease, but is restricted. Dust with thiram.

I have heard that soaking corms for thrips will delay blooming for 2 weeks. Is it true? (Wisconsin.) Disinfectants frequently have a slight retarding effect on growth and bloom; the length of delay varies with circumstances.

Are there any cultural practices which aid in the control of thrips? Digging early in the fall, before the corms are quite mature, and cutting off and burning the tops before the thrips can work down into the corms will help.

When bulbs are taken from the ground, a brown scale or spot appears. Is this a disease, and what steps may be taken? (Virginia.) This is probably scab, a bacterial disease that shows as circular black depressions with a raised margin. Clean off husks before planting in the spring. Discard corms where the scab has gone through to the corm itself and dust the rest with thiram.

The tips of the leaves start turning brown, and this continues down the stem until the plant dies and the corms rot. What will correct this? (Indiana.) This may be scab, although usually there are definite spots on the leaves. It may also be dry rot, a fungus disease that turns the leaves yellow and produces dark sunken lesions on the corms and root decay. Discard all spotted corms, treat before planting, and, if possible, practice a 4-year rotation—that is, do not replant gladioli in infected soil before 4 years.

How do you treat gladiolus corms for fusarium yellows? (Indiana.) You can't entirely prevent yellows by corm treatment. The fungus lives in the soil and is widely distributed throughout the Middle West. Some varieties are more resistant than others. Wait at least 4 years before replanting gladioli on diseased soil. Use only corms that bear cormels; treat as for scab.

If space is limited and you must replant gladiolus corms in the same place, is there any way of inoculating the soil against disease and thrips? (Mississippi.) You can't inoculate it, but you can disinfect a small area with soil sterilizers. (See Soil Sterilization.)

GLOXINIA (SINNINGIA SPECIOSA)

What causes gloxinia buds to blast when nicely started?   Sometimes a gray mold fungus, botrytis, of the same genus that causes peony buds to blast. Usually poor ventilation and excessive humidity are contributing causes. Remove all diseased parts as soon as noticed.

GOLDEN GLOW (RUDBECKIA)

My golden glow was eaten this year by beetles, light green with black spots. What were they? (Kansas.)   These were diabrotica, or spotted cucumber beetles. Dust with methoxychlor or spray with carbaryl.

GOURDS

How can I keep insects from ruining fancy gourds? (Georgia.)   Gourds are afflicted by the same pests and diseases as cucumbers. A combination spray of methoxychlor, malathion, and captan should take care of wilt, borers, cucumber beetles, aphids, and whiteflies more or less successfully. Start spraying when the plants are small and repeat at 10-day to 2-week intervals. For chewing insects alone, methoxychlor may be used as a spray or dust. Wipe the gourds with a disinfectant to prevent spotting after harvest.

HACKBERRY (CELTIS)

How can leaf galls in hackberry trees be eradicated? (Colorado.)   These galls are caused by plant lice. Spray with malathion or Orthene when the leaves are half out.

HAWTHORN (CRATAEGUS)

With what should red hawthorns be sprayed when red-cedars sur-

round them? (New York.)   Spray several times during May with wettable sulfur and ferbam.

What should I do about a sort of mildew that turns the leaves on my English hawthorn yellow and causes them to fall in midsummer? (Iowa.)   The orange rust will cause defoliation, and so will a fungus leafspot, to be controlled by spraying with zineb in May. If you have true mildew, a white coating on the leaves and buds, spray with Karathane or Benlate before the buds open and after the petals have fallen.

What is the remedy for the lesser borer in the trunk of Paul's scarlet hawthorn?   I am not sure which borer you mean. If it is one that brings sawdust to the mouth of holes, you can gas it with a few drops of Borerkil, sealing up the hole with putty or gum. If it is the flatheaded borer, keep your tree growing vigorously, paint pruning scars and other wounds, and treat with lindane to prevent future attacks.

HELENIUM

What shall I do for white grubs in the roots of helenium? (Michigan.)   There is not much you can do for plants where the roots are already eaten off. White grubs are usually worse in land recently taken over from sod. Perhaps you can transplant your heleniums to a bed that has been in cultivation for a long time. Spading a bed and leaving it rough during the winter will kill grubs. You can dust or spray diazinon or Dursban on the soil as a preventive measure.

What about the black "bugs" on helenium? (New Jersey.)   The chief offenders are small black snout beetles, which start chewing the young shoots in early spring and often keep working until flowering. Frequent spraying with methoxychlor keeps them fairly well in check. Later in the summer, black aphids may appear. You can add malathion to the spray or use a separate application of malathion.

HEMLOCK (TSUGA)

The hemlock branches turned brown and died until 4 or 5 had to be cut off. What can be the cause? (Tennessee.)   It might be spruce mite injury, or a fungus blight. You can dust with sulfur or spray with Kelthane for the former; for the latter, you can only cut out and burn the infected limbs.

HIBISCUS

What makes the leaves on Chinese hibiscus dry up and fall off? It is hard to say. There is a fungus blight, a stem rot, and a leafspot which might have such symptoms, but your trouble is more likely one of water relations—either too dry soil or one waterlogged from overwatering.

The buds on my hibiscus formed but before blossoming turned brown and dropped off. Why? (Maine.) If you had a spell of rainy weather, it might have been botrytis blight, gray mold, which possibly might have been prevented by spraying with captan.

HICKORY (CARYA OVATA)

What spray will kill the grubs that get in hickory nuts? (Ohio.) These are the larvae of the hickory-nut weevil in all probability. Spraying has not been recommended for the control of this pest. The larvae leave the nuts in the late fall and pass the winter in the soil, and it has been suggested that harvesting early may prevent them from producing weevils for another year.

HOLLYHOCK (ALCEA ROSEA)

What is the cause of the rusting, yellowing, and dropping of foliage of hollyhocks? (Maine.) Rust is due to the rust fungus, which produces its spores in little reddish pustules on the underside of the leaves. Yellow areas appear on the upper surface, and with a bad case of rust, the leaves turn yellow, wither, and may fall off. There are usually rust lesions on the stem as well as on the leaves.

Is there any way to prevent rust on hollyhocks? (Connecticut.) Remove infected leaves as soon as noticed, and clean up all old stalks and leaves in the fall. Dust with sulfur and ferbam or spray with zineb starting in early spring, being careful to cover the undersurface of the leaves.

I used dusting sulfur early on my hollyhocks but was unable to get more. What else could be used in place of it? (Maine.) Zineb.

My hollyhocks rot. Why? I've put cinders, lime, and peat moss in the soil, as the area is damp. (New Jersey.) Haven't you any well-drained place that has ordinary good garden soil? Any self-respecting plant might rot in such a mixture. Sand is the only thing you haven't tried, and that might work. Don't forget that hollyhocks are biennials. They usually die naturally after blooming.

HONEY LOCUST (GLEDITSIA TRIACANTHOS)

During July the leaves of my thornless honey locust gradually turn brown followed by severe leaf drop. What's the problem? This problem is widespread in the more temperate parts of the United States. It is caused by the honey locust mite, which quickly develops destructive populations beginning in mid-June. By spraying with Kelthane in late June or early July, leaf browning and defoliation can be prevented.

There has been some twig dieback on my two specimen honey locusts. I noticed that for 2 or 3 years the foliage had become increasingly webbed and brown as summer progressed each year. Is there any connection and what webs the leaves? (Virginia.) The mimosa webworm likes honey locust as well if not better than mimosa, which is on the decline due to mimosa blight. It is a moth in the adult stage, but the damage is caused by a small, green, half-inch-long, wriggly caterpillar. It can be controlled readily with carbaryl, diazinon, or Orthene in late June. Two or three generations occur, so a second spray would be advisable in late July or early August.

There are little nutlike growths on my honey locust where leaves should be. What is it? (New York.) Honey locust pod gall midge incites this growth. Though not severely destructive, it can be controlled with 2 or 3 biweekly sprays of diazinon beginning in early May.

HONEYSUCKLE (LONICERA)

How can I exterminate aphids on honeysuckle? (Kentucky.) It is rather difficult, for the aphids congregate on the young shoots in great numbers and dwarf the leaves. Even the flower buds may be injured. Spray frequently with malathion; start when you see the first few aphids and not the first few hundred.

HOSTA

My hosta last fall looked lacelike, the leaves were so badly eaten. What is the cause and what shall I do? (Ohio.) Slugs will have this effect on hosta leaves. A metaldehyde or mesurol bait is recommended, or beer in saucers. (See Slugs.)

HOUSE AND GREENHOUSE PLANTS

What are the white plant lice that look like cotton that appear on house plants? These are mealybugs, sucking insects like aphids. They are prevalent in greenhouses and on many house plants—coleus, croton, cactus, crassula, gardenia, poinsettia, rubber plant, and many others. A severe infestation is evidence of neglect.

What can be done to rid house plants of woolly aphids? These are mealybugs. It is easier to prevent them than get rid of them. Keep your plants frequently syringed or washed in a not too hot or dry atmosphere. Remove the first bit of white fluff you see with a tiny cotton swab wrapped around a toothpick and dipped in alcohol (omit the alcohol for cactus). Try a house-plant aerosol bomb.

How do you rid house plants of the white mealybug that leaves a sticky substance on the leaves? The sticky substance is honeydew, secreted by various sucking insects. If mealybugs get started despite your picking them off, spray with Orthene or malathion. Have the plants somewhat shaded from the sun and rinse with pure water several hours later. Malathion may injure crassula and some ferns; try a rotenone-pyrethrum aerosol bomb.

Should house plants with mealybugs be repotted after control? It is not necessary if you got control; if you did not, repotting would do no good. Of course, repot your plants if their growth requires it.

Do you know a home remedy good for plant lice? Just ordinary soap and water will do, but spraying is preferable. Aphids are not hard to kill if they are sprayed frequently. Or use a house-plant aerosol bomb.

My house plants show a brown scale and a sticky substance. Can the scale be avoided by treating the sticky substance? It's the other way around. You treat the scale and then it can no longer secrete the honeydew. Wash scales off in a strong soap solution, scrubbing them off with a brush, and then spray with malathion or Orthene spray, as used for aphids.

We are bothered with very small white bugs that suck the underside of leaves; when the plant is shaken, they fly off and settle back again. What are they? These are whiteflies. Spray the plants in the morning, before the flies get active, with resmethrin or Orthene, hitting the underside of the leaves.

What can you use to get rid of little white maggots in the soil? These are fly maggots, often present in soil with much humus or plants fed with organic fertilizers. Water the plants with a solution of malathion. Or the soil may be baked before using for potting.

What causes the small black flies on house plants, similar to fruit flies?   These breed from the maggots or eggs that came in with the potting soil. Some recommend watering the soil with lime water as for earthworms, or working in tobacco dust, or watering in any contact insecticide.

Is there any way to keep red spider off my indoor plants, other than constantly washing them off under running water?   A frequent bath is the best way to keep spider mites in check. A Kelthane spray, or houseplant aerosol bomb containing a miticide, will help fight spider mites, as will avoiding too dry an atmosphere.

How do you get rid of red spider in a greenhouse?   Frequent syringing with pure water is helpful and this may be followed with a sulfur dust. However, too much syringing in a greenhouse is often accompanied by increased plant disease, in which case spraying with a miticide or using an aerosol or smoke bomb would be more satisfactory.

A small insect inhabiting my greenhouse looks like a crab, and spins a web from leaf to leaf. I have tried dusting and the force of plain water. What shall I use?   If very small and if the leaves are turning yellowish, they may be spider mites. Otherwise they are probably some species of spider, harmless to plants.

Can insects, scale, etc., be controlled in a small greenhouse by fumigating only?   You will probably have to supplement with some spraying or aerosol smoke bombs. Nicotine fumigation is effective against aphids and does fairly well for thrips, but is not so good for whitefly and scale.

Is there a way to destroy angleworms in a potted plant?   Dust the surface of the soil with hydrated lime and water it in, or else water the plants with lime water. Earthworms do no damage in themselves, but they can clog up the drainage hole.

I am having trouble with soil nematodes in my house-plant soil. Can you recommend a procedure to be used on a small scale?   Dispose of infested soil and use sterilized soil or soilless mixes available in garden stores. Small batches of garden soil or used soil from pots can be baked in a preheated oven for 1 hour at 200° F. (See Soil Sterilization.)

What is the yellowish-brown scale that forms on the top of soil in pots?   An indication that your soil needs cultivating and a little oxygen allowed to get into it. Scratch it up with the tines of an old fork.

My jade plant, peperomia, and some others have a rust on the underside of the leaves. What is it?   Probably not an organic disease as much as a reaction to the environment, possibly too much water and not enough oxygen in the soil.

What causes powdery mildew to appear on house plants? This is a fungus growth that usually comes only when plants are kept in a too moist atmosphere—something that seldom happens with house plants. Dusting sulfur or a house-plant aerosol containing a fungicide for mildew will control it.

What will destroy or prevent wiggle-tails, or mosquitoes, in a water garden or pots in the greenhouse without injuring the plants? Try spraying with pyrethrum or rotenone. Do not let water stand in cans, pots, or other containers around the yard.

HYDRANGEA

What shall I use on my hydrangeas to prevent brown spots on the leaves? (Texas.) To control leafspot, spray with captan or zineb. Remove infected leaves.

What solution should be used for mildew on hydrangeas, or should the soil be treated? (Texas.) Treating the soil won't do any good for mildew. Dust with fine dusting sulfur or spray with Karathane or Benlate. Spraying with potassium sulfide has sometimes been recommended for the Southwest.

IMPATIENS

Why do my impatiens plants get a sticky substance on them? They have something like grains of sugar all over them. These grains of sugar may be honeydew secreted either by scale insects or aphids, but are more likely drops of exudate unrelated to insects. (See House Plants.)

IRIS

Some of my iris rhizomes are rotting. Although the shell seems dry, the inside, if opened before destruction is complete, is wet and slimy. What is this? (New York.) This is a perfect description of bacterial soft rot. You put your thumb on a supposedly firm shell only to have it sink into slimy, vile-smelling goo. The rot may start in the leaves, following punctures by young borers, and there is often a water-soaked appearance to the leaves.

What can I do to overcome soft rot in iris? (New York.) In the first place, take control measures against the borer (see below). Next, remove and destroy immediately any rotting rhizomes. Dig them out with surrounding soil and disinfect your trowel.

Will applying hydrated lime to our soil prevent the dying out and disappearance of bearded iris? (Georgia.) No. Iris is said to like lime, but so do the bacteria that cause soft rot. If the soil is slightly acid, it will deter the bacteria responsible for the disappearance of your iris.

How do you destroy the borer that attacks iris, cosmos, calendula, etc.? (Illinois.) It is not the same borer. The iris borer, a fat, flesh-colored caterpillar with a dark head, specializes in iris. In cosmos, it is probably the stalk borer. Sanitary measures are most important in getting rid of iris borers. If you are dividing the iris, do it early while the borer is still in the stalk and before it has eaten out the rhizome; in any case, before it has left the rhizome and pupated in the soil. The moth lays its eggs on old leaves and debris during the fall. Sometime in October or November, after a killing frost, clean up and burn all this old material, leaving only a clean fan of new leaves. In the spring, start spraying new growth with lindane once when first signs of feeding show on the leaves, or with dimethoate weekly for 3 to 4 applications.

Is there an effective means of controlling the iris borer? You have to start early in the spring to get the borers before they actually enter the leaves. Use dimethoate or lindane. Kill young borers already in the leaves by squeezing leaf sheaths between your thumb and finger.

What ate long holes or skeletonized my vesper iris seedlings during the summer? (New York.) My guess is that slugs were at work, but a zebra caterpillar also chews iris leaves. Spray or dust with methoxychlor for the caterpillar; use bait for slugs.

Do you know anything about the little round iris-wrecking beetle? I have fought it for years but never found it mentioned. (Connecticut.) A small, round, flat, dark weevil is said to eat iris pods and sometimes the petals. Try spraying with methoxychlor.

How can you lick thrips in iris? Does dark, rainy weather foster their growth? (Minnesota.) Thrips are especially disastrous to Japanese iris, but bearded iris may also be infested. You can try malathion or Orthene. Thrips are usually more numerous in hot, dry weather.

What is the meaning of brown spots on iris leaves? (Texas.) This is a fungus leafspot disease, usually fairly well controlled by cleaning up all old leaves in the fall, but occasionally requiring 2 or 3 applications of captan or Bordeaux mixture during the summer.

Why do iris leaves turn brown and dry during July and August? (Wyoming.) Crown or rhizome rot fungi may be the cause, or perhaps merely overcrowding and lack of water. If there are any signs of gray mold or white fungus threads with seedlike bodies, remove and destroy infected rhizomes. Sterilize the area with Vapam.

Why do my iris blooms last only 1 or 2 days and die? (Oregon.) The life span of a single iris flower is only a day or two; that's the way it is made. But if you mean that after 1 or 2 flowers come out your whole stalk withers and dies, that may be some fungus disease working at the crown, or possibly a very serious infestation of thrips.

My beautiful iris garden is being ruined by root-knot nematodes. What can I do? (Arkansas.) The root-knot nematode is one of the worst southern problems since it cannot be killed by winter cold or readily starved because it attacks so many kinds of garden plants. If you have any land that has not been growing nematode-susceptible plants, you can start a new iris garden there. You'll have to start with new rhizomes also. If you must use the same location, you can take out the iris and disinfect the soil with Vapam, methyl bromide, or ethylene dibromide. Or try Nemagon around living plants. (See Nematodes; Soil Sterilization.)

IVY, ENGLISH; GERMAN-IVY; AND GRAPE-IVY

What can be done to keep red spider from killing English ivy (Hedera helix)? Give it a weekly bath. Water is the very best deterrent for spider mites, and if the foliage is washed frequently, the creatures will never get started. If, however, the leaves are yellow and cobwebby, dip the vines in a Kelthane or other miticide solution.

My ivy gets a brown (looks like a flaxseed) sucking insect on it. I have tried repeatedly to eliminate it. What is it? If it is brown and thin, it is evidently the soft brown scale, and not the white oleander scale, which is equally common on ivy. Frequent spraying with malathion or Orthene when the young are hatching and the scales are vulnerable is supposed to keep them under control.

How do I get rid of the tiny brown slugs on the leaves of an ivy plant? These are probably scale. (See the previous question.) The best way to keep the plant free from them is to note the first one that appears and wipe it off with a soapy rag.

My English ivy was infested with scale in September; I picked off most of it and then noticed a sticky clear fluid oozing from the leaves. Is it from the scale? Yes, honeydew secreted by the insect. You will have to spray to clean it up.

My German-ivy (Senecio mikanioides) is defoliated by a minute black insect. What is it and how can I make it feel very unwelcome? It is a black aphid, very common on ivy. Spraying with, or dipping in, a solution of malathion will make this plant louse unwelcome. So will the weekly bath that keeps red spider in check.

What makes ivy plants wilt and the leaves turn yellow? Spider mites, usually encouraged by too dry an atmosphere, will cause leaves to turn yellow, but a bacterial disease, encouraged by too high humidity and too high temperatures, will also cause yellowing of leaves and sometimes their wilting if there are bacterial lesions on the petioles. This disease would be far more common in a greenhouse than in the dry air of the average home.

What causes new leaves on grape-ivy (Cissus) to dry and drop? Grape-ivy is susceptible to a fungus leafspot and dieback, which may kill the young leaves. Spraying with captan will control it. More probably your grape-ivy does not like its soil conditions. The new leaves will dry if the soil is either too wet or too dry.

JAPANESE CHERRY (PRUNUS SERRULATA)

Why did my two Japanese cherries die after the fourth blooming year? (Illinois.) It sounds as if they might have had a harmful spray. An oil spray too strong, or applied when it is too cold, can kill ornamental trees.

JUNIPER (JUNIPERUS)

What spray shall I use for juniper scale? (Pennsylvania.) If your bushes are not too close to any painted surface, spray with a 1 to 9 dilution of lime-sulfur before the new growth starts, about the first week in April in Pennsylvania. If your junipers are close to the house, this spray will discolor the paint and you should use a dormant oil or malathion during the summer. (See Dormant Spraying; also Evergreens.)

How can I keep bagworms off junipers? Does spraying do any good? (New York.) Yes. Spray with a contact insecticide or *Bacillus thuringiensis* after the young worms begin moving around with their bags and chewing, usually by mid-June. Pick off the bags during the fall and winter. (See Bagworms.)

How can I get rid of all the red spiders in my juniper? (Idaho.) Thorough spraying with Kelthane. Or dust with fine dusting sulfur. Dormant oil will work, but oil sprays sometimes injure junipers. (See Arborvitae.)

What causes my pyramid juniper to be slowly dying? The needles turn yellow-brown and drop off. Another juniper on the other side of my doorstep is just fine. (Wisconsin.) It may be spider mites, and a juniper near a wall, in a very warm place with little circulation of air, is far more susceptible to injury. The upright junipers very often get brown and unsightly in a few years, no matter what control measures are used.

Do windbreaks of Maryland pines or red-cedar trees (Juniperus virginiana) harbor diseases that may be transmitted to fruit trees nearby? (D.C.) Pines are not dangerous to orchard trees, although I am not sure what you mean by Maryland pine. Red-cedar harbors the cedar-apple rust fungus. Brown galls put out orange spore horns in the spring and infective material is carried to apples as much as a mile or more away, although the amount of infection is roughly proportionate to distance. In some apple regions, red-cedars are prohibited by law.

Some of the red-cedars in my hedge are developing brown patches; I suspect red spider. Can you prescribe a remedy? (Georgia.) It is very likely spruce mite. Try forceful spraying with Kelthane or Tedion, or occasional drenching with a strong stream of water from the hose.

LARKSPUR (CONSOLIDA)

What will kill little yellow lice on larkspur? (Arkansas.) Spray frequently with malathion.

Why does my larkspur turn yellow, soft at the base, and rot? (South Carolina.) This is probably crown rot or southern rot (due to *Sclerotium rolfsii*). Remove infected plants and soil. (See Delphinium.)

Why do my annual larkspur plants turn yellow and die just before or after the first blooms appear? (Massachusetts.) This may also be crown rot. The fungus starts working in warm, humid weather, which may coincide with the blooming time of the larkspurs. (See Delphinium for control.)

LAWN

How can I prevent neighbors' dogs from tearing up the grounds to get at moles, aside from getting rid of the moles? Why not attempt getting rid of the moles that attract the dogs? A fence around your property and a gate tightly latched may be the best solution to keep the dogs off your grass. Even if dogs are kept on leash, sometimes their owners walk them on the lawn side of the sidewalk rather than curb them.

How can I get rid of moles in the lawn? We have tried traps, the pitchfork, castor beans, cyanide gas, Mol-o-gen, and we still have the moles. (Ohio.) Traps have to be set with great care. Treat the lawn with diazinon or chlorpyrifos to eliminate grubs that attract moles. (See Moles.)

Can chinch bugs be controlled by applying tobacco dust around the edges of the lawn? (Massachusetts.) No. You have to cover the entire area very thoroughly. Use Aspon, Dursban, diazinon, or carbaryl. Make one application in June, and one in August for the second brood.

What caused white, slimy mildew spots on my lawn under red oak trees? (New Jersey.) There are several fungus diseases of turf, most common being large brown patch, dollar spot, or small brown patch, and spot blight of pythium disease. The latter may be your particular trouble. It occurs in warm, humid weather and where the air is stagnant, as it might be under an oak tree, but thiram or captan will probably check its spread. Avoid overwatering. Avoid also, in humid weather, letting the clippings remain on the grass.

What causes the half-circle formation of toadstools, killing the grass, and what can we do to correct it? (Washington.) This is a fairy ring of mushrooms rather common in lawns. The fungus mycelium starts in one spot and spreads in a circle, sending up the fruiting bodies at intervals. Fungicides are ineffective. Various chemicals have been suggested: 4 ounces of iron sulfate to 1 gallon of water; 1 ounce of potassium permanganate to 4 gallons of water; cut the grass close for several feet around the rings and wet the ground thoroughly.

LILAC (SYRINGA)

I have a gray scale on the twigs and branches of my lilacs with some branches already dead. What can I do to get rid of this pest? (Massachusetts.) If the scale is round, it could be scurfy scale, but more likely it is elongate and is oystershell scale. A dormant oil spray before buds break in the spring will help, but not eliminate it. Follow up with 1 or 2 contact sprays when the overwintering eggs hatch, usually in the end of May. This scale insect has many host plants, so have a careful look at other trees and shrubs in your yard to see if it has a start elsewhere. Remember, even when you do achieve control the dead scales will adhere to the bark for several months.

The bark on my lilacs is flaking off in large chunks, especially near

the larger crotches and on the trunk, with holes underneath the rough places. What causes this and what can I do? (New York.) Lilac borer adults (a clear-wing moth) lay their eggs on roughened bark, especially where there are wounds, branches broken off, or lawn-mower "burn." Tiny young caterpillars tunnel through the bark and bore into wood. It is important to prevent borers from getting in or reentering plants previously attacked. Three monthly sprays of lindane, beginning in mid-May, will help prevent lilac borer infestations.

How can I prevent lilac leaves from becoming mildewed during the summer? (Indiana.) The mildew, or white powdery coating over the leaves, comes from a fungus that grows over the outside of the leaves and so can be killed by dusting with fine sulfur or spraying with Benlate. Mildew usually appears in late summer. It is unsightly but has little permanent deleterious effect.

What shall I do for an insect that rolls up lilac leaves, leaving eggs and a web? Eventually the leaf is eaten through in this spot and the leaves are scalloped, but I think this is done by another insect. (Washington.) Probably 2 phases of the same insect, the lilac leaf roller, which is reported in the Puget Sound region. Spray with malathion, diazinon, or methoxychlor to kill the young larvae before the leaves are rolled.

What causes the foliage to turn brown and die shortly after blooming? Any one of several blight or leafspot fungi, a bacterial blight, a wilt from verticillium fungus in the soil, a graft blight due to grafting on privet stock, too much fertilizer, or not enough water.

Why did large lilac bushes develop black and brown spots on the leaves and fall off? Possibly a fungus disease, possibly weather, or a soil condition or graft incompatibility.

LILY (LILIUM)

What causes lily buds to have brown spots on them? (Illinois.) Presumably botrytis blight, a fungus disease, which produces oval, orange, or reddish-brown spots on the foliage, a bud blight, and sometimes stem lesions. The disease is more prevalent in rainy weather.

Can you spray the growing lilies with something to bring them through the blossoming period? (New York.) Spraying with benomyl (Benlate), or with Bordeaux mixture every 2 weeks, starting in early spring, should control botrytis blight sufficiently to obtain normal flowering. Pick off and burn each spotted leaf.

Just how does the lily-disease mosaic look on the foliage? (New

York.) The leaves of infected plants are patterned with light- and dark-green mottled areas, varying with the species. Mottling is accompanied by stunting, and leaves may die, from the base upward, prematurely.

How do you tell the difference between mosaic and chlorosis in lilies? (California.) Mosaic, the virus disease, shows up as a mottled green and yellow effect, while chlorosis, a physiological disease, often appearing in lilies grown with too much lime in heavy soil, is a yellowing of the entire leaf, except near the veins. Spraying with 0.5 per cent solution of ferrous sulfate, or applying iron chelates to the soil, will often bring back the green color.

My lilies were a complete failure last year. Leaves on gold-banded and pink-spotted varieties became yellow and twisted and the bud died. Can you advise procedures for next year? This may have been basal rot, due to a fungus, fusarium, which came to you in diseased bulbs. The lower leaves turn yellow and the plants seldom come to flowering. In buying new bulbs, make sure they are healthy. It is said that some control is obtained by immersing diseased bulbs in Formalin diluted 1 to 50.

Why do lily bulbs turn yellow and die after growing a few inches? Some never come through the ground. (Iowa.) This may be bulb rot from diseased bulbs, or stump rot, caused by phytopthora living in the soil and attacking the new growth as it emerges from the soil. Spraying with captan will help in the latter case.

What would you suggest is wrong with our regal lilies, which grow well, with firm stalks and buds, and then suddenly topple over with the stem withering halfway? (Minnesota.) There is a disease called limber neck, which seems to be due to unfavorable physiological conditions, but no one knows very much about it or how to prevent it.

Why have my Madonna lilies grown smaller and poorer in quality? They have small white insects on the bulbs when dug up. If these insects are very, very small, they are bulb mites, and doubtless responsible for your lilies getting poorer. Destroy infested bulbs; plant new ones in another place in a well-drained soil. If your insects are larger, they may be root aphids, and you may be able to kill them with a solution of malathion.

What can I use to keep bugs off lily blossoms? (Illinois.) There are several species of aphids that infest lilies, one of which, the cotton aphid, carries the mosaic virus. In addition to aphids on the buds, the leaves, especially in late summer, are very often completely covered with these plant lice. Spray with malathion, repeating as needed.

How can one protect Madonna lilies from a worm that hollows out the stem? (Indiana.) This is the common stem or stalk borer that attacks many garden plants. Clean up the weeds around and burn in the fall any plant tops suspected of harboring borers. It may be possible to save a lily in bloom by slitting the stem and killing the borer with a knife or injecting some borer paste.

How can I keep moles away from lilies? Plant bulbs in wire baskets, but moles don't eat lily bulbs, as they are carnivorous. Mice eat bulbs and are especially fond of lilies.

LOCUST (ROBINIA)

I have noticed large bulges in the bark of our flowering locust. Is this a disease? What do you suggest as a remedy? (Connecticut.) The swellings are caused by the locust borer, a devastating pest not readily controlled. The larvae live in the wood, and the adult, black, yellow-marked beetles come out in September to feed on goldenrod and lay their eggs in crevices in the locust bark. If the trunk is painted or sprayed with a lindane solution, it will kill all the young larvae that come in contact with it. This practice may be restricted to professionals in some states.

I travel the Northeast extensively and have noticed that all the black locusts along the interstate highways are brown in midsummer from New York down through western Virginia. Is this from the herbicides used along highways? (Pennsylvania.) Weed spraying is not responsible. The locust leafminer is the culprit. The larvae of that leaf beetle brown the leaves during June and July. Apparently the trees survive attack year after year, though weakened.

LUPINE (LUPINUS)

What causes a large, healthy Russell lupine plant to die late in August? (Washington.) It may have been a fungus stem, crown, or root rot, but it may also have been unfavorable soil conditions. Russell lupines have often been short-lived in this country. Some think a rather peaty soil, well supplied with organic matter and phosphorus, and testing pH 5.5 to 6.0, works best for lupines.

Can anything be done to Russell lupines to prevent aphids? I have sprayed with everything. (Massachusetts.) You can't exactly prevent aphids, but you should be able to kill the first few before they multiply with a contact insecticide such as malathion.

MAGNOLIA

My beautiful small magnolia seems to have scale. Is this usual? I sprayed with lime-sulfur last spring. Was I correct? Large blackish magnolia scales are not unusual. A dormant lime-sulfur spray at 1 to 8 dilution should have gotten the scales, but it is an unpleasant spray to use. Try a dormant oil. (See Dormant Spraying.) Crawlers of magnolia and tulip tree scales are both active on magnolia in late August and September. Spray them with malathion.

MAPLE (ACER)

Last spring, after leafing out, my Norway maple began to die out in the small branches, finally getting so thin you could see through it. What caused this? (Virginia.) Verticillium wilt, a serious fungus disease of maples, works that way, with the sudden dying of a branch. There will be green streaks, later turning black, in the sapwood. Maples sometimes recover from mild cases of wilt if the infected branches are promptly pruned out. Often, however, the tree must be removed and destroyed as quickly as possible, getting out the roots also. Plant another kind of tree in that location.

My silver maple tree is all eaten up by worms. What can be done? (New York.) If it is the green-striped maple worm, a caterpillar 1½ inches long with dark and yellow-green stripes alternating down the back, spray with carbaryl or methoxychlor when the caterpillars are young, probably in June. The forest tent caterpillar, blue-black with white diamonds, chews in May, and hence requires an earlier spraying.

What insect works on the leaves of hard maple trees? (Illinois.) The green-striped maple worm and caterpillars of the tussock moth are reported to feed on the foliage of hard maples in the Midwest.

Can you tell me how best to control maple aphids? (Massachusetts.) The Norway maple aphid, a large, greenish plant louse, not only wrinkles the leaves but drops its sticky honeydew on cars parked underneath. If you can afford it, have the tree sprayed with malathion. A tree expert with a power sprayer will be needed for large trees.

Our Japanese maple drops its leaves about the end of July; they seem to dry up. We give it plenty of water. What is the trouble? (Ohio.) It is possible to give it too much water. Aphids sometimes get so numerous that the leaves curl and dry. This maple must be sprayed cautiously, for it is susceptible to spray injury, which may cause the leaves to burn or fall. Malathion may be used on a not too hot day.

Why do the leaves of my Japanese maple get rust spots on them and roll up and fall off? (New York.) This may be sunscald or perhaps spray injury. (See the answer to the previous question.)

Is the spray used for leaf curl on peach trees injurious to dwarf red maples? (Oregon.) It depends on what was in the peach spray. Ferbam should not be injurious.

I have a bug that splits my maple tree limbs. (Ohio.) There are several maple borers, the work of any one of which would so weaken the tree that branches might be split off. The callus borer is marked by swellings and abnormal growths.

What do you do for borers? (New York.) If they are in the branches of small limbs, cut out the infested parts and burn. If the sugar maple borer is the problem, spraying with lindane may help prevent damage.

Last season we had trouble with worms under the bark of young maples, causing excessive bleeding. Is there anything we can do to prevent their appearance this season? (Ohio.) In Ohio, newly set maples are prey to the flatheaded borer. Trunks should be wrapped from the ground to the first branches with Kraft crepe paper or any good grade of wrapping paper. It may not be too late to wrap for another year.

Do maple trees normally require a yearly spraying? (New Hampshire.) One treatment with carbaryl or methoxychlor after the leaves are well out will give protection against chewing insects, such as the forest tent caterpillar or green-striped maple worm, but in some seasons of light infestation you may not need it. A yearly dormant spray is not necessary on maples, and oil sprays may even be injurious.

MARIGOLD (TAGETES)

What insect, triangular in form, spotted brown or gray, stings the tops of marigolds before buds appear so they are flat and empty? (New York.) The tarnished plant bug works on marigolds. It is oval, mottled brown, and stings the buds of many flowers. It is a sucking insect, subdued by malathion or carbaryl. Remove all nearby weeds.

Why do my dwarf marigolds turn brown and dry up after blossoming well for a month? It is not lack of water. (New York.) Perhaps you cultivate too close to them, perhaps it is a fungus stem or collar rot or wilt. If the latter, you must remove diseased plants and either sterilize the soil or use another location for your next planting.

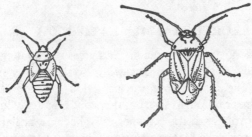

The tarnished plant bug attacks marigolds and many other garden flowers. It is triangular with brown or gray spots.

MATRIMONY-VINE (LYCIUM HALIMIFOLIUM)

What causes greenish warts on the leaves of matrimony-vines? I cannot see the insects. (Illinois.) This is a leaf gall caused by an insect you can't see because it is inside the gall. It is a mite anyway, and almost too small to see. Try spraying with Kelthane when the leaves are half out.

MONKEY-PUZZLE TREE (ARAUCARIA ARAUCANA)

What can I do for a monkey tree whose branches are turning and dropping? (Virginia.) The lower branches of the monkey-puzzle tree may be attacked by a fungus blight. All you can do is to remove dying wood.

MOUNTAIN-ASH (SORBUS)

How can I combat worms on my mountain-ash trees? They completely strip the foliage. (New York.) This is the work of the worm-like larvae of the mountain-ash sawfly, which feeds a couple of weeks ahead of the Japanese beetle. Spray with carbaryl in late May and get ahead of the worms.

What causes the leaves of my mountain-ash tree to look grayish or bronzed in June? (Virginia.) The European red mite is rather common on mountain-ash as well as fruit trees in the mid-Atlantic states and in the Northeast. A spray with Kelthane or Tedion should prevent this. Overwintering eggs on the twigs can be controlled with a dormant oil before they build up during the growing season.

MOUNTAIN-LAUREL (KALMIA LATIFOLIA)

What shall I do for blight when the leaves are spotted and burned, followed by slow death? (New Jersey.) You probably have two distinct troubles. The spotting is not often serious on mountain-laurel, but when the shrubs are brought in from the woods and stay in shady places under the drop of trees, the leafspot may become unsightly, in which case it may be controlled by spraying with zineb or ferbam. The burning is probably winter burn and sunscald, due to the drying effect of winter wind and sun. Death may be due to neither the leafspot nor the sunscald but to some unfavorable soil condition.

MYOSOTIS (FORGET-ME-NOT)

The stems of Myosotis scorpioides turned black from the soil toward their tips. What caused this? (New York.) A wilt due to a fungus, probably sclerotinia, in the soil. All you can do is remove the infected plants, digging out all surrounding soil and filling the hole with fresh soil from another location.

NARCISSUS (DAFFODIL)

What can I do to save my daffodils from destruction by a large, short grub, which eats the centers of the bulbs? (Idaho.) This is the larva, yellow-white and about ¾ inch long, of the narcissus bulb fly, which resembles a bumblebee and lays her eggs at the base of the leaves or in the neck of the bulbs. When the bulbs are taken up, infested ones will be of lighter weight and softer. Destroy those seriously infested.

Is there any specific spray for the control of the narcissus fly? Naphthalene flakes are not satisfactory. (Washington.) No, there is no spray or any satisfactory treatment for the bulbs. It is easier to burn all infested bulbs and purchase more.

My daffodil bulbs, which have been in the ground for several years, are now being destroyed by maggots. Someone gave us a lot of tankage. Would that be the cause? (New York.) The maggots are probably the larvae of the lesser bulb fly—yellowish-gray, wrinkled, about ½ inch long. There are usually several to a bulb, as opposed to the narcissus bulb fly, where there is usually one. The life history and control are about the same. The tankage did not bring your maggots but might provide a favorable medium for them, since they are not confined to living tissue. (See the previous section.)

If 'Von Sion' flowers come up green and yellow, instead of their original beautiful yellow, is the soil or the fertilizer to blame? (Georgia.) This particular narcissus often loses its original character after growing in gardens a year or two, but if the leaves were streaked with yellow along with the streaking of the flowers, you probably have mosaic, a virus disease, and the diseased individuals should be destroyed.

Why do my double white daffodils, just before opening, turn brown and black? I have tried lime, shallow and deep planting, and moist places. (New York.) These late-flowering double daffodils frequently blast before flowering. Lack of continuous moisture and hot weather have been blamed. Be careful of too much lime.

NASTURTIUM (TROPAEOLUM)

How do you control black aphids on nasturtiums? (New York.) By using malathion or other contact spray frequently, faithfully, and usually frantically. These aphids are very hard to kill. Use an angle nozzle to reach the underside of the leaves; start spraying early and continue through the season. Sometimes it seems simpler either to ignore the aphids and yellowing leaves or to omit nasturtiums.

What can I do to keep the plant lice formed by black ants off nasturtiums? (Michigan.) These black aphids (technically they are bean aphids) are not "formed" by ants and they may appear quite independently of them, but often they are protected from their natural enemies by ants, who feed on the honeydew secreted by the aphids. (For control, see the answer to the previous question.)

What do you use for cutworms among nasturtiums? (Michigan.) Not much, since paper collars are rather impractical for nasturtiums. Dursban or diazinon should be effective. (See also Cutworms; Slugs and Snails.)

OAK (QUERCUS)

My large oak is infested with borers. All summer small branches were falling off the tree and each branch had a large brownish worm. What can I do? (Connecticut.) This worm, the grub stage of a beetle, is known as the oak twig pruner because it cuts off the branches. Since the larvae winter in the fallen branches, your job is to clean up all these.

What can I do to put new life in an oak tree that was struck by light-

ning? (Maryland.)   If possible, have a tree expert go over it to note the extent of the damage, remove shattered limbs, and apply a wound dressing. Feed with a rapidly available fertilizer. Valuable trees should be equipped with lightning protectors—a very good form of insurance.

This fall there were loads of little white bugs clinging to the bark of our oak tree. Later they seemed to have disappeared. We are worried about the tree, which has not responded to treatment. (Kansas.)   These could have been the young stage of scale insects, several of which infest oak; or, if they were fluffy white bits, some sort of woolly aphid, or else, if on twigs, mealy flata (planthoppers), rather common on many trees in late summer and causing no particular damage. The poor health of your tree may be due to borers or to scale. Have it examined by a reputable tree expert.

OLEANDER (NERIUM)

How can I keep my oleanders free from insects?   Malathion will control the young, motile stages of the oleander, cottony cushion, hemispherical scales, and mealybugs. (See House Plants.)

What is destroying the leaves of my oleander shrubs in the yard? I saw some large reddish caterpillars. (Florida.)   The oleander caterpillar is often a problem and can be controlled easily with carbaryl if you find them when they are still young and small.

PALM

The soil of my potted palm seems to contain many small insects like soil lice. Do they hurt the roots and how can I destroy them?   Your description is too vague, but they sound like root aphids. Root aphids can be killed by making a depression around the plants and pouring in malathion, diluted as for spraying.

Little white spots form on the leaves of my palm. They can be washed off but reappear. What shall I do to prevent this?   The spots are probably mealybugs, or possibly one of the many species of scale. Keep the leaves syringed frequently and control ants, for they often carry around young insects. Try malathion or Orthene applications. (See House Plants.)

PANSY (VIOLA)

What can be used to prevent rabbits from eating pansies?

(Ohio.) Probably a wire fence around the pansy bed is the best method. If that is impossible, try moth balls or some other of the many repellents suggested under Rabbits.

What is the white moth, similar to the cabbage moth, that lays its eggs on pansies? These hatch into small black hairless caterpillars that eat foliage and stems; during the day they lie on the ground, climbing up the plants at night. (Washington.) You have described the sluglike larva of the violet sawfly, the adult of which is a four-winged black fly, so the moth you mention must be something else. Spray with methoxychlor or carbaryl for false slugs or sawfly larvae.

What is it that eats leaves and flowers of pansies? I have found one mahogany-colored worm with short hairs. (North Carolina.) The woolly bear caterpillar comes close to your description. It has a brown body, black at each end, and clipped hairs. It eats all kinds of garden plants. Spray or dust with methoxychlor if large numbers occur; woolly bears are seldom numerous enough to warrant spraying.

How do you prevent pansy plants raised indoors from getting infested with lice? Keep them syringed frequently. Treat with an aerosol plant bomb.

PECAN (CARYA ILLINOINENSIS)

What should I spray pecan trees with, and when? (Texas.) A suggested spray schedule lists a dormant oil spray for scale, and 4 applications of captan for scab, starting when the nuts set and repeating at 3-week intervals. Add malathion for aphids and methoxychlor or carbaryl for caterpillars and leaf-case bearers. Clean up and burn old hulls and infested nuts to control shuckworm and nut weevils. Consult your State Experiment Station or county agent through the Cooperative Extension Service.

What caused my trees to shed the pecans before they matured? (Louisiana.) Pecan scab, a fungus disease, causes the nuts to dry up and fall. Control by spraying with captan. In buying new trees, choose resistant varieties.

PENSTEMON

Why didn't my 'Garnet' penstemon bloom? The tips of the branches blighted and turned black instead of forming buds. (Texas.) Crown rot, caused in Texas by *Sclerotium rolfsii,* is common on penstemon and would blight the buds; but generally the whole plant would wilt and die. (See Crown Rot.) Penstemon likes a well-drained but not dry soil, and dies out in a year or two if not kept in full sun.

The tips of penstemon buds are webbed together and a small worm bores down the center of the stalks. What shall I do to prevent this? (Indiana.)   The tobacco bud worm reported on some garden plants is probably the pest you have. Spray thoroughly with carbaryl as the buds form. With the hydrangea leaf tier, also a bud worm, the leaves may be opened and the worm killed before it injures the flower buds.

PEONY (PAEONIA)

What causes peony buds to blight? (Michigan.)   A disease called botrytis blight, caused by *Botrytis paeoniae* and *B. cinerea,* and widely distributed across the United States. Young buds turn brown or black and fail to develop; irregular brown to black areas show on the leaves, and black pimples (sclerotia) form at the base of the stalks.

Why do stalks wilt and fall over? (Wisconsin.)   This is another symptom of botrytis blight. If the old stalks are left in the ground, the sclerotia will produce spores in the spring that infect the young shoots coming up. In wet weather, the shoots turn black and rot at the base, often being covered with a gray mold. If the weather is dry early in the season, the disease may not show up until the bud stage.

Why do peonies have brown spots on the petals? (Virginia.) Usually because of botrytis blight. The rain splashes spores from infected buds to opening blossoms, and everywhere a spore starts to germinate there is a brown spot on the petals. However, browning may also be due to thrips injury. (See Gladiolus.)

Is bud rot curable? (Wisconsin.)   Not curable, but often preventable. In the fall, cut down and destroy all peony tops, so the sclerotia cannot overwinter. With a sharp knife, cut each stalk just below the soil level. Never use the tops for mulching. Spray several times in the spring with benomyl, mancozeb, or zineb, starting when the reddish new shoots are 3 to 6 inches high, and again when 10 to 18 inches.

Why does the foliage turn black after the blooming period? (Tennessee.)   It may, in a wet season, be due to botrytis blight. Every infected bud or leaf should be cut off and every infected shoot carefully pulled up to prevent the spread of the fungus. Blackening may also be due to stem rot, a fungus disease characterized by blighted foliage, white film areas (mycelia) on the stem, and large black sclerotia in the pith.

What can be done for stem rot?   Remove the infected shoots very carefully so as not to drop out any of the sclerotia, which are formed loosely in the pith and fall out of the stalks. Destroy.

What would cause roots to rot? (Montana.) Possibly botrytis blight or stem rot; or sometimes a downy mildew which causes a wet rot of the crown. It may help to sprinkle a solution of PCNB (Terrachlor) over the soil. Peonies should not be planted in a too wet soil; if it is heavy clay, lighten it with coal ashes. Never leave manure on as a mulch so the shoots have to push up through it.

What insects or worms eat out the insides of roots? (New York.) Worms are probably millipedes feasting on tissue dying from some rot disease. They are not apt to be injurious to healthy roots. Eelworms, or root nematodes, may infest peonies and cause galls on the roots, but these worms are too small to be seen with the naked eye.

Is it natural for peonies to die during August? Should they be cut back at this time? (Wisconsin.) No, they should retain foliage all summer and not be cut back until late September or early October—just before frost. Your peonies may be afflicted with one of the diseases discussed above.

The foliage on my peonies turns a light color and looks blistered. What is wrong? What is the remedy? (Colorado.) Apparently a physiological disease called measles or edema and associated in some way with too much soil moisture or atmospheric humidity. There is no practical remedy known.

How can I control rose chafers on peonies? (Massachusetts.) There is no very satisfactory answer to this universal question. Pick off as many as you can and spray with carbaryl or methoxychlor. If it is any comfort to you, when the Japanese beetles get worse in Massachusetts, the rose chafers diminish.

Should one discourage the big black ants that come on buds? (Pennsylvania.) They do no damage themselves, but merely feed on the sweet substance exuded from the peony buds. Some authorities think they carry botrytis spores around with them.

PETUNIA

We are bothered with slugs and sowbugs eating petunia stems. We used bran bait, which killed birds but didn't kill the pests. Is there something safer to use? (Michigan.) Use mesurol bait, put it out in the evening, and place it under boards or in special traps (see Slugs and Snails) designed for the purpose so that birds cannot get at it.

The petunias in my flower boxes dry up and don't bloom well near

the end of the season. What is the trouble? (Ohio.)   It may be purely cultural difficulties—not enough water or poor soil conditions in the crowded box, but it may also be due to one or two fungi causing basal or root rots. Next time, be sure to use fresh soil.

By the end of June, insects start to eat petunia leaves in my window boxes. What kind of spray should I use, and how often? (Illinois.)   Spray with methoxychlor or carbaryl often enough to keep the new growth covered. Look for hairless caterpillars feeding after dark. It may be climbing cutworms, which can be controlled with diazinon.

PHLOX

What is the cause of phlox foliage drying up from the roots to the bloom? (Colorado, Kansas, Illinois, Michigan, Minnesota, Missouri, Ohio, Pennsylvania, Washington, Wisconsin.)   This question is almost as universal as the one about chrysanthemum foliage turning brown, and there is no real answer. It is evidently a physiological disease and not one caused by any specific organism. It may be due to a checking of the food and water movement at the point of union between current and old growth. In the fall or early spring, cut old stalks back to ground level.

Is there any remedy for phlox blight?   A liberal supply of water and cutting diseased stems back to sound wood may help. (See the above question.) Fungus leafspots may accompany the blight; these can be checked by spraying with captan, ferbam, zineb, or Bordeaux mixture.

What is the best remedy for rust? (Maryland.)   There is no rust common on phlox, gardeners all over the country notwithstanding. The reddish discoloration of the leaves termed "rust" is merely one phase of leaf blight. (For a definition of the fungus disease, see Rust.)

When our perennial phlox is in full bloom, a stalk or two in a clump suddenly shows green wilted leaves, and in a day or two the entire plant may be dead. What is the cause? (West Virginia.)   This may be the leaf blight discussed above, or death may be due to the fungus crown rot or southern blight. (See Crown Rot.)

How is mildew prevented? (New York, Texas.)   Dust or spray the foliage with Benlate or Karathane, being careful to cover the undersurface. Except for the phlox variety 'Miss Lingard', mildew on phlox in New York does not start much before July, so that treatment may be delayed until then. In Texas, start when the foliage is well out. Phlox that is crowded or shaded is more subject to mildew.

What can be done to prevent phlox from turning yellow before blooming? (Virginia.) If the foliage is really yellow (and not brown, as in leaf blight), spider mites are probably to blame. These can be seen in silken webs on the underside of the leaves. Spray with Kelthane. Frequent syringing with water or spraying with other miticides will also give control. (See Mites.)

A small, soft-bodied insect, orange with black stripes, attacks my phlox. Nothing seems to control it, and I have never been able to find out what it is. What is it? (Indiana.) Probably the phlox bug, a sucking insect with reddish or orange margins on the wings and a black stripe on the back. Kill the nymphs by spraying with malathion or carbaryl.

What shall I do for a striped flying beetle? (Virginia.) Striped cucumber beetles attack flowers. Spray or dust with carbaryl or methoxychlor.

PHOTINIA

Please tell me what causes scale on photinia, and what to do for it? (Texas.) Scale is a sucking insect. Usually, when adult, it is covered with a shell and attached to the plant, although the young scales may move around. In Texas, you can control scale by spraying with malathion when the young scales are crawling. Lacebugs are more common on photinia than scale, and can be controlled with the same spray. (See Scale Insects; Lacebugs.)

PIERIS (ANDROMEDA)

What can be done for lacebugs? (New Jersey.) Yellowed or speckled white leaves, with brownish bits of excreta on the underside, are sure signs of lacebug injury. Spray with malathion or carbaryl (Sevin) or another contact insecticide when the young bugs hatch (usually late May or early June) and repeat in 2 weeks. Pieris is most susceptible to lacebugs when in the sun. Moving the plants to partial or light shade (not *deep* shade) often helps. (See Lacebugs.)

PINE (PINUS)

There is white scale on my mugo pine. What is the proper treatment? (Iowa.) Lime-sulfur can be applied in the spring before new growth starts. If the pine is near a house, substitute dormant oil. Or spray with malathion when the young scales are in the crawling stage at the end of May and the end of July. (See Dormant Spraying.)

How can I save Scots pines that have an insect or worm in the buds? (Michigan.) The worm is the grub of the European pine-shoot moth; it emerges as a reddish, white-marked adult sometime in June. The easiest method of control on small trees is to break off and destroy the infested buds (readily told by light color, or crook, or mass of resin) before the moth comes out to lay her eggs. If the trees are too large, spray, about the middle of June and in early July, with methoxychlor and malathion or dimethoate.

Is there any control for the worm that starts boring through the new growth of pines, killing the very tops of the trees, if not found in time? (New York.) This may be the pine-shoot moth, but more likely is the white-pine weevil, the grub of which mines into and kills the leader of the tree. Cut out the infested shoot below the grubs between early June and mid-July. Remove some of the laterals and tie up one to replace the leader. Spray with lindane or Meta-Systox-R in early April.

Why are the needles chewed off my pine twigs, leaving only a brush of new growth at the tip? (New Jersey.) This is the work of a sawfly, which has become a very serious pest of pines in New Jersey. The larvae hatch from scalelike eggs on the needles in late April or the beginning of May. They work in groups and clean up one branch before moving to the next; but they feed only on the old growth, not the young needles. Spray with carbaryl at the first sign of feeding. There are many sawfly species working on pines in the spring and summer. One type webs the needles together. Spray at the first sign of feeding.

What insect works on white pine, boring small holes in the trunk? What is the treatment to save the tree? (Minnesota.) There are several bark beetles that make such holes. Treatment is difficult, and a badly infested tree should be cut and burned to prevent beetles migrating to other pines. Newly transplanted trees should have the trunks wrapped. Keep the trees fed and watered properly. (See Borers.)

What can I do to save my trees from the pine beetle? (Louisiana.) The southern pine beetle is distinguished by making pitch tubes midway up the trunk. The black turpentine beetle is at the base of the tree. Keep the trees well fed and watered, for these bark beetles work in weakened hosts.

How can pines be cleared of bagworms? (West Virginia.) Cut off all the bags you can reach. Spray with a contact insecticide or *Bacillus* when the young worms start feeding. (See Bagworms.)

What is the best insecticide for red spider? (Ohio.) Kelthane gives control of spruce mite, the common "red spider" on needled evergreens. (See Mites.)

What is the best way to get rid of white-pine rust? (Michigan.) Destroy all currants and gooseberries within 900 feet of the pines, as they serve as alternate hosts for the white-pine blister rust, probably the most important disease of this tree.

PLUM, ORNAMENTAL (PRUNUS)

I have a Prunus (pissardii) cerasifera 'Atropurpurea' which loses its leaves every summer. What causes this? How can it be corrected? (Pennsylvania.) Perhaps it was sprayed for the Japanese beetle, so prevalent on this host. This plum objects strenuously to many spray materials, dropping its leaves at the first treatment. Rotenone dust or methoxychlor will control the beetles without injuring the foliage. This tree often drops its leaves in unfavorable weather even when no spray has been used.

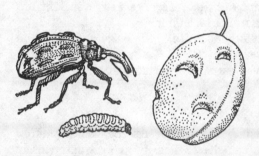

Plum curculio: a small, gray, humpbacked snout beetle.

POINSETTIA (EUPHORBIA PULCHERRIMA)

What can be done for mealybugs on poinsettias? Remove them singly with a toothpick. Spray with malathion, Orthene, or a house-plant aerosol bomb if the pest still persists. (See House Plants; Mealybugs.)

POPLAR (POPULUS NIGRA 'ITALICA')

What control is possible for a bug or beetle that works on the leaves of our Lombardy poplars? (Indiana.) If it is a yellowish beetle with black stripes or spots, and the grubs skeletonize the leaves, it is the cottonwood or poplar-leaf beetle at work. Control by spraying with methoxychlor or carbaryl in May.

A scale is forming on the trunk of our Lombardy poplar. Is there any cure? (Indiana.) The oystershell scale is common on poplar. Spray with a dormant oil, or with malathion for crawlers. (See Dormant Spraying.)

PRIVET (LIGUSTRUM)

What is the best spray for a brown scale our privet hedge gets every summer? (California.) Spray with malathion when the young are crawling. You may need to repeat the spray once or twice during the summer. A summer oil spray might help.

PYRACANTHA (FIRETHORN)

What causes the leaves of pyracantha to turn rusty brown and the berries to fall? (Texas.) Pyracantha is subject to fire blight, a bacterial disease that will suddenly kill branches. Cut diseased branches out and spray with streptomycin when in bloom. (See Fire Blight.) If the leaves are merely discolored and not dead, lacebugs may be sucking underneath. If so, spray with carbaryl or malathion.

My pyracantha has a weblike substance, with twigs and leaves in meshes on the limbs. What shall I do? (Arkansas.) It is probably pyracantha webworm. Spray with carbaryl or methoxychlor.

RHODODENDRON

How can I detect, and either prevent or destroy, rhododendron borers? (Pennsylvania.) You can detect them by the sawdust (insect frass) protruding from holes in the trunk or branches. They can be prevented by spraying the stems and trunks with lindane in early May and again in early June. (See Borers.)

How can we get rid of red aphids on rhododendrons? (New York.) Are you sure you have aphids? They are most unusual on rhododendrons. The best rule for aphids on any shrub is to spray with malathion.

What is the cause of a black film on rhododendron leaves? (New Jersey.) It is a fungus, sooty mold growing in the honeydew dropped by scale insects or aphids working on some tree overhead or nearby. There is little you can do for the rhododendrons, except scrubbing the film off. Having the trees sprayed for aphids or scales is usually expensive. Tuliptrees are the worst offenders.

How do I get rid of the pest that eats the margins of the rhododen-dron leaves? (Oregon.)   Any of several night feeders may do this, but the most important is the black vine weevil. Spraying plants and soil under the plants with chlordane in late June and 2 weeks later was the only control until it was canceled by the EPA. No insecticide is now registered, but keep in touch with your county agent for new developments.

My rhododendrons have a dry curling blight on the leaves. They eventually drop off. I have sprayed with rotenone, without results. What shall I use? (Massachusetts.)   This may be a fungus blight or canker, but it is more likely the effect of winter wind and sun. Spraying will not help in either case. Watering the rhododendrons thoroughly in the fall and providing some sort of windbreak over the winter will be most helpful.

Rhododendron leaves have dried up and turned brown. What can I do? (California.)   This can't be winter injury, as in Massachusetts, but it could be summer burning; or injury at the roots from the black vine weevil; or borer injury; or an attack of armillaria root rot; or injury from prolonged droughts. You'll have to call in some local expert for a real diagnosis, although it seems a little late to save your shrub.

What is the cause of large black spots on rhododendron leaves? The adjacent plant that gets more sun is healthy. (California.)   Sooty mold on the surface or fungus leafspots, which would be more likely to occur on a plant in the shade. It is probably not serious.

ROSE (ROSA)

The leaves of my roses have black spots. What is the cause? (New Jersey.)   The causative agent is a fungus. *Diplocarpon rosae,* which grows into the leaf and forms the black spots by its dark mycelial threads just under the cuticle. In a few days, little black pimples show up in the spots. These are the fungus fruiting bodies ready to discharge their spores, which are carried by rain or wind, by gardeners on hands, tools, or clothing, or even by beetles, to a healthy leaf. There they start another cycle if given 6 hours of continuous moisture for germination.

The leaves of roses turn yellow and all drop off before the summer is over. Why?   That's the way black spot works: first spotted leaves, then loss of color, and finally defoliation. There may also be lesions on the stems. Roses often put out a second set of leaves and lose these, too, thus weakening the plant so that it may not live through a hard winter.

What is an easy way to control black spot? (Nebraska.)   There is none. A control program means applying a summer spray or dust *weekly,* from the time the leaves come out until late frosts in the fall. It also means picking off infected leaves as soon as the spots appear.

What is an effective early spring treatment to kill the spots that may still be present on the canes? (New York.) A dormant spray of lime-sulfur, 1 to 9 dilution, just as soon as the roses are uncovered and pruned in the spring, is often recommended, but summer spraying is more helpful.

Does sulfur really control black spot? If so, how should it be applied —on the foliage or on the ground around the bushes? (Michigan.) It works very well, if used faithfully. It will do no good on the ground. Get a good dust gun and cover the plant with a fine film of dust, working from underneath and making sure that the lowest leaves are coated.

Is there a modern remedy for the prevention and cure of black spot? (Kansas.) Yes. Spray with folpet (Phaltan), Benlate, Daconil, mancozeb, or maneb. Despite the best of care, black spot is apt to show up by the end of the season. For encouragement, compare your roses with those of your neighbor who has done no dusting or spraying.

Is it harmful to pick off all leaves when all are infected? Yes, it probably is. Theoretically, you pick off every infected leaf, but this means starting early in the season and taking only an occasional one. If you wait until there is 100 per cent infection, the shock to the plant of sudden and total defoliation would be great. Pick off the worst leaves, remove all those fallen to the ground, and resolve to do better next year.

To control black spot, would it be wise to destroy all plants now in the garden and plant new stock? (West Virginia.) No, you are more than likely to get black spot with your new plants from a nursery. Buy whatever new plants you like, but do not destroy the old plants for this reason. Start your spraying program with the dormant spray.

To destroy black spot, would it help to remove 2 or 3 inches of topsoil, then sprinkle sulfur and put on new topsoil? No. This would remove some inoculum, old leaves rotting into the soil, but it might also injure some of the rose roots. Sulfur in the soil would not help much and might make the soil too acid.

Is there any way to sterilize the ground in a rose bed to prevent a recurrence of black spot? (Ohio.) No, and even if you could, the next new plant you bought could bring it back to your garden.

If rose leaves turn yellow and fall off with no sign of spot, is this black spot? (Pennsylvania.) Usually it is not. Leaves may turn yellow from too much moisture in the soil in early spring, or from drought in summer, or from nutrient deficiency.

Can cow manure cause black spot? (Virginia.) No.

Where no winter protection is required, what can be done through the winter to guard against black spot? (Maryland.) You might put on the 1 to 9 lime-sulfur spray in December, after the plants are dormant, and repeat in early March before growth starts, but this may be wasted effort. Spray regularly in summer.

Black spot has been unusually bad this year in spite of constant dusting with sulfur. Why? (Michigan.) The way the material is applied and the timing of the treatment before rains are important in control, but some seasons black spot flourishes in late summer despite the most careful control measures.

Does cold weather freeze black spot? (Indiana.) It kills the summer spores, but not the mycelia living in leaves fallen to the ground, or the special winter spores. In some states, probably including Indiana, the mycelia in lesions on the canes live through the winter and produce summer spores again the next season.

What causes mildew? (Utah.) The mildew fungus, which sends its white, felty, mycelial threads branching over the leaf or flower buds, gets its food by little rootlike suckers extending into the plant sap. The powdery effect comes from chains of summer spores growing upright from the mycelium. These spores are readily detached and carried by wind or rain to healthy leaves.

What was wrong with my polyantha roses this summer? The calyx was swollen and white, leaves wrinkled, stems white, bloom scanty. Is there danger of this spreading to a bed of hybrid teas? (Ohio.) Mildew will deform the buds, curl the leaves, and cover everything with a white coating. Ordinarily mildew is severe on certain ramblers and polyanthas in May and June, and may affect hybrid teas in late summer. If your hybrid teas are regularly sprayed with a fungicide throughout the summer, you need not unduly fear infection from the polyanthas.

Why does one of my climbing roses always have mildew, even the shoots as they come through the ground? (Missouri.) Some varieties are more susceptible than others. Either change your roses for others more resistant to mildew in your locality or make up your mind to keep them faithfully sprayed or dusted.

Can you tell me how to prevent blue mold from forming on my 'Dorothy Perkins' roses? I have cut back, every spring and fall, and sprayed, but it persists. (North Carolina.) Mildew is most persistent on 'Dorothy Perkins'. Cutting back shoots will do no good. The spores will come on the wind from somewhere. Start treating as soon as the leaves appear, and keep it up at least once a week through flowering, and occasionally thereafter. If it is a large arbor, you can probably get better coverage with a liquid spray than with a dust from a small dust gun.

What is the best treatment for white mold on rose climbers? (Massachusetts.) Benlate is very effective; Karathane and Actidione PM are specific mildewcides.

What kind of spray is effective against mold on rose buds? (California.) In California, you have a very special problem with mildew, and although sulfur dust is often recommended, spraying with Benlate or Karathane is sometimes more effective. Use a spreader and avoid spraying when temperatures are above 85° F.

How does one treat roses that build up big rust spots, like dust, on the stems of bush and buds, which finally kill the plant? (Michigan.) These dusty pustules are made up of spores of the rust fungus; they are orange early in the season, later turning dark brown. Clean up all fallen leaves; treat with dormant lime-sulfur in the spring; and spray weekly with zineb or mancozeb through the growing season.

What can be used to rid bushes of yellow fungus growth? (Wisconsin.) This is rust, which attacks the canes as well as the foliage. Prune out infected canes and follow the directions given above. Rust is prevalent in the Midwest, but is seldom seen on the East Coast, except sometimes north of Albany and Boston.

The foliage of my rambler rose is spoiled during the summer by brown spot on leaves. Spray controls this on later leaves, but the early leaves are infected while the plant is blooming and spraying then spoils the appearance of the plants. What is the trouble? (Illinois.) There are several fungus leafspots, in addition to black spot, which may occur on roses, but control would be the same. Many sprays are inconspicuous on roses and may be used during blooming.

What is the best treatment for brown canker on roses? (Ohio.) The very best treatment is to refuse to plant in your garden any rose that comes to you with its canes covered with little white spots with reddish margins. Next best is to remove all cankered canes at spring pruning, following this with the dormant lime-sulfur spray. Any treatment for black spot will reduce canker infection during the summer.

Some of my bush roses and climbers have long canes that turn brown at the ends, and eventually the entire cane dies. Why? (Illinois.) Probably due to a canker that has girdled the base of the cane and cut off the water and food supply. Or it may be winter injury. Clean out infected canes at pruning. Use the dormant lime-sulfur spray.

What causes roses, when cut back, to start getting brown on the stems, and this brown to travel down until the whole stem is dead? (Florida.) Canker fungi often follow pruning cuts, unless these cuts are clean and sharp and made close to an eye, and on a slant, so that water will not stand on the tissue. If you have much trouble, disinfect your pruning shears between cuts.

What is an effective control for peduncle necrosis, a disease quite prevalent here, chiefly in red roses? (Illinois.) Peduncle necrosis, a drooping of the flower pedicle and a reddish lesion on the upper part, seems to be some physiological disease for which no control is known. Possibly a feeding program can be developed to get these roses to hold their heads up.

What causes rose leaves to turn a pale yellowish-green, and what will prevent this? (Florida.) Spider mites will do this, but in Florida the trouble is probably too alkaline a soil, making iron unavailable. The soil can be treated with ferrous sulfate or iron chelates but it will be better to acidify the soil by adding sulfur. Send a soil sample to your State Experiment Station and ask for directions.

Why do my climbing roses turn black toward the stalk during the fall? (New York.) If roses are fed in late summer with an excess of nitrogen, so there is much succulent growth, this will turn black and soft at the first touch of frost.

Will lime-sulfur spray help roses? (New Jersey.) Sometimes, when used as a 1 to 9 dormant spray, just after pruning in the spring. It controls scale and may "burn out" overwintered cane lesions of black spot. It is not ordinarily used for a summer spray on roses.

What will kill scale on the wood of climbing roses? (Pennsylvania.) If the bushes are not against the side of a garage or a house with light paint, give the dormant 1 to 9 lime-sulfur spray. If staining painted woodwork must be avoided, substitute a dormant oil. (See Dormant Spraying.) But, in my experience, this is a poor substitute for lime-sulfur on roses.

How do you kill the green licelike "beasties"? (Pennsylvania.) The "beasties" are plant lice, or aphids, sucking insects readily killed by thorough application of most contact insecticides; malathion or Orthene is very effective, or use Meta-Systox-R.

How early should one start spraying to get rid of aphids on roses? (Michigan.) Fairly early in the spring. Since a contact insecticide is required, wait until the first few start working. Ordinarily, cool, rainy weather in the spring and the cooler weather toward fall encourage aphids, and they are not as numerous in midsummer. One cannot predict insect invasions accurately, but must be prepared to cope with them immediately.

How can roses (indoors) be freed of a small black insect pest? Malathion should take care of aphids. Try washing them off and then spraying the entire plant. (See House Plants.)

My rose garden is located near 2 old apple trees. Spraying with a rose spray twice weekly proved ineffective against a plague of whiteflies in September and October. What should I use? (Connecticut.) These whiteflies are apple leafhoppers, whose late-summer brood is often difficult to control. Try malathion, carbaryl, dimethoate, or Meta-Systox-R, directing your spray underneath the leaves. The stippled white leaves are unsightly, but there is no lasting injury from this late brood of leafhoppers. The early brood comes in May and is more readily controlled.

What is the best control of spider mites on rose leaves? (California.) No one is best. Kelthane, Tedion, Omite, or chlorobenzilate are all good, plus an occasional washing with the hose. They are most serious in enclosed gardens or on roses under overhangs where there is little air circulation.

How can I get rid of big insects on 'Paul's Scarlet'? They eat up every plant. These bugs work in pairs by the hundred. They fly. (New York.) You describe the rose chafer, sometimes called rose bug, which is a long-bodied, long-legged tan or grayish, rather soft beetle. They are often found in pairs, mating. They feed on the flowers and are a destructive pest for about 6 weeks in late May and June. Their numbers diminish with the advent of Japanese beetles.

How can one eliminate the rose chafer? (Rhode Island.) It is not easy; hand-picking is really the best control. Or spray with carbaryl (Sevin).

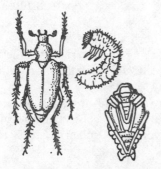

Rose chafer or rose bug is a tan beetle that attacks many garden flowers.

What is the best way to save roses from the Japanese beetle? How much insecticide is needed and when should I use it? (New York.) Carbaryl or methoxychlor in any combination spray or dust will keep rose foliage reasonably free from chewing by beetles. Pick them off the flowers. Beetles become numerous by the end of June and continue into September. To protect the new leaves, which the beetles prefer, a weekly treatment is required.

Japanese beetles destroy the buds of my roses. Should the buds be cut off shortly after they are formed, or would it be more beneficial to the stalk to leave the buds on? (Pennsylvania.) The plant does not care whether or not the buds remain; all it wants is plenty of green leaves to make more food. Leave the buds on until they show color, then cut them and enjoy them in the house. Cut in the morning or the beetle will get them before you do. Cut off fading, full-blown flowers, which attract beetles. When cutting, make a clean slanting cut just above an eye—as if you were spring pruning; it saves lots of canker trouble.

What is the Oriental beetle? What color is it; how can it be recognized and found? (Illinois.) It resembles the Japanese beetle in size and shape, but is duller in color, which varies—either light-brown, purplish-black, or mottled. The Asiatic garden beetle (another species) is copper-brown and feeds only at night. Both beetles are most dangerous in the grub stage, feeding on grass roots, and both are chiefly pests of the Atlantic seaboard.

Is the Oriental beetle the same as Fuller's rose beetle? (Oregon.) No, Fuller's rose beetle is a small gray snout beetle with grayish patches. It is also a pest of citrus trees on the West Coast. Spray with methoxychlor or malathion, and pick off by hand.

When rose buds open, you can see numerous very minute white insects running along at the bottom of the petals. What kind of disease is this? (New Jersey.) It is not a disease. The insects are thrips, usually the flower thrips, but sometimes onion or greenhouse thrips. They are rasping-sucking insects and injure the flowers rather than the foliage.

What makes my roses turn brown? Just before they open, the outside leaf is brown and dry, but if I take off the leaf, the bud will open. (Wisconsin.) Thrips very often cause roses to "ball" in this way. Sometimes the bud will open normally, and sometimes all the petals turn brown.

How are thrips on roses controlled? (New York.) Frequent spraying with malathion, dimethoate, or diazinon may help. They are hard to control. Thrips injury is usually worse in a dry season. After a wet spring, there is seldom a serious infestation of thrips in June.

I dug up some rose bushes this fall that had not thrived and found small white particles on the roots. What caused this? (New York.) If the particles were alive, you could have soaked the roots in a malathion solution, then poured the solution into the soil and replanted, for they may have been root aphids. If the particles were a fungus growth, it would have been too late to save the plants.

What is the trouble when new rose shoots die on the end and the buds dry and fall off when they are the size of small peas? (Pennsylvania.) The rose midge is to blame. The adult is a yellow-brown minute fly that lays her eggs in the leaf and flower buds; these hatch and the maggots burrow into the new growth, causing the result you describe. When each maggot reaches maturity (indicated by the orange color), it drops to the ground, where it pupates just beneath the surface and produces another midge. In warm weather, the whole life cycle takes only 10 to 12 days, so there are many generations in a season.

What is the control for rose midge? (Indiana.) DDT sprays once controlled them. Now Orthene is registered for this use. Remove infested shoots.

What can I do about the Asiatic beetle, which chews up my roses? (Michigan.) Are you sure you have the Oriental beetle? This one and its cousin, the Asiatic garden beetle, are chiefly distributed along the Atlantic seaboard and are not primarily pests of roses. Perhaps you have rose chafers or the rose curculio.

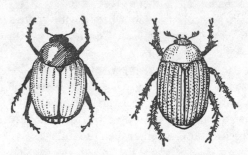

A Japanese beetle (left) and an Asiatic beetle (right).

How do I get rid of green beetles with black spots on them? They get inside my roses and ruin all the blooms. (Texas.) These are the diabrotica or 12-spotted cucumber beetles. They are controlled by the carbaryl or methoxychlor in your regular schedule.

Last year a little green worm (coiled) ate all the leaves off my roses. (Minnesota.) This is the coiled rose worm, a rose slug, controlled by spraying with carbaryl or methoxychlor and by cleaning up all decayed

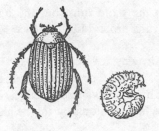

The Asiatic beetle feeds at night and attacks China-asters, zinnias, carrots, beets, peppers, and other plants. The grubs injure grass and vegetable roots.

wood and pithy stems in which the insect can hibernate during the winter.

Why do the leaves on my roses turn brown early in the summer? I find green worms on the underside; spraying does not seem to help. (Michigan.) These are rose slugs, not true slugs, but sawfly larvae, which skeletonize the leaves, eating out everything but the veins and so cause the browning. Slugs work in the early spring, starting almost as soon as the leaves come out, occasionally in midsummer, and they often have a late summer brood. Spraying will control them but good coverage is needed on the undersides of the foliage.

What kind of a pest eats holes in rose leaves and buds? (Missouri.) Perhaps the rose curculio, a red beetle with a black snout. Eggs are laid and larvae develop in the buds and young fruits, so pick off all dried buds. Spray with methoxychlor or carbaryl.

I have observed wasps chewing the edges of my rose leaves. Should I try to poison them? (Wisconsin.) This is the leaf-cutter bee taking circles from the leaf to roll into a cylinder for a nest and then coming back to cut a larger circle that fits exactly and forms the top of the nest. I am always so intrigued by the seeming intelligence of this insect—which really does little harm—I never want to poison it. It is also a good pollinator.

In pruning my roses, I found the branches dry and dead inside, and a small black beetle. What will exterminate this insect? (Oklahoma.) This is the rose cane borer or stem girdler. All that can be done is remove and burn infested shoots, cutting below the borer. Fall pruning sometimes encourages the insect. If you leave long canes in the fall and the borer works near the top, you can cut out the injured wood in the spring without any real damage to the bush.

What will kill ants around bushes and not kill the rose plants? (Missouri.) Try to find their nests and apply an insecticide. (See Ants for more suggestions.)

How can I keep moles from eating our rose bushes? (Mon-

tana.)   The eating is done by mice in the mole runs, but the tunnels can dry up the roots. Step on the mole runs around bushes. (See Moles; Mice.)

How can I prevent rabbits from destroying my rose bushes? (Pennsylvania.)   If you don't like the looks of a fence, or cannot get the materials, there are various chemicals that have an evanescent effect. Moth balls work for me, but I think they are helped along by the neighbors' cats. (See Rabbits.)

What is the best all-purpose spray for hybrid tea roses? I am not adept at diagnosing pests and diseases. How frequently should it be used? (New York.)   No one is best. I use Isotox Insect Spray (Sevin, Kelthane, Meta-Systox-R) plus Phaltan.

RUBBER PLANT (FICUS ELASTICA)

What is the cause of rust ruining the leaves of rubber plants?   There is a fungus disease, anthracnose, which appears as a scorching and tip burn of the leaves and has little rose-colored spore pustules; there is a true scorching from dry air in a too hot hothouse; and there is a red scale. Pick off spotted leaves; do not let drops of water stand on the leaves; keep the house cool and the atmosphere humid. Spray for scale with a contact insecticide.

SEDUM

What makes sedum rot off the top of the ground? (New York.)   Sedum is subject to both crown rot and stem rot, two fungus diseases. Remove the diseased plant and the surrounding soil and fill in the hole with fresh gritty soil before replanting; give perfect drainage.

SNAPDRAGON (ANTIRRHINUM)

Small brown dots appear on the underside of the leaves of my snapdragons. Is this rust? (Louisiana.)   Yes, the rust pustules are chocolate brown and show on the underside of the leaves.

How can I control and kill snapdragon rust? (West Virgina.)   It can't be killed, but spraying with zineb biweekly until the plants are 15 inches tall will help prevent new infections. By far the easiest way to control this disease is to grow rust-resistant varieties.

What causes snapdragon to wilt and die? (Texas.)   In Texas, southern blight, cotton root rot, verticillium wilt, stem rot, and some other diseases. Remove diseased plants and try to replant them in a new location.

SPRUCE (PICEA)

What is an effective remedy against spruce gall? (New York.) Spruce galls are caused by adelgid aphids. The one that causes the elongation and swelling of the tips of blue spruce has Douglas-fir as an alternate host. When new growth starts, the aphids work at the base of the leaves, causing each cell to become enlarged and the whole gall to look something like a small pineapple. The best control is to remove the galls in midsummer before they open and free the new aphids.

What kind of spray shall I use for spruce gall, and when is the proper time to spray? (New York.) For Norway spruce, where the galls are located at the base of the twigs, rather than at the tips where they are easily cut out, spray with malathion in the summer after the galls open to expose the aphids; spray in the spring, just before new growth starts, with a carbaryl or malathion solution. With the blue spruce, if it was impossible to cut off all the galls while they were closed, spray in early April with malathion or Meta-Systox-R.

Why do the needles of a Black Hills spruce turn brown and fall off? (Illinois.) All spruces are subject to infestation by spider mites, which suck the sap from the needles, turning them grayish, and later brown, and often causing defoliation. A dormant oil spray or a spring or fall spray of Kelthane has been recommended. (See Mites.)

What causes the needles of our Norway spruces to turn brown and fall next to the trunk? I have found a small moth hidden in the branches. (Illinois.) There are several small moths the larvae of which mine in the needles of spruces, feeding on them and webbing them together. Ordinarily they are not serious and the browning of the inner needles may be natural ripening. Spray with carbaryl or malathion if necessary to control the larvae.

What diseases get on Koster's blue spruce? Should they be sprayed? The most serious disease is a canker or dieback of the lower limbs, which is not amenable to sprays. Cut out the diseased branches. Rust may sometimes attack spruce but is not serious in ornamental plantings. In general, you do not need to spray spruce for disease control, but occasionally for gall aphids and spider mites. (See the above questions.)

A blue spruce suddenly drops all its needles with no apparent cause.

Would you suggest a spray? (New York.) No, never spray unless you have "apparent cause." A tree in that condition might be made sicker with a spray. It sounds like a drought reaction, but it could be too heavy, wet soil, or escaping gas, or too strong a spray or some other environmental cause.

Borers in my spruce trees cause white encrustations on the trunks. What spray should I use, and when? (Illinois.) If these are bark beetles, there is no spray that will help, and seriously infested trees should be cut and burned before the beetles escape to other spruces. Ask a tree expert to diagnose the trouble.

STOCK (MATTHIOLA INCANA)

Why can't I raise good-looking stocks? Mine are always spindly and buggy. Even when I spray them, they are small and sickly. (California.) Stocks in California suffer from several diseases. Young seedlings get a bacterial wilt, prevented by immersing seed in hot water held at 127° F. for 10 minutes and planting in a new location. A fungus crown rot appears on overwatered, poorly drained soil; mosaic stunts the plants. Remove the infected plants and spray to control aphids with malathion.

What can be done to control stem rot on stock? (Arizona.) Stem and root rot are caused by a soil fungus which yellows the lower leaves, girdles the stem, causing wilting, and rots the roots. Since the fungus spreads for several feet through the soil away from the plant, it is not removed by taking up diseased plants and surrounding soil. Sterilize the soil (see Soil Sterilization) or plant in a new location.

SWEET PEA (LATHYRUS ODORATUS)

How do you control mildew on sweet pea? (Washington.) Dust frequently with fine dusting sulfur, starting before mildew usually appears or spray with Karathane or Benlate. They can be combined with malathion to control aphids.

Will treating the soil prevent green lice on sweet peas? (Wisconsin.) Di-Syston granules or dimethoate on the soil may help. Usually you spray for aphids during the growing season, using malathion up to blooming time.

Will treating the soil prevent the blighting of sweet peas? (Wisconsin.) Soaking the soil with a benomyl solution before planting will help in the control of various root rot diseases that cause wilting or blighting of the plants. (See Soil Sterilization.)

What causes sweet peas to wilt just below the flower buds, then the whole plant turns greenish white and dies? (Connecticut.) A fungus disease called anthracnose, common on outdoor sweet peas, has this effect. The fungus also causes a disease of apples and lives during the winter in cankered limbs and mummied apples as well as on sweet pea pods and seed and soil debris. Spray with benomyl biweekly during the growing season. Clean up all plant refuse in the fall. Plant only those seeds that appear sound and plump.

Why do my sweet peas develop a curled and puckered appearance? I plant on new ground each year, treat seed with Nitragin, and give plenty of moisture. (Idaho.) This is probably mosaic, carried from plant to plant by aphids. Virus diseases are common in the Northwest and there is nothing you can do except try to control aphids by sprays and remove infected plants promptly.

SWEET WILLIAM (DIANTHUS BARBATUS)

What causes sweet Williams to rot and turn yellow? I do not over-water them. (California.) A stem rot caused by a soil fungus, usually most destructive during warm, rainy periods, which you don't often have in California. Change the location if you can or sterilize the soil; use a light soil; avoid wounding the stems in cultivating.

SYCAMORE (PLATANUS)

What causes sycamore leaves to turn yellow and drop all summer long? (Missouri.) The most common cause is the fungus disease known as anthracnose, scorch, or leaf-and-twig blight, but this usually appears as brown areas on the leaves and is serious, chiefly following a wet spring. It is controlled by spraying 2 or 3 times with zineb or benomyl in the spring and by cleaning up all infected leaves in the summer. Yellowing and leaf fall may be due to hot, dry weather rather than disease.

TIGRIDIA

What treatment should be given tigridia bulbs which, when lifted from the border, are found to be covered with aphids? (New Jersey.) This is probably the tulip-bulb aphid, which commonly infests gladiolus, a relative of tigridia. For gladiolus, a 2-hour soaking in malathion solution can be used. You will have to experiment to see if this treatment injures tigridia.

TRUMPET VINE (CAMPSIS)

What do you use for green lice on a trumpet plant? (Pennsylvania.) Spray with malathion, starting early, before the leaves curl.

What can be done about leaves curling up on the trumpet vine, caused, I think, by red spider? (Pennsylvania.) If the leaves are curled, it is more likely that aphids are at work. Spider mites are more apt to turn the leaves yellow and mealy. Spray with malathion or any other contact insecticide for aphids, with Kelthane for mites.

TULIP (TULIPA)

What causes tulip blossoms to blister? Is it a disease? Botrytis blight causes brown or water-soaked spots on the petals, which might be called blisters. This is a fungus disease, very contagious, often known as gray mold or tulip fire. The spores are carried by the wind and rain from infected leaves or blossoms to healthy ones. Small black sclerotia are formed on leaves and petals rotting into the soil, and on the bulbs, and serve to carry the fungus over the winter. Spray with zineb, benomyl, or mancozeb from early spring weekly until bloom is finished.

Can the bulbs of diseased tulips be dug up and treated and used again? (Maine.) If the blighted blossoms are picked off immediately, and if all blossoms are cut off as they start to fade; if diseased leaves are removed when seen, and all leaves are cut off at ground level as soon as they ripen, the fungus may never get down to the bulb, and it is safe to leave it in the ground. If the bulbs are dug, it is better to discard any showing sclerotia than to treat them. If healthy new bulbs are to be planted in old infected soil, then the soil should be treated. (See Soil Sterilization.) If tulips are seriously diseased early in the season, the bulb is also infected, and should be taken up and destroyed immediately without waiting for the normal digging time.

Why did my last year's tulips grow headless stalks? (New York.) Botrytis blight often causes blind buds. These usually come when the bulb itself was diseased in the ground, and not as the result of secondary infection from plants nearby.

Last spring most of my bulbs failed to grow; those that did were sickly-looking. Was this due to not mulching the bulbs or a disease? I

planted large, healthy bulbs. (Minnesota.)   It probably was disease. If you planted deep enough, there was no need to mulch. You either had botrytis blight from sclerotia in the soil or on the bulbs under the husk, so you did not see them, or else they had gray bulb rot. The latter also is a sclerotial disease; it is more often characterized by large numbers of tulips failing to come up than is the botrytis disease, which is characterized by a weak growth above the ground. Plant new bulbs in another location, and make sure there are no black bodies either on the surface of the bulb or under its outer covering.

Why do white or yellow tulip varieties seem not to be affected by the virus disease that causes "breaking" of the colors? (New York.)   The breaking is a depigmentation, and if there is no color pigment in the flower, or very little, it cannot "break." However, there is now known to be another virus that adds color to light-colored varieties.

How can I prevent my tulip bulbs from being eaten by very small insects? (Missouri.)   These are probably bulb mites, very small, yellowish-white spiders. A heavy infestation will pulverize the inside of a bulb. Discard all such bulbs; dip the rest in malathion, 1 tablespoon per gallon of water, for 10 minutes and replant in another location or in sterilized soil.

What are the thin white worms, ½ inch long, that eat bulbs in the ground? (Illinois.)   These are probably scavenger worms, feeding on bulbs rotting from some other cause. Seek for the original culprit.

What treatment do you recommend for the soil of tulip beds where ground aphids are present? (New Jersey.)   Soak it with a malathion solution according to the directions on the container.

Do moles eat tulip bulbs? (Washington.)   Moles are carnivorous, living on grubs and other animal life. Usually the mole makes the run to the tulip bed and mice follow along to do the actual eating. (See Moles; Mice.)

TULIP-TREE (LIRIODENDRON TULIPIFERA)

How can I save a tulip-tree that shows signs of fungus growth on the south side? (New Jersey.)   Consult a tree expert. If fungi are growing out from the trunk, it is a sign of internal decay.

Can anything be done for a tulip-tree, about 10 years old, that is badly infested with oystershell scale? (New Jersey.)   This may not be oystershell scale. The tulip-tree scale—oval, brown, ⅓ inch across—is far more common and injurious on this tree. A dormant oil, applied in early spring, should control it. (See Dormant Spraying.) The eggs of this scale hatch in late summer, so sprays for crawlers should be applied in late August or early September.

VIBURNUM

What treatment should be used on common viburnum to discourage pests that cause the leaves to curl? (Illinois.) This is the snowball aphid, and it starts curling the leaves almost as soon as they unfold. Spraying with Orthene or malathion when the buds first break will help to control this pest. Usually after you fight the aphid for a few years, you either ignore it or plant another variety of viburnum.

When a snowball tree or any other shrub is diseased, can one get it back to a normal, healthy condition or must it be replaced? (Minnesota.) That all depends on the disease, or the pest. The common snowball will curl up with aphids every season. You would have to select a different variety.

A bush of Viburnum carlesii has a deposit of rough white along the stems. Is it mealybug? What can I do to save the bush? (New Hampshire.) Probably not. Many woody shrubs in late summer are attacked by planthoppers, whose young leave flocculent white masses over the twigs. There seems to be no permanent injury. Spray with malathion and don't worry.

Each summer black spot comes on the leaves of my Viburnum carlesii and they drop off. What is the preventive? (Kentucky.) There is a bacterial leafspot listed for viburnum, but this may not be your trouble in Kentucky. Spraying with streptomycin may work. Try picking off infected leaves and cleaning up fallen leaves. Sulfur sprays may injure this species.

VIOLET (VIOLA)

What can be done to protect violets against caterpillars? (Louisiana.) Pick the caterpillars off by hand as far as possible. Dust with methoxychlor or carbaryl.

WALNUT (JUGLANS REGIA)

I have an English walnut that makes a new growth every spring and then the leaves drop off, and it is bare the rest of the summer. What causes this? (Pennsylvania.) It may be a leafspot disease, but more likely uncongenial surroundings. The English walnut is exceedingly particular as to soil requirements, being intolerant of wet soils but requiring very deep, fertile soil with no excess of alkali.

WILLOW (SALIX)

The beautiful willow on my lawn, which has reached gigantic proportions, keeps losing its leaves as a result of bugs. It seems a shame to cut down the tree. Is there something I could spray on the bark and branches within my reach? (Long Island, N.Y.) These are probably willow beetles. Have your tree sprayed once a year, in late May or early June, with malathion and carbaryl.

What can I do about the millions of dark red lice that get on our large weeping willow from midsummer to the time of frost? It is impossible to use the yard for my laundry. (Ohio.) Have your tree sprayed with malathion or another contact insecticide by a tree expert with power apparatus.

Will whitewashing a willow keep tree borers from attacking it? (Illinois.) It probably would have little effect. Wrapping the trunk with wrapping paper or Kraft crepe paper will keep borers out, but this is usually done only the first 2 years after transplanting. (See Borers.) Better get the advice of a reliable tree expert in your vicinity.

Is there any relation between scale insects and borers on pussy willow? What is the prevention? (Pennsylvania.) No relation. Spray for scale with a dormant oil. (See Dormant Spraying.) Cut down seriously infested trees and start over. Pussy willows grow fast.

YEW (TAXUS)

Are all insects injurious to yews controlled by applying chemicals to the surrounding ground? (Pennsylvania.) No. Chlordane was used to kill the grubs and adults of the black vine weevil, which is probably its most injurious insect pest. Now there is no registered control for this pest, but Orthene may be in the future. Yew is also subject to attacks by scale insects and mealybugs, which are controlled by spraying foliage with malathion.

YUCCA

What are the soft-bodied insects that infest yucca? What spray is there for control? (North Carolina.) Aphids are soft-bodied insects infesting yucca, but mealybugs—soft white creatures—are more likely to be the trouble. Spray forcefully with malathion. Repeat as necessary.

ZINNIA

What is the cause of the white, powderlike discoloration on zinnias? (New Jersey.)   This is powdery mildew, a fungus disease, which usually appears toward the end of the season and is chiefly of importance because of the unsightly foliage. Dust with fine dusting sulfur or spray with Benlate or Karathane.

What makes the leaves of zinnias curl up from the sides? (Vermont.)   Mildew sometimes has this effect. Or it may be a physiological condition.

My zinnias have been troubled by rust. What will stop it? Could it start from a narrow strip of brush and small trees adjoining my garden? (Massachusetts.)   There is no rust common on zinnias, but there is a bacterial, and also a fungus, leafspot that can cause reddish discoloration of the leaves in late summer. It is not usually serious, and it might be prevented by spraying with captan. You need not fear the strip of brush as far as "rust" is concerned, but if the weeds flourish, too, it would be a source of insect pests.

The roots of zinnias planted in open ground are covered with aphids; the plants withered after they had grown a few inches. How can we get rid of them? (Rhode Island.)   You can try making a shallow depression around each plant and pouring in a solution of malathion according to directions on the container; but if your soil is so badly infested, it would be better to plant more zinnias in another location. (See also Soil Sterilization.)

What should be used to get rid of tarnished plant bugs on zinnias and other plants? I have tried many sprays without success. (New York.)   Frequent applications of carbaryl or malathion spray might help. The first and most important step is getting rid of the weeds that harbor this plant bug.

This year my zinnias have been badly infested with stem borers, but there were no marks or sawdust visible on the outside. I cannot find material telling their life cycle or control. Can you supply me with information? (California.)   These probably are the common stalk borers, although they are listed as general only east of the Rockies. They winter as eggs on weeds and old stalks, so that the chief control measure is getting rid of these. (See also Borers.)

Vegetables

ASPARAGUS

Will rust-resistant asparagus always escape the disease? Not entirely. The 'Mary' and 'Martha Washington' varieties are reasonably rust resistant, but in some seasons in certain areas the red and black pustules show up on the leaves and stems, with yellowing of the tops. In that case, spray with maneb 3 times at 2-week intervals after the cutting season. Destroy old tops.

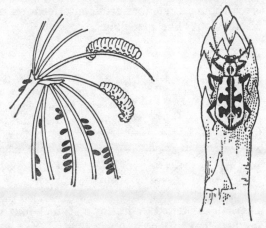

Asparagus beetles (right) eat tender shoots in the spring. Later the grubs feed on foliage (left) as they emerge from eggs.

Is there a spray or remedy of any kind for asparagus beetle? (Oregon.) This red, blue, and yellow beetle is chiefly controlled by clean cutting during the harvest season, although an occasional dusting with rotenone may be needed. After the cutting season, dust with carbaryl or methoxychlor.

Is it true that calendula plants interplanted with asparagus repel the asparagus beetle? No scientific evidence on record. Why don't you try it and judge the results yourself?

What about the Japanese beetle on asparagus? (New Jersey.) The

Japanese beetle may appear in swarms on asparagus foliage in mid-summer, but the injury is rarely sufficient to call for treatment.

BEAN (PHASEOLUS)

What is the chewing insect, colored yellow with black spots, shaped a little like the ladybug but longer? (Texas.) Either the Mexican bean beetle or the bean leaf beetle. The former looks more like a ladybug with its 16 small black spots, but it is larger, more convex, and coppery-yellow. Its spiny yellow larvae are also found on the leaves. The bean leaf beetle is prevalent in southern states. It is about the size of a ladybug, red to yellow, with 6 black spots and a black band around the wing covers. Its larva is a white grub which feeds on the stem and roots below the soil line. Both beetles are controlled by the same treatment. The yellow-green spotted cucumber beetle also feeds on bean foliage in Texas, and this, too, looks like a ladybug.

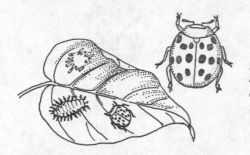

The Mexican bean beetle is cop-pery-yellow and has 16 black spots. Both adults and the spiny, dirty-yellow larvae feed on the undersides of foliage.

All known insecticides failed to destroy a ½-inch-long yellow creeper on my beans. It looks like a caterpillar. What is it? (Massachusetts.) Probably larvae of Mexican bean beetles, which are fat, soft, covered with black-tipped spines, and something under ½ inch long. They succumb to rotenone dust in this stage, or spray with diazinon or carbaryl. The larvae are easier to kill than the adult beetles.

Are little pests that look like a yellow bur on green beans the bean beetle? (Ohio.) Yes. That is a very good description of the larvae of Mexican bean beetle.

What are the time cycles of the Mexican bean beetle? With a succession of snap beans, I notice some plantings suffer more than others. (New York.) You are right. Beans planted in June in New York will mature in July between the two broods of beetles. The first beetles appear in May, when the early beans come up, feed for a week, and lay their eggs in orange-yellow clusters on the underside of the leaves. The larvae hatch in another week, feed for 2 to 5 weeks, pupate on the leaves, and in 1 more week produce the adults, which feed and lay eggs for the second generation. This is usually much more destructive than the first, untreated bean foliage being completely riddled during August and September.

How long a season has the bean beetle? (Virginia.) About as long as the beans are growing. In Virginia, the Mexican bean beetle will probably have 3 broods a season.

What is the cheapest and most effective way to destroy bean beetles without harming the plants? (New York.) Apply rotenone, preferably in dust form for ease of application and coverage, or carbaryl, diazinon, or methoxychlor as a spray.

Is daily picking of the bean beetles and eggs the easiest way to control them? (Virginia.) An occasional dusting will be a lot easier than daily picking off, unless there are very, very few beans. Combine the two methods, picking off as many as you can whenever you have time. Each female removed before egg laying, or each cluster of eggs burned up, means fewer beetles for the next brood.

Is there anything other than spraying, dusting, and hand-picking to control the Mexican bean beetle? (New York.) Yes, sanitary measures at the end of the season are very important. Clean up all plant debris, or else spade or plow it under deeply, and clean up all weeds and trash around the garden so there will be no hiding place for the overwintering females.

Is there anything to be done about such pests as bean beetles and cutworms during the winter? (Indiana.) Fall plowing or spading and keeping the garden clean during the winter will certainly help to discourage both of these pests.

What can I do for the little bugs that appear on lima beans? (Maryland.) The Mexican bean beetle is as destructive to lima beans as it is to string beans. Use the same control measures.

What will destroy the Japanese beetle on snap beans? (Massachusetts.) Rotenone dust or spray, or carbaryl, as recommended for Mexican bean beetle, will also take care of Japanese beetles.

How can I kill or prevent small green bugs with black dots on its back that eat bean foliage? I was afraid to spray on account of poisoning the vegetable. (California.) These are diabrotica, or 12-spotted cucumber beetles. You can safely spray with either rotenone or carbaryl.

My snap beans had little greenish bugs all over the plants all season.

What are these? How can I get rid of them? (New York.) The regular bean aphid is black; the pea aphid is green and sometimes attacks other legumes. A greenish leafhopper sometimes infests beans. Malathion or diazinon spray should keep any of these under control and may be applied almost up to picking time. Or rely on the rotenone used for beetle control.

What shall I use, and when, for very tiny whiteflies that rise in a cloud from snap beans? (California.) It is doubtful that whiteflies on beans are injurious enough to warrant control measures. They may be sprayed with diazinon or malathion up to within 5 days of picking to kill adults. Sprays must be repeated every 3 to 4 days until the adults are gone.

How does the bug called a weevil get into beans? (Massachusetts.) Eggs are laid on the pods while the beans are in the garden; these hatch into grubs, which burrow through the pod into the bean. There they change into the small, dull-gray adult weevils with reddish legs. Several broods may be produced in storage, ruining the beans for either seed or food.

The beans I raised last summer have little holes from which have come little beetles. What treatment should the vines have to prevent them? (Maine.) These are the bean weevils (weevil being merely the name given to a beetle with a little snout). There is no treatment for the vines except to clean them up. The beans have to be treated after harvest. (See the next question.)

How can I protect the beans from weevils during storage? There are several methods: (1) Spread out in pans and heat dry in the oven at 130° to 140° F. for 1 hour (some say 30 minutes). (2) Suspend seeds in a cloth bag in a kettle of cold water and heat to 140° F. Dry quickly. (3) Shake the beans thoroughly in a container, with 1 pint of lime to each quart of beans.

Does treatment injure the beans for food or seed? It should not, if directions are followed. The excess lime can be shaken off in a strainer and then the beans should be washed.

Last year my pole beans did poorly and when I pulled them up there were a lot of very small bugs on the roots. What were they? (Massachusetts.) Root aphids, in all probability. Push the soil away slightly from around each stem and pour in a cupful of malathion solution, 1 tablespoon to 1 gallon of water.

I had some fine 'Kentucky Wonder' beans, but after a while the leaves turned brown and the beans stopped growing. What caused this? (Massachusetts.) This might have been the root aphids just mentioned; or perhaps dry root rot, caused by a fungus that lives several years in the soil, necessitating a long rotation; or rust. (See below.) It could have been heavy, wet soil without the fungus. In our town, in an "experience meeting" at the end of a past season, we learned that pole beans did extremely well in the plots that were almost pure ashes, and hence well drained, and very poorly at the other end of town, where the soil was heavy clay.

Last summer I was bothered with "rust spots" on my green beans, varying from skin deep to the center of the pod. What was the trouble? (North Carolina.) Not true rust but a fungus disease called anthracnose or pod spot, which shows up as round sunken spots with dark borders and pinkish spore pustules in the center. Anthracnose cannot be "cured" but it can be prevented by planting seed from healthy pods or else seed grown in the West where the disease is not a problem. Avoid working with beans when they are wet, as this spreads the spores from diseased to healthy plants. Resistant varieties are chiefly of the shell-bean type. Maneb or zineb sprays will prevent its spread.

What causes blight on the leaf of green beans? (Ohio.) If there are small angular lesions and black veins, this blight is anthracnose. Look in catalogs for resistant varieties. If the blight shows up as irregular blotches on pods, it is bacterial blight.

How is bacterial blight controlled? (Ohio.) Use disease-free seed, either from healthy pods or western-grown. Do not work with wet plants. Spray with Fixed Copper. Some varieties are more or less resistant.

What is the treatment for rust that comes about midseason on pole beans? (Massachusetts.) True rust is a fungus disease that shows as reddish powdery pustules on the leaves. In Massachusetts it is generally serious only on pole beans, where it causes early death of the vines. The rust winters over on dead plants and on stakes. Destroy vines after harvest, and next year use new poles or soak the old ones in formaldehyde (1 to 100 dilution), and keep them wet overnight by covering. Spray with sulfur, zineb, chlorothalonil, or maneb.

What is the treatment for mosaic on green snap beans? (Washington.) There is no treatment. The virus usually comes in with the seed. Destroy plants with mottled light- and dark-green leaves. Choose resistant varieties like 'Topcrop', 'Tendercrop', or 'Greencrop'. In Washington, curly-top, another virus disease, may affect beans. Destroy dwarfed plants with puckered leaves.

Why do my snap beans mildew? (California.) Powdery mildew is a fungus disease very prevalent in California. It usually attacks beans in cloudy weather or toward autumn. Dust with sulfur; choose mildew-resistant varieties such as 'Greencrop'.

Does mildew appear on snap beans because of soil or atmospheric conditions? (California.) This is not a soil fungus; the spores are carried by the wind. For some reason, the California atmosphere is peculiarly conducive to mildew, not only on beans but many other vegetables and ornamentals.

BEET (BETA VULGARIS)

How are leafminers kept out of beet tops? (New York.) There is no spray that will surely prevent maggots from working inside the beet leaves, turning the tissues brown, but malathion may help. Pick off infested leaves and destroy the wild host, lamb's-quarters. Incidentally, lamb's-quarters when young is a perfectly delicious vegetable, preferred by many to spinach, so a good way to destroy it is to cook it for dinner.

What about beet webworms? There are several species of caterpillars which eat the leaves and web them together. Dust with 5 per cent methoxychlor dust or spray with malathion and remove weeds like lamb's-quarters.

Should beet seed be treated before planting to prevent damping off? Definitely. The rough beet seed may carry spores of several disease organisms. Thiram (Arasan) or captan is very effective for beets. (See Seed Treatment.)

What causes spots that resemble warts on beets? The same organism that produces potato scab. Do not grow beets on land that has grown scabby potatoes. If the soil is alkaline, make it slightly acid with sulfur, and avoid any alkaline agents such as lime and manure. Use a cover crop of rye in place of the manure.

How can I keep beets and spinach from blighting? Our soil is slightly alkaline. (Washington.) In Washington, blight probably means curlytop, a virus disease that used to be called western yellow blight, characterized by yellowing, stunting, and death. The virus is transmitted by the beet leafhopper, so that insect control with contact insecticides is important. There is little else you can do except destroy diseased plants immediately and keep down weed hosts. Soil acidity is not a factor, as it is in scab.

Is leafspot on beets prevented by spraying? Spraying with zineb can prevent the round, red-bordered spots from getting numerous, but in the small garden, picking off spotted leaves is ordinarily sufficient control.

BROCCOLI

How can I keep aphids off broccoli? (Oregon.) Spray or dust with malathion until the heads form, then treat with pyrethrum if necessary. Often the aphids cluster on a single head or leaf, which can be removed and burned. If aphids are numerous on a head, cut for eating, separate into flowerettes, and soak in strong salt water. The aphids will float out and can be poured off. Then rinse the broccoli well in pure water before cooking.

How are root maggots and worms controlled? See Cabbage. Broccoli is a member of the cabbage family, and while it is free from many cabbage diseases, it has its share of aphids, root maggots, and green worms eating the foliage and flower heads.

BRUSSELS SPROUTS (BRASSICA OLERACEA GEMMIFERA)

What is the best control for worms and aphids on Brussels sprouts? Rotenone dust or carbaryl is allowed for worms on Brussels sprouts and will keep the aphids down to some extent. *Bacillus thuringiensis* is excellent for cabbage worms. Or they can be sprayed or dusted with malathion. (See also Cabbage.)

CABBAGE (BRASSICA OLERACEA CAPITATA)

Is there any way to prevent white maggots from attacking the roots of cabbage plants? (Wisconsin.) When a young cabbage wilts and, upon being pulled up, discloses white maggots working on the underground stem and roots, it is too late for control. There are several ways of preventing maggot injury. Apply diazinon dust or spray to plant bases when the plants are set out.

The cabbage root maggot's eggs are laid on stems, near ground level, in early spring.

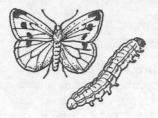

The cabbage worm is green. The adult is a white or yellow butterfly, a familiar visitor to the summer vegetable garden.

How are tar-paper disks, for control of root maggots, applied? Cut a 4-inch square or circle; make a hole in the center with a spike, and make a cut from the outer edge to the hole, so you can get the paper around the stem. Work gently, so as not to bruise the young seedling. The disk should stay flat on the ground and fit snugly around the stem.

What is the calomel treatment for seedlings? This treatment has been replaced by the more effective diazinon dust or spray treatment to plant bases.

What is the best way to control the black flea beetle on small cabbage plants? (Virginia.) These small but very active beetles do considerable damage to young plants, often riddling the leaves with tiny shot holes. Spray with carbaryl.

Is there more than one type of cabbage worm? There are 3. The true cabbage worm, a green caterpillar of the common white or yellow butterfly; the cabbage looper, a striped pale-green worm that moves like an inchworm and changes into a brownish-gray moth; and a small, greenish caterpillar that is the larva of the diamondback moth. All these are controlled in the same way. Spray with rotenone, carbaryl, or *Bacillus thuringiensis*.

Is lump lime good to destroy cabbage worms and those little dark worms that hold themselves in ring shape? (Maine.) Lime has been used to control cabbage clubroot, if your soil is acid, but would have no effect on cabbage worms. For clubroot, use Terrachlor, 6 tablespoons per gallon of water, 1 cupful in a hole when planting. The little dark worms are millipedes and not very injurious.

How can I control blue aphids on cabbage? (California.) By a malathion or diazinon spray, or dust, which can be used almost to harvest time.

What treatment is best to kill grasshoppers that attack garden vegetables such as cabbage and broccoli? (California.) Spray vegetables with carbaryl or methoxychlor. (See Grasshoppers.)

The leaves of my cabbage plants turned yellow and the cabbage died. Is anything wrong with the soil? (Wisconsin.) This is cabbage yellows, caused by a soil fungus—a species of fusarium—very common in your state. Either plant in a new location or grow varieties marked "yellows-resistant" in your seed catalog.

In order to grow cabbage, do I have to buy yellows-resistant seed? (New York.) Advisable, but it may not be necessary in New York. The disease is not so prevalent as in the Midwest, and if you have no previous record of cabbages dying or yellows on your soil, you need not worry much.

For years I have had trouble with cabbage plants. Just before they are ready to head up, the leaves turn yellow and drop off. The plant dies. There is no evidence of insect pests. (Delaware.) Your soil is apparently well inoculated with the "yellows" or fusarium wilt fungus. Plant resistant varieties.

What causes cabbages to rot off the stalk? (Iowa.) Black rot or blight, a bacterial disease, is one cause. The plants are stunted; leaves turn yellow to brown, shrivel and drop off; or the head may decay and fall off in a slimy mass. The vascular ring in the stem and the leaf veins are black. Use clean seed or disinfect with hot water (see Seed Treatment); plant in disease-free soil; remove diseased plants; clean up all cabbage refuse.

What causes the tops of the cabbage leaves to turn black, sometimes running through the entire head? (Wisconsin.) Either the black rot just discussed or a fungus disease called blackleg. There are dark areas with black dots on stems and leaves. If the stem is girdled near the ground line, the plants wilt and die. Use cabbage seed grown near Puget Sound, where the disease is rare, or treat with hot water. Practice sanitary measures given above and a 4-year rotation.

What is the best remedy for preventing clubroot in cabbage and cauliflower? (Michigan.) Clubroot is the name of a disease that causes grossly enlarged and malformed roots and stunted, sickly plants. If the disease has been present previously, treat the soil with fresh hydrated lime, 10 pounds to 100 square feet, and rake it in shortly before planting; or try a soil treatment with PCNB (Terrachlor) when planting. Use 6 tablespoons per gallon of water and put in 1 cupful per hole when transplanting.

What is the cure for cabbage wilt—curled tips of leaves, whitish color? (California.) This may be powdery mildew, with the fungus growing over the leaves and causing the white color. If so, you can dust with sulfur. If it is a chlorosis (an actual loss of color in the leaf tissue), then perhaps some chemical is lacking for good nutrition or your soil is too alkaline.

CARROT (DAUCUS CAROTA SATIVUS)

We have trouble with maggots in the carrots. Can you give any help in controlling this pest? (Washington.) In western Washington plant early carrots so that they can be harvested by July 15, and in small blocks so they can be screened and the rust fly prevented from laying her eggs. Do not plant late carrots before June 1. Use diazinon in the seed furrow.

Please advise me about the small worms that make burrows in carrots. Are they wireworms? (Oregon.) Probably these are the maggots of the carrot rust fly discussed in the previous question. Control measures for Washington should also apply for Oregon.

What grub or bug eats tunnels through the sides of carrots? (Iowa.) In Iowa, the carrot grub, which looks like the common white grub and eats pieces out of the carrots, and the rust-fly maggots, which make rust-colored tunnels, are the chief insect pests. Control both pests by dusting the ground along the row, as soon as the seed is planted, with diazinon. Rotating is helpful.

Can carrot worms be avoided by harvesting early or by adding lime to the soil? (Michigan.) By planting in June, the first brood of the rust fly can be avoided, and harvesting can be done before the second brood. Lime is sometimes recommended to drive away the carrot beetle but should not be used unless your soil requires it.

What are the insects that look like blue lice and infest my carrot roots? How can I get rid of them? (New York.) These are root aphids (plant lice); they look bluish because of a powdery coating. If the infestation is bad enough to require control, pour malathion, 1 tablespoon per gallon of water, around the stems after loosening the soil.

How do I keep ants from putting plant lice on carrot roots? (New York.) Find the nest if you can and treat with an insecticide. (See Ants.)

How can I keep my carrot crop from rotting in the garden? (Arizona.) Your carrots either have southern blight (see Crown Rot) or else bacterial soft rot, a bacterial disease that more often appears in storage, but occasionally in the garden. The fungi and bacteria are in the soil, so you must plant in a new location or treat the soil. (See Soil Sterilization.)

Is there a foliage disease of carrots? (New Jersey.) There is a leaf blight that produces spots on the leaves, after which they turn brown and die, but it is not ordinarily serious enough in the home garden to require more than cleaning up old tops. If necessary, spray with captan.

CAULIFLOWER (BRASSICA OLERACEA BOTRYTIS)

How are cauliflower troubles controlled?   Treat the seed and practice the same sanitary measures as recommended for cabbage. Occasionally there is a bacterial or fungus spot on the heads; for this there is no practical control.

CELERY (APIUM GRAVEOLENS DULCE)

Is blight on celery in the seed or the soil? (Indiana.)   Both. There are 3 blights: early and late blight caused by fungi, and a bacterial blight. The organisms are carried over in celery refuse in the garden and on the seed. Practice a 3-year rotation and either use seed that is 2 years old or treat it with hot water at 118° F. for 30 minutes. Then dry and dust with thiram.

How can celery blight be prevented? (Pennsylvania.)   Spray with maneb, benomyl, or chlorothalonil at weekly intervals in the seed bed; and at 7- to 10-day intervals after setting out in the garden. Blight is worse in a wet season and is spread by working with plants when they are wet.

Our celery is injured by slugs; is there any remedy? (Pennsylvania.)   Clean up hiding places such as loose boards and old plant debris; sprinkle lime on the ground. (See Slugs and Snails.) Slug bait is not registered for use on celery.

How can I get rid of beetlelike bugs in celery plants? (Pennsylvania.)   These are tarnished plant bugs and very difficult to get rid of. Clean up weeds and try pyrethrum or malathion dusts or sprays.

COLLARDS (BRASSICA OLERACEA)

How can one overcome insects on collards? (Alabama.)   See Cabbage.

CORN (ZEA MAYS)

How can one tell when corn has been stung by the corn borer moth? (New York.)   The yellow-brown moth of the European corn borer lays its eggs in groups of 20 or more on the underside of the leaves, and the larvae, tiny, flesh-colored borers, tunnel their way into the stalk, leaf stems, and ears. Their presence is shown by tassels bending over or broken, fine sawdustlike castings on the leaves, and small holes in the stalks, often with protruding borings.

When should corn be planted to avoid the borer? (Michigan.) There are 2 broods of the European corn borer. Extra-early corn will be injured by the first, and very late corn will be attacked by the second brood. Corn planted between the middle of May and the first of June will mature chiefly between the broods and thus escape much injury.

What is the latest on the control of corn borer? (Vermont.) That the treatments for the borer must be related to growth stages of the corn. Give the first dusting when tassels can be seen on half the plants by looking down into the tops. Dust into the tassel whorl and give two more treatments at 5-day intervals, using carbaryl or diazinon. Ryania dust is also used, but it is more expensive.

How else can one fight the borer? The corn borer feeds on more than 200 kinds of plants and winters, in the larval stage, in old herbaceous stems. It is extremely important to clean up in the fall, not only old cornstalks and stubble, but dahlia and gladiolus tops, and to clean up weeds, especially pigweed and smartweed.

Is the common stalk borer injurious to corn? Yes, especially at the edge of the corn patch near weeds or where wasteland has been recently turned into a garden. The young caterpillars are brown, white-striped, turning grayish as they increase in size. The moths lay their eggs in September on giant ragweed and many other weeds. Cleaning up is the best control measure.

Can worms in sweet corn be avoided? (Washington.) The corn-ear worm is more widely distributed than the corn borer, and the caterpillars are large, brown to green, and striped. The moths lay their eggs

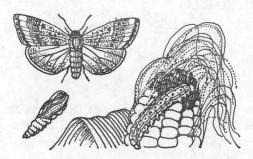

The corn-ear worm is a large, brown-to-green worm with distinct stripes.

chiefly on the corn silk, and the young larvae feed on that and the tip of the ear. Treat as for the corn borer. Repeat 3 to 4 times at 2-day intervals.

Can anything be done about Japanese beetles on sweet corn? (New Jersey.) They congregate on the silk, so the ear-worm applications will also control them.

How can squirrels be kept from eating corn? (Indiana.) Squirrels, and occasionally raccoons, are very destructive pests of corn, and there is little to be done except shoot them, which is not permitted in most localities. In my garden, the corn was planted in a square block. The squirrels started to eat on the outside row, and when this was left to them they ignored the rest of the corn patch.

How can I eliminate smut from sweet corn? (New York.) The only control measure is to cut off the large smut boil—from ear, tassel, or stalk—before it opens to discharge the black spores that will infect other corn. Avoid the use of manure likely to be infected, and burn up stalks after harvest. Spraying is not helpful and there are no resistant varieties.

Is there any other important corn disease? (New Jersey.) Bacterial, or Stewart's, wilt may be serious after a mild winter. There are discolored streaks in the leaves, and young plants wilt and die. The bacteria are spread by corn flea beetles. Many of the new hybrid varieties are resistant to this disease.

CUCUMBER (CUCUMIS SATIVUS)

What measures can be taken against striped cucumber beetles? They seem almost impossible to destroy. (Illinois.) They are hard to control, but there are many ways to fight these green, black-striped beetles: (1) Remove weed hosts, especially Chinese-lantern plants. (2) Protect young seedlings with Hotkaps or cheesecloth tents. (3) Plant extra seeds in the hills and discard the most injured seedlings. (4) As soon as the ground cracks over the seedlings, start dusting with rotenone, carbaryl, or methoxychlor. Repeat treatments as often as needed to keep plants covered with dust.

What causes bugs in the roots of cucumber plants? (Pennsylvania.) The larva of the spotted cucumber beetle works on the roots of many plants and is known as the southern corn rootworm. The beetle, green with 12 black spots, is controlled like the striped cucumber beetle. The spotted beetle also attacks many ornamental plants, where it is known as diabrotica beetle. "Bugs" may also be root aphids (see under Aphids).

A worm eats our pickle cucumbers. Is there a remedy? (Illinois.) The white or green pickle worm is especially destructive in southern states but is occasionally found as far north as Illinois. It bores into the ripening fruits. The dusts listed for the striped cucumber beetle should be helpful. Carbaryl will control but may injure cucumbers. Destroy all old vines.

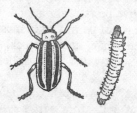

Striped cucumber beetle attacks cucumbers, melons, and squash. It is green with black stripes. The larvae attack roots.

What is the control for the large, flat, gray beetle that attacks cucumber, pumpkin, squash, and melon vines? I have used moth balls in the hills with the seed and it seemed to work. Was it by accident? (Arkansas.) Probably, although the moth balls might have some repellent effect on the squash bug. (See Squash for more details.)

How can I rid cucumber vines of lice? (Texas.) The melon aphid is very destructive to all cucurbits, causing leaves to curl, wilt, and brown; it attacks many other plants, including lilies, to which it carries mosaic. Spray or dust with malathion, being careful to get underneath the leaves.

How are whiteflies on cucumbers killed? (New York.) The treatments for aphids (see the previous question) should subdue them. They are often abundant on cucurbits, but of minor importance.

What pest or disease causes cucumber to wither, runner by runner, until the plant dies and semimature fruit shrivels up? (New York.) It is either the squash vine borer (see Squash) or wilt. The latter is a bacterial disease, very prevalent, disseminated by spotted and striped cucumber beetles, which carry the bacteria in their digestive tracts during the winter and deposit them in droppings on the leaves as they feed. The young vines can be sprayed or dusted to control the cucumber beetles. Malathion or methoxychlor will control the squash vine borer.

My pickles show mosaic. What can I do about that? (Michigan.) Control the weeds, such as burweed, milkweed, catnip, pokeberry, and groundcherry, which harbor the virus; control the melon aphids and cucumber beetles, which carry the virus from the weeds to the cucumbers. Try resistant varieties. Purchase treated seed.

My cucumber leaves look rusty and yellow. What causes this? (Massachusetts.) Bacteria produce angular leaf spots and fungi, brownish circles. Spray foliage with captan or maneb, especially in the latter part of the season. Clean up and burn all old vines.

EGGPLANT (SOLANUM MELONGENA ESCULENTUM)

How can one get an eggplant that does not die of wilt? (Alabama.) You have to set healthy plants grown from clean seed in soil that has not grown eggplant for 4 years. Eggplant wilt—also called foot rot, blight, leafspot, and wilt from its various symptoms—is so severe in the South that clean seed is rarely found. Soak in hot water, 122° F. for 5 minutes; then rinse in running water and dry thoroughly. Tie the seed in a cheesecloth bag before immersion. After drying, treat the seed with Arasan or captan. (See Seed Treatment.) To prevent fruit rot, use mancozeb or zineb every 7 to 10 days as the fruit ripens.

What makes eggplants wilt? (New Jersey.) In New Jersey, it is probably verticillium, which stunts the plants and turns the leaves yellow. The plant wilts in the heat of the day and the vessels are dark if the stem is cut. Use a long rotation that does not include tomatoes, potatoes, or raspberries. The fungus can live in the soil a long time. Or try soil sterilization with Vapam.

LETTUCE (LACTUCA SATIVA)

Why did my head lettuce rot after it was transplanted from the greenhouse? It was covered with a grayish fuzz. (New York.) This was botrytis blight, or gray mold disease, which infects seedlings if they are kept too wet in the greenhouse and shows up as bottom rot. Remove the plants carefully with the surrounding soil and soak the soil with a captan solution mixed according to container recommendations. Sterilize the soil used for flats in a greenhouse or cold frame. Plants can be sprayed with Botran. A similar rot, but starting from the top down, is called "drop," and is controlled in the same way.

MELON (CUCUMIS MELO)

How do you exterminate the small yellow chewing insect with black stripes known as the cantaloupe bug? (Texas.) The striped cucumber beetle frequently congregates on melon fruit. (See Cucumber for control.)

What insect kills my cantaloupes almost overnight? It is the same

color as the leaves, small and egg-shaped, and the leaves scald and brown. (Missouri.) The melon aphid almost fits your description. (See Cucumber for control.)

Can root rot on melon vines be prevented? (Vermont.) Fusarium wilt, a soil fungus, causes the plants to become stunted and yellowed. Long rotations reduce the amount of wilt. No fungicide is registered.

My muskmelons did well up to ripening, then wilted and died. Why? (Michigan.) Perhaps the fusarium wilt just discussed; or cucumber wilt (see Cucumber); or the squash vine borer (see Squash).

ONION (ALLIUM CEPA)

Is there a practical method (for a small garden) to keep onions raised from seed free from the onion maggot? (New York.) Treat the soil at planting with diazinon or malathion. Use shallow planting.

What causes onions to rot? Seemingly a worm or bug bores through the stalk. (Wisconsin.) This is the onion maggot discussed above. When damaged onions are put in storage, they decay and cause the surrounding bulbs to rot.

I pulled and stored my onions and found that the majority are going bad. Why? (Pennsylvania.) Fungi following after maggot injury are responsible. Onions should be stored only where there is free air circulation, either in a string bag or else with the tops left on and braided into chains to hang up on the wall. The latter method is easy and very successful, and you can always cut off just the size onion you want without rummaging through a bag.

What is the best means of control for onion thrips? (Connecticut.) It is very difficult to control this small sucking insect, which rasps the leaves and turns them whitish. Early planting is said to be helpful, for most thrips are present after July 1. Spray weekly with diazinon or malathion.

Can cutworms be prevented from injuring young growing onions? (New York.) Paper collars are impractical, so use diazinon if the cutworms are too numerous to destroy by hand-picking. (See Cutworms.) The maggot treatment will also take care of cutworms.

What is the black powdery mass on leaves and bulbs? Onion smut, a fungus disease. The easiest way to avoid it is to grow onions from sets, because they can be infected only in the young, seedling stage. In growing from seed, start in a clean, new seed bed and transplant, or else treat seed with Arasan or captan before planting.

PEA (PISUM SATIVUM)

How are damping off and root rots on peas prevented? (Connecticut.) Early planting helps get peas started before the root-rot fungi can get in their work, but treating with captan helps prevent root rot as well as damping off. Avoid heavy, low, and poorly drained soils. Use a 3- to 5-year rotation if possible.

How can I control the pale-green plant lice that suck the sap from the vines? The pea aphid is very difficult to control, but malathion or diazinon spray or dust is helpful.

How can moles be prevented from destroying green peas? I have read that moles eat only worms. If so, what becomes of the pea seed? (Washington.) Perhaps the seeds are consumed by mice that use the mole tunnels.

PEPPER (CAPSICUM ANNUUM)

What should be used to kill lice on pepper plants? (Nebraska.) Malathion or diazinon should be safe if the fruits are carefully washed; but pyrethrum or rotenone can be substituted as nonpoisonous materials. In general, peppers have the same pests as potatoes, and control measures are the same.

Why do my peppers turn brown and fall off as soon as they are formed? (Connecticut.) This is probably due to unfavorable weather, which sometimes causes not only blossom and fruit drop of many plants, but a blossom-end rot of the fruits after they were formed. (See Squash; Tomato.)

POTATO (SOLANUM TUBEROSUM)

How do I prevent potato leaves from curling and turning brown, and the vine from dying before the tubers are full grown? (New York.) This is late blight, the most destructive disease of potatoes. Plant only "certified" tubers, of a blight-resistant variety, and start spraying with maneb or chlorothalonil when the plants are 6 inches high; repeat every 10 to 14 days until the plants stop growing.

How can the home gardener, with no power-spray equipment, prevent late potato blight? (Massachusetts.) Spraying is preferable, and can be done with a 3-gallon compressed-air sprayer, but dusting can be substituted, using chlorothalonil or maneb dust.

When should blighted potatoes be dug? (Massachusetts.) If the vines are severely infected, dig as early as possible before the fungus gets down to rot the tubers.

Is there any treatment of the soil to prevent potato rot? (Connecticut.) No, it would not pay or help much to chemically treat soil for potatoes, and the best seed treatment is to make sure they are sound when cut for planting. The practice of hilling potatoes is in a sense a helpful treatment because it interposes more of a barrier between the fungus spores developing on the leaves and the tubers below.

What is the cause of scab on potatoes? (Vermont.) A common soil organism closely related to bacteria, *Actinomyces scabies*. It is unable to grow in an acid soil, but as the soil becomes increasingly alkaline, scab injury increases, varying from slight russeting to greatly roughened scabby areas on the tubers.

What can be done for potatoes that get rough, scabby hides? We put plenty of cow manure on. Do we use it too green, or too much, or too often, or is it the weather? We used to have lovely potatoes. (Kansas.) You use it too much and too often for soil infected with scab organism. Manure has an alkaline effect, like lime and wood ashes, and the more alkaline the soil, the better *Actinomyces* likes it. Resistant varieties are available.

What can be done with soil that produces scabby potatoes? (New York.) Get your pH (soil acidity) down to around 5.4. Adding sulfur will increase acidity. The amount needed varies with the original pH, but might run around 10 pounds per 1,000 square feet or 300 to 400 pounds per acre.

The government puts out some kind of solution for potato seed. What is it? (New York.) State Experiment Stations or county agents may arrange cooperative seed treatments for farmers but it is doubtful if the government gives out any such material. To control scab and rhizoctonia, uncut potatoes may be dipped in nabam solution (1 pint in 30 gallons of water) just before planting. The backyard gardener would do better to make sure he is using clean, sound potatoes for seed and omit the treatment.

How are potato bugs controlled? (New York.) Spray or dust foliage with methoxychlor or carbaryl to take care of these large orange-yellow, black-striped beetles and their enormous humpbacked, reddish larvae. This is the famous Colorado potato beetle, one of the pests to become resistant to DDT in the heyday of that insecticide.

How do you control the old-fashioned black potato bug?

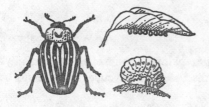

The potato bug is a double menace as both black-striped adults and fat, copper larvae feed on leaves.

(Ohio.) Blister beetles are hard to kill. Hand-picking is excellent. The potato beetle treatments should also work.

How shall I exterminate long-bodied gray or brown beetles that clean out a potato patch in one night? (Nebraska.) These, too, are blister beetles. They may be plain black, or striped, or margined, or brown or gray, but, in any color, they have voracious appetites. (See the previous question; also, Blister Beetles.)

We were warned that if we planted potatoes in soil where nothing had recently been grown they would be wormy. Why? (Ohio.) White grubs and wireworms are usually prevalent in sod land, and when this land is prepared for a garden, the worms remain until their life cycle is completed. Potatoes planted in newly broken sod land are very apt to have brown tunnels going through the tubers. If new land must be used, treat soil with diazinon. (See Wireworms.)

Last year my potatoes were scabby from wireworms. How can I raise clean potatoes in the same ground another season? (Ohio.) After one year of cultivation you may have fewer wireworms, but it would be safer to treat the soil before planting potatoes again.

Why do the edges of potato leaves get brown before the late blight season? (New Jersey.) This is a condition called hopperburn, due to the sucking of many leafhoppers. Carbaryl will control them.

What about virus diseases of potato? (New Jersey.) There are a great many, and the names describe the symptoms. Some of these are "yellow dwarf," "leaf roll," "mosaic," and "spindle tuber." Plant certified seed, or resistant varieties, and destroy any plant that seems to be infected. Control the aphids to prevent the spread of the disease.

Some of our potatoes had a layerlike black moss inside them. What caused it? (Virginia.) There are many causes of tuber discoloration: late blight and other fungus diseases, some bacterial and virus diseases, and a physiological disease called black heart. Your trouble may be the latter, and it comes from too great heat and lack of oxygen. If the potatoes stay out in bright sun after being dug, or if the storage place gets too hot, black heart may develop.

PUMPKIN (CUCURBITA PEPO)

How can cucumber beetles on pumpkins be controlled successfully? (Illinois.) Any of the treatments discussed under cucumber should be satisfactory on pumpkin.

How can the pumpkin vine borer be kept from entering vines as they are beginning to set fruit? (West Virginia.) For the control of the squash vine borer, and also squash bugs on pumpkin, see Squash.

RADISH (RAPHANUS SATIVUS)

What control is there for the light-green worm, like a caterpillar, that eats the leaves of radishes? (New Jersey.) This is probably the larva of the diamondback moth. (See Cabbage for control.)

Is it safe to eat radishes grown in soil treated with diazinon to eliminate wormy root crops? (Pennsylvania.) There should be no danger if the label directions for treatment were followed.

Why are my radishes small with a black spot up the middle? There is a disease called black rot of radish, caused by a fungus, but there is not much known in the line of control. Try a different location and the 'Red Globe' type of radish variety.

RHUBARB (RHEUM RHABARBARUM)

Why does rhubarb rot? (Virginia.) Phytopthora foot, or crown rot, causes sunken spots at the base of the leafstalks and a rot and wilting that progress from stalk to stalk until the whole plant dies. Dig out and burn diseased plants, being careful not to scatter infected soil. Disinfect the location with 1 to 50 formaldehyde. Plant only healthy roots.

What are the insects that bore holes in rhubarb stalks? (Pennsylvania.) Rhubarb curculios. Pick them off, because sprays do not seem to control them. They are yellow-snout beetles, which puncture stems and cause black spots. Destroy dockweed near the rhubarb.

SQUASH (CUCURBITA)

Is there any treatment for 'Hubbard' squash and the worms that burrow inside the stem? The squash vine borer is a white grub or caterpillar that works inside the vine, causing wilting beyond the point of attack, which is indicated by yellow excrement outside. The adult is a clear-wing moth. Spray or dust plant bases and stems with methoxychlor or malathion in late June and weekly in July.

Is there any way of exterminating the rather hard-shelled sucking insect, with a repugnant odor, which attacks squash plants first, then others? (Texas.) This is the squash bug, sometimes called stink bug, which is distributed all over the United States. The adults are brownish black, ⅔ inch long; they hide under the leaves and suck the sap, causing the vines to wilt. They attack all vine crops, but prefer squash. They can be killed with malathion, methoxychlor, or carbaryl sprays or dusts. Hand-pick the adults or trap them under boards. Destroy all old vines in the fall.

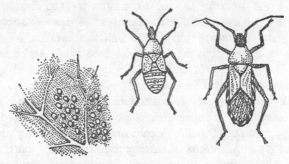

The squash bug is a large, lively rusty-black beetle, destructive at all stages, hatching from orange eggs on the undersides of leaves. It attacks squash and pumpkins.

What causes summer squash buds to drop off? (Connecticut.) Chiefly unfavorable weather conditions. However, the male and female flowers are separate on squash plants, and the male flowers, of course, drop off without setting fruit.

Why can't I raise crookneck squash? Something attacks the roots and prevents the fruits from maturing. (Michigan.) It may be a water relation rather than an organism at the roots. Blossom-end rot is common in squash, causing the small squash to wither at the blossom end, which is followed by secondary rot fungi. This disease is thought to be due to an insufficient or uneven water supply.

What caused about 8 out of 10 straight-necked squash to rot shortly after setting? (Connecticut.) The weather, and resultant dry soil, caused this blossom-end rot. (See the previous question.)

SWISS CHARD (BETA VULGARIS CICLA)

How can I control leafminers on Swiss chard and beet foliage? Spray with malathion every 7 days but wait 7 days before harvesting.

TOMATO (LYCOPERSICON LYCOPERSICUM)

What is the cause of blossom-end rot, which looks more like a fungus disease than a rot? It covers from ¼ to ½ of the fruit and is gray-black and quite firm. (Oregon.) Blossom-end rot does look like a fungus disease, and it is probably the most common tomato disease across the country, but it seems to be due to disturbed or uneven water relations. When the plant is growing rapidly in moist weather, and a hot dry spell follows, water is lost from the tissues faster than it can be taken up by the roots. The blossom end of the fruits, being farthest away from the roots, loses water first and the cells collapse and turn black.

What will prevent tomatoes rotting at the blossom end just before ripening? (Illinois.) Maintain an even water supply. A deeply prepared soil well supplied with organic matter helps; but plants that receive too heavy applications of nitrogenous fertilizers, particularly manure, are more subject to this rot. A balanced fertilizer high in superphosphate and available calcium decreases susceptibility. Calcium nitrate is good to use as the source of nitrogen. Although blossom-end rot usually shows up in periods of drought, it may appear when the soil has received so much rainfall that the small roots are killed for lack of aeration. Spraying with calcium chloride (1 tablespoon in a gallon of water) will help prevent blossom-end rot.

What causes rot inside perfectly good-looking tomatoes? (Connecticut.) Probably the same type of weather and soil conditions that cause the blossom-end rot discussed above.

Is tomato wilt carried on the seed or does it remain in the soil? (Mississippi.) Both. Primarily a soil organism, the wilt fungus may be carried on the seed.

What is the cause of blight on tomatoes that begins at the bottom of the plant and works up? The leaves curl; the fruit develops but does not come to completion; and the plant dies slowly. (Pennsylvania.) This is probably fusarium wilt, caused by a fungus that lives in the soil. At first, the leaves roll up and wilt in the middle of the day; later there is a permanent wilting, yellow leaves, and death.

If my tomato plants all succumbed to the wilt in a damp season last year, will they do so again this year when planted on the same ground? (Connecticut.) If you plant susceptible varieties, they are very likely to, for the fungus lives several years in the soil. Rotation or soil sterilization is necessary; also, cleaning up all tomato refuse.

My tomatoes wither and stop bearing about the first of August. What are wilt-resistant varieties? (Tennessee.) 'Better Boy', 'Heinz 1350', 'Campbell 1329', 'Supersonic', 'Roma', 'Louisiana Gulf State', 'Minalucie', 'Jet Star', and 'Springset' are reasonably resistant to fusarium wilt. Consult seed catalogs for others.

What are the causes and cure for the mosaic disease of tomatoes? (Pennsylvania.) The cause of mottled dark- and light-green misshapen leaves is a virus. The only cure is prevention: destroying diseased plants as soon as noticed, and also weed hosts, and controlling insect carriers.

What are the weed hosts of mosaic? Ground-cherry, horsenettle, jimsonweed, and nightshade are the most important. Tomatoes should also be grown as far away as possible from tobacco, petunias, and potatoes, for the same virus may be present in these plants.

Can tobacco dust or nicotine spray be used safely on tomato plants? I think I read somewhere that a virus disease results. (New Jersey.) The tomato mosaic virus is carried in ground tobacco, so that one should not smoke while working with tomatoes or use tobacco dust. However, nicotine sulfate used as a spray apparently does not carry the infective principle, and nicotine dust made from nicotine sulfate mixed with lime would also be safe. The gardener can carry the virus from plant to plant on his hands, which should be washed frequently with soapy water while working with tomatoes.

What can we do to overcome brown specks on our tomatoes? Will lime overcome this? (New Hampshire.) Brown spots on the leaves and sunken black spots on the stems and fruit may be due to early blight caused by a fungus (Alternaria). Look for resistant varieties in catalogs. It is better to use sprays without lime, because this causes blossoms to drop off (lime in the soil is a perfectly good recommendation). Spray weekly or biweekly with maneb, captan, zineb, or chlorothalonil. Use clean seed and practice crop rotation. Do not apply maneb or zineb later than 5 days before harvest.

What causes anthracnose on tomatoes? What is the remedy? (Indiana.) Anthracnose is a fruit spot rather common in the central states. The spots are dark, sunken, with concentric markings, and there are pinkish spore pustules in the center. The fungus lives in the soil, so that a 4-year rotation should be practiced. Avoid poorly drained soil and fertilize properly. Pick all ripe fruit as soon as possible. Spraying with maneb, zineb, captan, benomyl, or chlorothalonil is effective.

My tomatoes had an earthy flavor and were mushy. Was it the variety or the soil conditions? August was a wet month. (New York.) The rainy weather may have caused growth cracks in which one of the mold fungi grew to produce the mushiness and the flavor, which should not be charged against the variety. Staked tomatoes suffer less in a wet season. Pick tomatoes frequently, and remove and destroy all soft and rotting fruit.

What is the best formula to prevent rust on tomatoes in southern Florida? The "rust" is probably sunscald; there is no true rust common on tomatoes. Keep as much foliage as possible on the plants, so that the fruits are not exposed to the sun in hot, dry weather. Verticillium and other wilts that cause loss of lower foliage increase sunscald. A very light covering of straw over fruit clusters may reduce this disease.

Are there many diseases that attack tomatoes? There are many leaf and fruit spots, wilts, and blights; southern states have to contend with nematode root knot and southern blight, while virus diseases, curly-top, and spotted wilt are prevalent in the Northwest. Consult your Cooperative Extension Service if you need help. Despite diseases, tomatoes are an easy and prolific crop for the home gardener.

What is the easiest way to circumvent cutworms on tomatoes? A paper collar put around each seedling after it is transplanted. (See Cutworms.) Pouring ½ cup of diazinon spray mixture around each plant when transplanting is very effective.

What causes little holes in the leaves of tomato seedlings? (New Jersey.) Flea beetles. They may riddle the foliage if not controlled and seriously injure the young plants. Dust with rotenone dust or spray or dust with carbaryl. (See Flea Beetles.)

How can I get rid of the huge green caterpillars on tomatoes? (New York.) The large tomato hornworm is best controlled by picking off by hand. Or dust or spray with *Bacillus* or carbaryl. If the caterpillar is in the fruits, it is the corn-ear worm, also called tomato fruitworm. Destroy infested fruits as soon as discovered. The same treatment as for the hornworm will do, or use methoxychlor.

What is the pest on tomato leaves in August that looks like salt on the leaves and later turns into tiny flies? (Wyoming.) Your grains of salt are the nymphs of whiteflies, common on tomatoes in late summer,

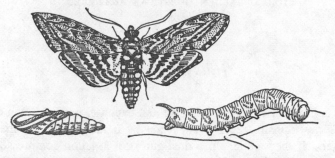

The tomato hornworm is a rather fierce-looking, large, and nervous green worm. It attacks tomato foliage and sometimes eggplants, peppers, and potatoes.

but not particularly injurious. Malathion or diazinon sprays or pyrethrum or rotenone dusts may control them. (See Whiteflies.) These insecticides kill only adults, so treat at 4-day intervals until eliminated.

How can I get rid of the yellow bug on tomato plants that looks like a ladybug? (New York.) The Mexican bean beetle occasionally wanders over to tomato plants but ordinarily does not require treatment there. (See Beans.)

A green bug, with shield-shape marking, stings and ruins our tomatoes. Is there a remedy? (Texas.) This is the green stink bug, a close relative to the squash bug. The nymphs are greenish with black markings and the adults are green or brown; they suck the sap of tomatoes, peas, beans, and other plants. Dust or spray with malathion or carbaryl when the young bugs first appear and repeat as needed. Also hand-pick.

Is there a way to get rid of the worm that enters the stalks of tomatoes in bloom so that the plant dies or falls over? (Missouri.) Getting rid of the weeds in the vicinity is the best and practically only way of getting rid of the common stalk borer. (See Borers.)

TURNIP (BRASSICA RAPA RAPIFERA)

What can be done about maggots in turnips? See Cabbage.

Why do yellow turnips rot in the ground? (New York.) Sometimes bacterial soft rot follows along with the maggots, especially in a wet season and if the plants are crowded together in the row. Thin your turnips early and space widely. See that the rows are far enough apart. Remove all diseased turnips immediately. Practice crop rotation.

Fruits—General

What is the least equipment, in size and expense, needed by an amateur to spray 12 fruit trees? (New Jersey.) It all depends on the size of the trees. If they are small, a dust gun or a 3-gallon compressed-air or knapsack sprayer might do the job for a while. For somewhat larger trees, you might manage with a slide (trombone) sprayer or a hose-end gun or a bucket or barrel pump on wheels. For 12 mature trees, you would need some sort of power sprayer.

For backyard fruit trees, what sprayings are really necessary? (Mississippi.) That depends on the backyard, but ordinarily several sprays including a calyx spray, when most of the petals have fallen, and a foliage spray 10 days to 2 weeks later are most indispensable. (See also discussions under the different fruit hosts.)

When should fruit trees be sprayed, just before or after the bloom opens? (Mississippi.) It depends on the fruit and the pests you want to control. In general, sprays are not applied when fruits are in full bloom for fear of preventing pollination. The farmer usually applies

The 3-gallon compressed-air sprayer, knapsack type, is convenient for spraying small fruit trees.

what is called a "pink" spray on apples just before blooms open; but the amateur can often wait until it's time for the calyx spray, when most of the petals have fallen.

What is the best simple spray for fruit trees? (Michigan.) There is no one best spray for all fruit trees but various commercial fruit spray mixtures are available, to be used according to instructions on the label. If you want to make your own, one multipurpose spray consists of 2 tablespoons of captan, 50 per cent W.P. (Wettable Powder); 2 tbsp. malathion, 25 per cent W.P.; and 3 tbsp. methoxychlor, 50 per cent W.P., to 1 gallon of water. Kelthane is added to this mixture as necessary for mite control. In addition, peaches might have a dormant spray of ferbam or Bordeaux mixture and other fruits might have a delayed dormant (green tip) of oil. Ask your own county extension agent or State Experiment Station for a spray schedule suitable for home gardeners in your area.

What is advisable to use as a general spray for apple, cherry, and plum trees, and grapes? (Illinois.) The mixture given above would be a general spray for your fruit trees. For grapes, spray just before and just after bloom, repeat 10 days later, and again after 14 days. Your county extension agent or Agricultural Experiment Station can send you a circular on spraying fruits in Illinois.

When is the best time for dormant spray of fruit trees? What spray can be used? Can this spray be the same for apples, peaches, plums, and cherries? (New York.) The dormant spray is best applied after the buds have begun to swell but before they show green at the tip. Probably you could safely use a 1 to 9 dilution of lime-sulfur on all these fruits, or even an oil spray, but you will get much better results if the spray is directed at specific pests for each kind of fruit and timed for these. (See also the discussion below under different hosts.)

How and when should fruit trees too small to have fruit or blossoms be sprayed? Bulletins tell about pre-blossom sprays, etc., but with no older trees around, how are you to know when to spray? (New York.) Having no fruit, you do not have to use all the different sprays, for they are chiefly intended to provide sound fruit. If scale is present, put on a dormant spray; later you can spray the foliage to control cankerworms, Japanese beetles, aphids, etc., if these insects appear and are injurious.

Do you know what will kill rose chafers without killing fruit trees and bushes, which they attack so furiously in June that we get no fruit? (Michigan.) Your county Cooperative Extension Service or State Agricultural Experiment Station says that rose chafers attack in the vicinity of sandy quackgrass sod. You must be on the alert to spray as soon as they appear. Carbaryl sprays will help keep them in check.

What is the best method to deal with Japanese beetles in a young orchard? (D.C.)   Spray with carbaryl.

How can I get rid of lice on my fruit trees? (Minnesota.)   Add 2 tablespoons of malathion to a gallon of spray mixed up for other purposes. Malathion should be especially added to a delayed dormant spray to control aphids.

Mice or rabbits gnaw the bark of my young fruit trees. What shall I do? (New York.)   Mechanical protectors such as wood veneer, tar paper, cloth, or ¼-inch galvanized wire are most satisfactory in protecting young trees from injury. The wire is best. Keep it away from the trunk except at the top of the wrap. Protectors must be 20 inches higher than the winter snow line. For repellents, see Rabbits.

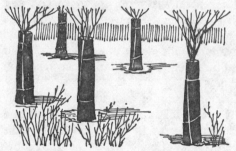

Young apple trees can be protected against injury from rabbits by tar-paper or hardware-cloth cylinders fastened around their trunks.

Is there any repellent I can put around young fruit trees to keep the deer and rabbits from eating the new leaves next spring?   Various repellents have been tried with success in some cases and no success in others. Contact your county extension agent or State Agricultural Experiment Station for regional help.

Specific Fruits and Their Pests

APPLE (MALUS)

How can I get 1 or 2 large apple trees effectively sprayed without spending more money than the fruit is worth? (Massachusetts.)   You cannot expect to get 1 or 2 fruit trees sprayed without its costing you much more than the fruit itself is worth. You have to balance the account by considering apples also as ornamentals and think of the fun you have picking your own fruit. The charge for several sprays must cover the time of 2 men, cost of materials, transportation of a special trip for only 1 or 2 trees, and the seasonal nature of the work. To save money, you must do the spraying yourself, which would not have much effect on a large tree, or else resign yourself to wormy apples. A surprising amount of pies and applesauce come from unsprayed apples. One unsprayed tree may provide 7 families one summer with all the applesauce they can set aside for winter. If trees are not sprayed, it is very important to clean up all dropped apples every week.

How many sprayings of apple trees are indispensable for reasonably satisfactory fruit in the home garden? When we have our trees sprayed 5 times, it is much cheaper to buy apples. (Ohio.) Five sprays are supposed to be the minimum for sound fruit: dormant, cluster bud, calyx, and first and second codling-moth sprays, but often the dormant spray may be omitted if there are no scale insects, and possibly one or two other sprays. The calyx spray, when 90 per cent of the petals have fallen, and the first codling-moth spray, 17 days after calyx, are probably most useful in providing reasonably clean fruits. Use a general-purpose spray.

About how many gallons of spray should be used to cover a 5-year-old apple tree and a 10-year-old tree—for dormant and full-leaf sprays? (New York.) A foliage spray for a 5-year-old apple requires 1 to 2 gallons; 10-year-old, 4 to 5 gallons; 25-year-old, 12 to 15 gallons. A dormant spray might take about half as much.

Can old apple trees that bear many infected apples ever grow sound fruit? (New York.) Yes, with a definite spraying program combined with rigid sanitary measures.

What is the easiest and best way to spray a few apple trees infested with codling moth? (Massachusetts.) There is no easy way, but in Massachusetts the calyx and second cover sprays are most important.

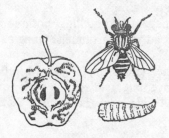

Apple maggot is a common pest. A small black and white fly is its parent.

What is a practical control of curculio on apples in the small garden? (Massachusetts.) Calyx and first cover sprays are most important in controlling curculio. (See the schedule below.) Gather and destroy dropped fruit every week.

My 'McIntosh' apples this year were covered with black spots, ⅛ to ¼ inch in diameter. The trees were sprayed. Can you identify it and suggest a remedy? It seems to be a local infection. (Massachusetts.) 'McIntosh' apples are very susceptible to scab, a fungus disease more prevalent following a wet spring. It is controlled by maneb, mancozeb, ferbam, captan, or wettable sulfur sprays, which must be carefully timed. (See the spray schedule below.)

A spray schedule for Massachusetts is as follows:

Delayed Dormant—Desirable spray if red mite or San Jose scale is present. Use dormant oil according to manufacturer's recommendations.

Pre-Pink—Desirable on 'McIntosh' and other susceptible varieties to control scab. Five level tablespoons of wettable sulfur or 2 tablespoons of captan and 3 tablespoons of methoxychlor to 1 gallon of water.

Pink Spray—Important for scab-susceptible varieties. Same mixture as pre-pink but add 1 tablespoon of malathion for aphids.

Calyx Spray—Important to control scab, codling moth, and curculio. When 90 per cent of the petals have fallen, apply 5 tablespoons of wettable sulfur or 2 tablespoons of captan and 3 tablespoons of methoxychlor to 1 gallon of water.

First Cover Spray after Calyx—Important to control curculio, leafhoppers, and scab. Apply when the temperature reaches 75° F., 5 or more days after calyx spray, using 5 tablespoons of wettable sulfur, 3 tablespoons of methoxychlor, with 1 tablespoon of malathion per gallon of water.

Second Cover Spray—Important to control codling moth, scab, and sometimes curculio. Apply 7 to 10 days after first cover spray, using same materials as first cover.

Third Cover—Important for apple maggot and scab. About July 10, when maggot flies appear, apply 5 tablespoons of wettable sulfur and 3 tablespoons of methoxychlor to 1 gallon of water.

Fourth Cover—Important for apple maggot and codling moth. Apply about July 25 to prevent maggot (railroad worm) tunnels. Same as for third cover.

What sprays should be used on an uncared-for apple orchard in New Jersey? About the same sprays as above, but send for the New Jersey Apple Spray Schedule from the State Agricultural Experiment Station, New Brunswick, N.J. 08903.

What causes brown spots through the interior of apples and what will prevent this? (New Jersey.) Probably the apple maggot, a slender white worm that feeds within the pulp and carries with it germs of a soft rot. The adult is a small black and white fly. The maggot winters in the soil as a small seedlike pupa; the flies come out in the summer, usually in July. The 2 sprays listed as third and fourth cover in the Massachusetts spray schedule above should work in New Jersey but check with the Experiment Station in New Brunswick or your county extension agent concerning the proper time to apply them. Cleaning up every rotten, dropped apple is very important in preventing more maggot trouble for another year.

How can I reclaim apple trees whose fruit is always badly infested with railroad worms or, I suppose, codling moth? (Vermont.) Railroad worms are apple maggots (see the preceding question) and quite different from codling moth larvae, which are larger, ¾ inch long, pinkish white with brown heads. The larvae winter in cocoons in the crotches and under the bark of trees. The moths emerge to lay their eggs in warm, dry weather about a week after the petals have fallen. The newly hatched caterpillars enter through the calyx cup of the fruit unless a poison spray is in place. Later-hatched caterpillars enter the fruit through the side. After 3 to 4 weeks inside the apple, the larva burrows through a mass of excrement to the surface and crawls down the branches for a suitable place for a cocoon. In addition to spraying, scraping the bark on the trunk up to 10 feet during the winter will be very helpful in reducing codling moth infestation. Chemically treated bands on scraped trees will collect larvae and prevent damage.

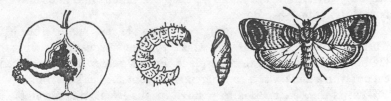

The codling moth is the parent of the worst apple pest.
The larvae are pinkish-white caterpillars, ¾ inch long,
and tunnel through apples and other fruits.

I spray my one apple tree 4 times as prescribed in all manuals, but recently the apples have brown spots throughout and are sort of knotty and misshapen. Why? (New York.) This is probably the result of apple maggot. You need a summer spray in addition, about June 25 to

July 1, which is a combined codling-moth cover spray and first apple-maggot spray. A second spray for maggots should go on about July 10 to 15. The misshapen, knotty apples are also occasionally the result of redbug punctures. Add malathion to the calyx spray if redbugs appear.

How do you prevent the apples from falling off the tree and getting wormy? (Illinois.) The 3 codling-moth sprays listed as minimum for Illinois are calyx, 17 days after calyx for the first brood, and 9 weeks after calyx for the second brood. Amounts of methoxychlor to use are given in the spray schedule for Massachusetts.

When and how often should I spray an old 'Baldwin' apple tree that bore very wormy apples this year? (New Hampshire.) For codling moth and railroad worms, the calyx, first cover, and third cover (about July 7) are most important. (See the Massachusetts schedule above for formulas.) Pick up all dropped apples and destroy them.

My apple trees are young but will soon need a spray. What can I use that will not be injurious to the bees? (Iowa.) Any insecticide may be injurious to bees; that is why spraying schedules call for treatment before the blossoms open or after almost all the petals have fallen.

I've had scale on an apple tree for more than a year. Will a dormant spray used next spring be effective to save this tree? (Illinois.) It should be. Unless there is an extreme infestation, scale insects will not kill a tree very quickly. Use a 3 per cent oil spray.

How can I raise apple trees without having them destroyed by borers? (New York.) Wrap the young trees when they are set out in Kraft crepe paper, starting several inches below the ground and going up to the lowest branch. Remove in August and rewrap in a few weeks for a second year. Wire wraps later will keep out rabbits and mice and check borer infestation. (See Borers.)

What should be done to borers deep in an apple tree? (New York.) Poke in a flexible wire where you see sawdust protruding from the bark and try to kill them in place. Borers nearer the outside can be cut out with a knife. Use a commercial fumigant such as Borerkil.

What is the best method to remove fungus from an apple tree? This runs from the ground to about 4 feet up. (New York.) If you mean a greenish moss on the trunk, that is of no consequence, but if you mean a collection of shelf fungi, they are indications of a heart rot inside the tree, which may or may not be worth saving by cavity treatment.

Why do red-cedar (Juniperus virginiana) evergreens harm apple trees? (Minnesota.) Because they form the alternate host for the cedar-apple rust. Spores are carried from the cedar galls in the spring to infect young apples and foliage, which will show rusty spots in midsummer. Maneb or ferbam sprays for apple scab will control rust. (See also Juniper.)

What is the cause and cure of blight on apple trees? (Illinois.) You doubtless refer to the bacterial disease known as fire blight, which kills back branches and blights blossoms so that they appear burned by fire, and produces cankers on twigs or the main trunk. Cutting out infected portions well below the visibly blighted area is most important, and so is breaking out blighted fruit spurs. If the disease is serious, apply a special full-bloom spray of streptomycin or a spray of Bordeaux (mixed according to instructions on container) to control the blight of blossoms.

What causes apples to rot on the tree and dry up? Is it a fungus disease or insects? What kind of spray should I use? (Illinois.) It sounds like black rot, a fungus disease characterized by mummied fruits and by frog-eye spots on leaves as well as a bark canker. Either ferbam, captan, zineb, or wettable sulfur in the regular pre-blossom sprays for apple scab should take care of black rot, provided that all mummied and rotting fruits are cleaned up. In southern Illinois, another fruit rot, called bitter rot, may be prevalent. The normal spray schedule will take care of this.

How can I get rid of powdery mildew on an apple tree? (Washington.) Cut out mildewed twigs at the time of pruning. Spray with 1 to 100 lime-sulfur or wettable sulfur in the cluster-bud and calyx stage and again 2 weeks after petal-fall stages. If a regular schedule for scab is being carried on, powdery mildew will be taken care of.

Is there anything that can be sprayed into the ground while the tree is in blossom to prevent 'Winesap' apples from ripening with specks and rottenness at the core? (Maryland.) Elgetol in earlier times was used to spray on the ground to eradicate the apple-scab fungus, but this would not be the cause of rottenness at the core. Rot and specks may be due to apple maggots, controllable by summer fruit spraying. Corky brown specks through the fruit sometimes come from lack of boron in the soil. In that case, you can apply powdered borax, ¼ to 1 pound, depending on the age of the tree. The larger amount is not safe on a tree under 25 years old. Apply it like fertilizer. One dose will last 3 years.

What is the cause and remedy of brown bitter spots on apples? (Wisconsin.) Either the bitter rot or boron deficiency previously discussed or a disease called bitter pit, due to some disturbed water relation with no very definite remedy.

What causes peculiar greenish sections in the flesh of some apples? (Connecticut.) Climate, variety, and water relations seem to have something to do with this physiological condition called water core. Maintain an even supply of water; maintain the proper balance between the root and the top by pruning; and pick the fruit at proper maturity.

My apples no sooner form in the spring than they become wormy and practically all drop off. (Long Island, New York.) This sounds like the European apple sawfly, a relatively new pest present in southeastern New York and Connecticut. This damage can be prevented by using a combination of malathion and methoxychlor in the calyx or petal-fall spray and in the first cover spray.

APRICOT (PRUNUS ARMENIACA)

What can be done against wormy apricots? A tiny worm starts eating around the stone and destroys the fruit. (Michigan.) This is the plum curculio, common also on apple, peach, and cherry trees. It is controlled by methoxychlor and malathion sprays and a stringent cleaning-up campaign. (See Plum.)

My apricot trees turn yellow and the fruit loses all its flavor. Is this a condition of the soil? (Utah.) In Utah it is probably a chlorosis due to a too alkaline soil, corrected by applying a fertilizer and equal parts of iron and aluminum sulfate, using 1 pound of mixture to each inch of diameter of the trunk. Apply beneath the branch spread, either in water solution or in holes 12 to 18 inches deep. Yellowing may also be symptoms of a virus disease. Consult your State Experiment Station.

BLACKBERRY (RUBUS)

How do you get rid of red rust in 'Alfred' blackberry? It acts like fungi but does not yield to sulfur; it is very contagious. (Missouri.) It is a fungus, officially named orange rust of blackberry. It lives all through the interior of the plant and cannot be controlled by fungicides as are other rusts. Remove diseased plants, getting out all roots, before the contagion spreads farther.

BLUEBERRY (VACCINIUM)

Why do my blueberry bushes have little pieces of wood, which look like worms, on the ground near the roots? (Massachusetts.) It sounds like frass (excrement) from a borer working in the stem. If you can find the hole, inject some borer fumigant, such as Borerkil.

CHERRY (PRUNUS)

When is the proper time to spray cherry trees to get better fruit and prevent insects? (New Jersey.) Write to the New Jersey Agricultural Experiment Station, New Brunswick, N.J. 08903 and request their extension bulletin on home-fruit-pest control.

After my cherry tree blossoms, the leaves curl up with aphids. When and with what will I spray? (New York.) A dormant oil spray helps to control cherry aphids. When the aphids first appear and before the young leaves curl, spray thoroughly with malathion, repeating as necessary.

How can I prevent the rot of cherries on trees? (Illinois.) Captan or benomyl will hold brown rot in check. Use captan in a multipurpose spray mixture at pink, petal-fall, and later stages, and also at full-bloom stage by itself. Insecticides must not be included during bloom; they kill the pollinators.

What causes cherry leaves to turn yellow in midsummer and drop off? What spray do you recommend? (Wisconsin.) This is a fungus leaf-spot, controlled by captan as in the preceding spray schedule.

What will kill worms that feed on the roots of cherry trees until the trees are killed? Will it be safe to plant another tree in this ground the following spring? (Michigan.) It is not clear whether you mean the peach tree borer, which works on the trunk under the soil surface, or the larvae of white grubs. Keeping the ground plowed and cultivated before replanting or treating for grubs will help get rid of the latter. The peach tree borer stays under the bark rather than in the soil; replanting in the same spot would probably be fairly safe. (See Peach.)

CURRANT AND GOOSEBERRY (RIBES)

Is gooseberry or any other berry harmful to pine trees? (New Jersey.) Gooseberries and currants are alternate hosts for the white pine blister rust. Where this disease is prevalent, they should be removed whenever they are found within 900 feet of white pines. Black currants are particularly susceptible to blister rust and should not be grown at all in rust areas.

Is there a disease-resistant currant? (Connecticut.) Variety 'Viking' is said to be resistant to white pine blister rust.

What causes red blotches on 'Red Lake' currant? (North Dakota.) Large reddish blotches on leaves of currants frequently indicate aphids working on the underside. If there are rusty patches on the underside of leaves, it may be white pine blister rust.

How can I rid currant bushes of aphids? (Illinois.) Add 1 tablespoon of malathion per gallon of water to any spray applied as soon as the foliage is developed, or put on a separate spray of malathion. Direct the spray toward the underside of the leaves.

What is the best insecticide for worms in gooseberries and currants? (Washington.) The currant fruit fly is a serious pest of currants and gooseberries in western Washington. White maggots feed inside the berry, causing the fruit to turn red and drop. Spray with malathion or contact your State Extension Service for the latest information on its control.

What is best to use on gooseberry bushes affected with leaf-chewing worms? (Indiana.) A combination spray of malathion and captan applied as soon as the foliage is well developed will take care of the currant worm (your "leaf-chewing" worm) as well as aphids and leafspot.

What causes leaves to turn brown in the early part of summer? (New York.) If there are dark spots on leaves and later defoliation, it is a fungus leafspot controlled by spraying with captan. If the whole shoot blights, it is caused by an internal fungus. There is nothing to do but cut infected canes at ground level.

GRAPE (VITIS)

What is the proper spray to use for black rot on grapes? (Ohio.) Black rot causes more loss than any other grape disease. The berries turn purple prematurely and change to hard, black, shriveled "mummies." Spray with captan, benomyl, or ferbam when new shoots are ½ inch long and again when they are 8 to 12 inches long; spray after blossoms fall with captan or folpet and repeat at 2-week intervals if the disease has been serious in other years.

What causes grapes to drop before they are ripe? (Pennsylvania.) Frequently the grape berry moth, which can destroy 60 to 90 per cent of the fruit on an unsprayed vine. Add 2 tablespoons of carbaryl to the ferbam spray applied just after petal fall, and again 10 to 14 days later. An additional spray might be necessary in late July or early August.

What do you do to keep Japanese beetles off grapevines? (Michigan.) Apply carbaryl when the beetles appear in numbers; repeat as needed.

How do you control rose bugs on grapes? (Massachusetts.) Cultivate the soil around the vines thoroughly in May and early June. Spray with 2 tablespoons of carbaryl to 1 gallon of water as soon as the beetles appear; repeat if necessary.

My grapevine is troubled with a small insect or fly early in the season, and a small bug or hopper in midseason. What spray should I use? (Wisconsin.) The early "fly" is probably a flea beetle, which will be controlled by the spray used for berry moths. Leafhoppers are sucking insects very injurious to grapes during the summer. Apply carbaryl in late June and early July.

How do you control mildew on grapes? (Michigan.) Spray with folpet, captan, benomyl, or zineb for downy mildew.

PEACH (PRUNUS PERSICA)

What is the white worm I find in the bark of my young fruit trees at the earth line? It buries itself in a jellylike mass. (New Jersey.) This is the peach tree borer, responsible for the death of many peach trees. The white, brown-headed worms, larvae of black and yellow wasplike moths, live in the bark from 8 to 10 inches above the soil to 3 to 4 inches below the surface. Control depends on chemical trunk treatments. Apply lindane as a drenching spray to the trunk from the first branch to the ground. Do not spray the fruit or foliage.

Is there anything we can do for the peach tree borer besides spraying? (Ohio.) You can fumigate in early fall after the young worms have hatched and are under the bark. The standard material is paradichlorbenzene. The crystals are placed carefully in a ring around the trunk, not closer than 1 inch or farther than 2 inches from the crown. The dosage must be very exact: 1 ounce for trees 6 or more years old, ¾ ounce for 5-year-old trees, and ½ ounce for 4-year-old trees. No treatment should be given to peaches set out for less than 3 years. Before placing the crystals, remove all grass, seeds, and debris from around the tree, and immediately afterward mound up with additional soil, being careful not to disturb the crystals. The time of treatment varies according to the state, usually September for New York and up to November 1 for the South. The soil temperature should not be much lower than 60° F. for effective results. After several weeks, the mound of soil should be leveled off. For more information, see Home and Garden Bulletin No. 211, *Control of Insects on Fruits and Nut Trees in the Home Orchard Without Insecticides* (USDA).

How do you get rid of the worms that make gum at the roots of peach trees? (Indiana.) If the trees are less than 3 years old, or there

A peach borer, a fat white grub, shown burrowing into a peach tree trunk. The adult moth, blue-black with an orange band, lays eggs at the base of tree trunks from early summer to fall.

are only 1 or 2, you can go after the worms with a knife or a wire, a process known as worming. See the previous questions and ask your own county Cooperative Extension Service for advice.

What, other than a borer, will cause peach trees to lose sap at the trunk and the tips of the branches to be coated with a gummy substance? (Pennsylvania.) The gum is one manifestation of brown rot, controlled with sulfur, captan, or benomyl sprays or dusts and also by cutting out diseased twigs and branches and destroying all infected fruit or old "mummies."

Shortly before the time for peaches to ripen, they rot on the tree and dry up. Is there danger of next season's crop being affected? If so, what is the treatment? (Pennsylvania.) There is very much danger of brown-rot infection from these mummied fruits on the tree or others that have fallen to the ground. Pick all the fruits and destroy them. Follow a spray schedule. (See Plum.)

What is the spraying program for peach trees? (Massachusetts.) Write to the Experiment Station, Amherst, Mass. 01002, or your local Cooperative Extension Service, and request their latest spray program for peach trees.

Red blotches on peach leaves are causing them to curl up. Why? (Massachusetts.) This is peach-leaf curl, a fungus disease. Its principal symptoms are much thickened distortions of the leaves, often followed by defoliation.

What is the best way to control peach-leaf curl? (Washington.) Spray before buds start to swell during the dormant season with ferbam or Bordeaux mixture according to the directions on the container.

Some insect I have never seen cuts a thin slice in the skin of each peach, from which oozes a colorless syrup. What is it? (Massachusetts.)   The cuts are made by the plum curculio, a snout beetle. (See Plum.)

The Oriental peach moth is attacking our 2-year-old peach trees, 3 different varieties. What remedy should be used? (Ohio.)   This small gray moth with chocolate markings is the Oriental fruit moth and lays her eggs in the leaves; the young worms bore in the twigs and later generations attack the fruit. Spray with malathion or methoxychlor with 3 applications—early July, mid-July, and early August.

The green tips of my peach trees died back all last summer; little white worms were inside the shoots. I was told that it was caused by the tarnished plant bug. Is there any control? (Indiana.)   Tarnished plant bugs do sting peach twigs and turn them black. There is little control except to destroy the weeds and sometimes to spray with carbaryl. However, since there were worms in the twigs, it was probably the Oriental fruit moth; this kills back the twigs also. (See the previous question.)

What should I do for yellows in young peach trees? (Alabama.)   Yellows may be due to a virus or to an alkaline soil. Ask your county extension agent for a diagnosis and help.

Why do our peach seeds split, causing the peach to rot? What is the remedy? (Washington.)   There is a physiological disease called split pit that results in rotting embryos and the gummosis of the fruit. The cause and remedy are not exactly clear, but the symptoms are more pronounced on a few varieties and in the years of a light crop. It is suggested that thinning be delayed 5 weeks after the pits start to harden.

What spray is used to prevent the dropping of premature fruits such as peaches? (Ohio.)   Hormone sprays are used to prevent the premature dropping of some fruits, usually apples. It is doubtful if they will work on peaches.

PEAR (PYRUS)

What is the cause of fire blight in pear and apple trees? (Iowa.)   Bacteria cause the disease but there are contributing factors. The more vigorous a tree, the more susceptible it is to fire blight because the bacteria prefer succulent tissue. Do not overfertilize (fall feeding is safer than spring), do not prune heavily, and do not cultivate around the trees. Some varieties, like 'Kieffer', are more or less immune.

Will spraying a pear tree while it is dormant check fire blight? There is no way to have all the diseased parts pruned out without ruining the tree. (New Mexico.)   You will lose the tree anyway if you do not have the diseased parts cut out, perhaps even if you do. The fire-blight bacteria are not on the outside, to be killed there by a spray, but are working down inside the twigs in the vascular system. Cut out *below* the infected portion of twigs and scrape away all dead wood from cankers on the main trunks and large limbs. Paint these wounds with Bordeaux paint, made by stirring raw linseed oil into dry powder. In the spring, the bacteria ooze out from the dead twigs and cankers in little droplets, which attract the bees. The bees, flying from blossom to blossom, carry around the bacteria and cause new infection. From blighted blossom clusters, the bacteria work down inside the twigs into the main branches. Spraying with streptomycin or Bordeaux mixture according to the instructions on the container when the blooms are open helps prevent this new infection. Break out all blighted blossom clusters.

Why did a few branches on my young pear tree die after the fruit was hanging on? (Pennsylvania.)   Probably fire blight. It may have been secondary infection from twigs or fruit blighted in primary early-spring infection.

Is there any practical remedy for curing fire blight on pear foliage? (Connecticut.)   No. If you see blighted foliage, you must cut the whole branch out 6 inches or more below the part that looks burned or blighted.

Is there anything that will cure pear blight? I had 4 dwarf trees. When the first one had it, I cut it down; the others all have it now. (Illinois.)   You cannot "cure" fire blight by any method. All you can do is to clean up infected parts and spray to prevent reinfection through the blossoms. Were you very careful to disinfect your tools after cutting down the diseased tree before working on the others?

I planted some pear trees in a 20-foot square space of apple trees. I am told that they will give the blight. Would you leave them, take them out, or use some spray to prevent it? (Indiana.)   Pears are much more susceptible to fire blight than apples, and if blight is in your neighborhood, which is more than likely, they will probably acquire the disease first, after which bees may carry it to your apple trees; your pruning shears will carry it unless you disinfect them between cuts. Formalin, at a 1 to 20 dilution, makes a good disinfectant. If you leave your pears where they are, plan on a blossom spray as described above.

What may I spray on a pear tree to kill a snail-like insect that kills the foliage? (Ohio.)   This is the pear slug, whose slimy dark-green to orange larvae skeletonize the leaves before they turn into sawfly adults.

If the pears are getting the regular apple-spray schedule, slugs will be controlled, or a separate spray of methoxychlor (3 tablespoons to 1 gallon of water) may be applied as soon as young slugs are noticed.

How can I get rid of the pear and plum leaf slugs? (California.)   The pear slug attacks pear, plum, and cherry trees. It can be killed by any kind of finely ground dust, but a 5 per cent malathion dust is preferable. It can also be killed by regular malathion, carbaryl, or methoxychlor sprays.

How can I get rid of bugs on a pear tree? Little worms are eating the leaves. (New York.)   See the two previous questions for the treatment of pear slug.

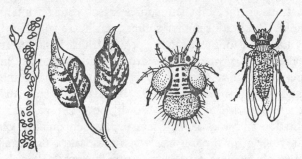

Pear psylla. The adult (right) is a reddish-brown fly with transparent wings.

Will you please give me information about pear psylla? (Massachusetts.)   The pear psylla is the most serious pest of pears, especially in the Northeast. The adult psyllids are only $\frac{1}{10}$ inch long, reddish-brown, with rooflike transparent wings. They live during the winter under the bark and in orchard debris, emerging in early spring to lay eggs in cracks in the bark and on the buds; the eggs hatch into yellow nymphs, which suck sap from the leaf and fruit stems and leaves. To control, spray with dormant oil at the green-tip stages. Use a multipurpose spray at pink, petal-fall, and then as needed.

About the first of August, the leaves of my young dwarf pear turned black and fell off. What caused this? (Maryland.)   The pear psylla, whose sucking causes defoliation. The black discoloration was due to a sooty mold, growing in honeydew surrounding the psylla nymphs. A summer spray of malathion is helpful if the psylla were not cleaned up by a dormant spray.

Is it proper to spray a pear tree in the winter that was covered with a

sort of mildew during the summer, or wait until spring? (Maryland.) If you mean a true mildew, i.e., a white coating on the leaves, summer sulfur sprays or dust will control it, but more likely you refer to the blighted effect produced by pear psylla. (See the above question.)

PLUM (PRUNUS)

A fungus gathers on our plums each year and the fruit rots on the tree as soon as it starts to ripen. Why? (Michigan.) This is brown rot of stone fruits, a fungus disease very common on peaches, plums, and cherries and sometimes injurious to apples as well. In early spring, spores are sent up from cup-shaped fruiting bodies growing out of old mummied fruits in the soil. The spores infect young fruits, producing grayish mold. These are summer spores, which are splashed by rain or carried by the wind to infect other ripening fruits. Diseased fruits wrinkle and either hang on the trees or drop to the ground as "mummies."

Will you please tell me how to spray plum trees so that the fruit will not rot and drop before ripening? (Illinois.) Captan or benomyl sprays are usually used to control brown rot. Write to your State Experiment Station and ask for their latest spray schedule for plums.

What do you do for a plum tree when the bark is dark and splitting and in a few places gum or a jelly is running out? (Virginia.) Gummosis is one of the symptoms of brown rot. (See the above question for advice.) Sanitation is even more important than spraying. Every mummied fruit fallen to the ground or left on the tree should be removed and burned.

How early do you spray plum trees? (Michigan.) If there is scale, especially San Jose scale, use a dormant oil spray, although this is needed only in occasional years. You can put on a pre-blossom or cluster-bud spray of captan, methoxychlor, and malathion, but for the home garden, the shuck or husk-split stage may be early enough to start spraying.

What is the chemical that is put around plum trees to prevent curculio? (Florida.) The curculio, a small, gray, hump-backed snout beetle, is the cause of wormy plums. There is no chemical for the soil, but keeping it well cultivated to destroy pupae and larvae in their earth cells and picking up and burning all dropped fruits are very important in controlling this serious pest. The methoxychlor recommended above is for the curculio.

What is the best spray for plums that will not be injurious to a small

apiary in an orchard? (Iowa.)   The spray schedule is so adjusted that there will be no poison on the open flowers when the bees go after nectar.

QUINCE (CYDONIA OBLONGA)

When and with what material should quince trees be sprayed? (New York.)   A spray schedule for New York State calls for a dormant oil spray if lecanium scale is present, and a pink spray and a calyx spray of captan, methoxychlor, and malathion to control leaf blight, leafspot, codling moth, and Oriental fruit moth. Repeat the spray at 3-week intervals until 3 weeks from harvest.

RASPBERRY AND BOYSENBERRY (RUBUS)

What are the various diseases that attack black raspberries? How can they be controlled? (Ohio.)   Virus diseases are green mosaic, yellow mosaic, leaf curl, and streak. Fungus diseases are verticillium wilt, orange rust, anthracnose, cane blight, spur blight, powdery mildew, leafspot, and bacterial crown gall. Most of these are controlled by sanitary measures—removing infected plants or plant parts. Many raspberry diseases are distributed in planting stock; order virus-free plants. A dormant spray of lime-sulfur, and pre-blossom and after-blossom sprays of ferbam or captan, will help control anthracnose and cane blight.

During the bearing season, we noticed overnight a bush or two stricken as if with heavy frost or a blowtorch, then turning black and drying up. We could find no insects. What caused this? (Michigan.)   This is cane blight, caused by a fungus that frequently enters through insect wounds. Remove the blighted parts immediately, destroy fruiting canes after harvest; avoid sites with poor air and soil drainage; control weeds; spray with lime-sulfur when the buds show silver, for a dormant spray, and with ferbam or captan 1 week before, again immediately after blossoming, and again after harvest.

How do I control orange rust on boysenberries? (New York.)   Orange rust is a systemic disease; that is, the rust fungus is found throughout the whole plant and not just on the leaves. Infected plants never recover; there is no control by spraying. Pull out diseased plants by the roots and destroy them before the rusty spores are shed to infect nearby brambles.

How can I rid my boysenberry vines of mildew? I used dry sulfur for 3 months but some of the runners died and the vines are all white.

(Washington.)   Try spraying with Karathane or with wettable sulfur with a sticker. Consult your county extension agent for the best spray for your locality.

How can I get rid of crown gall without having to throw away all of my berry bushes? (Illinois.)   You can't get rid of it. Even if you pull up these bushes, the bacteria will live in the soil for some years. Get healthy bushes and plant in a new location or sterilize the soil. Never bring in diseased stock from a nursery; refuse plants showing any signs of enlargements or galls.

What about insects on raspberries? (Wyoming.)   Raspberry pests in Wyoming include aphids, false chinch bugs, fruitworms, grasshoppers, leafhoppers, leaf slugs, legume bugs, mites, scales, strawberry leaf rollers, and root weevils. Your county extension agent will help you work out a schedule for control of pests most destructive in your garden.

Some insect cuts rings about ¼ inch apart on my red raspberry canes and deposits its eggs between. What is the insect and what is its control? (Ohio.)   This is the raspberry cane borer. The adult is a black and yellow beetle who deposits her eggs in new growth after first encircling the stem with 2 rows of punctures. The girdled tips wilt, and unless they are cut out, the young borers work down the canes. Remove all infested portions; cut out old canes after harvest.

Can red raspberries have little worms in the caps? (Ohio.)   Yes, these are the grubs of the raspberry fruitworm. The adult is a light-brown beetle that feeds and lays eggs on blossoms. Dust or spray with malathion or methoxychlor as the blossom clusters are forming; repeat in 10 days.

Is there anything that can be grown to attract Japanese beetles away from raspberry bushes? (New Jersey.)   They exert such a potent attraction that even soybeans may not entice them away. Pick your raspberries early in the morning, before the beetles are active, and keep the bushes dusted with rotenone.

STRAWBERRY (FRAGARIA)

How can you keep birds out of strawberry beds? (Illinois.)   Cover the beds with a fine-enough mesh netting so that the birds won't get caught and strangle themselves. Most garden centers and nursery catalogs sell a light net made for this purpose.

What is the strawberry weevil? (New York.)   The strawberry weevil, or blossom clipper, is a dark, reddish-brown to black, small snout beetle. It hibernates in rubbish in hedgerows and perhaps under the mulch in strawberry beds. It lays an egg in an unopened bud and causes it to fall by cutting the pedicel. The grub feeds on pollen and pupates inside the bud, going into hibernation in midsummer. Spray with carbaryl, malathion, or methoxychlor when the blossom buds appear and again before bloom. Dust with pyrethrum or rotenone after fruits start to form.

What causes strawberries to wilt and die just when they are in fruit? The roots turn yellow, brittle, and rot. (Wisconsin.) White grubs working on the roots will cause strawberries to wilt. These are most serious in land turned over from sod but may linger in soil in cultivation. They can be kept from injuring strawberries by treating the soil with Dursban or diazinon. Avoid planting strawberries immediately following sod. If no grubs are present, it can be a fungus root rot, in which case new plants should be set in fresh or sterilized soil.

What is the small black beetle that attacks our strawberries? (Illinois.) There are several beetle possibilities on strawberries. This one may be the adult of one of the strawberry root weevils. The grubs feed on the roots; later the weevils feed on the plants at night. Try a methoxychlor or carbaryl spray on the plants.

How do you deal with strawberry leaf roller? (Iowa.) This is a small greenish caterpillar that draws the leaflet together with a silken thread, feeds inside, and causes it to turn brown and die. Spray with diazinon or carbaryl in early spring just before the first blossoms open. Rotenone dust can be used after fruits form. Clean up the leaves after the crop is harvested.

Why do my strawberries turn white and the plants die? (Wyoming.) Chlorosis either from a virus disease or too alkaline soil. Send a specimen and a soil sample to your State Experiment Station, Laramie, Wyo. 82070.

14. Weeds

HOME GARDENERS, in common with farmers, nursery owners, golf greenskeepers, and others engaged in horticultural pursuits, are faced throughout the growing season with the problem of weed control. Keeping weeds out of garden areas where they compete with cultivated plants for nutrients and water is surely one of the most trying and time-consuming tasks of garden maintenance for the home gardener. While there has been much progress in the development of chemical weed-killers, the majority of them are for agricultural and professional uses and are often hazardous and may be of limited value to the home gardener and small property owner (see the second question below). The exception, of course, is in weed control in lawns, and here the home gardener is as much the beneficiary of modern technology as the nursery owner or greenskeeper.

The home gardener today, even though essentially still dependent on his own energy in controlling weeds among flowers, shrubs, and vegetables, can lessen his burden considerably by the use of mulches. Mulches look attractive, conserve soil moisture, improve plant growth, and contribute humus to the soil as they slowly decompose. In some home-garden situations, mostly in vegetable gardens, black plastic sheeting, available in rolls from garden centers or mail-order sources, is practical as a means of controlling weeds.

Q&A   General

How can you keep weeds down? By constantly attacking them while they are still young, and above all by preventing them from seeding. In borders and shrub plantings, use mulches; on cultivated ground, use a tiller and hoe, plus hand-weeding; on lawns, weedkillers and good culture will encourage desirable grasses; on drives and paths, use weed-killers.

I keep hearing about miracle chemicals that will take all the labor of weeding out of garden maintenance. And yet when I read the labels and instructions on containers of weedkillers in my garden center, I find the chemicals are for very special and restricted uses and situations—none of which seem to apply to my home garden. Is there one weedkiller I can use among my flowers, shrubs, and vegetables to kill weeds? Selective herbicides are chemicals developed to control some plants but not be harmful to desirable ones. It is not likely that you would find one that will rid you of all your weeds and be safe on all desirable plants. It is much easier for the large-scale farmer or nursery owner who grows many of a specific crop to solve a weed problem than the home gardener with a limited growing area and a wide variety of plants in a vegetable garden or in ornamental plantings. The home gardener may best rely on hand-weeding, hoeing, and the use of mulches. The hobbyist who specializes in one crop may well find herbicides to solve his problem. The major exception is weed control in lawns. You have to admit that the elimination of crabgrass seed germination by the use of pre-emergent chemicals is quite a miracle.

I have 6 acres, not worked for about 20 years, that are full of weeds. What is the best way to get rid of them? Is it best to till in the fall or spring? Consult your Cooperative Extension county agent for specific controls for specific weeds.

We intend to fence our lot in the spring. Adjoining are open fields. How can I keep down weeds at the base of the fence on the outside? If you are not planting too close to the inside of the fence and there are no roots of desirable trees under the fence, use one of the nonselective long-lasting weedkillers such as Princep, Pramitol, Hyvar X, Spike, or Aatrex.

Is there any method to kill weed seeds in a seed bed? The best method for most home gardeners is to keep the bed moist to encourage germination and then to cultivate 2 or 3 times (allowing 10 days between each cultivation) to destroy seedlings. Sterilization with Vapam is also effective, but it must be carefully applied according to instructions.

How can I get rid of weeds before and during the growth of parsley, besides weeding? Hand-weeding in the rows and frequent hoeing between the rows are the best methods for annual weeds. Stoddard Solvent Oil has been recommended. Consult your county extension agent for advice.

Is it possible to spray carrots to control the weeds? Yes. Stoddard

Solvent Oil can be used. For latest information in your area, consult your Cooperative Extension Service.

In August I put Turf-Builder around a privet hedge. Six weeks later a broadleaf weed came in thick around the hedges. Could it be the Turf-Builder? Turf-Builder is a proprietary plant food that certainly does not contain weed seeds. It probably stimulated the growth of weeds present in the soil, thus proving its efficiency as a fertilizer.

Is there anything that will kill weeds, yet not destroy flowers or vegetables? Cultivation sometimes followed by mulching is the safest approach. There is no herbicide safe on all flowers and vegetables. Dacthal and Vegedax are labeled for use on many established flower and vegetable plants to prevent weed seed germination—consult the label for specific crops and weeds. Adequate mulch may reduce weed seed germination sufficiently.

What can be done to keep a gravel drive free from weeds? This depends upon the weed problem, if there are tree roots under the drive, and where the surface water from the driveway drains. If the water from the drive does not flow onto desirable plants, including grass, some of the nonselective herbicides such as Pramitol, Hyvar X, Spike, or Aatrex can be used. Princep can be used over tree roots if they are not close to the surface. Use according to directions.

What is the name of a compound to put in paths between flower beds to eliminate weeds? There are two choices, the best of which is to use a herbicide that is safe in the flower bed at a slightly higher strength. The other alternative is to use a short residual herbicide such as Paraquat on growing weeds, making sure to keep it away from desirable foliage.

What is best to use in killing weeds in a brick drain? Providing the drain does not carry water into garden areas or into a pond or stream used by fish or animals, any commercial weedkiller should prove effective.

Is 2, 4-D dangerous to use? All herbicides can be dangerous unless used with extreme caution. It is best to use 2, 4-D and similar herbicides in a sprayer used only for lawn spraying because it takes special procedures to adequately remove them from a sprayer. Apply 2, 4-D as a coarse spray with low pressure on a day that the wind will not blow the droplets onto desirable plants. There are special applicators for lawn treating that are much safer than hand-spraying. Use low-volatile esters or amines to prevent fumes from causing damage to desirable plants.

How can I tell different kinds of weeds? See *Common Weeds of the United States* (Dover Publications).

I am planting a garden over an old asparagus bed and have tried many ways to kill the asparagus, even to digging up the crowns, but the asparagus persists. How may I rid myself of this nuisance? Keep digging. Every time an asparagus stem appears, dig out the root from which it arises.

Specific Weeds

How can one get rid of bindweed on a lawn without killing roses, trees, and shrubs? If the bindweed is actually growing in the lawn, spray with 2, 4-D. Digging out would be the only solution in the shrubbery.

How can I exterminate an extremely hardy vine resembling a morning-glory, having white flowers and seemingly endless roots? Doubtless hedge bindweed, a pernicious weed with deep thick underground stems and roots, every fragment of which can grow. Where it exists, either don't plant anything and constantly hoe, so that no leaves can build up a food store in the roots, or plant only low-growing crops that can be hoed frequently so that no vines can get started. Also it has been determined that repeated applications of 2, 4-D while the weed is actively growing can kill it nearly 100 per cent. Avoid spray or drift of 2, 4-D to desirable plants except grass.

How can I get rid of Bermuda grass? The U. S. Department of Agriculture recommends 8 tablespoons (¼ pound) of dalapon in each gallon of water. Apply 1 gallon of the mixture to each 1,000 square feet of lawn to be treated. Make one application in late June and another within 3 to 4 weeks to kill any remaining plants. Reseed 4 weeks after the second application if temperatures have been high and the area has been kept moist. Otherwise, wait 6 weeks before reseeding.

What can I do for Bermuda grass in flower borders? (Tennessee.) In borders it must be kept down by frequent hoeing and treating the invading Bermuda grass on the edges with dalapon.

How can I clear land of blackberry vines? Spray the vines during the growing season with a combination of 2, 4-D plus Banvel D (dicamba). If the vines show signs of recovery, repeat the treatment. The solution reaches the roots through the vines and kills them.

Can you name a formula to kill buckthorn or plantain? At what time of year should it be used? The plantains are easily controlled in a lawn by spraying with 2, 4-D in the spring or fall. Cultivation is very effective in the garden.

Narrow-leaf plantain (left), a deep-rooted weed in lawns. Dig up seedling plants. The broad-leaved plantain (right).

What is dicamba? Dicamba is 3, 6 dichlora—0 anisic acid, a growth regulator different in composition but similar in action to 2, 4-D, although affecting different weeds. It is used in combination with 2, 4-D for lawn weed and brush control.

What is more effective in controlling weeds, 2, 4-D or Banvel D (dicamba)? Both are effective, but 2, 4-D is best against dandelion and poor against chickweeds and clover, while Banvel D is more effective on chickweeds and clover but ineffective against dandelion.

We have some patches of Canada thistle in our garden. Is digging them up the best remedy? Yes, if the work is well done. Any pieces of root left in the soil will grow, however, and digging should be followed by repeated hoeings. You might also use a 2, 4-D formulation as a spray or aerosol to treat only the foliage of the Canada thistle.

We have a large hay field next to us with a few bad patches of Canada thistle. The seeds blow over into our garden. Can these patches be eliminated by spraying? Yes. Use 2, 4-D as a summer spray and again in early September when regrowth has occurred.

What is the best way to clean cattails and rushes from a lake's edge? The best practicable method is to dig them out completely. If the surface of the lake could be lowered for a considerable period, they might die out from lack of moisture. Also try spraying with Dowpon, for it has given good results, but first check with local authorities for safety to water.

What is the best method of fighting crabgrass after it has germinated? Pull every seedling as soon as it is big enough to recognize, thus preventing seeding (crabgrass is an annual). Postemergence sprays that have given good results are DSMA, MSMA, and AMA. Make 3 applications at 7- to 10-day intervals, the first soon after the crabgrass emerges.

Crabgrass is the bane of lawn-makers. (For   control,   see Lawns.)

How can creeping Jenny or moneywort be eradicated? This is the yellow-flowered *Lysimachia nummularia,* sometimes used as a ground cover. The herbicide 2, 4-D gives excellent control.

What is the best method for controlling dandelions? They can be pulled if the soil is soft from rain, but all the root must be removed as any piece can make a new plant. It is easier and more effective to spray with 2, 4-D or apply 2, 4-D with a rag or a cane with a herbicide applicator on the bottom.

Dandelion: To control occasional plants, cut the taproot well below the ground with a knife and prevent plants from forming seeds. Spray colonies of the plants with 2, 4-D.

How can one effectively destroy dock weeds? Specimens of small size can be pulled out when the soil is very wet. With larger plants, use the spot treatment with 2, 4-D recommended for dandelions.

What can be done to get rid of dodder? Dodder, also called love-vine, goldthread, strangleweed, desire's-hair, and hellbind, is a parasitic annual. Cut down and burn all infected plants before the dodder has a chance to seed, or treat the soil with Dacthal spray or in granular form before the seeds germinate.

What method of controlling chickweed do you recommend to the home gardener? There are several kinds of chickweed. The most frequently occurring ones are common chickweed, which is a winter annual, and mouse-eared chickweed, which is a perennial. Both are best controlled in the garden by frequent cultivation and in the lawn by spraying with mecoprop, MCPP, or Banvel D in early spring or fall. Do not use over the recommended amount of Banvel D once a year near trees.

Chickweed is one of the worst garden weeds. Control its spreading roots by cultivation or 2, 4-D.

Will you suggest a remedy for a much-branched, green, leafy weed with tiny daisy flowers, each having 5 white petals? I think it is called galinsoga. This is an introduction from tropical America. It is very sensitive to frost, but is an annual and so overwinters as seed. Hand-pulling large plants before seeds form and cultivation to kill young ones are the most practical remedies.

Is it possible to remove Johnson grass or quackgrass from a vegetable garden so that it will not be back the next season? These are two distinct species. Both may be eliminated by forking out as much as possible by hand, taking pains to get every root, and then by repeatedly cultivating the surface throughout the summer. Johnson grass is particularly resistant, and vigorous methods must be used. Attempts might be made to cover the Johnson grass or quackgrass with black polyethylene plastic. If properly done, this can kill it after two full growing seasons. As far as using chemicals on these two vicious spreaders in the vegetable garden, better write your State Experiment Station or call your county extension agent to see if there is anything new to be recommended. State regulations regarding herbicides differ.

The weed lamb's-quarters is common in my garden. How do you keep it down? This weed usually favors rich soils. It is controlled by cultivating and is easily hand-pulled. When the plants are young, lamb's-quarters makes excellent salad greens.

We have a shrub called Japanese-bamboo that is becoming a nuisance. How can it be eradicated? This is *Polygonum cuspidatum,* with the more accepted common name of Japanese knotweed. It is very difficult to control by digging because of its massive underground root system. If there are no trees nearby, repeated applications of dicamba will work. Otherwise it may be advisable to have a professional apply glyphosate (Roundup) to the foliage in late summer or early fall.

What will kill moon-vine or wild morning-glory? Dig out as much as possible, then keep the ground surface cultivated at frequent intervals so that no new shoot ever attains a height of more than 2 inches before being cut off. Spraying with 2, 4-D or 2, 4-D plus Banvel D also gives good control.

How can a fairly large patch of nettles in a field be eliminated? By repeatedly mowing so that the plants are never permitted to get more than a few inches high. Also, by spraying the plants when young with a commercial weedkiller.

Nut-grass is a troublesome weed in my garden. Can you suggest a means of eliminating it? This could be yellow or purple nutsedge, either of which are extremely difficult to control and practically impossible to eliminate because of the dormant tubers that can remain in the soil for many years before growing. In lawn areas, use AMA, DSMA, MAMA, MSMA, or basagran as a spray on growing plants. In garden areas, use the same treatment or incorporate Eptam in the soil to retard tuber sprouting.

What can be done to destroy petunia seedlings? I would like to plant something else in a former petunia garden, but the petunias come up by the hundreds each year. Hand-weeding or hoeing after the seedlings are up is the only practical treatment.

Can you suggest any means of getting rid of plantain (both narrow- and broad-leaved) in quantity? Very effective is 2, 4-D spray on turf.

How can I get rid of a patch of poison-ivy? On areas where no food crops will be grown, spray or use a brush to dab the foliage with amitrole. In areas with fruit trees or where vegetables will be planted, use Ammate. Do not handle or burn live or dead poison-ivy leaves, vines, or roots. Use gloves when treating poison-ivy.

How may I get rid of poison-ivy growing in a planting of lily-of-the-valley? Get someone immune to poison-ivy to carefully dig up the bed. Transplant lily-of-the-valley to another location for 2 or 3 years. Meantime, eliminate any poison-ivy that appears on the old site with commercial sprays such as Ammate or amitrole.

What is the poison-oak plant and how can it be destroyed? Poison-oak (*Rhus toxicodendron*) is similar to poison-ivy (*R. radicans*), but has more oaklike leaves. Spray with amitrole in nonfood-crop areas or

Ammate in food-crop areas. Keep off the foliage of desirable plants.

Every summer my garden is invaded by purslane. What can I do? This is an annual that develops rapidly in warm weather and rich soil. Attack vigorously with a hoe and cultivator while the weeds are still tiny. If the plants get large, rake them up and compost, otherwise they will root and grow again. Purslane, steamed in a little water, is an excellent potherb.

Which is the most effective way of ridding the ground of quackgrass? It grows in the soil around my shrubbery and cannot be exposed to anything that would harm these plants. Incorporate Eptam into the soil by cultivation immediately after applying the granules—see the container for rates. In the spring, work the whole area over with a spading fork and carefully remove all underground stems of the grass. Follow this throughout the summer by forking out every piece of the grass that appears before the leaves are an inch high. Or cover all the ground about the shrubs with black polyethylene film.

How can I eradicate redroot (pigweed)? This weed can be eradicated only by soil fumigation with Vapam, but usually adequate control can be secured by hoeing and hand-pulling.

How do you get rid of sandburs? Practice clean cultivation. The plant is an annual and can be controlled by clean cultivation or using the herbicide Dacthal before the seeds germinate.

How can I destroy sheep sorrel and at the same time use the ground for vegetables and flowers? Sheep sorrel is a sure sign of poor, infertile, and, usually, acid soil. Apply fertilizer generously and test for lime needs. Nitrogenous fertilizers are especially helpful.

Is there any method of destroying sumac other than digging it out? Spraying young foliage with a mixture of 2, 4-D and Banvel D (dicamba) when it is half mature in the spring, and a second time when regrowth is at about the same stage, has given good control.

I have an old trumpet-vine root in the ground and want to plant a fruit tree instead. How can I kill the heavy root so it won't take the strength from the fruit tree? Dig out the trumpet-vine root and turn over and fertilize the soil before planting the fruit tree. Or you can spray with a mixture of 2, 4-D and Banvel D (dicamba).

How can I get rid of white clover in my garden? White clover is best controlled in lawns by spraying with MCPP or Banvel D in the spring or fall. In garden areas, it is easily controlled by cultivation and hand-weeding.

What is the best method of getting rid of white snakeroot? Grub out the roots.

What is the best way to get rid of wild carrot? The plant is biennial and does not reproduce itself if it is cut down before it reaches the seedling stage. Also, 2, 4-D will control it.

Wild garlic is becoming troublesome. How shall I eliminate it? This is a most pernicious weed, once established. If the area is not too large, hand-digging, followed by destruction of every bulb, is best. Cultivate the surface frequently. Repeat spraying for several years with 2, 4-D in the spring when the garlic is tall, before the grass is cut. Dormant bulbs come up for a period of years, making repeated treatments necessary.

How can wild grapevines and poison-ivy be killed? These seem to cover every rock and bit of space on our farm. Goldenrod and milkweed mingle with these weeds. If the farm grows good crops, the poison-ivy can be controlled with Ammate. If there is poor control of the goldenrod and milkweed, use 2, 4-D on young foliage, repeated until control is adequate.

*Poison-ivy (left); Virginia-creeper (right),
often mistaken for it, has five leaflets.*

Can wild morning-glory be exterminated around the trunk of fruit trees without killing or damaging the trees? Maintain a circle of bare ground around the tree and keep this clean of all growth by scuffle hoeing every few days throughout two successive growing seasons. As an alternative, cover the infested area with black polyethylene plastic film for two seasons.

How can I get rid of wire grass? This name is applied to several distinct species of grasses, and also to a kind of rush. Several of these indicate soils low in fertility. Some are annuals; some are perennials. Frequent cultivation and prevention of seeding are recommended treatments. Dalapon spray is effective on many perennial grasses, sedges, and rushes.

I have a poplar tree, recently cut down, but the roots keep sending up suckers. How can I kill this 2½-foot stump once and for all without having to dig it out? Make a groove or hollow in the stump and place a half cupful of crystals of sodium sulfamate there. This will gradually dissolve in rainwater and be absorbed by the wood.

Can I spray brush while it is dormant in the winter and still expect a good kill? Yes, using a mixture of 2, 4-D and Banvel D (dicamba) in kerosene and directed to the base of the plants so that the stems are thoroughly wet on all sides.

In reading a trade magazine I saw an advertisement of a power company spraying brush along the power lines to kill the growth. Can I use this same material on my property? Certainly, it is usually a mixture of 2, 4-D and Banvel D (dicamba) mixed with water for use when plants are in leaf, and mixed with kerosene when plants are dormant. It is easily applied and very effective on many plants. It is easily obtained under the general name of brush killer. Keep off foliage of desirable plants.

We have an old pasture covered in spots with hawthorns as much as 6 inches in diameter. How can I best eliminate these plants without having to pull each one out with a tractor? Try spraying the lower base of the trees with a concentrated solution of 2, 4-D and Banvel D (dicamba) in oil in the winter while the trees are dormant.

We have a large flagstone terrace at the back of our house. Various low-growing plants—thyme, dianthus, etc.—grow between the stones, but are being crowded out by crabgrass. Is there a weedkiller to use that would not kill the desirable plants but eliminate the crab-grass? Spreading siduron or any other preemergent crabgrass herbicide in the spring over the terrace should nearly solve the problem. Use your lawn spreader to distribute the chemical, then use a broom to sweep the chemical particles from the flagstones into the soil spaces between the stones. While most crabgrass will be eliminated, a few plants can be expected.

We have many plants of poke-weed at our summer place. I have been told the plants are edible but others say they are poisonous. What is the truth? The truth is that the black berries, tap roots, and mature foliage (especially in late summer when it turns reddish) of the pokeberry (*Phytolacca americana*) are poisonous; but the emerging shoots in the spring are *not* poisonous and are delicious cooked in the same manner as asparagus.

Please give me a list of edible weeds. Pokeberry (see above); purslane; milkweed (*Asclepias syriaca*); dandelion; watercress; upland cress. For others see *Billy Joe Tatum's Wild Foods Cookbook and Field Guide* (Workman Publishing Company, New York, 1976).

How can I get rid of wild veronica in my lawn? There are many kinds of veronica (speedwell). You must have the veronica identified to determine which control measure to use. Consult your local county extension agent. Creeping veronica (*Veronica filiformis*) is best controlled at time of flowering by spraying with Dacthal.

How can I smother the unwanted growth of such woody brush as honeysuckle, Virginia-creeper, poison-ivy, and huckleberries that form patches in my woodland garden? I am afraid to use chemical brush killers as I have many groupings of wild flowers and shrubs, such as rhododendrons, yet the honeysuckle, etc., is too extensive for just hand-grubbing. This situation is not easily resolved. If you can use a rotary mower in such confined space, cut the brush as close to the ground as possible. Then pile on layer upon layer of newspapers. To hold the newspapers in place as well as conceal their presence, cover with half-rotted leaves, marsh hay, straw, grass clippings, or compost. Pull or cut any unwanted growth as it breaks through the papers and mulch. Eventually you will have a rich mixture in which to plant additional wild flowers, but in the situation as you describe it, there will always be a need for some hand-grubbing of alien growth. For one thing, birds, which are attracted to woodland gardens because of the shelter and food they offer, are bound to scatter seeds of the plants you wish to eliminate. Very cautious spraying of a herbicide such as amitrole on a day when there is no wind might be safe on the larger weed patches.

Describe the plant marihuana. Marihuana (*Cannabis sativa*), also known as hashish or Indian hemp, is a tall, rather weedy annual with narcotic properties. It is often found in waste areas or in fields. (It was once grown as an ornamental foliage plant in the British Isles.) It is native to Asia. It has alternate, compound foliage in a digitate arrangement of 3–7 leaflets which may be 9 inches long. The inconspicuous green flowers appear late in the summer, with male and female flowers being carried on separate plants as with holly. The tough fibers of the stems were once used to make rope.

Marihuana (Cannabis sativa) *is also known as hashish or Indian hemp.*

15. Regional Garden Problems

(*Arranged by States*)

CLIMATIC AND SOIL conditions, of course, do not follow state lines. Even within state boundaries such conditions may vary to a very great degree. Altitude, the direction of prevailing winds, the proximity of large bodies of water—all these and many other factors enter into the picture.

However, a certain amount of generalization based on the broad factors of latitude, topography, and the prevailing movements of large bodies of air can properly be applied to the climate of any given state. The relation of this fact to the growing of plants in any particular section of the country is obvious.

The residents of different states will find in these pages much information that will be of use to them. Also, much regional information for New England and Mid-Atlantic States has been given in other sections. But let us emphasize again, wherever some particular local problem is involved, the importance of consultation with some local authority, such as one's county extension agent or State Agricultural Experiment Station. The locations of the latter are given on page 1444. (The addresses and telephone numbers of county extension agents are found in the telephone directory, listed under your county and under the designation "Cooperative Extension Service.")

Alabama

What do you consider good group plantings of perennials and annuals, separately and mixed? Day-lilies and angelonia; physostegia and Shasta daisies; violets and zephyranthes; verbena and bouncing bet. For color combinations of annuals blended to taste, try pink cosmos behind deep-blue petunias; lupines edged with pansies. The possibilities are limitless.

What flowers can we grow to send to shut-ins during the winter months? Pansies in little grape or strawberry boxes, as well as in many leftover kitchen containers. Freesias, paper-white narcissus bulbs in small bowls of pebbles, wandering Jew in attractive little pots, and many different kinds of easy-to-grow but much-appreciated succulents.

What apple can be raised in Alabama as a successful commercial venture? In extreme northern Alabama, 'Delicious', 'Black Twig', 'Jonathan', 'McIntosh', and several other varieties of apples should grow successfully. Varieties developed largely in Israel are worth trying farther south. Consult local nurseries.

When is the best time to set out azaleas and in what type of soil, for best results in this state? It is the custom, but not essential, to move azaleas when they are in full bloom. Balled plants should be moved carefully into beds that have been prepared with rotted hardwood leaves, peat moss, and aluminum sulfate if the soil is not acid. The beds should be entirely free from lime. Be sure to set the plants at exactly the same level they grew in the nursery and water well.

I am told that my azaleas and camellias will do better if I mulch with oak leaves around them. Is this true? Yes. These plants succeed much better under a mulch than they do with clean cultivation. Oak leaves are excellent when applied about 4 inches thick. As the leaves decompose and the mulch becomes more shallow, pile on more leaves to keep the blanket up to the original thickness. A mulch retains moisture, prevents extremes of temperature, and discourages weeds.

What are some of the best bulbs for fall planting on the Gulf Coast? Calla-lily, hybrid amaryllis, iris species (native), leucojum, lily, butterfly-iris (*Moraea*), narcissus, and zephyranthes.

Will the cushion-type chrysanthemums succeed in the Birmingham area? Yes, these popular garden perennials do well in this locality.

What can I do for the powdery mildew on my crape-myrtle? At first signs, spray with Benlate or Karathane fungicides. Use 1 ounce to 25 gallons of water. Do not apply when the temperature is above 85° F. Dusting sulfur will do as well, but it must be carefully applied after each rain until the mildew is under control.

Are any day-lilies evergreen in southern Alabama? Yes, many of the choice hybrids are evergreen and are, therefore, of much value in the winter garden.

What sprays are recommended for various scales and insects common to fruit trees, and when should they be applied in Alabama? Combination or all-purpose sprays are available for use on fruit trees in the home garden. It is necessary, however, to spray a number of times each season to get satisfactory results. Spray as follows:

1. When leaves begin to bud out: apple, peach, plum, apricot.

2. When bloom shows color: apple, peach, plum, apricot, pear, quince, cherry.

3. When all petals have fallen: apple, peach, plum, apricot, pear, quince, cherry.

4. When shucks fall: cherry, peach, plum, apricot.

5. Every 2 weeks from petal fall to shuck fall: apple, pear, quince, cherry, peach, plum, apricot.

6. Two weeks before harvest: peach, plum, apricot.

7. After harvest: cherry.

Can fuchsia plants be left in the ground outdoors during the winter in the South? In certain areas and in certain well-protected places, fuchsias may be grown as garden perennials. If they are growing in the ground, they will be much hardier, of course, than if they are plunged in their pots. As potted plants they are quite likely to freeze. The plastic cones used for winter protection of roses can also be used on fuchsias.

When should gladioli be planted in Montgomery, Alabama? February or March, so that newly emerging flower scapes will miss the late frosts.

When should Bermuda grass seed be planted? Sow in early spring if it can be watered; during the summer rains; or in early autumn if winter ryegrass is not going to be used. When the grass shows definitely green, make a light application of a nitrogenous fertilizer and water in well. These feedings may be repeated at 4- or 5-week intervals during growing weather.

If grass (Bermuda or centipede) grows around the base of camellias

or azaleas, does it hurt them?   It is better to maintain circles free of grass around the bushes. A mulch of compost, bagasse, or leafmold placed on the ground surface is very beneficial.

How can I eradicate nut-grass?   Nut-grass is very difficult to eradicate in the lower South. It would be best to consult your regional county agent for recommendations based on your particular property.

What herbs are most suitable for southern Alabama?   *For fall:* anise, chives, winter savory, sage, and dill. *For spring:* sweet basil, summer savory, sweet fennel, coriander, thyme, and sweet marjoram.

What are the cultural requirements for Japanese iris in this state?   Japanese iris prefer a moisture-retentive soil of slightly acid reaction. The roots may be planted or transplanted after flowering or during the autumn and winter. Applications of a plant food in March, May, and July should take care of nutritional needs; a mulch is highly desirable.

What is the best fertilizer for nandina? I have strong, healthy plants, but the berries dry up and fall off before they turn red.   Any good commercial fertilizer mixture should suit nandina. An application in January, spread around the shrubs and lightly scratched into the soil, and another in June to mature the new growth, should be adequate under normal garden conditions. Keep the soil moist to avoid the drying of berries. Nandina berries will color best in full sun; they may be destroyed by very low temperatures.

Can oranges be grown along the Gulf in Alabama and Mississippi?   Yes. Satsuma oranges are dwarf citrus trees that belong to the kid-glove group. These are quite hardy, and when budded on hardy trifoliate stock, they will produce excellent early oranges along the upper Gulf Coast.

What is the proper method for growing pansies from seed in the South?   Pansies are cool-weather annuals and the seeds will not germinate well in the warm weather of early autumn. Seeds sown after the weather turns cool in October or early November germinate well and give flowering plants in April and May. Sometimes germination in warm weather can be hastened by placing a small seed flat, properly prepared, in the refrigerator for a week or so.

Will peonies grow well in Alabama? I was told that they grow best near salt water. We are quite inland.   Peonies are temperate-zone plants and in many parts of the lower South they will not succeed. It is not the proximity of salt water that assures success with peonies, but a combination of soil and a long, cold winter without warm breaks that will guarantee a complete dormancy in the peony crown.

Why are rhododendrons practically failures in the lower South, where soil conditions appear to be ideal, as both evergreen and deciduous azaleas and the white dogwood grow and bloom luxuriously? In the South there is not a sufficiently long or sufficiently severe winter season for most rhododendrons. Soil conditions may be ideal but climatic conditions are definitely not right for most rhododendrons. However, you can probably grow *Rhododendron chapmanii, R. ovatum,* possibly *R. fortunei,* and there may be possibilities for warm climate gardens in the rhododendrons from Malaysia.

What rock-garden plants will grow in partial shade in central Alabama? Most rock gardens are exposed to full sun, and the usual list of plants for rock gardens include few shade-loving species. There are many, however, that do excellently in partial shade. You could make a fine collection from the wildflowers of your locality. Deep pockets of earth may be prepared for hardy ferns, to be used as a dominant green note. Besides wildflowers, you could add sweet violets, viola, florists' anemones and ranunculus, alliums, zephyranthes, periwinkle, lily-of-the-valley, lady's-slipper orchids, and other native orchids of the Southeast.

What roses would you suggest for Alabama? In addition to the hybrid teas, you can grow such tea roses as 'Duchesse de Brabant', 'Sombreuil', and 'Maman Cochet', which are too tender for northern gardens.

What about planting roses deeper than usual in the South? In this locality tests have shown that it is much better to set roses at exactly the same depth that they grew in the nursery.

When should bush roses be pruned in central Alabama? In February or in March, just before growth commences. Head the canes back to 4 or 5 good strong eyes if you wish to prune low to produce a few perfect flowers. If you prefer tall, luxuriant bushes covered with masses of smaller blooms, prune as high as you wish, but remove all half-dead or diseased wood and cut each healthy cane back somewhat. Pruning cuts should be made about ¼ inch above a strong eye that points away from the center of the plant.

I have been told that I cannot grow tulips on account of the winter temperatures here. Is this true? Only partly true. Tulips cannot be successfully grown in the Deep South without special prior treatment. They require several months of cold weather and a cool spring to develop normally. Ask your supplier about specially treated bulbs. Do not, however, try to keep tulip bulbs in a refrigerator. Temperatures below

40° F. will start both root and top growth, spoiling the bulbs unless planted at once.

Alaska

We must move to Anchorage. Will it be possible for me to have a garden there? Yes, but because of the short summers (less than 100 days of growing weather), your choice of plants will be restricted. Most annuals do well—especially when started indoors under fluorescent lights. The University of Alaska (mailing address: Cooperative Extension Service, Fairbanks, Alas. 99701) maintains a display of ornamental plants suitable for home gardens in the region; you could write them for literature to study before your move. You will be able to obtain help and ideas from Anchorage's Parks and Recreation Department, which maintains a greenhouse and extensive public plantings.

What house plants can I grow in Alaska? Almost all the plants you can grow indoors in more benign climates. Your major concern must be with light and coping with the short days of winter. However, this is easy to remedy with the installation of fluorescent light fixtures, under which you can grow African-violets, succulents and cacti, orchids, coleus, geraniums, wax begonias, azaleas, asparagus-fern, chrysanthemums, etc. Greenhouses are very popular and, even though the amount of light is increased, many owners add fluorescent light units to improve plant growth and to make use of every bit of growing space. Many greenhouse owners also grow certain vegetables, such as tomatoes and cucumbers, which cannot produce fruits outdoors because of the short summers.

Where should I go in Alaska to see wildflowers? Mt. McKinley National Park, accessible from Anchorage and Fairbanks, is one of the best places. The park is open from June 1 to mid-September.

Arizona

What are the characteristics of the soils of Arizona, Colorado, and New Mexico? The whole Southwest region has, except for the mountain areas, few forests or other vegetation to provide humus. Hence, in general, the soil, whether sand, silt, clay, or caliche, requires the addition of much humus. The compost pile is very necessary here. Peat moss, rotted strawy manure, any decayed vegetation is useful. One successful gardener in central New Mexico began with a half acre of caliche—shale clay. She first put on a heavy layer of dairy manure and had a team plow and harrow this. Next came 20 bales of peat moss. A surface mulch of peat moss and manure each fall with constant additions from the compost pile kept her garden growing and blooming with a lushness unbelievable when one saw the surrounding soil and vegetation. The lack of humidity in the air, as well as low rainfall, makes much watering necessary. Incorporation into the soil of generous amounts of humus helps it to retain moisture and so reduces the labor of watering.

What are the best flowering plants to stand Arizona desert heat?   Perennials that flower early, followed by annuals that can stand heat and dry air. Native plants should be most satisfactory. Such early perennials as dwarf phlox, dianthus, iris, euphorbia, oenothera. Annuals: verbena, zinnia, marigold, mesembryanthemum, mirabilis, petunia, portulaca, salvia, Xanthisma texana (star of Texas), California-poppy, venidium, xeranthemum, and Texas bluebonnet.

What kind of flowers can be planted in the fall in a high altitude (7,000 feet) where it is very cold?   Fall planting of perennials is more successful in this climate if done early—even before the first killing frost. Plant shrubs and roses in either fall or early spring. For fall planting: lilies, narcissus, peonies, pyrethrum, iris, campanulas, tulips, phlox, dianthus, dictamnus, heliopsis. Hybrid tea roses can be planted, if covered during the winter. Polyantha and floribunda roses should be quite satisfactory, and will give a long season's bloom and require little or no winter protection. Among the sturdiest are 'Else Poulsen' and 'Spartan'. Climbing roses are more difficult, since in your climate they require protection from the winter sun. Some of the hardiest are 'Paul's Scarlet', 'White Dawn', 'New Dawn', 'Blaze'. Shrub roses include rugosa and rugosa hybrids, R. hugonis; and the best of the hybrid perpetuals. (See also Section 6, Roses.)

Can you advise me as to a good climber, either annual or perennial? I live in a hot, dry climate, and the season is long.   Annual: madeira-vine, coral-vine, Cobaea scandens, gourds, thunbergia, cardinal-vine, morning-glory, moonflower. Perennial: passion-flower, trumpet vine, Clematis texensis, Lonicera heckrottii, silver fleece-vine.

When is the best time to plant chrysanthemums in Arizona?   Spring. Even late-spring transplanting brings earlier and more profuse bloom than if the plants are left undisturbed. Divide old clumps in the spring.

Can wild Indian paintbrush be transplanted and if so, how and when? Indian paintbrush (*Castilleja chromosa*) is partially a parasite. To transplant successfully, its host must be transplanted with it. *Chrysothamnus* (rabbitbrush) is one host of *Castilleja chromosa*. Transplant any time when the ground is sufficiently moist to make a ball. They move easily in full bloom if kept well watered. Dig a trench around the plant, then lift it with a ball or clump not less than 1 foot in diameter, taking with it any other plants contained in the ball.

Can I grow Lilium bakeranum in Arizona? *Lilium bakeranum* is listed among the difficult ones. Since it is a stem-rooting species, bulbs should be planted about 3 times their own depth. To prevent drying, as well as alternate freezing and thawing, a mulch is necessary. In its western China home, it grows on steep, loamy slopes among shrubs and grasses.

When is the proper time to plant lily bulbs in our southern country? The time to plant lily bulbs is determined by the time of dormancy of the bulbs rather than by the climate of their new home. *Lilium candidum* is planted in August and September. Top growth begins immediately. Plant lilies whose bulbs mature later (the majority of species and hybrids), in September to November.

What climbing rose will do the best here? All the climbing forms of hybrid perpetuals and hybrid teas should do well. Some that are grown successfully in the Southwest are 'Blaze', 'New Dawn', 'Climbing Crimson Glory', and 'Climbing Talisman'. Protection from winter sun may be necessary on a southern exposure. Spruce branches or cornstalks may be woven into a rose trellis, or roses, support and all, may be laid on the ground and covered.

Arkansas

Will delphinium and Oriental poppies grow in this part of the country? Yes. *Delphinium* x *belladonna* is more likely to prosper than some of the fancy hybrids. Pacific Hybrid delphiniums can be grown in your area only as biennials.

What flowers can I plant in a coco-grass-infested area? Few plants have the persistence of these stoloniferous grasses. Some that may fight their way are goutweed (*Aegopodium* 'Variegatum'), Kenilworth-ivy, buttercup, strawberry, and moneywort (*Lysimachia nummularia*). Consult your county extension agent for a chemical control for hard-to-kill grasses.

Can I put poinsettia plants outdoors in the summer? They can be put out during warm weather, in a spot with sunshine, but sheltered from strong winds. Be sure to bring them inside in the fall before night temperatures drop below 55° to 60° F. (See Section 12.)

California

What can I mix with adobe soil to make a garden? Two very good materials to mix with adobe soil are decomposed granite and bean straw. A 3-inch layer of granite, dug in deeply, followed by a deeper layer of bean straw, also dug in deeply, will help greatly. Where available from electric utilities, steam cinders that have weathered over the winter make excellent soil conditioners. Decomposition of the straw should be permitted to advance well before planting is done. This treatment will not improve drainage, for adobe is generally too deep.

What kind of fertilizer is best for adobe soil? Have your soil tested. Follow the recommendations made according to the results of the test.

What is the treatment for hard, black soil near Los Angeles? (See Section 1.) The most important consideration of all is in respect to water. First, don't ever work adobe soil when it is wet, for it will cake and harden and be put out of condition for a long time. Second, do not overirrigate, for it drains poorly. Tile drainage, if not too costly, can be used to improve heavy soil. Check the soil to see how deeply it has dried, and aim to irrigate just enough to moisten the soil to that depth. Cultivate as soon as the soil surface is dry.

How can adobe soil be made to produce? See the previous questions. Alkalinity must also be considered. If the plants look yellow and stunted, there may be an alkaline condition. Soil sulfur or ferrous sulfate, at the rate of 2 pounds per 100 square feet, will reduce the alkalinity. More or less may be used yearly, after the first application is made as a test. Normally, adobe soil produces heavily.

It is cold and often foggy here, and this seems to slow plant growth down. Would an extra amount of fertilizer give plants beneficial warmth? No. Commercial fertilizers will not supply any warmth to the soil. However, nitrogen fertilizer will stimulate growth if the soil is not too cold, and phosphorus and potash may be used to hasten maturity.

We had to import soil for our garden, but now it is worn out. Can it be improved?   The lack of humus in most California soils is the cause. The imported soil may have had some, but the thin layer was stripped very soon. Soils wear out from lack of humus. Addition of bean straw, manures, or peat moss would have helped maintain the purchased soil. Follow a yearly program of planting the garden area to a cover crop of cow peas or other legumes, to be tilled under when 6 inches tall. This will provide a constantly increasing supply of humus. Add compost, and if available, animal manures mixed with peat moss. During the growing season, feed little and often with a complete plant food or with liquid fertilizer.

What can be done with soil spoiled by the oil from the pods, leaves, and bark of eucalyptus trees?   First, clean off all debris; then turn the soil as deeply as possible. Permit rains and heavy waterings to leach out the toxic oils. After lying fallow during the winter, the soil should be in fair condition. Constant raking must be practiced to keep off the debris.

My soil is light, has no clay subsoil, and requires too much water. How can I use less?   The problem is not one of using less as much as of *losing* less. Add as much humus as possible, preferably with peat moss. Cultivate as soon as the surface is dry. In irrigating, do not wet the soil too deeply for annuals, vegetables, or shallow-rooted plants, for the water will drain away. Trees and shrubs should be irrigated deeply and seldom, to encourage deep rooting. One solution is to dig out light soil to a depth of 12 inches and lay down plastic. Replace the soil with added compost.

What is a good book on soils and fertilizers for California?   Some of the very best information on the subject is to be found in bulletins of the State Agricultural College in Berkeley, Calif. 94720. Also consult your county Cooperative Extension Service.

Can one make an attractive garden with perennials alone?   It often seems like less work to grow perennials, but if results are desired, they involve about as much work as annuals. One should start off with a good shrub background, not too tall, to add to the appearance and break the wind. Then select perennials that are proven in your region. Select them for durability, successive blooming dates, and reasonably clean habit. Interplant with bulbs and corms like lilies, muscari (grape-hyacinths), watsonia, calla, and others that grow in your area for several years without lifting. Although perennials do create spectacular effects, annuals will usually produce more bloom all summer long with far less time and effort.

What are the best flowers for winter, spring, summer, and fall?   This could make a long list, but here are some good ones: *Spring:* freesia, calla, ixia, sparaxis, narcissus, minor bulbs, sweet peas, snapdragon, columbine, mesembryanthemum. *Summer:* geranium, heliotrope, lantana, fuchsia, dahlia, gladiolus, montbretia, tigridia, haemanthus, gaillardia, marigold, zinnia. *Fall:* hardy asters and chrysanthemums. *Winter:* sweet pea, calendula, snapdragon, stock, various kinds of dianthus, and wallflower.

What are some good border flowers or plants, not over 12 inches high? Annuals that might answer the purpose are lobelia, portulaca, ageratum, low-growing marigolds, sweet-alyssum, and *Phlox drummondii.* Perennials could be *Chrysanthemum mawii, Nierembergia hippomanica,* day-lily, coral-bells, *Aster* x *frikartii,* and gazania.

What flowers will grow in pots in the sun all day? The reason most plants fail under these conditions is the rapid drying of the soil. The soilless mixes tend to dry out more slowly although pots (in contrast to larger planters) usually need plenty of water under most circumstances.

What plants will hold adobe soil on hillsides? Nothing surpasses the common ice plant (mesembryanthemum) for this purpose; but other good ones would be honeysuckle, creeping lantana, geranium, and St. Augustine grass.

What are good plants for adobe soil, especially in the sun? As a general rule, the same plants will grow in adobe as in any other soil, but the difficulty caused by poor drainage eliminates some. The doubtful type of plant would include choisya, cistus, caesalpinia, helianthemum, leptospermum, and others known for their tolerance of dry conditions.

What flowers or shrubs would do well on the west side of a house where the temperature sometimes reaches 140° F.? In such hot, dry spots, one must have heat-loving plants. Leptospermum, oleander, lantana, bougainvillea, cistus, plumbago, *Cotoneaster lacteus,* diosma, felicia, helianthemum, leucophyllum, *Pittosporum tobira, Viburnum suspensum,* and *V. tinus* all should do well. For annuals, marigolds, petunias, portulacas, and tithonias will give summer color.

What low perennial may be planted in the shady strip between a drive and house? *Fragaria chiloensis* would be a happy choice. It is a creeper with bright-green foliage and bright-red fruits. *Campanula mayii* or *Bergenia crassifolia* would give some color, but would grow 12 inches to 15 inches tall. *Ajuga reptans* would also do very well.

What can be grown under eucalyptus trees? The heavy demand for food and water by the eucalyptus and the toxic effect of its leaves and bark make trouble for most plants. Grass, heavily fed and watered, is satisfactory, since debris can be easily raked off. English ivy is often used as a ground cover, but hand-picking of debris is necessary.

My house faces southwest, and the northeast corner gets little sun. What plants would do well there? This is an ideal spot for some of the shrubs that do not like full sun, especially camellia, azalea, gardenia, star jasmine, fuchsia, *Daphne odora,* hydrangea, eranthemum, ginger-lily, English holly, and nandina.

What flowers or vines will grow on the north side of our house, where it is shady all the time? There are many plants that grow well in the shade, the degree of shade being a limiting factor. Camellia, fuchsia, begonia, violet, fern, *Bergenia crassifolia* all do well in some shade. If very dense, use ferns, aucuba, sarcococca, and aspidistra.

We live under oaks, and find violets, iris, ferns, coleus, and begonias growing fine. What would do well in sunny spots in such soil? In sunny spots near oaks, most plants should thrive. If coleus and begonias overwinter, it would indicate a frost-free area, so try primroses, cineraria, calceolaria, and cyclamen for winter. In the shade azalea and camellia should do well. In the summer avoid rank-growing annuals, but try the rest.

What climber would grow on the wall of a summerhouse facing the ocean near Los Angeles? Few climbers compare with the blood trumpet vine (*Distictis buccinatoria*) under such circumstances. It has beautiful foliage, and for most of the year it produces huge red trumpets of bloom. It does not object to the salt breezes. It will need a trellis until it has something to hold on to.

What vine similar to trumpet vine can I put on the north side of my house? The trumpet vine itself, *Distictis buccinatoria,* does very well on the north, as will also *Bignonia violacea, Thunbergia grandiflora,* and *Distictis lactiflora,* all of lavender and blue shades. The Cape-honeysuckle, *Tecomaria capensis,* even more vivid than the trumpet vine, does well too. None of these like heavy shade, but normal conditions on the north are satisfactory. All are equally hardy.

How can I grow a beautiful dichondra lawn? The soil should be well enriched and perfectly graded. The plants are purchased in flats. They are divided with a knife into 2-inch or 3-inch squares. Planted about a foot apart, and well watered, these will soon spread. Frequent feedings with a balanced complete fertilizer and plenty of water are needed to keep the "lawn" green. It should be cut 3 or 4 times a year. A serious fault of dichondra is that chemical weedkillers will also kill the dichondra.

What time of year is the best for starting a lawn in Southern Califor-

nia? A lawn may be started at any time, but the best time is fall—September or October. This will establish the plants well before heavy rains and give a good turf before the summer's heat.

How do you renovate an old lawn infested with "devil grass"? It can hardly be eliminated, for a tiny piece of root starts a new plant. The customary procedure is to run a renovator over the lawn several times and rake out the roots as well as possible. This gives the new sowing a chance to fight the "devil grass" (Bermuda grass), though it will succumb again sooner or later. (Contact your local garden center.) Dalapon, a selective weedkiller, is the best chemical control to date.

How is a lawn of sagina moss made? *Sagina subulata* is not a moss but a flowering plant. It is used as a shade-tolerant ground cover. It must have light soil and good drainage. It may be planted at any time of the year, but preferably in the spring. Flats may be purchased at some nurseries, and the plants are divided and planted quite closely. It has a serious failing in that it turns yellow in spots and must be replanted, but it is fairly permanent. (See also Moss Lawns, Section 9.)

What shrubs would make a good flowering hedge? The list would be almost limitless in Southern California, but some of the best would be abelia, white and red, *Cassia splendida, Plumbago capensis, Murraya exotica, Choisya ternata,* cotoneaster, *Grewia caffra, Feijoa,* pyracantha, *Solanum rantonnetii, Viburnum suspensum* and *V. tinus,* and lantana. Properly cared for, a hedge of varicolored hibiscus can be beautiful. Oleander, with pruning, works out well.

How is a flowering hedge best planted? Except for hibiscus, the plants mentioned above could be planted from containers at any time. (Hibiscus should be well established before winter.) Allow plenty of room for each plant to develop into a good specimen. Drop a line, and stake out the center of each hole along it. Dig generous holes and add plenty of manure or humus. In the rear, leave a good irrigation ditch. By all means, carry on a program of pruning, so that the hedge does not become an eyesore.

What are good plants for green hedges? This would depend on the size required. For a very low hedge, nothing surpasses *Buxus microphylla* var. *japonica. Myrtus* 'Compacta' and *Ligustrum henryi* also make good low hedges. For a moderate-sized hedge (up to 5 feet), the wax-leaf privet (*Ligustrum lucidum*) is excellent. Boxwood is fine anywhere up to this height. For the tall hedge, *Pittosporum undulatum* outdoes any other. In hot, dry areas, *Ligustrum japonicum* is a tough, tall hedge.

Our dwarf eucalyptus windbreak blew over in a storm. What could

we use that would be sturdier? *Eucalyptus globulus* 'Compacta' is so shallow-rooted that it blows over easily. One good substitute is *E. cornuta*. Another would be *E. sideroxylon,* if it were topped out at about 20 feet. *Pittosporum undulatum* also makes a good windbreak if it need not be high.

What shrubs can be planted in Southern California in January and February? Since most shrubs are grown in containers, they can be planted at any time. Very tender plants, such as bougainvillea and hibiscus, are best planted later.

What are some shrubs that would make good foundation plants? Such a list should be made up of plants that will not cover the windows in a few years. Some good ones for sun are *Convolvulus cneorum, Correa reflexa, Juniperus* 'Tamariscifolia', *Turraea obtusifolia* —all of which grow very low. *Choisya ternata, Murraya paniculata, Viburnum suspensum, Myrtus* 'Compacta', *Ligustrum indicum, Abelia floribunda, Diosma ericoides, Gardenia, Pittosporum tobira*—all of which grow to moderate size, and can be kept low easily by pruning.

Will you name some shrubs that are quick to grow and easy to care for around a new home? This is really the worst thing to do in California, as quick-growing shrubs around the house in 3 or 4 years make a jungle and a mess. Be patient, and a permanent effect can be obtained by using slower-growing, more durable material.

My shrubs and trees grow too fast. How can this be prevented? Overwatering and overfeeding cause too rank a growth. Do not use fertilizer for several years, and water just enough to keep plants from wilting.

What are some good evergreen trees for a small home in the Los Angeles area? The evergreen elm, *Ulmus parvifolia* 'Pendens' (*sempervirens*), *Pittosporum undulatum,* and *P. rhombifolium* give beautiful fruits, as well as being good foliage trees. *Jacaranda acutifolia,* nearly evergreen, has a mass of blue flowers in the spring. *Calodendrum capense,* a mass of pink flowers in summer, is a good tree. *Magnolia grandiflora* is everyone's favorite. For certain types of homes, olive trees have a fine character.

What kind of tree do you suggest putting in a front yard only 40 feet wide? One of the finest trees is the evergreen elm, *Ulmus parvifolia* 'Pendens' (*sempervirens*). Care must be used in its purchase, for seedling forms vary too much. The best nurseries grow only from cuttings taken from fine trees.

What fruits are most likely to do well on the Pacific Coast? There is no fruit that does not do well somewhere on the Coast, except very tropical types. In the North, all the deciduous fruits, like apple, cherry, and plum, do very well. Farther south, the evergreen fruit area begins, and citrus, avocado, and other subtropicals do well.

How do you cure curly leaf on trees?   First, investigate for the presence of aphids. Most so-called curly leaf is the result of these plant lice. They are easily controlled by malathion, 2 teaspoonfuls of 50 per cent emulsion per gallon of water. If this is not the cause, it may be the curly-leaf virus. Consult your county extension agent.

Where can one obtain information on tropical ornamentals?   Not many truly tropical plants thrive in Southern California, where subtropicals are the rule. Tropicals generally demand a moist climate, with never any frost. They like light, moisture-retentive soils. They desire at least partial shade. Obviously, lath houses and conservatories are the answers. If attempts are to be made to grow them, contact one of the large nurseries in Southern California that specialize in exotic material, and the State Agricultural Experiment Station.

Would you please make suggestions for growing plants in a lath house?   On the whole, the plants that like shade prefer a light soil containing leafmold, which provides good drainage. This is often given by building raised beds and filling with prepared soil. Careful attention must be given to watering, but the results are worthwhile. Feeding should be done with cottonseed meal or an acid fertilizer. Do not grow heavy vines on the lath.

What plants are grown in lath houses?   Camellia, fuchsia, and begonia plants are raised by every lath-house owner. Other desirable subjects are gloxinia, streptocarpus, achimenes, caladium, anthurium, cyclamen, stephanotis, *Hoya carnosa,* and sarcococca. Many orchids also do very well.

What evergreen vine can I use over my lath house that will not freeze easily?   *Gelsemium sempervirens* is a good vine if the temperature does not drop below 15° F. It has a light growth that will not be too dense for the plants beneath, and in late winter is a mass of yellow bloom. It is very clean, and has refreshingly green foliage all year.

Why doesn't my almond tree bear?   A single tree never bears; 2 varieties must be planted together to get pollinization. Good combinations are 'Nonpareil' and 'Ne Plus Ultra', or 'Ne Plus Ultra' and 'I. X. L.'

I have an Arbutus unedo that blooms but does not set fruit. Why?   Some arbutus do not bear well. It would be well to investigate its environment before deciding that it is a poor type. The trees like good drainage. They do not like to be exposed to hot, dry winds; nor do they like an alkaline soil. If conditions are favorable and the tree is healthy, then the seedling is evidently a poor type.

I have an avocado tree 8 years old. Why do the blooms fall? There may be many factors. The tree may be still immature. Drainage may be poor. Overwatering or feeding before the fruits set may have forced off the bloom. Oil sprays are sometimes given at the wrong time, before the fruit is set.

My seedling avocado has fruit. Will it be good? There is a chance that it will be good. All the good varieties were once seedlings. For new plantings, seedlings are not worth the gamble, when there are such fine named varieties.

Should I destroy a seedling avocado with black fruit, growing 8 feet from another avocado? One tree or the other would be best removed, for the tops spread wide, and you would end up with 2 poor trees. The black fruit is typical of many fine kinds of avocados.

What time of the year should avocados be picked? Avocados are picked at any time of the year, depending on the varieties planted. For home use, they are best allowed to ripen on the trees. An avocado becomes somewhat soft when ripe.

Can azaleas be grown in Southern California? Evergreen azaleas do beautifully with proper care. They should never be planted in full sun. A large amount of peat moss should be mixed in the soil. Drainage must be perfect, and in heavy soils this means raising the plant above the surrounding soil. During the summer, water heavily and feed generously with cottonseed meal or other acid fertilizer.

How can I encourage bananas to ripen in the Los Angeles area? First, types that fruit in this area should be purchased. Plant in a rich, well-drained spot that is protected from hot, dry winds. Keep the plant growing in healthy condition and fruit should ripen.

Is there any special care for bird-of-paradise? Should it be pruned or divided? If you have it outdoors in your California garden, let it grow as it pleases. Remove only dead foliage and don't divide before the foliage dies. Feed and water plentifully during the summer.

How are blackberries grown in California? Blackberries grow fairly well here in heavy loam. Young plants are set out in early spring, about 3 feet apart. The first growth is pinched when a few feet tall to encourage branches that bear the fruit the next year. Each year canes that have fruited are cut out after harvesting. A mulch of manure or compost in the spring and copious watering in the growing season are desirable. In warm climates, blackberries are short-lived. Start new plants from root sprouts of existing plantings for replacement every 3 years.

Can blueberries be grown in California? There are some places where they should grow well, but they seldom do. If you have a moist climate and cool winters, write to an eastern nursery specializing in fruits, and try its recommendations.

What is the best care of boxwood? Boxwood is a very easily grown plant. It likes a fertile soil, with plenty of organic fertilizer. It must never be allowed to become dry or it will start to shed foliage. Frequent prunings or shearings will keep it dense. Be on the lookout for red spider, which mottles the foliage, and for scale. There are many sprays for red spider on the market, and scale is controlled by a 1½ per cent or 2 per cent oil spray or by malathion in June or July.

How are boysenberries grown? Plant in early spring, at least 5 feet apart. Allow the vines to grow on the ground. Be generous with water and fertilizer. Early the next spring, tie the vines on trellises. As the berries start ripening, cut out new growth. After harvesting, cut off the vines that bore the fruit and allow new growths to grow on the ground. These should be tied up early the following spring. Plenty of fertilizer in the spring and plenty of water in the summer will produce tremendous crops.

In the West, should ranunculus bulbs be lifted after flowering? Yes; when they are dormant, they resent the water given other plants. When the foliage is yellowed and dry, they are ready for digging. Seedling-grown ranunculus give far superior bloom but are troublesome to start.

What is the proper care for calla-lily in California? Calla-lilies are almost weeds here, except in bad frost areas. They enjoy partial shade but it is not necessary. They like a very rich soil and plenty of water and rich compost. They do not need a rest period. They can be divided at any time, but early fall is best.

Could you suggest a tree similar to the Deodar cedar? There are a number of fine coniferous trees for Southern California. The atlas cedar and its blue variety, the canary pine, the Aleppo pine, the stone pine, the Monterey pine, the coast redwood, and the California incense-cedar all do well in most areas.

When should chrysanthemums be planted, and how? New plants can be set out in the spring and planted about 12 inches apart to the same depth they were growing. They enjoy a rich soil and reasonably generous watering. Pinch several times in the summer to encourage branching and strong stems. Divide yearly, after blooming. Container plants are available nearly year-round.

We water our citrus trees by trenches and daily sprinkling. Is this too much? Citrus trees do not need much water when once established.

Overwatering forces growth at the expense of fruit and may kill the tree. A well-established tree need not be watered more than once a month. This will encourage deep rooting.

How old must a seedling citrus tree be before it bears fruit? This would be extremely variable, but a guess would be between 4 and 8 years. Seedlings are seldom worth growing.

Why does a young lemon tree produce hard lemons? The first fruit of citrus trees often has a very thick rind. If the tree is a seedling, there is a good chance that it is a hard type. Citrus is one fruit that responds to good care. Instructions can be obtained from your local county extension agent.

I have a lemon that is losing its leaves. Why? A very heavy crop of fruit often will strip a lemon of most of its foliage. Overwatering in poorly drained soil may cause the condition, but the poor health of the tree will be obvious. Less water and a feeding of commercial citrus food in the spring should bring it back. Lemon trees require very little water.

When should lemons be planted? Lemons and other citrus and evergreen fruits are best planted in a well-worked soil in the spring when cold weather is over and before summer's heat. A stake should be provided immediately, and some kind of shade on the south side to prevent sunburn on the trunk. Watering should be liberal the first year.

How are 'Meyer' lemons and dwarf limes grown? There are no true dwarf limes, though the 'Rangpur' (*Citrus* x *limonia*) is somewhat small. Lemons are quite hardy; limes (*Citrus aurantifolia*), definitely not. Where each can be grown, requirements are the same. Good drainage is essential. They want plenty of water when young, much less as they mature. Light feeding in the spring is beneficial. Most 'Meyer' lemon trees tend to overbear. Thin out fruits in clusters to a single lemon.

How can one tell the difference between young oranges and lemons? The best way is to note the foliage. The lemon has much paler foliage than the orange, if the orange has been growing well. It sometimes is very difficult, except for an expert, to tell.

How does one apply lime around orange trees? Lime is sprinkled on the soil rather heavily, as far out as the branches spread. It is cultivated in a few inches. Irrigation then carries it evenly through the soil. Ground limestone is the best form to use.

What do you spray oranges with? Under normal conditions, oranges are sprayed in the summer with a dormant oil, usually a 2 per cent solution of light medium. This will kill red spider, scale, aphids, etc. It should never be applied when the temperature is above 90° F. in the shade. A perfect coverage is essential.

How do you prune cotoneasters to get good berries? Cotoneasters fruit on 1-year-old wood. After the berries fall, the wood on which they were borne should be cut back about 6 inches from the ground. New growths for the following year's berries will spring freely from the stubs. Never be afraid to cut the sprays for decoration, for this can become a part of the pruning if the stems are cut back to about 6 inches.

My cotoneasters, though faithfully watered and fertilized for over a year, have had no berries. Could they be "duds"? Cotoneasters have perfect flowers and do not require pollination to set berries. Dead wood, caused by dieback from fire blight, usually strikes the stems bearing flower buds, causing sterility. Probably too much shade, too much water, too immature, or pruning off the flowering wood would be the difficulty. Since they are almost foolproof, patience will probably reward you with their showy berries. (See the previous question.)

My cypress tree yellows, then browns. It seems to be dying. Why? This is a disease called coryneum canker and has no permanent cure. Cutting out the first cankers to appear will retard the disease, as will a spray of Bordeaux mixed according to the instructions on the container. Monterey cypress is the most frequent victim. Forbes' cypress seems resistant.

What special culture is needed for tree ferns? The tree fern, *Alsophila australis,* is not a temperamental plant, but it must be treated as a fern. It likes shade, leafmold, perfect drainage, and must never be allowed to dry out, even for an hour. During the spring and summer, it likes feedings of dried blood or liquid fertilizer high in nitrogen.

How often should figs and peaches be watered? The texture of the soil decides this. Sandy soils need more water; heavy soil, less. During the growing season, deciduous fruits require a moist soil. Watering every 2 weeks in sandy soil might not be too much. On the other hand, 2 or 3 good soakings during the season might suffice in adobe soil.

What kind of soil and care do fuchsias require? They like protection from hot sun; the north and east sides of the house are good. If possible, provide a light, well-drained soil high in humus. They must never suffer from a lack of moisture. Regular monthly feedings of acid fertilizers are appreciated, the best being cottonseed meal. This feeding should be started in March and continued until September.

How should fuchsias be pruned when in the ground? In February or March, cut back hard, leaving only a little of the previous season's growth. The best plants are obtained if the new growth is pinched when about 6 or 8 inches long, thus making the plant bushy.

How are potted fuchsias cared for? Fuchsias are generally grown in 6-inch pots as rapidly as growth permits, and then shifted into 8-inch pots. If feeding is carried out, every 2 years should be often enough to shift plants to larger pots. During the growing season, they should be watered heavily and food applied monthly. Each February or March, they should be pruned hard to force new flowering growth.

How often should gerbera plants be divided? Do they require fertilizer? Gerbera plants really demand rich, well-drained soil. They particularly like organic fertilizer. Divide every 3 or 4 years in the early fall. They are subject to aphids, so spray with malathion.

In California, should gladiolus bulbs be lifted? Yes. They multiply fast and need separation; they should be kept dry when dormant. They can best be treated for thrips when out of the ground. After digging, keep them in a sack for about 2 weeks with naphthalene flakes to kill thrips, then remove them and screen or shake the naphthalene off. Store in a cool, dry place.

When should we prune grapes set out last spring? 'Tokay', 'Muscat', 'Ribier', and 'Zinfandel' all require hard pruning. Pruning the first winter is to restrict the plant to one stem to form the trunk. It should be the most vigorous branch and should be cut back to 2 eyes. (See Grape.)

What is the difference between strawberry guava and pineapple-guava? Although both belong to the myrtle family, they are different genera. The strawberry guava is *Psidium littorale;* this and its variety *littorale* make 2 fine fruits and very attractive plants with light-green, glossy foliage. The pineapple-guava (*Feijoa sellowiana*) has very pleasant fruit that is excellent for jam, and is a beautiful large shrub with silvery foliage and bright-red flowers. Both are well worth growing for fruit and ornament.

I am interested in a small herb garden. Can you suggest some herbs for it? Herbs do well in Southern California, especially in light soils. They like poor soil and little water. Except for mint, they will not survive in the shade. Plant in early spring. The plants should be renewed every 3 or 4 years. A good list would include sweet basil, thyme, sweet marjoram, savory (both winter and summer types), tarragon, sage, rosemary, lavender, chives, mint, and lemon balm. (See Herbs.)

Why is it that some people have such bad luck with English holly in California? English holly is grown to perfection in California, but it will not thrive in the full blazing sun in the summer. A slight shade must be provided.

What planting and care is necessary for iris in adobe soil?   Irises are exceedingly easy to grow. The only precaution to take in adobe soil is not to plant too deeply. Barely cover the rhizomes and do not water heavily. Every third year, clumps should be dug, saving only the new, strong rhizomes. Except in interior hot areas, this is best done as soon as flowers fade in the spring. In the hot areas, September is better. Feeding in spring and fairly generous watering until they flower will ensure good bloom.

How should jasmines be pruned?   True jasmines grow so abundantly that they should be severely pruned in the winter. Old stems should be cut out at the ground each year, as the bloom is much finer on young growth. The bad reputation of the yellow jasmine is due to its excessive growth, but it can be kept in bounds and attractive by regular pruning.

What lilacs would bloom here in Los Angeles County?   Eastern lilacs are unsatisfactory, suffering either from excessive heat or mildew. The lilac that does very well is the Persian lilac, *Syringa persica*. It has lavender flowers in the spring that are fine for cutting, and the plant is of graceful habit. Easterners who remember lilacs with nostalgia should plant the lovely species of *Ceanothus,* often called California-lilac.

When should lilies be planted in California?   Lilies should be planted as soon as they are available in the fall. They like full sun and rich soil, but resent poor drainage or fertilizer touching the bulbs.

Does lily-of-the-valley do well in the California coastal region?   There are a number of successful plantings here. They need shade and a light soil.

Can mangoes be grown in Southern California?   They can and are grown in frost-free areas. They need plenty of water and the soil should be constantly mulched.

What would be a good covering under oak trees?   Three very good ground covers would be the evergreen ornamental strawberry (*Fragaria chiloensis*), bugle-weed (*Ajuga reptens*), and English ivy (*Hedera helix*).

How are oleanders pruned to keep them vigorous and flowering freely?   After the plant is several years old, old stems, as soon as they have finished flowering, are cut off almost to the ground. No plant suckers more freely, so do not be afraid of harsh cutting.

Can papaya be grown in California?   Only in a few areas that never have frost. The trees are difficult to pollinate, and several trees must be planted. Though they are delicious and have been fruited, they are a gamble.

How are flowering peaches pruned? These plants have an unhappy life in the Southern California area because most people fail to cut them hard enough. They need the stimulus of hard pruning. They should be cut back each year after flowering, leaving only about 6 inches of growth of the previous year. If pruned right after blooming, there will be plenty of time for the plant to send out and mature strong growth for next year's bloom.

Is the peony plant a shrub? Will it grow in Southern California? Though there is a shrubby type, most peonies are herbaceous, dying to the ground in the winter. In Southern California, they grow well in only a few favored locations. The long, hot summer is too much for them. They are not a good choice. North of San Jose, tree peonies are reliable and beautiful.

What should I do to have success with perennial phlox? Hardy phlox grows well in Southern California, but it takes clean, healthy stock, planted in rich soil, with some little protection from the afternoon sun. They should be divided, in the fall, every few years. Flower heads should be removed immediately after fading.

What is the culture for Norfolk-Island-pine in order to get rapid development? This plant is not a rapid grower even in California. If your area is not subject to hard frost, treat like any other tree. It will not make more than 1 or 2 tiers a year.

How is the dwarf pomegranate grown? Dwarf pomegranates are grown chiefly for their decorative bloom. They require little care. Like most deciduous plants, they enjoy plenty of food and water during the growing season. Thinning out occasionally in the winter encourages better bloom. Do not allow fruit to mature on the plant. There are some new types that are really showy.

How should a 'Santa Rosa' plum be pruned? Pruning fruit trees is a long subject, well covered by bulletins obtainable from your county agent. Training should be started the first year and practiced every winter. (See Plums.)

How should pyracantha shrubs be pruned? Pyracanthas (firethorns) and cotoneasters have the same habits, and should be pruned much alike. After a plant is several years old, each berry-producing branch should be cut back to within about 6 inches of the trunk; each year thereafter the producing branches should be cut to within 6 inches of their bases. They should never be sheared, for it will result in a top-heavy plant. The time for pruning is when the berries fall or dry. Some species will grow into small trees if left unpruned.

When should roses be planted? When available in your region, probably about December 15 to May 1. Or buy container-grown plants, which can be planted anytime.

How should roses be planted? Holes generous enough to receive the roots without cramping should be dug. Mix a shovelful of rich compost or manure in the bottom, then hold the plant at the required depth (the bud union—the swelling between roots and branches—should be even with or an inch above the soil surface), pull in a little soil, and work it around the roots with the fingers. Gradually fill the hole, packing the soil around the roots. Water thoroughly.

How should roses be fertilized? A liberal dressing of a commercial rose fertilizer in early spring and again in June, with light applications of fertilizer, monthly, between April and August, will keep roses growing and blooming.

When should rosebushes be pruned? In Southern California, roses try to be everblooming. This is not in the best interest of the plants. Water should be withheld after September, and the plants allowed to become dormant. Then, in December, a severe pruning is in order every other year. Reserve only 3 or 4 stout canes and reduce these to about ⅓ their length. Proper cutting of buds and dead blooms, leaving only about 3 eyes below the cut, will take care of most of the pruning in the intervening 2 years.

How should large-flowered climbers be pruned? Climbers of this type differ from the hybrid teas in that wood of the previous season is required for bloom. They are best pruned after blooming. Old canes should be cut down low. The new canes may be shortened, and lateral growths restricted to 2 or 3 eyes. At this time, tying and training are best done.

What is the method of, and time for, pruning roses? They are generally pruned by cutting off buds and dead blooms. If these are cut so that only 2 or 3 eyes are left on each cane, and all weak and crossing growths are removed, little more will be needed. Any heavier pruning that seems required should be done in December and January.

How should I care for roses in tubs on a patio? Roses may be well grown in large tubs if feeding and watering are properly done. During the winter, cease feeding and reduce water. In the spring, a topdressing of fertilizer will be appreciated. Thereafter, feed monthly with a complete fertilizer. Because of the limited amount of soil in a tub, repotting with fresh soil every few years is a "must."

When are rose cuttings taken in California? Most roses are budded, for their own roots are weak. Understock roses are grown from hardwood cuttings inserted in the field in the winter. Greenwood cuttings may be rooted at almost anytime.

How many years before sapota and cherimoya bear fruit? Are 2 trees necessary for cross-pollination? Seedling sapotas take 7 to 8 years; budded stock takes 4 to 5 years. Seedling cherimoyas bear in 4 or 5 years; budded stock takes 2 or 3 years. Two trees are not necessary in either case, but some growers recommend hand pollinization of cherimoyas for greater yield.

What is the proper culture for schizanthus and wallflower? Neither plant is difficult to grow. Seed is sown from July to September. There may be difficulty with seed during the hot months, so the later date may be more convenient. When a few inches high, the seedlings should be moved to the spot in the garden where they are to grow. Shade them for a few days, until they take hold. Neither seems too fussy about soil outdoors.

When are strawberries planted, and what is their care? Strawberries in California may be set in the fall. They must have a well-worked soil with good drainage and are planted on raised beds about 2 feet wide, with a shallow irrigation trench. They need copious water during the summer for they are shallow-rooting. They are generally left several years without replanting. A feeding of manure or a complete fertilizer in the spring is advisable. However, fruiting will be heavier if runners are rooted in pots so that a new row can be planted about every 3 years.

What are tangelos? Tangelos are fruits resulting from crossing the grapefruit and tangerine. The old name of grapefruits was pomelo, hence the name tangelo. They grow the same as oranges, requiring identical care, and produce delicious tangy fruits in the winter. Several varieties are on the market that have fruiting periods from November until early summer.

Can the tea plant (Camellia sinensis) be safely planted outdoors in Southern California? The true tea plant is frequently found in Southern California, making a very attractive shrub. In adobe soil, plant it a little above the soil level. In sandy soils, plenty of water is necessary. Plant it in full sun. Acid fertilizer is most appreciated in the spring.

What vegetables may be planted in January and February? Among the many vegetables planted in Southern California in the winter are cabbage, broccoli, spinach, kohlrabi, beets, parsley, peas, turnips, carrots, and onions. In some areas, more favored by good drainage and mild climate, squash (under Hotkaps) may be planted at this time.

How are violets seeded or planted, and do they do well in Southern California? Violets do very well in California. They want a light soil, high in humus, and some shade. Though they must be divided every few years, they will become permanent if cared for. Try the huge flower type, 'Royal Robe'.

I have violets planted around an oak, growing and blossoming freely, but the whole plant heaves out. Why? Violets in California have this habit, and undoubtedly to a greater degree when leaves falling on them force them to grow upward for light. They should be divided every few years and replanted firmly, for they will lose vigor if growing too much on the surface.

How should walnuts be watered? Walnuts are irrigated more or less frequently, depending on the soil. Sandy soil may require monthly irrigation during the growing season, while adobe would need only one watering. Some experts claim that irrigation about two weeks before harvest makes shucking easier. If trees are grafted on black walnut stock, overwatering encourages black root rot.

Colorado

Our springs are dry and late in Colorado. Can you give me a list of annuals that can be planted in the fall? Larkspur, California poppy, calendula, echium, bartonia; in short, all of the hardy annuals. Cover the seed bed with a winter mulch. Remove when seeds germinate in the spring.

We live northeast of Colorado Springs, altitude 7,500 feet; I cannot get annuals to grow more than 6 inches high. Can it be the soil or cool weather? Cosmos and morning-glories do well. Since these annuals thrive this high in other parts of your region, your trouble may be poor soil, alkaline soil, or perhaps late planting.

How do you take care of boysenberry bushes during the winter in Colorado? Remove the canes from their supports, lay them flat and cover with straw, cornstalks, or spruce branches. It is advisable to spray first with lime-sulfur, or aluminum sulfate, to make them less attractive to mice. Or place mouse poison inside drain tiles laid between the canes.

We irrigate our land in Colorado. I have a bank that I wish to cover with some drought-resistant ground cover; it will have to depend on rain for moisture. What shall I use? *Sedum stoloniferum* can "take it," making a year-round cover. Burlap helps to hold the new surface if the bank is steep.

What treatment should be given monkshood (aconitum)? In any except subalpine regions in Colorado, aconitum would resent open sunshine and consequent dryness. Try changing to shade, or semishade, and deep, rich, peaty soil.

What can I do to raise pansies successfully in southern Colorado? Sow seeds in a prepared seed bed early in September. In colder areas, plants will survive better in a cold frame. Keep moist and mulch when the ground begins to freeze. Next May, transplant to a permanent bed of good loam enriched with rotted manure and peat moss and in open sun. Keep seed pods picked.

What are the best, showiest, and easiest grown perennials for late-summer blooming in this climate? *Anemone japonica,* anthemis, chrysanthemums, *Clematis heracleafolia,* eupatorium, helenium, *Heliopsis* 'Pitcherana', monarda, perennial asters, *Phlox paniculata, Physostegia virginiana,* ceratostigma, rudbeckia hybrids, *Salvia argentea, S. pratensis.*

What perennial, preferably a foliage plant, would make the best low-growing border for my garden in eastern Colorado? *Cerastium tomentosum* (kept within bounds), *Festuca ovina glauca, Euphorbia myrsinites*—all 3 have silver-gray foliage. *Teucrium chamaedrys,* kept shorn, makes a neat, green, miniature hedge, suggestive of boxwood edging.

Hybrid tea roses bloom prolifically in this climate but are hard to keep from freezing during the winter months. How would you advise to mulch and protect for the winter? Prune down to 6 or 8 inches in autumn, mound up soil or peat moss around each plant. Cover with a layer of any open material that will shade from the sun and permit air circulation, such as spruce or fir branches, or straw held down with wire. The plastic cones now available are unusually successful unless left on too late in the spring.

Will you suggest some hardy roses for high altitudes in Colorado? *Rosa hugonis, R. rugosa* and its hybrids; 'Harison's Yellow'; 'Frühlingsgold'; hybrid perpetuals 'Frau Karl Druschki' and 'General Jacquemot'.

Can you give some information on spring versus fall planting of roses, shrubs, and trees in Denver, a mile above sea level? In such regions of dry, sunny cold winters, the difficulties of watering and protecting newly planted woody material make spring planting preferable.

How can I grow sweet peas successfully in southern Colorado? In autumn dig a trench 12 inches wide and 12 to 18 inches deep. In the bottom put a 6-inch layer of rich compost or manure. Fill with good, rich, friable loam. Early the following March, sow seed. Unless sweet peas have been grown in the soil before, be sure to inoculate the seed with a suitable legume culture available from most mail-order seed houses or garden centers.

Florida

When is the best time to transplant amaryllis? Root action commences in late September or early October. The bulbs should be lifted, divided, and reset, therefore, in the early autumn. Bone meal or another alkaline plant food is suggested for these bulbs.

We must move to southern Florida. Can you recommend a gardening book for that area? *Florida Gardening Month by Month,* by Nixon Smiley (University of Miami Press, Coral Gables, Florida).

What is the best type of soil for blackberries in Florida? A sandy loam soil that has a relatively high organic content is best for the bramble fruits. A heavy hammock type is ideal, particularly if there is a constant water table 2 or 3 feet below the surface. A slightly acid soil is considered best.

How are caladiums grown? Plant the tubers in a partly shaded position that is sheltered from strong winds. The soil should contain an abundance of humus and should be reasonably moist at all times. Feeding with liquid fertilizer during the season of active growth is very beneficial.

What is the correct culture for calla-lilies in northern Florida? Callas are tropical bulbous plants easily injured by frost. The roots are usually received in November, and they can be planted at once in a rich, acid, mucky mixture in large pots or urns. These containers may be plunged under trees and taken indoors when frost is forecast. They can be held in a dormant state until the danger of frost has passed in March, and then planted in a rich acid bed out-of-doors. South of Bradenton, callas are best left in the soil permanently.

What is frenching and bronzing of citrus fruits, and how is it cured? Frenching is the result of a zinc deficiency and is corrected by adding zinc sulfate to the sprays. Bronzing results when there is insufficient magnesium available to orange trees. Dolomite in judicious amounts will usually correct a bronzed condition. Epsom salts and a potassium-magnesium sulfate will also correct the deficiency.

What causes oranges to split open before they are ripe, and how is this prevented? It is usually thought to be caused by a deficiency of copper. Small amounts of copper sulfate (bluestone) will tend to ameliorate the condition.

What are the brown dots on the undersides of orange leaves? Round brown dots with reddish centers are Florida red scale. This pest can be controlled with an oil emulsion spray, used according to the directions on the package.

What are some of the best climbers for central Florida? Bougainvilleas in their several attractive colors; the very colorful flamevine; herald trumpet—a rampant tropical creeper; queen's-wreath, with its gorgeous purple blossoms; *Quisqualis indica* (Rangoon-creeper); the luxuriant coral-vine; the fast-growing skyflower; and the fragrant Confederate jasmine, and several other climbing jasmines, are among the most popular of Florida's many vines.

What about columbines for central Florida? Although columbines are native to extreme western Florida, they do not grow readily in the peninsula. They can be flowered, however, with good culture. Get plants from the North and set them in a partially shaded place in November, feeding them a balanced plant food every 2 or 3 weeks as they grow. They need an abundance of water and must not have too much root competition for water or nutrients.

When should dahlias be planted in southern Florida? For spring and summer bloom, plant the roots in January or February; for autumn bloom, arrange to have roots held in cold storage and delivered in late August or early September.

How may good dahlias be grown in central Florida? The roots are procured in February or March and are planted about 5 inches deep in garden beds that have been enriched with compost and a commercial fertilizer. Drive a stout stake by the stem end of the root and tie the plant every 8 inches or so as it grows. Feed liberally every 3 or 4 weeks. Dust with sulfur or malathion at the first signs of red spider.

How can I have dahlias in central Florida? Set the roots in good soil about 5 inches deep; water and feed liberally as the plants grow. These roots will be difficult to carry over in Florida, so it is suggested that you treat them as annuals, starting over each autumn. Don't overlook the small-flowered types from seed grown as annuals.

Can I increase my very beautiful flame-of-the-woods? Yes, use softwood tip cuttings in June or July and insert them in clean white sand in a new box. Place cheesecloth over the box; set in on the north side of the house and sprinkle daily with a fine spray. The cuttings should root in 4 or 5 weeks.

Will foxgloves grow in northern Florida?   Possibly in the extreme western end of the state, but they are certain to be a disappointment in most areas. Like many other perennials, they need a long, cold winter for inducing an unbroken dormancy.

How shall I fertilize, water, and care for a lawn of centipede grass?   Centipede grass is one of the best lawn materials for the light, sandy soils of Florida. An application of a lawn fertilizer in March, another in June or July, should suffice. Water the fertilizer in as soon as applied, and irrigate often enough to keep the grass leaves from curling and turning gray-green. Frequent mowing is necessary for a good centipede turf. During the growing season, the mower must be used at least once each week.

Will heliophila grow in northern Florida?   Yes, these South African annuals, commonly known as cape-stock, should do well if the seeds are sown in flats in January, the seedlings grown in a not too moist soil, and the plants set out in March.

What can I do to have irises from Kentucky bloom in Florida?   Nothing! Excepting in extreme western Florida, bearded irises are not successful. The light, sandy soils and lack of sustained low winter temperatures do not suit these favorites of temperate gardens. Why not use native southern species that do succeed so beautifully?

When should I fertilize my lawn?   Early in March, apply a lawn fertilizer; then again when the rains start in June, make a second application. In all parts of Florida except the extreme north, additional small monthly feedings in January and February help to keep the grass green through the colder months and build it up for its spurt of spring growth.

Can old-fashioned lilacs be raised as far south as Jacksonville?   No, the light, sandy acid soils and lack of a real dormant season do not suit these popular temperate garden plants and they are certain to be disappointing. Why plant lilacs in Florida when the lovely crape-myrtle (*Lagerstroemia*) is available in a wider range of color?

When should a mulberry tree be pruned to be sure of a good crop in Florida?   Mulberry trees should be pruned directly after they have finished fruiting in the spring.

What is the best time to plant nasturtiums in Florida?   Nasturtiums must be grown in autumn in order to mature blossoms before frost; or in spring, by sowing after the last frost for blooming before hot weather sets in and kills the plants.

When should my oleanders be cut back?   Just after flowering. If plants are to be kept from getting very large, root prune them at this time by driving a spade deep in a circle about 2 or 3 feet from the plant.

Is peat from local bogs good for us to use on our gardens? Local peat is excellent if it comes from an inland bog. Be very certain that you do not buy muck from a tidal marsh, however, as this saline material will kill or injure plants.

Can peonies be grown successfully in the central part of Florida? Peonies are a complete failure in peninsular Florida. The light, sandy soil and the lack of continuously cold winter to assure complete dormancy combine to defeat our best attempts to make southerners out of these temperate garden favorites.

What roses do best in southern Florida? If you can give them good loam, with enough humus in it to hold moisture, grow the old teas like 'Lady Hillington' and 'Marechal Niel' and the more enduring of the hybrid teas such as 'Radiance', 'Red Radiance', and 'Crimson Glory'. Among floribundas, most will do well for a time, but especially recommended are 'Fashion', 'Floradora', and 'Pinocchio'. If the heat and sandy soil is too much for these, you may want to purchase inexpensive plants from Texas yearly and grow them as annuals.

I want to use old-fashioned roses. Which ones will do best with the least care? The old French rose grows well. Among our most dependable old roses are 'Louis Philippe', 'Safrano', 'Duchesse de Brabant', 'Marie van Houtte', 'Minnie Francis', 'Belle of Portugal', and 'Mme. Lombard'. Plants of these varieties will thrive in your southern garden long after plants of cutting varieties have succumbed. You will have trouble finding them, though. (See Section 6 for information on Heritage Roses.)

When is the best time of year to set rosebushes? Roses planted in December and early January will have time to make good root growth before top growth is started by the warm days of early spring. The earliest possible planting is considered best for Florida.

How far back should roses be trimmed, and what time of the year is best? Bush roses should be pruned, in January or February, to 4 or 5 strong eyes on each of 4 or 5 canes. Make the pruning cuts about ¼ inch above a strong eye that points away from the center of the plant. Ramblers can be pruned at the same time, using a renewal system to remove all of the canes more than 1 or 2 years old, as blossoms are borne from spurs on 1-year canes. As large-flowered climbers bloom on 2-year-old wood, merely prune out dead canes and cut flowering stems back to 2 or 3 eyes. Train canes horizontally to encourage many flowering shoots.

Will Centaurea moschata (sweet sultan) grow in northern Florida? Yes, very excellent sweet sultans have been grown and sold in this area. Sow seeds in a flat in October. The seed will germinate better if stored in a refrigerator for 2 weeks before planting. Transplant seedlings to well-enriched beds in midwinter. Plants should blossom in April and May. Red spiders must be forestalled with sulfur dust or malathion during dry periods.

Will violas succeed here? Yes, these miniature pansies do very well if plants are bought from a northern specialist in November and planted at once to grow through the cool winter.

What is the culture for watsonia in northern Florida? Watsonia, like gladiolus, can be planted in February in northern Florida. Set the corms about 3 inches deep in beds that have been enriched with compost and a commercial plant food. The blossoms should be produced in April and May.

Will the willow oak grow in Florida? Yes, the willow oak (*Quercus phellos*) is native to northern Florida and will succeed as a fast-growing, desirable tree as far south as the central part of the peninsula. Unless the upright growth of the willow oak is wanted, the live oak (*Quercus virginiana*) is a superior tree. It is evergreen with a majestic spreading habit.

Will the weeping willow grow successfully in Florida? It will grow in heavy soils close to watercourses in northern Florida, but it will not grow as well as it does farther north, nor can it be considered nearly as beautiful here as in the temperate states.

Can you tell us about Florida lawns? As new home owners from the North, we were appalled when we faced southern grasses for the first time. True, the first look at St. Augustine lawns can be something of a shock! Coarser than either crabgrass or quackgrass, abhorred in the North, it does seem an improbable substitute for bluegrasses. Once the shock is over, you will learn to live with St. Augustine grass; yes, even to love its springy texture underfoot. Florida soils, particularly the sterile coastal sands, present still further problems, for which new techniques are needed if grasses are to survive.

What grass should I use on my lawn in central Florida? The first choice of an inexperienced lawn owner should be St. Augustine. It is coarse, aggressive, and invasive, and far from smooth in appearance, but it is green, survives, and has few enemies. It is salt-resistant (a major problem in coastal areas) and can be quickly established from sprigs (short lengths of cut stems). It requires less fertilizer than do Bermuda and zoysia, which do make lawns more closely resembling those of the North. Most important, it is quite shade-tolerant. Its one weakness is its lack of resistance to chinch bugs.

Is there any control for chinch bugs? Malathion doesn't touch them. Diazinon (trade name Spectracide) is a specific control. The variety 'Floratan' is resistant, and where chinch bugs attack year after year, it should be planted in place of common St. Augustine.

Is 'Bitter Blue' St. Augustine superior to common? When first introduced, it was a darker, richer green, had shorter internodes with finer leaves, and produced a smoother, more attractive sod. Since then it has become mixed with common. If you are buying 'Bitter Blue', be sure to examine it in the field first, checking against common. Even better is 'Floratine' (not 'Floratan'), but more expensive. It has the finest stems, with short internodes. To get the genuine, be sure that the 'Floratine' has a blue state certification tag.

I am told that I must feed my fine-leaved Bermuda lawn often. How often and how much? For superior growth, the fine-leaved Bermuda grasses need to be fed about a pound of actual nitrogen per 1,000 square feet for every month they are in active growth, which usually means from March through November. This can be reduced by using slow-acting fertilizers that contain nitrogen in the form of IBDU, urea-form, or sulfur-coated urea. These must, of course, contain other nutrients in addition to nitrogen. They can be applied quarterly and will feed for about 3 months from each application.

Friends are urging me to plant Bahia grass. They say it looks more like Kentucky bluegrass than any other Florida grass. Bahia is being oversold. While it is freer from pests and other ills than most grasses, it is severely attacked by mole crickets. It must be mowed high, 2½ to 3 inches, which destroys the illusion of a bluegrass lawn. At this height it seeds heavily and must be cut every week to look even reasonably neat. This mowing cannot be skipped at any time between the end of April and Thanksgiving. It is tough and takes a powerful mower to cut. It does not form a true sod and the soil beneath is exposed. In alkaline soils it must be treated regularly with a solution of ferrous ammonium sulfate if it is to hold a deep-green color. Bahia is not all bad. It is fairly tolerant of light shade and will grow on acid soil. On clay soil, which it prefers, it is one of the hardiest of the warm-season grasses.

My friends tell me that the only grass that will do well on my poor soil is centipede. What do you advise? Centipede is also called lazy man's grass because it can stand more neglect than any other. It requires very little feeding and will actually die out if overfed. It is low-growing: the stems hug the ground so closely that it needs mowing only once every other week. It is not salt-tolerant and is damaged both by nematodes and ground-pearl scale. If you need a low-maintenance turf, this is it, but it won't be a model lawn.

I have heard that Florida lawns can be kept green all winter by overseeding. What seed do I use for this purpose?   Either Italian or common ryegrass is the usual grass used for overseeding. The newer fine-leaved ryegrasses are somewhat more vigorous but not superior in appearance. 'Highland' bent grass is fairly expensive, but the seed is so fine that it goes much farther and costs little more.

Is zoysia a good grass for Florida lawns?   Common zoysia from seed is worthless. The finer 'Emerald' zoysia and *Zoysia tenuifolia* are excellent but demand heavy feeding and liberal irrigation. *Zoysia matrella* (Manila grass) is spectacular as a shade grass but difficult to maintain.

My lawn is being destroyed by mole crickets. How can I control them?   Use baits containing Baygon, Dursban, or malathion placed on the lawn in June. Or spray with Baygon 70 per cent Wettable Powder, 1 or 2 ounces of solution to 1,000 square feet.

I am confused by catalog descriptions of citrus fruits. What are some good home-garden varieties?   You may have to ask your Cooperative Extension Service office for sources, since the better home-garden varieties are not grown commercially to any extent. Oranges: 'King', 'Ponkan' ('Chinese Honey'); tangelos: 'Orlando', 'Minneola', 'Seminole', 'Temple'; grapefruit: 'Marsh Seedless'; lemon: 'Meyer'. There are no named varieties of kumquat, calamondin, or tangerine.

Please list some noncitrus fruits for Florida.   Banana: 'Dwarf Cavendish', 'Lady Finger'; figs: 'Osborn's Prolific', 'Ronde Noire', 'White Genos', 'Celeste', 'Brunswick', 'Magnolia'; mango: 'Irwin', 'Fascell', 'Kent'. There are no named varieties, but the following fruits are delicious: papaya, Otaheite-gooseberry, Barbados-cherry, Natal-plum, Surinam-cherry, and sea-grape.

I have heard that apples can be grown in Florida, particularly a variety called 'Helm'.   'Helm' will fruit in Florida, but it is so poor that it isn't worth growing. See local garden centers for some of the warm-climate fruit varieties originated in Israel. To throw apple trees into dormancy so they will develop flower buds, you may have to defoliate them completely in mid-November, picking off every leaf by hand. The defoliants used for taking leaves off roses to put them into dormancy can also be used, but this is a tricky operation, better left to experts.

Georgia

What grows most satisfactorily in partial shade in this state other than azaleas and camellias? Oakleaf hydrangea (*H. quercifolia*), St. Johns-wort (*Hypericum*), heavenly-bamboo (*Nandina domestica*), stewartia, *Gordonia lasianthus,* and illicium are all excellent shrubs for the shady garden.

What is the best position and soil for amaryllis? Amaryllis grown outdoors in the South does well in a sunny or lightly shaded position in a well-drained fertile soil that is neutral or very slightly acid.

What are the cultural needs of amaryllis? Apply balanced fertilizer immediately after blooming; water well through dry periods during its growing season. In the fall, mulch with half-rotted leaves to which have been added some bone meal and dehydrated cow manure or compost.

The tops of my amaryllis are green all year. Some of the outer leaves turn yellow and soft, but they do not yellow like other bulbs. When should they be dug? They should be dug in late fall. If the foliage has not completely died down (and this does not happen with all amaryllis), it can be artificially ripened off by drying in a sunny, airy place.

About 20 months ago, I planted some amaryllis seeds, the plants from which have been green ever since, without blooming. What time of year should they be given a rest period? How? The best results are obtained if seeding amaryllis are grown on without rest until after they produce their first blooms. This is usually in from 18 to 36 months from the time of sowing. The giant-flowered hybrids may take up to 4 years to bloom.

My fancy-leaved caladium plants die down in the fall. What shall I do with them? In November, lift them; cut off the few remaining leaves; pack the tubers in peat, vermiculite, dry sand, or sawdust, and store the container in a frost-free place until spring.

What causes the black scum on my cape-jasmine bush, and how can I prevent it? This sooty mold on gardenia leaves follows the attacks of whitefly and can be corrected and prevented by occasional applications of an oil emulsion spray or malathion. One application in September, another 2 or 3 weeks later, and possibly a third during midwinter should prevent this condition. Your garden center will have oil sprays put up in small cans for your convenience.

I have read that daffodils of the North have longer stems than those of the South. What can I add to the soil to make my daffodils have longer stems? In all probability, the climate is responsible for the shorter daffodil stems, and even though your bulbs are adequately fed, there will be a tendency to shorter stems.

When do you plant dahlias in Georgia? In March and April. If the emerging tips are nipped by the latest spring frosts, no great damage will be done; but it is best to plan your planting so that there will be no frost damage.

When is the best time to transplant dogwoods, redbuds, and other trees from the woods? December through February, while the trees are dormant and without leaves. Remember that transplanting is a surgical operation and extreme care must be exercised to keep the roots covered and the trees protected from sun and wind during transport. Cut back moderately the lateral branches, plant at the same depth they formerly grew, and wrap the trunks with burlap or muslin as protection against sunscald and borers. Use trees under 8 feet in height rather than larger ones.

What is the best method of protecting gerbera plants from the cold? If gerbera plants are killed to the ground, you can cover the crowns with a light mulch of pine straw or oak leaves. If you are in the southern part of the state and wish to keep the plants from being killed on cold nights, cover with a heavy blanket of Spanish-moss, uncovering after the danger of severe cold has passed.

How are gerbera plants cared for? These South African daisies are not particular as to soil type, provided it is well fortified with plant food and plants have enough water. They will be benefited by a good mulch of oak leaves, compost, or similar organic material.

Should I use fertilizer when I plant my gladioli? A balanced commercial fertilizer can be scattered in the bottom of the 4-inch deep planting furrow and lightly cultivated in. Then set out the corms.

How can I grow gourds in a hot, dry location? If it is too hot and dry for gourds to thrive in your part of Georgia, get an early start with them and allow them to mature in midsummer. However, gourds should thrive in most sections of Georgia.

How are herbs grown in Georgia? Except for mint, herbs require a position in full sun on well-drained light soil for best flavor. It is believed that when grown in rich garden loam, herb flavor is less intense.

What herbs are best for middle and south Georgia? For fall planting: anise, chives, winter savory, sage, and dill. For spring planting:

sweet basil, summer savory, sweet fennel, coriander, thyme, and sweet marjoram.

What is the ivy that is so effectively used around the huge oaks in the Tallahassee and Thomasville area?   This is the Algerian ivy (*Hedera canariensis*), a relative of the English ivy. It is considered one of the very best ground covers for spots where grass will not grow.

Can I make a good lawn in a wooded area?   On the land, spread a layer of manure or compost, rotted oak leaves, together with some balanced lawn fertilizer. Spade or till this deeply; rake until level; plant as follows: In October or November, sow Italian ryegrass for a winter effect until warm weather, then plant sprigs of St. Augustine grass in rows about 12 inches apart. Always water well, as growing grass needs a great deal of moisture. St. Augustine grass goes dormant in the winter. It must be overseeded with Italian ryegrass in late fall if a green lawn in winter is wanted.

What is the best grass for a wooded lawn?   Italian rye, in the winter, if there is partial protection from fallen pine needles. In southern Georgia, St. Augustine grass is excellent for shady locations.

Why do nandina berries drop?   They will not drop if there has been good pollination at flowering time. If there is rain when the blossoms open, the pollen will be washed away, and there will be either no set or a poor one.

When is the proper time to plant nandina berries? How long does it take for them to come up?   Nandina berries can be sown when they are red or as they begin to fall from the plant. Germination is slow and the plantlets will probably not appear until the following spring or summer.

What can I use in place of pansies during the heat of the summer?   Torenia (wishbone-flower) is an excellent substitute for pansies to grow during summer months. Sow seeds in flats in April or May, and transplant to a garden when the pansies are pulled out.

Will peonies do well in this climate? Would you advise early, midseason, or late varieties?   None will succeed south of Atlanta. Use only tried early varieties in north Georgia.

How can we get perennial flower seed to come up in August and September when, in this area, it is so hot and dry?   Germination will be poor at this season. Hold the seeds until later in the autumn for best results. Even better, sow in well-prepared soil, just before freezing weather, to germinate in March or April.

Will perennial poppies grow year after year in this locality?   Possibly they will succeed in extreme north Georgia; from Macon southward, they are a failure.

Can roses be grown in the far South in sandy soil?   The sandy soils, warm winters, and the prevalence of disease make rose growing difficult in the far South. Large wholesale nurseries in eastern Texas have lowered the price of roses in recent years and many successful gardeners grow roses frankly as annuals. The plants are bought in the fall, planted well in very rich beds, and forced for blooms during the following spring. In the summer, they are usually discarded as worthless.

When should climbing roses be pruned?   From November to January in Georgia; a renewal system is used—old canes are cut low down, leaving this year's and last year's shoots only. Climbing roses flower from spurs that are borne on last year's canes. Old wood is not floriferous.

What is the name of the hardy red rose that grows so freely here? There is also a light blush pink that seems to thrive without any care.   The red rose is 'Louis Philippe', sometimes called the "cracker rose." The light, shell pink is probably 'Marie van Houtte'. 'Safrano', 'Minnie Francis', and 'Duchesse de Brabant' are also old-fashioned roses that will grow for many years in southern gardens.

When is the best time to transplant the red spider-lily?   This flower, *Nerine sarniensis* (often misnamed *Lycoris radiata*), is best transplanted in July or early August. It is also called the Guernsey-lily.

Will you give some suggestions as to the planting of shrubbery around small residences in the vicinity of Atlanta?   Plants that are evergreen, slow-growing, hardy, and resistant to drought would include azalea, camellia, podocarpus, box, Japanese holly, Chinese holly, boxthorn, cotoneaster, pyracantha, jasmine, wax or glossy privet (*Ligustrum lucidum*), and abelia. These are all suitable for foundation planting but use them sparingly. Small houses will soon be overwhelmed by most of these plants unless they are used with restraint.

When shall I prune shrubs that were injured by frost?   It is more tidy to cut the shrubs back as soon as the injured parts turn brown, repeating later if inspection shows that the injury extends farther than your first pruning.

Can you suggest pink- and blue-flowering shrubs and flowers for my town garden, and yellow, orange, and white for my country place?   For the town garden: camellia, rose, azalea, deutzia, weigela—all pink; buddleia, plumbago, althaea, vitex—all blue. For the country: yellow—hypericum, *Galphimia glauca,* forsythia; orange—jasmine, basket of gold alyssum, *Rosa hugonis;* white—gardenia, philadelphus, camellia, rose, althaea, ligustrum, azalea.

Can tulip bulbs in the South be grown and increased for a number of years, as are narcissus? They are not satisfactory beyond one season except for certain varieties of tulips in sections of the upper South. In the lower South, tulips of certain varieties must be placed in cold storage for 2 months and planted in December. If held below 40° F. for longer than 2 months, they will root in the package.

How can I grow large tulips in north Georgia? In extreme north Georgia, use only varieties that are recommended; plant in well-enriched beds.

Will verbena act as a perennial in the lower South? Yes, plants can be grown from seed or cuttings. Old plants can be lifted, divided, and reset in the winter for spring bloom. Red spiders must be controlled in hot, dry weather with sulfur dust or malathion.

Hawaii

I am interested in growing orchids. How should I begin? Visit the Orchidarium Hawaii, 524 Manono Street, Hilo, a half-acre botanical garden devoted to orchids and their culture.

How do I obtain information on home gardening in Hawaii, which will be my future home? From the University of Hawaii, Honolulu, Hawaii 96822. There are also many botanical and public gardens to visit that feature plants native to the islands as well as tropical plants from other countries.

Idaho

What perennial daisies, other than white ones, would you suggest for Idaho (elevation about 3,500 feet)? You might try golden marguerite, *Anthemis tinctoria,* which can be grown from seed or plants and can be purchased from most mail-order nurseries. Any of the earlier Michaelmas daisies (hardy asters) should be suitable. *Aster* x *frikartii* is more like a daisy and very lovely. Hardy chrysanthemums are very satisfactory where the season is long enough. Choose varieties recommended for far north gardens.

What are the names of some hedges that will stay green all year in this climate? Probably none except your native evergreens. Spruce and juniper make lovely hedges and can be kept within bounds by clipping.

Can you give a list of low-growing (not to exceed 12 inches) perennial flowers that will provide bloom from early spring to late fall? They would be in sun, no shade.   *Anemone pulsatilla; Campanula carpatica, C. pusilla;* heuchera, various; *Phlox subulata; Gypsophila repens; Iberis semperflorens; Thymus serpyllum; Saponaria ocymoides; Penstemon crandallii, P. caespitosus, P. humulis;* alyssum; arabis; aubrieta; lewisia; antennaria; helianthemum; dianthus, various; sempervivum; *Veronica spuria; Melampodium cinereum; Malvastrum (Sphaeralcea) coccineum; Linum flavum* and *L. alpinum; Oenothera caespitosa, O. lavandulifolia,* and *O. missouriensis; Ceratostigma plumbaginoides;* iris, dwarf varieties; *Abronia fragrans; Physaria didymocarpa; Teucrium chamaedrys.*

What causes red raspberry blight in irrigated ground?   If the blight referred to is the yellowing of the leaves, it is usually caused by too wet subsoils, especially heavy or clay soils. Install underground drainage or plant in lighter, better-drained soils.

I live in an area having neutral to slightly alkaline soil, at an altitude of 4,250 feet. It is irrigated country. There are many plants that will not do well, either because of the short growing season or because of water around the roots. Can you name some shrubs, besides lilacs, bridalwreath, and snowballs, that might thrive?   The following shrubs are suggested for trial: highbush-cranberry (*Viburnum opulus*); *Spiraea* x *arguta,* or *S. thunbergii;* buffalo berry (*Shepherdia argentea*); Austrian copper rose. Trees: river birch (*Betula nigra*); weeping willow; soft maple or silver maple; and possibly sycamore. Evergreens: blue or Black Hills spruce; and possibly *Juniperus scopulorum* and *J. pfitzerana.*

What hardy roses would you suggest for Idaho?   In the Boise Valley and near Lewiston below 2,500 feet, the species like *R. hugonis, R. setigera, R. rugosa* and hybrids thrive without winter protection.

Can the trumpet vine be grown where there are zero winters?   If you mean *Bignonia capreolata,* the answer is no. If you mean *Campsis radicans,* yes. Both are called trumpet vine.

Illinois

What are the best 4 or 5 apple trees for the Midwest and for the small home garden?   The best way to choose apples is to try the fruit and see what you like. For summer: 'Lodi', 'Jerseymac', 'Yellow Transparent'. For fall: 'Jonamac', 'Macoun'. For winter: 'Golden Delicious', 'Jonathan', 'Spigold'.

Why don't I have any success with asters? Is it the climate here in north Illinois? No, your difficulty (if by aster you mean the so-called annual China-aster grown from seed) is probably due to disease, either aster wilt or aster yellows. The answer to wilt is to use wilt-resistant varieties. For yellows, spray the plants with malathion to kill the leafhoppers, which spread this disease.

What pruning is required on azaleas in the Midwest? Only enough to keep them shapely. Such pruning as is required should be done immediately after blooming. Careless use of the pruning shears can destroy bloom for 2 or 3 years and spoil the natural shape of the bush.

How can I control orange rust in my blackberries? Eliminate wild brambles from the locality; remove diseased plants in the patch, including roots, as soon as the disease appears in early spring; plant a resistant variety.

Can blueberries be raised successfully in northwestern Illinois? Yes, provided you acidify the soil properly. (See Blueberry.)

Can blueberries be successfully raised in eastern central Illinois? Yes, provided good culture and soil acidification receive careful attention.

What is a sweet cherry for central Illinois? 'Black Tartarian' is most universally successful, but it is necessary to have 2 or more trees, as they are self-sterile, and sour cherry pollen does not fertilize them. Plant a 'Napoleon' with it.

Will crape-myrtle live through the winter in the latitude of Chicago? No, even the so-called hardy type will winter-kill.

What is the proper care for wintering perennial foxglove? If possible, handle in cold frames, with the glass on, covered with mats to shut out winter sun. Lacking this, use umbrellalike coverings that allow the air to get in, but not water and sun. It is a tricky species to grow in Illinois.

What plants will provide the most cutting flowers to be grown in a small garden in Chicago? Among the annuals, perhaps more blooms can be cut from marigolds and zinnias than from any others in this class. Petunias are excellent because they provide low edgings in the garden picture yet yield satisfactory flowers for cutting too.

For people who do not like the ever-present foundation plantings of evergreens, what do you consider the best substitute for my locality, near Chicago? It would have to be something that will do at least reasonably well in a good deal of shade. A neat, healthy, clean shrub that will grow in shade is a problem, but *Euonymus alatus* 'Compactus' comes pretty close to filling the bill. With clean, dark-green foliage and striking autumn color, it is a highly desirable semiformal shrub and would make an attractive accent near the house.

I have a home on Lake Michigan, and have plenty of sand in front down to the lake; what would you suggest for a ground covering of character?   If in sun, and if you incorporate plenty of leafmold or peat moss, this sounds like a place for the bearberry (*Arctostaphylos uvaursi*).

Where can we secure information on the best table grapes that will grow in this locality? (Winnetka.)   The New York Fruit Testing Association, Geneva, N.Y. 14456, or your local State Experiment Station, Urbana, Ill. 61801, will give you the information you want.

Which are the varieties of herbs most practical for growing in this latitude? How should the seed bed be prepared for best results in herb production?   *Perennials:* sage, thyme, chives, mint. *Annuals:* sweet basil, sweet marjoram, and dill. These are the easiest to grow, but since taste is such a personal thing, the only criterion is, after all, what you like. (See Herb Gardens.)

How far north will Kerria japonica grow?   Into southern Wisconsin.

I have trouble in growing perennial lupine. Is there any special treatment?   Yes. They are legumes and must have the special inoculating bacteria to form the nodules they require in order to extract nitrogen from the air. Also, while they require calcium, they need more iron than most legumes. The trick is to keep them at a pH of about 5.9 to 6.8, where by juggling iron and calcium you can give them what they want.

What magnolias are suitable for northern climes?   Only two magnolias are commonly grown in Illinois, the saucer magnolia (*M.* x *soulangeana*) and the star magnolia (*M. stellata*).

What pruning is required on magnolias in the Midwest?   In the Midwest, the problem is to get them to make adequate growth, not to cut out any excess wood. Throw away the pruning shears and you'll have better luck. Only if branches are badly placed or broken should they be touched.

How far north will nectarines bear?   While they will bear in Illinois, they are so subject to curculio damage that they are seldom successful there.

Can I be sure of a crop if I plant southern paper-shell pecans in Illinois?   Not as a general rule. Even in southern Illinois, the 'Stuart', one of the hardiest southern varieties, seldom matures its kernels.

How far north will pecan nuts grow? Southern Illinois is about the northern limit of the pecan.

What is the best time to plant peonies in southern Illinois? Specialists in this area try to plant as close to September 15 as possible.

Is it necessary to mulch such perennials as delphinium, phlox, or carnation in this latitude? They are better for a mulch if it is not too dense and soggy. Think of a mulch for these plants as protecting the ground from winter sun, not as a blanket of insulation to shut out all cold. Make it airy but shady. Allow the breeze to blow through. Evergreen boughs are ideal.

Why can't we keep perennials during the winter? We cover them for the winter months. They were probably killed with loving kindness: a dense covering of leaves or other compact material will smother rather than protect plants. Use light, airy mulches, but apply *after* the ground freezes, not before. Remove early in the spring (about March 15 in the Chicago area) to avoid damaging spring growth.

I have a rhododendron in a 15-inch pot. Can this be planted in the garden and safely left outside all winter? I live in a suburb near Chicago. Probably not, but it depends on how hardy a species or variety it is. It would need protection from cold, wind, and sun during the winter, especially its first few winters after planting.

Should roses be planted in full sunshine or in partial shade? Some of the delicate pinks and the types of red that "blue" in sunshine are better for light shade at midday. But they should have at least five to six hours of full sun, preferably early in the day.

Can roses be hilled up 6 or 8 inches with soil before the ground has frozen and before their leaves have fallen? I always wait for leaves to fall and wood to ripen; then the ground freezes suddenly and I don't get them covered. Choosing the right time to cover roses is one of those things that makes gardening interesting (and confusing). The leaves must be off before they are covered, which means after a good sharp freeze, but usually there is a warm spell after such a freeze which allows for pulling the earth around the plant. If you have only a few plants, you might try the old trick of saving a few bushels of unfrozen earth in the cellar and applying this after the wood has ripened. For larger rose gardens, place mounds of hilling soil or compost near the beds and cover with burlap or tarpaulins during the first cold night to prevent freezing. Then hill up the plants the following day. Where cost is not a factor, plastic rose cones (in most garden catalogs) are excellent. Since they often save their cost in roses, they are worth considering.

What bush roses are best suited for the Chicago area? All hybrid perpetual roses are suited to Chicago; in fact, they are much more so than the more favored hybrid teas. With hybrid perpetuals, choose any that strike your fancy: they're all hardy. Perhaps the most satisfactory of the true shrub roses is *Rosa rugosa.* Above all, avoid the overpromoted *Rosa multiflora,* a weedy species recommended for hedges.

What climbing roses can be left on a fence or trellis all winter with little protection? The old rambler types (which bloom on new wood) survive this sort of treatment, even though their condition horrifies the meticulous rosarian. The dead wood can be cut out after bloom. However, be prepared for the white mildew that attacks practically all roses of the rambler type.

How far north will spicebush grow? The spicebush, *Lindera benzoin,* makes satisfactory growth as far north as southern Wisconsin.

Are there any strawberry varieties resistant to the red stele root-rot disease? Yes, the 'Sparkle', 'Midway', and 'Red Chief' varieties are resistant. Check with your county extension agent for others.

How can I succeed in growing everbearing strawberries? It is not easy to grow these fruits well, especially during the heat of summer. They require very fertile soil of good texture and a continuous supply of water throughout the season. The ground should be mulched lightly to keep the berries clean. A protective winter mulch is also necessary. (See Strawberry.)

Is it possible to transplant the sweet-gum tree in central Illinois? I have been unable to do so successfully. Yes, but get a nursery-grown tree with fine, fibrous roots. Be sure you plant it in rich, deep land. It won't grow in dry soil.

Is the birch bothered with borers in central Illinois? The birch borer makes this beautiful tree all but impossible to grow in central Illinois. By the time the pest is discovered, the damage is done, and there is no preventive treatment.

Can espalier fruit trees be grown in Illinois? Yes, but do not expect too much from them. The training of fruit trees in special shapes was originated in Europe, so that they could be planted along stone walls where the heat would help ripen the fruit. In the Midwest, the problem is too much heat, not too little. Use espaliers for special ornamental effects, not where fruit in quantity is the object.

How late (in the fall) can fruit trees be planted in central Illinois? Planting can go on all winter long provided good cultural practices are followed, but March or April should be equally satisfactory. It is a question of convenience and comfort, not of the thermometer, which ends the fall planting season.

What are the best fruit and nut trees for the average property in this region? The best sure-fire fruit trees for Illinois are apples, crab apples, and sour cherries. Native walnuts are about the only nut trees that are really reliable, and these must have light, loamy soil and good drainage.

Are there any wildflowers, which can be developed from seed, that can be grown in northern Illinois? Most wildflowers depend on seed for their continuation. Many are perennials and require as much care as other perennial seeds. Some possibilities are: *Aquilegia canadensis,* many violets, goldenrod, Allegheny foamflower, butterfly-weed, wild asters, Dutchman's-breeches, *Phlox divaricata,* and many others.

Will a tree wisteria grow in Chicago climate? Yes, provided its other requirements are met. It grows in almost any soil, but thrives best in a deep, rich loam that does not get too dry.

Indiana

Can you tell me how to grow delphinium in Indiana? Delphiniums come from cold regions and resent hot summers. To coax them into good behavior, give them a deeply prepared friable loam and under each plant put a 4-inch layer of peat moss mixed with rich compost. Spray weekly with Kelthane to control cyclamen mite. Cut flower stems off before they begin to seed. Grow the beautiful Pacific Hybrids as biennials. Sow seed from the current season's crop as soon as 50° F. readings begin in autumn. Keep fresh seed in a refrigerator until planting time.

What are the most desirable flowers to plant in a rock garden in northern Indiana? See Plants for Rock Gardens, Section 2.

Can Smyrna fig plants winter in the backyard in this section of Indiana? Definitely not; but figs can be grown in tubs and carried over in a cool cellar (between freezing and 40° F.) and set out again in early May. These will *not* be the Smyrna fig (which requires a special wasp for pollination) but the mission type, which can be pollinated by American insects.

Is there an American holly to use in climates such as Indiana in order to have enough berries to be attractive in the winter? You can't grow holly such as you see on Christmas cards. The deciduous species *Ilex verticillata* (black-alder or winterberry) is deciduous but bears bright-red holly berries on bare stems well into the winter.

Can pecans, English walnuts, and filberts be successfully grown? What types are best? Only in the southern end of Indiana are pecans and English walnuts likely to succeed. Filberts can be grown in most of the state.

What kind of peach trees would be best for Indiana climates? Practically any varieties in commerce are successful in your state.

What is the best time to plant roses in southern and northern Indiana? Should plants be 1, 2, or 3 years old? Either late-fall or early-spring planting is satisfactory for roses of any age. Most roses sold commercially are 2 years old.

When is the best time to set out monthly blooming roses? Either late-fall or early-spring planting should prove satisfactory. Which is better depends upon what kind of a winter or summer follows planting—something no one can foretell. However, planting in the spring does save overwinter losses and is preferred by most gardeners.

What kinds of plants, shrubs, or evergreens shall I place on the north and west side of my house? Large shrubs of coarse texture are suitable near a big old structure; smaller, neater ones of fine texture are better for colonial or modern homes. Combine a few shrubs with ground covers rather than plant a solid line of shrubs.

What summer- and fall-blooming shrubs, especially evergreens, are particularly suitable for this locality? The soil is sandy loam. There are practically no evergreen shrubs that would have good flowers during the summer and fall in this locality. Most evergreen shrubs like *Pieris japonica, Kalmia latifolia,* and hardy evergreen azaleas bloom in the spring.

When is the best time to put out strawberry plants in this locality? Late March or early April, if you can get them into the ground.

Iowa

Has the bayberry, so common in coastal New England, ever been grown in midwestern gardens? Yes, but not successfully. It requires acid soil and a moist, cool atmosphere—conditions that cannot easily be supplied in Iowa.

Can blueberries be grown successfully in central Iowa? Yes, provided rules for cultivation and acidifying the soil are observed. (See Blueberry.)

Are flowering dogwoods hardy in south Iowa? Yes, although flower buds are usually killed in severe winters.

Is it possible to grow American holly (Ilex opaca) in northern Iowa? No, it is not winter-hardy in Iowa.

What could we plant on bare ground that would be lawn enough for our 15-month-old son to play on by June? It needn't be a permanent lawn. This is a question to make someone knowledgeable about lawns cringe, since the only answer is to recommend planting either timothy or oats. Both will cover the ground with a rough, haylike coating that can be mowed, but neither is really satisfactory. The only other possibility, perennial ryegrass, makes a very good temporary turf that lasts a couple of years.

Can I grow flowering magnolias here in Iowa? *Magnolia* x *soulangeana* and *M. stellata* do well on any rich, loamy soil well supplied with humus, but would probably need watering during summer droughts. Wrapping in burlap when small will protect buds from winterkilling, but when the plant attains tree size, you will have to be reconciled to losing bloom about every third spring.

Will nectarine trees survive southeast Iowa winters? No.

What nut trees are hardy as far north as central Iowa? Butternut, black walnut, and hickory. Central Iowa is the northern limit of all three.

Will the passion-flower (Passiflora) live out-of-doors in southeast Iowa? *Passiflora incarnata,* the passion-flower, will survive in Iowa, but it is not the exotic tropical beauty one might imagine from its name. The more showy species will not survive.

What kinds of peach and pear trees are most adaptable to Iowa? Among hardier peaches, there are 'Harbelle' from Canada and 'Reliance' from New Hampshire. Among pears are 'Maxine', 'Magness', and 'Moonglow'. Consult your county extension agent at the Cooperative Extension Service (under county government) for others.

What is a good low-growing perennial for the north side of a house? If you mean the dense shade north of a house, where no sunshine ever falls, no showy perennial will grow. If the shade is only moderately dense, with sunshine sifting through the foliage of trees, you might try *Phlox divaricata, Vinca minor,* dwarf irises, *Dicentra eximia,* dwarf columbines, *Campanula carpatica,* or various primroses.

Is there a red raspberry suited to this midwestern climate that will bear the first year? 'Latham' has been successful over a wide range of the Midwest, but should not be allowed to bear the first year, nor should any other variety be allowed to do so.

My black raspberries dried up on the plants this summer. The canes are weak and all pitted with gray spots. What can I do about this condition?   Your plants are infected with the common and serious disease known as anthracnose. Cut out the canes most badly infected; feed the plants with a straw-manure mulch or complete fertilizer in early spring; spray the canes carefully with either Bordeaux mixture or lime-sulfur at least twice a year, especially when the leaves are unfolding and just before the blooms open. Consult your Cooperative Extension Service for local recommendations.

Can roses and other shrubs be successfully planted in the fall in northern Iowa?   Yes, provided the normal precautions are taken. Fall planting is much preferred to late-spring planting, except for roses. But don't wait too long in the spring. Plant before apple trees are in bloom.

I understand that the large-flowered climbers should not be pruned. How should they be grown in northern Iowa? Must one take them down each fall?   This type does need pruning to keep in bounds and to cut out old, unproductive wood. But remember that the plants bloom on 2-year-old wood, and if all the old growth is cut away, you get no bloom. Protect in winter by laying them down and covering them with earth.

When is the best time to transplant strawberries in Iowa? I see some transplanted in the fall and some in the spring.   As early in the spring as the soil can be planted and worked is best. Only pot-grown plants have much chance to succeed if planted in late spring.

Should tritoma be stored for winter?   Yes, dig the clump with soil adhering to the roots and store in a cool (from 33° to 40° F.) cellar until late April.

Is vitex hardy in this part of Iowa? I have tried to grow it and it winter-kills.   It is not hardy outdoors without very heavy protection. Or it can be cut back and, taking up the clumps of roots, wintered in a cold frame.

Are Carpathian walnut trees hardy in Iowa?   No records are available, but they have survived severe weather in central Wisconsin.

Is the lovely low-growing yew suitable to our Iowa climate?   Practically all of the low-growing varieties of the Japanese yew are fully winter-hardy in your locality, provided drainage is good and suitable cultural practices are followed. Protect from harsh, drying winter winds.

Kansas

Should cherry trees be pruned each year to get larger fruit and better yield? If so, when? Cherry trees do not usually need or stand severe pruning. In early spring, remove diseased wood and broken branches and thin out crowding and crossing branches.

I have a good grapevine. How can I get more plants just like it? Most native grapes are propagated easily by cuttings. In early spring, cut several of the best 1-year-old canes into pieces about 15 inches long with 2 or more buds on each piece. Plant these in good soil, with at least 1 good bud above the ground. With good care, many of these cuttings will root and grow. The best plants may be reset in a permanent location the following spring.

We seeded a new lawn early this spring and have a good stand of grass. Should it be mowed or left to grow this year? It can be mowed, but not shorter than 2 inches. The final mowing height after midsummer will depend on variety (in bluegrasses). (See Lawns.)

Should grass clippings be raked off the lawn? It is not necessary unless the grass is exceptionally high. (See Lawns.)

We have been told that we should cut our grass high. How high is "high"? Leaving 2 to 3 inches is high-cut. Many bluegrass varieties can be mowed as short as 1 inch where this is desirable.

How can we raise good lupines? Lupines are cool-season plants that do well in acid soils and consequently cannot be expected to do well in your locality.

Why do monthly roses grow tall instead of bushy? Shade will draw up the plants somewhat. If the canes are very long and don't produce blooms, they are probably coming from the understock on which the monthly rose was budded. Canes of this kind should be cut out.

I have hybrid tea roses that I wish to transplant in the spring. When should this be done? Transplant as early as the soil can be worked. Prune the tops back, leaving only 3 or 4 inches. Take up a good ball of soil with each plant. (See Roses.)

A polyantha rose planted last spring did not have a bud on it all summer. What is the cause of its failing to bloom? Polyanthas normally bloom freely the first season. Possibly the polyantha top died and the understock on which it was budded came up and did not bloom. If the plant is producing long, straggly canes, it would be better to replace it.

What is the best winter protection for roses in western Kansas? Hill the soil up around the plants approximately 8 inches. Wait until the ground is frozen and then add straw or similar material several inches deep, so that all of the soil mounds and the level soil between plants are mulched.

How heavily shall I prune roses in the fall that were put out in the spring? Don't prune your roses in the fall. Wait until spring, and then prune out the wood that has been winter-killed. (See Roses.)

Kentucky

At what depth should freesia bulbs be planted? What month should they be planted? Freesias should be planted heavy end down, with the tips barely below the soil level. A good test for depth is to be able to feel the bulb tops without being able to see them. September is the best planting month for freesias. They must have a heavy (but airy) mulch during the winter. Even then they may not survive.

How can one get rid of Bermuda grass in this state? If it gets a start on either lawn or farmland, nothing else will grow. Where vegetables or flowers are planted, Bermuda grass must be constantly dug out until entirely eradicated. Several herbicides, used according to directions, will eradicate this. Consult your county extension agent.

How can I get pansies started in the winter? Pansies can be started in a cold frame or hotbed or in flats in the house during the winter. They cannot be successfully started from seeds outdoors after late summer or early fall. The plants themselves will be fairly hardy in your locality after becoming established, but winter-planted seeds outdoors would not germinate until the following spring.

Is it possible to have healthy perennial phlox plants in this vicinity, where we have very humid, hot summers? What soil conditions are suitable to them? The Ohio Valley has the above summer conditions, and freezing and thawing for 5 months in the winter. Perennial phlox can be grown in your area as successfully as anywhere else. They are entirely hardy and like good, rich soil. With established plantings, fertilizer may be put on the top of the ground during the winter. A mulch on the surface of the soil during the hot months of summer will keep the reflected heat from burning the lower foliage; watering should be done by laying the hose on the ground, soaking the soil but not sprinkling the leaves.

What is the proper culture for tritoma? Tritoma (*Kniphofia*) should go through the winter safely without extra protection. It is wise, however, to cut the foliage down after the first frost and cover the area with 6 or 8 inches of leafmold or other mulch. Tritomas are not particular as to soil, but an occasional fertilization will produce larger blooms. The usual method of propagation is from divisions of the old plants taken up in early fall and replanted promptly.

Louisiana

How can chrysanthemums be grown in northeastern Louisiana? Garden chrysanthemums are started from tip cuttings rooted in sand in April and set into beds of fertilized soil when they have become well rooted. If divisions of the old clumps are used, the plants can have a great deal of leafspot, and so cuttings are much to be preferred.

What is the proper time to trim crape-myrtle in northern Louisiana? When the leaves fall in the autumn. Crape-myrtle flowers on the current year's wood, so pruning must be done *before* growth starts, never after.

What are the best flowering evergreens to plant in the vicinity of New Orleans? Among the choicest evergreens for this area are the many beautiful varieties of azaleas and camellias, the last including the tea of commerce, a very beautiful flowering evergreen shrub. Others are illicium, banana-shrub, the poinsettia, and (in sheltered locations) the hibiscus.

What care and culture does gerbera require? If you can get fresh seeds, these will germinate well in about 2 weeks; if not, buy divisions of old plants, set them at the same depth at which they grew previously in beds that have been made rich by spading in compost. Use a mulch of oak leaves to cover the soil around the plants and apply a balanced plant food in January and June—watering well during all dry periods.

Should one take up gladiolus bulbs every year? Yes, it is by far the best practice to lift gladiolus corms every year, just after the foliage turns yellow. The tops are cut off, the mother corms are discarded, and the new corms are stored in shallow boxes in a cool, shaded place. (See Gladiolus.)

Should calla-lilies be left in the ground all winter? Mine did not bloom, but the leaves are still green. I planted them last February or March. In semitropical sections of Louisiana, calla-lilies can be left in the ground all year. The soil must be acid, mucky, retentive of moisture, and free from too much competition from the roots of large shrubs and trees.

When is the best time to move spider-lilies? White spider-lily (*Hymenocallis*), in early spring. Red spider-lily (*Lycoris*), July or early August.

Which roses thrive best in the Louisiana soil and climate? Many of the true tea roses, such as 'Safrano', 'Marie van Houtte', 'Minnie Francis', 'Duchesse de Brabant', and 'Louis Philippe' will survive for many years. It is best to grow the modern hybrid tea varieties as annuals, renewing a part of all of your rose bed each autumn.

How late can rosebushes be planted in central Louisiana? What is the best fertilizer to use? Early planting is recommended, and December to February is considered the best period. However, the latest possible date would be about April 1. Commercial rose mixtures are satisfactory.

What is the proper care for roses and the best time to plant in southern Louisiana? Roses should be set between December and February, the earlier the better, so that the root systems may become well established before the top starts to grow in the warm weather of spring. Have the beds fertilized in advance, plant at the same depth as they grew in the nursery, and water in well. Be sure that the plants never suffer from drought, and feed every 4 weeks during growing weather.

What is the best way to keep snapdragons during the winter in Louisiana? Young plants (less than 1 year old) should carry through the winter in the open ground without special preparation if the drainage and other conditions are normally good.

Michigan

Will chrysanthemums winter safely in northern Michigan, near Petoskey? Yes, with protection. A blanket of evergreen branches intermingled with leaves would be the best covering. Apply when the soil is slightly frozen. The soil should be well drained.

How late is it safe to plant crocus, hyacinth bulbs, and other early spring-blooming bulbs in southern Michigan? Crocus, scilla, and hyacinth bulbs can be planted safely as late as sound unshriveled bulbs are available, although earlier planting is preferable. Late-planted hyacinths will have to be mulched if they are to survive. Tulips, on the other hand, should not go in until about the middle of October. While most experts condemn late planting of narcissus, they can be planted as late as December 1 with good results by setting them 6 inches deep—over the *top* of the bulb. They bloom late, but with perfect flowers.

Can you suggest evergreens suitable for this climate? *Juniperus chinensis, J. pfitzerana, J. monosperma, J. scopulorum, J. horizontalis, J. sabina* 'Tamariscifolia'; *Picea pungens; Pinus aristata, P. mugo, P. nigra, P. ponderosa, P. strobus,* and *P. sylvestris; Taxus canadensis; Thuya; Tsuga; Abies lasiocarpa* and *A. concolor; Pseudotsuga menziesii; Rhododendron* in variety in southern Michigan.

Can you give me information on the raising of foxglove (Digitalis purpurea)? Plant seed in late May in a shaded cold frame. When fall rains start, put on the glass to protect from excess moisture. Cover plants with marsh hay or evergreen boughs after the first freeze and replace the glass. Transplant into a permanent situation (light shade and loose, loamy soil, with plenty of humus) toward the end of April or the first of May.

Can gum trees (Liquidambar styraciflua and Nyssa sylvatica) be grown in central or northern Michigan? *Nyssa sylvatica* (sour gum or black gum) is not considered hardy in central Michigan. It is difficult to transplant, unless nursery-grown stock is used. It likes low, damp soil with plenty of humus. It is hardly worth trying in this region. *Liquidambar* (sweet-gum) is hardy over most of the lower peninsula of Michigan, provided that conditions are right. This is the northern limit of its range. It must have deep, rich, moist soil and stand free from all shade. Neither species would attain full stature in Michigan.

Will you please give me, as nearly complete as possible, a list of herbs that will thrive in this vicinity? *Annual:* basil, borage, parsley, summer savory, anise, burnet, caraway, coriander, dill, and sweet marjoram. *Perennial:* balm, camomile, catnip, chives, horehound, lavender, mint, rue, sage, thyme, and yarrow.

Can Hibiscus rosa-sinensis be grown in Michigan? No, it is a tropical and will tolerate no frost whatever.

Will Ilex crenata be hardy in Grosse Pointe (Detroit), Michigan? The Japanese holly is not considered reliably hardy north of the Ohio River, though it sometimes survives a hundred miles north of there in well-sheltered spots. It is not a good bet for Michigan.

Can American holly (Ilex opaca) be grown in the northern states? No, it is not hardy in the North. It grows in protected spots in Massachusetts, but Michigan winters would be too hard on it.

Is there any shrub holly, 5 to 10 feet high, that is reliably hardy in

southern Michigan? The word "reliably" is the pinch. You probably mean an evergreen holly that is 100 per cent hardy and looks like the pictures on the Christmas cards. The answer to that is "No." There are three deciduous hollies, all of which have attractive winter berries: *Ilex glabra* (inkberry), *I. laevigata* (smooth winterberry), and *I. verticillata* (black-alder). The first species has black berries; the other two, red. All three need a humus-rich soil that retains moisture. Oregon holly-grape (*Mahonia aquifolium*) will give the foliage effect of true holly, but the fruit will be blue, not red.

Which are the best nut trees to plant in Michigan? Black walnut, hickory, and butternut. If you are near any of the Great Lakes, toward the southern part of the state, the hazels or filberts may do well for you.

Can 'Alberta' pears be raised successfully in lower Michigan? Do you mean the 'Elberta' peach? The southwestern corner of Michigan is one of the world's great peach sections. On the other hand, if the Canadian hybrid pears (like 'Tait-Dropmore' and 'Pioneer', or the Chinese sand pears grown in Canada) are meant, the answer is also "Yes." However, these pears are a compromise between hardiness and quality, and ought to be dropped from consideration for high-quality sorts that will do well in Michigan, such as 'Cayuga' or old favorites like 'Bartlett' and 'Seckel'.

Can perennial phlox be transplanted in the early spring in Michigan? Yes, this is the preferred time. Move as soon as the ground can be worked.

What plants are best for Michigan's climate? Only the hardier types. Investigate the large number of species and varieties being grown in the Nichols Arboretum of the University of Michigan, Ann Arbor, Michigan, and the Matthaei Botanical Gardens, also of the University of Michigan, Ann Arbor.

What low-growing rock-garden perennials are hardy in northern Michigan—30° to 40° F. below zero in the winter? *Hymenoxys acaulis; Androsace sarmentosa; Anemone blanda* and *A. quinquefolia; Aethionema*, various; *Callirhoe involucrata; Gypsophila repens; Campanula muralis; Hypericum reptans; Iberis sempervirens; Arenaria*, various; *Armeria laucheana; Aubrieta; Campanula pusilla; Dianthus alpinus; Heuchera sanguinea; Iris pumila; Linum alpinum; Aquilegia saximontana* and *A. alpina; Primula*, various; *Phlox subulata, P. bifida; Penstemon caespitosus, P. crandallii,* and *P. alpinus; Physaria didymocarpa; Saponaria ocymoides; Papaver alpinum; Veronica prostrata.*

Is it possible to grow rhododendrons successfully in Detroit, Michigan? Yes, but this is no tyro's job. Careful preparation of the soil is essential. Protection from winter sun and wind are particularly important. The best trick is to plant on the north side of a building or dense hedge, so that on June 21 the sun just touches the base of the stem. Then as the sun recedes to the south in the winter, the shade protection, such as burlap or wrapping in straw, will still be needed. Above all, don't neglect watering, even during the winter. And see that the soil remains acid. The following rhododendron species have been grown in the East Lansing area and are generally recommended for the Great Lakes region: *Rhododendron carolinianum; R. catawbiense; R. x laetevirens; R. maximum; R. micranthum; R. mucronulatum; R. racemosum; R. smirnowii; R. yakusimanum.* The following rhododendron hybrids are recommended: 'Boule de Neige'; 'Mrs. Charles S. Sargent'; 'Nova Zembla'; 'Pinnacle'; 'P.J.M.'; 'Ramapo'; 'Roseum Elegans'; 'The General'; 'Windbeam'.

When is the best time to set out hybrid tea roses in southeastern Michigan? There is no "best" time, since we cannot tell in advance what the weather will be. Plant as early as possible in the spring, or as late as possible in the fall. Many commercial growers and landscapers set out stocks during thaws in December and January. In fall planting, hilling up is necessary. Sometimes good pot-grown plants (7-inch to 8-inch pots) are available for late-spring and early-summer planting.

Is fall planting of hybrid tea roses considered safe in Michigan, in the area of Grand Rapids? If done *late* enough, fall planting is usually better than spring planting. Protection by hilling up the soil over the crowns of the plants is necessary.

Why can't roses in central Michigan be pruned in autumn? They can; but there is not much point in doing so, since the branches will have to be cut back to live buds in the spring, anyway, and the unpruned branches help hold snow in place, which forms a good mulch.

Is clematis hardy in northern Michigan? Most clematis are hardy, with proper culture.

What shrub or evergreen can you recommend for planting on the north side of a house where the soil is dry? Your native *Cornus sericea,* the red Osier dogwood, is a highly desirable and hardy shrub for just such a situation. Pfitzer's juniper is a desirable evergreen subject, but may need some watering to become established.

Minnesota

Will you please name several of the spring-flowering bulbs, other than tulips and narcissus, that we can grow here in southern Minnesota? Chionodoxa (glory-of-the-snow), crocus, galanthus (snowdrops), muscari (grape-hyacinth), ornithogalum (star-of-Bethlehem), scilla (squill).

How can I protect Canterbury bells for winter? Keep moisture out of the center of the rosette of leaves—this is where rot starts. They can be wintered satisfactorily in a cold frame. If this is not available, use a light straw mulch on the ground around the plants and under the leaves. Then place a thick layer of lightweight brush over the bed and cover this with straw or marsh hay. The brush is necessary to keep the straw from smothering the green leaves that remain all winter.

Will you give the name of a good cherry-plum tree that is suited to the climate in central Minnesota? The list of hardy varieties includes 'Oka', 'Sapa', and 'Sapalta'. The 'Compass' variety is an excellent pollinizer for the above.

I want to plant some currants. What is a good variety? There are several excellent varieties, including the old 'Perfection' and the newer 'Red Lake'. These are hardy in your state. In some localities, however, planting is restricted because of danger from the spread of the white pine blister rust. Consult your county extension agent at St. Paul.

We grow some dogwoods here, but not the beautiful large-flowering kind. Do you think that we could? The flowering dogwood of the South and East is not hardy in your area.

Our little evergreen trees don't look quite right, and we have been told that they have red spiders. Is there a cure? See Spider Mites.

When is the best time to prune evergreens like junipers and arborvitae? Wait until new growth is 3 to 4 inches long. Then snip off half the length of this new growth. This will avoid leaving dead stubs. Only Japanese yew retains live buds on wood older than one year. It can be cut back to old hardwood as late as July 15.

We have extremely cold winters here (over 30° below zero). I have never seen a forsythia this far north. Would one survive our winters? Some of the hardier forsythias may survive, but the flower buds are winter-killed when exposed to such low temperatures.

Can gladiolus bulbs be left in the ground if heavily mulched and well drained? I recently read an article where it was claimed that they were being successfully wintered that way, even here in Minnesota. Yes. Cover with a 12-inch mulch of compost or straw after the ground freezes. It is usually considered better and easier to dig, store, and replant the bulbs.

Is it necessary to give winter cover to grapevines here in southern Minnesota? Most of the standard grape varieties must be protected during the winter. The varieties 'Fredonia' and 'Beta' are usually winter-hardy if the wood is well matured before cold weather.

My arborvitae hedge is almost 7 feet tall, and I would like to have it just about 3 feet. Can it be cut back to that height? No. Evergreens like this should not be pruned back beyond the green, actively growing shoots. They do not renew themselves from old hardwood as deciduous shrubs do.

Even the hardiest privet hedges kill back here in the winter. What would you suggest for a clipped hedge about 6 feet tall? Consider *Cotoneaster acutifolia* or *Lonicera tatarica* and its varieties.

When and how is pansy seed sown? Sow the seed about August 1 in a seed bed well loosened up with leafmold or peat moss. When the seedlings are large enough, transplant to a cold frame, using a similar soil, where they are kept during the winter.

When should pansies be planted out in the garden? Pansies, if grown in a cold frame during the winter, will not be injured by the frosts and light freezing of early spring. Plant them in the garden as early as the soil can be worked.

Do you know the name of a good pear suited to the climate of central Minnesota? The University of Minnesota has originated several pear varieties. 'Parker' and 'Patten' are recommended. These 2 varieties planted together help, through cross-pollination, to ensure heavier crops.

We have read about mixing peat moss with soil to make it acid. There is a lot of peat moss near here. Could we use it? Not all peat moss is necessarily acid. The only way to be sure is to have it tested. It can be used as humus in your soil, however, whether acid or not. To acidify soil, add flowers of sulfur. (See Section 1.)

How deep should peonies be set? Cover the pink buds on root divisions about 2 inches, no deeper.

Will you give a list of hardy perennials for central Minnesota? Coreopsis, gaillardia, peonies, iris, delphinium, hosta, aquilegia, Shasta daisy, thalictrum, dictamnus, hardy asters, hemerocallis, hardy chrysanthemums, phlox, veronica.

What perennials would form a good backbone for a northern Minnesota garden where frost comes early and winterkilling is a problem? Coreopsis, gaillardia, peony, iris, delphinium, aquilegia, Shasta daisy, veronica.

Will black raspberries do well in this part of the country? Black raspberries are doubtfully hardy in the extreme north.

When is it best to plant roses—fall or spring? It is safer to plant roses in the early spring. If fall planted, they must be very well protected against severe winter temperatures.

What is the best way to protect a tree rose during the winter in Minnesota? Dig up the plant carefully so as not to injure roots. Lay it in a long trench and carefully work the soil around and over it. Cover with at least 6 inches of soil. After the ground freezes 1 or 2 inches, cover with several inches of straw or evergreen boughs.

How much of hybrid tea rose tops should you prune off in the fall? Don't prune in the fall. After they are uncovered in the spring, cut back to good, sound, live wood.

We have sandy soil and 40° below zero in the winter. Can I raise climbing roses? Yes, if they are given good winter protection. Take the canes off their support in the fall and tie them together to make one long bundle. Lay this bundle flat on the ground and completely cover with soil. Have 2 or 3 inches of soil over all the canes. Mulch over the soil with several inches of straw. Select such superhardy varieties as 'Viking Queen', 'White Dawn', and 'Blaze'.

What roses are best for northern Minnesota? Shrub roses like *Rosa hugonis, R. rugosa* and hybrids, and also the sub-zeros such as 'Queen O' The Lakes' and 'Arctic Flame'.

What causes climbing roses, after being uncovered in the spring, to die back to within 2 feet of the ground? The buds are alive, yet the canes die back. The canes are wrapped with marsh hay and waterproof paper. If there is a section near the base where canes are exposed or poorly protected, the canes will be killed from that point to their tips. Also canker, a fungus disease, may girdle the canes, producing similar results.

What fruit-bearing shrubs are hardy enough for our northern climate? Korean cherry, Juneberry, elderberry, American highbush-cranberry, and some of the flowering quinces are hardy, especially in favorable situations. Buffalo berry (*Shepherdia argentea*) produces fruit that many enjoy, but not everyone. It is particularly grown in western Minnesota.

Which of the cultivated varieties of walnut are hardy enough to be

planted in central Minnesota? The named varieties are not always winter-hardy in central Minnesota. Even in southern Minnesota, the standard varieties are recommended only for trial.

Mississippi

When is the best time to set out new chrysanthemum plants? Rooted cuttings of chrysanthemums should be set out in the garden in May or June. It is better to use cuttings than divisions from the old clumps, as in this way you will avoid carrying over infection of the leafspotting disease. Choose an overcast afternoon, water well, and shade for a day or two.

How can rain-lilies be made to bloom and thrive in the Delta section of Mississippi? These little flowers (*Zephyranthes*) of the West will usually succeed quite well in this state. With sufficient moisture, fertilizer, and freedom from severe competition, they should bloom profusely during the summer months.

How deep should gladiolus corms be planted? In light, sandy soils of the lower South, it is best to set gladiolus corms 3 to 4 inches deep. Thus, they will have better moisture and will not topple over when in bloom.

What grass is best suited for the Gulf Coast? There are several excellent lawn grasses for this area. For shade, under trees—St. Augustine. Poor soil, not much shade—centipede. Full sun, good soil—Bermuda. Good soil, lots of moisture—carpet grass or 'Meyer' zoysia, which must have plenty of water until well established but is then drought resistant (grows in sun or shade). (See also Florida.)

Could I trim a gardenia bush to shape? Would it bloom? When should it be cut? Prune, if necessary, just when growth begins in the spring, by thinning out crowded shoots and cutting back straggly branches.

Tell me why my white spider-lilies (Hymenocallis) will not bloom even though the foliage develops. They have been in the ground several years. Too much shade; lack of plant food (they are gross feeders and respond well to fertilizing); or lack of moisture during the growing season.

Will the loquat or "Oriental-plum" grow in the lower cotton belt? Yes, the loquat is a most ornamental evergreen tree, hardy in the Gulf Coast region. Ordinarily it bears large annual crops of delicious yellow fruits that are esteemed as fresh fruit and for pies, tarts, and conserves.

Can nandina be grown from cuttings? Attempts to grow nandina from cuttings will be disappointing, in spite of the best possible care. Propagate these shrubs by sowing ripened seeds in a flat. Care for them until the following summer, when germination should be complete.

When is the best time to plant roses on the Gulf Coast? Between December and February. Early planting is much to be preferred, as the root systems will then have time to become well established before top growth is forced out by the warm weather of spring.

What is the best soil for growing roses? A sandy loam or Delta soil that is fairly high in organic matter, retentive of moisture, and well fortified with readily available nutrients.

Is the old-fashioned moss rose obtainable? Where? You will find the moss rose listed by a few specialists in old roses. It is curious, rather than beautiful. Unless you are familiar with it, better see it in bloom before planting.

Missouri

I would like to know when to plant bulbs of Sprekelia formosissima, commonly known as Jacobean-lily, in Missouri—in early spring, or should I wait until May? What kind of soil and fertilization is needed? Plant after the danger of hard frosts has passed. It will thrive on a variety of soils but prefers a medium loam. The soil should be highly fertile; very old manure or compost and liberal supplies of superphosphate are good.

What annual can I plant that will bloom all summer in a north garden that gets sun in early morning and late afternoon? Annuals are notorious sun lovers. A few that will condescend to grow without full sunshine are balsam, impatiens, godetia, lobelia, nicotiana, *Centaurea imperialis* (sweet sultan), clarkia, *Cynoglossum amabile* (Chinese forget-me-not), petunia.

What care should I give perennial asters set out in the fall? A light mulch of straw, hay, or dry leaves during the winter is all that they need. Remove the mulch before growth starts early in the spring.

What azaleas will grow well in Jackson, Missouri? Consider the following: Knaphill and Exbury azaleas; Mollis azaleas; the flame azalea (*Rhododendron calendulaceum*); pinxterbloom azalea (*R. nudiflorum*);

snow azalea (*R. mucronatum*); varieties of *R. obtusum,* such as 'Amoenum' and 'Hinodegiri'.

What sweet cherries are hardy and satisfactory in the Midwest? Sweet cherries are not a reliable crop in the Midwest except in western Michigan. You might consider the variety 'Kansas Sweet', a red-fruited variety recommended for the Midwest. It should be planted with 'Montmorency' for cross-pollination. They lack hardiness, both as to heat and to cold.

What would be the best type of living Christmas tree for us? Colorado blue spruce or red-cedar.

How can one grow large chrysanthemums outdoors in Missouri? Most large-flowering commercial or greenhouse chrysanthemums do well outdoors in Missouri. Grow just 3 or 4 stems on each plant. Remove all side buds, letting only the top bud flower. Plenty of water, fertilizer, and cultural care are essential.

What shrubs and flowers would be good for a city garden in this state? Shrubs: *Cotoneaster divaricata* and *C. acutifolia; Deutzia* x *lemoinei; Kerria japonica; Philadelphus,* various; *Spiraea prunifolia; Viburnum carlesii.* Perennials: tulips; daffodils; ornithogalum; phlox, early varieties; Oriental poppy; dianthus; lupine; pyrethrum; linum; gaillardia; dictamnus; hybrid lilies; chrysanthemum; aster (Michaelmas daisy). Annuals: calendula; marigold; petunia; verbena; *Phlox drummondii;* gypsophila; larkspur; dimorphotheca; zinnia; calliopsis; *Mirabilis jalapa* (four-o'clock).

I have a Shasta daisy from Idaho. Its flowers there were very large, but mine are smaller. Does Missouri climate have something to do with it? Climate is not to blame. Shasta daisies need full sun, fertile loam soil, a good supply of water during the growing season, and a light mulch of straw or leaves during the winter.

Can we raise delphiniums in the Midwest successfully? Set out strong plants in the spring. A deep, fertile loam soil is required. Add a generous amount of ground limestone if the soil is acid. Full exposure to the sun and constant moisture at the roots during the growing season are essential. Cultivate frequently and provide good drainage to prevent winter injury. A light mulch of straw or hay during the winter may be beneficial. The striking Pacific Hybrids are best grown as biennials in your area, sowing fresh seed from the current year's bloom as soon as nighttime temperatures below 50° F. occur. Keep seed in the refrigerator if hot weather continues. A cold frame should be used during the winter.

What hardy ferns will succeed in Missouri, and how are they

grown? Ferns like a cool, shady exposure (northern). Any soil that contains a good supply of leafmold or peat moss, and constant moisture, will be satisfactory. Plant ferns in the fall before the ground freezes. Collect native species from your vicinity or purchase from a wildflower specialist.

What kind of herbs can we raise here? Anise, caraway, chervil, chives, coriander, dill, fennel, tarragon, lavender, sage, lemon balm, rosemary, spearmint, summer savory, sweet basil, thyme, sweet marjoram.

Can lavender be grown in Missouri? How is it cured (as used in sachet bags)? Yes, lavender can be grown in Missouri. Plants can be obtained from most nurseries. Hang small bunches of the flowers in a warm room or shed where they will dry quickly. They can be stripped from the flowering stems, put in sachet bags, etc., as soon as dry.

Is it possible to grow Magnolia grandiflora in the vicinity of St. Louis, Missouri? What soil does it prefer? Yes. Since St. Louis is about the northern limit for this tree, growth is slow and mature specimens are relatively small. A southern exposure with a north to northwest windbreak is most favorable. It grows best in a fertile clay loam soil. Flowers appear in July.

What culture is needed for hardy phlox in Missouri? Give full sun, a fertile loam soil containing a good supply of organic matter, adequate drainage to prevent winter injury, frequent cultivation, and irrigation during a dry growing season. Transplanting or dividing may be necessary after the plants have grown in one spot for 3 or 4 years.

What is the proper winter protection for rhododendrons and azaleas in Missouri? A 6- to 10-inch mulch of dry leaves, preferably oak leaves. Rhododendrons exposed to direct sun during the winter should have a burlap or lath screen to prevent the leaves from "burning" or turning brown.

Can tree roses be grown in central Missouri? Plant in the spring in fertile clay loam soil well supplied with humus. Cut back the top growth or "head" to 3 or 4 eyes, and tie the main stem firmly to a strong stake. Full sun and a constant supply of moisture are necessary. For winter protection, loosen the roots on one side, bend the plant over, cover the top with soil and a heavy straw mulch, first wrapping the main stem with burlap or paper. Uncover early in the spring before growth starts.

What is the best time to plant roses and when is the best time to prune? Set out roses in the fall if the plants are dormant; otherwise wait until early spring. Prune hybrid teas in early spring. Climbing roses are pruned after they flower. (See Roses.)

Why do my rosebushes grow so tall and have very few leaves? Any of the following might be the cause: too much shade; suckers from seedling stock at the base of the grafted plant; black spot, defoliating plants; excess nitrogen in the soil.

How much should a climbing 'Peace' rose be pruned each year (flowers are 5 inches in diameter—now 2 years old)? Also 'Blaze'? It depends on the type of trellis and the effect desired. For extensive coverage, remove only the dead wood and a few of the oldest canes each year. Drastic pruning results in few flowers until the plant gets reestablished. All large-flowered climbers bloom best on 2-year-old canes.

What flowers would be best for a shady garden, with some sun in the afternoon? Anchusa, balsam, impatiens, bleedingheart, spring-flowering bulbs, campanula, columbine, ferns, forget-me-not, fuchsia, eupatorium, godetia, day-lily, lobelia, mertensia, primroses, lily-of-the-valley, plantain-lily, tuberous-rooted begonia, thalictrum, tradescantia, vinca, violets.

Is it good or bad to cover strawberries with straw or leaves during the winter in Missouri? A straw mulch is recommended, especially for young plants just getting established. Leaves are all right if they are not permitted to remain excessively wet, pack down, and thus smother the plants.

How should Urceolina peruviana be cared for in order to have it bloom? This rare Andean bulb will probably not be hardy in Missouri. Grow it in a pot of light but rich soil in a sunny greenhouse or window. Rest it by keeping it quite dry after its leaves die away in the winter. Repot in the spring as growth begins.

Are there any large-flowered white or yellow violets that will grow well in a midwestern climate? *Viola blanda* (white), *Viola hastata* (yellow), and *Viola rotundifolia* (yellow). Violets need light shade, friable soil containing lots of leafmold or peat moss, and extra water during dry weather. Protect them with a light mulch of leaves or straw during the winter.

Montana

What are some good shade-tolerant flowers for the north of a house and under trees in this climate? *Brunnera macrophylla;* aconite; lily-of-the-valley; bleedingheart; hosta; mertensia; myosotis; primroses; *Phlox* *divaricata* and *P. carolina; Campanula carpatica* and *C. rotundifolia;* bloodroot; trollius; thalictrum; violet; *Epimedium grandiflorum.*

Our gladiolus bulbs seem to "run out." Is this because of the short season? Possibly the season is too short to mature the new corms. Rich, deeply prepared soil and sufficient moisture at the roots to keep them growing vigorously in an open sunny location, protected from the wind, should help to produce better corms.

What hedge is best suited to this climate? To form a neat shorn hedge, Amur River privet. For an informal taller hedge, Persian lilac, *Rosa hugonis, R. rubrifolia,* and Chinese elm.

Is the tree peony adapted to the northern Rocky Mountain region? Many tree peony varieties can be grown in Montana if altitude is not more than about 4,000 feet above sea level. They grow with coaxing, in Denver, Colorado, at 5,280 feet in altitude. Drying of the stems by winter wind and sun seems to be the difficulty.

Could you suggest perennials for a cold climate and a short growing season, at an elevation of 5,700 feet? Peony; iris; columbine; *Phlox subulata, P. divaricata, P. paniculata; Trollius europaeus; Mertensia virginica;* campanula; pyrethrum; *Papaver orientale, P. nudicaule;* primroses; delphinium; rudbeckia hybrids; *Centaurea macrocephala; Physostegia virginiana; Clematis integrifolia, C. recta, C. grandiflora; Monarda didyma.*

What can be done to control rust or blight in sweet peas? See Section 13. Where days are hot and nights are cool, do all watering as infrequently as practical, but always thoroughly and always before noon. Try the spring-flowering type.

Nebraska

Will you list some annuals that bloom most of the summer and can endure the heat and drought of Nebraska? Zinnia, marigold, petunia, portulaca, annual gaillardia, *Catharanthus roseus, Anchusa capensis,* annual phlox, scabiosa, cosmos.

Is boxwood out of the question in this locality? Boxwood is not hardy under your conditions.

Why did a hard November freeze kill Chinese elm and still not affect other trees in Nebraska? Most of the other shade trees used in your state go into a state of dormancy without the help of moderately cold weather in early fall. The Chinese elm apparently requires some cold weather to harden it off before it becomes dormant and is able to stand a hard freeze. The Siberian elm (*Ulmus pumila*) is a more reliable species. Chinese elms are semievergreen.

We have some evergreens planted against the front of our house. Do you advise mulching the ground there for winter? Yes, a loose mulch of peat moss mixed with compost, leafmold, or some similar material helps to conserve soil moisture and prevents too deep freezing. Since evergreens give off moisture even when the soil is frozen, it is important to water thoroughly before freezing occurs.

What annual herbs can be grown in Nebraska? Sweet basil is easily propagated from seed and very easy to grow. It makes a dense, bushy growth about 24 inches high. Sweet marjoram, dill, and lemon balm are propagated from seed and are also easily grown. (See Herbs.)

Will you name 3 perennial herbs that can be grown in Nebraska, and give their uses? Chives are onionlike plants having small stems that are cut several times during the year and used as flavoring or as a garnish. Sage is a commonly grown perennial herb. Its principal use is in the flavoring of sausage, in dressings for poultry or rabbit, and as sage tea. Lavender is a member of the mint family used as a natural perfume for silks and linens.

My tulips and narcissus do well, but my hyacinths always fail. Is there any special care they should have? Your experience appears to be typical. Hyacinths don't seem to be adapted to your area of the country.

I know that iris should be moved in the summer, but if it is necessary, can they be transplanted in early fall? Yes, though it is beyond the recommended planting season.

What lilies can we grow most easily here? Try the hybrids. (See Lily.)

What perennials can we grow that will stand heat and drought? Iris, perennial sweet pea, veronica, euphorbia, statice, gypsophila, hardy asters, liatris, physostegia, hemerocallis (day-lily).

When do you advise planting hybrid tea roses? Early spring is safer than fall planting in your area. If you plant early, just as soon as the ground can be worked in the spring, the plants will come along as rapidly as fall-planted stock.

Must I hill up the soil around hybrid tea roses for the winter? This makes good winter protection where temperatures drop low enough to freeze the ground deeply. After the ground freezes, add a mulch of some loose, light material.

On what date should I hill the soil around my hybrid tea

roses? About mid-October. It should be done just before the first hard freeze. If not done before the ground freezes, you will have trouble handling the soil.

What is the best kind of winter protection for roses in this state? Hill the plants 10 to 12 inches high. Fill the holes thus left with leaves and branches and cover the plants completely. Climbers should be hilled and branches laid down and covered completely with soil and mulch. Or use plastic rose cones available from mail-order nurseries and most garden centers. Be sure to uncover early but slowly in spring.

Will you tell me what to do after I uncover my hybrid tea roses? Hybrid tea roses should be pruned after they are uncovered in the spring. Cut back to good, sound, live wood. Ordinarily that leaves canes of 6 inches or less in length.

When is the best time to plant trees—spring or fall? Spring planting is safer than fall planting. Planting should be done very early to get the most good from spring moisture.

Nevada

Are there any azaleas hardy enough for this climate? Last winter the coldest was 16° below zero but temperatures sometimes go to 37° below zero. Azaleas require very acid soils and refuse to grow in soils that contain lime. Most western soils are filled with lime and for this reason azaleas will not thrive. It is doubtful if they would survive 37° below even if the soil were suitable.

When should one set out fruit trees? Plant in Nevada in early spring after severe cold is over but before the buds start to swell—the latter part of March or the first part of April, depending on the altitude.

Should rosebushes be trimmed back to 8 inches in the vicinity of Reno, Nevada? All roses except the shrub roses should be cut back to firm, healthy wood in early spring. Flowers come on the new growth and too much old wood will produce small and inferior flowers.

New Mexico

How long should dahlias be kept out of the ground before planting again? Only until climatic conditions permit replanting. They can be planted in the spring just before the last heavy frost is expected. Be ready to cover if an unusual late frost occurs.

What are the best bush fruits and when should they be planted? Raspberry, loganberry, boysenberry, strawberry, and grape. Plant in spring in the north; fall or spring in central and south New Mexico.

What are the best tree fruits to plant in this climate? In the higher-altitude regions of northern New Mexico: apple, crab, pear, plum, and cherry. Toward the south, and in lower altitudes: peach, apricot, cherry, pear, fig, persimmon.

What is the best lawn grass to plant in western New Mexico? In high-altitude regions of northern New Mexico: Kentucky bluegrass and varieties. Central and southern: Bermuda grass or zoysia.

Is there any grass that will stay green all year? In regions with sufficiently cool summers, yet not too extremely cold winters, Kentucky bluegrass keeps green all winter if well watered.

When would you make a lawn in New Mexico? March to June in the north; September to November in the south.

How can a lawn be kept in good growing condition? First, by providing a surface, at least 4 inches deep, of good loam containing adequate humus on which to seed or plant the grass. In the dry air of the Southwest, lawns keep in better growing condition when given a mulch in November of 50 per cent peat moss and 50 per cent compost or manure pulverized and raked in, followed by watering as needed to keep roots moist. 'Meyer' zoysia is drought-resistant when established. (See also the following questions.)

How often should grass be mowed here? A little, secluded, intimate lawn should be kept shorn more frequently and closely than is necessary for a large expanse. In general, lawns in New Mexico are better mown not too frequently or too closely, since the slightly longer grass helps provide shade and so prevents surface drying.

What fertilizer should I use for a lawn? Before seeding, apply a lawn fertilizer. If growth is not vigorous, give a second application in June. A feeding in September is probably the most important of the year. At this time old roots die off and new roots begin growth. Fertilize again during late winter to encourage growth.

How often should I water my lawn? In New Mexico, lawns need watering as frequently and as thoroughly, both summer and winter, as is necessary to keep the grass roots moist at all times. This is true of even the higher-altitude regions, except where snow covers the ground most of the winter.

When is the best time to plant roses in New Mexico?   Spring in the north; fall or early spring in the south.

What winter protection do roses need?   In the north, mound the plants up with soil or compost and peat moss; cover with spruce branches or cornstalks. In the center and south, no winter protection is necessary. No protection is necessary for shrub roses or polyantha-type roses anywhere below 7,000 feet altitude. Above that, they are hardly worth the necessary coddling.

When is winter protection necessary for roses?   Winter protection for hybrid teas and climbers can be applied after the surface inch or two of ground freezes.

What hybrid tea roses are continual bloomers here?   Almost all hybrid teas thrive and bloom where the altitude does not exceed 6,500 feet. Hybrid perpetuals do well in alkaline soil.

Will you name some shrub roses for northern New Mexico?   'Frühlingsgold', 'Harison's Yellow', *Rosa hugonis; R. setigera; R. rubrifolia; R. rugosa* and its hybrids.

What climbing roses are suitable for New Mexico?   Any and all climbers revel in the sun of southern New Mexico. Some that bloom most profusely are 'Silver Moon', 'Blaze', and all the climbing hybrid teas. In higher altitudes, the choice is more limited and climbers require protection from winter sun.

North and South Carolina

Will gardenias and camellias grow out-of-doors in this part of North Carolina?   Camellias should do very well for you, blooming profusely in March. Gardenias would remain alive but it is doubtful whether you would ever have any blooms. The gardenia will stand temperatures as low as 20° to 24°, but anything lower than this kills the plant back to the roots. Both must have wood at least a year old on which to bloom. Your best chance would be to grow them as tub or box plants, keeping them indoors and well watered during the more severe winter weather.

How often should camellias planted in boxes be watered during the winter months in a greenhouse? What are the best plans for building a greenhouse 12 × 20 feet especially for camellias?   Often enough to keep the soil always moist but never waterlogged. When water is applied, give enough to saturate the whole body of soil. Build the greenhouse where it receives full sunshine. Allow for ample ventilation both at the top and sides. Provide a heating system that keeps a deep-night temperature of 50° F.

Can I grow the double varieties of Camellia japonica outside in South Carolina? Yes.

Please give some hints on pruning or shearing evergreens. Also, what is the proper time? I live in western North Carolina. Evergreens are not pruned in the general sense of that word. They may be clipped or sheared during the growing season, beginning in spring. This should be done after new growth is 3 to 4 inches long. Then half of the new soft twig is snipped off. One exception to this is the Japanese yew and its varieties. It is the only evergreen that retains live but dormant buds on wood older than one year. Shear it at any time before mid-July. This encourages bushier, more compact growth, but any late-fall or winter shearing would increase the danger of winterkilling.

Can I grow grass in the shade? Ground covers are best in heavy shade. In light shade, plant a shady grass mixture recommended for your region.

What is the proper fertilizer to use on nandina to produce the maximum number of berries? Old rotted cow manure (if you have it) or rich compost and superphosphate. It needs a well-drained position and generous amounts of water in dry weather. (See the next question.)

Why doesn't my nandina have berries after having bloomed? Rainfall influences the production of berries. Cross-pollination from one plant to another is necessary. Plant in groups for this reason. There are chemical preparations that can be sprayed on the blossoms of nandina hollies and on many other plants. These usually produce heavier crops of fruits or berries. Try this on your nandina next spring.

Should I trim nandina plants? If so, when? Pruning is usually unnecessary. If, however, they are too large for the space you want them to occupy, the entire plant can be trimmed back; or the older, heavier shoots can be cut clear back to the ground. During the winter or very early spring, new shoots will appear from the roots.

Will pansy seeds planted December 1 bloom the following spring? If planted in a cold frame in October or in a hotbed the first of December, the plants will be large enough to set out in the open in early spring and will start to bloom almost immediately. Planted in the open ground the first of December, seeds will not germinate until spring, and would be several weeks coming into bloom. By planting both in a cold frame (for early bloom) and in the open (for late bloom), you can enjoy pansies over a longer period in the summer. Seed for October sowing should be held in the refrigerator for 2 weeks prior to sowing.

Do peonies in South Carolina require partial shade or full sun to best stand our hot summers?   Peonies will stand partial shade in temperate gardens, but do well only in the extreme northwestern corner of South Carolina. They require a long, cold winter to induce complete and unbroken dormancy and are a disappointment in most parts of the cotton belt.

What hardy perennials can be depended upon for summer bloom in the mountain region of western North Carolina?   You may almost take your choice from perennials listed in dealers' catalogs. Practically all well-known, and many unusual, perennials flourish in the western mountain section of your state. Pick the ones that appeal to you most, and plant them with full assurance that they will succeed for you there.

Will you please give information about the growing of all plants, especially roses, in this locality? Most articles are written for the states north of us or south of us, or the western part of the country.   You live in a latitude where all annuals grow rapidly and where practically every variety of perennial plant will do well. Only the doubtfully hardy ones need any winter protection and your main handicap in growing hybrid tea roses would be the false springs and late freezes that occur almost every year. When roses go dormant in early winter, hill the soil up around them to a depth of about 6 inches, and do not give any other protection. Your area is ideal for growing climbing roses and floribundas. The same rules for fertilization and spraying apply there as in every other part of the country.

Are there any roses that will grow on a fairly windy shore (eastern exposure) in eastern North Carolina? The soil is well drained, with a good sand-humus mixture.   You might not be able to succeed as well with hybrid tea roses as growers in other areas, but hardy climbers and floribundas adapt themselves perfectly to your locality, soil, and climatic conditions. *R. rugosa* and many of its hybrids like 'Max Graf' and 'Pink Grootendorst' are ideally suited to seashore conditions. A few of the more reliable hybrid tea roses are satisfactory if not given too much winter protection. This causes them to make premature growth in the spring, which frequently is killed back by late freezes.

Can you recommend quick-growing, medium-sized shade trees for lawns in this area?   The fastest-growing are Siberian elm, box-elder (*Acer negundo*), and weeping willow, but they are not among the most desirable or longest lived. Tulip-poplar, sweet-gum, and your native maple grow fast enough and are among the best of the permanent shade trees for your locality. Native evergreens do well if moved when small.

What are the fruiting shrubs and trees, semitropical and otherwise, that would grow and fruit in eastern North Carolina?   All kinds of barberries, cotoneaster, dogwood (both tree and bush forms), euonymus, hollies, honeysuckles, privets, and viburnums will give a varied display in fall and winter. Many shrub roses also bear attractively colored hips. The callicarpas have lilac and violet fruits; snowberries and coralberries bear profusely, as do the various types of Russian-olive, which have orange and silvery fruits. Among the trees, nothing is prettier than your native hawthorn, wild plum, magnolia, and mountain-ash. Several North Carolina nurseries list most hardy trees and shrubs.

When should I plant sweet peas in South Carolina? Sow the early-flowering or later kinds in November. Protect with litter—straw, rough compost, leaves—during severe spells. The early sorts should bloom in May; the late sorts, 2 or 3 weeks later.

North and South Dakota

How deep should I plant daffodils? Do they need any special winter protection? Cover bulbs with 5 or 6 inches of soil when planting. They can be protected with a loose mulch of straw or coarse hay. The mulch goes on after the ground is frozen.

When is the best time to sow Kentucky bluegrass seed? In early spring or in late summer.

How can one grow and winter lilies in North Dakota? Plant in the fall or early spring in well-drained soil. The top of the bulb should have about 8 inches of soil above it when planted. Mulch with 2 to 4 inches of straw after the ground freezes in the fall.

Where can hybrid nut seed or trees be obtained for trial in this locality (northern Great Plains)? Contact your State Experiment Station at Fargo, North Dakota, or the Experiment Station at Morden, Manitoba.

Can peonies be planted this spring or must we wait until fall? Fall is the better time to plant peonies, and you will be just as far ahead if planting is done then.

When is the best time to plant perennials in our cold country? Early spring. Good-sized clumps of the hardier sorts can be planted about the first of September, and if properly mulched they will winter well.

Will hybrid tea roses winter-kill in South Dakota? No tea or hybrid tea rose will winter successfully in South Dakota without being covered with a heavy mulch of earth. Some shrub roses like *R. hugonis, R. spinosissima, R. rugosa* and hybrids should winter without protection.

What is the best time to dig tulip bulbs in North Dakota? Two or 3 weeks after the foliage matures, dig the bulbs and leave the stems and foliage attached. Spread them out in shallow trays and store in a dry, cool place. The tops can be removed and the bulbs cleaned up in late summer.

How soon should tulips be replanted? They were dug in early summer. Replant these bulbs about October 1.

Ohio

What is the best type of soil for growing apples in central Ohio? What cover crop would you recommend while the trees are small? Central Ohio is largely a silty clay loam. Make sure that the soil is well drained. Sow soybeans in early June and plow under in September. Then sow ryegrass as a cover crop if the soil is not to be kept cultivated.

Can gerbera be wintered over in Sandusky, Ohio? How are the roots stored? If by "wintering over," outdoor culture is meant, this is theoretically possible, except that a mulch heavy enough to protect the plant will probably smother it. Gerbera plants can be lifted after a sharp frost has killed the leaves, with soil adhering to the roots, and stored in a cool place (above freezing, but it must not go above 40° F.) covered with damp sand or peat to retain moisture. Examine during the winter and sprinkle if needed. Plant out again in the spring when apples bloom.

Have you any suggestions for growing herbs for flavoring in Ohio? All of the annual and most of the perennial herbs can be grown in Ohio. In general, a rather poor sandy soil in full sunshine is their preference. (See Herbs.)

Will you please give me a list of some herbs that will grow here? *Annuals:* basil, chervil, coriander, caraway, dill, fennel, summer savory. *Perennials:* burnet, chives, hyssop, marjoram, mint, sage, sorrel, tarragon, winter savory.

What is the best rose collection to plant in this part of the country? All the hybrid teas can be grown in Ohio. Your State Experiment Station at Columbus is one of the best sources of information on roses anywhere.

What is the proper time to plant hardy shrubs and perennials in northern Ohio in the spring? Crape-myrtle, catalogs state, is hardy north of Virginia, with protection. What kind of protection is meant? Plant anytime before the leaf buds begin to open. "Protection" means some kind of burlap wrapping or screen, as of pine boughs, to protect them from winter winds. You will not find crape-myrtle as satisfactory as lilacs in Ohio.

How and when should I plant everbearing strawberries in central Ohio? Plant as early in the spring as the plants are available and the soil can be prepared. Avoid newly turned sod because of the danger of grub damage. Any good loam will grow strawberries; even light sandy soils, if fertilized.

Oklahoma

Can you give me pointers on how to grow the rose daphne (Daphne cneorum)? Daphne is propagated by cuttings and layers. *Daphne cneorum* seems to need a green finger. It will tolerate much sunshine, also partial shade; sometimes, but not always, it resents acid soil and likes a little lime, a friable soil, and a rock at its back.

How can I succeed with delphinium in Oklahoma? Delphiniums are cool-climate plants and dislike heat. Deeply prepared, friable, sandy loam is preferable. A layer of peat moss under their roots is also a good idea. Treat them as annuals or biennials.

What flowers, if any, can be grown as borders to shrubs in a shady lawn? Chiefly early flowers that do their growing before trees are in leaf: *Brunnera macrophylla;* bleedingheart; columbine; day-lily; daffodils; Oriental poppy; *Phlox divaricata; Ceratostigma plumbaginoides;* primroses; plantain-lily; *Trollius europaeus;* tulips; tuberous begonias; impatiens.

What flowers that are good honey producers will grow in an Oklahoma garden? Willow, linden, apple, plum, and pear trees. Crocus, nepeta, clover, Michaelmas daisy, and monarda (bee-balm).

Can you give a list of fruit trees, berries, and small fruits that do the best in this climate? Strawberry; boysenberry; dewberry; plums: Japanese varieties and 'Green Gage' ('Reine Claude'); cherry, early varieties; peach; apricot; apple; crab apple; and pear.

When shall I plant gladiolus in Oklahoma? First planting, between March 1 and 15. Successive plantings, every two weeks until mid-May.

Will you tell me how to get rid of Bermuda grass? Grasses are difficult to eradicate, since their narrow leaves do not succumb to most herbicides. An airtight covering of heavy building paper or black plastic is effective, as is persistent hoeing of grass blades as they appear. No plant survives long when smothered or sheared above the ground in its growing season. Consult your county extension agent concerning the use of dalapon (trade name, Dowpon) and other herbicides.

What would be the best grass for a lawn that will grow under trees and will stand dry weather? A shady lawn mixture containing a high percentage of one of the fine-leaved fescues, if it is to be sprinkled or irrigated; otherwise, buffalo grass or carpet grass; or if too shady for this, a ground cover such as *Vinca minor.*

Our lawn is barren of Bermuda grass in the shade of trees and where their tiny roots come to the surface. Will you recommend a grass or ground vine that will overcome this and withstand the hot winds of Oklahoma? *Vinca minor* is a presentable ground cover, tolerant of shade, heat, and some dryness.

How shall we care for peonies in the South? Peonies do not like a hot climate. Give them deeply prepared rich soil with a layer of peat moss below their roots. Plant with the eyes 2½ inches below the surface of the ground. For larger blooms, remove all side flower buds. They must have a long dormancy induced by cold weather.

What perennials will do well in partial shade and in full shade? If shade is caused by trees, enrich the soil and add leafmold or peat moss. Aconitum; anemones, several varieties; *Brunnera macrophylla**; columbine; bleedingheart; hosta*; lily-of-the-valley; *Mertensia virginica*; Phlox divaricata;* primroses; *Vinca minor**; violets*; *Uvularia grandiflora**; most ferns.*

What perennials will give color from spring to frost? Continuous bloom from spring until frost is possible from a succession of different varieties such as spring-flowering bulbs; mertensia; *Clematis davidiana;* peonies; irises; dictamnus; *Phlox divaricata, P. subulata, P. carolina,* and *P. paniculata; Campanula carpatica, C. persicifolia; Nepeta* x *faassenii;* eupatorium; monarda; chrysanthemum; Michaelmas daisies. However, if continuous bloom is really important, you will find annuals more satisfactory. There will be periods in any perennial planting without flowers. Buy bedding plants for earliest color; sow seed for midsummer-on bloom.

What perennials will grow best on the north side of a house in Oklahoma? Ferns, columbine, *Phlox divaricata, P. carolina, Trollius europaeus, Brunnera macrophylla,* primroses, campanula, bleedingheart.

Will you give some information on rose culture and protection in the

* These will grow in full shade.

Southwest? Roses in the Southwest need a deep, rich soil—a 6-inch layer of rotted manure, or compost and peat moss to keep their roots cool—and an open, sunny place with good air circulation. For winter protection, hill the soil up around them, and cover with spruce branches, straw, or any light covering that will protect them from winter sun. Or use the more reliable plastic rose cones if the cost is not a factor. They will save more roses, at least partially offsetting their higher cost.

When should roses be pruned back in the summer? How much pruning should they receive? As soon as the rush of summer bloom is over. A mulch of compost in midsummer encourages fall bloom. As soon as first fall buds form, feed a balanced fertilizer. Climbing roses and hybrid perpetuals bloom on 2-year-old wood. Leave all vigorous canes of last season's growth. Cut out at the ground all wood older than this.

Our new property is entirely without shade. What trees are the fastest-growing and make good shade? Siberian and Chinese elms will grow rapidly and provide shade. *Acer saccharinum* (the silver maple) is also a fast grower. Unless you are over 60, however, don't be too impatient. In a few years a pin oak will outgrow any of the less permanent trees.

Oregon

Can I grow camellias? Yes. (See Tender Shrubs.)

When should daffodil bulbs be planted in Portland? Throughout the fall months; the earlier, the better.

Should daffodils be lifted annually and the soil fertilized before planting? Lift only when the bulbs become overcrowded and the flowers begin to deteriorate—usually after being in the ground for 3 or 4 years or even more. Divide the bulbs after the foliage has browned; replant. The bulbs are rich feeders and should be fertilized annually.

Will you give a good list of hardy evergreens for 20° F. below zero; and the soil they require? Blue spruce, Norway spruce; Douglas-fir; concolor fir; Scots pine, ponderosa pine, Austrian pine, mugo pine; juniper, both upright and spreading; any of the American arborvitae. Deciduous: Western larch. They will grow in any good garden soil.

What annual herbs and perennial herbs are grown in Oregon? *Annuals:* summer savory, sweet marjoram, dill, chervil, pot-marigold, coriander, sweet basil. *Perennials:* chives, tarragon, sweet woodruff, lemon balm, curly mint, sweet cicely, wild marjoram, rosemary, winter savory, thyme.

Do perennial herbs require winter protection? In the colder areas, some of them do. (See Herbs.)

I was presented with a double red hibiscus plant sent from Southern California. A local nursery advises that it is hardy in this climate. I planted it on the west side of my house to protect it from east winds, but it looks sick. What do you advise? Herbaceous perennial species of hibiscus and the hardy shrub species (such as rose-of-Sharon) will grow outside in the Northwest, but not tropical shrub species. We cannot tell from your description which kind yours is. However, if it is ailing, chances are it is *Hibiscus rosa-sinensis,* which would not be hardy in Oregon.

Where, and how, shall I plant lilies-of-the-valley for good blooms? My plants thrive but have no blooms. On the north side, where they get plenty of light and filtered sunshine part of the day. Lily-of-the-valley, once established, becomes quite rampant. They like a rich, woodsy soil containing a little well-rotted manure or rich compost. Try confining your plants within an area with boards to force blooms.

Will magnolias live in northern Oregon? Deciduous magnolia can be grown. Some evergreen varieties succeed in milder parts, but are not recommended for colder areas.

Shall I plant nandina and Mexican-orange in the sun or shade? One source says in the sun and another says in the shade. I am perplexed. Plant them in full sun in the Pacific Northwest. Neither plant is given a high rating for hardiness, so both should be placed in a protected situation.

How shall I care for oleander that is 6 years old? It buds each year but never blooms. Is it too cold here? I have it outdoors all year. If the plant and buds do not suffer definite injury from frost, it is not too cold. Lack of sufficient light may cause a lack of bloom. Prune the previous year's shoots well back in the spring.

Shall I plant pernettya in the sun or shade? In the Pacific Northwest, the plants do much better when planted in full sun.

How can I make pernettya have more berries? Three or more plants must be grown together for cross-pollination; plants should be pruned annually, removing some of the old wood. Sometimes root pruning is necessary to prevent them from spreading and making too much sucker growth at the expense of fruiting.

When should roses be planted? Plant in the fall or spring (former, preferably) in holes sufficiently wide and deep to accommodate the roots without crowding. Set budded plants with buds about 2 inches below the surface of the soil. Prune the roots at the time of planting. Shorten the canes of fall-planted bushes; prune in the spring. Prune spring-planted ones at the time of planting. If the soil is dry, water well. Surface dress with fertilizer after the plants have become established.

Should rosebushes be planted in full sun, or where they have some shade?   A situation fully exposed to sun is best.

What makes Sagina subulata turn brown in spots?   Air pockets that form under the "moss." Remove the brown part and substitute a healthy piece of the plant, first placing a little fresh soil and fertilizer in the hole. Sagina must be kept well pressed to the ground to avoid brown spots and needs renewal occasionally to keep it in good condition.

Will you suggest a few shrubs that will grow well at the coast in the briny atmosphere?   *Hypericum* x *moseranum,* hydrangea, kerria, azalea, rhododendron, flowering quince, deutzia, weigela, symphoricarpus, *Ilex aquifolium, Jasminum nudiflorum,* kalmia, *Viburnum tinus.*

Can you suggest locations for planting some shrubs—deutzia, flowering quince, and pomegranate?   In your state, growing conditions are so good that most shrubs are easy. Deutzias like well-drained soil with a generous supply of humus, in the sun or partial shade. The quince does well in any good soil in full sun. *Punica granatum* (pomegranate) needs deep, heavy soil, sun, and elbow room. Fertilize, if necessary, when planting by incorporating rotted dairy manure or rich compost in the soil below the roots.

How shall I treat my violets to make them bloom?   They do best in good loamy soil containing a little old manure or rich compost, and leafmold. To encourage plenty of blooms, runners must be removed. After plants of good size have flowered, they should be lifted, divided, and replanted.

South Carolina (See page 1408)

South Dakota (See page 1411)

Tennessee

Will pink amaryllis grow outdoors in the climate of southern Tennessee? There are many so-called bulbous plants that belong to the amaryllis family. Those which are so frequently grown in pots are not reliable outdoor subjects. The best for your purpose is the one called "hardy-amaryllis," correctly known as *Lycoris squamigera*. The bulbs increase year after year in the open ground.

When should boxwood be pruned in Tennessee? It is not customary to prune established boxwoods unless special shaping is wanted. Sometimes the smaller ones will send out precocious shoots that are cut off to retain the symmetry of the bush. Where pruning or shearing is necessary, this should be done during the growing season. Fall or winter pruning increases the danger of winterkilling.

In Chattanooga, buddleias hold their green leaves all year. As they bloom on 1-year wood, where should they be cut back to make the most and the largest flowers? The old, heavy canes should be cut back to the ground in late fall or early winter. The strong younger shoots will bear larger blooms. If the entire plant is left undisturbed, you will have more blooms, but smaller ones.

If Canterbury bell seeds are planted in a seed bed during the latter part of winter, will they bloom that same summer? The Canterbury bell is a biennial plant and is best sown in early summer. Young plants can be transferred to the beds in early fall and given a light covering of leaves. These will bloom the following year. Seeds planted in late winter can be transplanted the following spring or fall for bloom the second year.

Will cape-jasmine stand the winters of this area (Johnson City) in Tennessee? The cape-jasmine or gardenia is not reliably hardy. It will stand 20° to 24° F. without damage. It blooms only on old wood, and if this is frozen back, there will be no blooms the next year, even though the roots remain alive and the plant continues to send out new growth. In your area it would be far better to grow gardenias as tub plants: outdoors in the spring, summer, and fall, and indoors during the cold winter months.

If dahlias are left in the ground during the winter, will the new shoots bloom and do as well as if the tubers had been taken up? Dahlias can be given extra covering and left in the open ground in your area. The clumps should be taken up in the spring, however, divided, and replanted; such divisions will bloom just as well as those taken up and stored. The only danger is an occasional extremely severe winter during which they might be frozen.

What winter protection should be given rose trees planted in the upper South, where temperatures go to zero? Only the grafted head of a tree rose is likely to be damaged by zero-degree weather. Dig up one side of the root, bend the plant down until the head touches the soil, and cover with mixed soil and leaves, pinning the mound down with a burlap sack. In the spring, this covering is taken off, the head pruned, and the soil packed around the roots to hold the tree upright again. In Tennessee, packing the standing tree in straw bound in by burlap would probably be sufficient protection.

Texas

Will Japanese anemone grow here? What location is best? What kind of soil is needed? A partially shaded situation, sheltered from strong, drying winds, is best. It requires a rich, moist soil, and a generous supply of water during dry periods.

Can I leave anemone corms in the ground after they bloom? Are they supposed to come up year after year? It is better to lift the bulbs and store them in peat moss or in dry sand until inspection shows that they are beginning to push for another season of growth.

Will you please give me some practical suggestions as to the means of winter storage of tender tubers and bulbs when basement or root-cellar facilities are not available? Tender bulbs can be lifted when the foliage turns brown or is frosted, and stored in containers of slightly moist peat, vermiculite, sand, bagasse, or rice hulls. The containers should be placed in a cool, shaded place. If they can be put in cold storage at about 50° F., they will keep very well.

When is the proper time to graft citrus fruit trees on trifoliate orange stock? When the bark will "slip" or separate easily from the wood; ordinarily after a good rain during May, June, or July.

Do you think columbine and bleedingheart can be grown in central Texas? With good care, columbine will succeed; and bleedingheart also, if the soil is slightly acid and a sheltered position is given.

Will you give the care for dahlias? Is late planting best for here? Set out tubers about 10 days before the average date of the latest spring frost. This will vary for different sections of the state, but March should be right for the warmer sections, April planting for sections farther north. Set roots about 5 inches deep in beds enriched with compost; tie plants to a stout stake as they grow; feed every 3 or 4 weeks with a balanced fertilizer. Dahlias must have plenty of water if you wish to cut an abundance of fine blooms.

Is it O.K. to leave dahlia bulbs in the ground until ready to plant in the spring, or should they be taken up in the fall after stalks die? Both systems work. If you have been successful in leaving them in the ground, well and good. But if too many clumps have been disappearing, lift and carefully store in peat, sand, or similar material in a cool, shady place. With either method, the clump should be divided into single roots, each with a bud or eye showing.

Can Shasta daisies be dug up in the spring to permit the soil's being turned over and limed? They can be lifted, divided, and reset in the spring, but autumn is much preferred, so the plants will have many well-established roots before warm weather.

Will dogwood grow in this state? Yes, with proper preparation. A neutral or slightly acid soil, a high amount of organic matter, and good drainage are essential. Water freely in periods of drought and wrap the trunks with burlap for the first season or two.

When is the best time to transplant dogwood? During early winter, when they are without leaves. Dig as much of the roots as you can, protect from the sun and wind, and set at the same level as they formerly grew. Wrap the trunks with cloth as a protection against sunscald and the entry of borers.

Will you list some of the best annual and perennial flowers for this section of the Gulf Coast? *Annuals and perennials treated as annuals, for winter:* sweet-alyssum, blanket flower, California poppy, calliopsis, carnation, delphinium, larkspur, lupine, pansy, petunia, phlox, poppy, statice, sweet pea. *Annuals, for summer:* cosmos, ageratum, marigold, morning-glory, nasturtium, portulaca, verbena, zinnia. *Perennials:* hemerocallis, Louisiana iris, blue sage, Stokes'-aster, violet, canna, chrysanthemum, four-o'clock, moraea, Shasta daisy, Transvaal daisy (gerbera), golden glow.

Which flowers are easily grown in the extreme South? (Gulf Coastal area.) Practically all annuals may be grown in the Gulf Coastal area if fitted into the season that suits their needs. Hardy annuals during the autumn and winter; heat lovers, like marigolds, cosmos, and zinnias, during the hot, humid summers. See seed catalogs.

What is the best time to plant flowers this far south? *Hardy annu-*

als: sweet-alyssum, calendula, calliopsis, carnation, pansy, petunia, statice, and sweet pea, in the fall in warmer sections. *Tender annuals for the summer:* cosmos, ageratum, torenia, portulaca, nasturtium, and zinnia, after the danger of frost has passed. Perennials should be divided in the winter or when they are through blooming rather than in the spring.

What is the correct time to plant seeds of annual flowers in Austin? When should I set out perennials? For the cool-weather group—such as calendula, snapdragon, and pansy—October through December. For the heat-tolerant group—such as marigold and zinnia—March to April. Perennials should be divided in the winter, December through February, or immediately after blooming.

Should leaves be left on perennial borders in our climate? Yes, but do not let them pack down heavily over the crowns of the plants. New leaves should be added as the mulch decomposes.

What are the best fruits for this climate? Oranges, grapefruit, peaches, pears, plums, bramble fruits, and figs.

How can I grow gardenias in Dallas? A slightly acid soil, rich in organic matter, a mulch of oak leaves, and facilities for watering during dry times are essential. An occasional watering with a solution of copperas will supply iron, and periodic spraying with an oil emulsion will control whitefly and sooty mold.

What is the best location for gladioli—partial shade or all sun? When is the best time to plant for this part of the country? Gladioli are sun-demanding; corms should always be set in full sun. The planting time should be gauged by the time of the latest killing frost for your area. Then plant about 2 or 3 weeks ahead of this date. Late February and early March for southern sections; 2 or 3 weeks later farther north in the state.

Is there a practical way to get rid of "nut" or coco grass? It is very difficult to eradicate once it gets beyond the hand-digging stage. However, there are herbicides available. Consult your local county extension agent for advice.

How can I kill Bermuda grass in my flower beds? There is no safe selective chemical for flower beds. Weed by hand.

When is the time to plant California privet hedge in central Texas? December to February. Cut the plants back heavily at planting time; set at the same level that the plants grew; water well at once.

What herbs would you suggest for Gulf Coast country, for growing on a commercial scale? Sage (*Salvia officinalis*) promises to be the best prospect for commercial production, following trials at the State Experiment Station in this area.

When should hibiscus be moved?   December to February. If the plant is frosted in early winter, cut it back severely and move it to the selected site.

What variety of holly that will bear berries can best be grown here? What soil and treatment are required?   The Chinese holly (*Ilex cornuta*), the Dahoon holly (*Ilex cassine*), American holly (*Ilex opaca*)— varieties of all of these species succeed in this locality.

My hydrangeas do not grow and bloom as they should. What kind of soil and fertilizer are best for them in southeast Texas? I used well-rotted leaves and animal manure. Are they too rich for them?   Your soil sounds all right, provided it is not strongly alkaline. Sulfur and alum will acidify the soil; rotting leaves should help. Be sure not to prune after the wood is mature, as flower buds would be removed. Pinch or prune no later than July.

How can I make hydrangeas, planted outdoors in Texas, bloom?   A soil not too alkaline, an abundance of organic matter, and water are essential. Severe competition from tree roots, winterkilling, or late pruning can cause failure to bloom, as the flower buds are formed before the plants go dormant in the fall.

How can I protect Dutch iris from the cold?   When low temperatures are forecast, cover plants with evergreen boughs or some other light mulch until the danger from that particular cold snap has passed. Generally, the plants should be uncovered after 2 or 3 days. Newspapers or a single thickness of cloth is of no value.

Why do tall bearded irises refuse to bloom along the Gulf Coast?   Our light, sandy soils and lack of a real and prolonged dormant season combine to rule out this popular perennial for the Gulf Coast. In some areas, 1 or 2 varieties seem to be pretty much at home, but not like the semitropical perennials that really succeed here. Try some of the Louisiana irises instead.

My yellow jasmine is a beautiful shrub, three years old, and has had only 1 small bloom on it. Can you tell me why?   Jasmine requires plenty of sunshine. Possibly too much shade is the cause of your trouble.

Are lilacs and rhododendrons suitable for moist coastal areas?   These temperate shrubs are sure to be disappointing to you here. They must have a complete dormant period (induced by long, unbroken cold) and a heavy, rich soil. Better stick to the beautiful semitropical flowering shrubs that succeed in your area. For example, try crape-myrtle (*Lagerstroemia*), which comes in a wider range of color than do lilacs.

What lilies will do well in semi-alkaline soil? Easter lilies, madonna lilies (*L. candidum*), *L. chalcedonicum, L. bulbiferum, L. martagon, L.* x *testaceum* and other European types should all succeed if your soil is not too basic (alkaline). Of course, the incorporating of acid organic materials will help in the culture of all of these and many of the modern hybrids.

Please advise if lycoris is adapted to this climate. What will make it bloom? *Lycoris squamigera* should flower in the northern section of Texas if the bulbs are properly fed and watered and do not suffer too much root competition. *Lycoris radiata* will probably succeed in the southern areas under conditions of good culture and freedom from too many roots.

Rice hulls make very light soil, but are they too rich for pansies? If so, what besides sand should be used? Mixed with sandy soil, rice hulls make a good compost for pansies.

How many species of passion-flower are there? Will any of these grow in Texas? There are about 400 species. The fruits and flowers are of many kinds; some few of the fruits are edible, most are not. *Passiflora caerulea* and *P. incarnata* should do well in gardens in southern Texas.

What is the best understock for peaches in the South, where root rot is prevalent in areas with high alkaline soil? Tennessee wild peaches are the most widely used understocks in all parts of Texas, but are not resistant to root rot.

Will peonies do well in central Texas in a black, waxy soil? If so, what varieties do best? No, peonies will not succeed in this climate. (See question on peonies in South Carolina, this section.)

What is the best time to divide and reset perennials in Austin? Autumn or winter; or immediately after flowering. In this way, the roots will be widespread and well established before spring growth commences.

What is the best time for planting perennials? Fall. Practically all herbaceous perennials can be lifted in late fall, or very early winter, and reset.

Should ranunculus bulbs remain in the ground year after year? It is better to lift them each year after the foliage has died down and store in a dry place.

Will you list some good rock-garden plants for use in this state? Probably the best groups are the true cacti and semitropical succulents that succeed out-of-doors in the South. The usual alpine rock-garden plants used in the North will be a disappointment to you in Texas.

What roses are best for southern gardens?   The teas do well if they have good care. Some old-fashioned roses, like 'Louis Philippe', 'Mme. Lombard', 'Minnie Francis', 'Duchesse de Brabant', and 'Safrano' will thrive long years after many choice cutting roses have succumbed to this climate. A few Texas nurseries specialize in these varieties for southern gardens. You can grow hybrid teas by treating them as annuals. They are produced by the millions commercially in Tyler, Texas.

What makes roses die so quickly here?   Black spot, dieback, crown gall, an excessively alkaline soil, lack of a distinct rest period—all contribute toward a short life for modern roses. In many southern gardens, hybrid teas are being grown as annuals.

Could I grow roses in a dry clay soil?   To do so successfully, it will be necessary to improve the soil by the addition of compost, rotted leaves, sand, and other materials. An abundance of water is essential, and frequent feeding during growing weather, with a balanced commercial fertilizer.

Will you tell me the proper time to set out new rosebushes in southern Texas?   Early planting is strongly recommended for the South, December to February being best by all odds.

Is fall or spring the best time to plant roses in west Texas?   Fall planting (or, more accurately, winter planting) is better by far. If the plants are set in December to February, roots can become established before top growth starts in the spring.

What is the cause of roses planted in either fall or spring growing and blooming all summer, apparently strong and healthy, then suddenly dying in the fall? The trouble starts with black patches on the stems, while 25 per cent of bushes are not affected. (Galveston.)   Patches on the canes are caused by the so-called dieback disease, for which no dependable control is known. Prune away diseased parts and mop the cuts with Bordeaux or sulfur paste. Black spots, followed by yellow areas on the leaves, are a manifestation of black spot, which can be controlled by a fungicide.

Will you please give some information as to the enemies of roses in the South and Southwest? Also, what kinds are best for this state?   The greatest trouble is black spot, a fungus disease that can be controlled by the frequent use of captan or maneb. In the Deep South, so-called dieback is a serious trouble for which no dependable control is yet known. Old-fashioned varieties in the tea group are most dependable.

What shrubs shall I plant in southwestern Texas, where there is a dry

climate, wind, and alkaline soil? It is best to use natives, and some of the best of these are *Leucophyllum frutescens; Tecoma stans; Diospyros texana; Rhus virens* and other species of sumacs; several species of *Acacia; Chilopsis linearis; Sophora secundiflora;* several species of salvia; *Clematis drummondii;* several species of juniper; several species of yucca and agave.

Can I have a list of flowering trees or shrubs for Houston? *Trees:* Magnolia, mimosa, huisache. *Shrubs:* crape-myrtle, pittosporum, photinia, privet, oleander, jasmine, forsythia, spiraea, weigela, pyracantha, camellia, azalea, and gardenia.

What are some of the best shrubs for foundation plantings? Azalea, camellia, podocarpus, euonymus, cotoneaster, pyracantha, Japanese box, Japanese holly, jasmine, abelia, feijoa, and hibiscus.

Utah

Can I have a list of rock-garden plants hardy in Utah? The following should be hardy in Utah, at altitudes below 6,000 feet: any of the sedums, pinks (*Dianthus*), dwarf phlox (*P. subulata*), bellflower (*Campanula carpatica*), saponaria, globeflower (*trollius*), coralbells (*Heuchera*), and violas. The last 3 should have partial shade.

Is there any fairly good climbing rose that will go through the winter without covering in a climate where the temperature occasionally goes from 10° to 15° F.? Try 'Blaze' and 'Dr. J. H. Nicolas'; a southern or eastern exposure is preferable. If its stems are trained horizontally, 'Climbing Peace' can be sensational. 'Queen of the Prairies', with large clusters of blush to rose, cupped, globular flowers, blooms late and only once each season but is very hardy. Ramblers would also probably survive without protection.

Do you have a list of flowering shrubs and trees that would grow in an altitude of 6,000 feet? Try French hybrid lilacs; they should do well at this altitude. Other good shrubs would be mock orange ('Virginal' or 'Galahad'); highbush-cranberry; wayfaring tree (*Viburnum lantana*); buffalo berry (*Shepherdia argentea*). *Small trees:* Colorado pink locust; hawthorn; or 'Hopa' flowering crab.

Washington

When and in what kind of soil and location should alstromeria be planted?   Plant tubers 5 to 6 inches deep in September or early October in a rich, well-drained soil, and in full sun or partial shade; place the little eyes up and the tubers down.

Does alstromeria require winter protection in the Pacific Northwest?   Alstromeria makes growth during the winter, and if the weather is cold, they should be mulched so that frosts do not freeze them down to the tubers, which are tender and will perish if once frozen.

What time should one take up dahlia tubers?   Lift as soon as early frosts have cut down the tops, usually in late October or early November.

Is there any secret to growing cutleaf weeping birch trees? Every season I notice a few die off here in Yakima. It's heartbreaking to grow one for 6 or 7 years and then see it wither and die.   The tree calls for no special culture. It likes a sandy loam soil. Being a shallow rooter, it must have plenty of moisture, particularly during dry periods. Leaf diseases and a birch borer are among its enemies. The borer is known to be somewhat prevalent in your area and could be responsible for the death of the trees. It is responsible for birches dying at the top, known as "stag heading."

When is the proper time to plant fruit trees in the Seattle, Washington, area?   December is the ideal time. Planting, however, may be carried on through January and February.

How do I trim boysenberry, loganberry, and grapes in Seattle?   Grapes—in February, cut back the previous year's growth to 2 or 3 eyes. Remove weak canes. Loganberry and boysenberry—cut back all the old wood to the ground as early as possible after the fruit has been picked. This gives new shoots, which produce the next crop, a better chance to develop. Thin these, leaving only the strong ones, and nip off the ends or tips.

I have heard of a plant called pearlwort, which is supposed to be a moss. Is it suitable to plant instead of grass?   This is *Sagina subulata,* a creeping perennial, evergreen, hardy, bearing little white flowers, and in habit of growth similar to moss; but it is *not* a moss. It is used as a ground cover, also for planting between steppingstones, and sometimes for making lawns. It's much inclined to get humpy and must be kept flat by rolling or tamping. If this is neglected, the humps turn brown. Grass makes a much superior lawn and requires only a little more care.

Is montbretia hardy in the Pacific Northwest? I lost mine last winter— the first time in 20 years. Montbretias are not always hardy, although in the milder parts of Washington they go through the average winter outside without being harmed. To be on the safe side, either mulch or lift and store them in frost-free quarters for the winter.

What are some nut trees that will grow in Spokane? The black walnut and hardy filbert. Others, such as butternut and English walnut, have been planted but do not survive for long.

Would a rhododendron be hardy in eastern Washington? Many fine rhododendrons may be grown in eastern Washington, provided that they are given an acid soil, good drainage, some shade, and protection from cold winds. The soil in this area is alkaline and must be replaced with one that is on the acid side and which is kept so by an occasional application of sulfur. Select only varieties of known hardiness.

What are a dozen or more good roses for a beginner in Washington? All the hybrid teas and floribundas do superbly well in your climate. Select varieties from the catalog of one of the famous West Coast rose breeders and growers. A few outstanding varieties of *hybrid teas* are: 'Mojave', orange; 'Helen Traubel', apricot-pink; 'Charlotte Armstrong', 'Chrysler Imperial', red. *Grandifloras:* 'Buccaneer', yellow; 'American Heritage', blend of yellows and reds; 'Queen Elizabeth', rose-pink; and 'Scarlet Knight', red. *Floribundas:* 'Circus', multicolored; 'Spartan', orange-red; 'Fashion', coral pink; 'Frensham', red.

In the Pacific Northwest, can roses be transplanted any time during the winter? Yes, but November and December are the preferred months.

Will a tamarix hedge grow well in a rainy climate? Yes. It grows very rapidly in the Pacific Northwest. It should be pruned annually.

What are some shrubs that will do well on a dry, hot hillside exposed to the south? Tolerance of widely varying conditions makes the following shrubs grow almost anywhere in the Temperate Zone: *Berberis thunbergii* and *B.* x *mentorensis; Cotoneaster acutifolius, C. divaricatus,* and *C. salicifolius; Amorpha fruticosa,* and *A. canescens; Holodiscus dumosus; Mahonia repens; Caragana arborescens; Colutea arborescens; Hypericum prolificum; Ceanothus fendleri; Lonicera; Potentilla fruticosa; Prunus besseyi* and *P. tomentosa; Rhus; Rosa spinosissima; Shepherdia argentea; Symphoricarpos orbiculatus; Philadelphus microphyllus; Jamesia americana; Prunus tenella.*

Will you suggest shrubs that will do well in moist shade? *Mahonia aquifolium* and *M. repens; Euonymus fortunei radicans; Cornus; Hydrangea; Rhodotypos scandens; Ribes; Rubus deliciosus; Symphoricarpos albus* and *S. orbiculatus; Viburnum lentago, V. carlesii,* and *V.* x *burkwoodii; Arctostaphylos uva-ursi; Physocarpus opulifolius; Ptelea trifoliata; Lonicera involucrata; Genista tinctoria; Amelanchier; Cotoneaster divaricatus, C. horizontalis, C. acutifolius,* and *C. franchetii.*

Wisconsin

How and when should chrysanthemums be given winter protection in Kenosha County, Wisconsin? Apply a light covering of dry leaves and top with evergreen branches when the soil is slightly frozen.

Are any varieties of azaleas or rhododendrons hardy as far north as Wisconsin? You might try 'P.J.M.' rhododendron and the Chinese azalea, *R. molle,* in protected parts of your garden.

Will bent grass thrive in north-central Wisconsin? Yes, provided you are willing to fuss with it. But for the home gardener, the less touchy, hardier grasses, such as bluegrass, are far more satisfactory.

Is the blue beech hardy in this midwestern climate? Yes. *Carpinus caroliniana* (blue beech or hornbeam) is native from Minnesota to Florida and is fully hardy. Plant it in rich, moist soil.

In this climate, what is the best time to plant seeds of Canterbury bells? Plant in late May to allow a full season's growth before the plants go through the winter. Carry over in the cold frame. Canterbury bells all belong to the species *Campanula medium,* and all varieties are equally hardy, but none is easy to grow.

Can I grow the large-flowered chrysanthemums in the garden? These chrysanthemums are neither hardy nor early enough for Wisconsin, but flowers of some of the University of Minnesota hybrids reach 3½ to 4 inches in diameter.

What is the proper method of planting and caring for Daphne cneorum in southeastern Wisconsin? *Daphne cneorum* likes a situation open to the sun but sheltered from winter winds. An opening in a planting of evergreens that faces south is ideal. Plant slightly deeper than the plant stood in the nursery, and fill up to the ground level with soil and leafmold or rich compost. A pH reaction of between 5.9 and 6.8 is satisfactory. Use balled and burlapped or container-grown stock and plant in the spring.

What fruits (cherries, plums, pears, grapes) are hardy in Wisconsin? All sour cherries are reasonably hardy, but where high winds prevail, better stick to the sand-cherry and plum hybrids, which, while not so high in quality, do make good jams and pies. Of the true plums, a series from the University of Minnesota is recommended. 'Superior' and 'Pipestone' are good. Add some cherry-plum hybrids, such as 'Sapalta', 'Compass', and 'Oka', for variety. The 'Beta' grape (a 'Concord'-wild-grape hybrid) is reliably hardy but should be used only if 'Concord' does not do well near you. 'Parker' and 'Patten' are good pears that can take it. Check with local nurseries to see if older, tested sorts are hardy in your neighborhood, since most of those mentioned above are recommended largely because they will not winter-kill, not for highest quality.

Is there an apricot that will withstand our winters? Two apricots from the University of Minnesota that have been developed for rugged climates are 'Moongold' and 'Sungold'. Plant one of each for cross-pollination.

What dwarf fruit trees will grow well in southeastern Wisconsin? Whatever standard varieties are hardy in your area. Dwarfness does not affect hardiness. Pears and apples, the two species most commonly dwarfed by grafting, should be 100 per cent hardy. However, don't overlook the possibility of growing full-sized varieties as semi-dwarfs, keeping them cut down to shrub forms. This is often more satisfactory for regions where apples do not do too well. Most apples in England are grown in bush form, by the way.

Can white or green grapes be raised in central Wisconsin? 'Minnesota 66' is a green grape that has gone through 40° F. below zero. Worth trying, but not too reliable, are the old green 'Niagara', yellowish 'Seneca', and early green 'Ontario'.

Can you tell me what grapes and nuts I can grow? The only grape that produces fair fruit and will survive your severe winter is the 'Concord'-wild-grape hybrid 'Beta'. You are about on the northern limit of black walnut, hickory, and butternut.

Will the shrub lantana thrive in Wisconsin's climate? What you mean by the shrub lantana is probably *Viburnum lantana,* the wayfaring tree, which is hardy at Lake Geneva and possibly north of that point; *Viburnum carlesii* is about the same for hardiness and is far superior in bloom and fragrance. *V. lantana* makes a splendid dense hedge. *Lantana camara,* the true lantana, is a tender shrub grown in the north under glass or as a bedding plant like heliotrope.

Are pansies hardy in Wisconsin? Not in the sense that they can be left outdoors without protection and survive. In Wisconsin, they can be started in cold frames, wintered with the glass on, and set out in the spring.

When and how should pansies be started from seed? Pansy seed does not germinate satisfactorily at temperatures above 65° F. This means late seeding (about August 20) in your area. Plant in a cold frame in well-drained soil, not too heavy, and not too rich in nitrogen. Potash (which promotes tougher growth) helps the plants to winter over. Wait until snow flies and cover lightly with pine or spruce boughs, or with marsh hay, and apply the sash to the frames. Remove the glass about April 1 and set the plants in a permanent position about May 1.

I have my rosebushes hilled up about 8 inches. Where and when should the tops be cut off? You might as well wait until spring. The tops will have to be cut back to live wood anyway, and one cut is easier to make than two. Also, the tops help catch and hold snow—the natural cover for roses.

Should a climbing rose be taken down from its trellis each year and covered with leaves during the winter? In Wisconsin, climbing roses should be laid down (a trellis hinged at the bottom so it can be dropped over without removing the canes is best) and covered. But do not cover with leaves; damp soil is much better. It keeps the canes moist and does not allow wind to blow off the covering.

Will you name the 12 best all-around varieties of hybrid tea roses for this area? The reliable rose specialists and large American nursery concerns usually offer collections that are made up of roses satisfactory over a wide range of territory, beautiful in flower, and reasonable in price. You can do far worse than to trust to their expert judgment in this matter of variety. (See Roses.)

What kinds of shrubs with red berries are hardy for northern Wisconsin? *Berberis thunbergii, Crataegus* (hawthorn); *Euonymus europaeus; Lonicera tatarica* (bush honeysuckle); 'Hopa' crab; *Prunus tomentosa; Rosa palustris; Sambucus microbotrys* (bunchberry elder); *Symphoricarpus orbiculatus; Viburnum lantana* (red to black berries); *V. opulus; V. trilobum.*

What perennials should I plant for a succession of bloom in Wisconsin for spring and summer? Achillea; aconitum; delphinium; aquilegia; *Artemisia lactiflora;* asters; *Dicentra spectabilis; Centaurea macrocephala;* chrysanthemum, earliest varieties; iris; dictamnus; peony; erigeron; hemerocallis; linum; lupine; *Papaver orientale* and *P. nudicaule;*

physostegia; *Phlox subulata, P. divaricata,* and *P. paniculata; Trollius europaeus;* thalictrum.

When is tree planting most successful—spring or fall?   Unless one has the gift of long-range forecasting, this cannot be answered categorically. For most trees, the best time to plant is as soon as possible, since waiting merely means delay in getting the tree established. But certainly fall planting (anytime after the leaves fall) is much preferred to the usual practice of waiting until the trees are in leaf in May before setting out. Exceptions are the thin-barked trees like sycamore and birches, and those with fleshy roots like magnolias, which do best when planted as early as practicable in the spring. Professionals, with the use of modern transplanting techniques and equipment, can move large specimens with huge balls of earth at any time of the year.

Can you suggest some reliable shrubs (flowering) for Wisconsin?   *Amelanchier; Berberis thunbergii* and *B.* x *mentorensis; Buddleia alternifolia; Desmodium; Euonymus europaeus; Exochorda racemosa; Hypericum prolificum; Lonicera; Physocarpus opulifolius; Prunus tomentosa* and *P.* x *cistena; Rubus deliciosus; Sambucus; Spiraea; Syringa; Viburnum; Rosa rugosa; R. rubrifolia.*

Wyoming

Should I mulch my bleedingheart or in any way give it extra protection this winter?   A mound of leafmold or coarse compost over its crown would be helpful but not absolutely necessary.

Please name some good perennials to grow in the different climates of the state of Wyoming.   Variation in climate seems less a difficulty in Wyoming than the quality and condition of the soil. The following grow successfully where some protection from the wind is possible: basket of gold; *Centaurea macrocephala; Saponaria ocymoides;* pyrethrum; peony; iris; oenothera; nepeta; lupine; linum; hemerocallis; *Heliopsis* 'Pitcherana'; gypsophila; euphorbia; *Phlox subulata* and *P. paniculata;* chrysanthemum; delphinium; aster; hollyhock; *Clematis integrifolia* and *C. recta;* anchusa.

What climbing roses would you recommend for Wyoming?   'Blaze', 'Dr. J. H. Nicolas', and 'White Dawn' are extra-hardy varieties. Try also the continuous bloomer 'Golden Showers'. 'Viking Queen' is another toughie.

What roses do well in Wyoming?   Floribunda roses do excellently in Wyoming and require little or no winter care. Among the best of these are 'Frensham', red; 'Eutin', red; 'Circus', multicolored; 'Spartan', orange-red; and 'Fashion', coral-salmon.

16. Sources for Further Information

Books

AFRICAN-VIOLETS AND OTHER GESNERIADS

African-Violet Handbook for Judges and Exhibitors. Ruth G. Carey. R. G. Carey, Knoxville, Tenn.

African-Violets. M. J. Robey. Barnes.

African-Violets. Sunset Editors. Lane.

All About African Violets (Revised Edition). Montague Free and Charles Marden Fitch. Doubleday.

Helen Van Pelt Wilson's African-Violet Book. Helen Van Pelt Wilson. Hawthorn.

Miracle House Plants: The Gesneriad Family. Virginie and George A. Elbert. Crown.

ANNUALS

Annuals. Brooklyn Botanic Garden.

Annuals. James U. Crockett. Time-Life.

Picture Book of Annuals. Arno and Irene Nehrling. Hearthside.

Woman's Day Book of Annuals and Perennials. Jean Hersey. Simon & Schuster.

BEGONIAS

Begonias: The Complete Reference Guide. Ed and Mildred Thompson. Times Books.

Begonias as House Plants. Jack Kramer. Van Nostrand.

Begonias for Beginners. Elda Haring. Bookworm Pub.

Tuberous Begonia. Brian Langdon. International Publications Service.

BIRDS

Bird Feeders and Shelters You Can Make. Ted S. Pettit. Putnam.
New Handbook of Attracting Birds. Thomas P. McElroy. Knopf.
Songbirds in Your Garden. John K. Terres. Hawthorn.
Trees, Shrubs and Vines for Attracting Birds. Richard M. De Graaf and Gretchin M. Witman. University of Massachusetts Press.

BOTANY

Botany. Taylor Alexander et al. Western Pub.
Introductory Botany. Arthur Cronquist. Harper & Row.
Introductory Plant Science. Henry T. Northen. Wiley.
Manual of Cultivated Plants. Liberty H. Bailey. Macmillan.
Manual of Cultivated Trees and Shrubs Hardy in North America. Alfred Rehder. Macmillan.

BROMELIADS

Bromeliads. Victoria Padilla. Crown.
Bromeliads for Home, Garden and Greenhouse. Werner Rauh. Sterling.
Bromeliads: The Colorful House Plants. Jack Kramer. Van Nostrand.

BULBS

Bulbs. James U. Crockett. Time-Life.
Bulbs. Sunset Editors. Lane.
Bulbs for the Home Gardener. Bebe Miles. Grosset and Dunlap.
Complete Book of Bulbs (Revised Edition). F. F. Rockwell, Esther C. Grayson, and Marjorie J. Dietz. Lippincott.
Hardy Bulbs. Louise B. Wilder. Dover.
Hardy Garden Bulbs. Gertrude S. Wister. Dutton.

CACTI AND SUCCULENTS

Book of Cacti and Other Succulents. Claude Chidamian. Doubleday.
Cacti. John Borg. Sterling.
Cacti and Other Succulents. Jack Kramer. Harry N. Abrams.
Cacti and Succulents. Time-Life Books Editors. Time-Life.
Plant Jewels of the High Country: Sempervivums and Sedums. Helen E. Payne. Pine Cone Pubs., Medford, Oregon.

CHRYSANTHEMUMS

Chrysanthemums. J. F. Smith. Hippocrene.
Chrysanthemums: Year Round Growing. Barrie J. Machin and Nigel Scopes. Sterling.
Pocket Encyclopedia of Chrysanthemums in Colour. Stanley Gosling. Arco.

CITY, SHADE, AND SEASIDE GARDENS

City Gardener. P. Truex. Knopf.
Gardening by the Sea. Daniel J. Foley. Chilton.
Gardening in the City. Carla Wallach. Harcourt, Brace, Jovanovich.
Gardening in the Shade. Brooklyn Botanic Garden.
Shade Gardens. Oliver E. Allen. Time-Life.
Successful Gardening in the Shade. Helen Van Pelt Wilson. Doubleday.
The Terrace Gardener's Handbook. Linda Yang. Doubleday.
Your City Garden. Jack Kramer. Scribner's.

CONTAINER AND HANGING PLANTS

Container and Hanging Gardens. Staff of Ortho Books. Ortho.
Container Gardening Indoors & Out. Jack Kramer. Doubleday.
Container Gardening Outdoors. George Taloumis. Simon & Schuster.
Hanging Plants for Home, Terrace and Garden. John P. Baumgardt. Simon & Schuster.
Window Box and Container Gardening. Judith Berrisford. Transatlantic.

EVERGREENS

Conifers for Your Garden. Adrian Bloom. Scribner's.
Evergreens. James U. Crockett. Time-Life.
Handbook on Conifers. Brooklyn Botanic Garden.

FERNS

Ferns. Philip Perl. Time-Life.
Ferns to Know and Grow. Gordon Foster. Hawthorn.
Handbook on Ferns. Brooklyn Botanic Garden.
Home Gardener's Book of Ferns. John Mickel and Evelyn Fiore. Holt, Rinehart and Winston.

FLOWER ARRANGEMENT AND PRESERVATION

Complete Book of Flower Preservation. Geneal Condon. Prentice-Hall.

Complete Flower Arranger. Amalie A. Ascher. Simon & Schuster.

Decorating with Plants. Time-Life Editors. Time-Life.

Flower Arrangements for Special Occasions. Winifrede Morrison. Hippocrene.

Flower Growing for Flower Arrangement. Arno and Irene Nehrling. Dover.

Flowers, Space and Motion. Helen Van Pelt Wilson. Simon & Schuster.

Keeping the Plants You Pick. L. L. Foster. Crowell.

FLOWER SHOW MANAGEMENT

Handbook for Flower Shows. National Council of State Garden Clubs. St. Louis, Mo.

FLOWERS IN GENERAL

Color Dictionary of Flowers and Plants for Home and Garden. Roy Hay and Patrick M. Synge. Crown.

FRUITS (See also Vegetables.)

All About Growing Fruits and Berries. Staff of Ortho Books. Ortho.

Fruit Trees and Shrubs. Brooklyn Botanic Garden.

Fruits for the Home Garden. Ken & Pat Kraft. Morrow.

Green Thumb Book of Fruit and Vegetable Gardening. George Abraham. Prentice-Hall.

GARDEN CONSTRUCTION, FURNITURE, AND ACCESSORIES

Book of Garden Ornament. Peter Hunt, ed. Architectural Book Publishing Company.

Complete Book of Garden and Outdoor Lighting. Bernard Gladstone. Hearthside.

Fences and Gates. Sunset Editors. Lane.

Garden Art and Decoration. Sunset Editors. Lane.

Garden Construction. Ogden Tenner. Time-Life.

How to Build Fences, Gates and Walls. Stanley Schuler. Macmillan.

Walks, Walls and Patio Floors. Sunset Editors. Lane.

GENERAL GARDENING

America's Garden Book. James Bush-Brown. Scribner's.

Complete Guide to Successful Gardening. Marjorie J. Dietz, ed. Mayflower.

Complete Illustrated Book of Garden Magic. Roy E. Biles and Marjorie J. Dietz. Ferguson and Doubleday.

Encyclopedia of Gardening. Norman Taylor, ed. Houghton Mifflin.

Reader's Digest Illustrated Guide to Gardening. Carroll Calkins, ed. Reader's Digest.

Rockwells' Complete Guide to Successful Gardening. F. F. Rockwell and Esther C. Grayson. Doubleday.

Standard Cyclopedia of Horticulture. Liberty H. Bailey, ed. 3 volumes. Macmillan.

Wyman's Gardening Encyclopedia. Donald Wyman, ed. Macmillan.

GERANIUMS

Geraniums. H. G. Fogg. Branford.

Joy of Geraniums. Helen Van Pelt Wilson. Morrow.

Miniature Geraniums. Harold Bagusi. Branford.

GLADIOLUS (See Bulbs.)

How to Grow Gladiolus. N. A. Gladiolus Council. Peru, Ind.

GREENHOUSES

Commercial Flower Forcing. Alex Laurie and others. McGraw-Hill.

Complete Greenhouse Book. Peter Clegg and Derry Watkins. Garden Way.

Garden Rooms and Greenhouses. Jack Kramer. Harper & Row.

Gardening Under Glass. Jerome A. Eaton. Macmillan.

Greenhouse Gardening. Henry and Rebecca Northen. Wiley.

Greenhouse Gardening. Time-Life Editors. Time-Life.

Winter Flowers in Greenhouse and Sun-heated Pit. K. S. Taylor and E. W. Gregg. Scribner's.

GROUND COVERS

All About Ground Covers. Staff of Ortho Books. Ortho.

Ground Cover Plants. Donald Wyman. Macmillan.

Ground Covers for Easier Gardening. Daniel J. Foley. Dover.

GROWTH REGULATORS

Plant Growth Substances. Folke Skoog, ed. University of Wisconsin Press.

Plant Growth Substances in Agriculture. Robert J. Weaver. Freeman.

HERBS

Complete Book of Herbs and Spices. Sarah Garland. Viking.

Gardening with Herbs for Flavor and Fragrance. Helen M. Fox. Dover.

Herb Gardening At Its Best. Sal Gilbertie. Atheneum.

Herbs and Their Ornamental Uses. Brooklyn Botanic Garden.

Herbs for Every Garden. G. B. Foster. Dutton.

Herbs: How to Grow Them and How to Use Them. Helen N. Webster. Branford.

Herbs: Their Culture and Uses. Rosetta E. Clarkson. Macmillan.

Herbs to Grow Indoors. Adelma Grenier Simmons. Hawthorn.

HOUSE PLANTS AND INDOOR LIGHT GARDENING

After-Dinner Gardening Book. Richard W. Langer. Macmillan.

All About House Plants (Revised Edition). Montague Free and Marjorie J. Dietz. Doubleday.

Complete Book of Houseplants Under Lights. Charles Marden Fitch. Hawthorn.

Decorative Gardening in Containers. Elvin McDonald. Doubleday.

Exotic Plant Manual. Alfred B. Graf. Scribner's.

Flowering House Plants. James U. Crockett. Time-Life.

Foliage House Plants. James U. Crockett. Time-Life.

Gardening Under Lights. Time-Life Books Editors. Time-Life.

House Plant Decorating Book. Virginie F. and George A. Elbert. Dutton.

Indoor Light Gardening Book. George A. Elbert. Crown.

IRIS

Iris Book. Molly Price. Dover.

Irises. Harry Randall. Taplinger.

World of Irises. Bee Warburton. American Iris Society, 6518 Beachy Avenue, Wichita, Kansas.

LANDSCAPING AND DESIGN

Art of Home Landscaping. Garrett Eckbo. McGraw-Hill.
How to Plan and Plant Your Own Property. Alice R. Ireys. Morrow.
How to Plan Your Own Home Landscape. Nelva M. Weber. Bobbs-Merrill.
Landscape Gardening. James U. Crockett. Time-Life.
Landscaping and the Small Garden. Marjorie J. Dietz. Doubleday.
Patios, Terraces, Decks, and Roof Gardens. Alice Upham Smith. Hawthorn.
Your Private World: A Study of Intimate Gardens. Thomas Church. Chronicle Books.

LAWNS

Lawn Keeping. Robert W. Schery. Prentice-Hall.
Lawns and Ground Covers. James U. Crockett. Time-Life.
Lawns and Ground Covers. Sunset Editors. Lane.

ORCHIDS

All About Orchids. Charles Marden Fitch. Doubleday.
Home Orchid Growing. Rebecca T. Northen. Van Nostrand-Reinhold.
Miniature Orchids. R. T. Northen. Van Nostrand-Reinhold.
Orchids. Alice F. Skelsey. Time-Life.
Orchids and How to Grow Them. Gloria Jean Sessler. Prentice-Hall.
Orchids for Home and Garden. F. A. Fennell, Jr. Holt, Rinehart & Winston.
Orchids You Can Grow. Harry B. Logan. Hawthorn.

ORGANIC GARDENING

Basic Book of Organically-Grown Foods. Organic Gardening & Farming Magazine Editors. Rodale.
How to Have a Green Thumb Without an Aching Back. Ruth Stout. Exposition.
Organic Gardening Under Glass. George and Katy Abraham. Rodale.
Organic Gardening Without Poisons. Hamilton Tyler. Van Nostrand.
Organic Vegetable Gardening. Joseph A. Cocannouer. Arc Books.
Weeds: Guardians of the Soil. Joseph A. Cocannouer. Devin-Adair.

PERENNIALS

Better Homes & Gardens Perennials You Can Grow. Better Homes & Gardens Editors. Meredith.

Gardening with Perennials Month by Month. Joseph G. Hudak. Times Books.

Low Maintenance Perennials. Robert S. Hebb. Times Books.

Perennials. James U. Crockett. Time-Life.

Picture Book of Perennials. Arno and Irene Nehrling. Hearthside.

PESTS AND DISEASES

Diseases and Pests of Ornamental Plants. Pascal P. Pirone. Wiley.

Gardener's Bug Book. Cynthia Westcott. Doubleday.

Handbook on Garden Pests. Brooklyn Botanic Garden.

Pests and Diseases. Time-Life Editors. Time-Life.

Plant Disease Handbook. Cynthia Westcott. Van Nostrand-Reinhold.

PLANT BREEDING

Plant Breeding. Kenneth J. Frey, ed. Iowa State University Press.

Plant Breeding for Pest and Disease Resistance. Gordon E. Russell. Butterworths.

Principles of Plant Breeding. Robert W. Allard. Wiley.

PROPAGATION

Plant Propagation. John P. Mahlstede and E. S. Haber. Wiley.

Plant Propagation in Pictures (Revised Edition). Montague Free and Marjorie J. Dietz. Doubleday.

Plant Propagation Practices. James S. Wells. Macmillan.

Step-By-Step Guide to Plant Propagation. Philip M. Browse. Simon & Schuster.

PRUNING AND BONSAI

Bonsai. Sunset Editors. Lane.

Bonsai, Saikei and Bonkei. Robert L. Behme. Morrow.

How to Prune Almost Everything. John Philip Baumgardt. Morrow.

Japanese Art of Miniature Trees and Landscapes. Yuji Yashimura and Giovanna M. Halford. Tuttle.

Pruning Manual. Edwin F. Steffek. Little, Brown.

Pruning Manual, based on *Bailey's Pruning Manual.* E. P. Christopher. Macmillan.

Pruning Simplified. Lewis Hill. Rodale.

Step-by-Step Guide to Pruning. Christopher Brickell. Simon & Schuster.

Sunset Pruning Handbook. Sunset Editors. Lane.

REGIONAL GARDENING

Florida Gardening Month By Month. Nixon Smiley. University of Miami Press.

Flower Growing in the North: A Month-by-Month Guide. G. E. Luxton. University of Minnesota Press.

Gardening in the Upper Midwest. L. C. Snyder. University of Minnesota Press.

Gardening Round the Year. Margaret T. Wheatly. (Santa Barbara) Woodbridge Press.

Southern California Month-by-Month Flower Gardening Book. Margaret Redfield. Tarcher.

The Southern Garden. Ben Arthur Davis. Mockingbird Books.

Way to Beauty: Planting and Landscaping in the Rocky Mountains. George W. Kelly. Pruett.

RHODODENDRONS AND AZALEAS

Dwarf Rhododendrons. Peter A. Cox. Macmillan.

Rhododendrons and Their Relatives. Brooklyn Botanic Garden.

Rhododendrons in America. Ted Van Veen. Van Veen Nursery, Portland, Oregon.

Rhododendrons of the World. David G. Leach. Scribner's.

ROCK GARDENING

Rock Gardens. Brooklyn Botanic Garden.

Rock Gardens and Water Plants in Color. Francis B. Stark and Conrad B. Link. Doubleday.

ROSES

Anyone Can Grow Roses. Cynthia Westcott. Macmillan.

Complete Book of Miniature Roses. Charles Marden Fitch. Hawthorn.

Modern Roses VII. McFarland Company, Harrisburg, Pennsylvania.

Old Roses. Ethelyn E. Keays. E. M. Coleman.

Peter Malins' Rose Book. Peter Malins and M. M. Graff. Dodd Mead.

Rockwells' Complete Book of Roses. Frederick F. Rockwell and Esther C. Grayson. Doubleday.

Rose Lover's Guide. Roland Browne. Atheneum.

Roses. James U. Crockett. Time-Life.

SHRUBS (See also Trees.)

Dwarf Shrubs. Donald Wyman. Macmillan.

Flowering Shrubs. James U. Crockett. Time-Life.

Guide to Garden Shrubs and Trees. Norman Taylor. Houghton Mifflin.

Nursery Source Guide. Brooklyn Botanic Garden.

Shrub Identification Book. George W. Symonds. Morrow.

Shrubs and Vines for American Gardens. Donald Wyman. Macmillan.

SOILLESS GARDENING

Beginner's Guide to Hydroponics. J. S. Douglas. Drake.

Hydroponic Gardening. R. Bridwell. Woodbridge Press.

Hydroponics. Dudley Harris. David Charles.

The Indoor Water Gardener's How-to Handbook. Peter Loewer. Walker & Company.

SOILS AND FERTILIZERS

Our Soils and Their Management. Roy L. Donahue, et al. Interstate.

Soil Fertility and Fertilizers. Samuel Tisdale and Werner Nelson. Macmillan.

Soils: An Introduction to Soils and Plant Growth. R. L. Donahue, et al. Prentice-Hall.

Soils That Support Us. Charles E. Kellogg. Macmillan.

TERRARIUMS

Complete Book of Terrariums. Charles Marden Fitch. Hawthorn.

Fun with Terrarium Gardening. Virginia and George A. Elbert. Crown.

Gardens in Glass Containers. Robert C. Baur. Hearthside.

Gardens Under Glass. Jack Kramer. Simon & Schuster.

Terrarium Book. Charles Evans and Roberta Pliner. Random House.

Terrariums and Miniature Gardens. Sunset Editors. Lane.

TREES

Evergreen Garden Trees and Shrubs. Denis Hardwicke and Alan R. Toogood. Macmillan.

Flowering Trees. Brooklyn Botanic Garden.

The Gardener's Basic Book of Trees and Shrubs. Stanley Schuler. Simon & Schuster.

Tree Identification Book. George W. Symonds. Morrow.

Tree Maintenance. P. P. Pirone. Oxford University Press.

Trees. James U. Crockett. Time-Life.

Trees for American Gardens. Donald Wyman. Macmillan.

Trees for Architecture and the Landscape. Robert Zion. Van Nostrand-Reinhold.

TULIPS

Book of Tulips. Tom Lodewijk. Viking.

VEGETABLES AND FRUITS

Food-Lover's Garden. Angelo M. Pellegrini. Knopf.

Garden-to-Table Cookbook. James Beard, et al. McGraw-Hill.

Home Vegetable Garden. Brooklyn Botanic Garden.

New Vegetable and Fruit Garden Book. R. Milton Carleton. Regnery.

Vegetables and Fruits. James U. Crockett. Time-Life.

VINES

Shrubs and Vines for American Gardens. Donald Wyman. Macmillan.

Vines. Richard H. Cravens. Time-Life.

WATER GARDENING

Garden Pools, Fountains and Waterfalls. Sunset Editors. Lane.

Gardening With Water, Plantings and Stone. Carroll Calkins. Cornerstone.

Water Gardening Indoors and Out. Reginald Dutta. Crown.

WEEDS

Common Weeds of the United States. U.S.D.A. Research Service. Dover.

Weed Biology and Control. T. J. Muzik. McGraw-Hill.

Weeds. Alexander C. Martin. Western Publishing Company.

Weeds of Lawn and Garden. J. M. Fogg, Jr. University of Pennsylvania Press.

Wild Green Things in the City. Anne O. Dowden. Crowell.

WILDFLOWER PLANTS AND GARDENS

American Wildlife and Plants. Alexander C. Martin, et al. Dover.

Feasting Free on Wild Edibles. Bradford Angier. Stackpole.

Field Guide to Wildflowers. Roger T. Peterson and Margaret McKenny. Houghton Mifflin.

Growing Wild Flowers. Marie Sperka. Harper & Row.

Growing Woodland Plants. Clarence and Eleanor Birdseye. Dover.

Handbook of Wild Flower Cultivation. Kathryn S. Taylor and Stephen F. Hamblin. Macmillan.

Pioneering with Wild Flowers. George D. Aiken. Countryman.

Using Wayside Plants. Nelson Coon. Hearthside.

Wild Flower Gardening. Time-Life Books Editors. Time-Life.

Wildflowers: Perennials for Your Garden. Bebe Miles. Hawthorn.

State Agricultural Experiment Stations

The addresses of state agricultural experiment stations are given below. They, often in cooperation with the U. S. Department of Agriculture, the various state agricultural colleges, and the county Cooperative Extension Service, offer regional gardening advice and publish bulletins, leaflets, and reports that are free or available at small cost. Addresses of the Cooperative Extension Service will be found in your telephone book under the county government. There are Cooperative Extension Service offices in 3,150 county seats. Lists of bulletins and leaflets published exclusively by the U. S. Department of Agriculture can be obtained from the Superintendent of Documents, U. S. Government Printing Office, Washington, D.C. 20402.

Alabama: Auburn, 36830
Alaska: Fairbanks, 99701
Arizona: Tucson, 85721
Arkansas: Fayetteville, 72701
California: Davis, 95616; Parlier, 93648; Riverside, 92502
Colorado: Fort Collins, 80523
Connecticut: Storrs, 06268; New Haven, 06504; Windsor, 06095
Delaware: Newark, 19711
Florida: Gainesville, 32601

Georgia: Athens, 30602; Tifton (Coastal Plain Station), 31794; Experiment, 30212

Guam: Agaro, 96910

Hawaii: Honolulu, 96822

Idaho: Moscow, 83843

Illinois: Urbana, 61801

Indiana: Lafayette, 47907

Iowa: Ames, 50010

Kansas: Manhattan, 66506

Kentucky: Lexington, 40506

Louisiana: Baton Rouge, 70893; Calhoun, 71225

Maine: Orono, 04473; Monmouth, 04259; Presque Isle, 04769

Maryland: College Park, 20742

Massachusetts: Amherst, 01002

Michigan: East Lansing, 48823

Minnesota: St. Paul, 55108

Mississippi: State College, 39762; Poplarville, 39470

Missouri: Columbia, 65201

Montana: Bozeman, 59715

Nebraska: Lincoln, 68503

Nevada: Reno, 89507

New Hampshire: Durham, 03824

New Jersey: New Brunswick, 08903

New Mexico: Las Cruces, 88003

New York: Geneva, 14456; Ithaca, 14850; Highland, 12528

North Carolina: Raleigh, 27607

North Dakota: Fargo, 58102

Ohio: Columbus, 43210; Caldwell, 43724; Ripley, 45167

Oklahoma: Stillwater, 74074

Oregon: Corvallis, 97331

Pennsylvania: University Park, 16802

Puerto Rico: Rio Piedras, 00928

Rhode Island: Kingston, 02881

South Carolina: Clemson, 29631

South Dakota: Brookings, 57006

Tennessee: Knoxville, 37901

Texas: College Station, 77843; Lubbock, 79401

Utah: Logan, 84322

Vermont: Burlington, 05401

Virgin Islands: Kingshill, St. Croix, 00850

Virginia: Blacksburg, 24061

Washington: Pullman, 99163
West Virginia: Morgantown, 26506
Wisconsin: Madison, 53706
Wyoming: Laramie, 82071

Horticultural and Special Plant Societies

African Violet Society of America, Box 1326, Knoxville, Tenn. 37901
American Amaryllis Society Group (see American Plant Life Society)
American Begonia Society, 10692 Bolsa St., Garden Grove, Calif. 92643
American Bonsai Society, 1263 W. 6th St., Erie, Pa. 16505
American Boxwood Society, Box 85, Boyce, Va. 22620
American Camellia Society, Box 1217, Fort Valley, Ga. 31030
American Daffodil Society, Tyner, N.C. 27980
American Dahlia Society, 1649 Beech, Melrose Park, Pa. 19126
American Fern Society, George Mason University, Fairfax, Va. 22030
American Fuchsia Society, Hall of Flowers, 9th Ave. and Lincoln Way, San Francisco, Calif. 94122
American Gloxinia/Gesneriad Society, Box 312, Ayer, Mass. 01432
American Gourd Society, P.O. Box 274, Mt. Gilead, Ohio 43338
American Hemerocallis Society, Rte. 2, Box 360, De Queen, Ark. 71832
American Hibiscus Society, 206 N.E. 40th St., Pompano Beach, Fla. 33064
American Horticultural Society, Mount Vernon, Va. 22121
American Hosta Society, 980 Stanton Ave., Baldwin, N.Y. 11510
American Iris Society, 2315 Tower Grove Ave., St. Louis, Mo. 63110
American Ivy Society, National Center for American Horticulture, Mount Vernon, Va. 22121
American Magnolia Society, 14876 Pheasant Hill Ct., Chesterfield, Mo. 63017
American Orchid Society, 84 Sherman St., Cambridge, Mass. 02140
American Penstemon Society, Box 450, Briarcliff Manor, N.Y. 10510
American Peony Society, 250 Interlachen Rd., Hopkins, Minn. 55343
American Plant Life Society & The American Amaryllis Society Group, Box 150, La Jolla, Calif. 92038
American Primrose Society, G. Fenderson, Grout Hill, Acworth, N.H. 03607

American Rhododendron Society, 617 Fairway Dr., Aberdeen, Wash. 98520

American Rock Garden Society, Rte. 1, Box 282, Mena, Ark. 71953

American Rose Society, Box 30,000, Shreveport, La. 71130

Bamboo Society, 1101 San Leon Ct., Solana Beach, Calif. 92075

Bonsai Clubs International, Box 2098, Sunnyvale, Calif. 94087

Bromeliad Society, Box 41261, Los Angeles, Calif. 90041

Cactus and Succulent Society of America, 2288 Highland Vista Dr., Arcadia, Calif. 91006

California Horticultural Society, California Academy of Sciences, Golden Gate Park, San Francisco, Calif. 94118

Chicago Horticultural Society and Botanic Garden, 18 South Michigan Ave., Chicago, Ill. 60603

Cymbidium Society of America, 1250 Orchid Dr., Santa Barbara, Calif. 93111

Epiphyllum Society of America, P.O. Box 1395, Monrovia, Calif. 91016

Garden Club Federations:
    There are three national federations of garden clubs: the Garden Club of America, the National Council of State Garden Clubs, and the Men's Garden Clubs of America. Each is listed here alphabetically, and names of member clubs may be obtained through their offices.

Garden Club of America, 598 Madison Ave., New York, N.Y. 10022

Herb Society of America, 300 Massachusetts Ave., Boston, Mass. 02115

Holly Society of America, 407 Fountain Hill Rd., Bel Air, Md. 21014

Horticultural Society of New York, 128 W. 58th St., New York, N.Y. 10019

Indoor Light Gardening Society of America, 423 Powell Dr., Bay Village, Ohio 44140

International Geranium Society, Dept. AHS, 6501 Yosemite Dr., Buena Park, Calif. 90620

International Lilac Society, Box 315, Rumford, Me. 04276

Marigold Society of America, Box 1776, Stillwell, Ind. 46351

Massachusetts Horticultural Society, 300 Massachusetts Ave., Boston, Mass. 02115

Men's Garden Clubs of America, 5560 Merle Hay Rd., Des Moines, Iowa 50323

National Chrysanthemum Society, B. L. Markham, 2612 Beverly Blvd., S.W., Roanoke, Va. 24015

National Council of State Garden Clubs, 4401 Magnolia Ave., St. Louis, Mo. 63110

National Fuchsia Society, 110 So. F. St., Oxnard, Calif. 93030

National Junior Horticultural Assoc., 384 Colonial Ave., Worthington, Ohio 43085

National Oleander Society, 5127 Avenue 01/2, Galveston, Tex. 77550

North American Gladiolus Council, 30 Highland Place, Peru, Ind. 46970

North American Lily Society, Box 40134, Indianapolis, Ind. 46351

Northern Nut Growers Assoc., 3100 Kane Rd., Aliquippa, Pa. 15001

Palm Society, 1320 S. Venetian Way, Miami, Fla. 33139

Pennsylvania Horticultural Society, 325 Walnut St., Philadelphia, Pa. 19106

Saintpaulia International, Box 549, Knoxville, Tenn. 37901

Southern California Horticultural Institute, P.O. Box 49798, Barrington Sta., Los Angeles, Calif. 90049

Botanical Gardens, Arboreta, and Public Gardens

Arboretum of the Barnes Foundation, 300 Latches Lane, Merion Station, Pa. 19066

Arnold Arboretum, The Arborway, Jamaica Plain, Mass. 02130

Arthur Hoyt Scott Horticultural Foundation, Swarthmore College, Swarthmore, Pa. 19081

Bayard Cutting Arboretum, P.O. Box 66, Montauk Highway, Oakdale, N.Y. 11769

Bellingrath Gardens, Theodore, Ala. 36582

Berkshire Garden Center, Stockbridge, Mass. 01262

Birmingham Botanical Garden, 2612 Lane Park Rd., Birmingham, Ala. 35223

Boerner Botanical Gardens, 5879 South 92nd St., Hales Corners, Wis. 53130

Bowman's Hill State Wildflower Preserve, Washington Crossing State Park, Rte. 32, River Rd., Washington Crossing, Pa. 18977

Boyce Thompson Southwestern Arboretum, P.O. Box AB, Superior, Ariz. 85273

Brookgreen Gardens, Murrels Inlet, S.C. 29576

Brooklyn Botanic Garden, 1000 Washington Ave., Brooklyn, N.Y. 11225

Callaway Gardens, Rte. 27, Pine Mountain, Ga. 31822
Cary Arboretum of the New York Botanical Garden, P.O. Box AB, Millbrook, N.Y. 12545
Colonial Williamsburg Foundation, Drawer C, Williamsburg, Va. 23185
Cornell Plantations, 100 Judd Falls Rd., Ithaca, N.Y. 14853
Dawes Arboretum, Rte. 5, Box 270, Newark, Ohio 43055
Denver Botanic Gardens, 909 York St., Denver, Col. 80206
Descanso Gardens, 1418 Descanso Dr., La Canada, Calif. 91011
Desert Botanical Garden, 1200 Galvin Parkway, P.O. Box 5415, Phoenix, Ariz. 85010
Duke Gardens Foundation, Rte. 206 South, Somerville, N.J. 08876
Dumbarton Oaks, 1703 32nd St., N.W., Washington, D.C. 20007
Fairchild Tropical Garden, 10901 Old Cutler Rd., Miami, Fla. 33156
Florida Cypress Gardens, P.O. Box 1, Cypress Gardens, Fla. 33880
Garfield Park Conservatory, 300 N. Central Park Blvd., Chicago, Ill. 60624
Hammond Museum Oriental Stroll Gardens, Deveau Rd., North Salem, N.Y. 10560
Hershey Rose Gardens and Arboretum, Hershey, Pa. 17033
Highland Park, 375 Westfall Rd., Rochester, N.Y. 14620
Holden Arboretum, 9500 Sperry Rd., Mentor, Ohio 44060
Huntington Botanical Gardens, 1151 Oxford Rd., San Marino, Calif. 91108
Longue Vue Gardens, 7 Bamboo Rd., New Orleans, La. 70124
Longwood Gardens, Kennett Square, Pa. 19348
Los Angeles State and County Arboretum, 301 N. Baldwin Ave., Arcadia, Calif. 91006
Magnolia Gardens, Rte. 4, Charleston, S.C. 29407
Marie Selby Botanical Gardens, 800 S. Palm Ave., Sarasota, Fla. 33577
Middleton Place, Rte. 4, Charleston, S.C. 29407
Missouri Botanical Garden, 2345 Tower Grove Ave., St. Louis, Mo. 63110
Morris Arboretum, 9414 Meadowbrook Ave., Philadelphia, Pa. 19118
Morton Arboretum, Rte. 53, Lisle, Ill. 60532
Mount Vernon Gardens, Mount Vernon, Va. 22121
New York Botanical Garden, Bronx Park, Bronx, N.Y. 10458
Norfolk Botanical Gardens, Airport Rd., Norfolk, Va. 23518
Old Westbury Gardens, P.O. Box 430, Old Westbury Rd., Old Westbury, N.Y. 11568

Pacific Tropical Botanical Garden, P.O. Box 340, Lawai, Kauai, Hawaii 96765

Phipps Conservatory, Schenley Park, Pittsburgh, Pa. 15213

Planting Fields Arboretum, P.O. Box 58, Planting Fields Rd., Oyster Bay, N.Y. 11771

Queens Botanical Garden, 43-50 Main St., Flushing, N.Y. 11355

Rancho Santa Ana Botanic Garden, 1500 N. College Ave., Claremont, Calif. 91711

Strybing Arboretum and Botanical Gardens, Golden Gate Park, San Francisco, Calif. 94122

Swiss Pines, Charlestown Rd., R.D. 1, P.O. Box 127, Malvern, Pa. 19355

U.S. National Arboretum, 24th & R Sts., N.E., Washington, D.C. 20002

University of Washington Arboretum, Seattle, Wash. 98195

Wave Hill, 675 W. 252 St., Bronx, N.Y. 10471

Winterthur Gardens, Rte. 52, Winterthur, Del. 19735

Some Sources for Plants and Seeds

ANNUALS (General)

Burpee Seed Co., Warminster, Pa. 18991; Clinton, Iowa 52732; Riverside, Calif. 92502

Henry Field Seed & Nursery Co., 407 Sycamore St., Shenandoah, Iowa 51602

Gurney Seed & Nursery Co., 2nd & Capitol, Yankton, S.D. 57079

Joseph Harris Co., Inc., Moreton Farm, Rochester, N.Y. 14624

Herbst Brothers, Seedsmen, Inc., 1000 N. Main St., Brewster, N.Y. 10509

J. W. Jung Seed Co., Randolph, Wis. 53956

Earl May Seed & Nursery Co., Shenandoah, Iowa 51603

Olds Seed Co., Box 7790, Madison, Wis. 53707

George W. Park Seed Co., Inc., Greenwood, S.C. 29647

R. H. Shumway, Rockford, Ill. 61101

Thompson & Morgan Inc., P.O. Box 100, Farmingdale, N.J. 07727

Otis S. Twilley Seed Co., Inc., P.O. Box 65, Trevose, Pa. 19047

World Seed Service, J. L. Hudson, Seedsman, Box 1058, Redwood City, Calif. 94064

ANNUALS (British Sources)

Samuel Dobie & Sons Ltd., Llangollen, North Wales, England
Suttons Seeds Ltd., Hele Rd., Torquay, Devon, TQ2 7Q5 England
Thompson & Morgan Ltd., London Rd., Ipswich, IP2, OBA, England

BULBS

Antonelli Brothers, 2545 Capitola Rd., Santa Cruz, Calif. 95062
Burpee Seed Co., Warminster, Pa. 18991; Clinton, Iowa 52732; Riverside, Calif. 92502
Connell's Dahlias, 10216 40th Ave. East, Tacoma, Wash. 98446
De Jager Bulbs, Inc., 188 Asbury St., South Hamilton, Mass. 01982
International Growers Exchange, Box 397-N, Farmington, Mich. 48024 (perennials)
John Messelaar Bulb Co., Box 269, Ipswich, Mass. 01938
Rex Bulb Farms, Box 774, Port Townsend, Wash. 98368
John Scheepers Inc., 63 Wall St., New York, N.Y. 10005
Van Bourgondien Brothers, 245 Farmingdale Rd., P.O. Box A, Babylon, N.Y. 11702
Wayside Gardens Co., Hodges, S.C. 29695
White Flower Farm, Litchfield, Conn. 06759

FRUITS

Alexander's Nurseries, 1225 Wareham St., Middleboro, Mass. 02346 (blueberries)
W. F. Allen Co., Berry Lane, P.O. Box 1577, Salisbury, Md. 21801 (strawberry, blueberry, raspberry, and blackberry plants, grapevines, asparagus)
Brittingham Plant Farms, Dept. 7, Salisbury, Md. 21801 (strawberries, blueberries, raspberries, grapes, blackberries)
Burpee Seed Co., Warminster, Pa. 18991; Clinton, Iowa 52732; Riverside, Calif. 92502 (general)
The Conner Co., Inc., P.O. Box 534, Augusta, Ark. 72006 (strawberries)
Farmer Seed & Nursery Co., 818 N.W. 4th St., Faribault, Minn. 55021 (general)
Henry Field Seed & Nursery Co., 407 Sycamore St., Shenandoah, Iowa 51602 (general)
Dean Foster Nurseries, Hartford, Mich. 49057 (general)
Gurney Seed & Nursery Co., 2nd & Capitol, Yankton, S.D. 57079 (general)

Inter-State Nurseries, 1423 E. St., Hamburg, Iowa 51644 (general)

Kelly Bros. Nurseries, Inc., Dansville, N.Y. 14437 (general)

Henry Leuthardt, Montauk Hwy., East Moriches, N.Y. 11940 (dwarf and semidwarf, espaliers)

J. E. Miller Nurseries, West Lake Rd., Canandaigua, N.Y. 14424 (general)

Rayner Bros., Inc., P.O. Box 1617, Salisbury, Md. 21801 (strawberries, blueberries, raspberries, grapes, asparagus roots)

Shasta Nursery, Inc., 165 Logan St., Watsonville, Calif. 95076 (strawberry plants)

Dave Wilson Nursery, Hughson, Calif. 95326 (dwarf, general)

HERBS

(Seeds are listed in most general seed catalogs. Plants may often be found in local garden centers. A few specialists are listed below.)

Comstock, Ferre and Co., Box 125, Wethersfield, Conn. 06109 (seeds)

Greene Herb Gardens, Greene, R.I. 02827 (enclose self-addressed, stamped envelope)

Merry Gardens, Camden, Me. 04843 (plants)

Nichols Garden Nursery, 1190 N. Pacific Hwy., Albany, Oreg. 97321

Tool Shed Herb Farm, Turkey Hill Rd., Salem Center, Purdy Station, N.Y. 10578

INDOOR PLANTS (House and Greenhouse)

Alberts & Merkel Bros., 2210 S. Federal Hwy., Boynton Beach, Fla. 33435 (orchids, bromeliads, foliage plants)

Arthur Eames Allgrove, Wilmington, Mass. 01887 (terrarium plants)

Antonelli Brothers, 2545 Capitola Rd., Santa Cruz, Calif. 95062 (tuberous begonias, dahlias, and others)

Buell's Greenhouses, P.O. Box 218DO, Weeks Rd., Eastford, Conn. 06242 (African-violets, gloxinias, gesneriads; also seeds)

Edelweiss Gardens, 54 Robb Allentown Rd., Robbinsville, N.J. 08691 (terrarium plants, orchids, ferns, begonias, and bromeliads)

Fennell Orchid Co., 26719 S.W. 157 Ave., Homestead, Fla. 33031 (orchids, bromeliads, ferns, rare tropical house plants, along with complete growing instructions)

Finck Floral Co., 9849 Kimker Lane, St. Louis, Mo. 63127 (orchids)

Fischer Greenhouses, Oak Ave., Linwood, N.J. 08221 (African-violets and related plants)

International Growers Exchange, Box 397-N, Farmington, Mich. 48024 (general)

Jones & Scully Inc., 2200 N.W. 33rd Ave., Miami, Fla. 33142 (orchids)

Kartuz Greenhouses, Inc., 1408 Sunset Dr., Vista, Calif. 92083 (gloxinias, African-violets, begonias)

Logee's Greenhouses, 55 North St., Danielson, Conn. 06239 (begonias, rare plants, geraniums, herbs)

Lyndon Lyon Greenhouses, Inc., Dolgeville, N.Y. 13329 (African-violets, miniature roses, and house plants)

Matsu Bonsai Nursery, Livingston Manor, N.Y. 12758 (bonsai plants, tools, and containers)

Rod McLellan Co., 1450 El Camino Real, South San Francisco, Calif. 94080 (orchids)

Merry Gardens, Camden, Me. 04843 (geraniums, ivy, fuchsia, and many others)

George W. Park Seed Co. Inc., Greenwood, S.C. 29647 (plants, seeds, lights, and materials)

John Scheepers Inc., 37 Wall St., New York, N.Y. 10005 (mostly bulbs)

The House Plant Corner Ltd., Box 617, Kennett Square, Pa. 19348

Ed and Mildred Thompson, P.O. Drawer PP, Southampton, N.Y. 11968 (begonias)

Tinari Greenhouses, 2325 Valley Rd., Box 190, Huntingdon Valley, Pa. 19006 (African-violets)

Volkmann Bros. Greenhouses, 2714 Minert St., Dallas, Tex. 75219 (African-violets)

Wayside Gardens Co., Hodges, S.C. 29695 (bulbs)

Wilson Bros. Floral Co. Inc., Roachdale, Ind. 46172 (geraniums and others)

PERENNIALS (General)

Bluestone Perennials, 7231 Middle Ridge, Madison, Ohio 44057

Burpee Seed Co., Warminster, Pa. 18991; Clinton, Iowa 52732; Riverside, Calif. 92502 (seeds)

Inter-State Nurseries, 1423 E. St., Hamburg, Iowa 51644

Lamb Nurseries, E. 101 Sharp Ave., Spokane, Wash. 99202

George W. Park Seed Co. Inc., Greenwood, S.C. 29647 (seeds)

Spring Hill Nurseries, Reservation Center, P.O. Box 1758, Peoria, Ill. 61656

Wayside Gardens Co., Hodges, S.C. 29695
White Flower Farm, Litchfield, Conn. 06759

PERENNIALS (Specialists)

Cooley's Gardens, P.O. Box 126, Silverton, Oreg. 97381 (iris)
Eden Road Iris Garden, P.O. Box 117, Wenatchee, Wash. 98801 (iris)
Far North Gardens, 15621 Auburndale Ave., Livonia, Mich. 48154 (primroses)
Huff's Garden Mums, Box 187, Burlington, Kan. 66839 (chrysanthemums)
Klehm Nursery, 2 E. Algonquin Rd., Arlington Heights, Ill. 60005 (peonies)
Melrose Gardens, 309 Best Road S., Stockton, Calif. 95205 (iris, daylilies, daffodils)
Oakhill Gardens, 1960 Cherry Knoll Rd., Dallas, Oreg. 97338 (sedums and sempervivums)
Savory's Greenhouses, 5300 Whiting Ave., Edina, Minn. 55435 (hosta)
Schreiner's Gardens, 3625 Quinaby Rd., N.E., Salem, Oreg. 97303 (iris)
Louis Smirnow & Son, 85 Linden Lane, Glen Head, P.O. Brookville, N.Y. 11545 (peonies)
Gilbert H. Wild & Son, Sarcoxie, Mo. 64862 (iris, peonies, day-lilies)

ROSES

Armstrong Nurseries Inc., 1239 S. Palmetto, Ontario, Calif. 91761
Inter-State Nurseries, 1423 E. St., Hamburg, Iowa 51644
Jackson & Perkins Co., Medford, Oreg. 97501
Roses of Yesterday & Today, 802 Brown's Valley Rd., Watsonville, Calif. 95076
Wyant Roses, Inc., 200 Johnny Cake Ridge, Mentor, Ohio 44060 (old and new)

TREES, SHRUBS, AND VINES (General)

Burgess Seed & Plant Co., Bloomington, Ill. 61701
Farmer Seed & Nursery Co., 818 N.W. 4th St., Faribault, Minn. 55021
Earl Ferris Nursery, 811 4th St., N.E., Hampton, Iowa 50441
Henry Field Seed & Nursery Co., 407 Sycamore St., Shenandoah, Iowa 51602
Girard Nurseries, P.O. Box 428, Geneva, Ohio 44041
Gurney Seed & Nursery Co., 2nd & Capitol, Yankton, S.D. 57079

H. G. Hastings Co., Box 4274, Atlanta, Ga. 30302
Inter-State Nurseries, 1423 E. St., Hamburg, Iowa 51644
Kelly Bros. Nurseries, Inc., Dansville, N.Y. 14437
Mellinger's, 2310 West South Range Rd., North Lima, Ohio 44452
Musser Forests, Inc., Box 340, Indiana, Pa. 15701
Wayside Gardens Co., Hodges, S.C. 29695
Western Maine Forest Nursery Co., Fryeburg, Me. 04037
White Flower Farm, Litchfield, Conn. 06759

TREES, SHRUBS, AND VINES (Specialists)

Alexander's Nurseries, 1225 Wareham St., Middleboro, Mass. 02346 (lilacs)

Armstrong Nurseries Inc., 1265 S. Palmetto, Ontario, Calif. 91761 (deciduous fruit and shade trees)

Baldsiefen Nursery, Box 88, Bellvale, N.Y. 10912 (rhododendrons and azaleas)

California Nursery Co., Box 2278, Fremont, Calif. 94536 (fruit and nut trees, grapevines)

D. S. George Nurseries, 2491 Penfield Rd., Fairport, N.Y. 14450 (clematis; mostly wholesale)

Nuccio's Nurseries, 3555 Chaney Trail, Altadena, Calif. 91001 (camellias and azaleas)

Orinda Nursery, Bridgeville, Del. 19933 (camellias and rhododendrons)

A. Shammarello & Son Nursery, 4508 Monticello Blvd., South Euclid, Ohio 44143 (rhododendrons and azaleas)

VEGETABLES

Burgess Seed & Plant Co., Bloomington, Ill. 61701
Burpee Seed Co., Warminster, Pa. 18991; Clinton, Iowa 52732; Riverside, Calif. 92502
Comstock, Ferre and Co., Box 125, Wethersfield, Conn. 06109
DeGiorgi Co., Inc., P.O. Box 413, Council Bluffs, Iowa 51502
Farmer Seed & Nursery Co., 818 N.W. 4th St., Faribault, Minn. 55021
Henry Field Seed & Nursery Co., 407 Sycamore St., Shenandoah, Iowa 51602
Gurney Seed & Nursery Co., 2nd & Capitol, Yankton, S.D. 57079
Joseph Harris Co. Inc., Moreton Farm, Rochester, N.Y. 14624
Johnny's Selected Seeds, Albion, Me. 04910
J. W. Jung Seed Co., Randolph, Wisc. 53956

Earl May Seed & Nursery Co., Shenandoah, Iowa 51603
Nichols Garden Nursery, 1198 Pacific, Albany, Oreg. 97321
Olds Seed Co., Box 7790, Madison, Wisc. 53707
George W. Park Seed Co. Inc., Greenwood, S.C. 29646
R. H. Shumway, Rockford, Ill. 61101
Stokes Seeds Inc., 737 Main St., Box 548, Buffalo, N.Y. 14240
Thompson & Morgan Inc., P.O. Box 100, Farmingdale, N.J. 07727

VEGETABLES (British Sources)

Samuel Dobie & Sons Ltd., Llangollen, North Wales, England
Suttons Seeds Ltd., Hele Rd., Torquay, Devon, TQ2 7Q5 England
Thompson & Morgan Ltd., London Rd., Ipswich, IP2, OBA, England

WATER-LILIES

Lilypons Water Gardens, 10000 Garden Rd., Lilypons, Md. 21717;
    839Q FM 1489, Brookshire, Texas 77423
Paradise Gardens, Bedford and May Sts., Whitman, Mass. 02382
Slocum Water Gardens, 1101 Cypress Gardens Rd., Winter Haven, Fla.
    33880
William Tricker Inc., Box 398, Saddle River, N.J. 07458; Box 7843,
    Independence, Ohio 44131
Van Ness Water Gardens, 2460 North Euclid, Upland, Calif. 91786

WILDFLOWERS

Gardens of The Blue Ridge, Box 10, Pineola, N.C. 28662
Putney Nursery, Putney, Vt. 05346
Siskiyou Rare Plants Nursery, 2825 Cummings Rd., Medford, Oreg.
    97501 (plants only, for alpine, rock, or woodland gardens)

Index

Abelia, 356–57
Abelia x grandiflora, 357
Abeliophyllum, 357
Abscission layers, 341
Abutilon (flowering-maple), 287, 1036–37
Acacia, 287–88, 435
Acanthopanax sieboldianus, 357–58
Accessories, garden, 131–33; books on, 1436–37
"Acclimatizing" plants, 282
Acephate, *see* Orthene
Achimenes, 501
Acidanthera, 501
Acid phosphate, 13
Acid soil, 10, 18, 36–41, 309, 907, 959; clay, 19; plants that grow well (pH 5.0 to 5.5), 37; plants that prefer pH 6.5 to 7.0, 37–38; reason for, 38–39; rock plants, 161; testing for, 45–46; vegetables, 785–86
Aconitum, 141, 630–31, 1200–1, 1367
Acorn squash, 879
Actinomyces scabies, 872, 1302
'Adams' elderberry, 957
Adder's-tongue, *see* Dogtooth-violet
Adiantum, 293
Adlumia fungosa, 452
Adobe soil, 1350, 1352, 1362
Aechmea fasciata, 1079
Aerosols, 1145–46
African-daisy, 667

African-lily, 502, 1122
African-violet, 651, 1037–42; bloom, 1038–39; books on, 1433; insects and diseases, 1040–41; leaf cutting of, 197; pest control, 1201; propagating, 1041–42; soil, 1037–38; watering, 1038
Agapanthus (African-lily), 502, 1122
Ageratum, 666–67, 677, 1201–2
Agricultural drain tiles, 18, 28, 34, 35
Ailanthus (tree-of-heaven), 326
Air-layering, 253
Air-plant (*K. pinnata*), 1117
Ajuga, 88
Akebia, 454–55
Alabama, 676, 996, 1210, 1218–19, 1220, 1299, 1323, 1343–47
Alaska, 1347
Alder buckthorn (*R. frangula*), 440
Alfalfa, 37, 56, 59
'Alfred' blackberry, 1318
Algae, 50, 131
Algerian ivy (*H. canariensis*), 1377
Alkaline soil, 10, 41–42, 959; vegetables, 41, 785
Allium, 146, 467–68, 847
Allspice tree, 288
Almond, 357, 993, 1356
Alpine (*F. vesca*), 981
Alpine plants, 161–62
Alsike clover, 38
Alstroemeria, 502, 1426
Althaea, 620

Aluminum sulfate, 11, 41, 45, 373, 535
Alyssum (*A. saxatilis*), 592; pest control, 1202; *See also* Gold alyssum; Sweet-alyssum (*L. maritima*)
Amarcrinum, 1202
Amaryllis belladonna, 502
Amaryllis formosissima, 529
Amaryllis hallii, 490
Amaryllis (*Hippeastrum*), 288, 502–3, 1122–25, 1202, 1368, 1375, 1418
Amazon-lily (*E. grandiflora*), 293, 518, 1125
American beech, 324
American Begonia Society, 463
American cranberry, *see* Cranberry-bush
American Dahlia Society (A.D.S.), 463, 518
American elm, *see* Elm
American Gloxinia and Gesneriad Society, 463
American holly (*I. opaca*), 426, 428, 1387, 1393
American hybrid lily, 483–84, 489
American Rock Garden Society, 154
American Rose Society, 531, 533, 552–53, 566, 560, 574
Amino acids, 12, 13
Ammonium sulfate, 11, 40, 72
Amorpha, 357
Amorphophallus (snake-palm, hydrosme), 503, 1132
Ampelopsis, 455–56
Amsonia tabernaemontana, 592
Amur privet, 380
Anchusa, 593
Andromeda, 37, 39, 430–31, 1263
Anemone, 175, 468, 1202–3, 1419
Anemone blanda, 468
Anemone nemorosa, 468
Anemone peony, 638–39
Angelica, 142
Angel-wing begonia, 1045
Angleworms, 1163, 1243

Animal manure, 6, 973
Anise (*P. anisum*), 142, 1034
Annuals, 82, 652–88; African-daisy, 667; ageratum, 666–67; balsam, 668; bells-of-Ireland, 669; books on, 657, 1433; browallia, 669; ca-lendula, 669–70; campanula, 670; candytuft, 670; Cape-marigold, 672; castor-bean, 670; China-aster, 667–68; city garden, 204; cleome, 670–71; coleus, 671; cornflower, 671; cosmos, 671; culture, 664–66; cuttings, 661–62; dahlia, 672; dianthus, 672; in dry, sunny areas, 228–29; everlastings, 672–73; flowering cabbage, 669; four-o'clock, 673; fragrant, 187; gloriosa daisy, 673; godetia, 673; as house plants, 1065–67; impa-tiens, 673; kochia, 674; larkspur, 674; lobelia, 674; marigold, 674–75; meaning of, 653; nasturtium, 675; nicotiana, 675; nierembergia, 675; periwinkle, 675–76; petunia, 676–79; poppy, 679–80; portulaca, 680; propagation, 655–62; rectan-gular garden plan, 661; roof gar-den, 188; salpiglossis, 680; salvia, 680–81; sandy soil, 222; scabiosa, 681; seashore, 223; in a shady lo-cation, 227; snapdragon, 681–83; soil problems, 21; sources for, 1450–51; specific plants, 666–88; stocks, 683; sweet-alyssum, 667; sweet pea, 683–86; tall and spindly, 23; tithonia, 686; transplanting, 662–64; verbena, 687; in wet soil, 230; what to grow, 653–54; wish-bone flower, 686–87; zinnia, 688; *See also* Biennials
Annual vines, 452–54; *See also* Vines
Anthemis, 16
Anthemis nobilis, 38, 143–44
Anthracnose or pod spot, 1289, 1307–8

Anthurium, 288, 1042
Antibiotic drugs, 1195
Antirrhinum, *see* Snapdragon
Ants, 813, 1294; control of, 1146
Aphids, 900, 931, 1023, 1151, 1185, 1202, 1206, 1215, 1220, 1224, 1227, 1242, 1252, 1253, 1266, 1271–72, 1284, 1291, 1292, 1319, 1320; control of, 1147
Apple, 37, 895–96, 906, 921–33, 1311, 1323, 1374, 1380–81, 1412; age to plant, 908; best and quickest-growing, 932–33; blooming date, 929; clay soil, 20; difference between budding and "grafting," 919–20; failure to bear fruit, 927–28; fertilizer, 907, 923; harvesting, 916; insects and diseases, 930–32; mulching, 926; pest control, 1312–18; premature dropping of, 928; preserving an old tree, 928–29; productive life, 915; pruning, 923–26; rootstocks, 904; seeds, 919; spur-type, 921–22; storage, 917–18; time to plant, 923; transplanting, 923; varieties of, 902; waxing, 917
Apple blotch, 932
Apple maggot, 900, 1313, 1315
Apple mint (*M. suaveolens*), 149
Apple sawfly, European, 1318
Apple scab, 932
Apricot, 933, 1318, 1429; varieties of, 902
Aralia, 357–58, 1073–74
Arbor, 131–32, 964–65
Arboretum, 175, 323, 1448–50
Arborvitae (*Thuja*), 396, 400–1, 444, 1396, 1397; pest control, 1203
Arbutus, *see* Trailing arbutus
Arbutus unedo, 1356–57
Arctotis (African-daisy), 667
Aristolochia species, 289, 459
Arizona, 1154, 1278, 1294, 1347–49
Arizona desert, cacti from, 595

Arkansas, 368, 1203, 1246, 1248, 1266, 1298, 1349–50
Armadillos, 1147
Armillaria root rot, 1147–48
Armyworms, 1148
Artichoke, 813–14
Artificial light, *see* Light
Artificial soil, 80–83
Arugula, 876
Arum, 468
Arum palaestinum, 1126
Asarum europaeum, 146
Ashes: burned leaves and grass cuttings, 63; clay soil and, 18
Asiatic beetle, 1148–49, 1274, 1275
Asparagus, 37, 814–17, 1068–69; pest control, 1285–86
Asparagus beetle, 1285
Asparagus knife, 809–10
Asparagus 'Sprengeri,' 1069
Aspidistra elatior (cast-iron plant), 1069, 1204
Assassin bugs, 1151
Aster, 16, 37, 1381, 1400; China- (*Callistephus*), 666, 667–68, 1204–5; hardy, 593
Astilbe, 289, 593
'Astrachan' apple, 927
Aubrieta, 167
Auratum lily, 484
Aurinia, 592, 1202
Australian silk-oak (*G. robusta*), 1069
Austrian briar, 558
Austrian pine, 398, 407–8
Automobile driveway, 111–13
Autumn care, house plants, 1009, 1017–18
Autumn foliage, 324; shrubs, 356
Avens, 37
Avocado, 1069–70, 1357
Avocado pit (seed), 1070
Azalea, 37, 39, 40, 44, 45, 46, 53, 289, 358–60, 416, 417, 421–22, 1010, 1015, 1083–84, 1343, 1357, 1381, 1400–1, 1402, 1406, 1428;

Azalea (*cont'd*)
  acidity for, 11; books on, 1441; in
  foundation plantings, 217; as a gift
  plant, 1083–84; pest control,
  1205–7; *See also* Rhododendron
Azalea flower-spot disease, 1205

Babiana, 503, 529
Baby's-breath, 16, 37, 594
Baby's-tears (*S. soleirolii*), 1070
Bachelor-button, 671
Bacillus popillia (milky disease),
  1145, 1149
Bacillus thuringiensis, 871–72, 1145,
  1149, 1152
Backyard garden, 767–68
Bacteria, 3, 4, 58
Bacterial (or Stewart's) **wilt,** 1297
Badminton court, 128
Bagasse (sugarcane pulp), 53
Bagworms, 1150, 1231, 1247, 1264
Bahia grass, 700, 1373
Balance, garden, 93
'Baldwin' apple, 1316
Balloon flower (*Platycodon*), 644
Balm, *see* Lemon-balm
Balsam, 37, 402, 668
Bamboo, 1070–71
Banana, 1357
Banks: northeast exposure, 219; plan-
  ning and landscaping, 104–5;
  plants for, 224–25; seashore, 224
Banvel D (Dicamba), 1334
Barberry (*Berberis*), 309, 313, 344,
  360–61
Bark borers, 1227–28
Bark grafting, 263, 919
Bark (tree), 53; interesting types of,
  323; patterns, 307; rabbit destruc-
  tion, 1187, 1312; vandalism attack,
  328
Barley, 37
Barnyard manure, 68
Barrels for growing plants, 208
'Bartlett' pear, 940, 941

Basal rot, 488
Basement, raising vegetables in, 811
Basil (*Ocimum*), 143, 1034
Basket-of-gold (*Aurinia*), 592, 1202
Bathtub water, 210–11
Bayberry (*Myrica*), 361, 1386
Bay tree, 435, 1071
Bean beetle, *see* Mexican bean beetle
Beans, 37, 58, 766–67, 770, 785,
  804–5, 808, 818–24; broad or
  Windsor (*V. faba*), 818, 823; bush,
  753, 754, 818–20; castor-, 670;
  'Kentucky Wonder,' 819, 1288;
  kidney, 819; lima, 819, 820–22,
  1287; mung, 823–24; pest control,
  1286–90; pole, 753, 818–20, 1289;
  snap, 819, 1286–87, 1289–90; soy,
  37, 56, 57, 59, 805, 819, 822–23,
  1187; stringless, 820
Bean sprouts, how to grow, 824
Bean weevil, 1288
Bearberry (*A. uva-ursi*), 361
Bearded iris, 622–26, 627; "dwarf,"
  "lilliput," and "intermediate," 629
Beaucarnea (bottle-palm), 1071
Beaucarnea recurvata, 1071
Beauty-bush (*K. amabilis*), 317,
  361–62
Bechtel crab apple, 342, 1219
Beech, 1428
Beech grove, growing wildflowers in,
  171
Beech leaves, 67
'Beefsteak' tomato, 889
Bees, 968
Beet, 37, 49, 50, 753, 754, 777, 783,
  785, 807, 824–25, 1290
Beetles, *see* names of beetles
Beggar weed, 37
Begonia, 289, 1018, 1042–48, 1353;
  Angel-wing, 1045; best for the
  house, 1047; books on, 1433–34;
  care of, 1043–44, 1046; Christmas,
  1044–45, 1046, 1048; cuttings and
  propagation, 1046; Lorraine, 1208;

Begonia (*cont'd*)
pest control, 1207–8; soil, 1042–43; transplanting, 1047; tuberous-rooted, 503–5; wax, 659, 1045, 1046

Begonia grandis, 1046, 1048

Begonia sutherlandii, 1046

Belamcanda chinensis, 469

Bells-of-Ireland, 669

Bench (metal, wood, or cement), 132

Benlate (Benomyl), 1138, 1144, 1150–52

Bent grass, 37, 700, 1428; colonial, 703, 723; creeping, 703

Benzoin (spice-bush), 362, 1384

Bergamot, 666

Bermuda grass, 700, 1333, 1344–45, 1373, 1390, 1413–14, 1421

Bermuda onion, 859

Bibb lettuce, 854

Biennials, 688–94; best garden use of, 689; bloom, 689; Canterbury-bells, 690–91; foxglove, 691; as house plants, 1065–67; pansy, 691–93; rose campion, 694; specific plants, 690–94; Sweet William, 693–94; wallflower, 694; when to sow, 688–89; *See also* Annuals

Bigleaf maple (*A. macrophyllum*), 333

Bigtooth maple (*A. grandidentatum*), 333

Billbergia zebrina, 1079

Bindweed, 1333

'Bing' sweet cherry, 935

Biological control, 1144, 1149, 1152

Birch, 97, 307, 326–28, 1384, 1426; pest control, 1208; weeping, 327, 1208; white, 37, 327, 328, 1208; wildflowers among, 171

Bird bath, 131

Birdfoot violet (*V. pedata*), 650

Bird houses, gourds suitable for, 847

Bird-of-paradise (*Strelitzia*), 297, 1064–65, 1357

Birds, 325, 936, 952, 968, 990; books on, 1434; dust baths, 660; gardens to attract, 184; keeping away, 1152, 1328–29; shrubs to attract, 184, 355

'Bitter Blue' St. Augustine, 1373

Bitter rot, 1317

Bittersweet (*Celastrus*), 456–57, 1208

Black beetle, 1205

Blackberry, 37, 984–86, 1318, 1357, 1368; pruning, 988; varieties of, 903

Blackberry-lily (*B. chinensis*), 469

Blackberry vine (weed), 1333

Black-calla, 1126

Black flea beetle, 1292

Black gumbo soil, 21–22

Black Hills spruce, 1277

Black Leaf 40, *see* Nicotine sulfate

Black-lily-of-the-Nile (*A. palaestinum*), 1126

Black locust (*R. pseudoacacia*), 352

Black locusts, 1252

Black oak, 337

Black plastic, as a mulch, 804

Black raspberry, 987, 991, 1388

Black rose, 558

Black rot disease, 968, 1226, 1304, 1320

Black spot, 1226, 1267–68, 1269, 1282

'Black Tartarian' cherry, 935

Black tupelo, *see* Sour gum

Black walnut, 996–97; fruit trees and, 906–7

Bleedingheart (*D. spectabilis*), 293, 594, 1419, 1431

Blight, 1256, 1260, 1267, 1289, 1290, 1295, 1306, 1317, 1404

Blister beetle (potato bug), 871, 1152–53, 1217, 1302–3

Blood-lily, 526, 1131–32

Bloodroot (*S. canadensis*), 170, 171, 176
Blooms: in a cold frame, 267; pinching to force, 242; rose, 561; shrubs, 102, 355–56
Blossom-end rot, 1306
Bluebeard (*Caryopteris*), 364
Blueberry, 37, 39, 362, 898, 948–53, 1318, 1358, 1381, 1386; bird protection, 952; cuttings, 950; difference between huckleberries and, 953; fertilizer, 949–50; leafmold soil mixture, 40–41; mulching, 952; soil, 948–49; soil test conditions and, 46; varieties of, 903, 953
Blue clay soil, 19
Blue-flowering hydrangea, 37, 373
Bluegrass, *see* Kentucky bluegrass; Rough bluegrass
Blue pansy, 693
Blue rose, 558
Blue scilla, 491
'Blue Spires' veronica, 650
Blue spruce, 410, 411, 1277–78
Bluestar (*A. tabernaemontana*), 592
Bluestone path, 114
Bluet (*Houstonia*), 177
Board-on-board fence, 110
Bog: humus from, 51–52; peat from, 1371
Bog garden, 172–73, 181
Bog orchid, 173
Bokhara, 37
Bone meal, 13, 66, 544
Bonsai, 85, 185, 1033, 1034; books on, 1440–41
Books, 1433–44
Borage (*B. officinalis*), 143
Bordeaux mixture, 1137, 1143, 1153–54, 1226, 1233
Borders: annuals, 654; with bricks, 687; control of, 1154; herb planting, 136–37; perennial, 577, 579, 581, 582; rose, 559; spray schedule for, 1194; sweet pea, 684;

vegetables and flower beds, 768
Borers, 628, 931, 1223, 1245, 1254, 1258, 1278, 1316; *See also* types of borers
Boron, 50
Boston daisy (*C. frutescens*), 1060
Boston fern, 293, 1099, 1100, 1233
Boston-ivy, 1103
Botanical gardens, list of, 1448–50
Botany, books on, 1434
Botrytis blight, 488, 1280, 1299
Bottle gardens, 1031
Bottle or closed gentian (*G. andrewsii*), 179
Bottle-palm (*B. recurvata*), 1071
Bottom heat, 792
Bougainvillea, 289–90, 1027
Bouquet tulip, 499–500
Bouvardia, 289
Bowiea volubilis (climbing-onion), 1126
Box barberry (*B. thunbergii* 'Minor'), 360
Box-elder, 333, 1154
Boxes for plants, 188; vegetables in, 812
Boxwood, 422–23, 444, 1209, 1358, 1404, 1418
Boxwood canker, 1209
Boysenberry, 986–87, 1327–28, 1358, 1366, 1426
Bracted plantain, 742
'Bradford' pear, 350
Brambles, *see* Cane fruit
Breadfruit plant, 294
Brick drain, killing weeds in, 1332
Bricks, 687
Brick walk, 114–15
Brick wall vines (in the city), 206
Bridalwreath (*S. prunifolia*), 312, 383
Bridge grafting, 263
Briquette ashes, 36
Broad-leaf weed, 743

Broad-leaved evergreens, 414–35; azalea, 421–22; boxwood, 422–23; camellia, 424; culture, 414–19; daphne, 424–25; elaeagnus, 425; euonymus (wintercreeper), 425–26; holly, 426–29; leucothoe, 429; magnolia, 429; mahonia, 429; mountain-laurel, 430; pieris, 430–31; propagation, 420–21; pyracantha, 431–32; rhododendron, 432–33; skimmia, 434; specific kinds of, 421–35; viburnum, 434–35; winter protection, 419–20·

Broad-leaved plantain, 742, 1334, 1337

Broad or Windsor bean, 818, 823

Broad-spectrum insecticides, 1157

Broccoli, 38, 753, 771, 825–26, 1291

Broccoli raab, 826–27

Brodiaea (*Triteleia* and *Dichelostemma*), 469

Brome grass, 38

Bromeliads, 1048–49; books on, 1434

Broom (*Cytisus*), 363

Browallia, 669, 1065–66; pest control, 1209–10; for window gardens, 1066

Brown canker, 1270

Brown rose, 559

Brown rot, 900, 944, 1326

Brown scale, 1024, 1237, 1242

Brown soil, 26

Brussels sprouts, 37, 827, 1291

Buckeye, *see* Horse-chestnut

Buckhorn plantain, *see* Narrow-leaf plantain

Buckthorn (*R. cathartica*), 440, 1334

Buckwheat, 37, 56, 57

Budding, 262–63, 919–20; rose, 553

Buddleia, 290, 363–64, 1418

Buddleia asiatica, 290

Buddleia farquharii, 290

Bud stick, 262

Bugs, defined, 1154; *See also* Insects; Pest control; names of bugs

Bulbs, 462–529; books on, 1434; city garden, 204; in a cold frame, 267; culture, 464–67; fragrant garden, 187; greenhouse, 290; hardy bulbs, 464–500; hardy (for forcing), 1118; hardy (spring-flowering), 1119–21; pest control, 1210; phosphorus use, 13; propagating, 248–50; rest period in pots before replanting, 500–1; rock garden, 165–66; rodents and, 467; sources for, 1451; South African, 529; specific hardy bulbs, 467–500; tender, for indoors, 1122–36; tender types of, 500–29; what to grow, 464

Burford holly, 428

Burlap, 550

Burning bush (*Chaenomeles*), 381

Bush bean, 753, 754, 818–20

Bush rose, 1270

Bush squash, 753

'Buttercup' squash, 879

Butterflies, difference between moths and, 1181

Butterfly-bush, *see* Buddleia

Butterfly-weed (*A. tuberosa*), 177

Butternut, 993

Buttonball, *see* Sycamore

Cabbage, 37, 669, 753, 754, 781, 790, 806, 808, 828–30, 1291–93

Cabbage looper, 1151

Cabbage moth, 1259

Cabbage rose (*R. centifolia*), 559

Cabbage worm, 1292

Cabin, 100

'Caco' grapevine, 959, 964

Cacti, 594–95; Arizona desert, 595; books on, 1434–35; Christmas, 292, 1112–14, 1210–11; culture (indoors), 1109–11; difference between succulents and, 1115; Easter, 1112–14; for indoors, 1108–14; jungle, 1111–12; night-blooming, 1111–12; orchid, 1111–12; peanut,

Cacti (*cont'd*)
1110; pest control, 1210–11;
prickly-pear, 1210; soil (indoors),
1108–9; spineless, 595; Thanksgiving, 292, 1112–14
Cactus scab, 1210
Caladium, 505, 1126–27, 1211,
1368, 1375
Caladium esculentum, 506
Calanthe orchid, 294–95
Calceolaria, 290, 291, 1049
Calcium carbonate, 42, 72
Calcium cyanamide, 43
Calcium sulfate (gypsum), 18, 43,
728
Calendula, 82, 149–50, 291, 669–70,
1211, 1245, 1285
California, 366, 445, 528, 529, 823–
24, 828, 835, 871, 875, 933, 937,
959, 969, 1021, 1090, 1147–48,
1149, 1160, 1166, 1170, 1172,
1177, 1181, 1183, 1188, 1190,
1204, 1205–6, 1213, 1223, 1224,
1225–26, 1234, 1235–36, 1251,
1266, 1267, 1270, 1271, 1278,
1279, 1284, 1287, 1288, 1289–90,
1292, 1325, 1350–66
California-poppy (*E. Californica*),
16, 679
California privet hedge, 1421
Calla-lily (*Zantedeschia*), 1044,
1048, 1127, 1207, 1211, 1358,
1368, 1391–92
Calliopsis, 16
Calochortus, 469
Calomel treatment, 1292
Calyx rose, 1269
Camassia, 469–70
Cambium layer, 194
Camellia, 37, 424, 435–37, 1343,
1408, 1415; as indoor house plant,
1091–92; pest control, 1212
Camellia japonica, 1409
Camomile (*A. nobilis*), 38, 143–44
Campanula, *see* Canterbury-bells

Campanula isophylla (Ligurian
harebell), 1049–50
Canada, 994
Canada thistle, 1334
Canadian hemlock hedge, 441
Candytuft (*Iberis*), 38, 595, 670,
1212
Cane (or bramble) fruits, 982–91;
fertilizer, 982
Cankerworms, 1155, 1164
Canna, 505–6, 1172
Cannel-coal ashes, 36
Cantaloupe, 855–57, 1299–1300
Canterbury-bells (*Campanula*), 670,
690–91, 1212, 1396, 1418, 1428
Cape Cod house, 98, 214
Cape-cowslip, 527, 529
Cape-jasmine, 437, 1375, 1418
Cape-marigold (*Dimorphotheca*),
672
Capillary mats, 281
Captan (fungicide), 79, 1155
Caragana (pea-shrub), 445
Caraway (*C. carvi*), 140, 144
Caraway thyme (*T. herba-barona*),
153
Carbaryl (Sevin), 1138–39, 1155
Cardinal-flower (*L. cardinalis*),
170, 173, 177
Carnation (*Dianthus*), 38, 69, 82,
167, 291, 595–97, 672, 1213,
1340, 1383
Carolina rhododendron, 433
Carpathian walnut, 1388
Carrot, 37, 753, 754, 777, 783, 785,
807, 830–32, 1294–95, 1331–32;
wild, 1338–39
Carson, Rachel, 1137
Caryopteris (Bluebeard), 364
Cascade chrysanthemum, 608
Cast-iron plant, 1069, 1204
Castor-bean, 670
Catalog descriptions, 211–12
Catalpa, 328–29

Caterpillars, 932, 1196–97, 1206–7, 1308, 1329; gypsy moth, 1167–69
Cat manure, 54
Cats: insecticide spraying and, 1174; keeping away from garden, 1155–56
Cattails and rushes, 1334
Cattleya orchid, 295
Cauliflower, 38, 753, 754, 781, 832–33, 1293, 1295
Cedar, 30, 37, 401, 406; deodar, 1358
Cedar, red-, see Juniper; Red cedar
Cedar-of-Lebanon (C. libani), 401
Celastrus, 456–57, 1208
Celeriac, 833
Celery, 38, 754, 781, 795, 807, 833–36, 1295
Celery blight, 836
Cellar: growing mushrooms in, 854; raising vegetables in, 811
Centaurea, 660, 671
Centaurea moschata (sweet sultan), 1372
Centipede grass, 700, 1344–45, 1370, 1373–74
Centipedes, 1156
Ceratostigma plumbaginoides, 644–45
Ceriman (M. deliciosa), 294
Certified seed potatoes, 869
Chamaedorea elegans, 1076–77
Charcoal, 70
Chard, 38, 753
Chaste-tree, 364–65
Chayote, 836–37
Cheesecloth, 916
Chemical fertilizer, 71–72
Cherianthus cheiri, 694
Cherimoya, 1365
Cherry, 38, 341, 933–36, 1190, 1311, 1319, 1389, 1429; age to plant, 908; clay soil and, 20; fertilizer, 933–34; ground cover around, 221; harvesting, 916; imperfect bloom,

935–36; insects and diseases, 936; productive life, 915; pruning, 934; rootstocks, 904, 934; seeds, 919; varieties of, 902; See also Sour cherry; Sweet cherry
Cherry-laurel (P. laurocerasus), 446
Cherry plum, 944, 1396
Cherry tomato, 889–90
Chervil (A. cerefolium), 144
Chestnut, 994
Chicken manure, 68, 536
Chicken wire, 751–52
Chickweed, 1336
Chicory, 38, 837–38
Children's gardens, 183–84
Chimney soot, 71
China-aster (Callistephus), 666, 667–68, 1204–5
Chinch bugs, 746–47, 1156, 1249, 1373
Chinese cabbage, 753, 754, 807, 838–39
Chinese chestnut, 994
Chinese corktree, 329
Chinese elm, 1228, 1404–5
Chinese-evergreen (A. modestum), 1020, 1072
Chinese hibiscus, 173, 1095–96, 1240, 1393, 1422
Chinese jujube (or date), 969–70
Chinese-lantern (P. alkekengi), 1213–14
Chinese primrose (P. sinensis), 293, 1063
Chinese scholar tree, 338
Chinese witch-hazel (H. mollis), 389
Chionodoxa, 470
Chipmunks, 1157, 1195
Chives, garlic (A. tuberosum), 847
Chives (A. schoenoprasum), 144, 839
Chlorine, 50
Chlorophyll, 47
Chloropicrin (larvacide), 79–80, 1184

Chlorosis, 378, 1251, 1329
Chlorothalonil, 1157
Chlorpyrifos (Dursbar), 1144
Christmas begonia, 1044–45, 1046, 1048
Christmas cactus, 292, 1112–14, 1210–11
Christmas pepper, 1089
Christmas-rose (*H. niger*), 597–98
Christmas trees, 402–3, 412, 1401
Chrysanthemum, 38, 82, 291–92, 599–608, 1084–85, 1344, 1348–49, 1358, 1391, 1392, 1401, 1428; bloom, 602, 605, 607–8; books on, 1435; as corsages, 608; as a gift plant, 1084–85; pest control, 1214–17; planting, 600; pruning and disbudding, 603–4; seeds, 607; soil, 599–600; transplanting, 600
Chrysanthemum balsamita, 145
Chrysanthemum coccineum (pyrethrum), 647, 1186
Chrysanthemum x superbum (shasta daisy), 648, 1217, 1401, 1420
Cinder bed, 114
Cinders, 17, 18, 26, 35–36, 69
Cineraria (Senecio x hybridus), 37, 292–93, 1050; culture for, 292
Cinquefoil, 167
Citrus fruit: frenching and bronzing of, 1368; as house plants, 1092–93; pest control, 1217; *See also* Fruits and fruit trees; names of trees
City gardens: annuals, 204; backyard, 203, 767–68; best plane tree for, 339; books on, 1435; bulbs, 204; community gardens, 771–72; compost in plastic bags, 64; concrete containers, 185, 186; dog problems, 207; environment problems, 203–7; evergreens, 204–5; ground covers, 205; hedges, 440–41; humus, 206–7; indoor plants requiring little or no sunshine, 1028; keeping soil in good condition, 24; lawns, 205; organics and nitrogen, 57; perennials, 204; rock garden, 205; on the roof, 187–89; rooftop vegetables, 812; shade, 204; small or mini-gardens for small properties, 208–13; trees, 205–6; vegetable storage, 808; vines, 206; window-box, 190–91, 1027–30; *See also* Gardens; Herb gardens; House plants
Clapboard fence, 107
Clary (*S. sclarea*), 144
Clay pots, 1012
Clay soil, 17–20; dry, acid, and heavy, 40; hillside, 23; vegetable garden treatment, 775–76
Cleatis x jackmanii, 1217
Cleft grafting, 263–64
Clematis, 457–59, 1217, 1395
Cleome, 670–71
Climate, importance of, 195
Climbing fern (*L. palmatum*), 178–79
Climbing minis, 568
Climbing nasturtium, 454
Climbing-onion (*B. volubilis*), 1126
Climbing rose, 296, 550, 560, 1269, 1270, 1271, 1349, 1378, 1384, 1398, 1408, 1425, 1430, 1431; large flowered, 532; rambler type, 542; support for, 571
Clippings, grass, 62, 725, 1389
Clivia, 506, 1127
Cloning by tissue culture, 257–58
Clothes drying, 130–31
Clover, 38, 57, 58
Club moss, 180
Clubroot, 1293
Coal ash, 17, 35–36, 783; purpose of, 21
Coal gas, 1021
Cockscomb, 16
Coco-grass, 1349–50, 1421

Codling moth, 900, 942, 1152, 1313, 1315

Cod-liver oil, 82

Coffee grounds, 70

Coiled rose worm, 1274–75

Colchicum, 465, 470

Cold, from windows, 1021

Cold frames, 264–68, 682; advantages of, 265; best way to use, 266–67; difference between a hotbed and, 268; how to make, 251, 264–65; indoor vegetable sowing, 791–92, 793; self-ventilating, 659–60; vegetables, 811–12

Coleus, 662, 671, 1018, 1072, 1218, 1353

Collard, 38, 1295

Colocasia (elephant's ear), 506–7

Colocasia esculenta (dasheen), 845

Colonial bent grass, 703, 723

Colonial house, 100

Colorado, 1225, 1261, 1262, 1366–68

Colorado blue spruce, 411–12

Colorado potato beetle, see Potato bug

Columbine (*Aquilegia*), 38, 170, 178, 608–9, 1218–19, 1369, 1419

Columbine borer, 1219

Columnar Japanese cherry, 341

Columnberry barberry, 360

'Comice' pear, 942

Commercial fertilizer, 74–77

Community garden, 771–72

Competition (for food, light, and air), 195

"Complete plant food," 778

Compost and composting, 4–8, 53, 59–62, 75; building, 60; diseases, 65; garbage, 61–62; grass clippings, 62, 725, 1389; hickory hulls, 62; leaves, 5–6, 63; materials, 4–7; pests and diseases, 65; special problems, 63–64; techniques of, 7–8;

treating to combat insects and diseases, 1157

Compressed-air sprayer (knapsack type), 1310

'Concord' grape, 899, 960–61, 962, 968

Conditioning, soil, 21

Cones, rose, 549–50

Coniferous, defined, 389

Connecticut, 362, 384, 422, 669, 677, 923, 1021, 1149, 1173, 1177, 1195, 1200, 1203, 1209, 1240, 1245, 1252, 1258, 1272, 1279, 1300, 1301, 1302, 1305, 1306, 1317–18, 1319, 1324

Conservation laws, wildflowers and, 175

Contact insecticides, 1157, 1170

Container gardening, 185–87; books on, 1435

Containers: for mini-garden, 208; pebbles or broken pots in bottom of, 208; quickest drying out, 213; soil for, 210; vegetable transplants, 212

Convallaria majalis (lily-of-the-valley), 470–71, 1119, 1337, 1362, 1416

Cooking gas, 1021

Copper, 50

Coriander (*C. sativum*), 144–45, 1034

Corktree (*Phellodendron*), 329

Corms: propagating, 248–50; tender, 500–29; See also Bulbs; Tubers

Corn, 16, 37, 753, 759, 766–67, 781, 839–42, 1295–97; See also Sweet corn

Corn borer moth, 516, 1295–96; European, 1223

Corn-ear worm, 841

Cornelian cherry (*C. mas*), 88, 367

Cornell Mix, 80

Cornflower (*Centaurea*), 660, 671

Corn smut, 841–42

Corsages, 608

Cosmos, 38, 660, 671, 1219, 1245, 1366

Costmary (*C. balsamita*), 145

Cotoneaster, 365, 1360

Cotton, 38

Cotton or Phymatotrichum root rot, 1198

Cottonseed meal, 13, 52, 57, 66, 72, 544

Cottony cushion scale, 1189

Cow manure, 54, 55, 1269; substitute for, 57

Cowpea, 37, 56

Crab apple, 87, 341–42, 914; flowering, 313, 341–42; pest control, 1219–20; varieties of, 902

Crab-claw or claw cacti, *see* Thanksgiving cactus

Crabgrass, 708, 742, 1335, 1340; prevention, 743

Crab meal, 69–71

Cranberry-bush (*V. trilobum*), 386, 953–54

Cranberry (*V. macrocarpum*), 37, 953–54

Crape-myrtle (*Lagerstroemia*), 309, 357, 365–66, 1093–94, 1344, 1381, 1391; pest control, 1220–21

Crassula (Jade plant), 1115–16

Crawfish, 1158

Creeping bent grass, 703

Creeping bluet (*H. serpyllifolia*), 177

Creeping cranberry, *see* Cranberry

Creeping fig (*F. pumila*), 1103

Creeping Jenny (*L. nummularia*), 178, 1335

Creeping veronica (*V. filiformis*), 1341

Creeping wintergreen (*G. procumbens*), 183

Cress, 753, 754, 842–43

Crimson clover, 37, 56, 59

Crinum, 502, 1127–28

Crocosmia, 529

Crocus, 165, 465, 471–72, 1221, 1392–93; rodents and, 467

Crookneck squash, 1305

Crops in rotation, 763–64

Croquet lawn, 129

Cross-pollination, 914, 939, 967, 1365

Crotalaria, 56

Croton (*Codiaeum*), 1072

Crown gall, 1158, 1216, 1328

Crown imperial (*F. imperialis*), 480

Crown-of-thorns (*Euphorbia*), 1116–17

Crown rot, 617, 1158, 1218–19, 1225, 1259–60, 1304

Crown vetch, 23

Crows, 841

Cryptanthus cultivars, 1079

Cryptanthus (earth star), 1072–73

Cryptomeria, 401

Cucumber, 37, 753, 754, 843–45, 1297–99

Cucumber beetle, *see* Striped cucumber beetle

Cucumber tree (*M. acuminata*), 347, 348

Cultivation, 33–34, 231; benefits of, 199–200; vegetable, 800

Culture, 664–66; annuals, 664–66; broad-leaved evergreens, 414–19; bulbs, 464–67; cacti (indoors), 1109–11; disbudding and pinching, 242–43; ferns (indoor), 1097–1101; hardy bulbs, 464–67; herb, 138–39; house plants, 1010–17; mulches, 33, 231–37; narrow-leaved evergreen, 392–93; ornamentals, 230–45; perennials, 582–89; pruning, 201–2, 239–42; rock garden, 157–58; root-pruning, 243; rose, 534–52; supports, 202–3, 243–45; vines, 449–52; *See also* Water and watering

Cup-and-saucer vine (*C. scandens*), 453

Curb, ground cover between sidewalk and, 219–20

Curculio, 1314, 1326

Curing herbs, 139–40

Curly cress, 842–43

Curly leaf, 1356

Currant, 38, 898, 954–57, 1319–20, 1396; varieties of, 903

Cushion chrysanthemum, 600, 601, 602, 603, 605

Cut-leaf birch, 1208, 1426

Cuttings, 250–57; annuals, 661–62; leaf, 197, 256–57; narrow-leaved evergreens, 399–400; ornamentals, 250–56, 257; perennials, 590–91; propagating by, 196, 197, 250–57; root, 250, 254, 256–57; rose, 554–56

Cutworms, 36, 525, 1158–59, 1257, 1300, 1308

Cyclamen (*C. persicum*), 37, 1085–86, 1221

Cyclamen mite, 1221, 1227

Cypress, 445, 1360

Cypripedium acaule, 181

Cypripedium calceolus pubescens, 181

Cypripedium candidum, 181

Cypripedium montanum, 181

Cypripedium reginae, 41, 180–81

Daffodil, 37, 165, 204, 466–67, 472–79, 1121, 1376, 1411, 1415; best time to plant, 473–74; difference between narcissus and, 477; division or classification of, 477–78; fertilizer, 473; moisture requirements, 474–75; pests and diseases, 476–77; seeds, 476; soil, 472; with tulips, 474; won't bloom, 475

Dahlia, 38, 507–18, 672, 1369, 1376, 1406–7, 1418–20, 1426; bloom, 510, 511, 513, 514; catalog listing, 509, 518; clump division, 515, 516; diseases and pests, 516–17; easiest to grow, 518; fertilizer, 508; lack of bloom, 513; miniature, 1223; pest control, 1221–24; planting, 508, 509, 510; pruning, 510; seeds, 514; soil, 508; storage, 511–12

Dahlia "stunt," 1222

Daisy, 1379; African, 667; Boston (*C. frutescens*), 1060; gloriosa, 673; Marguerite (*C. frutescens*), 1060; Michaelmas, 593; shasta (Chrysanthemum x superbum), 648, 1217, 1401, 1420; *See also* Gerbera

Damask rose (*R. damascena*), 560–61

Damping off, 1027, 1159–60

Damson plum, varieties of, 902

Dandelion, 742, 743, 796, 845, 1335, 1340; soil test conditions and, 46

Daphne, 366, 424–25, 1224

Daphne cneorum (Rose daphne), 424, 425, 1413, 1428

Daphne mezereum, 366

Daphne odora, 425

Dasheen (*C. esculenta*), 845

Date, 969–70

Date palm, 1076–77

Davallia, 293

Day-lily (*Hemerocallis*), 609–11, 1344; perennials with, 577–78; varieties of, 611

D-D (soil fumigant), 1184

DDT, 1137, 1160, 1274

Deciduous trees and shrubs, 306–41; care of, 314–16; general information, 306; killing tree roots, 319–21; propagation, 321–23; pruning, 316–18; soil and fertilizers, 306–9; transplanting, 309–14; winter protection, 318–19

Decorating, house plant, 1027–30

Deer, 467

Delaware, 452, 619, 1209, 1212, 1293

Delphinium, 38, 69, 141, 588, 611–18, 1349, 1383, 1385, 1401, 1413;

Delphinium (*cont'd*)
 colors, 617–18; fertilizer, 613; pest
 control, 1224–27; planting, 613;
 seedlings, 614, 615, 616–17; soil,
 612
Delphinium cardinale, 615
Deodar cedar, 1358
Depleted soil, 22
Derris, 1160
Desire's-hair, 1335
Deutzia, 312, 366, 1417
Devil grass, 1354
Dewberry, 37
Diabrotica beetles, 1160, 1216
Dianthus, *see* Carnation
Diazinon (Spectracide, Gardentox),
 1144, 1304
Dibble (planting gadget), 851
Dichelostemma, 469
Dichondra, 715, 1353
Dicofol (Kelthane), 1144, 1161
Dicotyledonous (broad-leaf) pests,
 707–8
Dieffenbachia (dumb-cane), 1073
Digging soil, 31–32
Digitalis, *see* Foxglove
Dill (*A. graveolens*), 145
Dimethoate (Cygon, De-fends),
 1144, 1161
Dimorphotheca (Cape-marigold),
 672
Dioecious flowers, 194
Diospyros virginiana, 971
Dipper-type gourd, 847–48
Disbudding, 242–43
Diseases: books on, 1440; compost
 heap, 65; fruits, 900; greenhouse,
 285–87; house plants, 1023–24;
 how to diagnose, 1140; lawn, 744–
 46; *See also* Pest control; names of
 diseases
Dish gardens, 1033–34
Dish water, 210–11
Dittany of Crete (*O. dictamnus*), 145
Division, perennials, 591

Dizygotheca (False-aralia), 1073
Dock weed, 1335
Doctrine of Signatures, 140
Dodder, 1215, 1335
Dog manure, 54
Dogs, 1248–49; keeping away, 207,
 1161, 1231
Dogtooth-violet, 176, 479–80
Dogwood, 45, 87, 325, 342–45, 367,
 1227–28, 1376, 1387, 1396, 1420
'Dolgo' crab apple, 342, 926
Dolomitic limestone, 43
Doorway, 99–100
Dormant, defined, 239
Dormant spraying, 1161–62
'Dorothy Perkins' rose, 1269–70
Double daffodil, 478
Double day-lily, 611
Double grafting, 260
Double peony, 638–39
Double red hibiscus, 1416
Doubling of flowers, 24
Douglas-fir, 324, 398, 1234
Dracaena marginata, 1029
Drainage: flower pots, 1015; soil, 23,
 34–35; surface, 105–6; vegetable
 garden, 751
Dried blood, 13, 66–67, 72, 780
Dried manure, 55
Drill, defined, 795
Driveways, planning and landscaping,
 111–13
Dry, sunny areas, plants for, 228–29
Dry well, 105
'Duchess' pear, 941
Dumb-cane (Dieffenbachia), 1073
Dursban, 1162
Duster (garden), 1162
Dusting, 1162–63
Dust mulch, 231
Dutch elm disease, 101, 329, 1229–
 30
Dutch iris, 621, 624, 1422
Dutchman's breeches (*D. cucullaria*),
 171, 178

Dutchman's-pipe (*A. macrophylla*), 459

Dwarf Alberta spruce, 392

Dwarf apple, 930, 945; rootstocks, 904

Dwarf citrus, 1217

Dwarf conifers, 391

Dwarf daphne, 425

Dwarf dianthus, 597

Dwarf fruit trees, 895–97, 922–23; 944–48; care of, 944; fertilizer, 946; in pots, 947; pruning, 945

Dwarf Japanese yew, 421

Dwarf lemon, 1093, 1217

Dwarf lime, 1359

Dwarf nectarine, 922–23

Dwarf needle evergreen, 89

Dwarf orange, 1217

Dwarf palm, 1076–77

Dwarf pea, 803

Dwarf peach, 922–23

Dwarf pear, 940, 1325

Dwarf phlox, 643

Dwarf pomegranate, 1363

Dwarf red maple, 1254

Dwarf shrubs, 353–54

Dwarf vegetables, 210

Dwarf yew, 412

Early cabbage, 754

Early (Klondyke) cosmos, 671

'Early Rose' potato, 872–73

Earth mounds (on the lawn), 727

Earth star (*Cryptanthus*), 1072–73

Earthworms, 24, 727, 1163

Earwigs, 516, 1163, 1224

Easter cactus, 1112–14

Easter lily (*L. longiflorum*), 485, 489

Eaves, 215

Echeveria, 1117

Eelworms, *see* Nematodes

Eggplant, 38, 753, 795, 845–46, 1299

Eggshells, 70

Egyptian tree (*A. cepa proliferum*), 860

8–5–3 fertilizer, 75

8–6–6 fertilizer, 859

Elaeagnus, 383, 425

'Elberta' peach, 938

Elderberry, 957

Elephant-foot (*B. recurvata*), 1071

Elephant's-ear (*Colocasia*), 506–7

Elm, 38, 67, 87, 329; ground cover around, 221; pest control, 1128–30; *See also* Chinese elm; Dutch elm disease; Siberian elm

Elm scurfy scale, 1229

Endive, 37, 807, 846

Endymion, 478

English bluebell, 478

English border carnation, 595–96

English hawthorn, 346, 1239

English holly, 427, 428, 1361–62

English iris, 624

English ivy (*H. helix*), 1103–4, 1246–47; for low cover, 221–22

English-type home, 99

English walnut, 998–99, 1282–83, 1386

Enkianthus campanulatus, 368

Entrances, planning, 96–100

Environment, 203–13; city conditions, 203–7; house plants, 1020–22; importance of, 194–96; small or mini-gardens (for small properties), 208–13

Environmental Protection Agency (EPA), 1137, 1138

Epsom salts, 56, 80

Eranthis (winter-aconite), 479

Eremurus (foxtail-lily), 38, 479, 618–19

Ericaceous, defined, 414

Eroded soil, 22–23

Erythronium, 479–80

Escarole, 846

Espalier plant forms, 110–11; fruit trees, 944–48, 1384; pruning, 111; supports, 244

Eucalyptus, 1351, 1352–53

Eucharis (Amazon-lily), 293, 518, 1125

Euonymus scale, 1230

Euonymus (wintercreeper), 224–25, 425–26, 330, 368, 459, 1230–31

Eupatorium (hardy-ageratum), 619

Euphorbia, 649, 1116–17

Euphorbia pulcherrima (poinsettia), 1089–90, 1265, 1350

Evergreen-bittersweet, see Winter-creeper

Evergreens: to attract birds, 184; books on, 1435; broad-leaved, 414–35; in the city, 204–5; dwarf needle, 89; foundation area, 214, 215, 216, 218; low-growing, 391–92; narrow-leaved, 389–413; pest control, 1231–32; rock garden, 166; seashore, 223–24

Everlastings (annuals for drying), 672–73

Exclusion, pest control by, 1142

Exposure, house plants, 1019–20

Fairy rose, 567

Fallowing, purpose of, 34

Fall season: applying fertilizers in, 77–78; limestone, 44; plowing, 31

Fall webworms, 1164

False-aralia (Dizygotheca), 1073

False-cypress (Chamaecyparis), 402

Fatsia japonica, 1073–74

Featherock, 156

Feathery stevia, 296–97

Federal Environmental Pest Control Act, 1138

Federal Insecticide Fungicide and Rodenticide Act (FIFRA), 1137, 1138

Feeding house plants, 1013–14; See also Fertilizer

Fence posts, creosote-treated, 811

Fences: crops on a wire fence, 211; planning and landscaping, 106–10

Fennel (F. vulgare), 145–46, 847

Ferbam, 1164

Fern-leaf peony (P. tenuifolia), 639

Ferns, 37, 178–79, 1010, 1353; as-paragus, 1068–69; books on, 1435–36; in a conservatory, 293; culture (indoors), 1097–1101; house plant, 1097–1101; pest control, 1233–34; See also Foliage plants (indoors)

Ferrous ammonium sulfate, 14

Fertilizer, 65–79, 235–36, 778; add-ing to topsoil, 27; applying, 77–79; bacteria and, 4; best time to add to soil, 31; books on, 1442; cacti (in-doors), 1108–9; clay soil, 18; com-plete, 74–77; deciduous trees and shrubs, 306–9; difference between manure and, 778; fruit trees, 907–8; green manures, 58; hedges, 442; house plants, 83–84, 1005–6; inorganic, 64, 71–74; lawn, 735–40; low in nitrogen, 23; numbers on packages of, 1014; organic, 65–71, 737, 778; peat value, 52–53; perennials, 583–84; rock garden, 155–56; roof garden, 188; roses, 543–44; sandy seashore, 224; shrubs, 304–5, 309; side-dressings of, 779, 780; trees, 304–5; vege-table, 40, 778–85; vines, 304–5; ways to apply, 781; when to apply, 21; wildflower planting, 170–71

Fescue, see Fine fescue

Fiberglass pools, 124

Field mice, 467

Fig, 957–59, 1360; creeping, 1103; fiddle-leaved, 1080

Filbert, 995, 1386

Fine fescue, 700, 743; improved varieties of, 703

Fineness, soil, 33
Fir, 37, 402–3, 1234; Douglas-, 324, 398, 1234; Nikko, 402; soil around, 30
Fire blight, 940, 942, 1323–24
Firecracker plant (*D. ida-maia*), 469
Fireplace ashes, 36
Firethorn, 431–32, 1266, 1363–64
Fish pond, 124
Fish trimmings, 70
'5-in-1' apple tree, 929, 930
Five-leaf aralia (*Acanthopanax*), 357–58
5–10–5 fertilizer, 56, 76–77, 778, 780, 781, 816, 848, 859, 973
5–10–10 fertilizer, 56, 781, 816
Flagged walk, 163
Flagstones, plants between, 163
Flag terrace, 119
Flame azalea (*R. calendulaceum*), 359
Flame-of-the-woods, 1369–70
Flats, 655–56, 658, 790; preplanted, 794; removing annuals from, 663
Flax, 38
Flea beetle, 871, 887, 1164–65, 1308, 1321
Flora-tea rose, 563
Florence fennel (or finocchio), 146, 847
Floribunda rose, 530, 532, 541, 561–62
Floriculture, 193
Florida, 345, 953, 1164, 1179, 1219, 1221, 1233, 1258, 1271, 1308, 1368–74
Florida maple (*A. barbatum*), 333
Florida red scale, 1369
Flowering cabbage, 669
Flowering crab apple, 313, 341–42
Flowering house plants, 1036–65; abutilon, 1036–37; African-violet, 1037–42; anthurium, 1042; begonia, 1042–48; bromeliads, 1048–49; calceolaria, 1049; campanula

isophylla, 1049–50; cineraria, 1050; fuchsia, 1050–51; gerbera, 1058; gesneriad, 1058–59; heliotrope, 1059; impatiens, 1059–60; marguerite or Boston daisy, 1060; neomarica, 1060–61; orchid, 1061–63; primrose, 1063; shrimp-plant, 1063–64; strelitzia, 1064–65; sweet-olive, 1065
Flowering peach (*P. persica*), 350
Flowering quince (*Chaenomeles*), 380–81, 1190, 1417; *See also* Quince
Flowering spurge (*Euphorbia*), 649
Flowering tobacco (*Nicotiana*), 588, 675
Flowering wintergreen (*P. pauci-folia*), 183
Flowers: to attract birds, 184; in the backyard, 208; books on, 1436; catalog description, 211–12; clay soil and, 17, 20; darkening color, 50; greenhouse, 276–77; high altitude (7,000 feet), 1348; hotbed, 269; knowing when soil is right, 33; lime and, 43; reproduction, 194; rodents and, 467; shrubs with fragrance, 355–56; soil for, 23–24; specialization, 192; topsoil and, 26; wet ground, 229; *See also* Gardens; names of flowers
Fluorescent lights, 657, 1001, 1022, 1057; starting seeds under, 1027; vegetable seedlings, 791
Focal point, 93–94
Foliage plants (indoors), 1067–83; asparagus, 1068–69; Australian (silk-oak), 1069; avocado, 1069–70; baby's-tears, 1070; bamboo, 1070–71; bay tree, 1071; bottle-palm, 1071; cast-iron plant, 1069; Chinese-evergreen, 1072; coleus, 1072; croton, 1072; cryptanthus, 1072–73; dumb-cane, 1073; false-aralia, 1073; fatsia japonica, 1073–

Foliage plants (*cont'd*)
74; general information, 1067–68;
holly, 1074; leopard-plant, 1074;
mango, 1074–75; maranta, 1075;
monstera, 1075; nephthytis, 1075;
Norfolk-Island pine, 1075–76;
palm, 1076; peperomia, 1077;
pick-a-back, 1078; pineapple,
1078–79; pomegranate, 1079; redwood burl, 1080; rubber plant,
1080; sago-palm, 1080–81; schefflera, 1081; screw-pine, 1076–77;
sensitive-plant, 1081; snake-plant,
1081–82; spider-plant, 1082;
strawberry-geranium, 1082;
umbrella-plant, 1082; variegated
plants, 1082–83; weeping fig,
1074; *See also* Ferns
Folpet (Phaltan), 1144, 1165
Foot candles for growth, 286
Forget-me-not (*M. sylvatica*), 293,
1066, 1256
Formaldehyde (Formalin), 73, 80,
737, 1165
Forsythia, 88, 312, 313, 368–69,
1396
Foundation planting, 44–45, 88–89;
entranceway, 96–100; for problem
areas, 213–19
Fountains, 123
Four-o'clock (*Mirabilis*), 666, 673
4–12–4 fertilizer, 76, 778
Foxglove (*D. purpuria*), 38, 146,
691, 694, 1370, 1381, 1393
Foxtail, 38, 479, 618–19
Fragrant gardens, 187; from roses,
562
Franklinia alatamaha, 345
Freesia, 500, 519, 1128–29, 1390
French chateau-type house, 99
French endive, 807, 837–38
French hybrid lilac, 375, 377
French hydrangea (*H. macrophylla*),
370, 371–72
French Intensive Method, 211

French lavender, 1034
French lilac, 376
French pussy willow, 312
French Roman hyacinth, 480–81
French rose, 562–63
Fringed gentian (*G. crinita*), 179
Fringetree (*Chionanthus*), 345
Fritillaria, 480
Frost-hardy vegetables, 761
Fruit flies, 900
Fruits and fruit trees, 894–999; in
the backyard, 208; books on, 1436,
1443; cane or bramble, 982–91;
dwarf, 895–97, 922–23, 944–48;
espalier, 944–48, 1384; failure to
bear fruit, 905; fertilizer, 907–8;
general-purpose spray mixture for,
1194; heavy clay for, 20; herbicides and mulching, 904–5; for the
plants, 1092–93; insects and
home garden, 921; indoor house
diseases, 900–1; mulches, 910–11;
nut trees, 992–99, 1411, 1427;
orchard, 905–21; pepper plants,
867; pest control, 1217, 1310–29;
planting, 899–900; pollination,
903, 914–16; pruning, 911–12;
reason for growing, 894–95; rootstocks, 904; sandy soil, 16; selection of varieties, 901–3; shrubs,
354; small fruits, 897, 948–81; soil
and site, 898–99, 905–7; sources
for, 1451–52; spraying, 910,
1310–11; training, 911–12; yews,
413; *See also* names of berries;
fruits
Fuchsia, 619, 1018, 1050–51,
1234, 1344, 1360–61
Fuchsia magellanica, 619
Fuller's rose beetle, 1273
Fumigant, 1170
Fungicides, 1143–44, 1166; when to
apply, 1144; *See also* names of
fungicides

Fungus, 872, 1165–66, 1302, 1316, 1326
Furniture, books on, 1436–37; patio, 119
Furrow, defined, 795

Gaillardia, 1234–35
Galanthus (snowdrop), 480
Galinsoga, 1336
Gall, 1216, 1232
Gallica rose, 562–63
Game areas, 128–30
Garage, rock garden and shrubby plant background, 167
Garbage, 61–62, 70
Garbage cans, 131
Garden cart, 810
Garden duster, 1162
Gardenia, 437–38, 1399, 1408, 1421; as indoor house plant, 1094–95; pest control, 1235
Gardens: accessories, 131–33, 1436–37; backyard, 767–68; balance, 93; birds, 184; books on, 1436–37; in a bottle, 1031; children's, 183–84; community, 771–72; container, 185–87; design principles, 91–96; dish, 1033–34; edge of a lake, 24; features and accessories, 131–33; first, preparing land for, 21; fragrant, 187; herb, 133–39, 1034–36; humus available for, 51; knot, 134–35; lighting, 121; meadow wildflower, 172; miniature, 1030–36; mini-type, 208–13; moraine, 162; organic, 812–13; patio, 120; pools and water gardens, 121–26; rock, 154–69; and sandy soil, 16; soilless, 82–83, 197, 210; special types of, 133–91; sunken, 189, 654; tray, 1033–34; vegetable, 749–893; vertical, 209–10; wall, 163–65; wildflower, 169–83; window-box, 190–91, 1027–30; *See also* City gardens

Garden steps, 116
Garlic (*A. sativum*), 146, 847
'Garnet' penstemon, 1259
Gates, planning and landscaping, 109; *See also* Fences
Gelsemium sempervirens, 1356
Genista (*C. canariensis*), 1086
Gentian, 169, 179
Georgia, 181, 358–59, 506, 996, 1150, 1183, 1217, 1238, 1245, 1248, 1256, 1375–79
Geranium, 136, 293, 1016, 1018, 1051–58; beetle destruction, 1172; books on, 1437; cuttings, 662; easy to grow, 1058; for fragrance, 187; house plants, 1051–58; pest control, 1235–36; propagating, 294; scented, 136
Gerbera (Transvaal daisy), 294, 619–20, 1058, 1361, 1376, 1391, 1412
Germander (*Teucrium*), 134
German-ivy (*S. mikanioides*), 1104, 1246–47
Gesneriad, 1058–59
Ghent azalea, 358
Gift plants, 1083–91
Ginger-lily (*Hedychium*), 526–27
Ginger (*Z. officinale*), 146
Ginkgo, 324, 330–31
Glad-anthera, 526
Gladiolus, 38, 41, 519–26, 1344, 1361, 1376, 1391, 1397, 1399, 1404, 1413, 1421; best way to increase, 524; bloom, 523; books on, 1437; color changes, 524; miniature, 525–26; onions near, 861; pest control, 1236–38; planting, 521, 525; seeds, 524–25; setting out, 521; soil, 520–21; varieties, 525; watering, 522
Glenn Dale hybrid azalea, 422
Globe artichoke, 813–14
'Gloire de Lorraine' (Christmas) begonia, 1044–45, 1046, 1048

Gloriosa daisy (*R. hirta*), 673
Glory-lily (*Gloriosa*), 526, 1129
Glory-of-the-snow (*Chionodoxa*), 470
Glory-of-the-sun (*L. ixiodies*), 527–28
Glossy abelia, 356–57
Gloxinia (*Sinningia*), 1129–31, 1238
Goat manure, 55
Godetia (satin flower), 673
Gold alyssum, 167
Gold-banded lily (*L. auratum*), 488
Golden arborvitae, 401
Golden-chain laburnum (*L. anagyroides*), 324, 347
'Golden Delicious' apple, 927
Golden glow (*Rudbeckia*), 1238
Golden-rain-tree (*K. paniculata*), 346
Goldenrod, 1339
Golden-sunflower (Heliopsis), 620
Goldfish, 123
Gold star-grass (*H. hirsuta*), 481
Goldthread, 1335
Gooseberry, 38, 898, 954–57, 1319–20; varieties of, 903
Gophers, 727, 1166
Gordonia, 345
Gourds, 847–49, 1238, 1376
Grafting, 260–64, 919–20; reason for, 261; rose, 556
Grafting wax, 967
Grandiflora rose, 530, 532, 563
Grape, 38, 959–69, 1311, 1320–21, 1361, 1382, 1426, 1429; cross-pollination, 967; cuttings, 967–68; failure to bear fruit, 961–62; fertilizer, 959; flowers, 964; grafted vines, 967; ideal location, 959–60; insects and diseases, 968; planting, 960; pruning, 962–63, 965–66; seeds, 919; soil, 959; sun and, 960; training, 965; varieties of, 902, 968–69
Grape berry moth, 1320

Grapefruit, 1217
Grape-hyacinth (*Muscari*), 490–91
Grape-ivy (*Cissus*), 1104–5, 1246–47
Grapevine, 1389, 1397
Grass clippings, 62, 725, 1389
Grasshoppers, 1216, 1224, 1232, 1292
Grass (lawn), 699–703, 713–21; basic needs of, 696–98; "best," 713; green plant dyes, 717; improved varieties of, 701–3; northern, 700–1; "nurse," 714–15; shade, 715; soil importance, 703–5; southern, 699–700; sowing seed, 717–21; sprinkler systems, 719–20; watering, 734–35; for winter color, 716; *See also* Lawns
Gravel culture, 81, 82
Gravel path, 114, 115; keeping free from weeds, 1332
Gravel soil, adjusting for growing vegetables, 16
Gray birch, 97; bark patterns, 307
Gray mold, *see* Botrytis blight
Gray santolina, 134
Green ash, 324
Greenhouse, 272–97; books on, 277, 1437; bulbs, 290; compared to a plant room, 1021; construction and energy-saving ideas, 272–75; diseases, 285–87; gravel culture, 82; humidity, 281–82; insects, 284–85; light, 272–73; mealybugs, 1177; perennials, 589; pest control, 1242–84; plant rest, 284; potted plants in, 279–81; repotting plants, 283–84; rose, 564; solar, 275; specific plants for, 287–97; temperatures, 278–79; vegetables, 276; ventilation, 284; watering, soils, and general care, 279–82; what to grow, 276–78
Green lice, 1280

Green-manure crops, 6, 19, 56–59, 786–88
Green moss, 25
'Green Mountain' potato, 872–73
Green rose (*R. chinensis viridiflora*), 563–64
Green santolina, 134
Grevillea robusta, 1069
'Grimes Golden' apple, 927
Ground beetles, 1166–67
Ground corn cobs, 5
Ground covers: between sidewalk and curb, 219–20; books on, 1437–38; city garden, 205; for problem areas, 219–22; rose, 564
Growth regulators, books on, 1438
Grubs, 746, 1198–99, 1202, 1239, 1328, 1329
Guinea hen flower (*F. meleagris*), 480
Gummosis, 1326
Gum tree, 1393
Gypsum (plaster of Paris), 18, 43, 728
Gypsy moth, 1167–69

Hackberry (*Celtis*), 1238
Haemanthus (blood-lily), 526, 1131–32
Hairy vetch, 37
'Halehaven' peach, 937
Half-hardy annual, 653
Half-ripe wood cuttings, 250
Hanging baskets, 191; books on, 1435; raggedness look, 212–13; soil, 210
Hardening-off, 267–68
Hardwood cuttings, 250
Hardy-ageratum (*Eupatorium*), 619
Hardy annual, 653
Hardy aster, 593
Hardy bulbs, 464–500; for forcing, 1118–19; for indoors (spring), 1119–21
Hardy fuchsia (*F. magellanica*), 619

Hardy herbaceous perennial, 576
Harlequin bugs, 1160–70
Harvesting: herbs, 139–40; orchard fruits, 916–18; vegetables, 804–5
Hashish, *see* Marihuana
Hawaii, 1379
Hawthorn, 346–47, 1238–39, 1340; English, 346, 1239; pink, 206
Hazelnut, 370, 995
Head lettuce, 852, 853
Heaths and heathers (*Erica* and *Calluna*), 403–4
'Heavenly Blue' morning-glory, 454
Hedges, 439–48; arborvitae, 444; barberry, 444; boxwood, 444; caragana, 445; cherry-laurel, 446; in the city, 440–41; fertilizers and planting, 442; hemlock, 445–46; lilac, 446; Monterey cyprus, 445; privet, 446–47; Rosa multiflora, 447; rose, 564–65; for screening, 101; Siberian elm, 445; specific plants, 444–48; spirea, 447; spruce, 448; tamarisk, 448; trimming and training, 443; what to grow, 439–42; white pine, 446; willow, 448; yew, 448
Hedychium (ginger-lily), 526–27
Helenium, 1239
Helianthus, 38
Heliophila, 1370
Heliopsis (golden-sunflower), 620
Heliotrope (*Heliotropium*), 1059
Hellbind, 1335
Helleborus niger, 597–98
'Helm' apple, 1374
Helxine soleirolii, 1070
Hemerocallis (day-lily), 577–78, 609–11, 1344
Hemlock, 37, 311, 404–5, 441, 445–46, 1239; wildflowers and, 171–72
Hemp, 38
Hepatica, 179
Hepatica acutiloba, 179
Hepatica americana, 179

Herb gardens, 133–54; annuals and perennials, 133; books on, 1438; border planting, 136–37; cement blocks, 211; container garden, 185; culture, 138–39; in foundation planting, 208; harvesting, curing, and storing, 139–40; in the house, 135; kitchen-window garden, 1034–36; knot garden, 134–35; ornamental, 134; potpourris, 140–41; in pots, 134, 137–38; on the roof, 188; in shade, 136; soil, 138, 1035; sources for, 1452; space, 137; specific herbs for, 142–54; for tea, 134; water, 139; what to grow, 133–37; wheels, 141–42

Herbicides, 236–37, 1331; animal life and, 744; and mulching, 904–5; *See also* names of herbicides

Herb Society of America, The, 136, 149

'Heritage' raspberry, 983

Heritage Roses Group, 531, 574

Hermerocallis flava, 610, 611

Hibiscus, 173, 647–48, 1095–96, 1240, 1393, 1416, 1422

Hickory, 995, 1240

Hicks yew, 413

Highbush-cranberry, *see* Cranberry-bush

Hill, defined, 795–96

Hillside soil, 23; vegetables, 762

Hills-of-snow hydrangea, 317

Hindu lotus, 126

Hippeastrum, *see* Amaryllis

Holly fern, 1100

Holly-grape, Oregon, 429

Holly-grape (Mahonia), 88, 89, 429–30

Hollyhock, 588, 620, 1240–41; beetle destruction, 1172

Holly (*Ilex*), 426–29, 1074, 1422; *See also* American holly; Burford holly; English holly; Japanese holly

Honey locust (*Gleditsia*), 331, 1241

Honeysuckle (*Lonicera*), 370, 459–60, 1241, 1341

Hoop supports, 803

Hops, 38

Hornbeam (*Carpinus*), 331

Horse-chestnut (Buckeye), 331–32

Horse manure, 55, 543, 737

Horse-radish, 38, 849

Horseshoe pitching, 128–29

Horticultural societies, list of, 1446–48

Hosta, 1241

Hotbeds, 268–72; difference between a cold frame and, 268; indoor vegetable sowing, 791–92, 793; manure, 270–71; ventilation, 271

Hotkaps, 799, 811

House plants, 1000–36; in Alaska, 1347; annuals and biennials, 1065–67; in autumn, 1009, 1017–18; books on, 1438; cacti, 1108–14; citrus fruits, 1092–93; culture, 1010–17; decorating with, 1027–30; environment, 1020–22; exposure, 1019–20; feeding, 1013–14; ferns, 1097–1101; fertilizer, 83–84, 1005–6; flowering plants, 1036–65; foliage plants, 1067–83; functions of, 1000; gift plants, 1083–91; hardy bulbs for forcing, 1118–19; hardy spring bulbs, 1119–21; humidity, 1002–3; insects and diseases, 1023–24; miniature gardens, 1030–36; pest control, 1242–84; potting, 1012–13; propagation, 1025–27; pruning and training, 1005; repotting, 83, 84, 1006–7, 1012–13; rest period, 1010; in sand culture, 82; sanitation, 1024–25; shrubs, 1091–97; soils and fertilizers, 77, 83–84, 1005–8, 1010–12; sources for, 1452–53; succulents, 1115–18; summer quarters, 1008–9, 1017; temperature, 1001–2, 1015–16;

House plants (*cont'd*)
tender bulbs for indoors, 1122–36;
vacation care, 1018–19; ventilation, 1004–5, 1016–17; vines,
1101–8; watering, 1003–4,
1014–15
Hoya, *see* Waxplant
'Hubbard' squash, 1304–5
Huckleberry, 37, 1341
Hulls, hickory and walnut, 62
Human manure, 54–55
Humidifiers, 1002
Humidity: greenhouse, 281–82;
house plants, 1002–3
Humus, 8–9, 18, 50–52, 780; city
garden, 206–7; function of, 51;
recognizing types of, 50–51
Hungarian clover, 38
Hyacinth (*Hyacinthus*), 466–67,
480–81, 1132, 1392–93
Hybrid blueberry, 948–49, 950, 953
Hybridizing: perennials, 591–92;
roses, 557
Hybrid sweet corn, 842
Hybrid tea rose, 530, 532, 549, 565–
66, 1367, 1389, 1395, 1398,
1405–6, 1411, 1430; all-purpose
spray for, 1276; compared to
hybrid perpetuals, 565
Hydrangea, 53, 69, 294, 312, 370–74,
460–61, 1015, 1087–88, 1422; as
a gift plant, 1087–88; pest control,
1244
Hydrangea 'Bluebird,' 1087–88
Hydrated (or slaked) **lime,** 42, 43
Hydroponics, 81, 83
Hydrosme, 503, 1132
Hydroxyquinoline sulfate, 1170
Hymenocallis (Peruvian-daffodil,
Ismene), 527
Hypoxis hirsuta, 481
Hyssop (*H. officinalis*), 146

Iberis (candytuft), 38, 595, 670,
1212

Idaho, 499, 681, 1204, 1247, 1256,
1279, 1379–80, 1401
Illinois, 870, 906, 1152, 1161, 1186,
1187, 1203, 1204, 1205, 1215,
1219, 1220, 1223, 1225, 1226,
1227, 1230, 1231–32, 1236, 1245,
1247, 1250, 1251, 1253, 1255,
1262, 1270–71, 1273, 1277, 1278,
1281, 1282, 1283, 1297, 1298,
1304, 1306, 1311, 1316, 1317,
1319, 1320, 1326, 1328, 1329,
1380–85
Immunization, 1141–42
Impatiens (patience-plant), 673,
1059–60, 1244
Imperial crimson lily, 485
Incandescent light, 1021
Inchworms, 1155
Indiana, 678, 1216, 1226–27, 1236,
1250, 1252, 1260, 1263, 1265–66,
1269, 1287, 1295, 1297, 1307,
1320, 1321–22, 1323, 1324,
1385–86
Indigobush (*A. fruticosa*), 357
**Indoor Light Gardening Society of
America,** 1022
Indoor plants, *see* House plants
Indoor vegetable sowing, 789–93
Inoculant powders, 59
Inorganic fertilizers, 71–74; in compost, 64; difference between organic fertilizer and, 778
Insecticides, 741, 1143–44; biological, 1144, 1149, 1152; broad-spectrum, 1157; contact, 1157,
1170; how it works, 1170–71;
when to apply, 1144; *See also*
names of insecticides
Insects: beneficial types, 1150; fruits,
900–1; greenhouse, 284–85; house
plants, 1023–24; lawn, 746–47;
meaning of, 117; *See also* Pest control; names of insects
Intercropping, 764–65

Iowa, 71, 1174, 1181, 1213, 1224, 1225, 1239, 1251, 1293, 1294, 1316, 1323, 1327, 1329, 1386–88
Ipomoea, 1067
Iris, 38, 620–29, 1118, 1190, 1353, 1362, 1370, 1405, 1422; bloom, 623, 629; books on, 1438; classification of, 628; color, 626, 629; diseases, 628; division, 626; fertilizer, 622; medal for, 626; pest control, 1244–46; planting depths for, 622; rock garden, 167; roots, 625; seeds, 627–28; soil, 621; wild, 179
Iris borer, 1245
Iris cristata, 179
Irish juniper, 309, 405–6
Iris prismatica, 179
Iris verna, 179
Iris versicolor, 179
Iron, 14, 39–40, 50
Iron deficiency, 14
Iron sulfate, 50, 83
Ironwood tree, 97
Irrigation: lawn, 733–35; vegetables, 802; See also Drainage
Ismone, 527
Italian rye grass, 1377
Italian turnip, see Broccoli raab
Ivy, 191, 461, 1016, 1103–4; Algerian, 1377; Boston, 1103; English, 221–22, 1103–4, 1246–47; German, 1104, 1246–47; Grape-, 1104–5, 1246–47; Kenilworth, 1105; pest control, 1246–47
Ivy-leaved geranium, 1054
Ixia, 527, 529, 1133

Jack-in-the-pulpit (A. triphyllum), 179, 1073
Jacobean-lily, 529
Jade plant (Crassula), 1115–16
Japanese anemone (windflower), 1202–3, 1419

Japanese-bamboo (P. cuspidatum), 1336–37
Japanese barberry, 360
Japanese beetle, 910, 1151, 1272, 1285–86, 1297, 1312, 1320, 1328; control of, 1171–74
Japanese cherry (P. serrulata), 1247
Japanese clover, 38
Japanese flowering dogwood (C. kousa), 342
Japanese holly (I. crenata), 1393
Japanese honeysuckle, 23
Japanese iris, 621, 622, 623–24, 625, 628, 1345
Japanese maple, 1253–54
Japanese pagoda tree (S. japonica), 338
Japanese peony, 638–39
Japanese plum, 943; varieties of, 902
Japanese quince, 309
Japanese red maple, 334
Japanese rubber (C. argentea), 1116
Japanese snowball (V. plicatum tomentosum), 386
Japanese spurge (Pachysandra), 222
Japanese temple-cedar (Cryptomeria), 401
Japanese walnut, 998
Japanese yew, 412–13
Jasmine, 438, 1362, 1422
Jerusalem-artichoke, 814
Jerusalem-cherry (S. pseudocapsicum), 1088
Jiffy-7's, 198
Joe-Pye-weed, 173, 619
Johnson grass, 1336
Jonquil, 472, 477
Jujube, Chinese, 969–70
Jumping plant louse, 942
June beetle, 1174
Juneberry (Amelanchier), 970
Jungle cactus, 1111–12
Juniper, 318, 319, 405–7, 1034, 1231, 1247–48, 1396
Juniper scale, 1247

Juniperus virginiana 'Glauca,' 407
Juno iris, 629

Kalanchoe, 1088–89, 1117
Kalanchoe blossfeldiana, 1117
Kale, 38, 771, 807, 850
Kangaroo vine (*C. antarctica*), 1105
Kansas, 42, 371, 679, 686, 687, 870,
  1169–70, 1186, 1205, 1208, 1225,
  1233, 1234, 1258, 1262, 1268,
  1303, 1389–90
Karathane, 1174
'Katahdin' potato, 872
Kelp, 71
Kenilworth-ivy (*C. muralis*), 1105
Kentucky, 343, 523, 667, 681, 682,
  1156, 1216, 1241, 1282, 1370,
  1390–91
Kentucky bluegrass, 700, 1373, 1411;
  improved varieties of, 701–2
'Kentucky Wonder' bean, 819, 1288
Kerria japonica, 374, 1382
Kidney bean, 819
Kitchen-window herb garden,
  1034–36
Knaphill azalea, 359
Knob celery, 833
Knot garden, 134–35
Kochia, 674
Kohlrabi, 38, 850–51
Korean barberry (*B. koreana*), 360
Korean lespedeza, 712
Koster's blue spruce, 1277

Labor saving, 200–3
Laburnum (golden-chain tree), 324,
  347
Laburnum x watereri, 347
Lacebug, 431, 1174, 1263
Lace fern, 1100
Lachenalia (Cape-cowslip), 527, 529
Lady beetle, 1151
Ladybugs, 1223
Lady's finger, 38

Lady's-slipper, 41, 180–81, 295;
  pink, 181
Lady Washington geranium, 1054,
  1056
Lamb's-quarters, 1336
Lamps for garden lighting, 121
Lancaster rose, 561
Land plaster, 43
Landscape design principles, 91–96;
  See also Planning and landscaping
Lantana (*L. camara*), 1018, 1096,
  1429
Lapeirousia, 529
Larch, 332
Larkspur (*Consolida*), 38, 660, 674,
  1248
Larvacide, 79–80, 1184
Latana cuttings, 662
'Latham' raspberry, 991
Lath houses, 1021, 1356
Lavandula angustifolia, 147
Lavender, 134, 147–48, 1402
Lawns, 69, 695–747; animal damage,
  727; best deciduous trees for, 325–
  26; blemishes, 728–29; books on,
  1439; city, 205; contained (restrained at borders), 726–27; diseases, 744–46; fertilizers, 735–40;
  game area, 128–29; grading, 708–
  10; insect pests, 746–47; irrigation,
  733–35; landscape scheme, 106;
  lime sprinkling, 45; maintaining,
  706–8, 724; manure, 737–38; mistakes to avoid in planting (for
  landscape effect), 95; modern type
  of, 695–96; "moss," 747–48, 1426;
  mowers and mowing, 729–33;
  planting vegetatively, 721–23;
  seeding and sodding, 705–6; soil
  importance, 703–5; sowing, 710–
  13; spiking, 729; tending, 724–29;
  tree leaves on, 729; weed and pest
  control, 740–47, 1248–49; *See also*
  Grass
Layering, 258–59, 556

Lead arsenate, 1175
Leadwort (Plumbago), 644–45
Leaf curl, 1254
Leaf cuttings, 256–57; propagating by, 197
Leafhoppers, 931
Leaf lettuce, 753
Leafminer, 128, 1290, 1306
Leafmold, 5–6, 30, 40–41, 49, 51, 53, 63, 67, 233, 400
Leafspot, 1290, 1319; how to diagnose, 1140
Leather dust, 70
Leaves: blistered or puckered, 1218; burned ashes of, 69; clay soil and, 18; for compost, 5–6, 63; on the lawn, 729; as manure, 233; for producing acid soil, 40; silvery effect, 324; as soil conditioner, 67
Leek, 38, 753, 807, 851
Legume-Aid, 59, 630
Legumes, 44, 58, 59
Leguminosae family, 58, 823
Leguminous green-manure crop, 58
Lemon, 1093, 1359; dwarf, 1093, 1217
Lemon-balm (M. officinalis), 142–43, 1034, 1035
Lemon-lily (H. flava), 610, 611
Lemon oil, 1175
Lemon-verbena (A. triphylla), 148, 1034, 1035
Lentil, 38
Leontopodium, 168
Leopard moth, 931
Leopard-plant (L. tussilaginea), 294, 1074
Lespedeza, 56
Lettuce, 38, 753, 754, 771, 790, 796, 851–54, 1299; gourmet varieties, 765
Leucocoryne (glory-of-the-sun), 527–28
Leucocrinum (star-lily), 481
Leucojum (snowflake), 481

Leucojum vernum, 481
Leucothoe, 39, 88, 89
Leucothoe fontanesiana, 429
Liatris, 16
Lice, 628, 1208, 1220, 1227, 1235, 1248, 1257, 1259, 1278, 1294, 1301
Light and lighting, 1021–22; fluorescent, 657, 791, 1001, 1022, 1027, 1057; garden, 121; greenhouse, 272–73; house plants, 1001
Ligurian harebell, 1049–50
Lilac, 87–88, 312, 446, 1362, 1370, 1422–23; chlorosis in, 378; darkening color, 50; difference between lilac species and, 374–75; pest control, 1249–50
Lilac "graft blight," 378
Lilium bakeranum, 1349
Lilium longiflorum, 485, 489
Lilium philippinense, 489
Lilium speciosum 'Rubrum,' 484
Lily, 37, 482–89, 1190, 1405, 1423; applying wood ashes to, 68–69; best time to plant, 483; clay soil and, 20; cultural requirements, 486; diseases, 488–89; fertilizer, 482–83; hybrid, 483–84, 489; indoors, 1118–19; pest control, 1250–52; planting and care, 485; rodents and, 467, 488–89; seeds, 487; soil, 482; stem-rooting, 484; stems, 486–87
Lily-of-the-valley (C. majalis), 470–71, 1119, 1337, 1362, 1416
Lima bean, 819, 820–22, 1287; supports, 802
Limber neck, 1251
Lime, 19, 28, 40, 42–45, 584, 613, 622, 633, 728, 740, 907–8, 973, 1292, 1359; best time to add to soil, 31; on a lawn, 727–28; onions and, 859–60; telling need for, 25; in a vegetable garden, 774–75;

Lime (*cont'd*)
  when to add to the soil, 43; when
  to apply, 21
Limestone, 18, 40, 728
Lime-sulfur, 1175
Lime-sulfur spray, 1271
Lime tree, dwarf, 1359
Liming, lawn, 727
Lindane, 1138, 1175
Linden, 38, 318, 332
Lindera benzoin (spicebush), 362,
  1384
Liquidambar (sweet-gum), 333,
  1384, 1393
Liquid fertilizer, 508
Liquid house-plant foods, 77
Liquid manure, 56, 1014
Living stones (*Lithops*), 1117
Lobelia, 38, 173, 674, 1066
Lobelia cardinalis, 170, 173, 177
Loblolly bay (*G. lasianthus*), 345
Location, vegetable garden, 750,
  768–71
Locust (*Robinia*), 1252
Loganberry, 1426
Lombardy poplar, 338, 1265–66
Long Island, New York, 150, 425,
  434, 502, 797, 906, 958, 1283,
  1318
Long Island Sound, 71
Loose-leaf lettuce, 852
Loquat (oriental-plum), 1399–1400
Lorraine begonia, 1208
Lotus, Hindu or sacred, 126
Louisiana, 606, 1172, 1193, 1204,
  1205, 1220, 1259, 1264, 1276,
  1282, 1391–92
Lovage (*L. officinale*), 148
Lovevine, 1335
Lungwort, 140
Lupine (*Lupinus*), 37, 629–30, 1252,
  1382, 1389
Lycopodium (club moss), 180
Lycoris, 502, 1423
Lycoris radiata (spider-lily), 528

Lycoris squamigera (resurrection-
  lily), 490
Lye, 69

Macadamia, 995–96
'McIntosh' apple, 896, 926, 1314
Madonna lily, 486, 487, 488, 1251,
  1252
Maggots, 1175–76, 1242–43, 1291,
  1294, 1300, 1309
Magnesium sulfate, 83
Magnolia, 347–50, 429, 1382, 1387,
  1416; pest control, 1253; tree
  companion, 323
Magnolia acuminata (cucumber
  tree), 347, 348
Magnolia fraseri, 347
Magnolia grandiflora, 429, 1402
Magnolia hypoleuca, 347
Magnolia kobus, 347
Magnolia macrophylla, 347
Magnolia stellata, 350
Magnolia virginiana, 347, 349
Magnolia x soulangiana, 348–49
Magnolia x soulangiana 'Lennei,' 347
Mahonia (holly-grape), 88, 89, 429–
  30
Maidenhair fern, 293, 1100, 1233
Maine, 59, 181, 335, 427, 837, 953,
  984, 992, 1030, 1240, 1280, 1288,
  1292
Malathion (Cythion), 1144, 1176
Malling 9 ('M9') rootstocks, 896,
  899–900
Malus floribunda, 1220
Mammoth clover, 38
Mancozeb (Manzate 200, Dithane,
  Fore), 1144, 1176
Maneb (Manzate D, Dithane M-22),
  1144, 1176
Manganese, 50
Mangel wurzels, 38
Mango (*M. indica*), 1074–75, 1362
Manure, 13, 54–59, 536, 780, 782,
  783–84, 907; animal, 6, 973;

Manure (*cont'd*)
difference between "fertilizer"
and, 778; green, 6, 19, 56–59,
786–88; in a hotbed, 270–71; for
the lawn, 737–38; leaves as, 233;
liquid, 56, 1014; spent mushroom,
5
Maple, 38, 67, 96, 333–35; ground
cover around, 221; pest control,
1253–54
Maranta leuconeura, 1075
Maranta (prayer-plant), 1075
Marguerite daisy (*C. frutescens*),
1060
Marigold, 38, 660, 665, 674–75, 688,
1184; pest control, 1254, 1255
Marihuana (*Cannabis*), 1341
Mariposa-tulip, 469
Marjoram, 148–49, 1034, 1036
Marl, 43
Marsh hay, 158
Marshlands, 173
Marsh-marigold (*C. palustris*), 173,
180
Maryland, 645, 660, 796, 958, 1176,
1178, 1197, 1228, 1232, 1258,
1262, 1269, 1287, 1317, 1325,
1326
Maryland pine, 1248
'Mary Washington' asparagus, 817
Massachusetts, 153, 345, 347, 372,
385, 387, 402, 426, 440, 821, 865,
893, 933, 984, 989, 1149, 1155–
56, 1179, 1195, 1199–1200, 1221,
1230, 1248, 1249, 1252, 1253,
1261, 1267, 1270, 1284, 1286,
1287, 1288–89, 1298–99, 1301,
1302, 1312–13, 1314, 1318, 1320–
21, 1323, 1325; spray schedule
for, 1314
Matrimony-vine (*L. halimifolium*),
1255
May Day tree, 346
Mayflower, *see* Trailing arbutus
Meadow grass, 38

Meadow oat, 38
Meadow wildflower garden, 172
Mealybugs, 1023, 1201, 1202, 1210,
1218, 1235, 1242, 1265, 1282;
control of, 1176–77
Melon, 753, 805, 1298, 1299–1300
Mennonites (religious sect), 970
Mentha requienii, 149
Mertensia (*M. virginica*), 171, 180
Mesh wire supports, 803
Methoxychlor, 931, 1178
Mexican bean beetle, 820, 1216,
1286–87, 1309
Mexican-orange, 1416
Mexican sunflower (*Tithonia*), 686
Meyer juniper, 407
'Meyer' lemon, 1359
Mice, 488–89, 499, 547, 913; control
of, 1178
Michaelmas daisy, 593
Michigan, 343, 349, 378, 424, 427,
812, 842, 880, 953, 1029, 1035,
1205, 1214, 1220, 1227, 1236,
1239, 1256, 1260, 1261, 1262,
1264, 1265, 1268, 1269, 1270,
1271, 1274, 1275, 1294, 1296,
1298, 1305, 1311–12, 1318, 1319,
1320, 1321, 1326, 1327, 1392–95
Mignonette, 38
Mildew, 866, 1211, 1223, 1225–26,
1239, 1244, 1249, 1250, 1262,
1269, 1278, 1289–90, 1317, 1321,
1327, 1344; control of, 1179;
reason for, 1178–79
Milkweed, 16, 1339
Milky disease, 1145, 1149
Millet, 37
Millipedes, 1179
Mimosa (*A. julibrissin*), 378
Mimosa pudica (sensitive-plant),
1081
Miniature gardens, 1030–36; kitchen-
window, 1034–36; terrarium,
1030–32, 1099; tray and dish,
1033–34

Miniatures, *see* under names of flowers
Mini-gardens (for small properties), 208–13
Minnesota, 181, 550, 691, 889, 1179, 1209, 1218, 1225, 1236, 1245, 1251, 1262, 1264, 1274–75, 1280–81, 1282, 1312, 1316–17, 1396–99
Mint (*Mentha*), 149, 1034
Mississippi, 682, 1203, 1209, 1224, 1238, 1306, 1310, 1345, 1399–1400
Missouri, 178, 327, 829, 852–53, 865, 889, 997, 1166, 1202, 1215, 1216, 1262, 1269, 1275, 1279, 1281, 1300, 1309, 1318, 1400–3
Mist, rooting cuttings by, 251–53
Mister with a spray, 1003
Mites, 1161, 1179–80
Moccasin plant, 181
Mock-orange (*Philadelphus*), 309, 312, 317, 379–80
Moerheim blue spruce, 411
Mole crickets, 1180, 1374
Moles, 467, 498–99, 727, 1180–81, 1249, 1252, 1275–76, 1281, 1301
Mollis azalea, 1206
Molybdenum, 50
Moneywort, *see* Creeping Jenny
Monkey-puzzle tree (*A. araucana*), 1255
Monkshood (*Aconitum*), 141, 630–31, 1200, 1367
Monocalcium phosphate, 83
Monstera deliciosa, 294
Monstera (Swiss-cheese plant), 1075
Montana, 921, 1213, 1222, 1261, 1275–76, 1403–4
Montbretia, 1427
Montbretia (*Tritonia*), 529
Monterey cyprus (*Cupressus*), 445
Moonflower, 453, 666
Moon-vine, 1337
Moraine garden, 162
Morning-glory, 16, 453–54, 666,

1366; wild, 1337, 1339; in window gardens, 1067
Mosaic disease, 488, 516, 628, 990, 1250–51, 1289, 1298; weed hosts of, 1307
Mosquitoes, 1244
Moss, 39, 115
"Moss" lawn (pearlwort), 747–48, 1426
Moss rose, 568, 1400; miniature, 567
Mossy soil, 29
Moth balls, 1298
Mother-of-thyme (*T. serpyllum*), 153
Moths, 1181–82
Mountain-ash or rowan-tree, 206, 335–36; pest control, 1255
Mountain fringe, 452
Mountain-laurel, 37, 39, 40, 318, 415, 430; pest control, 1256
Mowers, lawn, 729–33
Muck, 51
Mud-pie test, 34
Mugo pine, 409, 1263–64
Mulberry, 970–71, 1370; varieties of, 903
Mulches and mulching, 33, 231–37; benefits of, 199–200; fruit trees, 910–11; herbicides and, 904–5; ornamentals, 231–37; roof garden, 188; roses, 544–45; shrubs, 303–4; trees, 303–4; vegetables, 804; vines, 303–4; woodland wild plants, 170
Mullein pink (*L. coronaria*), 693
Multiplier onions, 860
Mung bean, 823–24
Muriate of potash, 14, 74
Muscari (grape-hyacinth), 490–91
Mushroom, 811, 854–55; books on, 855
Muskmelon, 38, 754, 843, 855–57, 1300
Mustard, 753, 754, 796
Mustard-seed fungus, 1166

Myosotis (forget-me-not), 293, 1066, 1256
Myrtle, 88, 191, 1105; *See also* Crape-myrtle

Nandina, 309, 1345, 1377, 1400, 1409, 1416
Nanking cherry (*P. tomentosa*), 341
Naphthalene, 1225, 1237, 1256
Narcissus, 472–79, 1133–34, 1379, 1405; difference between daffodil and, 477; pest control, 1256–57
Narcissus fly, 1256
Narrow-leaf plantain, 742, 1334, 1337
Narrow-leaved evergreens, 389–413; arborvitae, 400–1; books on, 389–90; cedar, 401; Christmas tree, 402–3; cryptomeria, 401; culture, 392–93; cuttings, 399–400; false-cypress, 402; fir, 402–3; heaths and heathers, 403–4; hemlock, 404–5; juniper, 405–7; low-growing, 391–92; pine, 407–9; propagation, 399–400; pruning, 397–98; specific kinds, 400–13; spruce, 409–12; transplanting, 393–97; what to grow, 389–90; winter protection, 398–99; yew, 412–13
Nasturtium (*Tropaeolum*), 675, 1067, 1257, 1370
Native mountain andromeda (*P. floribunda*), 430–31
Nebraska, 1219, 1267–68, 1301, 1303, 1404–6
Nectarine, 939, 1382, 1387; dwarf, 922–23; varieties of, 902
Neglected soil, 24–26
Nematodes (eelworms), 747, 1182–83, 1184, 1214, 1243, 1246
Neomarica, 1060–61
Neomarica gracilis, 1061
Nephthytis (*S. podophyllum*), 1020, 1075

Nettles, 1337
Nevada, 22, 1406
New Hampshire, 184, 402, 441, 659, 1229, 1254, 1307, 1316
New Jersey, 179, 332, 336, 361, 402, 446, 502, 680, 681, 683, 828, 865, 892, 920, 952, 953, 969, 992, 1016, 1018, 1044, 1149, 1187, 1199, 1200–1, 1206, 1215, 1216, 1217, 1222, 1225, 1228, 1234, 1235, 1239, 1240, 1249, 1256, 1263, 1264, 1266, 1267, 1271, 1273, 1281, 1282, 1284, 1285–86, 1294–95, 1297, 1299, 1303, 1304, 1310, 1315, 1319, 1321, 1328
New Mexico, 1324, 1406–8
Newspapers, as mulch, 804
New York, 127, 137, 153, 157, 191, 327, 334, 340, 343, 359, 365, 371, 395, 398, 403, 408, 415, 419, 422, 431, 468, 491, 502, 560, 642, 659, 676, 682, 764, 790, 920, 926, 933, 942, 989, 993, 1035, 1092, 1148, 1156, 1166, 1171, 1181, 1182, 1195, 1204, 1207–8, 1209, 1216, 1222, 1225, 1227, 1229, 1231, 1232, 1236, 1239, 1241, 1244, 1245, 1247, 1250–51, 1253, 1254, 1255, 1256, 1257, 1261, 1262, 1264, 1266, 1268, 1273, 1274, 1276, 1277, 1278, 1280, 1281, 1284, 1286–87, 1288, 1290, 1293, 1294, 1295–96, 1297, 1298, 1299, 1300, 1301, 1302, 1308, 1309, 1311, 1315–16, 1319, 1320, 1327, 1328–29
New Zealand spinach, 753, 795, 805, 877–78
Nicotiana (flowering tobacco), 588, 675
Nicotine, 1307
Nicotine sulfate, 1184
Nierembergia, 675
Night-blooming cactus, 1111–12
Nikko fir, 402

Nitragen, 59
Nitrate of soda, 13, 18, 72, 907
Nitrogen, 12–13, 47–48, 779; effect on plant growth, 47; soil excess, 48–49
Nitrogen deficiency, 47–48
Norfolk-Island-pine, 1075–76, 1363
North American Gladiolus Council, 463
North American Lily Society, 463
North Carolina, 178, 191, 344, 440, 953, 1158, 1209, 1212, 1235, 1259, 1269–70, 1283–84, 1289, 1408–11
North Dakota, 782, 1152, 1319–20, 1411–12
Northern lawn grasses, 700–1; basic needs of, 696–98; suggested mowing height, 733; *See also* names of grasses
North-side foundation, 218
Norway maple, 334–35, 1253
Norway pine, 408
Norway spruce, 410–11, 412, 1277
Nucleoproteins, 47
Nurse grass, 714–15
Nut-grass, 1337, 1345, 1421
Nutrients, 11–14, 47–53; humus, 50–52; lawn fertilizer, 735–36; minor, 14; nitrogen, 12–13, 47–49; peat moss, 52–53; phosphorus, 13, 49; potash, 49; potassium, 13–14; trace elements, 50
Nutrient solution (for soilless gardens), 83
Nut trees, 992–99, 1411, 1427; almond, 993; black walnut, 996–97; butternut, 993; chestnut, 994; general information, 992–93; hazelnut, 995; hickory, 995; Japanese walnut, 998; macadamia, 995–96; pecan, 996; Persian walnut, 998–99; pistachio, 996
Nyssa sylvatica (sour gum or black gum), 339, 1393

Oak, 53, 67, 97, 337, 1353, 1362, 1366; ground cover around, 221; lime on lawn and, 45; pest control, 1257–58; soil around, 30; wildflowers and, 171–72
Oakleaf hydrangea, 371, 372
Oak leafmold, 40–41
Oak wood ashes, 69
Oats, 37, 57
Offsets, 250
Ohio, 332, 333, 427, 670, 676, 767, 777, 859, 879, 952, 1150, 1156, 1177, 1190, 1200, 1206, 1207, 1212, 1214, 1223, 1224, 1226, 1228, 1229, 1232, 1240, 1241, 1249, 1253–54, 1259, 1262, 1264–65, 1268, 1269, 1270, 1283, 1286, 1289, 1303, 1313, 1320, 1321, 1323, 1324–25, 1327, 1328, 1412–13
Oil sprays, 1184–85
Oklahoma, 595, 684, 685, 1203, 1236, 1275, 1413–15
Okra, 857–58
Old garden rose, 532
Oleander (*Nerium*), 438, 1096–97, 1258, 1362, 1370–71, 1416
Oncocyclus iris, 624
Onion, 38, 753, 754, 804–5, 807, 858–61, 1236, 1300; summer-flowering, 468
Onion sets, 858–59
Onion smut, 1300
Orange, 1345, 1359–60, 1369; dwarf, 1217; house plant, 1093; mock-, 309, 312, 317, 379–80
Orange flies, 1209
Orange lice, 1227
Orange peels, for compost, 62
Orange quince, 38
Orange rust, 985, 1327, 1381
Orchard fruit, 905–21; apple, 921–33; apricot, 933; best sites for, 899; cherry, 933–36; exhibiting, 918; fertilizer, 907–8; harvesting

Orchard fruit (*cont'd*)
and storing, 916–18; mulches and
cover crops, 910–11; peach, 936–
40; pear, 940–42; planting, 908–
10; plum, 942–44; pollination and
fruiting, 914–16; propagation,
918–20; protection, 913; pruning
and training, 911–12; soil, 905–7;
spraying, 910; what to grow, 920–
21; *See also* Fruits
Orchard grass, 37
Orchid, 37, 82, 1061–63, 1379;
books on, 1439; in a terrarium,
1032; wildflower, 180–81
Orchid cactus, 1111–12
Oregon, 1153, 1181, 1204, 1246,
1267, 1273, 1284, 1291, 1294,
1306, 1415–17
'Oregon Evergreen' blackberry, 984
Organic fertilizers, 65–71; in compost, 64; difference between inor-
ganic fertilizer and, 778; for the
lawn, 737; leafmold, 67
Organic gardening, 812–13; books
on, 1439
Organic insecticides, 1171
Organic material, importance of, 2–4
Oriental beetle, 1148–49, 1273; *See
also* Japanese beetle
Oriental bittersweet, 1208
Oriental fruit moth, 900, 939, 972
Oriental peach moth, 1323
Oriental plum, 1399–1400
Oriental poppy, 645–46, 1349; perennials planted around, 578
Ornamental pepper (*C. annuum*),
1089
Ornamental plants, 192–297; bulbs,
corms, and tubers, 248–50; city
conditions, 203–7; cloning and
tissue culture, 257–58; cold
frames, 264–68; cultivation and
mulching, 199–200, 231; culture,
230–45; cuttings, 250–56, 257;
disbudding and pinching, 242–43;

dry, sunny areas, 228–29; enemies
of, 203; environmental importance, 194–96; environmental
problems, 203–13; foundation
material for problem areas, 213–
19; as garden material, 192–94;
general-purpose spray mixture for,
1194; grafting, 260–64; ground
covers for problem areas, 219–22;
home greenhouse, 272–97; hotbeds, 268–72; labor saving, 200–3;
layering, 258–59; mulches, 231–
37; pest control, 1200–41; propagation, 196–97, 245–64; pruning, 201–2, 239–42; root and leaf
cuttings, 256–57; root-pruning,
243; sandy soil, 222–23; seashore,
223–24; seeds, 245–48; in shade,
226–28; slopes and banks, 224–26;
small gardens for small properties,
208–13; suckers, stolons, and
runners, 259–60; supports, 202–3,
243–45; transplanting, 197–99;
tropical, 1356; watering, 201, 237–
39; in wet ground, 229–30
Ornithogalum arabicum, 491, 1134
Ornithogalum (Star-of-Bethlehem),
491, 529, 1049–50, 1134
Orthene, 1185
Ostrich-plume fern, 1101
Outdoors, planning, 86–87
"Overliming" injury, 43
Own-root lilac, 374
Oxalis, 528, 1134–35
Oyster-plant (salsify) (*T. porrifo-
lius*), 38, 876
Oystershell scale, 1281

Pachysandra, 88, 222
Pacific dogwood, 344–45
Palm, 1076–77, 1258
Pandanus (screw-pine), 1076–77
Pansy, 38, 141, 191, 295, 650, 691–
93, 1258–59, 1345, 1367, 1377,
1390, 1397, 1409, 1423, 1430

Papaya, 1362–63
Paper garden plan, 87–88
Paper-white narcissus, 1134
'Paradise' asparagus, 817
Parking space, 112
Parsley, 37, 149, 795, 861–62, 1016, 1034, 1035–36
Parsnip, 38, 753, 862–63
Parthenocissus, 455–56
Partridge-berry (*M. repens*), 182
Passion-flower (*P. caerulea*), 1105–6, 1387, 1423
Paths, planning and landscaping, 114–16
Patience-plant, 673, 1059–60, 1244
Patio, 1364; furniture, 119; gardens, 120; location, 117; planning and landscaping, 89–90, 116–21; roses for, 572–73; screening, 121; shade, 118; *See also* Terrace
'Paul's Scarlet' climber, 560, 1272
Paul's scarlet hawthorn, 347, 1239
Pavement planting, 163
PCNB, *see* Terrachlor
Pea, 37, 58, 753, 754, 766–67, 795, 808, 864–67, 1301; dwarf, 803; everlasting, 38; perennial, 639–40; supports for, 803, 865–66
'Peace' rose, 1403
Peach, 38, 906, 936–40, 1254, 1311, 1360, 1363, 1386, 1387, 1423; age to plant, 908; approximate life of, 937; domesticating wild-grown, 938; dwarf, 922–23; failure to bear, 937; fertilizer, 907; flowering, 350; pest control, 1321–23; productive life, 915; propagation, 939–40; pruning, 938–39; rootstocks, 904; seeds, 919; spur types, 937; varieties of, 902
Peach borer, 1321, 1322
Peach-leaf curl, 1322–23
Peanut, 37, 863
Peanut cactus (*C. silvestri*), 1110
Pear, 38, 350, 940–42, 1387, 1397,

1429; age to plant, 908; clay soil and, 20; dwarf, 940, 1325; harvesting, 916; pest control, 1323–25; productive life, 915; pruning, 941–42; rootstocks, 904; seeds, 919; soil and fertilizer, 940; varieties of, 902
Pear blight, 1324
Pearlwort (*S. subulata*), 747–48, 1426
Pear psylla, 942, 1325
Pear slug, 1324–25
Peat moss, 4–5, 19, 57, 535, 536, 612, 780, 1010, 1054, 1397; fertilizer value, 52–53; and sand (50–50 mixture), 80–81
Pebbles, bottom of container, 208
Pecan, 996, 1259, 1382–83, 1386
Peduncle necrosis, 1271
Pennsylvania, 333, 348, 397, 485, 688, 814, 854, 969, 993, 1037, 1171, 1177, 1181, 1186, 1190, 1215, 1218, 1223, 1226, 1247, 1252, 1261, 1262, 1265, 1266, 1268–69, 1271, 1273, 1274, 1276, 1280, 1282–83, 1295, 1297, 1300, 1304, 1306, 1307, 1320, 1322, 1324
Penstemon, 168, 631
Peony, 69, 588, 631–39, 1260, 1345, 1363, 1371, 1377, 1383, 1397, 1409–10, 1411, 1414, 1423; bloom, 634; disbudding, 634–35; division, 637–38; fail to bloom, 637; fertilizer, 633; foliage, 636; planting, 633–34; scored and rated, 637; seeds, 638; soil, 632–33; tree-peony varieties, 639–40
Peperomia, 1077, 1243–44
Pepper, 37, 753, 790, 867, 1301
Pepper-grass (*L. virginicum*), 153
Pepperidge, *see* Sour gum
Peppermint, 38, 149
Perennials, 575–651; alyssum (or basket-of-gold), 592; amsonia (or

Perennials (*cont'd*)
bluestar), 592; anchusa, 593;
aster, 593; astible, 593; baby's-
breath, 594; bleedingheart, 594;
books on, 1440; cacti, 594–95;
candytuft, 595; carnation, 595–97;
Christmas-rose, 597–98; chrysanthemum, 599–608; city garden,
204; clay soil and, 18; columbine,
608–9; culture, 582–89; cuttings,
590–91; darkening color, 50; day-
lily, 609–11; delphinium, 611–18;
division of, 591; in dry, sunny
areas, 228–29; eremurus, 618–19;
eupatorium, 619; fertilizers, 583–
84; fuchsia, 619; gerbera, 619–20;
hardy herbaceous, 576; heliopsis,
620; hollyhock, 620; hybridizing,
591–92; irises, 620–29; kitchen
herb garden, 133; lupine, 629–30;
monkshood, 630–31; Oriental
poppy, 645–46; penstemon, 631;
peony, 631–39; phlox, 641–43;
planting and transplanting, 584–
86; platycodon, 644; plumbago,
644–45; primrose, 645–46; propagation, 589–92; pyrethrum, 647;
rose-mallow, 647–48; salvia, 648;
sandy soil, 222; scabiosa, 648;
seashore, 223; seeds, 589–90;
shade, 103, 217, 227, 228, 578–79;
shasta daisy, 648; soil preparation,
582–83; sources for, 1453–54; for
special purposes, 578–82; specific
plants, 592–651; spurge, 649;
sterilizing soil for, 80; tall and
spindly, 23; tradescantia, 649;
tree peony, 639–40; tritoma, 649;
veronica, 650; viola, 650; violets,
650–51; in wet soil, 230; what to
grow, 577–82; "wild sweet pea"
(perennial pea), 639–40; winter
protection, 587–89; yucca, 651
Perennial tree onion (*A. cepa proliferum*), 860

Pergola, 132
Periwinkle, 675–76
Perlargonium, 136
Pernettya, 1416
Persian lilac (*S. persica*), 376, 378,
1362
Persian walnut, 998–99
Persimmon, 971–72
Peruvian-daffodil, 527
Pest control, 1137–1329; biological,
1144, 1149, 1152; evergreens,
1231–32; ferns, 1233–34; fruits,
1217, 1310–29; house and greenhouse plants, 1242–84; how to get
information, 1170; importance of
diagnosis, 1139–41; lawn, 740–47,
1248–49; oil sprays, 1184–85;
ornamentals, 1200–41; roses, 545–
47, 1267–76; seed treatment, 1189;
soil sterilization, 1191; spray
materials, 1193–94; types of,
1141–45; vegetables, 1285–1309;
See also names of animals; bugs;
diseases; insects
Pesticides, 741, 1137, 1138–39; for
a greenhouse, 285; and public
health, 1185; *See also* names of
pesticides
Pests, books on, 1440
Pet litter, 81
Petunia, 38, 661–62, 676–79; beetle
destruction, 1172; grown indoors,
1067; pest control, 1261–62;
seedlings, 1337
Pfitzer juniper, 392, 407
pH, 9–10; modifying, 11; testing for,
45–46
Philodendron, 1106–7
Phlox, 16, 38, 168, 641–43, 661,
1383, 1402; perennial, 1363, 1390,
1394; pest control, 1262–63; rock
garden, 168
Phlox subulata, 168
Phosfon, 604
Phosphate rock, 13

Phosphorus, 13, 49, 777; effect on plant growth, 47
Phosphorus deficiency, 49
Photinia, 1263
Photosynthesis, 14
pH scale, 10
Phyllophaga, 1174
Phylloxera, 904
Pick-a-back (*Tolmiea*), 1078–79
Picket fence, 107, 109
Pickles, 1298
Pie-plant, *see* Rhubarb
Pieris (*Andromeda*), 37, 39, 430–31, 1263
Pieris japonica, 431
Pinching, 242–43
Pinching back, 665
Pine, 37, 398, 407–9, 1231; pest control, 1263–65; soil around, 30; white, 408, 446, 1264
Pineapple (*Ananas*), 1078–79
Pineapple-guava (*F. sellowiana*), 1361
Pine bark, 115–16
Pine beetle, 1264
Pine mice, 467
Pine needles, 45, 53, 67; mulching with, 234
Pink dogwood, 343–44
Pink hawthorn, 206
Pink hydrangea, 373
Pink lady's-slipper (*C. acaule*), 181
Pinks, 167, 596, 597, 672
Pinkshell (*R. vaseyi*), 359
Pin oak, 14, 337
Pinxterbloom (*R. nudiflorum*), 358, 359
Pipsissewa (*C. umbellata*), 183
Pissard (or purpleleaf) plum, 350
Pistachio, 996
Pitcher plant (*S. purpurea*), 173, 182
Pit house, sun-heated, 274
Plane, *see* Sycamore
Planning and landscaping, 85–191; to attract birds, 184; banks, 104–5;

bonsai, 185; books on, 1439; children's gardens, 183–84; container gardens, 185–87; design principles, 91–96; driveways, 111–13; entrances, 96–100; espaliers, 110–11; fences, gates, and walls, 106–10; foundation, 88–89, 96–100; fragrant gardens, 187; game areas, 128–30; garden features and accessories, 131–33; garden lighting, 121; herbs, 133–54; influences on, 85–86; lawns, 106; outdoors, 86–87; on paper, 87; paths and walks, 114–16; patio or terrace, 89–90, 116–21; pools and water gardens, 121–28; for privacy and comfort, 92; recreation areas, 90–91; rock gardens, 154–69; roof gardens, 187–89; screening, 100–1; shade, 102–4; sun deck, 90; sunken gardens, 189; surface drainage, 105–6; tool houses and utility areas, 130–31; trees and shrubs, 87–88, 101–2; wildflower gardens, 169–83; window-box, 190–91
Plantain, 743, 1334, 1337
Plant breeding, books on, 1440
Plant food, *see* Fertilizers; Manure
Plant injury, how to diagnose, 1140
Plant lice, *see* Aphids; Lice
Plant nutrition, *see* Nutrients
Plant room, compared to a greenhouse, 1021
Plant societies, list of, 1446–48
Plastic molded pools, 122–23
Plastic pots, 1012
Plowing, soil, 31–32
Plugs (biscuits of sod), 722
Plum, 38, 350, 943–44, 1265, 1311, 1325, 1326–27, 1429; age to plant, 908; European, 902; productive life of, 915; rootstocks, 904; seeds, 919; varieties of, 902
Plumbago (leadwort), 644–45
Plum curculio, 900, 1318, 1323

Pocket gopher (ground rat), 499, 1166
Pod spot, 1289, 1307–8
Poinsettia (*E. pulcherrima*), 1089–90, 1265, 1350
Poison-ivy, 32, 1337, 1339, 1341
Poison-oak, 1337–38
Poisonous plants, 471, 691, 871, 1073, 1088
Poke-weed, 1340
Pole bean, 753, 818–20, 1289
Polianthes (tuberose), 528
Pollination, fruit trees, 903, 914–16
Polyantha rose, 532, 541, 568, 1269, 1389
Polyethylene and cuttings, 251, 254
Pomegranate, 438–39, 1079, 1417; dwarf, 1363
Pompom chrysanthemum, 602, 603
Ponytail (*B. recurvata*), 1071
Pools and water gardens, 121–26; fencing in, 129; flowering plants, 125
Poor soil, 26–27
Poplar, 338, 1265–66, 1339–40
Poppy, 38, 679–80, 1377–78
Porous hose, 810
Portulaca, 16, 680
Post-and-rail fence, 108
Potash, 13–14, 47, 49, 69, 777–78
Potash deficiency, 49
Potassium, 13–14
Potassium nitrate, 83
Potato, 37, 49, 753, 754, 766–67, 781, 804–5, 867–73; pest control, 1301–3
Potato blight, 1137, 1301–2
Potato bug, 871, 1152–53, 1217, 1302–3
Potato rot, 1302
Pothos (*S. pictus*), 1107
Pot-marigold (*C. officinalis*), 149–50
Potpourris, 140–41
Pots and potted plants: for annuals, 656; dwarf fruit in, 947; green-house, 279–81; herbs in, 134, 137–38; house plants, 1012–13; roses in, 538–39; soil, 210; sterilizing soil, 80; vegetables in, 812; watering, 201
Potting soil, 1010
Poultry manure, 54
Prayer-plant, 1075
Praying mantis, 1151, 1186
'President Grevy' lilac, 377–78
Prickly-pear cactus, 1210
Primrose (*Primula*), 168, 295, 646–47, 1063
Primula malacoides, 295
Primula obconica, 295
Primula sinensis, 295, 1063
Princess-pine, 180
Privet (*Ligustrum*), 374–78, 380, 446–47, 1266, 1397
Problem areas: foundation material for, 213–19; ground covers for, 219–22
Propagation, 196–97, 245–64; annuals, 655–62; books on, 1440; broad-leaved evergreens, 420–21; bulbs, corms, tubers, 248–50; cloning and tissue culture, 257–58; by cuttings, 196, 197, 250–57; deciduous trees and shrubs, 321–23; grafting, 260–64; house plants, 1025–27; layering, 258–59; leaf cutting, 197; narrow-leaved evergreens, 399–400; orchard fruits, 918–20; ornamentals, 196–97, 245–64; perennials, 589–92; roses, 552–58; seeds, 245–48; shrubs, 252, 321–23; suckers, stolons, and runners, 259–60; trees, 321–23; wildflowers, 173–74
Protection, control by, 1143–44
Pruning, 201–2, 239–42; books on, 1440–41; deciduous trees and shrubs, 316–18; difference between shearing and, 239; espaliers, 111; fruit trees, 911–12; grape,

Pruning (*cont'd*)
962–63, 965–66; house plants,
1005; narrow-leaved evergreens,
397–98; orchard fruit, 911–12; ornamentals, 201–2, 239–42; root-,
243; roses, 539–43; shrubs, 202,
301–2, 316–18; tools necessary
for, 241–42; trees, 202, 301–2,
316–18; vines, 301–2
Prunus (pissardii) **cerasifera 'Atro-
purpurea,'** 1265
Pteris, 293, 1090
Public gardens, list of, 1448–50
Pulverized granite (granite meal), 72
Pumice rock, 156
Pumpkin, 37, 211, 754, 766, 806,
807, 873, 1298, 1304
Pumpkin vine borer, 1304
Purple-fringed orchis (*H. psycodes*),
181
Purple-leaf plum, 943, 1190
Purple lilac, 446
Purple raspberry, varieties of, 903
Purslane, 1338, 1340
Puschkinia, 491
Pussy willow (*S. discolor*), 387, 1228
Pyracantha coccinea 'Lalandei,'
431–32
Pyracantha (firethorn), 431–32,
1266, 1363–64
Pyramid juniper, 1248
Pyrethrum (*C. coccineum*), 647,
1186

Quackgrass, 743, 761, 1336, 1338
Quarantine laws, 1142
Quince (*C. oblonga*), 972–73, 1327;
productive life, 915; varieties of,
902

Rabbit-eye blueberry (*V. ashei*), 953
Rabbits, 180, 467, 516, 913, 939,
990, 1258–59; control of, 1186–
87; keeping away, 1312
Rabbit's-foot fern, 1100–1

Raccoons, 1195
Radish, 37, 753, 754, 766–67, 873–
74, 1304
Rain-lily, 1399
Raisins on the vine, 968
Rambler rose, 560, 1270; support for,
571
Ranch-type house, 100
Ranunculus, 295–96, 500, 528, 1135,
1358, 1423
Rape, 38
Raspberry, 37, 767, 897–98, 986,
987–91, 1327–28, 1387, 1398;
everbearing, 984, 989, 991; insects
and diseases, 990; mulching, 989;
planting, 987–88; pruning, 988;
varieties of, 902–3
Raspberry cane borer, 1328
Rats, control of, 1178
Raw ground limestone, 42
**Rebuttable Presumption Against
Registration** (RPAR), 1138
Recreation areas, planning, 90–91
Red and white amaryllis (*Hip-
peastrum*), 502
Redbud (*Cercis*), 351, 1376
Red-cedar, 37, 406, 412, 932, 1232,
1248, 1316–17
Red clay soil, 19
Red clover, 38, 56, 57
Red currant, 955, 956
'Red Delicious' apple, 926
'Red Lake' currant, 1319–20
Red oak, 37, 337
Red pine, 407–8
Red raspberry, 897–98, 906, 984,
989–90, 991; varieties of, 902
Red raspberry blight, 1380
Redroot (pigweed), 1338
Red rust, 1318
Red spider-lily, 1378
Red spider mite, 516, 1023–24, 1180,
1209, 1243, 1247, 1264–65, 1280
Red top, 37
Redwood burl, 1080

Refuse, compost heap, 60, 61–62
Regional gardening: books on, 1441;
   problems (arranged by states),
   1342–1432
Repellent, 1170
Repotting, 283–84; house plants, 83,
   84, 1006–7, 1012–13
Residual contact insecticide, 1170
Resmethrin, 1188
Rest period: greenhouse plants, 284;
   house plants, 1010
Resurrection-lily, 490
Retaining wall: planting, 164; roses
   for, 574
Retinosporas, 390
Rhamnus cathartica, 440, 1334
Rhizomes, 623, 625
Rhode Island, 761, 1213, 1219, 1220,
   1272, 1284
Rhododendron, 37, 39, 40, 44, 45,
   46, 66, 318, 415, 416, 417, 418,
   421–22, 432–33, 1341, 1346,
   1383, 1394–95, 1402, 1422–23,
   1427, 1428; books on, 433, 1441;
   from cuttings, 434; in foundation
   plantings, 217; with fragrant flowers, 433–34; hardiest hybrids, 433;
   pest control, 1205–7, 1266–67
Rhubarb, 37, 874–75, 1304
Rhubarb curculios, 1304
Rice hulls, 1423
Rock gardens, 154–69; books on,
   1441; bulbs, 165–66; city, 205;
   construction, 156; culture, 157–58;
   evergreens, 166; fertilizer, 155–56;
   moraine, 162; pavement planting,
   163; planning, 154; planting and
   culture, 157–58; with pool, 125–
   26; shrubs, 166–67; soil and fertilizer, 155–56; specific plants for,
   167–69; wall, 163–65; watering,
   158; what to grow, 158–61
Rock maple, 325
Rocky clay soil, 19–20
Rocky Mountain cherry, 935

Rodents, *see* names of rodents
Roman hyacinth (*H. orientalis
   albulus*), 480–81
Roof gardens, 187–89; vegetables,
   812
Room humidifier, 1002
Root celery, 833
Root cuttings, 256–57
Root knot, 1047
Root-knot nematode, 1183–84
Root lice, 1212
Root maggots, 879, 1291–92
Root-pruning, 243
Root rot, 1198, 1204, 1234, 1300
Roots: cuttings, 250, 254, 256–57;
   function of, 193; tree, killing,
   319–21
Rootstock, fruit trees, 904
Roquette or rocket salad, 876
Rosa damascena (Damask rose),
   560–61
Rosa multiflora (Living Fence
   Rose), 447
Rose, 69, 82, 296, 309, 317, 530–74,
   1228, 1346, 1364–65, 1367, 1371,
   1378, 1380, 1383–84, 1386, 1388,
   1389–90, 1392, 1395, 1398, 1400,
   1402–3, 1406, 1408, 1410, 1412,
   1414–15, 1416–17, 1419, 1424,
   1427, 1430, 1431–32; applying
   wood ashes to, 68–69; beetle destruction, 1172; best time to plant,
   536–37; books on, 1441–42; borders, 559; budding, 553; city garden, 205; color categories, 533;
   cones, 549–50; culture, 534–52;
   cuttings, 554–56; darkening color,
   50; displaying, 551–52; early
   bloomers, 561; for every purpose,
   558–74; fertilizing, 543–44; fragrance, 562; grafting, 556; greenhouse, 564; ground covers, 564;
   hedges, 564–65; as house plant,
   1091; hybridizing, 557; hybrid perpetuals, 565; hybrid sweetbriars,

Rose (cont'd)
572; hybrid teas, 530, 532, 549, 565–66, 1367, 1389, 1395, 1398, 1405–6, 1411, 1430; importing, 567; insects and diseases, 1190–91; layering, 556; miniature, 296, 532, 550, 567–68; moss, 567, 568, 1400; mulching, 544–45; organizations, 574; pest control, 545–47, 1267–76; planting, 536–39; potted, 538–39; propagation, 552–58; pruning, 539–43; ratings, 569; sandy soil, 16; seeds, 557; selecting plants, 532–34; shrubs, 570; soil preparation, 534–36; sources for, 1454; species, 570–71; spraying, 546–47; standard grades, 533; summer care and problems, 547–48; supports, 571; terraces and patios, 572–73; transplanting, 539; tree (standard), 573–74; types and classes of, 532–33; understocks, 557–58; walls, 574; watering, 545; winter protection, 548–51; See also names of roses
Rose-acacia (Robinia), 381–82
Rose campion (L. coronaria), 693
Rose chafer (or rose bug), 1272, 1311, 1320–21
Rose daphne (Daphne cneorum), 424, 425, 1413, 1428
Rose-mallow (H. moscheutos), 647–48
Rosemary (R. officinalis), 150, 1034, 1036
Rose midge, 1274
Rose-of-Sharon (H. syriacus), 313, 382
Rose petals, 140
Roseshell azalea, 358–59
Rotary sprinklers, 810
Rotation, crop, 763–64
Rotenone, 1139, 1160, 1188, 1267
Rough bluegrass, 703
Rubber plant (Ficus), 1080, 1276

Rubus, 982
Rue anemone (A. thalictroides), 175
Rue (R. graveolens), 150–51
Rugosa rose, 569
Rugosa shrubs, 570
Runners, propagating by, 259–60
Russell lupine, 1252
Russian mulberry, 970
Russian-olive (Elaeagnus), 383, 425
Russian statice (P. suworowii), 294
Rust on plants, 1188–89, 1211, 1219–20, 1226, 1233–34, 1240, 1254, 1262, 1284, 1308, 1404
Ruta graveolens, 150–51
Rye, 37, 56, 57, 58
Ryegrass, 56, 57, 701; improved varieties of, 702–3; Italian, 1377

Sacred lily-of-India, 1132
Sacred lotus (N. nucifera), 126
Sage (S. officinalis), 151, 1016, 1034, 1035
Sagina moss, 1354
Sagina subulata, 1417
Sago-palm (C. revoluta), 1080–81
Saikei, 1033–34
St. Augustine grass, 700, 1372
St. Brigid anemone, 500
Salad burnet (P. sanguisorba), 151
Salpiglossis, 296, 680
Salsify or oyster-plant, 38, 876
Saltpeter, 56
Salvia, 680–81
Salvia pitcheri, 648
Salvia sclarea, 144
Sand, mixing in clay soil, 17–18
Sandbox, 119; play area, 129–30
Sandburs, 1338
Sand culture, 82
Sand (or cherry) plum, 944
Sandy slopes and banks, 224–25
Sandy soil, 16–17, 906; fertilizer, 783; herbs, 138; lawn, 710; plants for, 222–23; vegetables, 16–17, 761, 771, 777, 813

Sanitation, house plants, 1024–25
San Jose scale, 931, 942
'Santa' Rosa plum, 1363
Sapota, 1365
Sassafras, 338
Satin flower (Godetia), 673
Saucer magnolia (Magnolia x
 soulangiana), 348–49
Savin juniper, 407
Savory, 151–52
Savoy cabbage, 828–29
Sawdust, 6, 53, 70, 234–35
Saxifragas, 168, 1082
Scab, 872, 1302
Scabiosa, 648, 681
Scale insects, 1243, 1249, 1253, 1263,
 1271; control of, 1189
Scarlet runner bean, 452–53
Schefflera (B. actinophylla), 1081
Schizanthus, 1365
Scion (cion), 260–61
Sclerotium delphinii, 1215
Sclerotium rot, 1225
Scotch broom, 363
Scotch rose, 570
Scots pine, 396, 1264
Scraggly plants, 23–24
Screening (or enclosing) a yard,
 100–1; patio, 121; utility area, 131
Screw-pine, 1076–77
Scrub oak, 37
Scuffle hoe, 810
'Scuppernong' grape, 966–67, 969
Sea kelp, 71
Sea-onion, 1202
Seashore, plants for, 223–24
Seaside, books on, 1435
Seaweed, 71
'Sebago' potato, 872
'Seckel' pear, 941
Sedge peat, 52–53
Sedum, 169, 1117–18, 1276
Seed boxes, counteracting sour soil
 in, 39–40
Seedlings, transplanting, 199, 247

Seeds: damping off disease, 1159–60;
 green-manure crops, 56; house
 plants from, 1026; lawn area,
 705–6; lawn grasses, 717–21;
 narrow-leaved evergreens, 399–
 400; ornamentals, 245–48; perennials, 589–90; propagation, 245–
 48; rose, 557; starting, 207, 246–
 47, 249, 1027; stratification of,
 248; treating, 1189; vegetable,
 788–97; vermiculite, 81; wildflower, 174
Seed sowers (tool), 810
Semesan, 1237
Sensitive-plant (M. pudica), 1081
Septic tank, vegetable garden and,
 812
Serbian spruce, 398
7–7–7 fertilizer, 56, 76, 859
Sevin, 1144
Sewage sludge, 5, 45
Shadblow (Amelanchier), 351
Shade: books on, 1435; city garden,
 204; foundation material for, 217–
 19; grasses, 715; herbs, 136; ornamentals, 226–28; patio, 118; per-
 ennials, 103, 217, 227, 228, 578–
 79; planning and landscaping for,
 102–4; planting in, 226–28; and
 soil, 28; trees, 101, 325, 326; vege-
 tables and, 769–70; wild plants
 under, 170; for window boxes, 190
Shaded soil, 29–31
Shaded stream, wildflowers, 173
Shagbark hickory (C. ovata), 995
Shale ground, 27
Shallot, 860; See also Onion
Shasta daisy (Chrysanthemum x
 superbum), 648, 1217, 1401, 1420
Shearing, difference between pruning
 and, 239
Sheep manure, 584, 1338
Sheep's fescue, 38
'Sheridan' grape, 968
Shinleaf (P. elliptica), 183

Shirley poppy (*P. rhoeas*), 679–80
Shooting-star (*D. meadia*), 182
Showy orchis (*O. spectabilis*), 181
Shredded redwood bark, 53
Shrimp-plant (*J. brandegeana*),
 1063–64
Shrub rose, 533, 570
Shrubs: abelia, 356–57; abeliophyllum, 357; acacia, 435; almond,
 357; amorpha, 357; aralia, 357–58;
 aromatic foliage, 356; to attract
 birds, 184, 355; azalea, 358–60;
 barberry, 360–61; bayberry, 361;
 bay tree, 435; bearberry, 361;
 beauty-bush, 361–62; benzoin,
 362; berried, 354; berries, 354;
 birds and, 355; bloom, 102, 355–
 56; blueberry, 362; books on, 1442;
 broom, 363; butterfly-bush, 363–
 64; camellia, 435–37; care of, 314–
 16; caryopteris, 364; chaste-tree,
 364–65; city garden, 205; in containers, 185, 186; cotoneaster, 365;
 crape-myrtle, 365–66; daphne,
 366; deciduous, 306–23, 353–56;
 deutzia, 366; dogwood, 367; dry,
 sunny areas, 228–29; dwarf, 353–
 54; enkianthus, 368; euonymus,
 368; fertilizing, 304–5, 309; foliage, 356; forsythia, 368–69; foundation area, 214, 215, 216, 218;
 for fragrance, 187; gardenia, 437–
 38; hazelnut, 370; honeysuckle,
 370; hydrangea, 370–74; indoor
 plants, 1091–97; jasmine, 438; kerria, 374; lime and, 43; mimosa,
 378; mistakes to avoid in planting
 (for landscaping effect), 95; mock-
 orange, 379–80; mulching, 303–4;
 oleander, 438; planning and landscaping, 101–2; planting time, 301;
 pomegranate, 438–39; privet, 374–
 78, 380; propagation, 252, 321–
 23; pruning, 202, 301–2, 316–18;
 quince, 380–81; in red clay soil,
 20; rock garden, 166–67; rose-
 acacia, 381–82; rose-of-Sharon,
 382; Russian-olive, 383; sandy soil,
 222; seashore, 223; selecting, 87–
 88; shaded place, 228; snowberry,
 383; soil and fertilizers, 306–9;
 sources for, 145–55; specific kinds
 of, 356–89; spirea, 383–84; stephanandra, 384; sumac, 384; sweet-
 shrub, 384–85; tamarisk, 385;
 tender shrubs, 435–39; transplanting, 309–14; viburnum, 385–86;
 watering, 302–3; weigela, 387; in
 wet soil, 230; what to grow, 353–
 54; when to buy, 299–300; windbreaks, 448–49; winterberry, 388;
 witch-hazel, 388–89; *See also*
 Hedges
Siberian elm, 324, 329–30, 445, 1228,
 1229, 1230
Siberian iris, 621, 624
Siberian squill (*Scilla*), 491
Siberian wallflower (*Erysimum*), 694
Sidedressings, fertilizer, 779, 780
Silent Spring (Carson), 1137
Silverbell (*Halesia*), 351–52
Silver juniper, 407
Silver leaf, leaves of, 67
Silver maple, 324, 1253
Simples, 140
Skimmia, 37, 434
Skimmia japonica, 434
"Slop culture," 81
Slope: excessive moss on, 29; for
 grapes, 959–60; plants for, 224–25
Sludge, 67–68
Slugs, 866, 1246, 1261, 1295; control
 of, 1190–91
Small gardens (for small properties),
 208–13
Smoketree, 352
Smyrna fig, 1385
Snails, 516, 1213; control of, 1190–
 91

Snake-palm (or hydrosme), 503, 1132
Snake-plant (*Sansevieria*), 1081–82
Snakes, 219
Snap bean, 819, 1286–87, 1289–90
Snapdragon (*Antirrhinum*), 82, 288–89, 661–62, 666, 681–83, 1067, 1276–77, 1392
Snap pea, 866–67
Snout beetle, 1323
Snowball, 312, 386
Snowberry bush (*S. rivularis*), 383
Snowdrop (*G. nivalis*), 480
Snowflake (*Leucojum*), 481
Snowhill hydrangea, 372
Soapy water, 70
Sod, 721, 722, 911
Sodded lawn, 721–22
'Sodus' purple raspberry, 989
Sod webworm, 746
Softwood cuttings, 250
Soggy soil, 28; drainage, 35
Soil Blender (electric-powered unit), 810
Soil grubs, *see* Grubs
Soilless gardening, 82–83, 197, 210; books on, 1442
Soils, 1–80; acidity, 10, 18, 36–41, 309, 907, 959; adobe, 1350, 1352, 1362; alkalinity, 10, 41–42, 959; artificial, 80–83; books on, 1442; cacti (indoors), 1108–9; for containers, 210; deciduous trees and shrubs, 306–9; digging or tilling, 772–74; drainage, 29, 34–35; fruit, 898–99, 905–7; greenhouse, 279–82; hanging baskets, 210; for herbs, 138, 1035; hotbed, 270; for house plants, 77, 83–84, 1005–8, 1010–12; lawn grasses, 703–5; nutrient elements, 11–14, 47–53; nutritional value of, 15; orchard fruit, 905–7; for perennials, 582–83; pH, 9–10, 11; plowing and digging, 31–32; preparation, 31–36; prob-

lems, 21–31; rock garden, 155–56; for roses, 534–36; sterilization, 79–80, 1191; terrarium, 1030; testing, 1–2, 45–46; tray or dish garden, 1033; types of, 15–20; vegetables, 772–88, 813; water and plant growth, 14–15; wildflower planting, 170–71, 174; for window boxes, 190; *See also* Compost and composting; Cultivation; Humus; Manure; Soilless gardening; types of soil
Soil-testing kit, 45–46
Solar energy, 269
Solar greenhouse, 275
"Solar pod" hotbed, 269
Solomon's-seal, 140
Soot, 71
Sooty mold, 1192
Sophora japonica (Japanese pagoda tree), 338
Sorghum, 38
Sorrel (*R. scutatus*), 877
Sour cherry, 915, 935
Sour gum, 339, 1393
"Sour soil," 39–40
South African or "Cape" bulbs, 529
South Carolina, 53, 316, 1248, 1408–11
South Dakota, 178, 680, 1411–12
Southern lawn grasses, 699–700; basic needs of, 696–98; suggested mowing height, 733; *See also* names of grasses
Sowbugs, 1192, 1261
Sowing: vegetables, 758; vegetable seeds, 758, 788–97
Soybean, 37, 56, 57, 59, 805, 819, 822–23; rabbit destruction, 1187
Soybean meal, 52, 57, 72
Spade, 809
Spading, 32, 1172–73
Spading fork, 809
Spanish iris, 624
Sparachetti, *see* Broccoli raab

Sparaxis, 527, 529
Sparrows, 866
Sparrow trap, 1152
Spathiphyllum, 1064
Spearmint, 38, 149
Spent mushroom manure, 5
Sphagnum moss, 81–82
Sphagnum peat, *see* Peat moss
Spice-bush, 362, 1384
Spider chrysanthemum, 608
Spider-lily (*Hymenocallis*), 1392, 1399
Spider-lily (*L. radiata*), 528
Spider mite, 1151, 1180, 1219, 1224, 1232, 1272
Spider-plant (*C. comosum*), 1082
Spiking a lawn, 729
Spinach, 38, 753, 754, 877–78, 1290
Spineless cacti, 595
Spirea 'Anthony Waterer,' 383–84
Spirea (*Spiraea*), 312, 383–84, 447
Spittlebugs, 1192–93
Split daffodil, 478
Split pit (disease), 1323
Sport, 571
Spotted wintergreen (*C. maculata*), 183
Sprayers (garden), 1194–95
Spraying, 1254; fruit trees, 910, 1310–11; roses, 546–47
Spray materials, 1193–94
Sprekelia formosissima (Jacobean-lily), 502, 529, 1400
Sprigs (stem fragments), 722
Spring beauty (Claytonia), 182
Spring season: applying fertilizers in, 77–78; cold frame, 267; rock-garden plants, 157
Springtails, 1024
Sprinklers, 123
Sprinkler systems, 719–20; for vege-tables, 801–2
Spruce, 37, 409–12, 448, 1277
Spruce gall, 1277
Spurge, flowering (*Euphorbia*), 649

Spuria iris, 624
Squash, 37, 804–5, 807, 878–80, 1298, 1304–5; acorn, 879; bush, 753; 'buttercup,' 879; crookneck, 1305; summer, 753, 805, 878, 880; winter, 753, 754, 806, 878–79, 880; zucchini, 880
Squash bug (stink bug), 1305, 1309
Squash vine borer, 1298, 1304–5
Squirrels, 499, 1221, 1297; control of, 1195
Staghorn fern, 1233
Staking plants, 244
Stalk borers, 879, 1216–17
Stalks, plowing under, 32
Stapelia, 1118
Star-lily or sand-lily (*Leucocrinum*), 481
Star-of-Bethlehem (*O. umbellatum*), 491, 529, 1049–50, 1134
"Starter" or "transplanting" solution, 778–79
State agricultural experiment sta-tions, list of (by state), 1444–46
Statuary, 132
Stem-rooting lily, 484
Stem rot, 1235, 1260, 1278
Stems, plant, 193–94
Stephanandra, 384
Stepping stones, 115
Steps, 116
Sterilization, soil, 79–80
Sternbergia, 465, 492
Stock, 38, 666, 683, 1278
Stoddard Solvent Oil, 1331–32
Stolons, 722–23; propagating by, 259–60
Stomach poison, 1170
Stone dust, 72
Stones, placing, 105
Stony soil, 27
Storage: herbs, 139–40; tools and equipment, 130
Strangleweed, 1335
Stratification of seeds, 248

Strawberry, 37, 767, 897, 906, 973–81, 1365, 1384, 1386, 1388, 1403; European, 981; everbearing, 979–80, 1413; failure to bear fruit, 977; fertilizer, 973; hill method of growing, 975; keeping birds away, 1152; matted-row method of growing, 975–76; mulching, 978–79; pest control, 1328–29; planting in a barrel, 980–81; propagation, 977; runnerless, 981; runners, 976, 977–78; setting out, 974–75; soil, 973; starting a patch, 974; varieties of, 903, 981; weeding, 976–77; wild, 981

Strawberry-geranium (*S. stolonifera*), 1082

Strawberry guava (*P. littorale*), 1361

Strawberry leaf roller, 1329

Strawberry weevil (or blossom clipper), 1328–29

Straw mulch, 870–71, 910

Strelitzia, 297, 1064–65, 1357

Streptomycin, 1195

Stringless bush bean, 820

Striped cucumber beetle, 879, 1263, 1297, 1298, 1304

Striped peperomia (*P. argyreia*), 1077

Structure of the plant, 193

Subsoil, 26, 35

Succession planting, 764–66

Succulents: books on, 1434–35; difference between cacti and, 1115; indoor house plants, 1115–18

Suckers, 841, 985; propagating by, 259–60

Sudan grass, 56

Sugarcane pulp, 53

Sulfate of ammonia, 13, 72–73

Sulfate of potash, 14

Sulfur, 40, 45, 1196, 1211, 1269

Sulfur dust, 1143, 1227

Sumac, 384, 1338

Summer-hyacinth (*G. candicans*), 480

Summer-lilac, 364

Summer phlox, 641–43

Summer savory (*S. hortensis*), 151–52

Summer season: fragrance in, 187; house plants, 1008–9, 1017

Summer-spinach, *see* New Zealand spinach

Summer squash, 753, 805, 878, 880

Sun deck, 90, 120

Sundew (*Drosera*), 173

Sundial, 132

Sunflower, 38; Mexican, 686

Sunken gardens, 189, 654

Sunrose (*Helianthemum*), 169

Superphosphate, 13, 56, 73–74, 780

Supports, 202–3, 243–45; for roses, 571; for vegetables, 802–3

Suppression, pest control by, 1142–43

Surface drainage, 105–6

Surface soil, cultivation, 231

Sweet alyssum (*L. maritima*), 38, 666, 667, 1065

Sweet bay (*M. virginiana*), 347, 349

Sweetbriar hybrid rose, 572

Sweet cherry, 915, 933, 935, 1381, 1401

Sweet Cicely (*M. odorata*), 152

Sweet clover, 56

Sweet corn (*Z. mays*), 805, 839–42, 1296–97; hybrid, 842; *See also* Corn

Sweet flag (*A. calamus*), 152

Sweet-gum, *see* Liquidambar

Sweet marjoram (*O. majorana*), 148, 1016, 1034

Sweet-olive (*O. fragrans*), 1065

Sweet pea (*L. odoratus*), 38, 204, 297, 683–86, 1278–79, 1367–68, 1404, 1411

Sweet pepper, 867

Sweet potato, 37, 753, 806, 807, 880–82, 1107
Sweet-shrub (*Calycanthus*), 384–85
Sweet sultan (*C. moschata*), 1372
Sweet vernal, 38
Sweet violet, 651
Sweet William (*D. barbatus*), 38, 693–94, 1279
Sweet woodruff (*A. odorata*), 152
Swimming pool, 129
Swiss chard, 882–83, 1306
Swiss-cheese plant, 1075
Sword fern, 1101, 1233–34
Sycamore, 338, 339, 1279; bark patterns, 307
Syringa persica (Persian lilac), 376, 378, 1362
Syringa reticulata (Japanese tree lilac), 374
Systemic (or chemotherapeutic) agents, 1196
Systemic insecticide, 1170

Tail fescue, 38
Tamarisk (*Tamarix*), 385, 448, 1427
Tampala, 753
Tamper, 656
Tanbark, substitutes for, 115–16
Tangelo, 1365
Tankage, 68, 72
Tank farming, 82–83
Tarragon (*A. dracunculus*), 152, 1034, 1036
Tazetta daffodil, 478
Tea herbs, 134
Tea plant (*C. sinensis*), 1365
Tea rose, 572; mauve hybrid, 566
Temperatures: greenhouse, 278–79; house plant, 1001–2, 1015–16
Tender bulbs, 500–29; for indoors, 1122–36; potting, 1013
Tennessee, 1209, 1231, 1239, 1260, 1307, 1333, 1418–19
Tennis court, 129
10–6–4 fertilizer, 75

Tent caterpillars, 932, 1196–97
Tepee supports, 803
Terminal bud, 243
Termites, 1197, 1217
Terrace, 1340; annuals, 654; difference between patio and, 116; dwarf fruit trees, 947–48; planning and landscaping, 89–90, 116–21; roses for, 572–73; shapes and styles, 117; soil erosion and, 22–23
Terrachlor (PCNB), 79, 1158, 1197, 1261
Terrariums, 1030–32, 1099; books on, 1442; soil, 1030
Texas, 28, 491, 686, 692, 1178, 1182–83, 1189, 1199, 1210, 1212, 1216, 1217, 1223, 1245, 1259–60, 1262, 1263, 1266, 1274, 1276–77, 1286, 1298, 1305, 1309, 1419–25
Texas root rot, 1198
Thalictrum dipterocarpum, 590
Thanksgiving cactus, 292, 1112–14
Thatch, 725–26
Thinnings, 797–98
Thin plants, 23–24
Thiram, 79
'Thornfree' blackberry, 986
Thornless honey locust (*G. triacanthos* 'Inermis'), 331
3–5–50 Bordeaux mixture, 1153
Thrips, 525, 861, 1202, 1224, 1237, 1238, 1245, 1273, 1300, 1340
Thyme (*Thymus*), 153, 1034, 1340
Tigerflower, 529
Tiger lily, 489
Tigridia, 529, 1237, 1279–80
Tilth, 33
Timothy, 38
Tinted spring tree foliage, 324
Tip burn, 853
Tissue culture, 258
Tithonia (Mexican sunflower), 686
Toadstools, 39, 1249
Tobacco, 37; nicotiana, 588, 675
Tobacco dust, 1249, 1307

'Tokay' grape, 964
Tomato, 37, 753, 762, 766–67, 770, 781, 790, 883–90; best for home garden, 888; "determinate" varieties, 883; fertilizer, 883; greenhouse disease, 286–87; hotbeds, 268; insects and diseases, 887–88; mulching, 886; night temperature and, 213; pest control, 1306–9; planting, 883–85; pruning, 885–86; resistant varieties, 889; seedlings, 885; soils, 883; staking, 885; supports, 802, 803; vine-ripened, 888
Tomato hornworm, 1309
Tomato juice, 890
Tool houses, 130–31
Topiary, 132–33, 241
Topsoil, 3–4, 26–27, 711; adding fertilizer to, 27; for flowers and vegetables, 26; on sandy ground, 16
Torenia (wishbone flower), 686–87
Town-house garden area, 96
Townsend moles, 1181
Trace elements, 50, 778
Tradescantia, 649
Tradescantia fluminensis, 1107–8
Trailing arbutus (E. repens), 37, 176
Training: fruit trees, 911–12; grape, 965; hedges, 443; house plants, 1005; orchard fruit, 911–12
Transplanting: annuals, 662–64; art of, 197–99; deciduous trees and shrubs, 309–14; layering and, 258–59; narrow-leaved evergreen, 393–97; ornamentals, 197–99; perennials, 584–86; roses, 539; seedlings, 247; trees and shrubs, 309–14; vegetables, 798–99
Transvaal daisy, see Gerbera
Tray garden, 1033–34
Tree fern (A. australis), 1360
Tree-of-heaven (Ailanthus), 326
Tree peony, 639–40, 1404

Trees: ailanthus, 326; air-purifying capacity of, 206; aphids on, 1147; to attract birds, 184; bark patterns, 307; birch, 326–28; books on, 1442–43; broad-leaved evergreens, 414–35; care of, 314–16; catalpa, 328–29; cherry, 341; city garden, 205–6; corktree, 329; crab apple, 341–42; cutting limbs, 240; deciduous, 306–41; decorative flowering, 341–52; with decorative fruit, 325; dogwood, 342–45; dressing a wound, 240–41; elm, 329–30; euonymus, 330; fertilizing, 304–5; franklinia and gordonia, 345; fruit, 895–97, 922–23, 944–48; ginkgo, 330–31; golden-rain-tree, 346; greedy roots, 323; ground cover around, 221; hawthorn, 346–47; honey locust, 331; hornbeam, 331; horse-chestnut, 331–32; laburnum, 347; larch, 332; linden, 331; liquidambar (sweetgum), 333; magnolia, 347–50; maple, 333–35; mountain-ash, 335–36; mulching, 303–4; narrow-leaved evergreens, 389–413; oak, 337; pear, 350; planning and landscaping, 101–2; planting time, 301; plum, 350; poplar, 338; propagation, 321–23; pruning, 202, 301–2, 316–18; redbud, 351; in red clay soil, 20; roots, killing, 319–21; sandy soil, 222; sassafras, 338; seashore, 223; selecting, 87–88; shadblow, 351; shade, 101, 325, 326; shapes of, 308; silverbell, 351–52; smoketree, 352; soil and fertilizers, 306–9; sophora, 338; sources for, 1454–55; sour gum, 339; for special purposes, 323–26; specific kinds of, 326–41; sycamore, 339; transplanting, 309–14; tulip tree, 340; watering, 302–3; in wet soil, 230; when to buy, 299–

Trees (*cont'd*)
300; willow, 340–41; windbreaks, 448–49; yellow-wood, 352; *See also* Christmas trees
Tree (standard) rose, 573–74
Trellis, 967, 983, 988
Trench, defined, 795
Tribasic copper, 1153–54
Trillium, 170, 182–83
Trillium grandiflorum, 182
Trillium ovatum, 182
Trillium nivale, 182
Trillium viride luterum, 182
Trimming hedges, 443
Tritelia, 469
Tritonia, 529, 649, 1388, 1391
Trout-lily, 479–80
Trumpet vine (*Campsis*), 1280, 1338, 1353, 1380
'Trysomic Seven-week' stock seed, 683
Tuberose, 528
Tuberous begonia, 1207–8
Tubers: propagating, 248–50; tender, 500–29; *See also* Bulbs; Corms
Tubs: dwarf fruit trees in, 947–48; soil, 210; vegetables in, 812
Tulip, 165, 466–67, 492–500, 1121, 1346–47, 1379, 1405, 1411–12; bloom, 290, 495–96; books on, 1443; with daffodils, 474; diseases, 498; fertilizer, 493; for indoor bloom, 290; most satisfactory for average garden, 500; pest control, 1280–81; rodents and, 467; seeds, 498; soil, 493; time to plant, 494; transplanting, 497; types available, 499
Tulip tree (*L. tulipifera*), 340, 1281–82
Tupelo, *see* Sour gum
Turf area, *see* Lawns
Turf-Builder, 1331–32
Turnaround, for a car, 112, 113
Turnip, 37, 49, 753, 754, 777, 807, 890, 1309
Twelve apostles, *see* Neomarica
2, 4-D herbicide, 707, 724, 741, 744, 1332, 1334
2–10–10 fertilizer, 76, 780

Umbrella (catalpa) tree, 328–29
Umbrella Kniffin, 965
Umbrella-plant (*C. alternifolius*), 1082
Understock, 261, 557–58, 1423
U. S. Department of Agriculture, 1137
Upland cress (*B. verna*), 154, 842–43, 1340
Urceolina peruviana, 1403
Urea, 73, 737
Ureaform (uraform), 73
Urginea maritima (sea-onion), 1202
Utah, 343, 1190, 1214, 1226, 1269, 1318, 1425
Utility areas, 130–31

Vacation care, house plants, 1018–19
Vallota, 502, 1135
Vandalism, 772
Vanhouttei spirea, 313
Vapam, 80
Varicolored corn, 842
Variegated plants, 1082–83
Vegetables, 749–893; acidity, 785–86; adjusting gravel soil for, 16; in alkali ground, 41, 785; auto exhaust fumes and, 207; in the backyard, 208; basement or cellar, 811; books on, 1443; catalog description, 211–12; clay soil and, 20; in cold frame, 811–12; community gardens, 771–72; considerable space requirements, 753; cultivation, 800; difficult to grow, 754; digging or tilling, 772–74; drainage, 751; dwarf, 210; equipment, 752, 760, 809–11; for exhibition

Vegetables (*cont'd*)
purposes, 808–9; fertilizers, 76,
778–85; frost-hardy, 761; general-
purpose spray mixture for, 1194;
in gravel or water culture, 82;
greenhouse, 276; green manures
(cover crops), 786–88; harvesting,
804–5; hotbed, 269; indoor sowing, 789–93; intercropping, 764–
65; irrigation, 802; Japanese beetle
destruction, 1174; keeping birds
away, 1152; knowing when soil is
right, 33; least space requirements,
753; lime requirements, 774–75;
location, 750; maintenance, 797–
809; mini-garden containers, 209;
mulching, 804; in the North (when
to plant), 763; organic, 812–13;
pest control, 1285–1309; planning
ahead, 754–56; planning the garden, 758–72; planning for winter
supplies, 756; preparing the
ground, 756; protection, 751–52;
reasons for growing, 749–50; roof
garden, 188, 812; rotation, 763–64;
sandy soil and, 16–17, 761, 771,
777, 813; septic-tank factor, 812;
shade, 769–70; short season requirements, 754; size of plot, 750–
51; in soggy soil, 28; soil preparation, 772–88, 813; sources for,
1455–56; sowing and planting,
758, 788–97; specific vegetables,
813–93; starting a home garden
(steps to take), 768; succession
planting, 764–66; supports, 802–3;
10 x 16-foot garden, 757; that yield
most, 753; thinnings, 797–98; topsoil and, 26; transplanting, 798–99;
20 x 30-foot garden, 757; use of
space, 766–68; watering, 801–2;
weed killers, 800–1; what to grow,
752–54; window-box, 853–54;
winter storage, 806–8

Vegetable spaghetti (*Cucurbita*),
891
Vegetative plantings, lawns and,
721–23
Veltheimia viridifolia, 1135–36
Velvet-plant (*G. aurantiaca*), 1083
Ventilation: greenhouse, 284; hot-
bed, 271; house plants, 1004–5,
1016–17
Verbena, 661–62, 687, 1379; lemon-,
148, 1034, 1035
Vermiculite, 18, 81
Vermont, 170, 312, 560, 601, 653,
691, 852, 983, 1084, 1223, 1284,
1296, 1300, 1302, 1315
Veronica, 650, 1341
Vertical gardens, 209–10
Vesper iris, 1245
Vetch, 37, 38
Viburnum, 385–86; evergreen, 434–
35; pest control, 1282
Viburnum carlesii, 386, 1282
Viburnum dilatatum, 386
Viburnum opulus 'Roseum,' 386
Viburnum plicatum tomentosum, 386
Vine maple (*A. circinatam*), 333
Vines, 452–62; for "accent points,"
245; akebia, 454–55; ampelopsis,
455–56; annual, 452–54; to attract
birds, 184; bittersweet, 456–57;
books on, 1443; city garden, 206;
clematis, 457–59; culture of, 449–
52; Dutchman's-pipe, 459;
euonymus fortunei (wintercreeper), 459; fertilizing, 304–5;
honeysuckle, 459–60; hydrangea,
460–61; for indoors, 1101–8; ivy,
461; mulching, 303–4; parthenocissus, 455–56; planting time, 301;
pruning, 301–2; roof garden, 188,
189; sources for, 1454–55; watering, 302–3; what to grow, 450–52;
when to buy, 299–300; wisteria,
461–62; woody, 453–62

Violet (*Viola*), 37, 183, 267, 650–51, 1282, 1353, 1365, 1373, 1403, 1417
Virginia, 191, 345, 674, 681, 865, 996, 1159, 1162, 1192, 1195, 1206–7, 1230, 1236, 1241, 1252, 1253, 1255, 1260, 1263, 1287, 1292, 1303, 1304, 1326
Virginia-creeper, 455, 1339, 1341
Virus diseases, 900–1, 936, 1303, 1307, 1327
Vista, 94
Vitamin B₁, 255
Vitex, 364–65, 1388
'Von Sion' flowers, 1257

Walks, planning and landscaping, 114–16
Wallflower, 694, 1365
Wall gardens, 163–65
Walls: planning and landscaping, 109–10; plant supports for, 244–45; roses for, 574
Walnut, 38, 1282–83, 1366, 1398–99; English, 998–99, 1282–83, 1386
Wandering Jew, 1107–8
Wardian case, 1099
Washington, D.C., 528, 817, 1209, 1215, 1312
Washington State, 69, 404, 672, 863, 999, 1233–34, 1249, 1250, 1252, 1256, 1262, 1278, 1281, 1289, 1294, 1296–97, 1301, 1317, 1320, 1322–23, 1328, 1426–28
Wasps, 968, 1151
Waste water, 28–29
Water and watering, 83, 237–38; capillary mat system, 281; dish or bathtub, 210–11; in excess, 15; after fertilizing, 79; greenhouse, 279–82; herb garden, 139; houseplants, 1003–4, 1014–15; lawn grass, 734–35; ornamentals, 201, 237–39; and plant growth, 14–15;

potted plants, 201; rock garden, 158; roses, 545; time of day, 213; trees and shrubs, 302–3; vegetables, 801–2; vines, 302–3; wick method of, 281; *See also* Culture
Watercress, 38, 153–54, 891–92, 1340
Water gardening, books on, 1443
Water lily (*Nymphaea*), 126–28; sources for, 1456
"Waterlogged soil," 27
Watermelon, 37, 754, 892–93
Water softener, 286
Watsonia, 1372
Wattle fence, 106
Wax begonia (*B. semperflorens*), 659, 1045, 1046
Waxplant (*Hoya*), 1108
'Wealthy' apple, 927
Weather vanes, 132
Webworms, 746, 1164, 1290
'Wedgwood' iris, 1118
Weedkiller, 207, 236, 707, 1331; for vegetables, 800–1
Weeds, 1330–41; books on, 1443; for composting, 6; edible, 845, 1340; general information, 1330–33; growth and soil type, 25–26; soil preparation, 25; specific kinds of, 1333–41
Weeping birch, 327, 1208
Weeping fig (*F. benjamina*), 1074
Weeping lantana, 1096
Weeping willow, 340–41, 1372
Weevil, 1288
Weigela, 317, 387
"Well-drained soil," 27
West Virginia, 190, 1165, 1206, 1262, 1264, 1268, 1276, 1304
Wet ground, planting in, 229–30
Wet marshland, 173
Wet potpourri, 140–41
Wet soil, 27–29, 34
Wheat, 37
Wheelbarrow, 810

Wheels, herb, 141–42
Whip grafting, 264
White birch, 37, 327, 328, 1208
White cedar, 37
White clay soil, 20
White clover, 38, 715, 716, 1338
White damask rose, 561
Whiteflies, 1024, 1188, 1201, 1220, 1234, 1235, 1272, 1288, 1298
White flowering dogwood (*C. florida*), 343
White forsythia, 357
White-fringed orchis (*H. nivea*), 181
White fungus, 1166, 1218
White grubs, *see* Grubs
Whiteleaf Japanese magnolia, 347
White lice, 1233
White mold, 1226
White oak, 38, 337
White pine, 408, 446, 1264; sawdust of, 70–71
White-pine rust, 1265, 1319
White snakeroot, 1338
Whitewash, 913
Wick method, 281
Widows' tears (*T. virginiana*), 649
Wild blackberry, 986
Wild blue phlox (*P. divaricata*), 182
Wild carrot, 1338–39
Wild columbine (*A. canadensis*), 178
Wildflower garden, 169–83; bog, 172–73; books on, 174, 1444; collecting plants, 175; fertilizer, 170–71; meadow, 172; propagation, 173–74; sources for, 1456; specific kinds of flowers, 175–83; woodland, 169–72
Wildflower mixture, 174
Wildflower preserve, 175
Wild garlic, 1339
Wild-ginger (*A. canadense*), 146
Wild grapevine, 1339
Wild Indian paintbrush, 1349

Wild marjoram (*O. vulgare*), 149
Wild morning-glory, 1337, 1339
Wild red raspberry, 989–90
Wild strawberry, 981
Wild sweet pea, 639–40
Wild veronica, 1340–41
Willow, 30, 38, 340–41, 448, 1283, 1372
Willow amsonia, *see* Bluestar
Willow oak, 1372
Wilt disease, 516, 1221–22, 1247, 1293, 1297, 1298, 1299, 1306, 1307; how to diagnose, 1141
Windbreaks, 206, 448–49, 1248, 1354–55
Windflower (Japanese anemone), 1202–3, 1419
Window-box garden, 190–91, 1027–30; mealybugs in, 1177; New York City, 191; vegetable, 853–54; winter protection, 191
Windows, cold from, 1021
Windsor bean, 818, 823
Wine grape, varieties of, 902
'Winesap' apple, 1317
Winged euonymus (*E. alata*), 368
Winter-aconite (*Eranthis*), 479
Winterberry (*I. verticillata*), 388
Wintercreeper (*Euonymus*), 224–25, 425–26, 330, 368, 459, 1230–31
Wintergreen, 37, 183; flowering (*P. paucifolia*), 183; spotted, 183
Winter green-manure crops, 57
Winter protection: broad-leaved evergreens, 419–20; cold frame, 268; deciduous trees and shrubs, 318–19; narrow-leaved evergreens, 398–99; perennials, 587–89; roses, 548–51; wall garden, 164
Winter savory (*S. montana*), 151–52, 1016
Winter squash, 753, 754, 806, 878–79, 880
Wire fence, vegetables, 762
Wire gates, 109

Wire grass, 1339
Wireworms, 525, 1199
Wisconsin, 400, 408, 690, 1192, 1204, 1207, 1217, 1224, 1226, 1227, 1236, 1248, 1260, 1261, 1262, 1270, 1273, 1275, 1278, 1279, 1292–93, 1300, 1317, 1319, 1321, 1329, 1428–31
Wishbone flower (*Torenia*), 686–87
Wisteria, 38, 461–62, 1385
Witches'-brooms, 1199–1200
Witch-hazel (*Hamamelis*), 38, 388–89
Witloof (*C. intybus*), 837–38
Wood anemone (*A. quinquefolia*), 175
Wood ashes, 14, 43, 68–69, 544, 740, 783; on heavy clay soil, 17; purpose of, 21
Woodbine, 38
Wood chips, 6, 115
Woodchucks, control of, 1200
Wood coke, 69
Wooden containers, types of, 186
Wooden-sapling fence, 107
Wood for layering, 259
Wood-hyacinth, 478
Woodland soil, 29–31
Woodland wildflower garden, 169–72
Wood soil, 51
Woody vines, 454–62

Woolly thyme (*T. pseudolanuginosus*), 153
Worms, 64, 829, 1210, 1254, 1259, 1261, 1281, 1291, 1294, 1296–97, 1298, 1300, 1301, 1318, 1319, 1320, 1321–22, 1325, 1328
Wyoming, 693, 1245–46, 1308–9, 1328, 1329, 1431

Yard, screening or enclosing, 100–1
Yellow clay soil, 20
Yellow clover, 38
Yellow-flowered cytisus (*C. racemosus*), 293
Yellow-fringed orchis (*H. ciliaris*), 181
Yellow herbaceous peony, 639
Yellow wax bean, 818
Yellow-wood (*C. lutea*), 352
Yew, 318, 412–13, 448, 1283, 1388
York rose, 561
Yucca, 16, 651, 1283–84

Zantedeschia, *see* Calla-lily
Zebrina pendula, 1107–8
Zephyranthes, 1237
Zinc, 50
Zinnia, 37, 650, 665, 1284
Zoysia, 700, 716–17, 1374
Zucchini squash, 880